Politics & Society
in the Contemporary
Middle East

SECOND EDITION

Politics & Society

in the Contemporary

Middle East

edited by
Michele Penner Angrist

LYNNE
RIENNER
PUBLISHERS

BOULDER
LONDON

Published in the United States of America in 2013 by
Lynne Rienner Publishers, Inc.
1800 30th Street, Boulder, Colorado 80301
www.rienner.com

and in the United Kingdom by
Lynne Rienner Publishers, Inc.
3 Henrietta Street, Covent Garden, London WC2E 8LU

Library of Congress Cataloging-in-Publication Data
Politics and society in the contemporary Middle East / edited by Michele
Penner Angrist. — Second edition.
     pages cm
  Includes bibliographical references and index.
  ISBN 978-1-58826-908-9 (alk. paper)
1. Middle East—Politics and government—1979– 2. Middle East—Politics
and government—1979– —Case studies. I. Angrist, Michele Penner, 1970–
  JQ1758.A58P655 2013
  320.956—dc23

                                                            2013003035

British Cataloguing in Publication Data
A Cataloguing in Publication record for this book
is available from the British Library.

Printed and bound in the United States of America

         The paper used in this publication meets the requirements
   ∞   of the American National Standard for Permanence of
         Paper for Printed Library Materials Z39.48-1992.

     5   4   3   2   1

Contents

v

Part 2 Cases

Part 3 Conclusion

Tables and Figures

Tables

Figures

Acknowledgments

The need for a second edition of this text arose much more quickly than was expected, and I owe a great debt of thanks to all of its contributors for their willingness to reengage with the project and revise its substance on comparatively short notice. This collaborative effort is one that I am privileged to be a part of as I continue to study and reflect on this important region with so many distinguished colleagues. We all remain cognizant of the central role played by the late Marsha Pripstein Posusney in launching the book, and we honor her memory as we work to keep it current.

—*Michele Penner Angrist*

1

The Making of
Middle East Politics

Michele Penner Angrist

The regional uprisings that came to be known as the "Arab
Spring" began unfolding just four months after the first edition of this text
appeared. That volume described and analyzed the predominance of authoritarian forms of rule in the Middle East and speculated—not especially op-
timistically—about prospects for change in the direction of freer and more
plural politics. Beginning in December 2010 and throughout 2011, as
demonstrators confronted dictators across the Arab world demanding more
accountable, more participatory, and less corrupt governance, it seemed
everything was changing. After decades in office, presidents fell from
power in Tunisia, then Egypt, then Libya and Yemen, while another engaged in a desperately violent attempt to cling to power in Syria. Serious
political turbulence struck monarchies as well, as citizens in Bahrain, Morocco, and Jordan called for thoroughgoing changes to the rules of the political game. These developments were broadcast on Al-Jazeera and other
satellite channels, while social media vehicles like Twitter and Facebook
also played a role in the mobilization, coordination, and dissemination of
political dissent. The original edition of this text appeared to be woefully
out of date.

Yet as 2012 came to a close the picture was more variegated. To be
sure, the Middle East is not the same as it was prior to the uprisings. Everywhere the political calculus of those who rule and those who are ruled has
been changed by the dramatic wave of demonstrations and their aftermath.
Still, two years now since it began, the Arab Spring has dramatically altered
political systems in only five of the region's twenty countries. As of this
writing, one can be reasonably optimistic about the prospects for more
competitive, freer politics in just two or perhaps three of those five cases.

Thus, plenty of authoritarian polities remain to study and understand—even if their leaders now have new challenges to navigate as they strategize to shore up their rule.

With the Arab Spring uprisings as a backdrop, then, this text introduces readers to the contemporary comparative politics of the Middle East. What does it mean to study the *comparative* politics of this region? Scholars of comparative politics study the internal political dynamics of countries (rather than relations between or among countries, which is *international* politics). So, for example, instead of exploring when and why countries in the region go to war with one another, we will explore how Middle Eastern governments are structured, who opposes those governments and why, how oppositions work to bring about change, and so forth. Some comparativists tackle this task by deeply mastering the internal politics of one country. Others study a country's domestic politics while also comparing and contrasting what they find with what is happening in other national contexts. Comparativists typically ask themselves what political trends are similar across countries—but also what differences exist, and why? Why did many authoritarian regimes buckle in the face of Arab Spring uprisings, while many, many more survived? Some buckled relatively peacefully, while significant blood was shed elsewhere—why? What political, social, economic, and other factors help us to understand both the similarities and the differences that we observe? This is the stuff of comparative politics. We learn about broader political science processes by studying a collection of countries' politics individually as well as in relation to one another. This text allows the reader to do both.

With comparative politics thus explained, let us now turn to defining the Middle East. What the Middle East is turns out to be a complex question. The name *Middle East* was not attached to the area by its residents themselves. Rather, beginning in the nineteenth century, political elites in Europe and the United States coined the terms *Near East* and *Middle East* to refer to (various delineations of) territories that lay between Western Europe and the *Far East* (China, Japan, etc.). Because the term *Middle East* was bestowed on the region by outside powers according to their own particular political, strategic, and geographic perspectives, it has been criticized as West- or Euro-centric. Still, it is in wide use today and typically refers to the geographic region bounded to the north by Turkey, to the east by Iran, to the west by Egypt, and to the south by the Arabian Peninsula (see Figure 1.1). In addition to Egypt, Turkey, and Iran, the Middle East thus includes Saudi Arabia, Yemen, Oman, the United Arab Emirates (UAE), Qatar, Bahrain, Kuwait, Israel, Palestine, Jordan, Iraq, Syria, and Lebanon.

The material in this book also encompasses North Africa, referring to the northernmost tier of African countries that border the Mediterranean Sea: Morocco, Algeria, Tunisia, and Libya. Definitions of *North Africa* vary

Figure 1.1 Map of the Middle East and North Africa

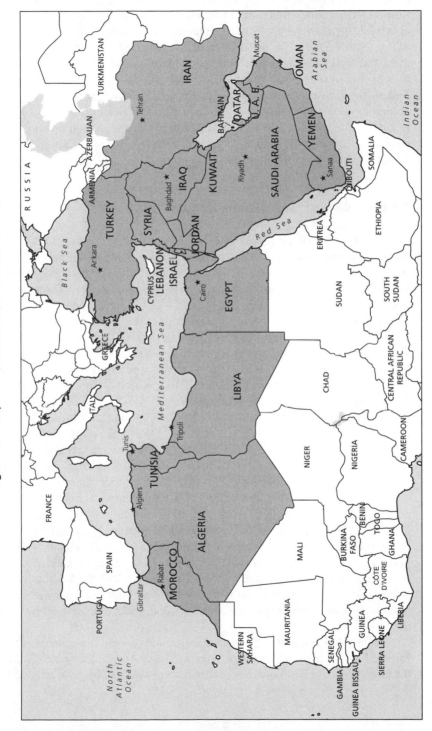

somewhat; for instance, in its definition of *Northern Africa,* the United Nations (UN) includes Sudan and the Western Sahara (a disputed territory controlled primarily by Morocco). Others sometimes include Mauritania within North Africa. We delimit North Africa as we do primarily because these four countries share a great deal in common with the political dynamics of the countries of the Middle East—and this is much less the case with Sudan, the Western Sahara, and Mauritania. *MENA* is a commonly used acronym referring to the Middle East and North Africa thus delineated, and readers will encounter it in this text. For simplicity's sake, in this book the term *Middle East* will refer to the countries of the Middle East and North Africa (those highlighted in Figure 1.1).

An Overview of States in the Region Today

The Middle East encompasses twenty countries that are home to approximately 460 million people. Most of these countries are Arab, meaning that their citizens speak the Arabic language and perceive that they have a shared historical, cultural, and social experience as Arabs. Three of the twenty countries are not Arab, however.[1] The national language of Israel is Hebrew, and while many Israelis speak Arabic, the historical, cultural, and social bond for the majority of Israelis emerges from their identity as Jews. Turkey and Iran also are not Arab countries. Turks are a different ethnic group and speak Turkish, a language that linguistically is unrelated to Arabic. The dominant language in Iran is Farsi, which—although written in Arabic script—also is unrelated to Arabic.

Many unwittingly think that the "Middle East" and the "Muslim world" are one and the same. Certainly, the vast majority of people living in all Middle East countries save Israel are Muslim. At the same time, religious minorities—especially Jews and Christians—are to be found in most of them. For example, Christians of a variety of denominations (Maronite Catholic, Greek Orthodox, and others) make up perhaps as much as 40 percent of the Lebanese population. Nearly 10 percent of Egyptians are Coptic Christians, and approximately 6 percent of Jordanians are Christian, most of them Greek Orthodox. Meanwhile, the Muslim world extends well beyond the Middle East. Muslim-majority countries are found in sub-Saharan Africa, Central Asia, and South and Southeast Asia. So the Middle East is just a small slice of the Muslim world in terms of both geography and population. Indeed, a majority of the world's Muslims live outside of the Middle East.

Table 1.1 provides basic statistical information about the countries of the Middle East. In terms of sheer size, Algeria, Saudi Arabia, Libya, and Iran are the largest Middle East countries; Bahrain and Palestine, by contrast, occupy

Table 1.1 Statistical Snapshot of Middle East Countries

Country	Land Area (sq. km)	Population 2011	Urban Population (% of total) 2011	Fertility Rate, Total (births per woman) 2010	GDP per Capita (constant 2000 US$) 2009	Literacy Rate, Adult Female (% of females ages 15 and above) 2005–2009
Algeria	2,381,740	35,980,193	73	2	2,193	64
Bahrain	760	1,323,535	89	3	11,601	90
Egypt	995,450	82,536,770	44	3	1,912	58
Iran	1,628,550	74,798,599	69	2	2,162	81
Iraq	434,320	32,961,959	67	5	752	70
Israel	21,640	7,765,700	92	3	21,602	n.a.
Jordan	88,780	6,181,000	83	4	2,577	89
Kuwait	17,820	2,818,042	98	2	23,116	92
Lebanon	10,230	4,259,405	87	2	6,350	86
Libya	1,759,540	6,422,772	78	3	7,885	82
Morocco	446,300	32,272,974	57	2	1,797	44
Oman	309,500	2,846,145	73	2	11,192	81
Palestine	6,020	4,019,433	74	4	1,056[a]	92
Qatar	11,590	1,870,041	99	2	30,547	93
Saudi Arabia	2,149,690	28,082,541	82	3	9,294	81
Syria	183,630	20,820,311	56	3	1,509	78
Tunisia	155,360	10,673,800	66	2	3,084	71
Turkey	769,630	73,639,596	71	2	4,969	85
United Arab Emirates	83,600	7,890,924	84	2	22,507	91
Yemen	527,970	24,799,880	32	5	583	45

Source: World Bank, *World Development Indicators*, various years (Washington, DC).
Notes: a. This value is from 2005.
n.a. indicates data are not available.

tiny pieces of territory. In terms of population, Egypt, Turkey, and Iran are the region's powerhouses, with populations upward of 70 million, while tiny Bahrain has a population of just over 1 million. More than 90 percent of Israelis, Kuwaitis, and Qataris live in urban areas, compared to only 32 percent of Yemenis and only 44 percent of Egyptians. Populations are growing most rapidly in Iraq and Yemen, where the average number of births per woman is five; by contrast, ten Middle East countries have fertility rates of just two births per woman. On a per capita basis, the economies of Qatar, Kuwait, the United Arab Emirates, and Israel produce the most. Yemen is the region's poorest country measured in terms of economic output, followed by Iraq and Palestine. Finally, the proportion of adult females who are literate ranges from just 45 percent in Yemen, to around 65 percent in Algeria, to 93 percent in Qatar. Clearly, there is considerable variation in the region when it comes to land, population, and indicators of development.

One of the main things the discipline of comparative politics studies is the type of governmental system a country has. Often referred to as a *regime,* a governmental system refers not to the particular group of individuals filling key offices at a given point in time—this is simply a *government*—but rather more broadly to the processes by which leaders are selected (election? dynastic succession? military coup?) and how those leaders in turn exercise power (in consultation with others according to a rule of law? individually and arbitrarily? somewhere in between?). For decades and until the Arab uprisings of 2010–2011, systems of government in the Middle East were, almost without exception, authoritarian. Moreover, for the last quarter of the twentieth century and the first decade of the twenty-first, the region was a global outlier in that, while every other area of the world saw (at least some) dictatorships fall and democracies erected in their stead, dictatorships in the Middle East stood firm and persisted. By 2011 this was no longer the case, and this chapter will close with an introduction to the Arab Spring, but the prevalence and endurance of authoritarian rule in the region prior to 2011 are a crucial context for understanding contemporary politics in the Middle East.

What, generally, does "authoritarian" rule look like? Leaders are not selected through free and fair elections, and a relatively narrow group of people control the state apparatus and are not held accountable for their decisions by the broader public. Although there is variation from case to case, political rights and civil liberties are generally quite limited. Political rights refer to norms such as free and fair elections for the chief executive and the legislature; the ability of citizens to organize in multiple political parties and compete in elections free from interference by the military, religious, or other powerful groups; the absence of discrimination against cultural, ethnic, religious, or other minority groups; and transparent, accountable, noncorrupt government. Civil liberties refer to freedom of expression and belief, freedom of association and organization, the rule of law, and individual rights.[2] Table 1.2 lists the rankings given to Middle East countries for political rights and civil liberties in 2008 and 2011 by Freedom House, a prominent nongovernmental organization (NGO) that gauges such rights globally.

Table 1.2 demonstrates that in 2011 only three countries—Israel, Turkey, and Tunisia—scored between 1 and 3 on the political rights scale and thus could be considered relatively free. Meanwhile, 16 of 20 countries scored a 5, 6, or 7—on the "not free" end of the scale. Kuwait, where a dynastic monarchy and an assertive parliament struggle for power, scored an "in-between" 4. While many countries have slightly better civil liberties scores, the overall civil liberties picture is very similar to that for political rights.

While most Middle Eastern regimes remain authoritarian, they are not homogeneously so. Dictatorship takes more than one form in the area. The two main variants are monarchies and republics. The monarchies are led by kings whose reigns are not conferred by elections; instead, when incumbents die or become incapacitated, leadership is passed down hereditarily

Table 1.2 Political and Civil Rights in the Middle East According to Freedom House

Country	Political Rights		Civil Liberties	
	2008	2011	2008	2011
Algeria	6	6	5	5
Bahrain	5	6	5	6
Egypt	6	6	5	5
Iran	6	6	6	6
Iraq	6	5	6	6
Israel	1	1	2	2
Jordan	5	6	4	5
Kuwait	4	4	4	5
Lebanon	5	5	4	4
Libya	7	7	7	6
Morocco	5	5	4	4
Oman	6	6	5	5
Palestine	5	6	6	6/5[a]
Qatar	6	6	5	5
Saudi Arabia	7	7	6	7
Syria	7	7	6	7
Tunisia	7	3	5	4
Turkey	3	3	3	3
United Arab Emirates	6	6	5	6
Yemen	5	6	5	6

Source: Freedom House.
Notes: Scale is 1–7, with 1 denoting "most free," and 7 denoting "least free."
a. 6 is for the Gaza Strip; 5 is for the West Bank.

through ruling families. In monarchies, power rests in and emanates from the ruling family and those elites who are allied to it. The region's monarchies are Saudi Arabia, Qatar, the UAE, Morocco, Kuwait, Bahrain, Jordan, and Oman.

The region's authoritarian republics are led by presidents, whose terms in office are conferred by elections. Elections are not free or fair, but they are held, usually at regular intervals, both for the chief executive position and for national parliaments. In these republics, political power typically emanates from preponderant political parties that are headed by the president, are backed by the military, and have access to large amounts of state revenues. Syria, Algeria, and Yemen are the Middle East's authoritarian republics—though as of this writing Syria is plunged in civil war while Yemen is navigating a political transition whose ultimate end point is uncertain. Prior to the Arab uprisings, Tunisia and Egypt also were authoritarian republics.

There is now a growing number of exceptions to authoritarian rule in the Middle East. The region comprises a number of countries with political systems wherein outsiders or opposition parties can successfully oust incumbent chief executives in elections—something that is simply not possible in the monarchies and authoritarian republics. Israel boasts free, fair, competitive, multiparty elections for seats in its parliament; for the past several decades, the prime ministerial position has changed hands regularly, alternating among two or three leading political parties. Turkey too can be labeled democratic: since 1950, free, fair, competitive, multiparty elections have determined which parties sit in the Turkish parliament and make up the cabinet; the prime ministerial office has rotated among several political parties on the left and the right of the political spectrum, and of late there has been alternation at the level of the presidency as well. Lebanon and Iraq hold competitive elections to determine the composition of parliaments and cabinets, which then set policy in those countries. And during the Arab Spring, Tunisia, Egypt, and Libya held multiparty elections to select parliaments, constituent assemblies, and/or presidents—though only time will tell if this method of leadership selection will continue to be the norm in those countries. As will be noticed in Table 1.2, the Freedom House scores for Lebanon, Iraq, Egypt, and Libya—and to a lesser extent Turkey and Tunisia—are below that of Israel, a fact attributable to the existence of ongoing limitations on liberties in those political communities. However, on the basic matter of whether or not incumbent chief executives are able to be removed and replaced through elections, these countries can be considered democratic—or at least "protodemocratic."

Iran's political system constitutes a category of its own, one which features both democratic and authoritarian elements. In the Islamic Republic of Iran, citizens go to the polls regularly to elect a president and parliament.

Historically, such polls have been fair and have featured competition among distinct political camps. Moreover, the presidency has rotated among these camps over the course of the past generation. Yet an institution called the Council of Guardians sits atop these elected bodies and controls their membership through its power to vet all would-be candidates for office. The council also can veto legislation passed by Iran's elected bodies. Ultimate power lies in the hands of Iran's (indirectly elected) Supreme Leader, who controls that country's armed and security forces, judiciary, and media outlets. That Iran's 2011 Freedom House political rights score was a 6 indicates that the authoritarian strands of Iran's political system overpower and marginalize its democratic strands.

This overview is just an introductory taste of contemporary political dynamics in the region. The chapters that follow go into much more detail, both by theme—government-opposition relations, the impact of international politics, economics, civil society, religion, identity, and gender—and by country. The remainder of this chapter provides essential historical knowledge regarding the crucial historical legacies that bear on Middle East politics and society today.

Essential Historical Background

Islamization and Arabization

How did the Middle East come to be predominantly Muslim in terms of faith and predominantly Arab in terms of language and ethnicity? The establishment and spread of Islam began in the seventh century C.E., and it was this process that also Arabized large portions of the region. Prior to the rise of Islam, two empires dominated the Middle East. The Sasanids ruled Iraq and Iran, while the Byzantines ruled the Anatolian Peninsula (modern Turkey), northern Syria, and parts of North Africa, Egypt, and those territories that lie immediately east of the Mediterranean Sea (modern-day Lebanon, Israel, and Palestine). In 610 C.E., a young caravan trader named Muhammad began receiving revelations. He would become the Prophet of Islam, a new faith that was born in Mecca and Medina (cities in what is today Saudi Arabia).

Islam was strictly monotheistic, which stood in contrast to the pagan beliefs of the majority of the tribes who inhabited the Arabian Peninsula at that time. It exhorted those tribes—which often were at war with one another—to see themselves as brothers instead, and to submit to the one true god, Allah. Islam also preached the importance of justice and of caring for the weak in society (the poor, the sick, orphans, and the like). Although Muhammad encountered considerable initial resistance from those to whom his prophecy represented a threat, by the end of his lifetime he had built a considerable new Muslim community, earning—through genuine conversion, diplomacy, and force—the loyalty of most tribes in the Arabian Peninsula. Upon the Prophet Muhammad's death, the realm of Islam exploded geographically. Arabian tribesmen, with zeal inspired both by their conversion to a new faith and by the prospect of new power and wealth, carried the banner of Islam northward out of the Arabian Peninsula into the "Fertile Crescent" (today's Lebanon, Syria, Iraq, Jordan, Israel, and Palestine), then eastward to Iran and westward across North Africa and even into Spain. These expansions destroyed part of the Byzantine and all of the Sasanid empires and paved the way for the creation of two successive Islamic empires: the Umayyad Empire (661–750), with its capital at Damascus, and the Abbasid Empire (750–945), with its capital at Baghdad.

Prior to Islam's emergence, Arabic-speaking tribes lived primarily in the Arabian Peninsula. With the Arab-Muslim conquests into the broader Middle East and subsequent building of empires, however, the pace of Arab peoples moving into the region picked up. Arabic, the language of the conquering empires, became the language of written communication with regard to administrative, religious, and cultural affairs. Non-Arabs gradually adopted the tongue as a result. Over an even longer period of time than Arabization consumed, a majority of people in the lands conquered by Muslim armies became converts to the new faith. These were not forced conversions, however. These Islamic empires allowed Jews, Christians, and Zoroastrians to practice their religions unimpeded as long as they paid special taxes. Conversions occurred slowly over time, out of political expediency (to be of the same faith as the ruling elite had its rewards), due to commercial interest (Islamic law and networks facilitated trade), as well as out of a sense of shared cultural and social experience that was acquired over time.

The Ottoman Empire

The last great Islamic empire was the Ottoman Empire, founded by Turkic tribes (thus Turkish- rather than Arabic-speaking) beginning in the thirteenth century and centered on the imperial capital Istanbul. At their peak in the mid–sixteenth century C.E., the Ottomans controlled a breathtaking swath of territory, extending from deep into southeastern Europe, eastward to the Iranian border, southward through the Levant and parts of the Arabian Peninsula, and across North Africa to the Moroccan border. The Ottoman leader, or sultan, controlled a professional army and sat atop a substantial bureaucracy that administrated imperial affairs. He was also the caliph of the Islamic *umma* (community or nation) and used Islam to legitimate his rule. *Sharia* (Islamic law) constituted a core element of Ottoman law, and the *ulama* (clerics) staffed the empire's court and educational systems. Yet while the Ottomans were an Islamic empire, other religious communities were allowed considerable leeway in terms of freedom of worship and control over local community affairs such as education and social services.

For the purposes of modern politics, two things are crucial to understand about the Ottoman Empire. First, it represented the last era in world history when the Middle East constituted a politically, economically, and militarily more powerful entity than "the West" (meaning, for that time period, Europe and Russia). During the 1500s the Ottomans challenged Venice, Italy, and Spain for supremacy in the Mediterranean. The Ottoman Empire also laid siege to the Habsburg capital of Vienna twice—once in 1529 and again in 1683. While it was victorious neither time, it did implant a pronounced sense of threat among Europeans.

The second critical point is that the tables began to turn in the seventeenth century as European states became increasingly powerful while the Ottoman Empire weakened. European powers successfully challenged the Ottomans for control over lucrative trade routes and penetrated the Ottoman Empire with European-controlled operations that imported European products and exported raw materials. These developments harmed the Ottomans economically, reducing revenues accruing to Ottoman coffers. Politically, modern nation-states emerged in Europe, as did nationalism, defined by James Gelvin as the "belief that because a given population shares (or can be made to share) certain identifiable characteristics—religion, language, shared history, and so on—it merits an independent existence" (2008: 56). Nationalism became a powerful ideology that undermined the multiethnic Ottoman Empire by inspiring many of its subject peoples to attempt to secede. Finally, by the turn of the nineteenth century, European armies had become more professional and deadly, utilizing new technologies, tactics, and organizational strategies. Meanwhile, internal to the empire, the quality of sultans was declining and the central government was weakening relative to provincial power-holders. Military morale and discipline too were waning, in part because the inflation that struck Eurasia at this time devalued troops' pay.

Ottoman elites were painfully aware of this turn of events. In the late 1600s the Ottomans lost territories to Russia, the Habsburgs, Venice, and Poland. Indeed, in 1656 the Venetians destroyed the Ottoman naval fleet. In the late 1700s the Russians repeatedly and successfully advanced on the Ottomans. The Ottomans were now following the Europeans in terms of culture as well. They imported architectural and painting styles, furniture—even tulips. By the 1800s, encouraged by Russia and other European powers, nationalist movements had arisen in Serbia, Greece, Romania, and Bulgaria, and these successfully seceded from the Ottoman Empire.

Ottoman elites were alarmed, of course, and as early as the 1600s began to wonder if and how they could reform the empire in order to better compete with their European rivals. As the Ottoman community engaged in deep intellectual debates, one camp concluded that if the Ottomans were to become a match for the Europeans, they would need to adopt European innovations in military technology and training and tactics, and political institutions like parliaments. A second camp reached a quite different diagnosis of the problem, however, concluding that Ottoman weakness was a reflection of declining faith. The answer, then, was a return to a reinvigorated and purified Islam, not the mimicking of European ways.

The former camp won out, for a time anyway. During the late eighteenth century and through much of the nineteenth, Ottoman sultans attempted to radically restructure the empire's operations to defend against expected further European encroachment. They changed how their subjects were taxed, both to increase loyalty and to increase revenues flowing to the empire's coffers. They created an Ottoman parliament, modeled after the British and French institutions—in the hope that more inclusive, consultative governance would make for improved subject loyalty and better policy. They brought in European advisers to train new army units in modern warfare techniques, and they overhauled their educational, legal, and bureaucratic systems.

Ultimately, it would be too little, too late. The reforms implemented during the nineteenth century faced significant internal resistance and thus their effectiveness was limited. What's more, the Ottomans could not stem the tide of nationalism and the desire of many Ottoman subject peoples to have their own state. When World War I ended, the Ottomans were on the losing side and would soon be extinguished as an empire.

European Imperialism in the Middle East

The Ottomans' painful experience of decline vis-à-vis an increasingly powerful set of European countries was only the first of a series of conflicts between the Middle East and Europe. The second was an era of direct rule by various European countries over territories in the Middle East. Specifically, beginning in the nineteenth century and continuing through the end of World War I, Britain, France, and Italy took control of the vast majority of the region. Table 1.3 illustrates which European power controlled what Middle East territory (identified by contemporary country names). Sometimes geostrategic affairs motivated the colonizers. Britain's footprint in the Middle East turned on two main concerns: securing access to regional oil supplies and protecting key access routes to India, the "jewel" of the British Crown. Depending on the case, France generally was motivated by its relations with Christian communities and by commercial interests. Intra-European rivalry and the prestige that was attached to overseas colonies also motivated both powers.

Table 1.3 European Imperialism in the Middle East

Country	European Power	Type of Authority	Years
Algeria	France	Colonial	1830–1962
Bahrain	Britain	Treaty	1880–1971
Egypt	Britain	Colonial	1882–1936
Iran	n.a.	n.a.	n.a.
Iraq	Britain	Mandate	1920–1932
Israel	Britain	Mandate	1920–1948
Jordan	Britain	Mandate	1920–1946
Kuwait	Britain	Treaty	1899–1961
Lebanon	France	Mandate	1920–1943
Libya	Italy	Colonial	1911–1951
Morocco	France	Colonial	1912–1956
Oman	n.a.	n.a.	n.a.
Palestine	Britain	Mandate	1920–1948
Qatar	Britain	Treaty	1916–1971
Saudi Arabia	n.a.	n.a.	n.a.
Syria	France	Mandate	1920–1946
Tunisia	France	Colonial	1881–1956
Turkey	n.a.	n.a.	n.a.
United Arab Emirates	Britain	Treaty	1892–1971
Yemen, South	Britain	Colonial	1839–1967
Yemen, North	n.a.	n.a.	n.a.

Note: n.a. indicates not applicable; territory was never controlled by a European power.

The degree to which European powers took over the reins of power in their respective Middle East holdings varied substantially. In part this depended on the type of intervention. Generally, holdings acquired prior to World War I were colonies, territories that European powers conquered unapologetically and exploited for their own purposes in the context of global great-power competition. Holdings acquired after World War I, however, were awarded by the League of Nations under the mandate system in the context of new, more restrictive international norms regarding European control over distant lands. In places where they acted as mandatory powers, Europeans ostensibly had an obligation to protect natives' welfare and prepare them for independence. In the Persian Gulf, British imperialism took the form of a series of treaty relationships negotiated with the ruling families of the small states that lined the coast.

In what ways did European power impact the region during this era? On one end of the spectrum, in Kuwait and the UAE, for example, Britain controlled foreign policy and port operations while leaving domestic political arrangements in those countries largely alone. In Morocco, the French took over domestic affairs—but did so by penetrating and harnessing existing indigenous institutions (like the monarchy), leaving them intact. By contrast, in Algeria, France uprooted and resettled tribes, destroyed domestic religious institutions, confiscated land, settled more than 150,000 Europeans, and ultimately annexed the entire country (as three separate French provinces). Perhaps even more dramatically, at World War I's end, France and Britain literally drew the modern-day boundaries of Lebanon, Syria, Iraq, Jordan, and Israel/Palestine; engineered their respective political systems; and—in Iraq and Jordan—selected which kings would be placed on their respective thrones.

European rule had dramatic socioeconomic impacts as well. France and Britain used their colonies as export markets for cheap European manufactured goods that competed with locally made products, hurting domestic artisan and craftsman classes. European powers also relied on their imperial holdings as a source of raw materials (cotton, wheat, etc.). These dynamics integrated the Middle East into global markets in a dependent manner as exporters of agricultural or primary (raw material) products, a fact that was an obstacle to future development and prosperity. While European control shaped Middle East states' economic trajectories in key ways, the European powers' disposition toward their Middle East subjects was one of superiority and contempt. France and Britain legitimized their foreign holdings in part with the idea that they had a "civilizing" mission in the region. In particular, they looked down on Islam and facilitated the entrance of Christian missionaries into Middle East societies. Another key impact of the colonial period was a domestic divide that emerged in Middle Eastern countries between urban elites who were exposed to and often adopted the ideas and culture of the French and the British, on the one hand, and the rural masses who remained more oriented toward Arab-Islamic culture, on the other.

Several countries in the region escaped the yoke of direct European rule. Turkey was the successor state to the Ottoman Empire in its core Anatolian Peninsula territory. While European powers had clear designs on that land in the wake of World War I, an Ottoman army officer named Mustafa Kemal organized Turks into a national movement and fought an independence war to establish the borders of what today is Turkey. In Iran, the Qajar dynasty ruled from the late 1700s through the early twentieth century, when power shifted into the hands of Reza Khan and subsequently to his son, Mohammad Reza Shah Pahlavi. Saudi Arabia is the product of the state-building efforts of the Al Saud tribe, which beginning in the early 1700s sought to expand and consolidate its power in the Arabian Peninsula. The campaign had its ups and downs, but by 1932, Saudi Arabia was a nation-state and it has been independent ever since. Prior to its unification in 1990, Yemen had existed as two separate countries for over a century and a half: Britain ruled South Yemen as a colony, while North Yemen escaped European control. The Gulf state of Oman did as well.

Creation of the State of Israel

If Europe was the source of imperialist policies that left a strong imprint on the borders, politics, economies, and cultures of the Middle East, so too did it provide the beginning of the modern story of the emergence of Israel. In the late nineteenth century, in the face of various forms of discrimination against Jews—the worst being violent pogroms against Jewish communities in Russia and eastern Europe—a man named Theodor Herzl began to advance the Zionist case that Jews constituted a nation, one that needed its own state in order to ensure that Jews could live in security and dignity in a land where they constituted a majority. He and like-minded Jewish leaders then worked to make this vision a reality. They built institutions to raise awareness about and funds for the project, and they also sought the diplomatic support they knew would be crucial if they were to somehow obtain their own state. Zionist diplomatic overtures ultimately found success with Britain, which in the 1917 Balfour Declaration lent its support to the creation of a Jewish national "home" in Palestine.

That support took concrete form at the close of World War I when the League of Nations portioned out the lands east of the Mediterranean Sea to France and Britain as mandates. The legal document establishing the Palestine Mandate included the language of the Balfour Declaration. The pace of subsequent Jewish migration from Europe to Palestine, which had already begun in the late 1800s, began to pick up, with major *aliyot*—or waves of migration—occurring after World War I and in the 1930s. Tens of thousands of European Jews purchased land, settled, and began building new lives, new communities, and new institutions (including collective farms, a labor federation, schools, hospitals, and social services) in Palestine. At that time, however, the vast majority of the existing inhabitants of Palestine (90 percent in 1917) were Arab. They saw Zionism and the influx of Jewish immigrants as threatening to Arab political, economic, and cultural interests.

For a generation, from 1920 to 1947, Britain attempted to manage what would prove to be an intractable conflict. The number of Jews in Palestine grew, as did the amount of land owned and worked by Jews. A rise in Arab landlessness and poverty followed, as the Arabs who had worked the lands purchased by Jews were forced to find employment elsewhere. The Arab community grew increasingly frustrated and despairing. Serious violence between Jews and Arabs broke out in the late 1920s and again in the mid-1930s. The economic strains of the Great Depression, and then Hitler's execution of millions of Jews during World War II, magnified and sharpened the conflict. In 1947, Britain, exhausted by the war and unable to reconcile Jews and Arabs, informed the world it would take its leave of Palestine and turn the problem over to the newly created United Nations.

After sending an investigatory team to Palestine, the United Nations proposed that the territory of the Palestine Mandate be partitioned into two states, with Jerusalem—a city dear to Jews but also to Arab Christians and Muslims—as an international protectorate. The proposed Jewish state would have enclosed 55 percent of the land at a time when Jews represented approximately 32 percent of the population and owned just 6 percent of the total land area. While the Jewish community accepted the partition plan, Palestinian Arabs saw it as unjust and inequitable—and rejected it. This impasse would mean war. With the international community unable to effect a solution, those on the ground prepared to fight. During the mandate years the Jewish community in Palestine had built a military organization, the Haganah, which now went into action seeking to secure the territories the partition plan had designated for the Jewish state. On May 14, 1948, Zionist leaders proclaimed the State of Israel. Almost immediately, the surrounding Arab countries invaded. Israel would be victorious in this war, extending the lands under its control beyond what would have been its borders according to the UN partition. The conflict between the newly created Jewish state and its Arab neighbors continues to the present.

Pathways from Colonialism

Israel was becoming a reality in the Middle East at about the same time that Middle Eastern populations were preparing to throw off the yoke of European domination. Egypt and Iraq achieved independence relatively early, in the 1930s (see Table 1.3). A wave of independence achievements then came during and after World War II, with Lebanon, Jordan, Syria, Libya, Morocco, and Tunisia becoming independent—in that order—between 1943 and 1956. Kuwait, Algeria, and (South) Yemen became independent in the 1960s, and Bahrain, Qatar, and the UAE followed in 1971.

Forcing the French and the British to take their leave was a task that varied in difficulty depending on the setting. Kuwait and the UAE had it relatively easy, as British domestic political discontent with the costs of imperialism prompted a more or less unilateral withdrawal. More often, independence was the product of nationalist movements that arose across the region, called on France and Britain to depart, and put pressure on them to do so. These movements tended to take the form of political parties—for example, the Wafd in Egypt, the Neo-Destour in Tunisia, and Istiqlal in Morocco. In Jordan, Iraq, Syria, and Egypt, nationalist movements used a variety of approaches to get their point across. These ranged from simple entreaties and signature-gathering campaigns, on the one hand, to demonstrations, protests, strikes, boycotts, and sometimes even riots, on the other. The goal was to show France and Britain that attempting to retain control over their Middle East holdings was going to be an increasingly difficult endeavor—and that the costs of staying outweighed the benefits. In all of these cases, the approaches seemed to work. France and Britain came to the negotiating table and granted independence to these countries—all with little to no violence.

Nationalist movements in Tunisia and South Yemen faced comparatively stiffer resistance from France and Britain, respectively. In those cases, nationalist contests dragged on longer and involved more violent methods, including bombings and assassinations. By far the most bitter independence battle, however, took place in Algeria. France was willing to let go of Syria—a League of Nations mandate that it was officially obliged to prepare for independence—without too much of a fight after having been the mandatory power there for approximately a generation. But Algeria was a colony, not a mandate, and France had been in control there for well over a century. Algeria had been politically integrated into France, and tens of thousands of French citizens had settled there. When in the 1950s a nationalist party called the National Liberation Front (FLN) took shape, it met stiff French resistance. Algerian independence came in 1962, but only after a bloody, eight-year war that took some 700,000 lives.

In the wake of the physical departure of the imperial powers, however, the extent to which Middle Eastern countries were independent was debatable. Often, nominally independent states maintained political, economic, and military ties to their former masters. While this may seem counterintuitive—after all, there was a great deal of ill will and anger toward the Europeans—newly independent Middle East countries were often too weak to do otherwise. In some instances, they were simply unable to force Europeans to leave completely. For example, while Egypt technically became independent in 1936—becoming a member of the League of Nations that year—Britain still controlled Egyptian foreign policy and the Suez Canal. In other instances, leaders maintained those ties more voluntarily, understanding that they could benefit from ongoing political-military support from and trade relations with their former masters. The postindependence Iraqi regime, for example, received significant British military aid, equipment, and assistance, and allowed Britain to retain basing rights in the country. In Jordan, a British officer, Sir John Bagot Glubb, remained commander of the Jordanian army until 1957.

In many cases, these postindependence ties to European powers either endure to the present day or have been redrawn to the United States, which, with France and Britain exhausted at the end of World War II, rose to become the preeminent Western power and a pivotal external player in Middle East politics. Morocco, Tunisia, and Algeria maintained close political, economic, and cultural ties with France, for example. Jordan maintained close ties to Britain, but also cultivated increasingly strong links with the United States over time. Mohammad Reza Shah Pahlavi made Iran a key US political and military ally in the region. And in the Gulf, Saudi Arabia and the smaller Gulf states came to depend on the United States for security in the wake of the British departure.

In Syria, Egypt, and Iraq, however, lingering ties to European powers after independence did not survive the powerful domestic dissent they generated. In those societies a power struggle emerged that pitted conservative, established elites who had served France or Britain and presided over enduring ties to their former masters against a younger, "challenger" generation (often civil servants, workers, students, and peasants) who disagreed with conservative elites on a variety of issues. For example, while conservative elites were content with the economic status quo, challenger forces— often organized into socialist and communist parties—typically were pushing for land reforms, the nationalization of industry, and other redistributive policies designed to remedy what they felt was an intolerably skewed distribution of wealth in their societies. Challenger forces also strongly objected to conservative elites' enduring ties to Europe. For challengers, European imperialism was a humiliating chapter in the history of their nations, one they could not close the book on until those ties were broken. Such ties were especially difficult to stomach in the wake of British support for Zionism. When in 1948 Arab armies were humiliated by Israel, tensions reached a breaking point. Challenger forces blamed conservative elites for having failed to shepherd national economic, political, and military development in ways that would have allowed Arab states to stand truly independent and militarily victorious in the region.

What followed in Syria, Egypt, and Iraq was a series of coups that reoriented domestic politics and foreign policy for decades. For challenger forces, the task at hand was figuring out a way to oust conservative elites from power. While multiparty elections were being held during these years, conservative elites (rightly) felt threatened by challenger forces and either rigged elections sufficiently to ensure conservative victories or simply ignored their results if they were not favorable. Given that the electoral route to power was closed, the solution challengers often hit upon was the army—where officers and recruits often were sympathetic to challenger views and wielded the coercive power to overthrow the existing regime. Military coups unfolded in Syria in 1949, in Egypt in 1952, and in Iraq in 1958. The political systems established in their wake cut ties to the West, established ties with the West's Cold War rival, the Soviet Union, and pursued redistributive economic policies.

The Structure and Dispositions of "Founding" Regimes After Independence

What, then, did Middle East regimes or political systems look like, after all the dust had settled in the wake of the imperial powers' departure? Here our task is to understand the structure and basic policy orientations of "founding" regimes in the region—meaning the first set of stable, patterned, and lasting processes by which leaders were selected and how those leaders in turn exercised power. Regime-formation processes in the postimperial Middle East would sort countries into three basic categories: single-party dictatorships, monarchical dictatorships, and democratic (or semidemocratic) regimes.

Single-party systems. Political systems dominated by single, preponderant political parties emerged in Syria, Iraq, Egypt, Algeria, Tunisia, and South Yemen—all of which were republics ruled in dictatorial fashion by presidents. In most cases, presidents hailed from militaries, which had been key institutions of upward mobility for the lower classes. The political support of the military was a core anchor for these political systems. But preponderant, ruling political parties also served presidents in their exercise of power. These parties were massive, with systems of branches organized throughout these nations' territories as well as, often, in universities and workplaces. Presidents typically drew from party cadres to fill key positions in the bureaucracy in order to ensure that those in charge of implementing policy were loyal. Presidents also used these parties to distribute patronage (jobs and other material perquisites such as food, attractive terms for loans, etc.) to supporters, to socialize young people into the ideals of the regime, and to mobilize people into demonstrations of public support for the regime on important political occasions. Finally, presidents typically structured "elections" so that their ruling parties won either all or the vast majority of parliamentary seats—making parliaments rubber-stamp institutions.

These regimes adopted a state socialist economic development agenda. They used the power of the state to restructure and grow national economies: they nationalized numerous industries; they invested capital in industrialization campaigns; they implemented land reform programs that broke up the estates of large landholders and redistributed them to peasants; and they built massive state bureaucracies to guide and manage the economy and to deliver social welfare services to the masses. Their twin goals were to augment national power by building a thriving economic base and to see to it that all citizens—not just the elite—benefited.

The single-party dictatorships in the postimperial Middle East also subscribed to the ideals of pan-Arab nationalism as articulated by Egypt's president Gamal Abdel Nasser. He blamed the West for facilitating the emergence of Israel and for dividing Arabs into a number of artificial states after World War I. This weakened Arabs when, according to Nasser and many intellectuals in the region, Arabs in fact constituted their own nation and should have had their own comprehensive state. To restore Arab strength, and to return the whole of the Palestine Mandate to the Palestinians, the divisions wrought by European interference would need to be overcome, and

Arab political systems would need to be unified. How this would be accomplished in practice was never clear—and an experiment in Egyptian-Syrian union begun in 1958 ended in failure just three years later—but the ideals resonated among Arabs, whose hopes were raised that a renaissance of Arab power and dignity would soon be in the offing. As these single-party systems matured through the 1950s and 1960s, the Cold War was building into a crescendo of bipolar competition. With the United States evolving into Israel's most important ally, the Middle East's single-party regimes moved in the direction either of strategic neutrality or of alliance with the Soviet Union.

Monarchies. In the Middle Eastern monarchies—Saudi Arabia, Qatar, Kuwait, the UAE, Oman, Morocco, Jordan, and Iran—the right to rule stemmed not from elections but rather from claims about the legitimacy of specific families' indefinite monopoly on power. Depending on the country, such claims revolved around a family's historic role in founding the state (Saudi Arabia and Kuwait) and religious lineage (the royal families of several regional monarchies trace their ancestry back to the Prophet Muhammad, for example). In addition to such arguments about the legitimacy of family rule, royal families relied on a variety of other mechanisms for staying in power. Trusted individuals (often family members) headed up the army, the secret police, and the cabinet. And the oil-rich monarchies used portions of their wealth to provide their subjects with elaborate social welfare benefits (free schooling, health care, etc.) to bolster subjects' political loyalty.

Like the single-party dictatorships, Middle Eastern monarchies tended to pursue state-led economic development. The state took the lead in making investments and building industry. The (many) monarchies with oil wealth used a portion of that wealth to establish large public sectors and elaborate extensive social welfare services. Yet while the monarchies followed economic strategies similar to those of the single-party regimes, they did so without the populist and redistributionist ethos that often characterized the single-party cases. Neither did the monarchies subscribe to pan-Arab nationalist ideals. Iran was not an Arab country and thus was marginal to that discourse. The Arab monarchies were threatened by Arab nationalism, in part because in two of the states that advocated Arab nationalism most ardently, Egypt and Iraq, monarchs had been dethroned in very recent memory. In addition, the republican and socialist ethos of those regimes was anathema to traditional ruling royal families and their wealthy, elite political allies.

Thus, while Egypt, Syria, Iraq, and Algeria courted Soviet assistance during the Cold War years, Middle East monarchies tended to ally with the United States. For example, Iran under Mohammad Reza Shah Pahlavi

(1941–1979) became a US client in the Middle East, advancing US foreign policy objectives in the region and buying US military equipment. Resource-poor Jordan relied on the United States for economic assistance and security guarantees. And while the oil-rich monarchies didn't need US economic aid, they did rely on the United States for security guarantees. Rivalries between the Middle East's single-party dictatorships and monarchies thus constituted an important Cold War dynamic in the region.

Democratic and semidemocratic systems. When surveying founding regimes in the postimperial Middle East, in just three countries did citizens have the capacity to potentially vote incumbents out of office through elections: Israel, Turkey, and Lebanon. All three countries' structures featured a president (with Lebanon's and Turkey's having more constitutional authority relative to Israel's primarily ceremonial post) alongside a prime minister and cabinet constituted from an elected parliament. In all three countries, parliamentary elections were organized in such a way that parliaments reflected domestic constituencies in proportional fashion. Israel and Turkey had multiparty systems wherein parties gained parliamentary seats proportionate to the percentage of the vote share each won in elections. In Lebanon, electoral districts and seat allocation practices were designed to represent the country's myriad religious and sectarian groups. Israel and Lebanon were democratic, while significant military influence in politics made Turkey semidemocratic.

Israel and Turkey followed state-led economic development trajectories similar to those selected by single-party and monarchical regimes. In both Israel and Turkey during the 1950s, 1960s, and 1970s, the state played a major role in the economy—owning substantial assets and directing the priorities and pace of development. Lebanon, by contrast, was a regional exception during this time, in that it preserved a largely market economy during the heyday of state socialism in the 1950s, 1960s, and 1970s. In terms of foreign policy, Israel and Turkey were part of the Western "camp" during the Cold War—Turkey as part of the North Atlantic Treaty Organization (NATO) alliance, and Israel with its superpower backer, the United States. Lebanon was split between forces seeking to orient politics toward the West and others seeking to make Lebanon part of the pan-Arab nationalist fold; indeed, this divide was one of many stresses that sent Lebanon into fifteen years of civil war beginning in 1975.

The (Poor) Performance of Founding Regimes Through the Late 1970s

While state socialist economic development, Arab nationalism, and the confrontation with Israel dominated the rhetorical and policy landscape beginning in the 1950s, by the 1970s their collective failure had become evident.

State socialist economies did not produce economic growth and material prosperity over the long run for the Middle Eastern countries that adopted them. Instead, many countries faced bankruptcy and the need, beginning in the 1970s and 1980s, to radically restructure the way their economies functioned. Neither did pan-Arab nationalism produce its intended effects. Intra-Arab rivalries—including those between the conservative monarchies and the more radical single-party republics—undermined the dream of Arab unity and strength. The failure of pan-Arab nationalism was underlined—and the ideology discredited—when Arab states suffered another devastating loss to Israel in the 1967 Six Day War. Nearly two decades after Arab states had failed to vanquish the forces of the Jewish state in 1948, in the 1967 war Israel captured the Golan Heights from Syria, the West Bank and East Jerusalem from Jordan, and the Gaza Strip and Sinai Peninsula from Egypt.

These developments undermined the legitimacy of Middle Eastern regimes—especially the single-party republics. Many analysts have argued that Nasser and the leaders of other single-party states (Syria, Iraq, Algeria, etc.) had made an implicit bargain with their peoples in the 1950s that the regimes would provide their citizens with economic prosperity and victory over Israel—but not political participation, free elections, and accountable government. Now, with regimes failing to deliver on their part of this bargain, citizens in the Middle East became politically restive. Because the monarchies had promoted neither populism nor pan-Arab nationalism, they were not as jeopardized by their failure. Still, the resource-poor monarchies were in difficult economic straits. And *all* Arab monarchies' citizens saw themselves at least in part as Arabs rather than just simply as "Saudis" or "Kuwaitis." Arabs' inability to overcome Israel perplexed, demoralized, and led many (in monarchies and republics alike) to attempt to diagnose the roots of Arab weakness.

The Iranian Revolution and the Rise of Political Islam in the 1970s

With the region filled with politically dissatisfied citizens trying to discern the reasons Arab regimes failed to deliver, many settled on variations of one basic answer: that Arab governments and society had distanced themselves too much from the teachings and traditions of Islam. The Arab single-party regimes in particular, while paying lip service to Islam, were quite secular in outlook and practice. Meanwhile, Arab societies, especially their middle- and upper-class urban strata, had adopted Western, secular mores and popular culture—including with respect to ways of dressing, decorating, consuming, recreating, and relating to the opposite sex. To critics, these developments undermined Arabs' Islamic heritage, in turn corrupting and handicapping them in their quest for dignity, prosperity, and power. Such "Islamist" thinkers harkened back to the days when the Umayyads, Abbasids, and Ottomans—empires that explicitly incorporated Islam and Islamic law into the public sphere—were in their glory, reasoning that political success stemmed from Islamic foundations.

In countries across the Middle East, Islamic movements emerged. In the very influential Egyptian case we should really say that Islamic movements *re*emerged, because the Muslim Brotherhood—the region's first and still one of its most important movements—was founded there in 1928. Established by Hassan al-Banna, a schoolteacher who rejected British political, economic, and cultural penetration of Egypt, the Muslim Brotherhood sought to return Egyptians to more pious lifestyles through educational and charitable activities, with the long-run goals of liberating Egypt from European domination, reconstituting the Egyptian state according to sharia law, and pursuing social and economic development. Nasser outlawed the Muslim Brotherhood, but his successor, Anwar Sadat, allowed it to return to action in the late 1970s to counterbalance his leftist opponents. Egypt's Muslim Brotherhood inspired branches in Syria, Jordan, and Palestine. Similar movements appeared elsewhere, including Tunisia's Islamic Tendency Movement and Algeria's Islamic Salvation Front.

These movements received a considerable momentum boost in 1979 when, in Iran, Shiʻite cleric Ayatollah Ruhollah Khomeini brought down Mohammad Reza Shah Pahlavi by building a broad political coalition under the umbrella of politicized Islam. From the late 1950s through the 1970s, the Shah had presided over a secular, repressive, Westernizing dictatorship that was tightly allied with the United States, had diplomatic relations with Israel, and gravely mismanaged the Iranian economy despite that nation's considerable oil wealth. In making those choices, the Shah alienated numerous sectors of Iranian society. Khomeini deftly drew upon Islamic symbols and values to formulate a powerful critique of the Shah's regime, temporarily unify a wide variety of political factions, and move millions of everyday Iranians to protest the Shah's regime—at considerable personal risk—in wave after wave of massive demonstrations that ultimately wore down the will of the Shah's armed forces to resist. On January 16, 1979, the Shah left Iran and headed into exile. Khomeini returned to Iranian soil on February 1, 1979, and proceeded to build a new political system: the Islamic Republic of Iran.

Iran's Islamic Revolution sent a shock wave through the Middle East. For incumbents, the success of an oppositional Islamist movement was very bad news. For Islamists, the revolution supplied powerful encouragement that there was hope for their cause. Indeed, much of the "stuff" of domestic politics across the Middle East from the 1980s to 2011 pitted regimes against oppositional forces dominated by Islamist parties or movements.

The comparative strength of Islamist actors—vis-à-vis both incumbents and other oppositional groups—varied from country to country, as did the tactics Islamists espoused. Some groups chose violent trajectories and sought to directly overthrow incumbent regimes, while others rejected violence and bided their time, "working within the system" as they focused on building their influence in society and in the institutions of the state. With few exceptions, however, Islamists were—and are—a political force to be reckoned with, regionwide.

Economic Reform and Democratization Pressures

The rise of political Islam was not the only new reality in the Middle East in the 1970s. Regimes also confronted two additional phenomena that constrained rulers' options and put pressure on their positions. First, beginning in the late 1970s and continuing into the 1990s, nearly every Middle Eastern country had to reform its economy, decreasing the state's role and integrating with the global market economy. Countries have done this to varying degrees—and always reluctantly, because loans from the World Bank and the International Monetary Fund (IMF) designed to facilitate economic restructuring come with potentially politically destabilizing conditions attached, such as policy changes that may cause serious hardships for citizens at the same time that they deprive regimes of key tools of political influence and control. Second, also beginning in the late 1970s and continuing into the 1990s, a wave of democratizing regime change swept through Southern Europe, Latin America, the Soviet Union and Eastern Europe, and parts of Asia and sub-Saharan Africa. Everywhere, political freedom seemed to be on the march.

For the Middle East's mostly authoritarian incumbent rulers, a new global democratic ethos was unwelcome, as it served to further delegitimize regimes whose constituents were already discontented and who faced increasingly significant Islamist oppositions. Meanwhile, all rulers—democrats and dictators—struggled with painful economic reform processes and worried about how the "losers" would react politically. Yet in the face of these multiple pressures—from Islamists, economic reform, and global democratizing norms—incumbent authoritarian regimes survived for decades, employing a variety of political strategies. Leaders in oil-rich states distributed their largesse in ways that kept key clienteles loyal and muted socioeconomic grievances. Leaders in less wealthy states tended to combine real and systematic repression carried out by the intelligence and security services with "façade" democratization—licensing opposition parties and holding elections that looked competitive while in reality playing fields were very uneven and the positions candidates were elected to were devoid of actual power. Leaders also exploited the fears of many constituencies, both domestic and foreign, who worried about Islamists' power and what they would do with it if allowed to rule. Their argument essentially was, "better the devil you know."

The Arab Spring and Beyond

In December 2010, incumbent Arab authoritarian regimes began, for the first time, to be vulnerable. Massive, territory-wide, peaceful popular demonstrations in Tunisia were triggered by the self-immolation attempt of a desperate young man, Mohamed Bouazizi, and facilitated by labor activists and social media. These protests overwhelmed the security forces, and, when the Tunisian army refused to enter the fray on his side, President Zine el Abidine Ben Ali fled to Saudi Arabia. A single-party dictatorship erected in 1956 and sustained for 55 years by just two presidents had crumbled in one month's time. The Arab public watched this breathtaking turn of events on satellite television, and within weeks similar protests erupted across the region, expressing economic grievances while demanding more participatory and less corrupt governance.

By the end of 2011, when the dust began to settle, three dictators had fallen: Ben Ali in Tunisia, Husni Mubarak in Egypt, and Muammar Qaddafi in Libya. In each of these countries, the stuff of politics then shifted to the election of new, more representative assemblies that took up the herculean task of crafting new constitutions. In Yemen, protests forced President Ali Abdullah Salih to yield power to his vice president. Unlike Ben Ali, Mubarak, and Qaddafi, however, Salih remained part of the political game and a participant in an ensuing national dialogue as head of his political party, the General People's Congress. In the spring of 2010, Bahrain's monarchical regime violently repressed protesters—including with help from Saudi and Emirati forces—and during the ensuing years continued to confront persistent dissidence with arrests, detention, trials, and occasional violence. In Syria, protests precipitated a bloody and protracted civil war.

While in the spring of 2011 all Arab dictatorships seemed vulnerable, as of this writing nine (Algeria and all of the monarchies) appeared to have weathered the storm comparatively unscathed. These regimes were not passive in the face of regional protests. Saudi Arabia led the countercharge, suppressing its own dissidents, sending troops to Bahrain, brokering the agreement that eased Salih out of power in Yemen, and shoring up the poorer monarchies, Jordan and Morocco, with financial and political support. The Moroccan king appeared to have preempted more thoroughgoing political change by offering a set of constitutional amendments that liberalized—but by no means democratized—the monarchy, and then holding new elections. Still, the dictatorships that avoided collapse in the first two post–Arab Spring years nevertheless confronted a new political reality wherein

publics perceive authoritarian rule as less inevitable and less invulnerable—
and autocrats undoubtedly will be seeking new methods of shoring up their
regimes in the years to come.

Importantly, the Arab Spring's repercussions were not limited to Arab
states. In hindsight, mass protests in Iran following a fraudulent presidential
election in June 2009 may have been a precursor to the Arab Spring, and incumbent Iranian conservatives no doubt had the Arab Spring on their mind
as the 2013 presidential election approached. The fall of Mubarak in Egypt
and Ben Ali in Tunisia deprived Israel of two of its most moderate Arab in-
terlocutors while empowering Islamists with a more critical position vis-à-
vis the Jewish state. In mid-2011 Israel experienced its own set of serious
mass demonstrations, which saw economic grievances take center stage.
Meanwhile, the upheavals presented Turkey with diplomatic headaches as
it tried to manage the impact of political change on its commercial relationships with Arab states. At the same time, civil war in Syria meant that
Turkey (as well as other neighboring states) was burdened with a significant refugee flow as well as worries about resurgent Kurdish demands for
autonomy should the Syrian state fracture.

In a heady time, then, this book equips the reader with the general and
specific knowledge essential for making sense of contemporary Middle East
politics. Part 1 of the book contains seven chapters, one each on an essential
dimension of politics and society in the Middle East. These chapters provide
an overview of the patterns, trends, and dynamics that characterize the region as a whole, across a number of core topics. Chapter 2, "Governments
and Oppositions," analyzes the extent to which citizens can—or cannot—
hold their governments accountable through periodic, democratically meaningful elections and the alternation in power of multiple political parties.
Chapter 3, "The Impact of International Politics," offers a framework for
understanding how dynamics and pressures outside states' borders have
shaped the domestic politics of countries in the Middle East. Chapter 4,
"Political Economy," analyzes how states have tried to spur economic
growth and development, how politics has influenced the substance of economic decisions, and how economic realities in turn impact political dynamics and decisionmaking.

Chapter 5, "Civil Society," examines how citizens in countries of the
Middle East organize outside the explicitly political sphere for philanthropic purposes and to advance their political, economic, and social interests—as well as why and how the Middle East's mostly authoritarian regimes have sought to control, curtail, and contain such activities. Chapter 6,
"Religion and Politics," explores the three monotheistic faiths that emerged
in the Middle East, the extent to which states in the region are religious,
and the main forms of politicized religious activism in the region. Chapter
7, "Identity and Politics," considers how various types of attachments—to

religion, language, lineage, and geographic homeland—matter politically. Finally, Chapter 8, "Gender and Politics," looks at the ways that women's (and men's) roles in society have been constructed and contested in the Middle East.

Part 2 of the book builds on these thematic chapters by presenting eleven case studies of contemporary political dynamics in twelve of the region's twenty countries: Algeria, Egypt, Iran, Iraq, Israel, Jordan, Kuwait and the United Arab Emirates, Palestine, Saudi Arabia, Syria, and Turkey. Each of these chapters opens with a historical overview and description of the contemporary political structure of the country in question. Each then examines the seven arenas presented in Part 1 and explicates what specific dynamics animate each arena in each country case.

As the volume will illustrate, a number of key problems, dilemmas, and issues dominate politics in the contemporary Middle East. First, after decades of authoritarian rule, Tunisia, Egypt, and Libya are endeavoring to join Israel, Turkey, Lebanon, and Iraq in crafting political systems in which competitive electoral competition determines who rules. In all seven of these cases, to varying degrees, political actors confront the arduous task of writing, amending, and/or living up to constitutions that allow actors with very different political preferences to make decisions and resolve conflicts through the ballot box rather than via diktat or violence—an enormously difficult and complex political challenge. In the meantime, authoritarian rule persists through large swaths of the region. Where it does, those who rule and those who are ruled will continue to engage in political struggles that will determine the prospects for more participatory and accountable governance.

Second, central to understanding politics in the Middle East is the realization that citizens' self-identification with respect to language, lineage, place, and faith inform their political goals and tactics. These identities often divide political communities in ways that affect contests about the shape of politics. For example, across the Middle East's Muslim-majority states and also in Israel, actors debate whether political rules will be based on secular or religious principles. Until the Arab Spring uprisings, regional dictatorships tended to be quite secular but faced (and repressed) potent Islamist opposition movements; in many places, violent confrontations took place between the two. In the wake of the Arab uprisings, once-banned Islamist parties won elections in Egypt and Tunisia and assumed key roles in governance and the writing of new constitutions. Given the gulf in political perspectives deriving from very different identities, Islamist-secularist interactions and negotiations have been complex, heated, and difficult. Religious, sectarian, and ethnic divides complicate pluralist politics in similar ways in Lebanon and Iraq. In the meantime, many of the region's remaining dictatorships—including Bahrain, Algeria, and Saudi Arabia—discriminate

against sections of their populations whose political identities represent unwelcome challenges to the status quo.

Third, the Middle East faces daunting economic problems that influence political dynamics and are in turn affected by politics. Regime type
aside, the goal of generating prosperity that is broadly shared by citizens
has eluded even the richest of Middle East states in recent decades. Socioeconomic grievances were a key driver of Arab Spring protests, and newly
established governments will be judged in large part by whether and how
quickly they can chart a more prosperous course. Indeed the democratic vi-
ability of new regimes in Tunisia, Egypt, Libya, and (potentially) elsewhere
will depend heavily on economic factors. In the meantime, surviving autocrats have more reason than ever to worry about economic performance,
living standards, and unemployment.

Fourth, an important dilemma for the region's leaders and peoples is
how to relate to the West, and particularly the United States. European actors exercised imperial control over the region in the nineteenth and early
twentieth centuries, only to be overtaken by the United States as the major
Western hegemon after World War II. Today, Western countries are major
(and not always welcome) military players on the ground in the region at
the same time that they control the purse strings of global financial institutions and offer democracy as a political model—one that some aspire to and
others reject altogether. What the content of diplomatic relations with the
West should be and whether Middle East states adhere to Western policy
exhortations (regarding economics, family law, human rights, etc.) constitute extremely sensitive political issues that divide and antagonize political
parties and civil society actors.

All of these domains—the shape of political regimes, identity politics,
economic challenges, and regional relations with the West—help explain
women's status in the region and will continue to influence the outcomes of
struggles over gender norms. Significant intraregional variation notwithstanding, women in the Middle East participate in the labor force and political institutions at a far lower rate than do their male compatriots; regional
norms prescribe a primarily domestic role for women; and women's legal
rights in the area of family law are distinctly circumscribed. While for
many (male and female) this state of affairs is acceptable, others work to
achieve increased legal parity, economic autonomy, and political voice for
women.

While these dynamics and challenges animate politics in the region,
they are not unique to the Middle East. Indeed, they are on the political
agenda of nations throughout the non-Western world. Moreover, within the
Middle East there is a diversity of experience: rich states and poor states,
democracies and dictatorships, countries that have cooperative relationships
with the West and countries that vigorously confront the West, places where

women can't drive and a place where a woman has served as prime minister. This text helps readers navigate this "messy reality" to comprehend both broad patterns and trends in the Middle East as well as the diversity of experience that exists within the region.

Notes

1. Note that there are five additional Arabic-speaking countries not included in the Middle East as defined by this text, because their politics do not align with dominant patterns and trends in the region: Mauritania, Sudan, Somalia, Djibouti, and Comoros.

2. These characterizations of political rights and civil rights are adapted from Freedom House's methodology statement, available at http://www.freedomhouse.org.

Part 1

Contemporary Dynamics

2

Governments and Oppositions

Mona El-Ghobashy

The Arab Spring brought hundreds of thousands of citizens out into the streets to demand social justice, freedom, and democracy. They were calling for democracy in its most essential form: the ability of citizens to have a say in the decisions that affect their lives. But this commonsense notion of democracy is very difficult to translate into concrete practices. It means that citizens should be able to control governments, usually by participating in periodic elections. For most of human history, however, it has been governments that have controlled their subjects. Governments possess armed forces, essential information, and the control over state organizations that give them huge advantages over ordinary people. This was the situation in the Arab countries on the eve of the popular uprisings in winter 2010. Governments supported by international powers such as the United States controlled their countries' economic resources and political arenas, ensuring that domestic opposition did not threaten their hold on power.

Then, a small event in a small town in Tunisia set in motion a series of startling developments. A policewoman confiscated the cart of a twenty-six-year-old fruit vendor named Mohamed Bouazizi. When he went to the municipality to complain and retrieve his wares, he was barred from entering the building. He left and then returned and planted himself outside the municipality gates, doused his body with gasoline, and set himself on fire to protest how ordinary people like him are mistreated and then ignored by government officials. Bouazizi's plight resonated with his fellow townspeople and then with hundreds of thousands of Tunisians. Their protests led to a cascade of ever-larger demonstrations that spread from various Tunisian cities to the capital, Tunis, and from there to the provincial cities and capitals of Egypt, Libya, Yemen, Algeria, Morocco, Jordan, Syria, and Bahrain. A people's uprising had begun, demanding more representative governments and a fairer distribution of national wealth. At the heart of the protests was the unified demand for an end to dictatorial governments and the start of a new era in which citizens get to choose their governments and then keep an eye on them through peaceful, legal opposition parties.

This chapter takes up the issue of how citizens come to control their governments, especially in circumstances where governments historically had the upper hand, neither representing nor serving the people. Elections have become the primary method by which citizens choose their rulers, returning them to office if they serve their interests and removing them from office when they do not. What's more, during the time when elected officials are in office, they're kept in check by legislatures, opposition parties, and an independent press, all of which make it their business to monitor the behavior of the government to ensure that officials do not abuse their power. In all of the countries in the Middle East, including the non-Arab states of Israel, Turkey, and Iran, politics revolves around the struggle to keep governments honest and accountable, both through free and fair elections and through the creation of legal opposition political parties.

Distinguishing Among Three Key Political Science Concepts

State: The permanent organizations of bureaucracy, the military and police forces, the legislature, the judiciary, taxation structures, economic regulation agencies, communication agencies (e.g., postal services and railways), penal institutions, and so forth.

Government: The group of people who control and manage state organizations. Governments attain power in a variety of ways—through popular election, selection by a narrow elite, military coup, or hereditary rule—depending on the kind of relations they establish with the societies they rule.

Regime: The set of rules for determining how key public offices are filled. These rules are determined by governments through bargaining and struggle with opposition groups, societal interest groups, and even international actors, including foreign governments. Regimes can be democratic, nondemocratic, or somewhere in between.

The Idea and Practice of Opposition

The democratic idea that people should choose who governs them is an ancient notion, but the practice is fairly recent. For most of human history, people had no say in who ran the political community they lived in. Even rarer is the practice of a government accepting opposition as a regular and protected feature of the political system. As political scientist Robert Dahl noted, "The fact that a system of peaceful and legal opposition by political parties is a comparative rarity means that it must be exceedingly difficult to *introduce* such a system, or to *maintain* it, or both" (1966: xiv, emphasis in original). If we assume that government officials seek to maintain their hold on power and minimize opposition, what would give rise to tolerated opposition parties? And how do such parties survive and become an accepted feature of a country's political life?

It seems reasonable to posit that governments would tolerate opposition only if they are compelled to do so. One circumstance in which governments may feel so compelled is when they recognize that in order to get things done, they need the cooperation of a broad segment of the population. Take the issue of taxation. All governments need taxes to fund public works projects such as roads and bridges and to underwrite massive ventures such as wars and systems of national defense. To induce people to pay taxes, governments need the consent of the governed; otherwise they risk antitax revolts or revolutions. Consent cannot be given orally or informally; instead, it must be hammered out within permanent institutions. Enter legislatures, the formal place where government officials bargain with representatives of the people over the terms of taxation. Hence the famous phrase from the American revolution: no taxation without representation. The process of negotiations over taxation and other major public policies is one concrete example of governments conceding the need for societal participation to get things done.

How does opposition come into play? Legislatures house representatives of the citizenry who negotiate on its behalf, but they are also places where critics of government performance bide their time until the next elections, when they can make a bid to become the government. Thus, opposition parties are not just groups of people who oppose the government. Their main goal is to win the public's confidence through elections and to become the government. The key idea is for different parties to *compete* before the public for the prize of exercising government power. Voters are the arbiters, choosing which of the competing groups will get to assume public office for a set term (usually four or five years). The party that wins the public's vote becomes the government while the party that loses moves into the ranks of legislative opposition until the next round of elections. Rotating government power in this way ensures that no single group captures state organizations and uses them to benefit only its supporters and clients.

It turns out that rotating political power—while desirable in theory—is very difficult to implement in practice. It took centuries of protracted crises, civil wars, and revolutions for today's advanced democracies to become countries where power changes hands peacefully and regularly via elections. As political sociologist Charles Tilly wrote, "Over the past few centuries of Western history, for example, whole clusters of regimes underwent a momentous shift from millennia of being simply unavailable for democratic change to frequent oscillation between democratization and de-democratization" (2007: 17). Thus, even when a political system reaches the point of peaceful, regular transfer of power, there is no guarantee that it will remain there. Democratization is not a one-way street. It can be reversed, especially if a party refuses to abide by the rules of the game and decides to monopolize governmental power indefinitely. In the Middle East, on the eve of the Arab Spring uprisings, the majority of countries suffered from a monopoly hold on government power by a single leader and his family and cronies. They used this power to enrich themselves while the impoverished majority like Mohamed Bouazizi led hardscrabble lives, with no opportunities for political participation.

Clearly, elections are important for the distribution and rotation of power. But how can we tell if an election is free and fair? How do we know if elections are moments of real competition between rival parties? After all, it's easy for rulers to hold elections and then manipulate them so thoroughly that incumbents can never be defeated at the polls. In fact, all over the world leaders have so frequently manipulated elections and other ostensibly democratic instruments such as parliaments and constitutions that political scientists have coined a special term for such political systems: *electoral authoritarian regimes* (Schedler 2002). These are political systems that have regular elections, but the function of elections is to thwart rather than deepen democratization.

How is it possible that elections can subvert democracy instead of advancing it? Scholars have tracked the diverse tactics used by autocratic leaders to game elections so thoroughly that they can never lose. Among other tricks, rulers design electoral rules that discriminate against the opposition (Robinson 1998; Posusney 2002); write vast powers for themselves into the constitution (Brown 2002); and purposely structure elections in ways that make opposition forces appear weak and hapless in front of the public (Schmitter 1978). Steven Heydemann summarized these tactics as employed in the Arab world with the pithy phrase "authoritarian upgrading" (Heydemann 2007). He points out that Arab rulers were not cartoonish dictators who simply repressed their opposition. Over time, they upgraded outdated forms of dictatorship with smarter, more efficient versions of autocratic control using elections.

Since elections are so easily manipulated to ornament autocratic rule, it's crucial to be able to discern whether any given election, anywhere, is really democratic. Remember that the key to meaningful elections is that government power changes hands periodically and peacefully. Different groups of people ought to take turns being in power, so that no single group entrenches its dominance and monopolizes the political arena. To be even more concrete, political scientists have developed a four-part litmus test to assess the democratic significance of an election (Przeworski et al. 1996):

1. Can incumbent parties lose the election?
2. If so, would the winners be allowed to form a government?
3. Would the winners be able to govern (i.e., make and change laws)?
4. Would elections be repeated?

If you think about these four questions carefully, they all get at the same concern: Is there some entrenched power bloc behind the scenes that distorts elections and prevents the periodic transfer of power? This is all-important since, as we've seen, elections can be staged to give the appearance of competition while the outcome is predetermined and the ruler(s) can never lose. By asking if dominant parties can lose and challenger parties can govern, the questions appraise whether elections really are the currency of political power, or whether they're a sideshow and power is actually concentrated in the hands of irremovable, unaccountable individuals.

Governments and Oppositions in the Middle East and North Africa

Before considering how elections in the contemporary Middle East fare under our criteria, let's take a closer look at the political lay of the land. What types of political systems exist in the region? To what extent can opposition parties form and contest the conduct of the government, and what are their chances of having a go at *being* the government? The region's political systems can be classified into three main types: republics led by presidents and/or prime ministers; monarchies ruled by kings; and the hybrid system of Iran, which is led by both a president and a high-ranking Shi'a cleric (ayatollah), a very powerful figure dubbed "the Leader" in Iran's constitution.

Historically, republics such as Tunisia, Algeria, Libya, Egypt, Yemen, Syria, and pre-2003 Iraq all were governed by powerful presidents who often rose from humble social backgrounds to the summit of political power through service in the military or police forces. The presidents consolidated their rule through tight control over two principal organizations: the armed forces and a single ruling party that dominated the political scene. Ruling parties performed a variety of crucial functions and explain why many of these presidents remained in power for years on end. Using their control over government resources, presidents used single parties as a patronage delivery system that distributed jobs, money, import licenses, and a host of other perks to cronies and their constituents. Ruling-party branches were spread out over the country to monitor the population, recruit young people to fill the party's ranks, and provide a space where ambitious party cadres could compete with each other to rise through party ranks and gain access to the president's inner circle.

During national legislative elections, ruling parties swung into action, ensuring that opposition parties did not make significant gains at the ballot box. Ruling-party cadres organized campaign rallies for the party's candidates, bought off voters with cash or foodstuffs, and faced off with popular opposition-party candidates in the streets and at the polling booth to maintain the party's crucial majority in parliament. Ruling-party legislators were the president's eyes and ears within parliament, controlling the post of parliamentary speaker, ensuring the smooth passage of all bills proposed by the president, and standing up to opposition legislators if they attempted to block legislation or assert their oversight role over the government.

Presidents in Tunisia, Egypt, Algeria, Syria, and Yemen even put themselves up for election in stage-managed contests with handpicked challengers. In 2004, Tunisia's president Zine el-Abidine Ben Ali extended his seventeen years in power by an election where he netted 94.49 percent of votes. Presidents engaged in such elaborate spectacles to legitimize their prolonged hold on power and claim broad popular acclaim for their rule. The ruling parties were indispensable on these occasions as well, organizing massive campaign rallies for the incumbent, orchestrating promotional appearances for him in the government-controlled media, and preventing independent monitors from observing the balloting on the ground to mask fraud, rigging, and voter intimidation. Finally, presidents frequently amended their countries' constitutions to prolong their rule, acts made possible by their ruling parties' majorities in parliament. For example, in 2000, Syria's constitution was amended to lower the minimum age for the president from 40 to 34, the age of current president Bashar al-Asad when he inherited the post after the death of his father Hafiz al-Asad.

As was noted in Chapter 1, the Arab Spring uprisings altered politics drastically in several of the region's republics. Dictatorial presidents fell in Tunisia, Libya, Egypt, and Yemen, while Syrian president Bashar al-Asad's determination to cling to power regardless of the cost plunged that country into a prolonged civil war. Tunisia, Libya, and Egypt went on to hold strikingly free and competitive elections for new assemblies and/or leaders to guide those countries through complex and uncertain transitions away from what had been long-standing authoritarian regimes. While hopes were high that democratic systems might be erected and sustained in their stead, as of this writing much uncertainty surrounds what their ultimate political trajectories will be. What *is* clear, though, is that the region's republics today are a much more heterogeneous group of countries—ranging from quite authoritarian (e.g., Algeria) to reasonably democratic (e.g., Tunisia, for now).

Moving on from the republics, one of the most striking facts about the Middle East is the presence of eight monarchies. The survival of monarchies in the Middle East is a puzzle because monarchs who actually rule and not simply reign have otherwise become extinct in the contemporary world. Yet, far from being antique holdovers from a traditional age, Arab monarchies are quite modern in their origins and their techniques of rule. Arab would-be kings first gained a foothold on power by forming alliances with the British and French colonial states that wielded enormous power in the Middle East during the late nineteenth and early twentieth centuries. Indeed, the monarchies of Saudi Arabia and Jordan would scarcely have retained their power had they not been sponsored and supported first by the British and then by the US governments. The one exception is the Moroccan monarchy, which has ruled the country since 1649.

When they were anointed, the monarchs built and sustained their hold on power using the "authoritarian upgrading" strategies identified by Heydemann. But there is one key difference in how monarchs manage the political arena as compared to the autocratic presidents of republics. Instead of establishing a large ruling party to dominate the political arena and win elections over and over again, monarchs often encourage pluralism among social groups and political parties, promoting ethnic, regional, and religious diversity. These "linchpin monarchies" (Lucas 2004), as in Morocco and Jordan, construct the position of the king as the essential node that holds the system together, standing above all societal divisions, protecting religious or ethnic minorities, and uniting the nation.

This familiar strategy of divide and rule is coupled with ideologies emphasizing the monarchies' noble origins in a storied past. Members of the Kuwaiti Al Sabah dynasty, rulers of Kuwait for over 200 years, underscore that their rule is responsible for the country's sovereign independence from the Iraqi threat (Herb 1999: 159). The Jordanian monarchy claims descent from the Prophet Muhammad, asserting on its official website: "Direct descendants of the Prophet Muhammad, the Hashemite family is a unifying factor interwoven into the life of modern Jordan."[1] By contrast, the Saudi monarchy does not claim descent from the Prophet but emphasizes instead its services to Islam: the Sauds title themselves "Custodians of the Holy Places," referring to the Muslim pilgrimage cities of Mecca and Medina. The Sauds also stress the exceptional qualities of Abdul Aziz al-Saud, who united the Arabian Peninsula and proclaimed the Kingdom of Saudi Arabia in 1932, citing his "shrewdness, courage, farsightedness and horseman-ship."[2] As with all founding myths of modern governments, the monarchies' official ideologies are best analyzed as instruments of rule rather than accepted as statements of fact.

The Islamic Republic of Iran is a hybrid system where political power is divided between elected politicians in the presidency and parliament and indirectly elected clerics such as the Leader and the powerful institution of the Guardian Council. The twelve clerics on the Guardian Council vet all candidates for presidential and parliamentary candidates, often disqualifying opposition candidates. Clerics must also approve all bills passed by parliament, and have the power to block bills if they consider them inconsistent with the constitution and Islamic law. In this way, the scope of political competition is significantly limited to groups approved by self-appointed clerical gatekeepers.

Beyond the republic–monarchy–Islamic Republic distinction, another major difference among the region's political systems is the extent to which they allow organized opposition parties to form and participate in honest elections. The two countries with the most well-developed competitive multiparty systems are Israel and Turkey. Israel's is a parliamentary democracy with a relatively large number of political parties. Of the 120 seats in the Israeli parliament (Knesset), 61 are required to form a government. Since 1948 when Israel was founded, no political party has secured the full 61 seats, and thus elections have instead produced coalition governments composed of several political parties. From 1948 to 1977, Israel was a "dominant-party democracy," where the same large party (the left-wing Labor Party) repeatedly won elections and led coalition governments. This changed in 1977 when the right-wing Likud party displaced the Labor party as the winner, making Israeli politics more competitive by inaugurating the practice of power rotation between different parties. Turkey has had a competitive multiparty parliamentary democracy since 1950, with political parties of various ideologies taking turns running government, often in coalition as in Israel. Until recently, Turkish politics had long been constrained by the interventionist stance of the military, which aborted the democratic process three times, in 1960, 1971, and 1980. The role of the military as an unelected veto player will be discussed further in the next section.

Before the 2011 uprisings, in none of the Arab countries could citizens choose their governments, much less control them. Both Arab kings and presidents thoroughly monopolized their countries' political systems, permitting some opposition parties while banning others, and ensuring that the tolerated opposition parties never threatened their hold on power. The leaders' monopoly on the political system was so complete that several Arab presidents were grooming their sons to succeed them as president in stage-managed elections. Syria's Hafiz al-Asad started the trend shortly before he died in 2000, and Husni Mubarak (Egypt), Muammar Qaddafi (Libya), Saddam Hussein (Iraq), and Ali Abdullah Salih (Yemen) were marching in al-Asad's footsteps before the US invasion in 2003 toppled Hussein and the popular insurrections of 2011 toppled the other presidents. The absence of any meaningful opportunities to replace the government via elections or even make the existing government responsive to the public is one reason why armed opposition groups developed in the region. In Egypt, an armed insurgency formed against the rule of Mubarak in 1992 that he eventually crushed in 1997. In Algeria, when the military canceled elections in 1992, insurgents took up arms and fought government forces in a full-scale civil war.

Today, in the wake of the Arab Spring, the status of opposition still varies from country to country. To give you a sense of the spectrum, 2011 elections in Tunisia, Egypt, and Libya saw a wide range of political parties given the freedom to compete in elections. Jordan and Morocco, on the other hand, have semi-opposition parties that are neither fully repressed nor fully empowered. And a handful of countries such as Saudi Arabia, Qatar, and the United Arab Emirates (UAE) blatantly ban all political parties. As the next section will demonstrate, the quality and competitiveness of elections also varies widely across Arab countries as well as within the same country over time—such as in Egypt and Tunisia before and after the toppling of their autocrats in the winter of 2011.

Iran is a very interesting halfway house between the cases of Turkey and Israel on the one hand and the (historically) noncompetitive Arab states on the other. Before 1979, Iran was ruled by a shah or king whom the people did not choose and could not replace. The Shah outlawed nearly all forms of opposition, which drove some of his opponents underground into armed groups (Abrahamian 1980). A spectacular popular revolution developed against the Shah's despotism in 1978–1979 and drove him out of Iran, establishing a new political system that marginally increased the Iranian people's ability to choose their government. Iranians simultaneously do and do not elect their leaders. This is because government power is divided between elected lay politicians (the president and members of parliament) and indirectly elected clerics. As Chapter 11 on Iran shows, the political system is quite complex, because the people elect the clerics who in turn choose the Leader and other important clerical decisionmakers. The intricate patchwork of institutions that make up the Iranian state means there's a built-in, constant tension between elected officials, such as the president, and indirectly elected officials, such as the Leader. Unlike Arab citizens before 2011, Iranian citizens are able to oppose and change some of their leaders and are now struggling to change the rules so that they can choose all of their leaders.

Elections in the Middle East and North Africa

Now that we have a sense of the structure of political power in the region's countries, let's take a closer look at the quality of regional elections by subjecting them to the four-part litmus test used in this chapter (see Table 2.1).

It might come as a surprise to learn that even before the Arab uprisings, all of the region's countries held some form of elections. Saudi Arabia used to be the holdout, until it began holding municipal elections in 2005 and gave women the right to run and vote in the next municipal elections, scheduled for 2015. Still, it matters whether or not a country has full-suffrage elections for a *national*-level legislature. One strategy of electoral authoritarianism is to have elections only for municipal bodies, so that incumbents can monopolize both executive and law-making powers at the national level. Refer to Table 2.1 and note that all of the region's countries have held national-level elections except three: Saudi Arabia, Qatar, and the UAE. Even within these three cases there are differences. In Saudi Arabia, there is a national legislature called the Consultative Council, but its 150 members are appointed by the Saudi king. In Qatar, there are only municipal elections, and in the UAE, there are elections to a national legislature, but the electorate is narrow and selected by the rulers of each of the seven emirates.

At this juncture it is crucial to point out that elections are not the only means of doing politics in the Middle East. Refer to the second column of Table 2.1 and note that in Syria, Libya, Yemen, Lebanon, Iraq, and Palestine various forms of political violence are also a prevalent feature of domestic politics. Political reputations and the distribution of power are determined not only at the ballot box but also in armed conflict between the government and insurgents, or between rival militias, or between a fledgling government and an occupation force as in the West Bank and Gaza Strip. Thus, for our purposes here it will be useful to add a fifth question to the four posed previously: Are elections the *only* currency of politics? If they are not, and if foreign armies and/or domestic insurgents or militias figure prominently in politics, the democratic significance of elections clearly is tempered. One way to think about the development of democracy is the extent to which political violence is minimized in a society over time. Political violence is never fully expunged from any political system, but in democratic states, armed conflict is reconfigured such that major policies and issues are decided by peaceful if hard bargaining between rival political parties—rather than by bullets.

Can Incumbents Lose Elections?

To assess the democratic significance of any given election, the first and most important question that must be asked is: Can ruling parties lose elections?

Table 2.1 The Democratic Significance of Elections in the Middle East

	Are Full-Suffrage National Legislative Elections Held?	Are Such Elections the Only Currency of Politics?	Can Incumbents Lose Elections?	Can (Nonincumbent) Winners Form Governments?	Can Elected Governments Actually Govern?	Are Elections Repeated at Regular Intervals?
Israel	✓	✓	✓	✓	✓	✓
Turkey	✓	✓	✓	✓	✓	?
Tunisia	✓	✓	✓	✓		?
Egypt	✓	✓	✓	✓	Military	✓
Morocco	✓	✓	✓	✓	Monarch	✓
Iran	✓	✓	Until 2009	Until 2009	Clerics	✓
Kuwait	✓	✓	✓			✓
Algeria	✓	✓				✓
Bahrain	✓	✓				✓
Jordan	✓	✓				✓
Oman	✓	✓				✓
UAE	✓					
Qatar	✓					
Saudi Arabia						
Iraq	✓	Insurgency	✓	✓	✓	✓
Lebanon	✓	Militias	✓	✓	✓	✓
Libya	✓	Militias	✓	✓	✓	?
Syria	✓	Civil war				?
Yemen	✓	Militias, insurgency	?	?	?	?
West Bank	✓	Occupation	?	?	?	?
Gaza Strip	✓	Occupation	?	?	?	?

For elections to be considered serious, the group of people who govern must be able to be unseated if they have lost the public's confidence. Otherwise, if elections are held but power-holders never lose despite widespread political discontent, then polls serve as grand spectacles that project the government's power rather than meaningful procedures that allow citizens to choose their governments. Elections-as-spectacle are precisely what many former Arab presidents engaged in. In 1989, Tunisia's then president Zine el-Abidine Ben Ali staged elections in which he won 99 percent of the vote and his party, the RCD, won all 141 seats in parliament. Such contests, in which opposition parties have no real chance of winning due to government manipulation, can be thought of as opportunities for the rulers to flaunt their power rather than occasions for citizens to choose their rulers.

The third column in Table 2.1 shows that roughly half of the countries that hold elections meet this criterion of incumbent parties losing. A defining moment in Middle East politics when a dominant party lost elections and gave up power peacefully occurred in Turkey in 1950, when the Republican People's Party lost to the opposition Democrat Party, ending the hegemony of the party established by the founder of republican Turkey, Mustafa Kemal Atatürk. A second such defining moment was in 1977 in Israel, when the dominant Labor party lost to the rising Likud party, established just four years earlier.

In Iran, the 1997 presidential election was important because it was the first time that the candidate favored by the Leader lost. The relatively unknown reformist Mohammad Khatami won with 70 percent of the vote in an election that saw 80 percent turnout (the previous presidential election had only 50 percent turnout). This presidential election upset was followed by more victories for upstart reformists, who captured 75 percent of the vote in local elections in 1999, 80 percent of the vote in parliamentary elections in 2000, and a second term for Khatami as president with 80 percent of the vote in 2001 (Abrahamian 2008: 188). Eight years later in 2009, perhaps seeking to avoid a reprise of the Khatami phenomenon, Leader Ali Khamenei and other conservative clerics in Iran's government blocked the popular reformist presidential candidate, Mir-Hossein Mousavi, from winning by actively working for the victory of their favored candidate, incumbent Mahmoud Ahmadinejad. The maneuver led to massive street demonstrations and the formation of the Green Movement as an oppositional social movement.

Iran in 2009 is not the only example of incumbent leaders refusing to lose elections. Perhaps the most famous case in the Middle East is that of Algeria in 1991–1992, an instance where that nation's first competitive legislative elections were aborted altogether when an opposition party was poised to win. After gaining independence from France in 1962, Algeria had a one-party political system that banned opposition parties. This changed in 1989 when massive popular protests against unemployment and inflation compelled Algeria's leaders to legalize multiple political parties and allow opposition parties to contest elections. An Islamist party called the Islamic Salvation Front (FIS) captured 55 percent of the vote in local elections in 1990 and 47 percent of the vote in the first round of the parliamentary elections in 1991. The FIS was poised to get an absolute majority of seats in the legislature in a second round of voting, but the military quickly stepped in, canceled the elections, and banned the FIS. Civil war between the military-led government and armed insurgent offshoots of FIS then broke out, lasting ten years and claiming 150,000 lives. The case of Algeria demonstrates the lengths to which some incumbents will go to avoid being unseated in elections.

Can (Nonincumbent) Electoral Victors Form Governments?

It seems counterintuitive, but winning an election is no guarantee that the victorious party will actually get to form a government, that is, appoint cabinet ministers—or, if the country has a parliamentary system, seat a prime minister from the winning party. Refer to the fourth column of Table 2.1. The case of the constitutional monarchy of Kuwait is interesting here. Since its independence from Britain in 1962, the country has possessed the Gulf's most politically assertive parliament, elected in robust national elections. The fifty-member parliament has the power to vote cabinet ministers out of office, including the prime minister, but does not have the ability to appoint the government, a prerogative claimed by the ruling Al Sabah dynasty. Since 2006, the elected parliament has been locked in battle with the Kuwaiti emir over the right to fill top cabinet positions, a battle that has seen the resignation of nine governments. The struggle has spilled out into massive street demonstrations that peaked in November 2011, when 50,000 demonstrators demanded the resignation of the prime minister (a nephew of the emir). In a sign of the increasing influence of both parliamentary opposition and youth-led social movements, the emir acceded to the protesters' demands and replaced the prime minister with another member of the royal family. But that did not appease the opposition, which is not backing down from its core demand to appoint the government. As Kristian Coates Ulrichsen observes, "The gloves have now come off on both sides, with the rising tide of opposition demanding nothing short of an elected government and a game-changing end to Al Sabah dominance of executive power" (2012b).

Can Elected Governments Actually Govern?

The protracted power struggle in Kuwait reveals a fundamental dynamic of democratization: struggles between elected and unelected branches of government. Recall the theme of this chapter, how citizens come to control their government. We know that elections are one means by which citizens control governments, by choosing the people who exercise government power and holding them to account. But what about powerful institutions of government that are not elected, such as monarchs, judiciaries, clerics, and militaries? In theory, elected branches of government serve as watchdogs over these unelected institutions, but what happens when the unelected parts of the government control the elected parts?

This is the problem addressed by the third criterion of our four-part litmus test. Refer to the fifth column of Table 2.1 and observe how rare it is for elected governments to actually be able to govern in the Middle East and North Africa. Why should this be? Remember that the underlying point of the four criteria is to identify whether or not entrenched, unelected power blocs subvert the purpose of elections. We can imagine a scenario where elections are held, incumbents lose, winners are congratulated and even allowed to form a government, yet their efforts are swiftly short-circuited or their ability to govern is seriously circumscribed by powerful unelected institutions or elites. Let's consider this dynamic of antidemocratic obstruction according to the type of elite that intervenes.

One familiar culprit is a politicized military elite that puts itself above the political fray but seeks to control the normal political process so that it always has the last word. Since canceling elections altogether—as the Algerian military did in 1992—is costly and incurs domestic and international condemnation, military generals who don't like the results of elections sometimes pursue more subtle means of intervention. One tactic is to let an election run its course, allow the winners to form a government, but then manipulate events to force the government out of office. This is what happened in Turkey in 1997. As Chapter 19 on Turkey shows, the military high command engaged in a "postmodern" coup. Rather than deploy tanks to oust the elected prime minister Necmettin Erbakan, the generals compelled him to adopt unpopular policies that eventually forced him to step down. Soon after, the promilitary Constitutional Court closed Erbakan's Welfare Party. The unelected parts of the Turkish government colluded to overturn the will of voters, because the party chosen by the electorate threatened the interests of entrenched state elites. The situation in Turkey is very different today. Since 2002, elected governments have steadily reduced the prerogatives of the military in the political arena and successfully passed constitutional amendments to roll back military interference.

A meddling military has yet more tricks up its sleeve to limit the reach of elected branches of government. It can allow an opposition party to win elections and form a government, but it can then "fence off" particular policy areas and government positions from oversight by elected officials. This is what political scientist Samuel Valenzuela calls creating "reserve domains" and "reserve positions" (1990). After Egypt's uprising, Egyptian military generals pursued these tactics when they realized that they could not rig the 2012 presidential elections the way their former leader Husni Mubarak had. Soon after polls closed on June 17, 2012, the generals issued a decree that stated that declaring war and appointing constitution-writers was their domain, not the elected president's, and that the minister of defense would be a position reserved for one of their own, not a civilian presidential appointee. Egyptian politics looked set to be a military-managed affair until the newly elected president, Mohamed Morsi, turned the tables on the generals a couple of months later and wrested back presidential powers. This will not be the end of the struggle within the Egyptian state between elected and unelected components, as each tries to amass for itself as much power as it can.

It is not only military generals who seek to limit the reach of elected officials. Monarchs too are very wary of elected parliaments and their demands to appoint and dismiss cabinet officials, as we have seen in the case of Kuwait. Thus, kings wall off sensitive government positions from control by elected bodies. A pertinent case here is Morocco, where King Mohammed VI hastily organized constitutional reforms and presided over parliamentary elections in 2011 to avoid the diffusion of regional protest fever to his country. Under the new constitution, the king relinquished his sacred status and agreed to pick a prime minister from the majority party in parliament. In the November 2011 legislative elections, the Islamist Justice and Development Party won the election and its chief was duly asked by the king to form a government. But with that same constitution, King Mohammed VI reserved for himself key policy domains and positions, retaining control of the religious establishment, the military, and the security services, as well as veto power over all ministerial appointments. All laws must still be confirmed by the king (Lust 2011). It will be interesting to observe whether the new opposition-led Moroccan parliament will follow the example of its Kuwaiti counterpart, link up with the youth-led protest movement, and begin to demand more powers from the king—or whether Mohammed VI has successfully stabilized his control over Morocco with the 2011 constitutional reforms and elections.

Somewhat more unusual is interference by clerics in the workings of elected governments. The relevant case here is Iran. Unlike Turkey's and Egypt's military generals, who intervened in the democratic process *after* elections brought to power political parties that threatened their interests, Iran's clerics control key steps *before* elections. For example, in the 2004 parliamentary elections, to avoid a repeat of the 2000 elections when reformists won 195 of 290 of Majles (parliament) seats, clerics disqualified 2,300 candidates out of more than 8,000 (Tezcür 2008: 58). In effect, Iran's clerics control both the input and output sides of elections, controlling who runs in elections and, for good measure, also having the final say on laws

that elected bodies produce. The Leader has vast reserve domains, appointing the heads of the judiciary, the armed forces and police, radio and television, prayer leaders in city mosques, and the Supreme National and Security Council. It is no surprise that the dynamics of contemporary Iranian
politics revolve around the struggle for freer and fairer electoral rules, as a
pathway into the longer-term struggle to empower elected branches of the
Iranian government over its unelected parts.

One of the most unusual and dramatic instances where an opposition
party won general elections, formed a government, but was prevented from
governing was in early 2006, when the Palestinian militia–cum–political
party–cum–social welfare organization Hamas defeated the dominant
standard-bearer of Palestinian politics, Fatah. The upset was particularly dramatic because Hamas had never before participated in national legislative
elections, having rejected them as a charade of the Oslo Peace Process, which
it had taken up arms to oppose. The obstructing actors here were not military
generals, monarchs, or clerics threatened by an opposition party coming to
power but rather a coalition of powerful international powers that had supported the losing incumbent Fatah party. The governments of the United
States, Israel, and the European Union boycotted the Hamas government for
its refusal to recognize Israel and give up its armed wing, depriving it of the
international aid on which the Palestinian Authority government had historically relied. To further strangle the fledgling government, Israel withheld
Palestinian tax revenues, resulting in widespread discontent among 150,000
state employees (including doctors, teachers, and security personnel) who
received only half their salaries in 2006. Power-sharing agreements between
the losing Fatah party and Hamas failed, and a civil war ensued that split the
Palestinian Authority into a Fatah-controlled Palestinian National Authority
in the West Bank and a Hamas government in the Gaza Strip.

The case of the 2006 Palestinian legislative elections and that of the
1991 Algerian elections illustrate the lengths to which entrenched powers
will go to reverse the outcomes of democratic elections, even if the cost is
a debilitating civil war. The ability of citizens to choose their governments
unsettles established networks of power and influence and upends existing
hierarchies. It is no surprise that incumbent elites do everything possible to
limit the transformative potential of democratic elections.

Are Elections Repeated at Regular Intervals?

The fourth and last criterion for democratic elections is that they are repeated at regular intervals (see the sixth column of Table 2.1). To consider
a political system meaningfully democratic, elections must be held at regular intervals and not be subject to cancellation or delay by incumbents. All
eyes, therefore, are on the Arab Spring countries of Tunisia, Egypt, and

Libya to see whether their first democratic elections in 2011–2012 will be repeated after the writing of new constitutions, or whether vestiges of the old rigged and limited elections will return.

Why does repeatability matter? In the same way that unelected power holders can game the workings of elections to their liking, they can also decide to delay or suspend elections at whim, so it is especially important for the electoral process to be fully transparent and organized at regular intervals. Elections lose meaning as means of popular control over government if their scheduling is opaque or erratic. For example, Jordan's King Hussein postponed general elections from 1967 to 1989 and closed parliament from 1974 to 1984. And recall how in the Algeria example, the military swiftly canceled elections in 1992 and repressed the main legal opposition party, prompting splinter groups to take up arms and wage a guerrilla war against the government in a devastating decade-long civil war. Ironically, both presidential and parliamentary elections continued to be held during the Algerian civil war. But with such pervasive political violence, one must question how meaningful such elections were, not least since they were held under the supervision of a military that showed itself to be incapable of accepting the outcome of a free vote.

This brings us back to the issue of political violence. How do we make sense of elections in political systems where there is considerable political violence, waged either by armed forces of the state or armed militias outside state control? How do we classify countries where the currency of political power is *both* elections and political violence? Recall that political violence can never be fully expunged from a political community. The challenge is to prevent the conditions leading to violence so that it occurs at the margins of the political process, not at its core. That requires that the political process be inclusive enough to accommodate all of a country's interest groups and factions. Since most political violence involves struggles to control or get access to the state, the establishment of legal opposition parties is crucial for channeling competition over the state into peaceful forums. Power-sharing and the creation of opportunities for different groups to take turns being in government is the key to reducing political violence. Table 2.1 illustrates just how difficult this is, for, as we move from left to right, there are fewer and fewer countries that meet all of the criteria for meaningful democratic elections.

Conclusion

Citizens who took to the streets in Tunisia, Egypt, Libya, and the rest of the countries that experienced massive popular protests in 2011 may not have explicitly called for free and fair elections (although many did). Their demands were phrased in more abstract and more basic terms, centering on popular participation in government and a say in how public policies are made. On the third day of the eighteen-day Egyptian uprising that would eventually topple Mubarak, a twenty-nine-year-old glass factory worker told a reporter, "It's our right to choose our government ourselves. We have been living 29 years, my whole life, without being able to choose a president. I've grown bald, and Mubarak has stayed Mubarak," he said, rubbing his bare scalp (Dziadosz 2011). Nearly two years later in Jordan, during large, unprecedented demonstrations calling for the ouster of King Abdullah II, a 22-year-old medical student said to a journalist, "When the people choose their government, they will accept the government's decisions—even a price hike—because then it is a decision of the people, too. It is not just a matter of money. It is about the will of the people" (Kirkpatrick 2012).

When protesters did cite elections, they were keen to distinguish between the rigged polls used by autocratic leaders and the free, fair contests citizens wanted to see. In October 2011, thousands of Moroccans demonstrated against the parliamentary elections announced by King Mohammed VI. "It is obvious that the polls will bring to power the same figures who have for years been plundering the wealth of the country and holding hostage the future of the Moroccan population," an activist from the February 20 protest movement said. Protesters chanted, "The elections are a charade; you will not fool us this time" (Karam 2011).

Citizens in the Middle East and North Africa have long struggled against the abuse of elections by autocratic leaders, either resisting openly by protesting in the streets and braving government intimidation to cast votes for opposition candidates, or staying home and refusing to participate in sham contests. The extraordinary wave of popular empowerment surging through the region has given new momentum to long-standing efforts by citizens to control their governments and keep them in check. First-time honest, competitive elections in Tunisia, Egypt, and Libya have renewed citizens' resolve to repeat the elections until they become routine features of their countries' political systems, and to work toward empowering the elected institutions of government against the obstructionist, interventionist ambitions of unelected power centers. Opposition parties are being created anew or remodeled to respond to citizens' thirst for political alternatives and watchdogs over government performance. As sociologist Charles Tilly would point out, the work of crafting representative, responsive governments is a herculean collective endeavor. It can be reversed, or come up against persistent roadblocks, or break down altogether, or turn into reconstructed forms of autocratic rule. The idea of democracy is attractive in theory but very difficult to implement in practice, since it threatens very powerful interests and established hierarchies. As you read through the rest of the book and learn more about additional factors affecting government-opposition relations, keep in mind Robert Dahl's two key questions: What would it take to introduce a system of peaceful legal opposition in environments where it does not exist? And what would it take to maintain such a system?

Notes

1. "The Hashemites: Jordan's Royal Family," King Hussein I, February 28, 2013, http://www.kinghussein.gov.jo/hashemites.html.
2. "King Abdul Aziz Al Saud," The Saudi Network, February 28, 2013, http://www.the-saudi.net/al-saud/abdulaziz.htm.

3

The Impact of
International Politics

F. Gregory Gause III

The domestic politics of Middle Eastern states are affected by their regional and international environments in numerous ways. These outside influences do not all push in one direction. Some external effects strengthen existing states and regimes; some others undermine them. There are foreign influences that can mobilize social groups and empower political opposition, while other external factors bolster incumbents. This chapter catalogues the various ways that external contexts can affect the domestic politics of Middle Eastern states. It categorizes external influences into two broad groups: those resulting from the region's placement in the global political-economic system and those resulting from the region's own international politics.

The Global System and the Middle East

The Middle East is located in three intersecting global systems, each one exerting its own pushes and pulls on the local states: the international economic system, the international geopolitical system, and the new global normative structure in which Western standards of human rights and governance are increasingly enshrined in international covenants and their observance is considered the entrance price for participating in some international institutions.

The International Economic System and the Middle East

Globalization is not a new phenomenon in the Middle East. The region has a long historical role as an entrepôt and middleman in East-West trade.

Since the beginning of the nineteenth century, more of its trade was directed toward an ascendant Europe than toward South and East Asia, which had been the dominant trading pattern previously. Middle Eastern and North African producers of agricultural and primary products geared production for the European market. Egyptian cotton, Syrian and Lebanese silk, and Algerian wine were exported to Europe. As noted in Chapter 1, European economic strength and political influence combined to open Middle Eastern markets to European manufactured goods, displacing local industry in many cases. European capital poured into the region in the nineteenth century, building the Suez Canal, railroads, and ports, and financing the deficits of the Ottoman, Egyptian, Tunisian, and Persian governments (Issawi 1982: chaps. 2, 4). These trade and capital flows pulled the region more closely into the European orbit, facilitating and justifying European interventions in local politics throughout the century.

Regions less integrated into the European-based global economy in the nineteenth century, particularly the Arabian Peninsula, became more so with the development of their oil resources in the twentieth century. While many of the newly independent Middle Eastern states adopted statist, if not autarkic, policies in the early and middle twentieth century to reduce the influence of outside powers in their countries (Turkey and Egypt are leading examples), Middle East oil exporters were becoming important parts of the global capitalist economy. Foreign capital developed the energy resources of Algeria, Libya, Iraq, Saudi Arabia, Iran, and the smaller Gulf states, providing governments with the money to build larger and more extensive states. While these governments benefited from their oil riches, the role of foreign oil companies in their politics excited nationalist opposition, which in turn led the home governments of these companies to try to intervene in local politics to protect these strategic investments. The most notorious of these interventions was the US-British intelligence operation in Iran in 1953 that led to the overthrow of Prime Minister Mohammad Mossadeq, who had nationalized the Anglo-Iranian Oil Company (now British Petroleum) in 1951, and the restoration of the Shah of Iran to power. While the United States was motivated more by Cold War concerns, British intervention was clearly aimed at preserving economic interests (Gasiorowski and Byrne 2004).

All of the Middle Eastern energy producers took control of their oil industries from the international energy companies in the 1970s and 1980s, as part of the revolution in world energy markets that drove up prices and shifted power from the consumer to the producer countries. They remain highly integrated into the world economy, though the levels of their exports as a proportion of their gross domestic product (GDP) tend to fluctuate both with the price of oil and with political factors like civil and regional wars (see Table 3.1). The governments in the oil states reaped enormous revenues

Table 3.1 Exports as Percentage of GDP, 1970–2010

	1970	1975	1980	1985	1990	1995	2000	2005	2010
Nonenergy economies									
Egypt	15	18	28	18	20	23	16	30	25[a]
Israel	31	33	44	44	34	29	38	45	37
Jordan	8	31	39	37	63	52	42	52	46[a]
Morocco	18	23	15	20	24	23	26	32	33
Syria	17	21	18	12	28	31	36	42	29[a]
Tunisia	22	31	41	33	43	45	45	48	49
Turkey	6	7	7	21	20	20	24	27	21
Energy-exporting economies									
Algeria	24	34	34	24	24	27	42	48	38
Iran	20	41	13	8	15	22	23	29	28
Saudi Arabia	59	84	71	36	46	38	44	59	58

Sources: International Monetary Fund, *International Financial Statistics Yearbook 1994* (for 1970–1990 data), *International Financial Statistics Yearbook 2007* (for 1995–2005 data), and *International Financial Statistics Yearbook 2012* (for 2009–2010 data) (Washington, DC, 1994, 2007, and 2012). Percentages calculated from lines 90c and 99b of the country tables in these yearbooks.
Note: a. 2009 data is the latest reported.

from both the price increases and their new control of their natural resources. These windfalls allowed them to build "rentier" states, relying on
revenues that accrued directly to their state treasuries from the international
economic system to fund their budgets rather than having to tax their own
populations. It is generally agreed that vast oil wealth strengthens authoritarian tendencies and reduces the chances of democratic development in
rentier states (Ross 2001; Anderson 2001; Bellin 2004). Beyond that, there
are important debates about the specific political consequences of great oil
wealth, referenced in greater detail in Chapter 4, on political economy.

While the Middle Eastern oil states were being integrated intensely into
the world economy in the twentieth century, many of the nonoil states of
the region were trying to decouple themselves from the world economy and
pursue development strategies that emphasized local industrialization and
de-emphasized reliance on international trade. However, as Chapter 4 explains, these strategies, while generating impressive economic growth rates
in the 1950s and even into the 1960s, by the 1970s were unable to sustain
the economic growth necessary to keep pace with population growth in the
region (Richards and Waterbury 2008: chap. 8; Henry and Springborg 2001:
chaps. 1–2). A number of Middle Eastern states then shifted their development strategies toward export-led growth and sought to reintegrate into the
global capitalist economy. The emirate of Dubai in the United Arab Emirates (UAE) has gone the furthest in this regard, attempting to become a
global center for trade, tourism, and services on the model of Hong Kong

and Singapore (Davidson 2008)—though the financial and debt crisis Dubai experienced in 2009, as a result of the global economic downturn, will probably take some of the shine off the "Dubai model."

Among the larger economies, Israel, Turkey, Morocco, and Tunisia took the most dramatic steps to adopt the "Washington Consensus" by aligning their economies with the recommendations of international financial institutions like the International Monetary Fund (IMF) and the World Bank. In each of these four cases, outside actors played a major role in both encouraging these policy changes and providing financial support for the transition. In the 1980s, the United States essentially midwived the Israeli switch by making emergency aid to Israel, which was mired in an inflationary economic crisis, contingent on the adoption of more liberal and market-oriented policies. The United States and the European Union (EU) opened their markets to Turkish exports and provided foreign aid to Turkey to cushion its economic transition, while the hope of EU membership pushed Turkish politicians to liberalize the economy further. Tunisia and Morocco benefited from preferential access to the EU market and various EU programs aimed at encouraging economic development along the Mediterranean rim (Richards and Waterbury 2008: chap. 9). (See Table 3.1 for the increasing role of exports in these countries' economies.)

While a few of the nonoil Middle Eastern states followed the zeitgeist of the late twentieth century and adopted policies of the Washington Consensus, many of them did not, or did so only in a halting and halfhearted way. The government of Egypt, to take one case, was fearful of the domestic political consequences of fully liberalizing its economy. Lifting food subsidies had led to riots on more than one occasion in the country. Opening the country fully to imports from abroad risked undercutting state-protected industrial manufacturers in Egypt and thus imperiling the jobs of Egyptians employed in this sector. So Egypt moved very slowly on economic reform. One of the reasons it was able to avoid the kind of wrenching economic transition other countries have experienced is the amount of foreign aid it received from the United States since it signed a peace treaty with Israel in 1979. For decades, Egypt used its strategic position to extract military aid, economic aid, and other concessions from great powers and regional neighbors.

A good example of how Egypt was able to avoid the kind of fiscal crisis that frequently accompanies the statist policies it had followed, while dodging pressures for full-scale implementation of Washington Consensus policies, occurred during the Gulf War of 1990–1991. The government of Egyptian president Husni Mubarak had run up a considerable foreign debt during the 1980s, postponing hard economic choices and subsidizing consumption. By the end of the decade, it was facing a serious debt crisis. Normally, the kind of debt relief Egypt needed would come only from international financial institutions, with stringent requirements for implementation of Washington Consensus policies. Then Saddam Hussein invaded Kuwait in August 1990. Egypt's support was so central to the construction of the US-led international coalition that expelled the Iraqis from Kuwait that Mubarak was able to get billions of dollars of official debt forgiven by the United States and European countries, negotiate more favorable repayment terms on Egypt's debt to Western private sector creditors, and garner billions in aid from the Gulf oil states. Economic crisis averted!

But Egypt's ability to play the strategic card was not unbounded. Pressures built for more serious implementation of Washington Consensus policies. After the appointment of Prime Minister Ahmad Nazif in 2004, Egypt took more serious steps to reduce consumer subsidies and dismantle the state sector of the economy. Egyptian exports as a percentage of GDP increased from the high teens and low twenties in the 1980s and 1990s to 30 percent in 2005 (see Table 3.1). The consequences included increased labor unrest and further limitations on political activism, preparing the ground for the upheaval of 2011 that forced Mubarak from office (Richards and Waterbury 2008: chap. 9; Henry and Springborg 2001: chap. 5).

It is interesting to note that the first two governments to fall in the Arab Spring of 2011 were Tunisia and Egypt, where economic liberalization had progressed further than in many other Arab countries. While the Washington Consensus agenda did lead to economic growth in both, it did little to address issues of unemployment, inequality, and corruption. How the new governments emerging from the uprisings of 2011–2012 in the Arab world will address their economic challenges and the extent of their integration into the global economy remains to be seen.

The Egyptian case illustrates the fact that most Middle Eastern states, because of their energy resources, their strategic locations, or their close ties with outside powers, retain some bargaining power in the international economy. They are not in a situation of dependency, where they are subject to the vagaries of international economic forces with little or no power to influence how those forces affect them. But they are not economic powerhouses. Their bargaining leverage is limited. They find themselves in a situation of asymmetric interdependence with the major players in the world economy, policy "takers" more than policymakers, but still able to affect the terms of their integration into the world economy.

Turkey's candidacy for membership in the European Union is the most far-reaching effort by a Middle Eastern state to integrate into the larger global economy by joining an international organization. Turkey applied for membership in 1987, with the EU officially granting Turkey candidate status in 1999. But the negotiations on actual membership have dragged on since then, and Ankara is beginning to give up hope of ever achieving full membership status. Still, in order to advance its candidacy, Turkey has made substantial changes in its economic and legal systems to bring them into accord with EU standards. It has also enjoyed the benefits of trade access to the EU, which since the mid-1980s has allowed Turkish industries to reconfigure themselves to serve the European market (see Table 3.1). Even if it does not gain full EU membership, Turkey has come to enjoy many of the trade benefits of membership and has reconfigured its economy toward integration into Europe.

The Turkish effort to join the EU is the most important international integration step by a Middle Eastern country, but it is not the only one. The United States has negotiated free trade agreements with a number of Middle Eastern states: Bahrain, Israel, Jordan, Morocco, and Oman. Negotiations with other states are ongoing. Only six Middle Eastern states are not members of the World Trade Organization (WTO) (Algeria, Libya, Syria, Yemen, Iraq, and Iran). These international negotiations have led to changes in the economic policies of the states involved, toward greater openness to the world economy. Iran, closed out of a number of international economic organizations and agreements for political reasons, has looked toward the Indian Ocean and East Asia for economic integration. Trade and other economic agreements with these states do not require the kinds of liberalizing domestic economic change that free trade agreements with the United States or the European Union do. Even Syria, one of the least "reformed" economies of the region, saw the role of exports in its economy grow, though almost 50 percent of its exports in the 2000s went to Iraq and Lebanon, two countries whose recent political circumstances gave Syria a larger role in their economies than would probably have been the case otherwise (see Table 3.1). The ongoing Syrian civil war reversed those tentative steps toward a more export-focused economy.

Trade and finance are not the only means by which Middle Eastern states are integrated into the world economy. Labor movements across regional lines also tie the economies of the sending and receiving regions together. The sending countries usually receive labor remittances from their nationals working abroad; receiving countries frequently experience social problems when integrating large foreign worker populations into their societies. Foreign workers can also develop new political identities when living abroad. The fact that the September 11, 2001, terrorist plot was hatched in Hamburg, Germany, among Arabs sympathetic to al-Qaeda working there is an indication that labor migration is not just an economic phenomenon. Middle Easterners working in Europe are a key regional linkage. In the early 2000s there were an estimated 1.4 million Moroccans, 1.3 million Algerians, 436,000 Tunisians, and 3.2 million Turks living in the European Union. Remittances accounted for 8.5 percent of Morocco's GDP and 5.1 percent of Tunisia's GDP in 2004. A second important linkage is between the Arab states of the Persian Gulf and the Indian Subcontinent. In 2002 it was estimated that 3.2 million Indians, 1.7 million Pakistanis, 820,000 Bangladeshis, and 705,000 Sri Lankans were working in the states of the

Gulf Cooperation Council (GCC) (Richards and Waterbury 2008: chap. 15). There are also important intraregional labor migration patterns, discussed later.

The degree of integration of Middle Eastern states into the international economy has had a significant effect on their own economies and thus their politics. Oil countries have benefited from their integration into the world petroleum and financial systems, reaping enormous windfalls during high price periods and being able to sustain programs that subsidize consumer goods and provide state employment to their citizens. However, oil states have suffered economically and, on occasion, found themselves victims of political instability when oil prices turned down. Some nonoil Middle Eastern countries, with the encouragement and assistance of international actors, adopted the liberal economic policies urged by Washington and the international financial institutions in the 1980s and 1990s, significantly changing their political economies. Other nonoil states resisted those pressures for liberal market reforms and received support from international patrons that helped them sustain elements of their more statist economics for longer than would have been the case otherwise. In all cases, both the position of Middle Eastern states in the international political economy and their relations with specific outside actors help explain their domestic political economies.

The International Geopolitical System and the Middle East

Because of geographical proximity and the importance of transit routes to the east, the Middle East has been entwined with the European international political system for centuries. Before the nineteenth century, the relationship was more between equals, with European intrusions into the region (the Crusades) balanced by Middle Eastern intrusions into Europe (from the Muslim conquest of Spain in the eighth century to Ottoman advances into southeastern Europe through the seventeenth century). But since Napoleon's conquest of Egypt in 1798, it has been the European powers (and the United States) that have been doing the intervening in the Middle East. Except for northern Yemen and central and western Arabia, every part of the Middle East was under European military control at some time in the twentieth century. European balance-of-power rivalries were played out in the Middle East in the nineteenth century and the first half of the twentieth. In the second half of the twentieth century it was the United States and the Soviet Union that competed for influence in the region. The oil resources of the Persian Gulf have attracted great-power interest since the beginning of the twentieth century. The September 11, 2001, attacks on the United States, perpetrated by nineteen Arab men affiliated with al-Qaeda, provided another reason for outside intervention in the region.

The most consequential effect of these outside-power interventions on the domestic politics of many Middle Eastern states was the very creation of those states. Libya, Jordan, Syria, Lebanon, Iraq, and the United Arab Emirates had never existed as independent political entities, in their current or any other borders, before they were created by Italian, French, and British colonial authorities. Even states that had some claim to an independent, precolonial history saw their borders drawn and their modern state governments created by European colonialism. Egypt and Iran, ancient civilizations with millennial state histories, were occupied by European powers whose interventions set the course of their modern politics. The same can be said of Morocco, a kingdom with a centuries-long history of independence before the twentieth century. Only Turkey and Saudi Arabia owe their modern foundations primarily to indigenous political movements— Mustafa Kemal Atatürk's nationalist movement in the wake of World War I and Abd al-Aziz Al Saud's religious-dynastic campaign in the first three decades of the twentieth century. In both cases, European pressures helped to determine the borders of the new states and European recognition cemented the two statebuilders' achievements. In the Saudi case, British financial support was an invaluable contribution to Abd al-Aziz's success. While history in the Middle East did not begin with European colonialism, European colonialism basically drew the map of the modern Middle East.

While as described in Chapter 1 the age of direct European control of the region basically ended in the two decades after World War II, the emergence of independent Middle Eastern states did not end the interest of outside powers in the region or their interventions in its politics. Great-power involvement in the area did not have uniform consequences, however. In some cases, outsiders overthrew Middle Eastern governments and, in the case of the US occupation of Iraq in 2003, completely restructured a Middle Eastern state. But many Middle Eastern regimes were able to use outside powers' strategic interest in the area to gain resources and support for their domestic and foreign policies, sometimes for their very survival. Skillful (and lucky) Middle Eastern rulers could play international politics in ways that bolstered their rule; unskillful (and unlucky) Middle Eastern rulers lost their thrones, their offices, and even their lives because they crossed a world power.

The examples of outside-power interventions that brought down leaders are dramatic and clear. During World War II, British and Soviet forces occupied Iran in 1941 and deposed its ruler, Reza Shah Pahlavi, whom they (rightly) suspected of contacts with Nazi Germany. The occupiers placed his young son, Mohammad Reza, on the throne as the new Shah. As mentioned, in 1953, US and British intelligence operatives coordinated an effort to bring down Iranian prime minister Mohammad Mossadeq, who had nationalized British oil interests in 1951 and who the United States feared would bring Iran into the Soviet orbit. Not all Cold War intelligence operations in the Middle East were so successful, however. Efforts by the Central Intelligence Agency (CIA) to destabilize what Washington saw as pro-Soviet leaders in Egypt and Syria in the 1950s and 1960s backfired. With the collapse of the Soviet Union and the opening of its archives, we will undoubtedly discover similar failed Soviet intelligence efforts to bring down pro-US Middle Eastern rulers.

The end of the Cold War did not end great-power meddling in the domestic politics of regional states. The US invasion of Iraq in 2003 was explicitly aimed at replacing the regime of Saddam Hussein and his Baath Party. Having accomplished that in relatively short order, the United States took on the more ambitious task of restructuring not just the ruling regime but the entire Iraqi state, disbanding the Iraqi army and gutting the Iraqi bureaucracy through decisions made a few months after the invasion (Ricks 2007). US occupation authorities and military commanders attempted to rebuild Iraqi military and civilian institutions, with mixed success, up until the US military withdrawal in 2011. The ultimate results of the US occupation of Iraq remain to be seen, but there is no denying that the intervention has dramatically changed the course of Iraqi political history. Another example of outside actors altering the political trajectory of a Middle Eastern state is the US, British, and French air support that was essential to the victory of the Libyan rebels who brought down Muammar Qaddafi in 2011.

Less obviously but no less importantly, great-power policies have also on occasion contributed to the strengthening of Middle Eastern states and regimes. Middle Eastern states occupy important strategic locations, and they have been able to use great powers' interests in them to extract resources from those powers. The Cold War competition between the United States and the Soviet Union provided the context for a number of regional leaders to obtain economic and military aid and political support from the superpowers. Egypt is an excellent example of how local rulers exploited the Cold War rivalry to their benefit. In the 1950s, Egyptian president Gamal Abdel Nasser received economic aid from both superpowers and military supplies from the Soviet Union, as Moscow and Washington tried to bring the largest Arab state into their orbit. When Egypt was attacked in 1956 by Israel, Great Britain, and France after Nasser's nationalization of the Suez Canal, both the United States and the Soviet Union supported him and helped him turn a military defeat into a political victory. As Nasser became more tightly allied with the Soviet Union in the 1960s, US aid dried up, but the Soviets supplied him with military equipment and helped him build the Aswan Dam (Rubinstein 1977). As the Soviet economic model faltered and Egypt's need for foreign aid grew, Nasser's successor, Anwar Sadat, skillfully repositioned Egypt as an ally of the United States. By making peace with Israel and cooperating with US political and military plans in the region, he was able to make Egypt the second-largest recipient of US foreign aid (after Israel) in the world (Karawan 1994).

While Egypt played the superpowers against each other in the 1950s and switched sides in the 1970s, benefiting all along, other Middle Eastern states picked a Cold War side early and were compensated for their loyalty. Under Soviet pressure for political and military concessions immediately after World War II, Turkey looked to the United States for support, which was forthcoming under the Truman Doctrine. Turkey joined the North Atlantic Treaty Organization (NATO) in 1951 and remains a member of the Western alliance to this day. During the 1950s, Turkey was a major recipient of US military and foreign aid. Morocco and Jordan are also longtime US allies and recipients of US foreign and military aid. Syria, beginning in the 1950s, and Iraq, beginning in the 1960s, were Soviet allies, exploiting the Soviet desire for strategic footholds in the region in order to extract aid from Moscow. Other Middle Eastern states also played the Cold War game and benefited from the superpowers' willingness to trade money and guns for political considerations.

Israel's relationship with the United States also developed in the Cold War context but is buttressed by the strong connections many Americans feel with the Jewish state. US military aid to Israel began in a serious way in the 1960s and major economic aid began in the 1970s as Washington gave up hope (temporarily) of drawing Egypt away from the Soviet orbit. US policymakers saw Israel as a counter to Soviet allies in Cairo and Damascus and an asset in the larger contest for Cold War influence in the region. After the Egyptian-Israeli peace treaty of 1979, Israel became far and away the largest recipient of US foreign and military aid in the world. The end of the Cold War did not change the relationship, though its original strategic rationale had ended. Support for Israel among the American public generally and from important organized political groups like American Jewish and fundamentalist Christian supporters of Israel ensured that US aid would continue to flow to Israel. (For differing views on the drivers behind US support for Israel, see Mearsheimer and Walt 2007 and Organski 1990.)

The US strategic interest in Middle East oil provided regimes in the Persian Gulf with military, economic, and political support from Washington. Saudi Arabia has been the centerpiece of US policy in the area since the end of World War II. US companies developed the Saudi oil industry and, from the 1940s through the 1960s, supplied the Saudi state with invaluable financial and technical assistance to consolidate Saudi family rule in Arabia (Vitalis 2007). The US government built and supplied the Saudi armed forces and provided military protection directly to Saudi Arabia when it was threatened by Egypt's involvement in the Yemen civil war in the 1960s and by Iraq's invasion of Kuwait in 1990. Indeed, Kuwait would not be a Middle Eastern state today had the United States not constructed an international military coalition to turn back Iraq's annexation of the country and fought the Gulf War of 1990–1991.

Yet strong external political support and military and financial aid were no guarantee of regime stability. Mohammad Reza Shah of Iran—installed on his throne by Great Britain and the Soviet Union, restored to power by US and British intelligence agents, recipient of US economic and military aid, and strong ally of the United States—was overthrown in the Iranian revolution of 1978–1979, and the United States, in the words of revolutionary leader Ayatollah Ruhollah Khomeini, "could not do a damn thing." The socialist government of South Yemen, an independent state from 1967 to 1990, relied heavily upon Soviet economic aid and political support. When Mikhail Gorbachev abandoned the Cold War competition with the United States, the South Yemeni leadership chose to unify with North Yemen and, in the process, lost its political clout. Egyptian president Husni Mubarak's close ties to the United States did not help him face down the popular uprising that led to his overthrow in February 2011. In the end, the United States supported the Egyptian military when it removed Mubarak from office. So, close ties with great powers do not guarantee protection for Middle East leaders. But some have been able, at various times and in various ways, to exploit outside-power interest in the region in order to extract resources and gain political and military support from those powers, helping them to build their states and solidify their regimes.

The International Normative System and the Middle East

International norms are much less tangible than military interventions or economic aid, but they do have some effect on the domestic politics of some Middle Eastern states. By the "international normative system" I mean the growing belief that ideas regarding human and individual rights, international law, and governance standards that have developed in the West have universal applicability. Some of these norms are embodied in international covenants (like the UN's Universal Declaration of Human Rights) signed by almost all Middle Eastern states. Others, like the global democracy trend, do not have an international legal basis but set a powerful normative standard that appeals to many people in the region. External governments hold Middle Eastern governments to account for their deficiencies in meeting these standards on occasion, but not frequently. Nongovernmental organizations like Human Rights Watch and Amnesty International call the attention of the world's media to violations by Middle Eastern governments of the rights of their citizens and try to support human rights activists in Middle Eastern countries. New communications technologies bring examples of democratic uprisings in other parts of the world directly to the citizens of

Middle Eastern states. While very few Middle Eastern governments live up
to these international norms, they can no longer ignore them as they formulate their domestic governing strategies.

The best example of how the international normative system can affect
the domestic politics of Middle Eastern states is Turkey. The Turkish ambition to join the European Union has meant that Turkish governments over
the past two decades have had to change a range of domestic laws and policies in order to comply with EU standards. Aside from the fundamental political-economic change from the Atatürkist state-directed economy to a
more liberal, export-oriented approach, Turkey has also extended new legal
rights to the Kurdish minority, abolished the death penalty, and adopted
other social legislation to meet EU requirements.

None of the other Middle Eastern states has as compelling a carrot as
EU membership in front of it as a spur to accept these new global norms.
But there are other efforts by outside powers to create institutional incen-
tives for these states to better respect human rights and move toward
democracy. The EU's Barcelona Process uses economic incentives to prod
Middle Eastern states not only to reform their economies but also to im-
prove their domestic governance and promote regional peace and stability
(European Union 2008). After the September 11, 2001, terrorist attacks, the
United States created a number of programs, including the Middle East Partnership Initiative and, with its Group of Eight (G8) partners, the Broader
Middle East and North Africa Initiative, to encourage Arab states to liberal-
ize and democratize (Wittes 2008).

Given the strategic importance of the region to outside powers, Middle
Eastern governments are better positioned than their colleagues in other
world areas to resist external pressures for domestic reform. But Middle
Eastern leaders have demonstrated that they do not think they can simply
ignore these global trends. In response, numerous authoritarian Arab
regimes felt compelled to have "freer" elections than they had in the past
three decades or to institute elections where none had existed. Direct US
pressure post-9/11 explains some of this movement, but not all of it. Saudi
Arabia reinstituted municipal elections in 2005. Bahrain, Qatar, Oman, and
the UAE all instituted some form of elections to a national and/or municipal
assembly after 1990. In 2005, Egypt conducted the freest parliamentary
elections since the military coup of 1952 and changed its constitution to
allow for direct election of the president. Jordan restored its elected parliament in 1989. Algeria has conducted a number of elections for parliament
and the presidency since its civil war wound down in the late 1990s. Morocco has held two relatively open parliamentary elections, both in the
2000s. In all these cases, authoritarian rulers manipulated the rules and used
their power to limit the effects of these democratic experiments (Brumberg
2002; Heydemann 2007). How important the global democracy trend and
these tentative democratic steps were to the revolts of the Arab Spring re-

mains an open question, as do the democratic prospects of the Arab states where authoritarian rulers fell. However, it is important to note that every Arab Spring revolt was made in the name of democracy and that free and fair elections followed the fall of dictators in Tunisia, Egypt, and Libya.

The effects of global norms on Middle Eastern politics should not be exaggerated. Human rights are abused from the Atlantic Ocean to the Persian Gulf and from the Black Sea to the Indian Ocean. Women's roles in society and politics are buffeted among international standards, Islamist groups' interpretations of religion, and local cultural practices. Oil money and strategic location allow Middle Eastern leaders to resist and deflect external pressures for reform. We saw this most recently in Bahrain, where the government suppressed Arab Spring demonstrations with very few international repercussions. The political effects of the global communications revolution are not yet clear, but they do not seem to pressure uniformly in the direction of more democratic politics. Yet we must recognize these external pressures on Middle Eastern governments to adhere to global standards of governance, and note that Middle Eastern activists themselves are increasingly using these global standards to call their leaders to account. These standards are now part of the global environment in which Middle Eastern states must function, and, if the democratic changes in Egypt, Tunisia, and Libya are consolidated, part of the regional environment as well.

The Domestic Effects of Middle East Regional Politics

The global system is not the only international context in which Middle Eastern states have to operate. Their own regional interactions can have powerful effects on their domestic politics as well. Middle Eastern states—particularly the Arab states but to some extent other members of the system as well—are tied together by cross-border linkages of ethnicity, language, religion, sect, and tribe. Identity crosses borders, as the dramatic spread of popular demonstrations across the Arab world during the Arab Spring attests. These transstate identities are a cause of regional conflict and, to a lesser extent, of regional integration. Both the conflicts and the integrative effects are important for understanding the domestic politics of Middle Eastern states.

Regional War and Domestic Politics

There has been no shortage of regional conflict in the Middle East since the end of World War II (see Table 3.2): nine Arab-Israeli wars (depending on how one counts them); the Iran-Iraq War; Iraq's invasion of Kuwait; regional interventions in civil wars in Yemen, Oman, Lebanon, Iraq, and Syria; and border skirmishes and troop buildups at one time or another on

Table 3.2 Middle East Wars and Conflicts, 1948–2012

Conflict	Years of Conflict	Major Players
Arab-Israeli Wars		
Israeli War for Independence	1948–1949	
Suez War	1956–1957	
Six Day War	1967	
War of Attrition (Israel-Egypt)	1969–1970	
Yom Kippur/Ramadan War	1973	
Israeli incursion into southern Lebanon	1978	
Israeli invasion of Lebanon (final withdrawal in 2000)	1982	
Israel-Lebanon border war	2006	
Israel-Hamas war in the Gaza Strip	2008–2009	
Gulf Wars		
Iran-Iraq War	1980–1988	
Gulf War	1990–1991	
Iraq War	2003–2011	
Civil Wars		
North Yemen (Yemen Arab Republic)	1962–1970	Egypt, Saudi Arabia, Great Britain, United States, Soviet Union
Jordan	1970–1971	PLO, Syria, Israel
Oman	1970–1975	Iran, South Yemen, Great Britain
Lebanon	1975–1991	Syria, Israel, PLO, Iraq, Iran, Libya, Saudi Arabia, United States, Soviet Union
Algeria	1992–early 2000s	France
Iraq	2003–present	United States, Iran, Turkey, Syria, Saudi Arabia
Syria	2011–present	Turkey, Iran, Saudi Arabia, Qatar, United States
Other Persistent Militarized Disputes		
Western Sahara	1975–present	Morocco, Algeria, Mauritania, Polisario
Kurdish issue	1920–present	Turkey, Iraq, Iran, Syria, and Kurdish groups in each country seeking autonomy and/or independence
Israeli-Palestinian issue	1947–1948, 1987–1991, 2000–present	Israel, PLO, Palestinian Authority, Hamas

almost every international border in the region. War can make the state, in that war forces a state to develop administrative capacities and can generate patriotic feelings that link society to the state. But war can break the state— or the regime—as well, particularly if that regime is on the losing side.

War-making has undoubtedly strengthened the Israeli state and affected its development. Born in war and involved in war almost continuously since its birth, Israel has built a citizen army whose influence pervades Israeli political life. Service in the army is the path to advancement in Israeli society and politics. It has also served as an integrating mechanism for Israel's disparate Jewish communities. The Israeli state developed as a wartime state, with large-scale state control over economy and society (Barnett 1992). It was only in the 1980s that Israel adopted more liberal economic policies. The particular history of the birth of Israel, in the wake of the Holocaust and amid Arab rejection, has forged a tight bond of patriotism between the state and its Jewish citizens. At the same time, this focus on the threat from the Arab world has made problematic the status of Israel's large Arab citizen minority within Israel's democratic political system. In addition, since 1967, the question of what to do with the territories captured in that war, particularly the West Bank, and how to govern the Palestinians who live in those territories, has been the dominant issue in Israeli politics.

Defeat in war has shaped Palestinian political identity in a similar way. The loss by Palestinians to the Zionist movement in the civil war of 1947– 1948 meant that they would not get their own state in their own territory. The refugee exodus from that war and the subsequent Arab-Israeli war of 1948– 1949 dispersed Palestinians across the region, with substantial communities in Jordan, Lebanon, Syria, and Kuwait. This experience of defeat and dispersion created a strong Palestinian identity, nurtured later by the Palestine Liberation Organization (PLO), founded in 1964. Palestinian communities in both Jordan and Lebanon provided a base for the PLO and its armed units to set up shop in those countries and contributed to tensions that eventually led to civil wars in both places. Like Israeli identity, Palestinian identity has been forged by war (Kimmerling and Migdal 1993; Khalidi 1997).

Israel and Palestine are states (or potential states) and identities born in war. The other Arab states do not owe their existence to Arab-Israeli wars, but the course of those wars has greatly affected their own political histories. While Israel's Arab neighbors have been motivated to become involved in the conflict by normal geopolitical incentives—such as territory, regional dominance, and balance-of-power concerns—popular support for the Palestinians also has driven them to fight the Israelis. The common Arab identity has led citizens in Egypt, Jordan, Syria, Iraq, and across the Arab world to sympathize with the Palestinians and see Israel's creation as an affront to Arabism. The Arab states were in part driven by popular pressures to enter into the war against Israel in 1948 (Rubin 1981). Defeat in that war contributed to political instability in Syria, with three military coups in 1949, and to the Egyptian military coup of 1952. The Syrian military government's desire to bolster its own domestic credentials by escalating the confrontation with Israel helped to drive the crisis that culminated in the 1967 Arab-Israeli war, in which Egypt lost the Sinai Peninsula and Gaza Strip, Jordan lost the West Bank, and Syria lost the Golan Heights. Jordan's entry into the 1967 war, despite Israeli guarantees of nonaggression if the Jordanians stayed out, was driven by King Hussein's belief that to stay on the sidelines while the Arab world confronted Israel would lead to a popular uprising against his regime. It was only with the weakening of pan-Arabism as a political ideology after the 1967 war that Egypt (1979) and Jordan (1994) were willing to risk signing peace agreements with Israel. (The Oslo Accords between Israel and the PLO in 1993 also removed a major barrier to Jordan's willingness to sign a peace treaty with Israel.)

War also greatly affected the political development of the Islamic Republic of Iran. The revolutionary regime that came to power in 1979 was able to use the Iran-Iraq War, launched by Iraq in 1980, to consolidate its control domestically. With Iraq's attack, the regime's domestic opponents could be portrayed to the Iranian public as traitors to the nation. War mobilization allowed the government to extend its control over society and the economy while rallying the Iranian public to its side. The new regime's success in turning back the Iraqi attack and recovering lost Iranian territory by 1982 helped to legitimate it to the Iranian public. Continuation of the war for six more years, in an (unsuccessful) effort to bring down Saddam Hussein's regime in Iraq, helped make the Islamic Republic—and make it in a particular way: as a centralized, dirigiste state (Milani 1994).

Regional conflicts gave Middle Eastern regimes a readily understandable, and for some of their population even an acceptable, pretext to consolidate authoritarian rule at home, under the slogan (coined by Egyptian propagandist Mohammad Hassanein Heikal) that "no voice could be louder than the voice of battle." The threat from neighbors, real and imagined, was used by other regional regimes as well to justify building police states and severely restricting political rights and freedoms. War and preparation for war might help make a state, but they rarely lead to more liberal politics. War preparation has also skewed the economies of Middle Eastern states toward more centralized control and led to disproportionately high rates of military spending as a percentage of the total economy (see Table 3.3).

Transstate Identities as Challenges to States

Identities cross borders in the Middle East, and the mis-fit between the borders of states and political communities creates important challenges to the

Table 3.3 Defense Expenditures as Percentage of GDP, 2010

Middle Eastern countries	
Algeria	3.59
Bahrain	3.27
Egypt	1.94
Iran	2.56
Iraq	6.04
Israel	6.46
Jordan	5.42
Kuwait	3.53
Lebanon	4.16
Libya	3.62
Morocco	3.50
Oman	7.26
Qatar	2.45
Saudi Arabia	10.10
Syria	3.94
Tunisia	1.22
United Arab Emirates	5.32
Yemen	5.82
Middle East average	5.01
Other countries and regions	
Brazil	1.61
China	1.30
East Asia and Australasia	1.44
NATO (excluding United States)	1.61
Non-NATO Europe	1.06
Nigeria	0.76
Pakistan	3.24
Russia	2.84
South and Central Asia	1.94
South Korea	2.48
United States	4.77
Global average	2.43

Source: International Institute for Strategic Studies, *The Military Balance 2012* (New York: Routledge, 2012).

consolidation of state authority and the development of citizen loyalty to the state (see Halliday 2005; Hinnebusch 2003; Lawson 2006) (see Figure 3.1 for an outline of the variety of cross-border identities in the region, and chapter 7 for much more on identity and politics). People in many Middle Eastern states do not see loyalty to their state as the ultimate expression of their political identity. Cross-border identities provide an avenue for intervention in the domestic politics of neighboring states. Ambitious regional leaders have used regional identities to mobilize support for themselves and against other leaders, destabilizing the domestic politics of their targets and sometimes bringing down other regimes. Here we use the terms *transstate* and *cross-border* to indicate any such identity; *transnational* to indicate

Figure 3.1 Transnational and Cross-State Identities and Organizations in the Middle East

---

Transnational Identities
Pan-Arabism or Arab nationalism
   Arab Revolt/Hashimite Arab nationalist movement (1917–early 1950s, including Iraqi "Fertile Crescent" plans and Jordanian "Greater Syria" plans)
   Baath Party, founded in 1943 with branches in many countries of the Arab East and, as of 2013, still the ruling party in Syria, whose platform calls for Arab unity
   Gamal Abdel Nasser's pan-Arabist movement (1954–1967, whose high point was the union of Egypt and Syria in the United Arab Republic, 1958–1961)
Islam
   Shi'i Islamist movements with ties to Iran (e.g., Hezbollah in Lebanon, Islamic Supreme Council of Iraq)
   Muslim Brotherhood, a centralized, Sunni political organization with branches in Egypt, Palestine, Jordan, Syria, Iraq, Kuwait, and elsewhere
   Salafi Sunni Islamist movements, including al-Qaeda
   Shi'i "sources of emulation" (*al-marja' iyyat*) (e.g., Ayatollah Ali al-Sistani of Najaf, who has followers not only in Iraq but also in Iran, Saudi Arabia, Bahrain, and elsewhere)
   Sufi brotherhoods

Cross-State Identities
Kurdish identity, with Kurdish communities in Turkey, Syria, Iraq, and Iran
Palestinian identity, with significant Palestinian communities in Israel, the Palestinian Territories, Jordan, Lebanon, and Syria
Tribal identities (e.g., Shammar tribal confederation, with members in Saudi Arabia, Kuwait, Iraq, Jordan, and Syria)

---

identities that are region-wide, or close to it, transcending existing state borders; and *cross-state* to describe identities that are of a state or substate character yet cross over one or more existing borders.

Arab identity was a serious challenge to state consolidation in the Arab East in the early decades of independence. In the immediate aftermath of the creation of the Arab states, important political movements emerged arguing that the division of the Arab world by the colonial powers was illegitimate and that the former Arab provinces of the Ottoman Empire should form a united Arab state. The Hashimite monarchs of both Iraq and Jordan, whose family led the "Great Arab Revolt" against the Ottomans, put forward various Arab unity plans in the interwar years. The creation of Israel added an emotional, popular element to the pan-Arab agenda. Arab nationalism was used to justify interventions into the politics of weaker Arab states like Syria by Iraqi politicians looking to encourage "Fertile Crescent" unity. Gamal Abdel Nasser of Egypt took up the banner of "progressive" Arab unity in the mid-1950s, using the new technology of the transistor radio to speak directly to Arabs in other countries, urging them to oppose their own governments and follow the Nasserist line. Nasser was able to mobilize support across borders and destabilize fellow Arab governments. The high point of Nasserist pan-Arabism was the union of Syria and Egypt in 1958 in the United Arab Republic (UAR), with pro-Nasser officers in the Syrian army in effect conducting a coup and offering the country to Nasser. While it did not last long, breaking up in 1961, the UAR actually redrew the map of the Middle East. Even when they were not crowned with such success, Nasser's efforts to mobilize support for himself and his local allies in other Arab states encouraged domestic discontent and instability up to the 1967 war (Seale 1987; Kerr 1971). Even after the heyday of Arab nationalism, common Arab identity was used as a pretext by the Baathist regimes of Syria and Iraq to interfere in each other's domestic politics and in the politics of other Arab states (Kienle 1990). While the popularity of Arab unity has faded, common Arab identity remains an important element of regional politics. The speed with which the Arab Spring demonstrations of 2011 spread from Tunisia to Egypt, Yemen, Bahrain, Syria, Libya, and (less disruptively) elsewhere in the Arab world attests to the fact that Arabs look across their borders and are affected by what their fellow Arabs in other states are doing.

In a similar way to Nasser, Ayatollah Khomeini used the larger Islamic identity and the narrower, sectarian Shi'i identity to mobilize support in Arab states and pressure Arab governments that opposed the Islamic Republic of Iran. Revolutionary Iran encouraged fellow Shi'a abroad to oppose the secular Baathist regime of Saddam Hussein and the pro-US monarchies of the Persian Gulf. While Khomeini was unable to bring down any of these regimes, agitation among Iraqi Shi'a contributed to Saddam Hussein's decision to launch his war against Iran in 1980 and contributed to the heightening of sectarian identities in Iraq. Pro-Iranian groups in Kuwait and Bahrain launched attacks against those governments in the 1980s. After the Israeli invasion of Lebanon in 1982, Iran created Hezbollah in conjunction with local allies there as an arm of its Shi'i Islamic revolution (Ramazani 1986).

States with weak administrative structures and multiple identity groups are particularly vulnerable to this kind of cross-border political intervention. Almost every major regional state, at one time or another, sponsored a group or party in Lebanon. Saudi Arabia and other regional powers have supported political and ideological allies in Yemen over the decades. Iraq after the US invasion of 2003, with its army disbanded and its state apparatus dismantled, was an open field for regional political interventions. Iran in particular took advantage of the weakness of the Iraqi center and its ties to various Iraqi Shi'i political groups to increase its influence there. As Syria descended into civil war in 2011, an array of regional powers, including Iran, Turkey, and Saudi Arabia, sought to advance their interests by supporting local factions. Strong nationalist sentiment among Kurds provides a ready point of access for states looking to pressure Iraq and Iran. The Shah's Iran, supported by the United States and Israel, encouraged Iraqi

Kurds to oppose the Baghdad government in the early 1970s. During the Iran-Iraq War, both countries tried to stir up the Kurdish populations of the other. Both Iran and Turkey, fearful of the autonomy Iraq's Kurds have enjoyed since 1991, have intervened in Iraqi Kurdish politics by building client relations with local politicians and parties. Turkey has also intervened militarily in Iraqi Kurdistan on a number of occasions (McDowall 2004).

The importance of cross-state identities in the Middle East has made it more difficult for states to consolidate their control over their territories and to develop patriotic links between citizens and their government. These identities offer an avenue for intervention by outsiders in the domestic politics of targeted states. They make neighbors acutely interested in what happens across their borders, for fear that identity politics will spill back into their own domestic politics. Cross-state identities can exacerbate regional tensions and lead to conflicts, which in turn can have their own effects on the politics of the states involved.

Transstate Identities and Regional Integration

Regionally, the destabilizing effects of cross-border identities far outweigh their integrative effects. However, Arab identity encouraged large-scale labor migrations within the Arab world during the oil boom of the 1970s and early 1980s. Millions of Egyptians went to work in Libya and Iraq, and hundreds of thousands went to the Gulf and Saudi Arabia. Hundreds of thousands of Yemenis worked in Saudi Arabia. Hundreds of thousands of Jordanians and Palestinians found work in the Persian Gulf states and Saudi Arabia. These massive labor migrations helped to redistribute some of the oil bounty from the resource-rich Arab states to the resource-poor states (Kerr and Yassin 1982). By lessening the pressures on domestic economies to employ their growing populations, the oil-fueled labor migrations took some of the economic and political pressure off governments in the labor-exporting countries. Labor remittances helped to sustain balance-of-payments deficits in the labor exporters as well. Migrants also brought home new political ideas. The Saudi brand of *salafi* Sunni Islam spread in the Middle East in part by Arab migrant workers picking up these ideas in Saudi Arabia and bringing them back home.

The second oil boom, of the 2000s, has not had the same effects in Arab labor markets. The political divisions created by the Gulf War of 1990–1991, with Iraq, Jordan, Yemen, and the PLO on one side and the Gulf states and Egypt on the other, disrupted the migration patterns that had developed in the 1970s. Egyptians left Iraq; Yemenis left Saudi Arabia. The restored Kuwaiti government made it clear that Palestinians were no longer as welcome, leading to the forced exodus of most of what had been the most prosperous and long-established Palestinian community in the Gulf region. Since that time, the oil-rich Gulf states have looked more to South and Southeast Asia for labor. These foreign labor communities, unable to develop links with the local community through Arab identity and the Arabic language, are easier to control politically and present less of a threat to the ruling regimes in a crisis. However, there are still large numbers of fellow Arabs working in the oil-rich Gulf states, including almost 1.5 million Egyptians and hundreds of thousands of Palestinians, Lebanese, Jordanians, and Yemenis (Richards and Waterbury 2008: chap. 15).

Conclusion

Both global and regional contexts affect the domestic politics of Middle Eastern states. These international and regional effects are not, however, one-dimensional. They can help to solidify states and regimes; they can weaken states and regimes. Recent global economic forces push toward more open and liberal domestic economies, but some Middle Eastern states have been able to trade their strategic positions for outside aid and support, enabling them to sustain inefficient statist economies longer than would have been possible otherwise. The region is not immune to the global normative pressures of human rights and democracy, as the Arab Spring clearly demonstrated, but many Middle Eastern states have been successful at avoiding serious domestic political reform urged by outsiders. While it is not possible to present one simple argument about the overall impact of global and regional influences on any particular Middle Eastern state, no Middle Eastern state can be analyzed in isolation from those influences. The task of the analyst is to appreciate how global and regional forces specifically play into the domestic politics of each of the states in the region.

4

Political Economy

Pete W. Moore

One of the most popular sociocultural stereotypes of Arabs is their predisposition to business and trade. After all, the Prophet Muhammad was a successful businessman and the region has long been geographically defined by its great urban trading centers. This is a stereotype that many Arabs embrace and even joke about. To wit: "The math teacher asks a Lebanese student, 'What is two plus two?' The student responds, 'It depends, are you buying or selling?'" Few, however, see business or making money as divorced from politics. Following the money—or exploring the political rationale for particular investment decisions—is the stuff of everyday discussion, whether among the urbanites of the oil-rich Gulf states or among rural populations in North Africa. Indeed this critical disposition animates not only the field of political economy but also emerged as a prominent theme in the 2011 uprisings. Whether it was bread-wielding Tunisians, marching Suez workers, or Yemeni protesters chanting against corruption, the 2011 Arab uprisings put political economy issues front and center. Protesters asked, where did all the money go and who decided? Individuals and interests who had profited from close connections to rulers were widely targeted by populations weary of decades of poor economic development. At the scholarly level, the study of political economy basically can be defined as investigating the effect of political variables on economic outcomes (how does authoritarian rule affect economic development?) or analyzing the effect of economic change on political outcomes (do oil profits impede the development of democracy?).

While many approaches in political economy borrow from both directions, scholarly biases favoring political or economic arguments are common. This chapter stresses the political foundations of economies and their effects, but the economic arguments are not ignored. Specifically, we cover four themes that bind the Middle East region:

- *Political power and economic policies:* Since the end of World War II, political leaders in the Middle East have crafted and implemented economic policies with clear political imperatives to maintain their rule and the socioeconomic privileges of their supporters.
- *Oil and politics:* The discovery and exploitation of oil in the region have interacted with the domestic politics of countries as well as relations between states in the region.
- *Reform and liberalization:* There has been a tension between state-dominated economies, which have been the norm for most of the post–World War II period, and the regional and international drive in the past twenty years to reform and liberalize those same economies.
- *The 2011 uprisings and their aftermath:* While socioeconomic grievance was far from the only complaint to drive protesters in 2011, it was prominent. This should not be surprising, given that protests infused with bread-and-butter concerns have characterized the region since the late 1970s. Moreover, the political transitions set in motion in 2011 will undoubtedly have wide-ranging economic effects.

All the countries of the region have gone through similar periods of growth and stagnation. In the aftermath of World War II, optimism and enthusiasm for political independence influenced political leaderships to embark on grand plans to catch up to the rest of the world in economic terms and with regard to infrastructure development. From about the mid-1960s until the early 1980s, the region witnessed what can be termed "the boom period," in which increasingly high oil prices and growing public investment flooded domestic economies with significant capital and finance. The clearest expression of this was the region's impressive annual growth in gross domestic product (GDP) in the 1970s (see Table 4.1). In particular, urban growth was significant, as was migration to cities. Highway systems, ports, and communications networks were put in place; public education was expanded; and government bureaucracies swelled. Given that all of this investment was guided by regimes of unelected monarchs and presidents, there was a clear political subtext. Money and the ruler's economic privileges could be used to buy loyalty or weaken one's political adversaries.

But this bubble was destined to burst. Starting in the early 1980s, oil prices dropped quickly, public budgets went into debt, and in parts of the region with persistent violent conflicts, instability combined with these dislocations and led to what has been termed "the bust period." This meant GDP growth rates stagnated (see Table 4.1) and unemployment increased. Promises of socioeconomic equality gave way to increasing inequality, both

**Table 4.1 GDP Growth in the Middle East and North Africa, 1975–2009
(average percentage per period)**

1975–1979	1980–1984	1985–1989	1990–1994	1995–1999	2000–2004	2005–2009
6.2	1.8	1.1	5.1	3.6	4.1	4.5

Source: World Bank, *World Databank, World Development Indicators and Global Development Finance,* various years, includes all income levels Middle East and North Africa, http://data.world bank.org/data-catalog (Washington, DC).

economically and politically. From the late 1970s and increasing into the 1980s, protests among workers and others adversely impacted by these shifts took place in Egypt, Morocco, Jordan, and Tunisia, foreshadowing the mass uprisings of 2011. In response, some states attempted austerity measures—like increases in prices and reductions in welfare subsidies—but often this led again to public disturbances and protests. For much of the 1980s and 1990s, states muddled through.

Not all countries, however, have failed to achieve productive economic development. Turkey, Israel, and Tunisia (for a time) have upgraded work-force skills and capitalized on exports in niche industries. Among the Gulf oil states, Dubai in the United Arab Emirates (UAE) has launched unprecedented efforts at diversification away from oil reliance. Still, for most of the region, boom and bust have gone hand-in-hand, and periodic economic growth has not led to productive or sustainable development. Since the turn of the century, the pendulum has again swung wildly. A new oil boom was followed by the 2008–2009 global financial crisis, which sent prices plunging and increased regional fears of financial contagion. While at first it appeared the region generally escaped the worst of the crisis, the 2011 uprisings put socioeconomic issues back on the table. The following sections examine the legacies of colonial rule that shaped independent states' policies, the years of economic growth or boom, oil politics, the bust period that followed, and the current situation of the region's political economies in the context of the 2011 uprisings.

The Colonial State and Political-Economy Legacies

Chapter 1 chronicles how most of the region's states achieved formal political independence from the European powers after World War II. Prior to European domination, the Ottoman Empire had controlled the region's people and economies. None of these external powers were interested in establishing responsible governance or developing productive economies. Instead, policies directed at the people and societies within a foreign power's control were designed to serve external strategic and commercial aims, often in competition with other outside powers. These legacies meant that newly independent rulers were hardly working from a blank slate when it came to their political economies. Hundreds of years of foreign rule, punctuated by two world wars in the twentieth century, left their impact in three ways.

First, when foreign governors and military forces departed, they left behind institutions that governed the collection of revenue, import and export practices, the distribution of investment, and the adjudication of private property rights. Colonial rulers generally did not invest in developing states' administrative capacities to tax residents or businesses. Rather, grants from the European capital typically funded the operations of the colonial enterprises. This left an important legacy in that political elites had important leverage over merchants and citizens, since rulers did not rely on them to generate public funds. Colonial powers determined import and export monopolies whereby selected business elites were given special access to imported goods—often from the colonial homeland (Vitalis and Heydemann 2000). This weakened domestic producers of the same good (often agricultural products) as well as other domestic private sector elements, which were left out of the special deals. Where large settler or foreign merchant communities existed (Algeria, Palestine, Egypt, and Turkey), colonial rule supported and extended those communities' economic privileges, thereby setting the stage for political backlash after independence. Colonial officials also favored the creation or continued existence of large landowning elites in the rural areas of countries like Egypt, Syria, and Iraq. The existence of these (often absent) landlords dampened development in rural agriculture, increased rural inequities, and provided resistance to industrialization and better collection of public revenues through taxation. But because these rural elites supported colonial rulers, their interests were protected (Gerber 1987). Finally, where external powers did establish profitable businesses within the indigenous economies (particularly in the oil sector and Egypt's Suez Canal, for example), continued foreign control even after political independence would ensure future political conflict.

Second, the creation of new states and borders limited the choices available in building economies or imparted strong incentives to build one's economy in a specific direction. In the most basic sense, the creation of new borders recognized by the United Nations (UN) meant some new states had natural resources while others did not—oil reserves being the most obvious. Where whole new political entities were created, as in Lebanon and Jordan, labor markets, private sector alignments, and domestic markets were completely remade. In the preindependence years, for example, merchants (especially in the Gulf) could migrate to other areas if relations with local political rulers soured. Once new borders were established, this form of exit was cut off (Crystal 1995). In short, the regional state system determined by departing colonial powers meant local leaders inherited a geographic and political economy terrain that could be changed little.

Third, how political independence from colonial rule unfolded often left consequential political legacies. Turkey's achievement of independence under the leadership of Mustafa Kemal Atatürk proved an early model for the economic development of other states later in the century. Atatürk's policies of the 1930s that established significant state control over the economy and financial sectors would be replicated by Gamal Abdel Nasser in Egypt twenty years later (Richards and Waterbury 1990: 187–193). The violent Algerian war of independence from France led to a subsequent political arrangement in which a strong Algerian state dominated by the victorious National Liberation Front (FLN) would guide economic decisions. Another violent conflict, which resulted in the creation of the State of Israel in 1948, had profound effects on regional political economies as neighboring states Jordan, Syria, and Egypt directed precious resources away from social development and toward military spending.

All Middle East states inherited political economic institutions and factors shaping their future development. This did not mean trajectories could not be changed or that destinies were set; however, decisions in the new environment of political independence were circumscribed. Moving sharply against these legacies would not be easy or politically profitable in most cases.

The Boom Years, 1950s–1970s

For many in the Middle East, the end of World War II marked an optimistic change. The instability of the end of Ottoman rule and the dislocations from European dominance under the mandate system were in the past. Formal political independence seemed to promise control over the future. The challenges of building new states and economies, however, were daunting. Political leaders had to build new state bureaucracies from the remnants of previous colonial rule, craft national identities and attachments for populations that were sometimes very socially diverse, and construct national economies with a promise of higher living standards for all. Rulers pursued all of these tasks simultaneously within a highly unequal global economy dominated by Western countries. Moreover, attempts to address one of these tasks would surely affect the prospects of completing the others. To add further complication, countries faced these challenges from different starting points or levels of preparation.

Some of the resource-poor countries, like Syria, Jordan, and Lebanon (as well as resource-rich Iraq), had complex societal divisions, which meant

that economic decisions that favored one part of society over another were
bound to have adverse political effects. A number of the smaller Gulf countries did not face such divisions, but having wholly new political borders
and limited urban populations brought other challenges. Where they enjoyed an advantage was with close European and US support for building
their oil-based economies right from the start. By contrast, a state like
Egypt had a more developed bureaucracy and civil service inherited from
British rule, yet that same colonial legacy meant Egypt's finance and trade
sectors were dominated by foreign interests (the British- and French-owned
Suez Canal, for example). Perhaps the best-prepared states could be found
in Turkey and Israel after 1948. In both cases, but for different reasons
(Turkey because foreign rule was thwarted and Israel because foreign support undergirded Jewish rule), these states enjoyed comparatively more
autonomy from external economic influences than did their neighbors. Domestically, political leaders in these states also faced less entrenched socioeconomic interests (particularly the absence of large landowning elites)
that could block efforts at economic development and industrialization, as
often occurred in other parts of the region. Despite different levels of preparation, all countries built their economies with significant state leadership.
All would realize decades of economic expansion and growth, but uneven
productive development would characterize the experience of most Arab
countries.

In the 1950s, a consensus emerged that economic development required strong state guidance. The argument followed that investment and
public finance would have to be injected to kick-start growth. Strong national leadership was required to guide the process and generate a national
commitment to large-scale public enterprises. Again, Atatürk's Turkey provided the model that Egypt and a number of other Arab states would follow.
Coupled with the rising tide of anticolonial movements in the region, these
statist policies became wrapped in a collectivist ideology. State-led development and socialist means of production—meaning significant public
ownership of leading economic sectors—had the declared goal of guaranteeing that all classes of Arabs would benefit from growth. Rural peasants
would be liberated from serflike conditions and urban workers would join
with students in moving toward greater social equality. That an Egyptian,
Syrian, or Algerian state would control the key economic assets of the
country would free countries from foreign economic control. These ideas
were not particular to the Middle East; they generally were embraced across
the developing world. Moreover, these views dominated economic policy
discourse well into the 1970s and contributed to widely shared economic
policies across the region, including growth of the public sector, state-
directed finance and creation of state-owned enterprises (SOEs), nationalization of leading economic enterprises, and rural land reform and agricultural

expansion. In fact, it is no coincidence that the 2011 protests often articulated commitments to equality and fairness, which have for so long gone unfulfilled for much of the region's people.

Building the capacity of the public sector entailed the wholesale expansion of government agencies and quasi-state institutions. In the 1950s and especially the 1960s, the size and scope of government ministries expanded. The logic was that since the economies of the region were "underdeveloped," modern civil servants and state capacities were needed to guide and encourage economic growth. An important complement to public sector expansion was the treatment of labor unions and professional associations. With few exceptions, labor unions and professional associations of doctors, lawyers, and engineers were brought under some form of state control (Moore and Salloukh 2007). In countries with mass-based political parties— like the FLN in Algeria, the Baath parties in Syria and Iraq, and the Arab Socialist Union in Egypt—unions and associations came under the sway of parties. To get a business license or practice in one's field, membership in such associations or the party was required. As a consequence, unions and associations in the Middle East were large, but had limited autonomy and ability to influence economic development or worker rights. This does not mean labor or associational activity has been marginal; rather, their roles in domestic political economies have often been limited by political leaders (Posusney 1997). In part, the significant role organized labor played in Egypt and Tunisia's 2011 uprisings was built upon a history of labor activism and state repression. Once that repression began to give way in 2011, labor, along with other social allies, was primed to keep pushing.

States also moved aggressively to nationalize leading industries and financial enterprises. Among the countries without significant oil reserves, the first sectors to be nationalized were industry, agriculture, and transportation. This typically entailed state purchase of company assets from foreign and domestic shareholders. The most famous of these nationalizations was Nasser's nationalization of the British and French–owned Suez Canal in 1956. Such sequestrations were replicated across the region. While some countries, like Jordan, professed a "free market" commitment even in these early years, all countries, including Israel and Turkey, allowed for significant state involvement in the economy. The oil-exporting nations followed similar patterns; however, national oil companies that had been controlled by European and US firms were the primary targets of nationalization. By the 1970s, all major oil-exporting countries had completely taken over their oil industries. In addition to the takeover of resident firms, states also created wholly new public industries and utilities, such as national airlines, telecommunications, and transportation companies. These SOEs enjoyed subsidized inputs and protection from external competition. Located in urban areas, these industries were also designed to provide employment for growing urban populations. Once protected industries developed their own capacities and efficiencies, the idea went, protections could be removed and these domestic firms would then compete in regional and international markets.

Not all economic policies were directed at cities. A number of policies, generally referred to as land reform, targeted rural areas. While the small Gulf oil countries generally lacked populated rural areas and therefore focused on urban growth, it will be recalled that Egypt, Syria, and Iraq had inherited significantly unequal and impoverished rural areas from colonial rule. Peasants *(fellahin)* often worked land—owned by large, mostly absent landlords—for increasingly marginal returns. In many countries, these landed elites had supported previous colonial rule and often inherited state institutions after independence; therefore, once revolutionary regimes took power, these elites became popular political targets. Land reform took many forms, but the aim was to break up large rural landholdings and redistribute the parcels to peasants. States were then to help small farmers prosper through the provision of irrigation, fertilizer, and road networks. Agricultural production would increase as a result and rural inequity would be alleviated—at least that was the idea.

Behind these ambitious policies and rapid changes, political constraints and opportunities were at work. As the great social historian Ibn Khaldun once remarked, no king is powerful alone; he requires people to support his rule. Economic policies, then, were a principal means of securing that support. Three basic political imperatives were at work: fashion a political coalition to support the ruling regime; weaken domestic rivals to that regime; and compete for ideological and sociocultural authenticity at home and abroad.

Expanding government agencies and the civil service directly employed large portions of the labor market. This gave people, especially in urban areas, a tangible stake in a regime's political rule. In countries with new revolutionary regimes, mass-based political parties evolved into gatekeepers to employment and economic gain. Party membership and civil service employment overlapped, so that the most likely path to social and economic advancement came through party allegiance. In the monarchical states and smaller Gulf countries, political parties were effectively outlawed or handicapped, so ruling families directly expanded public sector employment. By the 1980s, public sector employment, including in the military, was among the largest components of the workforce in most countries. Outside the public sector, state management of labor unions and professional associations limited the ability of political rivals or activists to mobilize through these venues. And while the letter of the law professed various labor rights in most countries, in practice these rights were not upheld, as strikes were not allowed and union leaders had little autonomy.

State control over leading economic firms, trade protection, and subsidies gave political leaders the tools to reward political allies. In other words, economic control translated into political patronage. Rulers could assign their allies, or clients, to sit on corporate boards and award public works contracts to favored businesses. By the 1970s, public-private shareholding companies formed in which the state would maintain a controlling ownership, with smaller—but very profitable—shares allowed for private sector allies. The sale or transfer of public land, particularly in booming urban areas, provided another way to route patronage to political allies. Finally, by controlling credit allocation and strictly licensing who was allowed to import and export, rulers could select allies to receive incredibly lucrative monopolies over luxury goods as well as basic staples. Imagine the money that can be made if one has the exclusive right to import, say, BMW motorcars or Apple computers to Saudi Arabia or Egypt. By signing one's name to the import bill, millions are made with little effort. Scholars refer to these mechanisms as "side payments," a euphemism for payoff (Waterbury 1993).

Last, in tone and in proclaimed intent, these policies corresponded to broad ideological as well as local sociocultural sentiments of the day. Arab nationalism, equality, and collective advancement were more than just slogans for many in the region. Though separate from Arab nationalism, Turks, Israelis, and Iranians identified with this collectivist spirit as well. Consequently, state efforts to limit foreign capital and guide the domestic private sector comported with conceptions of fairness and justice. Early efforts at land reform and redistribution in rural areas in particular expressed these attributes. Since the situation of peasants and rural inequality had been aggravated under colonial rule, it was no surprise that revolutionary movements in Syria, Iraq, Egypt, and Algeria drew much of their early support from these areas.

Through these various forms of patronage, regimes built coalitions of support and sidelined rivals in ways that would be economically consequential (Waldner 1999). In Algeria, Iraq, Egypt, and Syria, private sector elites who had been aligned with the previous colonial regimes were pushed out or co-opted through state-mediated side payments. In the Gulf states, ruling families were able to build massive bureaucracies that left marginal room for the private sector. However, a caveat is necessary. Highlighting the political and social sources of economic policy is not to argue that such considerations automatically impair economic development or interfere with the market. On the contrary, state provision of regulation, infrastructure, and investment is a requirement of efficient market operation, not an impediment. Middle Eastern countries were, after all, emulating the policies and strategies that had led to Europe's successful economic development a century earlier (Gerschenkron 1962), and economic policies that reflect social conceptions of justice can be found in all national economies. The question of the political underpinning of economic policies is not about political direction per se, but about who is to benefit from such policies. Are investments designed to broaden economic participation? Increase opportunities and capacities to advance? Distribute resources so as to include more and more sectors of society? Or are policies designed to enrich only a narrow stratum of society? The 2011 uprisings focused in particular on this last question.

Despite looming problems, some of the optimism of these decades was rewarded. In terms of real GDP growth per capita, the Middle East outperformed all other parts of the developing world, excluding East Asia, until 1979 (IMF 2003). State policies in these decades led to the construction of urban infrastructure, expanded road networks, new power grids, and modernized port facilities. Expansion of public education succeeded in boosting literacy, and increased public employment allowed women into the workforce in large numbers for the first time. Unfortunately, these were gains that could stagnate or be reversed.

Oil Politics

Shaikh Ahmed Zaki Yamani, Saudi Arabia's second oil minister, was reported to have once remarked, "All in all, I wish we had discovered water" (Karl 1997: 188). Reference to the perils of oil may clash with the perceived wealth of many oil-producing countries today; however, the interaction between oil and politics is anything but a clear success story. As the Ottoman Empire came to an end and Western dominance took hold, a group of seven US and European oil companies (the so-called seven sisters) came to control the region's oil resources through what were termed concession agreements. Typically, these agreements meant oil companies would finance oil exploration, but in return the seven sisters essentially owned the natural resource, could dispose of it as they saw fit, and only remitted a small portion of the profits to the host government (Parra 2004). Additionally, these contracts could not be adjudicated under the host country's legal system, creating conditions ripe for exploitation by the oil companies. The history of Western oil companies in the Middle East, therefore, is hardly a happy one (Vitalis 2007).

After independence, oil-exporting countries gradually turned the tables and organized so that in 1960 the Organization of Petroleum Exporting Countries (OPEC) was founded in Baghdad. From 1970 to 1973, the last three major exporters, Algeria, Libya, and Iraq, nationalized their oil industries. States, not companies, now controlled the development and use of their oil resources. In the wake of the 1973 Arab-Israeli war and US support for Israel, the OPEC states embargoed oil shipments, sparking the oil crisis of the 1970s. The rapid spike in the price of a barrel of oil transferred historically high profits directly to rulers and the nationalized oil companies they controlled. This has meant that oil profits compose the largest part of gross domestic product as well as the majority of government revenue in these countries. However, not all oil exporters in the region are similar.

One of the basic distinctions is size. The larger oil states, Algeria, Saudi Arabia, Iraq, and Iran, all have populations over 20 million. By contrast, the smaller Gulf oil states average populations of 1 million or less (see Table 4.2). Distributing oil profits over a larger society versus a smaller one leads to important differences. Consequently, the smaller Gulf states are among the world's wealthiest in terms of per capita income and GDP, whereas Saudi Arabia, the world's largest oil exporter, has seen its per capita GDP decline since the 1980s as its population has grown. It is easy to appreciate, then, that with such wealth, politics is close by. The interaction of oil and politics can be assessed from two vantage points: domestic and regional.

How oil has affected the internal politics of countries has long been a focus of scholarly debate. Until the 1970s, it was common for Western academics to argue that authoritarianism in the Arab Middle East was due to Islam or an unchanging "Arab character." Such simple connections persist today, but they have consistently been critiqued in the past several decades. A focus on the role of oil, instead of strictly religion and culture, was one of these critiques. The most prominent set of these arguments, known as the "resource curse" or "rentier state" theories, holds that the way a state earns its money (in this case through oil export) determines its basic politics.[1]

Table 4.2 Oil Production and Population Statistics, 2011

	Production (million barrels per day)	Population (total residents/ nonnationals in millions)
Algeria	1.9	37/negligible
Iran	4.2	78/negligible
Iraq	2.6	31/negligible
Kuwait	2.6	2.6/1.2
Libya	0.5	5.6/0.16
Qatar	1.6	1.9/0.55
Saudi Arabia	11.1	26/5.5
United Arab Emirates	3.0	5.3/3.0

Source: CIA World Factbook, https://www.cia.gov/library/publications/the-world-factbook (accessed November 2012).

Note: Production is distinct from exports, which is lower in most cases due to domestic consumption.

Rulers with exclusive access to oil profits enjoy what are called soft budget constraints; that is, far more money than required for public expenditure was available year in and year out due to high oil prices. In turn, rulers were free to distribute this wealth through a myriad of means to co-opt political allies and sideline rivals. In the logic of the rentier framework, since rulers did not have to exploit domestic resources to fund their states (that is, tax citizens), they were not compelled to grant political representation either; hence the twist on a well-known maxim, "no taxation, no representation." The expectation is that such polities should experience declining political opposition and subdued civic association, since gaining individual favor with the ruler becomes the name of the game. In this way, rentier theory argued that lack of democracy was not caused by religion or culture, but by economic factors, that is, easy oil profits. Lavish lifestyles for rulers, public budgets that dwarfed private interests, well-funded internal security apparatuses, and militarily powerful foreign patrons all gave the rentier state an appearance of fierce political strength. Yet here is where the "curse" part comes in, for there are costs to this type of political economy.

States built on distribution and not extraction (i.e., an income or corporate tax) are argued to have underdeveloped administrative capacities. For example, consider all of the information the government needs to tax a paycheck. All of those deductions and accounting procedures require lots of information that is constantly updated; this in turn requires state agencies with vast administrative skills to generate, monitor, and authenticate that information. Straightforward revenue distribution does not require such information-gathering skills. So while typical oil-state agencies appear numerous, expansive, and well staffed, they are flabby in terms of actual capacities and capabilities. They can't do much. Moreover, oil-dependent economies suffer from what economists term "the Dutch disease," a condition in which an economy is flooded with external revenue, depressing incentives to manufacture products while increasing the ability to purchase imported products. The result is a one-dimensional economy in which little is manufactured locally. Hence in theory, when the price of oil drops, the oil-dependent state does not have much to fall back on and political crisis is expected to follow. What happens when the rentier state is then forced to turn to domestic taxes? No taxation without representation?

As far as these arguments go, there is a degree of logic and plausibility. However, scholars have lately come to question the simplistic formula that oil causes political outcomes. First, oil does not spend itself; political rulers choose how to control and deploy these assets (Okruhlik 1999). As discussed previously, state-led development in the region has had clear political rationales. Likewise, Gulf rulers deployed their oil wealth not just to generate economic growth, but also to secure political rule. Certainly, having exclusive control over massive oil monies makes it easier to thwart political opponents and reward allies, but something more than just oil revenue generated society's support for or acquiescence to nondemocratic rule in the Gulf and beyond. For one thing, though oil prices declined precipitously in the 1980s and 1990s, no oil exporters embarked on democratization, and where some political liberalization did take place, it was marginal (Gause 1993). And though the exportation of oil seems an important similarity between, say, Libya and Iran, oil exporters are hardly uniform. For instance, Kuwait, a small oil-rich state with a ruling family, has had a freely elected parliament with a well-organized opposition since 1961. Though the Kuwaiti parliament's legislative powers are circumscribed, its latitude of political action is far greater compared to legislative bodies in neighboring countries. And in 2006, Kuwait extended suffrage to its female citizens, the first among the Gulf Arab monarchies to do so. Indeed, Algeria, Saudi Arabia, Qatar, Oman, Bahrain, and the UAE all have nondemocratic regimes that enjoy monopoly access to oil and gas revenues, yet their politics and societies are hardly similar. That mass political protest in 2011 struck Libya and Bahrain to a greater extent than the other resource-dependent countries reinforces the point of divergence among the Arab oil exporters.

The oil boom of the 1970s also had profound effects on the region as a whole and the relations among its states. Since many of the smaller oil states experienced inflows of finance that they could not hope to fully invest domestically, there was much capital to invest elsewhere. From the 1970s onward, Gulf states provided billions of dollars in bilateral aid, loans, grants, and development assistance to other Arab states that lacked oil resources. This financial power has positioned donor states, like Saudi Arabia, as important players and decisionmakers regarding a number of regional diplomatic issues. Such funds also became important sources of external financing for Egypt, Syria, Lebanon, Palestine, Morocco, and Yemen. In return, as the oil boom fed growth and expansion, large numbers of citizens of these countries migrated to the Gulf states to staff professional and middle-management positions in the government and private sector. The money they earned was often sent back to their families at home. Like development aid, these worker remittances became important sources of finance for the resource-poor countries of the Middle East.

In short, oil and politics have historically shaped one another, and since oil is a finite resource in continual demand, this relationship is sure to endure for many more decades.

The Bust Years, 1980–2000

Beginning in the early 1980s, most countries of the Middle East experienced stagnant or unstable economic growth and mounting public debt.

Much of the dissatisfaction with socioeconomic conditions that was manifested in the 2011 uprisings originated in this period. While expansion and economic growth took place until the late 1970s, more tangible *development,* through investments yielding productive returns and labor upgrading, failed to take root. After decades of mounting expectations, the economic crunch contributed to public discontent across the region. Sharp increases in the price of basic staples in Egypt, Jordan, and Morocco led to public protests in the 1980s, often ending in violent clashes with security forces. The increasing gap between rich and poor, and overt displays of elite consumption, contrasted sharply with regimes' rhetoric regarding equality and social justice. Where state programs and public investment were launched as means to fight inequality, they instead became exclusive venues for those few who had enough political access to realize significant benefit. Investment in education and upgrading labor skills quickly atrophied, because while such expenditures pay benefits for many in the long term, they pay few short-term political benefits. State-owned industries failed to become competitive and instead siphoned off declining public assets to continue operation. The private sector, though surviving the nationalizations and restrictions of the 1960s and 1970s, reacted by investing little in domestic enterprises and instead sent its capital overseas. Cities that had grown rapidly became overburdened with new arrivals, social services weakened, and urban planning ceased in many areas.

Rural areas fared little better. Promised land redistribution either never materialized or was piecemeal. Where peasants actually took control of land, state support arrived infrequently, forcing farmers to turn for loans to some of the same large landowners whose land was sequestered in the first place. Instead of a productive agricultural sector developing, rural debt increased and countries were forced to import many food products. Rural discontent was reflected in growing political opposition as well as cultural critique. For example, Yusuf al-Qa'id's popular novel *War in the Land of Egypt* depicted the failure of Nasser's land reform and the peasant oppression that followed. Among the Gulf oil exporters of the 1980s, the financial cushions were greater, but for the first time since political independence public debt became a reality. The conspicuous wealth of the ruling families led to critical questioning about the destination of oil profits. Here too, discontent expressed itself through popular novels like Abdul Rahman Munif's trilogy *Cities of Salt,* which depicted the social dislocations caused by oil exploitation in a small Gulf country.

These socioeconomic strains took place at the same time population growth remained high across the region. Since economic growth was not keeping up with the need to produce jobs, unemployment increased. Previous decades of growth and expansion without genuine economic development and investment succeeded in producing only low-quality jobs and uncompetitive industries. While sectors of the Turkish and Israeli populations achieved higher living standards in the 1980s, and previously underdeveloped South Korea and Taiwan began producing cars and electronics, Arab countries remained wedded to industries with low worker skills or sectors of economic activity that required little fixed investment (like transportation, trade, and services) and little upgrading or educational investment. Thousands of university graduates were coming into the labor market with few prospects beyond a mundane career in the public sector. Only for the few who were politically connected, or for the children of private sector elites, were there more opportunities for the future.

What explains such a big turnaround? The spark is commonly attributed to the long decline of oil and commodity prices from their highs in the 1970s to their lows in the 1990s. As oil producers witnessed reductions in their public revenue, bilateral aid and worker remittances to the resource-poor states declined accordingly. Egyptian, Palestinian, Jordanian, and Yemeni workers in the Gulf sent less money back home. The reduction in regional finances put serious strains on states' ability to continue their expansive economic policies. However, while oil prices certainly played a role, the problems of the bust decades went deeper.

A major reason for the economic downturn was found in the political rationales for the boom policies in the first place. As noted earlier, many economic policies corresponded to the needs of political elites to maintain ruling coalitions; thus, the webs of political patronage that followed were not easily changed. Clients of political patrons were expected to deliver political loyalty, not more valuable goods, more skilled workers, or more efficient factories. SOEs and shareholding companies that had been fostered through state patronage and protection had no incentive to wean themselves or invest in upgrading. Instead, state-owned factories became employment vehicles of last resort and sources of easy profit for the politically connected. Private sector elites cushioned by trade protection and easy profits from public contracts had little incentive to switch to more risky investments in domestic production.

Another reason for the bust was that competition in the international marketplace became fiercer. While the post–World War II global market was dominated by North America and a recovering Western Europe, the global economy of the 1980s saw the East Asian economies arrive as serious competitors. Exposing SOEs and shareholding companies to such competition would have had dire social ramifications. Domestic currencies that had been overvalued to aid industry and support urban consumer purchases of imports came to be an obstacle to economic adaptation. Lowering the value of one's currency (thus lowering the cost of exports but increasing the cost of imports) is one way to compete internationally, but that would carry political costs that rulers were not willing to undertake.

Stuck between the rock of political survival and the hard place of economic crunch, how did rulers and states respond? By implementing selective and limited economic reform, reaching out to international lending agencies for support, and allowing elements of limited political liberalization. At first, nearly all states in the early 1980s avoided any reductions in public spending or price supports. They simply kept going in the hope that conditions would improve. Such avoidance is common to most governments in the world, because what politician wants to be the first to call for austerity? However, as the downturn in world oil and commodity prices continued, public debt mounted, particularly among the resource-poor countries.

Countries like Yemen, Egypt, Jordan, and Morocco had problems financing their debts while maintaining high public budgets. Controlled experiments to lower public subsidies and let prices rise resulted in public unrest, limiting those options. A number of countries announced economic reform policies, or what generally became known as *infitah* (economic opening). Egypt, Tunisia, and Turkey led the way by announcing policies to increase the role of the private sector, increase foreign investment, and boost exports. Eventually, most countries in the region announced similar intents, but their experiences varied. Whereas Turkey and Tunisia would achieve some success in boosting manufactured exports and attracting investment, Egypt generally failed in its efforts. Openings to the private sector were selective and geared toward retaining political clients. Removing the modest welfare provisions that many states had created in the 1970s risked pushing more people toward the political opposition, which came to be dominated by the increasingly popular Islamist parties in the 1980s and 1990s. For rulers, the political costs of decentralizing economic control and resources were just too great.

By the late 1980s, some of the non–oil exporters were compelled to turn to international lending agencies like the World Bank and International Monetary Fund (IMF) for assistance. In what was known as the Washington Consensus, these international agencies offered funds to debt-burdened developing states, including Middle Eastern states, but required specific policy reforms in return. These reforms went beyond earlier *infitah* policies and included privatization of state assets, trade liberalization, currency liberalization, elimination of foreign investment restrictions, and public sector reform. But such reforms could cut support to clients, increase unemployment, and endanger private profits, all of which threatened the political loyalty and social stability that these policies were intended to generate in the first place. Rulers were wary of going down this road, and, as critics of the Washington Consensus argued, it was far from clear that such policies would restore growth and lead to meaningful development (Rodrik 1997).

Nevertheless, a number of Arab states (Algeria, Egypt, Jordan, Morocco, and Tunisia) signed loan agreements with the IMF. Interestingly, these states have been able to avoid or limit implementation of many of the reforms required by the loan agreements. Since the Middle East is viewed as strategically crucial for the United States and Europe, which are the IMF's largest contributors, there was a geostrategic interest in advancing loans to lessen political pressure on friendly regimes. In other words, when push came to shove, there was little interest on the part of Western donor countries to compel reforms or withdraw funding in ways that might endanger the stability of friendly regimes, especially in Jordan and Egypt (Harrigan and El-Said 2009: 10–11). Just as regimes in the region relied on different forms of state involvement in the economy as one means to ensure their political rule, leaders in the West needed those same regimes to stay in place to ensure their own political interests, like guaranteeing access to oil and normalizing relations with Israel.

The resource-exporting countries faced similar financial pressures, but most did not need to turn to international lenders. Iraq survived its war with Iran but then faced decaying economic conditions at a time of declining oil revenues. Saddam Hussein was able to survive until 2003 in part because of oil smuggling and circumvention of import restrictions through neighboring countries. Saudi Arabia witnessed a dramatic reduction in per capita income as its population continued to grow while its oil money decreased. Along with Saudi Arabia, the smaller oil producers met hard times as well, but the Gulf enjoyed a larger toolbox of responses to avoid turning to the IMF. These states could endure longer periods of debt financing and avoid serious austerity as private lenders were all too happy to extend loans (without reform conditions) to countries with significant oil revenues. Thus, none of the oil states were forced to turn to international lending agencies.

Finally, faced with tough social dislocations, some states entertained limited moves toward political liberalization as a last resort. Jordan reinstituted its elected parliament in 1989; Kuwait did the same after being liberated from Iraq in 1991; and Yemen followed suit after its brief civil war in the mid-1990s. The more conservative Gulf states promised various forms of appointed consultative councils—though these were well short of elected bodies. While not exactly a form of political liberalization, Saddam Hussein's Baath Party in Iraq devolved economic and political power to provinces in the south and west in order to cope with international sanctions in the 1990s. Finally, press freedoms were relaxed in a number of countries as new forms of media made their appearance in the 1990s. All of these shifts influenced some observers to expect that political liberalization would deepen as the economic downturn continued (Anderson 1995). Perhaps economic liberalization can be part of broader democratization, but this was not to be.

Liberalizations remained limited and genuine political decentralization rarely occurred. In Egypt, Jordan, Morocco, Kuwait, and Tunisia, press and associative freedoms were reversed in the mid-1990s. State security agencies increased their surveillance of opposition groups, while periodic arrests of opposition figures and general intimidation silenced those who might voice more opposition. Consequently, the region's regimes survived the bust decades politically intact. Economically and socially, however, there were great costs. Infrastructure decayed in many cities, living standards stagnated, and some measures of inequality increased. Though opposition movements had been blocked, the socioeconomic reasons for discontent remained unaddressed and would make themselves felt in 2011.

A New Century and the Road to 2011

The turn of the century has seen a region seemingly accustomed to shocks and sudden shifts witness even more. In this period a new oil boom took place, approaching the highs of the 1970s. The survival of the United States as the sole superpower directly affected the region's political economies through the "war on terror," the invasion of Iraq, and closer economic relations with a number of Arab regimes. The 2008–2009 global financial crisis had its effects, but the region largely escaped entanglement with America's bursting bubble. Instead, it was the 2011 uprisings that rocked the region with ramifications that we have only begun to grasp. Three trends from 2000 to the present are consequential for the near future: (1) increased international and bilateral pressures to liberalize economies, (2) deepening socioeconomic decay and inequality in a number of countries, and (3) the mass political uprisings and regime instabilities that followed. Taken together, these factors are remaking the region in profound ways. No longer can we speak of a single regional economy, one developmental path, or shared strategies. Instead, different parts of the region are moving in diverse directions, and disparities in wealth among as well as within countries are growing more pronounced. The road to 2011 was paved with these tensions.

In one sense, the start of the 2000s seemed to have provided much-needed fiscal cushion to the region's states. External actors, international lending agencies, multinational corporations, and world trade organizations increased investment and aid. Rulers in strategically important Middle Eastern countries could expect to bide their financial time through increased bilateral and military aid from the West, particularly the United States. In pursuing the "war on terror," US financial assistance to Jordan, Egypt, Yemen, and Morocco has increased significantly since 2000. Just like oil monies that flow to the Gulf's ruling families, Western budgetary and security assistance flows directly into the coffers of allied regimes, allowing them to shore up their rule without addressing underlying socioeconomic dislocations (Peters and Moore 2009). Indeed, depending on how it is measured, the Middle East is either the most aid-dependent region in the developing world or second only to sub-Saharan Africa (World Bank 2008: 366; Rivlin 2009: 33).

Additional external support has come from multilateral institutions offering potential benefits like membership in the World Trade Organization (WTO) and bilateral trade agreements with the European Union and the United States. Since the 1980s, the United States has signed free trade agreements with Israel, Jordan, Bahrain, Morocco, and Oman. These agreements require varying levels of openness to external investment, adherence to intellectual property rights, and even minimal labor rights. In theory, Arab countries that sign will gain privileged access to Western consumer markets, but in return Western exporters and investors should realize unfettered access to the signers' domestic markets. In general, these bilateral trade agreements signaled more political support than actual economic development, although Jordanian and Israeli exports to the United States have increased. Thus the general impression of the region on the eve of the 2011 uprisings was one of slow but progressing economic development—not great but better than some other parts of the developing world.

Returning to our theme of the domestic political foundations of economic development, we can begin to appreciate a different perspective in the lead-up to 2011, one that emphasizes socioeconomic discontent built on decades of uneven development. After all, little of the external aid awash in the region since 2000 seems to have filtered down, a fact not lost on much of the region's peoples. Public opinion surveys over that same period consistently ranked the economy and corruption as the top two concerns of most Arab citizens. Countries that already had young and impoverished populations, such as Yemen, Egypt, and Morocco, remained the same. Syria and Jordan faced many of the same problems, as income levels, infrastructure, and overall development have not advanced much past their levels in the mid-1980s. For example, though the Middle East exports more fuel than any other region, it also exports fewer manufactured goods than any other region, including sub-Saharan Africa (see Table 4.3).

Table 4.3 Manufactured vs. Fuel Exports by Region, 2009 (percentage of merchandise exports)

	Fuel	Manufactures
Europe and Central Asia	8.9	72.6
Latin America	21.0	50.2
Middle East and North Africa	67.8	24.5
South Asia	10.5	68.1
Sub-Saharan Africa	38.2	29.0

Source: World Bank, *World Databank, World Development Indicators and Global Development Finance,* includes all income levels Middle East and North Africa, http://data.world bank.org/data-catalog (Washington, DC).

The region entered the new century with some of the highest unemployment rates, particularly among youth, in the world. It was no surprise, then, that organized labor emerged as a prominent actor in the 2011 uprisings. While measures of inequality did not increase significantly, other measures of poverty and living standards did worsen. For most of the region, expanding job opportunities, improving public education, and upgrading urban infrastructure remained significant challenges. If one travels to Cairo, Amman, or Rabat today, it is easy to see pockets of wealth replete with conspicuous consumption, prestige vehicles, and Western retail chains. For the vast majority of citizens, these luxuries are far out of reach, leading to the conclusion that while new wealth is apparent in the region, it remains poorly invested and unevenly distributed. Those with political connections profit, and those profits tend to be spent on consumption and overseas bank accounts, not on productive domestic investments. Those without such connections struggle to give their families a better life. Not surprisingly, then, among developing regions, Arab countries consistently rank high on indexes measuring perceptions of corruption (UNDP 2004: 136–141).

Deficient economic development has been an even greater problem for countries suffering from political violence. Iraq, having experienced war with Iran, a decade of international sanctions, and then invasion by the United States in 2003, is the starkest example of reversed development. Though the country was the economic and social powerhouse of the region in the 1970s, the subsequent political and economic hardships have taken their toll. Large parts of Baghdad remain ethnically cleansed, hundreds of thousands of civilians have been wounded or killed, and over 4 million have been displaced. Iraqis now constitute the region's largest refugee population since the displacement of Palestinians during the creation of the State of Israel in 1948. The occupied Palestinian territories have also experienced regression. Israeli blockades and frequent violent conflict have scared away foreign investment, leaving Palestinians worse off than before the Oslo peace process began in 1993 (Roy 2007: 250–293). The wrenching civil violence in Syria suggests similar socioeconomic reversal for that country as more lives are lost, infrastructure is destroyed, and hope for a peaceful resolution fades.

All told then, political opposition and discontent with socioeconomic conditions came together in 2011 across the region. As we have reviewed, few of these conditions were new; in fact, there was a long history of socioeconomic protest met with state repression. While a full account of the 2011 uprisings will require more analysis, it was clear that protests in every country were infused with popular anger at corruption, inequality, poor job prospects, and most importantly, the accumulated privileges of regime leaders and their cronies. In Tunisia, protesters targeted Leila Ben Ali's real estate holdings and "Mr. 10%" Slim Chiboub and his Carrefour grocery chain. In Egypt, it was Ahmed Ezz's steel and the Mubaraks' Palm Hills. In Yemen, student protesters highlighted the ruling Salih family's trade monopolies; in Syria, the target was Rami Makhlouf's mobile phones and hotels; and in Jordan, public disgust was directed at Marouf Bakhit and his Dead Sea casino project. In these ways, decades of inequality and corruption came out into the open, linking places, monopolies, and regime cronies to give citizens no shortage of symbols of protest.

What then of the oil exporters for whom the socioeconomic issues might be different? At first glance, the 2011 uprisings seemed to have bypassed the major Arab resource exporters: Saudi Arabia, Kuwait, Qatar, Oman, and the UAE. On the other hand, Bahrain and Libya did witness large-scale protest infused with many of the same socioeconomic grievances of the less resource-rich countries. For Libyans, the corruption of the Muammar Qaddafi regime and vast inequality in how oil money was invested in the country animated protest. Bahrain had seen its resource exports decline at roughly the same time promises by the ruling Al Khalifas to allow greater political participation failed to materialize. That many of the country's poorest were also those most politically disenfranchised proved a combustible mix. Both countries attracted external intervention: North Atlantic Treaty Organization (NATO) intervention in Libya to hasten the fall of the Qaddafi regime, and Saudi and UAE intervention in Bahrain to preserve the ruling family there. And if we look closer, Saudi Arabia, Kuwait, and the UAE were not as calm in the face of 2011 as widely assumed. While the kind of sustained protests seen in Tahrir Square did not sweep the Gulf states, these smaller societies did witness historically unprecedented unrest. Saudi Arabia responded to organized protests with violence in its eastern provinces; Kuwaiti protests in parliament and mass street protests took place, forcing the Emir Shaikh Sabah al-Ahmad al-Sabah to shut down parliament; and in response to dissent voiced by some prominent Emiratis, UAE authorities arrested scores and exiled others. But despite these protests, the oil exporters again benefited from a much larger set of tools with which to respond and survive.

Staggeringly high oil prices until 2008 buoyed public budgets across the Gulf and allowed new forms of investment such as sovereign wealth funds (SWFs). These funds consist of percentages of oil revenues put aside each year. The resulting fund is controlled by the state and invested, usually overseas and without transparency, to earn returns so that in a future without oil reserves, national wealth can be preserved. These SWFs have grown in value into the hundreds of billions of dollars, making Kuwait, the UAE, and Saudi Arabia important global financial players with significant investment in Western government securities and private equities. The new oil boom also ensured continued military purchases from the West at a high pace, reinforcing the deep financial ties between Washington and the Arab

Gulf's ruling families. In addition to the use of force in responding to 2011, the oil exporters also deployed their new financial muscle to quell dissent. As Egypt's protests mounted in early 2011, Saudi Arabia, Kuwait, and the UAE announced massive new social spending and civil service pay increases. As protests spread from Egypt and Tunisia, the Gulf oil exporters then promised similar financial support to allied monarchies in Jordan and Morocco. The message was clear: continued ruling family control in the Gulf required the survival of monarchies in the entire region. The rentier state model discussed earlier has gone regional. And perhaps owing to their financial linkages and importance, Washington and Europe have been content to pick and choose where to step in—supporting regime opponents in Libya and Syria but supporting the regimes in Bahrain and Saudi Arabia.

For the time being, revenue and repression has worked for the Gulf states and their allies in Jordan and Morocco. Yet, it's important to note that little of this addresses the underlying socioeconomic grievances that have been at play for decades and loomed large in 2011.

Conclusion

As observed at the opening of this chapter, Arabs and Muslim society in general have historically been closely associated with commerce. Yet as post–World War II patterns demonstrate, the Middle East's potential for development has not been realized. While much of the region has experienced periods of economic growth, there has been little productive development. The growth that has occurred has often meant little more than increased consumption and expansion of money, coming and going with boom and bust. Development, on the other hand, requires higher value added, more complex manufacturing, competitive exporting, and increasing the skills, education, and security of domestic labor. Once begun, development is harder to reverse and tends to build upon itself. With few exceptions, these developmental benchmarks have not been achieved. The millions of Arab citizens who took to the streets in 2011 did so in defiance of a history of economic stagnation and political despotism. Their victory was to achieve tangible hope for greater, meaningful change, but this change will not be easy. For the countries whose mobilized protests toppled incumbent leaders and whose governments appear to be in transition, new political leaders are likely to emphasize ways to turn the external revenue faucet back on and avoid serious economic restructuring. The intensity and scope of the political demands of a newly empowered citizenry might outstrip the pace of economic recovery and reform. Fears of precocious democratization could strengthen the old guard and arguments for limited liberalization. For countries that have not yet witnessed sustained protest threatening incumbent leaders, many of the same socioeconomic grievances are still in play, suggesting that the 2011 uprisings may not be over.

Note

1. Rentier theory refers to rents. The classic definition of *rent* is income in the form of *reward* rather than something that is *earned*. Rent often derives from monopoly control of an asset. Some forms of commodity extraction, especially oil, require very little labor and capital investment after the initial drilling, and hence the price of a barrel of oil far exceeds the actual cost of production. Given that oil is state owned in most countries (a monopoly), the difference between low production costs and high world prices is the rent income.

5

Civil Society

Sheila Carapico

What role does civil society play in the mostly authoritarian polities of the Middle East? Civil society is a classic social science construct, broadly defined as an associational space situated between governments and households, and also between the public state sector and the commercial economy. Thus when we think of civil society, we think of professional associations, charities, universities, interest groups, media outlets, book clubs, and community betterment drives; of public gatherings or displays in civic-minded parades, concerts, or museums; and of suffrage, labor, civil rights, antiwar, and environmental movements. Often called the nonprofit, nongovernmental, or "third" sector, civil society is driven by neither the motive of businesses to profit nor the ambition of political parties or revolutionary movements to take over the state. The civic realm is a place for voluntarism, philanthropy, public-spirited activism, and civil discourse; it's a metaphorical public square.

According to many theorists, civil society is a distinctively modern phenomenon that gradually replaced primordial associations grounded in ascriptive bonds of caste and clan with individuals' voluntary memberships in the organizations of mass, literate, largely urban, bourgeois society. In many conceptualizations, a vibrant civic associational network and a lively public intellectual domain are the sine qua non for democratic development; to function fully, democracy needs a watchdog "fourth estate" in the press, organized groups to articulate interests and protect rights, and the free flow of ideas and information. Some take this argument a step further to assert that the test of civil society is its enabling of democratic transitions; without democracy, in other words, civil society cannot exist. By this criterion, many regarded civil society in most of the Middle East as impotent, or perhaps disabled. Even after mass mobilizations drove several tyrants from power in 2011 and 2012, some insisted that the test of civil society was whether the uprisings led directly to liberal democracy.

Yet we have known all along that when circumstances demand, civil society can enable communities to cope with physical or political adversity, to navigate bureaucratic obstacles, and even to breach authoritarianism. Indeed, comparative and historical research in Europe, the Americas, and elsewhere shows that civil society is not a constant, unchanging cultural attribute but rather a variable that changes shape and scope according to political and economic circumstances. At different moments, German civil society marched for Nazism, cowered from a police state, and breached the Berlin Wall, for instance. In the United States, civil society operated differently during colonial days, the Jim Crow era, the Great Depression, World War II, the Vietnam protests, and the age of electronic networks, and still assumes different forms in contemporary rural Wyoming, urban Manhattan, and flooded New Orleans. Civic networks in the old Soviet Union were deeply penetrated from top to bottom by the central government and security police. Yet writers, intellectuals, and regular folk found enclaves within totalitarian establishments, for instance in scientific institutes, theatrical companies, or religious and cultural establishments. Histories of postcolonial Africa document the various and varying ways that churches, Sufi orders, ethnic associations, and folk traditions contribute to the public civic sphere even in the absence of democratic governance, and sometimes amid very dire socioeconomic conditions or even bloody conflict. Finally, as the examples of the United States, Germany, France, Russia, and Kenya or Sierra Leone remind us, even if we demand of civil society that it practice civility, we should not assume that it is inherently liberal (in the American sense of the term); without ideological diversity and a spectrum of ideas, tolerance isn't of much use.

This chapter explains, in broad strokes, the forms and variability of activism in public civic spheres in the Middle East, even, or especially, in the absence of democracy. It is divided into five main parts, following a roughly chronological outline. The main argument is that civic engagement is shaped by and responds to material and political conditions: to constraints and opportunities. It isn't just "there" or "not there" and can certainly persist in the absence of liberal democracy. The first section shows that, contrary to Orientalist stereotypes, there was a strong tradition of voluntarism, philanthropy, and civic activism in the precontemporary Middle East that constituted a public civic realm if not modern civil society. The second and third sections are about the surge of civic associational activity around the middle of the twentieth century and how hard new national governments worked for decades to contain, co-opt, or suppress independent public organizing. The ways that individuals and groups operate within, evade, and protest authoritarianism are the subject of the fourth section, which is in many ways the heart of the chapter. Finally, we examine some ways in which the historic surge of public activism in 2011 constituted a civic revolution even if the near-term outcome in individual countries is not liberal democracy.

The Traditional Public Civic Realm

One formerly prominent but now outmoded viewpoint insists that civil society is a cultural characteristic of Western civilization, largely absent from the Islamic world, save perhaps among its Christian and Jewish minorities. Whole societies and individual organizations either are or are not civic, according to this rather essentialist, nearly racist line of reasoning. For some Orientalists, that which is Islamic cannot be simultaneously civil, nor can either indigenous initiatives rooted in ethnic, kinship, or aristocratic identities, or philanthropy based on Muslim or tribal impulses, be seen as examples of civic spiritedness. This perspective eliminates in one fell swoop all religious and communal charities, libraries, academies, coffeehouses, guilds, foundations, and municipal services as inherently different from the forebears of Euro-American civil society. This is odd because in the West we do count parochial universities, Knights of Columbus, Jewish community centers, and a host of other faith-based or sectarian institutions as civic on the basis not of their identities but of their activities.

The essentialist view of civil society as a historical and cultural constant rather than a variable breaks down easily under scrutiny. So does the claim that Islam, in contrast with the Judeo-Christian traditions, lacks concepts of public spirit, civic engagement, and charity. Inside the Middle East, and of course especially in Jerusalem, the three great religions historically provided great and small public services in fundamentally similar ways. In Islam, the concept of *maslahah,* the common good, is well developed. So is *khayriyyah,* meaning welfare, and across the region most communities historically had some kind of community welfare society, often named for the "sons" of the region. *Zakat,* a charitable tithe, is one of the five pillars of Islam. In some places and times (including in some places today), the tithe has been spent by community *zakat* committees. Philanthropy by wealthy men and women was, of course, political as well as pious. *Waqf* (or *hubus*) endowments historically supported public drinking fountains, baths, canal systems, schools, mosques, and other community services; marketplaces and caravanserais; and great libraries and universities. *Waqf* constituted social as well as considerable economic capital. Educational facilities, in particular, were important sites of the premodern public civic realm, insulated from state penetration, at least in the interim, by their protected endowments, bound by the wishes of the benefactor. The concept of *sadaqah,* meaning alms or charity, is almost identical in its spelling and its meaning in Hebrew and Arabic. The point of all this is not that Islam is all about charity but that Islam has a philanthropic tradition.

Regardless of religion, the regions south of the Mediterranean, down the Red Sea and the Persian Gulf, and stretching to the Indian Ocean, have a very rich urban history. More to the point, the Middle East has a history of municipal development and local self-help. In urban centers, clusters of religious scholars, judges, and officials interacted in architecturally rich public spaces. Chambers of commerce and guilds represented traders and tradesmen, often offering services to members and their families. Rural villages, tribes, and neighborhoods likewise collectively owned and supported meager but necessary services: water supplies, basic education, justice, and marketplaces. There were also judicial and scholarly communities, and Sufi orders. These inhabited a sort of public civic sphere whose role varied, considerably, across geographies and over time. The most pronounced and profound changes occurred in the modern era alongside the expansion of state authority and big business.

The "development" of civil society was certainly not a linear evolution from a primordial civic realm of *waqf,* caravanserais, and tribal water management into a modern civil society of journalist syndicates and feminist advocacy, however. There was always political struggle in and over the civic realm. Colonial rulers and leaders of postcolonial nation-states strove to mobilize or constrain civic institutions and movements. For centuries, there had been constant, multilayered contestations for control of *zakat* revenues between and among the Ottoman (and earlier) caliphates; the kings, muftis, and imams of vassal polities and provinces; and municipalities and neighborhoods. While religious scholars on royal payrolls asserted the inseparability of Islam from governance as justification for appropriation of the *zakat,* jurists in provincial academies often cited the "poor amongst you" clause of the quranic duty to tithe, in defense of the principle that revenues be spent locally. Tax revolts were not uncommon, especially when Ottoman and other rulers imposed nonquranic surcharges on the *zakat.* There were protracted disputes over control of *waqf* bequests, often vast downtown complexes of public buildings together with the commercial property whose revenues subsidized them. The centralization of independent foundations and their real estate under Ministries of Awqaf (the plural of *waqf*) was a long, politicized process in every country. Usually this was tied up with the nationalization of formerly independent educational institutions, whose individual curricula, traditionally designed by faculty, were replaced by centrally determined lesson plans. There was a parallel struggle over the amalgamation by colonial and postcolonial governments of heretofore locally autonomous judicial training institutes and the superseding of religious and tribal courts by justice ministries and legislative law.

The mostly precapitalist public civic realm had functioned without a modern state to provide goods and services—water, education, justice—subsequently subsumed, in a politically fraught manner, under the authority of emerging states. Of course its forms and practices were not identical to those in Italy or New England, because the physical topography, economic relationships, and political landscapes were very different. In the Middle East, for instance, ecological conditions necessitated complex institutional, legal, and infrastructural arrangements for the management of scarce water resources. Inherently localized, these varied across the Nile valley, desert Arabia, Mesopotamia, the mountains of Kurdistan, and the Mediterranean coast; among cities, towns, and villages; and according to rainfall and groundwater supplies available for households, animals, and crops. Yet nearly everywhere, water management accorded mosques a vital function beyond ablutions for prayer, gave special prominence to public baths, required complex cooperation among farmers, called for elegant engineering solutions like canal systems, was continually litigated under Islamic and tribal law, and was often handed to specialized committees. These indigenous, nonprofit, extragovernmental mechanisms and institutions had no direct counterpart in soggy Ireland.

In Yemen, which even northern Arabs consider a primitive backwater, countless examples of communities of residence, profession, tribe, and nation acted collectively on social and political issues under changing political, economic, and legal circumstances. To name just a few of these from the mid–twentieth century: students at a *waqf* academy in Hadramaut staged a protest play; political prisoners in the Hajjah jail penned political poems; labor unions staged strikes in Aden; migrant committees financed local schools and water projects in Hujuriyyah; merchants in Hodeida instituted commercial taxes to pay for street improvements; shaikhs mobilized volunteers to clear vehicular tracks up the mountains in Mahweit; a series of national and regional conferences unfolded in places, including the city of Ta'iz and the town of Amran; and Yemeni exiles in Cairo established a dissident press. These were transitional initiatives, vacillating between customary and contemporary activism, both a sign of socioeconomic change and an engine of that change: community roads, for instance, radically remade the countryside and its relationship to ports and capital cities (Carapico 1998).

Modern Civic Associations

The transformations wrought by the interaction of European imperialism and regional dynamics on old social systems were earth-shattering. From the late nineteenth century through the first half of the twentieth, new states were carved from the dying Ottoman Empire, and enclaves of capitalist development emerged in cities like Aden, Alexandria, Algiers, Basra, and Beirut. Political parties spanning the spectrum from the Communists on the left to the Muslim Brotherhood on the right appeared in the political arena, and large corporations grew in the economic sphere. The body of secondary and university students expanded exponentially. These and other changing circumstances expanded and shaped the space for civic activism, creating new exigencies, possibilities, and constraints. Let's consider some of the new associational trends, and then turn to the ways in which nascent national governments tried to harness their energies in the service of governance.

Professional associations emerged as the most important, distinctly modern element of civil society in terms of rank-and-file membership numbers. The transition to capitalism stimulated some old trade guilds and merchants' associations to reorganize; more important, it produced new kinds of class- or work-based unions, associations, and cooperatives. Business associations promoted innovative public works conducive to commerce while cultivating contacts with transnational firms and national governments, often wielding political as well as economic clout. Syndicates representing the professions—physicians, attorneys, engineers, teachers, pharmacists, architects, journalists, and other educated, middle-class fields—rose to national prominence. Likewise, especially in and around cities like Aden, Baghdad, and Cairo, labor unions organized to represent workers, particularly in large transportation and manufacturing enterprises. In more rural areas, farmers formed agricultural cooperatives and peasants' associations. Finally, student unions gave voice to university campuses that were growing into large public spaces. Among these, labor unions were especially well positioned to engage in large-scale demonstrations such as strikes, but farmers, students, women, and professionals organized as such also staged marches, other public events, petition drives, publicity campaigns, and the like.

The second quite noticeable advance, also directly connected to changing economies, was the appearance of new kinds of charities and welfare societies. Many, but not all, were faith based. Among those with a spiritual mandate, new and different Christian and Jewish models imported from Europe by missionaries and settlers made their mark in education, health, and the creation of the Jewish state. Muslim charities combining European, Ottoman, and indigenous practices expanded the range and number of their projects. Free health clinics, soup kitchens, women's centers, orphanages, parochial and secular education, and other welfare services were provided by volunteers utilizing charitable cash donations. Although many donors were motivated by piety, teams of social scientists, feminists, and communists, to name just a few secular labels, also joined social welfare movements in the Levant, North Africa, and Mesopotamia.

It is also important to note that civil society, in the sense of a public realm for discussion and debate, expanded with advances in education and the media. The print press, followed by radio, television, cassette tapes, cable stations, and the Internet, all spawned new communities of information and of shared interest. Because it is the lingua franca of what became, in the interwar era, more than twenty countries, broadcasting and publishing in Arabic were of special importance, spreading ideas and information out from Cairo, Baghdad, and Beirut, the media centers. Arabic-language radio and later television had a huge impact on public discourses, even in the most literal sense of contributing to the creation of something called Modern Standard Arabic. During this time, in cities across the Arab world as well as in Turkey and Iran and among the immigrants to what would become Israel, intellectual life experienced a renaissance. Communities of socially conscious artists, writers, performers, educators, and other professions formed clubs and salons, started schools and newspapers, wrote treatises and manifestos, and influenced both social and political life. National and international conferences of intellectuals, such as international women's conferences held in Damascus and Baghdad, made special contributions to the public civic sphere.

Last, let's look, if only briefly, at the spread of sports leagues, recreational clubs, and large sporting events. Many sociologists have observed that teams, games, and fan clubs are among the kinds of public experiences that generate social solidarity and social networks, notably across neighborhood and municipal lines. Sports, especially soccer, draw huge crowds to big games and millions of players to smaller public spaces. They're especially important to Middle Eastern youth. Sports teams are potent symbols of their nations.

Many or all of these elements of civil society mobilized, en masse on occasion, especially in moments of upheaval, disaster, or transition. Especially during the movements for national independence, syndicates, unions, sports clubs, medical charities, sororities, campuses, media, and other networks became conduits for mass participation. Now and then, enthusiasts filled downtown streets. In the 1930s and 1940s, Cairo and Baghdad were hotbeds of public civic engagement on the part of intellectuals, workers, feminists, professionals, and others. The long anticolonial struggles in Algeria and South Yemen during the 1950s and 1960s engaged peaceful demonstrators alongside independence fighters. Elsewhere, in countries like Kuwait and Jordan, where sovereignty was granted rather than won militarily, the public civic sphere was galvanized by the pending transfer of power, and in its immediate aftermath. Other such places and moments of extraordinary, even frenzied, levels of public civic involvement included Turkey in the early days of its republic, and, later, Iran in the dying days of the Shah's reign, Yemen immediately after unification, and Palestine in the mid-1990s when hopes were high that a state would be created in the West Bank and Gaza. But just as engagement overflowed around propitious historical events, it subsided at other times, especially in the face of ascendant police states.

Curtailing Civil Society

After independence, governments sought to rein in civic energies. Too often, newly installed monarchs and strongmen consolidated national power by attempting to obliterate alternative loci of legitimacy and harnessing community energies toward the central statebuilding project. In Turkey, Iran, Saudi Arabia, Egypt, and elsewhere, governments sought to undermine or curtail previously powerful clerical, judicial, academic, and commercial institutions. As explained in other chapters in this book, military officers gained power and established ruling parties in most of the newly established republics after independence: Egypt, Algeria, Tunisia, Syria, Iraq, Libya, and both Yemens. The Baath in Syria and Iraq, the National Liberation Front in Algeria, the Socialists in South Yemen, and the Arab Socialist Union (later renamed the National Democratic Party) in Egypt laid claim to representing their entire populations via the party's incorporation of civic organizations into its ranks. Although practices and institutional arrangements varied, the prevailing strategy was to give a veneer of legitimacy to centralized authoritarian governance by bringing most voluntary associations and other institutions under ruling-party control, and simultaneously to stifle existing or new autonomous organizations and media through regulation and censorship.

In effect, just as businesses like banks, industries, and the properties of the old aristocracies were nationalized, so too were universities, media enterprises, unions, syndicates, popular associations, charities, and even mosques. Agricultural cooperatives and community development associations were amalgamated into pyramidal nationwide federations, and membership became mandatory. National leagues of women, youth unions, and peasant associations were brought under the wing of ruling parties, and sometimes given token parliamentary representation. The professional syndicates of the educated middle and upper-middle classes were centralized under ruling parties or governmental agencies. With the nationalization of transportation and industry, port workers, rail workers, and factory workers became state employees, represented by national unions affiliated with or subsumed within ruling parties. In many fields, membership in the national federation or union, a precondition for employment or benefits, effectively mandated party membership. Charities were bureaucratized. Not only academic curricula but in many places even congregational sermons were made to conform to the official line. Ministries of education, health, labor, agriculture, industry, and information wielded inordinate power over the entire labor force in their sectors.

In a second prong of the same strategic centralization of social capital, independent civic organizing was effectively curtailed by draconian laws of association, often known in English as nongovernmental organization (NGO) laws, and by ministries of social affairs that were empowered to approve or dissolve social organizations. The history of Egyptian legislation in this regard is worth elaborating, because Egypt generated the model for laws of association throughout the Arab region. North Yemen, Algeria, Jordan, and later the incipient Palestinian Authority and even the Coalition Provisional Authority in Iraq (in Order 45 of 2003) borrowed language and restrictions from Egyptian associational law. Egypt's Ministry of Social Affairs was created in the 1930s to oversee social reform experiments and pilot community services being operated by organizations as diverse as the Egyptian Society for Social Studies, the Muslim Brotherhood, the Communist Party, and the Daughters of the Nile. Law 49 of 1945 gave the ministry authority to register, oversee, audit, and dissolve all associations. The nationalist military officers who abolished the pro-British monarchy, promised free universal services, and embarked on a program of nationalizations were suspicious of elitist charities, politicized associations, and independent social activism, whether foreign-influenced or indigenous, politically conservative or progressive. They banned both the Communists and the Brotherhood and enacted legislation to rein in freelance social work. The notorious Law 34 of 1964, emulated elsewhere, suspended the 4,000 associations already registered, pending their reorganization under new, complex regulations that empowered the Ministry of Social Affairs to merge, suspend, reorganize, or freeze the assets of any organization for reasons not specified. The ministry did exercise this power.

In the 1990s the notion of the NGO came into vogue among international donors and democracy brokers. North American, European, and United Nations (UN) agencies budgeted funds to be distributed as grants to civil society advocacy organizations, often known in the aid industry as CSOs. Indeed, among professional development brokers and the staff of international NGOs, it became the convention to equate "civil society" with NGOs, and to use the two terms more or less interchangeably. In fact, the expression *NGO,* written and pronounced exactly as in English (or alternatively, in the French version, as *ONG*), made its way into written and spoken Arabic. In turn, donor agencies developed very precise criteria for NGOs to be eligible for small grants and inclusion in NGO conferences and networks. To register as an observer at a UN convention, for instance, or to obtain funds from European or US agencies, NGOs needed to submit paperwork documenting goals expressly consonant with those of the sponsor, at least three years' worth of financial records, elections for its board of directors, and a suitable program or plan of activities. Those so qualifying for civil society funding—formal organizations with professional translators and accountants and a liberal organizational mandate—could compete for dollars and euros.

Authoritarian governments resisted this perceived intrusion by various methods. One strategy that governments or their ministries deployed to reinforce their monopolies on both foreign aid and ideological discourse was known as cloning: the creation of state-backed nongovernmental organizations, also called GONGOs (government-organized NGOs). Yemen's ruling party, the General People's Congress, encouraged party members to found NGOs to compete with autonomous organizations for international assistance and domestic publicity. The Tunisian government created a number of "front" NGOs, like Lawyers Without Borders, that often were infiltrated by security police. So-called RONGOs (royally organized NGOs) headed or endowed by members of the ruling Hashimite family, especially its princesses, multiplied in Jordan. A similar phenomenon took place in Morocco.

In Jordan, Morocco, Tunisia, Algeria, Egypt, Yemen, and the Palestinian Authority, NGO laws and other legislation, including censorship regulations, were deployed to block direct receipt of foreign funds by counterelites. Often it seemed that the executive branches of these aid-dependent governments were determined to maintain control of patronage networks and disbursements of development assistance monies. The Egyptian government took particular umbrage with professional advocacy organizations like the Arab Women's Solidarity Association, the Egyptian Association of Human Rights, and the Ibn Khaldun Center, whose Egyptian-American director and Sudanese accountant were imprisoned for making a European-financed documentary that Cairo charged was "harmful to Egypt's reputation." Indeed, after several lawsuits, and despite vigorous criticism from Egyptian activists and international agencies, Law 34 was tightened, nearly four decades after its initial promulgation, explicitly to forbid political campaigning and labor activism by associations registered under the law, and to close loopholes that had enabled some organizations to evade ministerial oversight by registering as nonprofit civil companies. Associations Law 84 of 2002 specifically forbade NGOs from engaging in either labor advocacy or political campaigning, tightened ministerial micromanagement, and empowered the Ministries of Social Affairs and State Security to prohibit activities, probe finances, force closure, freeze assets, and criminally prosecute violations.

Along with even cruder devices like spying on citizens, banning public meetings, outlawing criticism of the head of state, arbitrary detention, and physical brutality, these measures certainly curtailed civic activism, or kept it within mostly closely controlled confines. In Syria and Iraq under the Baath; in Libya and Turkey under the generals; in Iran under the Shah; in the Palestinian territories under Israeli occupation; and to a considerable extent in Tunisia, Egypt, Yemen, and the Islamic Republic of Iran in the early twenty-first century, the ever-watchful national security establishment penetrated deep into the public civic realm. Gatherings of more than a handful of people outside their homes required a special permit in many countries. It was nearly impossible to operate under police radar. Progressive and left-leaning or labor-oriented politicking was most stringently suppressed. In some circumstances, such as occupied Palestine and Baathist Iraq, religious congregations or tribal associations, though not entirely insulated from government interference, were the safest outlets for civic impulses, charity, and self-help. This was true in Iran under the Shah, too, which helps explain why religious authorities gravitated to the center of the power vacuum that was created after the fall of the monarchy; ironically, the Islamic Republic subsequently instituted particularly stringent restrictions on religious institutions and associations for the same reason.

Civil Society in Action

Under such constraints, short of armed insurrection, what can ordinary people and educated elites do? This section considers various forms of civic engagement under the less than democratic conditions that prevail across most of the Middle East in the early twenty-first century. They can be grouped under three headings: the quotidian ways that people engage in the public sphere or work for their slice of the common good, either by working within the system or by finding enclaves outside it; the more exceptional, take-to-the-streets moments of mass civic involvement; and ways in which citizens pursue their causes transnationally and in cyberspace.

Working Within the System

There are various ways of participating within the bounds of authoritarian political systems. First, millions of people belong to tens of thousands of licensed and registered labor unions, professional syndicates, women's federations, cooperatives, sports leagues, municipal betterment clubs, welfare funds, chambers of commerce, farmers' bureaus, alumni organizations, research centers, student governments, benevolent societies, theatrical groups, parent-teacher associations, and a host of other voluntary organizations. In many countries, syndicates for faculty, journalists, physicians, engineers, and other professions are strong middle-class lobbying and voluntary associations. All these organizations hold meetings, elect officers, put out newsletters, recruit participants, march in parades, sponsor fundraising drives, hold street fairs, and respond to humanitarian emergencies. Moreover, organizations of the sort we think of as the epitome of civil society, professional think tank–type advocacy groups dedicated to causes such as human rights, women's issues, or social reform, mushroomed in virtually every country in the Middle East, from Iran to Morocco. They hold authorized conferences and public service events all the time, which nonmembers also attend. Staff or volunteers write essays and give lectures. While the most vocally political projects may rankle authorities, people in cities, towns, and rural areas tackle less controversial projects on a regular, ongoing basis.

Second, cultural and customary venues offer a different sort of civic outlet in many settings, or under certain circumstances. Funeral processions or fortieth-day commemorations, normally apolitical ceremonies, have been known to take shape as protest displays, as in Iran when the Shah's forces murdered protesting seminarians and then more students who gathered to mourn the seminarians as martyrs, and again decades later when the same murder-mourning-punishment cycle was repeated: here, extraordinary circumstances infused a religious ritual with protest energies. Day-to-day social gatherings in coffeehouses or other venues can also have civic content, especially if there is sustained intellectual exchange about public affairs. In the affluent Gulf monarchies, where formal organizations with any sort of political agenda are inhibited, the customary cultural institution of the *diwaniyya* is an important site for public-spirited debate and deliberation. A *diwan* is a room, typically adjacent to the main house, where guests gather; the *diwaniyya* is the name for that gathering. It's a space that is physically within the domestic realm of the household, or the private sphere—but also a public space where men or women (usually not both together) gather for coffee or tea and conversation. In Yemen the corresponding venue is the qat chew, also a public gathering inside the home (the room is still called the *diwan*), where the chewing of this slightly stronger stimulant elicits even livelier conversation. These are informal institutions, unregulated societal customs authenticated by "tradition." What makes so many observers conclude nonetheless that these rather quaint semipublic gatherings, typically gender-segregated, are part of civil society is not only the kinds of discussions that take place, but also the sheer ubiquity and frequency of the meetings, whose repetitive, alternating, and interlocking attendance seems to link a huge swath of the national citizenry in a common conversation.

Another institution that is not inherently civic, but can be a vehicle for civic activism, is the tribe. Yemeni and Iraqi tribes are grounded in a region or locality, say a valley, mountain, or plain; the tribe's members are the ranchers and farmers of the region bearing the tribe's name. In many places the management of community property—water sources, grazing lands, market trails, and sometimes marketplaces—was organized historically through the tribe, in the name of the locality. Some tribes authorized committees to collect the *zakat* for expenditure within the locality. Many tribal groups raised cash contributions or work crews via a tribal rallying call. By extension, in the era of modernization tribal institutions took charge of upgrading water delivery systems and roads, or lobbied the state to do so. Thus community betterment associations can be organized on tribal principles, or through tribes, or be virtually indistinguishable from tribes because of their identical names and memberships. But there's more to it than that, for during major periods of political ferment, tribes and tribal institutions repeatedly organized peace mediations and conferences calling for justice, nonviolence, curbs on corruption, and long lists of other civic virtues. So, while almost no one considers tribes themselves civic associations, neither can they be dismissed as vestiges of a precapitalist primordial civic realm: tribal networks can sometimes be mobilized for what is otherwise known as grassroots organizing.

The Middle Eastern charitable endeavors we hear the most about are the faith-based initiatives, especially Islamic welfare societies, many of which combine traditional motifs with thoroughly modern practices. As discussed in Chapter 6, the contemporary Islamist political movement is multifaceted. It includes legal and illegal political parties that attempt, either via elections or by use of violence, to assume local, provincial, or national leadership. Parts of the partisan movement are situated, somewhat insulated, inside mosque congregations and religious academies. There's a violent wing, too, in many countries and across the region. As a definitional matter we should distinguish civic participation from either partisanship or religious worship, and also, obviously, from militancy. But old and new Islamic institutions do qualify as part of civil society in the same way that Jewish, Coptic, or Maronite welfare associations, think tanks, community centers, and philanthropic foundations do. There's no question that the clampdown against leftists and progressive forces across the Middle East in the 1970s and 1980s indirectly empowered more conservative, pious institutions associated with the Islamist movement toward the turn of the millennium. Islamist institutions are many, varied, and vibrant, and they include both contemporary versions of traditional practices like *zakat* committees or *waqf* endowments and thoroughly modern hospitals, benevolent associations, and universities. Denominational charities and welfare associations have provided particularly crucial services where states failed to function as such, particularly in Lebanon during the civil war, the West Bank and Gaza, and wartime Iraq, but also offer an essential social safety net in the poor countries of the Middle East.

People also network without joining formal organizations, or take on small, short-term projects that marshal limited resources. Poor women are especially inclined to associate via informal reciprocity networks of friends and neighbors. Unregistered, largely invisible, and comprising both men and women, these networks support rescue squads, community welfare funds, cleanup days, and neighborhood watch committees. Parents cooperate to work with or beyond schools and pool their resources for child care, tutoring, playgrounds, and other youth-oriented educational and recreational activities.

Artists and other intellectuals also find ways to articulate frustrations and aspirations within the bounds of censorship. Arabic and Persian verbal arts like poetry, song, storytelling, and jokes provide fictionalized satirical commentary on politics and society in the guise of parables about lions or pharaohs. These are passed by word of mouth; shared among friends inside homes, classrooms, or *diwans;* or distributed via cassette, CD, or, more recently, Facebook, Twitter, and YouTube. Nowadays, rap and *rai* musicians animate the imaginations of youth and concertgoers with their political lyrics. In addition, researchers and educators produce and disseminate socially and politically conscious materials for use by activists, and scholars hold workshops and seminars. Consider the work of women writers, scholars, and performers, for example, or a concert in Cairo in April 2008 by popular activist singer Marcel Khalifa, who performed songs with messages of labor solidarity and the works of Palestinian poet Mahmoud Darwish.

Organized interests find some room within semiauthoritarian systems to lobby parliaments for political reform. Not that it's easy to achieve the desired reforms. In the century-long struggle of Egyptian women, there were suffragette marches in the 1930s, and women's groups staged a sit-in at the parliament during the ferment leading up to the 1952 revolution. Writers, performers, and political figures publicized women's issues in the 1960s, 1970s, and 1980s. In one of a long series of focused campaigns involving complex coalition building, feminists called hundreds of meetings, and enlisted jurists, historians, and a new generation of young female scholars, to find religiously based arguments to repeal clauses in Egyptian family law that prohibited women from initiating a divorce; in 2001 they won a modest but significant legislative victory.

Protest Activities

When the legal avenues for complaint and lobbying are exhausted, when conditions become intolerable, or amid crises, people take to the streets, often in organized fashion, sometimes spontaneously. Even prior to the phenomenal confluence of Arab uprisings in 2011, three sets of issues seemed to prompt mass protests, which usually started off peacefully but were often confronted by police armed with laws prohibiting mass gatherings.

First, and frequently, people gather to protest wars. Demonstrations almost always erupt across the Middle East in response to Israeli and US military actions in the Arab region; some of these demonstrations have government support, but others face riot police. The Anglo-American invasion of Iraq beginning in March 2003, and each bloody encounter between Israeli forces and Palestinian or Lebanese fighters in the early twenty-first century, all prompted mass rallies and marches. For six weeks in March and April 2002, during the Israeli incursion into the West Bank, protesters streamed into Amman's streets, where they were confronted with tank cordons. The following spring, when the US-led coalition invaded Iraq, some 20,000 demonstrators filled downtown Cairo shouting antiwar slogans and scorning George W. Bush and Tony Blair; a few hundred activists, lawyers, journalists, and students then held a sit-in in front of the national bar association to demand the release of protesters who had been dragged off to jail. In both 2002 and 2003, similar scenes played out in cities across the region. Millions marched against Israel's incursion into Lebanon in 2006 and Gaza in early 2009. In the face of war, people don't just voice disapproval, however. Like Westerners, Middle Easterners also organize charitable and medical donations via private voluntary associations for war victims in Afghanistan, Bosnia, Palestine, and elsewhere.

Second are economic protests, which come in two forms that are both defiant of government policies: labor activism by employees and demonstrations against economic conditions by consumers. Both are mostly confined to the low-income countries, although there have been a few labor actions among usually passive immigrant workers in the Gulf as well. A wave of strikes gripped Egypt, the most populous country in the region, in 2006–2007. The most dramatic, protracted industrial action involved 30,000 textile workers at the Spinning and Weaving Company in Mahalla. In another episode, 2,000 members of the pharmacists' syndicate rallied to protest police raids on drugstores and privatization of the national pharmaceutical company. In June 2007, Al-Azhar University professors demonstrated for better pay. Over 50,000 Egyptian property-tax collectors engaged in a lengthy work stoppage and a ten-day sit-in in front of the national cabinet office, demanding salaries commensurate with other public sector white-collar workers. In 2008, a wheat and bread crisis led to more mass protest. In Yemen during 2005 and beyond, a series of demonstrations and protest marches, including a few that turned into riots, resisted policies like the lifting of subsidies on diesel fuel and the raising of taxes as the government passed the costs of its fiscal crisis on to consumers and citizens. All these and many other protests took different forms depending on context.

Third, people organize and agitate for political reform. Algerians wracked by economic crises and fed up with political conditions networked, protested, and lobbied in the late 1980s, pressing the ruling party for openly contested elections. In Yemen between unification in 1990 and the first national elections in 1993, and between the 1993 elections and the outbreak of civil war in 1994, a series of regional conventions drew tens of thousands of participants into what became known as a national dialogue: a solidarity conference in 1990, a cohesion conference in 1991, half a dozen other tribal conferences in rural areas, and urban meetings in Ta'iz and other cities, all complete with working papers written by scholars and petitions for better public health care, local and national elections, proper judicial procedures, and other reforms. In between, scores of colloquia and academic workshops generated resolutions and proposals that were published and distributed nationwide. The National Dialogue of Political Forces, a broad coalition led by two or three dozen nationally prominent political figures from across the ideological spectrum, was supported by countless weekly seminars and antiwar vigils on university campuses.

Other important protest movements and civic activities are described in other chapters in this book. The first Palestinian intifada was especially noteworthy. Three decades after Iranians deposed the Shah in a mass uprising only to find themselves constrained by a new form of authoritarianism, students and others gathered repeatedly to protest the closure of newspapers, attacks on intellectuals, the fraudulent trial of an outspoken professor, and the less-than-transparent reelection of an increasingly unpopular president.

Neither the Algerians nor the Yemenis were able to thwart the eventual outbreak of domestic armed conflict in the early nineties (a short war in Yemen and protracted murderous strife in Algeria). In both cases, civil society proved an insufficient bulwark against ruling military establishments, and activists eventually became disheartened by the resort to violence. The crushing of the first intifada and the greater resort to violence in the second were very sobering. The multifaceted surge of activism by judges, workers, students, and others in Egypt during the middle of the first decade of the twenty-first century, including the Kifaya (Enough) and April 6 movements, took years to reach a tipping point. The limits to the so-called Cedar Revolution in Lebanon, the brutal crackdown against protesters in Iran, the sporadic nature of demonstrations in Jordan, and the limited success of other popular movements analyzed elsewhere in this volume explain why so many observers in and beyond the Middle East were—until the Arab uprisings at least—rather pessimistic about the prospects for civil society to generate sustained, meaningful political reform. Civic openings when huge numbers of people tried to initiate meaningful change were often short-lived as authorities managed to restore what they called law and order. Nonetheless, people in virtually every country continually found tools and spaces for civic activism.

Transnational Public Civic Realms and Cyberspace

Besides the outlets for their civic energies people find in the everyday world of parent-teacher associations and in exceptional take-to-the-streets moments, two other virtual arenas for activism are available to speakers of Arabic, English, or French. First, there are extraterritorial conference circuits where rights defenders and other activists can take their complaints and claims to the transnational arena. Second, in the twenty-first century the Internet offers new possibilities for expression and networking. Available mainly to highly educated and/or relatively privileged elites, these very contemporary spaces for expression and agitation can at least partly evade state censorship and restrictions on assembly. Because of the lingua franca and a common media sphere, inter-Arab networks show particular vibrancy.

Sometimes relying on donor resources, Arab (and sometimes Turkish, Israeli, or Iranian) intellectual elites and rights advocates from different countries find common cause in regional NGO networks, women's organizations, bar associations, journalists' clubs, and other groups that hold annual or more frequent conferences. These ephemeral two- or four-day meetings are typically offshore, in deluxe five-star hotels or convention centers either in the region (Beirut, Casablanca, Doha, and Sharm al-Sheikh are key destinations) or abroad. These facilities are booked year-round with specialized conventions.

As an example, consider the conference circuit dedicated to gender issues and female empowerment, which was set in motion by the 1995 Beijing Conference on Women and a host of preparatory and follow-up activities around the globe, and specifically in the Middle East. Scores of intergovernmental, governmental, and nongovernmental organizations, machineries, and agencies are networked into a vast associational complex that operates on several scales simultaneously: the global, the regional, the national, and the local. This complex has specialized branches dealing with, among a host of other things, family law, honor crimes against women, labor rights, and gender images in media. Scores of Arab and other Middle Eastern women's groups participate in this network, attending global and regional plenary meetings and then conveying lessons learned once back home in workshops and training sessions. This material serves as the basis for national campaigns to reform divorce or criminal law or propose gender quotas for parliamentary elections in many Middle Eastern countries. Women's groups from Islamic countries also provide feedback to international women's organizations on what many of them regard as Orientalist stereotypes of passive, powerless Muslim women. Even when conferences take place in Cairo, Rabat, Amman, Doha, Ankara, or other Middle Eastern cities, and of course especially when women travel to Europe, North America, or Asia, the dialogue is extraterritorial and multilingual. This is an intermittent expansion of the public civic sphere beyond national boundaries.

Comparable networks unite judicial and rights communities in the Middle East and abroad that convene to discuss matters of law and the relationship between national and international law. For instance, the Union Internationale des Avocats, a consortium of some 200 national bar associations, held its annual meeting at the Jnan Palace Hotel and the Fez Congress Centre in 2005 around the theme "Lawyers of the World: A Single Code of Ethics?" This huge conference, with simultaneous translation into French, Arabic, Spanish, and English, was an event both in North Africa (specifically, Morocco) and in the transnational sphere. A 2006 conference titled "The Role of the Judiciary in the Process of Political Reform in Egypt and in the Arab World" in Cairo was organized by the Cairo Institute for Human Rights Studies in coordination with the Euro-Med Network for judges, advocates, lawyers, and scholars from Morocco, Algeria, Tunisia, Sudan, Saudi Arabia, Bahrain, the United Arab Emirates (UAE), Syria, Lebanon, Yemen, and Egypt, plus French, German, and US counterparts. Literally scores of such meetings help form a transnational community of Arab jurists and advocates with a common language, modern standard legal Arabic. They help, in other words, to create epistemic communities of legal practitioners who may be equally critical, for instance, of the egregious offenses of the Saddam Hussein regime and the US occupation that followed it. Pan-Arab and transnational solidarity building networks thus enable some activists to take reform agendas outside the realm of sovereign dictatorship.

Another kind of extraterritorial space for civic engagement exists on the Internet and in the blogosphere. The World Wide Web, of course, is a virtual rather than a physical public sphere. People type on their computers, sitting at home or in an Internet café, rather than conversing face-to-face or massing in the streets. Yet as others have noted, the scope and reach of websites, blog posts, and text-messaging are wide, even infinite; the capacity to disseminate messages, in words and in video, including video captured on cell phones, is unprecedented.

In the early twenty-first century, Middle Easterners have deployed the power of the Internet to communicate political messages to their countries and the world. Examples include Riverbend (riverbendblog.blogspot.com), the Baghdad blogger who fiercely resisted the Anglo-American occupation of Iraq, and Egyptian dissidents who created the enormously famous "We Are All Khalid Saʻid" Facebook page to protest police brutality against innocent civilians. Iranian and Israeli peace activists have also reached beyond linguistic and national boundaries to get in touch with comrades abroad and even with each other. During Israel's Gaza campaign of early 2009, the Arabic blogosphere lit up with messages nearly as critical of Arab governments as of the Israeli Defense Forces. Many outsiders have dubbed the Arab uprisings a Facebook revolution. Inside Tunisia, Egypt, Yemen, and other affected countries, people who communicated face-to-face or via cell phone found this silly, because the Internet was really not a tool of mass mobilization on the domestic level. Instead, the World Wide Web, YouTube, and even elite conference networks were mediums of international exchange. They helped communicate what was happening in Tunisia to Egyptians and then Yemenis, Bahrainis, Libyans, Syrians, and the world at large. Technology and globalization did not mobilize Yemenis, who by 2011 had been protesting for years, but direct contact with Tunisians and Egyptians did embolden the youth movement and broaden the pan-Arab discursive sphere.

Civic Revolutions

Yemenis had been staging political rallies around the country for years and finding other ways to challenge an increasingly authoritarian and corrupt government. Beneath the facade of stability Egypt was in foment. Tunisians, Libyans, Bahrainis, and Syrians seethed with frustration. Across the region flash protests appeared and seemed to vanish. Now and then seemingly apolitical soccer fans took over whole cities. Living standards had been deteriorating, except perhaps for members of bloated national security establishments. Meanwhile more human rights groups undertook more professional investigations into the instruments of repression wielded against dissidents and those making demands on government. In recognition of millions of Arab citizens demanding social justice, the 2011 Nobel Peace Prize was awarded to Tawakkul Karman, head of an association called Women Journalists Without Chains. She had been arrested and released shortly before emerging as a spokesperson for the movement to drive Ali Abdullah Salih from power.

In retrospect it was not surprising that a seemingly minor incident ignited mass indignation in Tunisia; that millions of Egyptians took to the streets after a blatantly fraudulent election and so much police and security abuse; that tens of thousands of Yemenis decided to camp out until some basic political demands were addressed; or that, after peaceful marches were met with brute force, Libyan and Syrian dissidents took up arms against two of the most despicable of Arab dictatorships. The unpredictable surprise was that all of these things happened in such rapid succession, or simultaneously, and galvanized Arab civic imaginations and Western perceptions in heretofore unthinkable ways.

The improbable spark for the whole so-called Arab Spring was when a street vendor in provincial Tunisia set himself on fire after an all-too-common altercation with a police officer. His friends and their friends and then their contacts and others who heard of what was happening decided to take a stand. An ordinary event spawned extraordinary public reaction, and after a month of popular protests a dictator who had been in power for more than three decades fled with his family to Saudi Arabia. Meanwhile the mother and friends of a young man murdered at a police station, Khalid Sa'id, invited Egyptians to show their defiance on Police Day, January 25, 2011. The turnout was huge. Three days later, on January 28, sports fans accustomed to claiming the streets joined political dissidents and civic activists and other angry citizens in breaking through police barricades. Throngs of people occupied Tahrir Square for another fifteen days before another lifelong dictator abdicated. By this time Yemenis mobilized protests that blended slogans from Tunisia and Egypt—"the people want the downfall of the regime" and "leave!"—with indigenous national or local chants, symbols, performances, manifestos, and other forms of political expression. In all three cases, civil society constituted itself not only by gathering in public places but also in organizational efforts to provide sanitation, protection, food, and Internet access to protest encampments and to maintain order and safety in neighborhoods. In Cairo, neighborhood watch and cleanup committees engaged energies that may or may not have been sympathetic to the revolt against Husni Mubarak. Against incredible odds, Yemeni protesters persevered for over a year in tent cities in Sana'a, Ta'iz, and other towns before the dictator finally relinquished power.

In the meantime, videographers, artists, bloggers, high school students, rappers, journalists, and others from across the entire region contributed thousands of socially conscious images, essays, and songs to the public civic sphere. Archivists collated these forms of creative expression for historical posterity. Public art and gallery exhibitions were commemorative, decorative, and inspirational. Interest groups convened and strategized. Labor and professional syndicates replaced leaders. There were more strikes and other job actions than ever. Human rights organizations worked overtime. University faculty insisted on electing deans. Schoolchildren demanded better lunches. More parents joined more educational committees. Thousands of Web initiatives and YouTube videos were launched.

Whether the cumulative result of these and other actions is a series of transitions to full-blown liberal democracy (inside individual countries or across the Middle East and North African region) remains to be seen. The outcome of so much civic activism might or might not be orderly or pretty. There are plenty of historical examples of civic uprisings that resulted in more tyranny rather than more freedom. In the 1979 Iranian revolution, for instance, citizens mobilized against one form of tyranny only to find themselves trapped in another—which was even more vigilant against mass assembly. This is a sobering analogy.

By the same token, the uprisings that swept across the Arab region in 2010–2012 demonstrated the collective power of disparate elements of civil society—bilingual elites, sports fanatics, wage laborers, rural smallholders, women's rights activists, students and graduates, neighborhood watch volunteers—to assert custodianship of public spaces. This was by no means the power of formal professionalized NGOs. It was the power of the multitudes. Even if security establishments and crony capitalists retain their respective strangleholds, in the wake of the uprisings they are aware of their tenuous control over the streets. Looking in particular at the three countries where mostly nonviolent resistance toppled long-entrenched strongmen—Tunisia, Egypt, and Yemen—we can see something that might be characterized as civic revolutions. Ordinary citizens occupied public civic realms even if they did not take control of the state apparatus or seize the ill-gotten gains of the ruling classes.

Conclusion

The argument in this chapter has been that civic activism is a variable, not a constant. If it were an immutable cultural characteristic with no historical or geographical variation, as some Orientalists used to assert, there would be no differences across time and place. Instead, we see that in the Middle East, as elsewhere, civil society advances and retreats, and changes scope and shape, responding to constraints and opportunities. There are historical antecedents aplenty to civil society in traditional public civic realms, and this historical reality refutes the opinions of those who (viewing the region from afar) see only the most European societies of Turkey and Israel as capable of proper civic activism. There is a pattern of late colonial and post-colonial civic efflorescence centered in almost every country on national independence, and its subsequent co-optation to a centralized, hierarchical, often stifling nationbuilding project. As detailed in other chapters, governments resorted to banal repression to curtail civil society.

And yet we have also seen how, in ordinary ways and crisis-driven outbursts, people organize, animate, and debate, sometimes within legal channels and sometimes by challenging restraints on assembly and expression. New technologies and conference networks enabled some activists to transcend some confines of censorship, policing, and legal restrictions on associational life—by organizing in extraterritorial, denationalized spaces or in cyberspace. More importantly, multitudes of ordinary people occupied public squares across much of the Arab world—and in fact inspired "occupy" movements across the globe. These developments do not necessarily predict a gloriously teleological outcome of democratic development on the near horizon, because we are cautioned by the numerous failures of reform movements to bring about better governance. The evidence does not call for excessive optimism or lead us to expect a linear progression toward democracy and social justice. Neither, however, are there grounds for ruling out the possibilities for democratization in the Middle East. Rather, civil society operates, even within autocratic polities, because citizens continually do struggle for rights, liberties, and a decent life.

6

Religion and Politics

Jillian Schwedler

Much of the politics of the Middle East has been viewed by those inside and outside the region as driven by religious differences. From the Arab-Israeli conflict to the Iranian revolution to the emergence of extremist groups such as al-Qaeda, religion has indeed been at the center of major political struggles in the region, with regimes, opposition groups, and everyday citizens routinely invoking religious rhetoric and symbolism. Religious groups have emerged as major players following the Arab uprisings that began in late 2010, with a range of Islamist parties in Egypt and Tunisia winning the largest blocs in those states' first truly free elections. Politics, at its heart, is about power, and political actors of every ilk bring their own understandings of the causes of injustice and the appropriate means for political change. Religion is also a central part of daily life in every Middle Eastern country, informing the ways in which most ordinary citizens understand politics as well as their own place in the world. But Western countries have also seen a resurgence of debate around religion, from its appropriate place in national politics to the growing number of religious revivalist movements. In this regard, politics in the Middle East are not necessarily about religion any more than are politics in Western countries.

In this chapter, I examine the major religions in the Middle East and the resurgence of politicized religion, from the creation of a powerful Islam-state alliance in early twentieth-century Saudi Arabia and the popular revolution in Iran that led to the creation of an Islamic state there in 1979, to the early Zionist movement that led to the establishment of the Jewish state of Israel in 1948, to the explosion of Islamic revivalist movements that emerged to challenge existing regimes in the latter quarter of the twentieth century, to the new roles in governance won by Islamist parties through free elections since 2011. I focus on two main categories of politicized religious activism, both of which advocate for political communities to adopt practices more closely shaped by their core religious values. The first includes religious groups working within existing regimes, a category that encompasses the vast majority of politicized Islamist groups. These groups engage in formal political processes to realize gradual political, social, and economic reforms. They do so within authoritarian states as well as in the transitioning states that have adopted more democratic practices since the Arab uprisings. The second category includes religious groups that reject existing regimes; these extremists seek immediate political change and frequently aim to rapidly overthrow the existing political order, through the use of violence if necessary. Though far fewer in number, extremists have left their mark on regional as well as global politics. Given that the vast majority of Middle Eastern people are Muslim—followers of the Islamic faith—both categories of religious activism are dominated by Islamist groups. However, it is important to remember that other religious groups also fall into each category.

The Historical Role of Religion in the Middle East

The Middle East is the birthplace of the world's three Abrahamic religions—Judaism, Christianity, and Islam—and thus the politics of the region have long been intertwined with struggles framed and inspired by religious differences. This does not mean that Middle East politics are religious in nature, but rather that political struggles—understood here as conflicts over the control of particular lands and the resources they hold—are often couched in terms of religion. As we will see, this distinction is crucial for understanding the historical role of religion in the Middle East as well as current debates about religious conflicts in general and Islamist groups in particular.

Judaism

Established more than 4,000 years ago, Judaism is the first of the three great monotheistic religions. According to Hebrew tradition, Moses led the Jewish people, with God's guidance, out of their slavery in Egypt and brought them to the Holy Land to establish a Kingdom of God (around 1450–1250 B.C.E.). Christians and Muslims share this vision of Judaism's origins, as each recognizes its faith as part of the same religious lineage (Judaism to Christianity to Islam) and believes in the same God. God revealed to Moses the first five books of the Hebrew Bible, called the Torah, which, together with the Talmud (a secondary text that includes interpretations of Jewish law, called the *halakah,* and the Torah), is the basic source of religious principles for the Jewish faith.

In 70 C.E., Jews were forced out of Jerusalem and Judea by the Romans, who also destroyed the Second Temple, which had been built on the site of Solomon's Temple (the First Temple). Exiled Jews settled in many directions yet maintained a strong identity as a single community that would one day reunite. In the Diaspora they maintained their religious practices and rituals, sustaining their identity through close-knit communities. In the late nineteenth and early twentieth centuries, increased violence and discrimination against Jews in Europe led to the emergence of a Jewish nationalist movement—Zionism—that aimed to establish a Jewish homeland and possibly even a Jewish state on the lands of historical Israel. Thousands of Zionists emigrated to Palestine over the next fifty years, sometimes living in peace with the indigenous Christian and Muslim Palestinians, and sometimes clashing, particularly over the control of land. The Jewish state of Israel was formally established in 1948.

Many of the first Zionists were secular and even Marxist in orientation, viewing Judaism as an identity and Zionism as a means for this religious-racial community to live on the land to which it felt strong historical connections. Today, the political left in Israel views the Israeli state more as a protector of the Jewish community than as a strictly religious state. On the right, Zionism is broadly viewed as an effort to realize God's intention that the Jewish people establish a Kingdom of God on that specific land. Today, Judaism has some 14 million adherents worldwide. In the contemporary Middle East, most Jews live in Israel, although small communities remain in Iran, Iraq, Morocco, Syria, Tunisia, and Yemen.

Christianity

Christianity is the largest religion in the world, with 2.2 billion followers. It finds its roots in the teachings of Jesus of Nazareth, a Jew whose followers later came to believe he was also the Messiah and the Son of God. Jesus was born in Bethlehem (circa 7–2 B.C.E.) and crucified by the Romans in Jerusalem (circa 26–36 C.E.). Jews (and thus early Christians) were exiled from Jerusalem in 70 C.E. by the Romans, migrating primarily to lands along the eastern Mediterranean, though often remaining under the repressive authority of Roman administrators. Christianity spread rapidly over the next 300 years and continued to thrive in Europe following the Islamic conquest of the Middle East beginning in the seventh century, though Christian communities remained active throughout the Muslim world.

The period before the Reformation was marked by the concerted efforts of European leaders to shape Middle Eastern politics in the name of religion. The Crusades were not a single campaign, but nine major European military invasions into the region from the eleventh to the thirteenth centuries. Early successes were followed by numerous defeats. Following the capture of Jerusalem by Christian forces in 1099, the invading army formally pardoned those who surrendered, then continued on to massacre all remaining Muslim survivors. Muslims recaptured Jerusalem in 1187 under the leadership of Saladin, and the last Crusader stronghold in the Holy Land, in Acre, fell to Muslim control in 1291.

Foreign Christian intervention in the Middle East returned in great strength during the European colonial period. In addition to direct political intervention by the governments of the predominantly Christian countries of Britain and France, colonialism brought Christian missionaries, who opened schools, publishing houses, and hospitals, and who proselytized Muslims at every opportunity. Given this historical connection of Christianity and colonialism, it is not surprising that many independence struggles against colonial powers in the Middle East were fought in the name of religion—specifically, Islam.

Today, Christians make up significant populations in Lebanon and the West Bank and Gaza, and have smaller communities in Egypt, Iran, Iraq, Jordan, and Syria. The number of Christians (and particularly Catholics) in the Middle East has increased significantly in recent decades as a result of the presence of large numbers of foreign workers, including laborers and domestic workers.

Islam

The third of the Abrahamic faiths is Islam, founded in the early seventh century when Muhammad of Mecca (570–632 C.E.) received the last revelations of God (beginning in 610 C.E.) via the angel Gabriel. Muhammad was ordered to spread a simple message: that there is only one God (in Arabic, Allah), and no other god is worthy of worship. This message was the same as that revealed to Abraham, Moses, and Jesus, among other prophets. Muhammad was to be the last prophet, however, delivering God's final set of instructions to humankind. A follower of the Islamic faith is called a Muslim, meaning "one who submits" to the will of God.

From the outset, Islam gained followers not only for the simplicity and clarity of its message but also because its orthodox strand declared—contrary to centuries of Christian domination in Europe—that individual believers needed no intermediaries between themselves and God. Following Muhammad's emigration *(hijra)* from Mecca in 622 C.E., the first Muslims recaptured Mecca against much stronger armies, a success that facilitated the first of many large-scale conversions to Islam by demonstrating that God was on Muhammad's side. Jews and Christians were declared to be protected religious communities, or *dhimmi,* and (at least officially) were not to be targets of conversion (though voluntary conversion was welcome). In practice, of course, Jews and Christians often experienced discrimination, though at times they prospered under Muslim rulers, many of whom were relatively more tolerant of Jews than were Christian rulers in Europe. Because literacy is central to Islam, Muslim leaders supported the creation of numerous centers of higher education—the oldest continuously operating university in the world is Al-Azhar University in Cairo, still a major center of Sunni learning. Early Muslim scholars were also responsible for preserving the classic texts and histories of the Greek and Roman periods, and for reintroducing them to Europe during the Middle Ages.

There are several divisions within the larger Muslim *umma,* or global community, although Muslims view these differences as having varying degrees of importance. The most significant divide came early in Islam's history, when a dispute emerged over authority within the first Muslim community following the death of Muhammad. The majority view—what has come to be called the orthodox view by that virtue alone—was that authority should be shared and that a new leader, to the extent one was needed, should be selected from among the community. The followers of this view are called Sunni Muslims. The alternative view is that authority should have passed to direct blood descendants of Muhammad's family through his nephew, Ali. These followers or partisans of Ali, literally Shi'at Ali, are the Shi'a (or Shi'ites, as sometimes written). The series of leaders through this bloodline are called imams, and different Shi'i communities follow the line of imams to different points. For example, some follow only through the seventh imam, some to the tenth imam, and still others through the twelfth imam, who is believed to have disappeared from Earth and will return one day to bring justice to the world. Shi'a are today located throughout the Middle East, but have significant communities (and sometimes majorities) in Iraq, Bahrain, Saudi Arabia, Lebanon, Yemen, and Iran.

For all Muslims the basic text of Islam is the Quran, or "recitation," and unlike the Hebrew and Christian bibles, it is believed to be the literal word of God as conveyed to Muhammad through the angel Gabriel. The Quran and the Sunna—the sayings (hadith) and practices of the Prophet Muhammad—together provide all the guidance a Muslim needs in life and form the basis of sharia. The term *sharia* is conventionally translated as meaning "Islamic law," but is more akin to a set of guiding principles derived from the Quran and the Sunna. Within Sunni Islam, there are four main schools of interpreting sharia. Individual Muslims may choose to follow the school they find most compelling, and while they may draw guidance from scholars who study sharia, they are ultimately responsible to Allah for making their own decisions. Islamic scholars of sharia, sometimes called jurists, clerics, or mullahs, are often asked by followers to issue an opinion, or fatwa, on a particular topic. Many Islamic scholars over time have cultivated personal followings, but their opinions and interpretations are never binding on individual Muslims.

The Islamic conquest spread quickly throughout the Arab world and beyond; by the sixteenth century three great empires were Islamic: the Turkic Ottomans (who dominated the Arab world), the Safavids in Iran, and the Moguls on the Indian Subcontinent. While Muslim rulers gradually lost control of the far reaches of these empires—Muslim Andalusia in southern Spain was lost in 1492—the Islamic faith is today the world's fastest-growing religion, with its 1.8 billion adherents rapidly approaching Christianity's 2.2 billion.

Religious States

Most countries in the Middle East can be defined as religious in the sense that a specific religion is given the status of official state religion. What this means in practice, however, varies dramatically. There are formal religious states (such as Saudi Arabia and Iran) that prioritize the full application of religious law in some combination of political, social, and economic matters. There also are more nominally religious states, where either the ruling elite claim authority based on direct descent from the bloodline of the Prophet Muhammad (such as in Jordan, Morocco, Saudi Arabia, Bahrain, and Kuwait), or the constitution specifies an official state religion and requires the head of state to be a member of that religion (such as in Egypt, Yemen, Syria, prewar Iraq, Libya, Algeria, Oman, and Tunisia). Israel is also a religious state to the extent that it claims legitimacy in part as a national homeland for Jewish people, though as we shall see, religious authorities do not dominate the political sphere.

Most regimes in the Middle East claim their legitimacy at least in part based on religion. We think of Saudi Arabia and postrevolutionary Iran as Islamic states and of Israel as a Jewish state, but religion is actually written into the constitution of most states in the region. With the Arab uprisings, many states have undertaken major revisions of their constitutions, but in no case have references to formal state religion been eliminated. Indeed, in Egypt and Tunisia, the status of religion has been hotly debated, with many secularists pushing for a reduced role for religion while Islamist parties push for an increased role. These debates are an important indicator of the centrality of religious values in the region, though it says little about the relationship of religion and politics in practice. It is crucial to remember that regimes as well as their challengers often seek to associate themselves with the most popular ideas of the time, and the language of religion is used in diverse ways by a wide range of actors, including state officials.

The State of Israel and the Symbolism of Jerusalem

In the late nineteenth century, the desire to establish a Jewish homeland spread among Jews throughout Europe, particularly after the first Zionist conference was held in 1897. When the Ottoman Empire was dismantled after World War I, Britain gained control of most of Palestine and was convinced by European Zionists to draw up the Balfour Declaration. This 1917 document, which was accepted by the League of Nations, called for the establishment of a Jewish national home in Palestine. Hundreds of thousands of Jews migrated to Palestine, largely from Europe but also from Arab, African, and other non-Western countries. The United Nations (UN) passed a resolution in 1947 that divided Palestine and called for the creation of the State of Israel. In the months before May 15, 1948, when the British mandate over Palestine was set to expire, Zionists and Arabs in Palestine fought a bloody civil war that drove many Palestinians into exile. Israel declared independence on May 15, forming a modern nation-state with an overtly religious identity.

The question of Israel as a Jewish state cannot be divorced from struggles over the sovereignty of Jerusalem, a city claimed by both Israelis and Palestinians as their capital, and by all three Abrahamic religions as historically and symbolically central to their faiths. With the establishment of Israel in 1948, Jerusalem was divided, with the western (Christian, Jewish, and Armenian) quarters under Israeli control, and the eastern (Arab) quarters (including the Western Wall and the site of the Temple Mount [which Arabs know as the Haram al-Sharif]) under Jordanian control. Israelis and Jews worldwide celebrated the reunification of the city when Israel recaptured the eastern quarters in the 1967 Six Day War. The status of the city remains contested under international law, and the Israeli claim of Jerusalem as its capital is not recognized by most nations.

For Christians, too, Jerusalem is a city of tremendous symbolic significance. Christianity originated in Jerusalem, where Jesus preached, died, and is believed to have been resurrected. Millions of Christians make pilgrimages to holy sites in Jerusalem each year, as well as to other holy sites in the West Bank (notably Bethlehem and Nazareth) and Jordan (notably the Baptismal Site on the East Bank of the Jordan River). Jerusalem is also the third-holiest place in Islam, after Mecca and Medina (both in present-day Saudi Arabia). Muhammad is believed to have ascended to heaven from the site of the rock on the Haram al-Sharif where Abraham was willing to sacrifice his son Isaac to God. (Jews built the First and Second Temples on the site for the same reason.) The loss of Jerusalem to Jewish control in the twentieth century is viewed by many Muslims as a dire warning from God to renew and deepen their faith. Indeed, many Islamic revival groups view the success of foreign powers in colonizing and dominating Muslim lands as a result of the widespread loss of faith among Muslims. Only by returning to the fundamental teachings of their faith, they argue, can Muslim peoples ever hope to gain dignity and control over their destinies.

Viewing Israel as a religious state, however, can sometimes obscure more than it illuminates. While it is true that its Law of Return grants citizenship rights to all Jews or those of Jewish lineage, at least 20 percent of Israel's Jewish population self-identify as secular and even atheist. While marriages and divorces are overseen entirely by religious courts (Jewish, Muslim, Christian, and Druze), Israel's legal system combines Jewish law with elements of British common law and civil law. Religious law does not dominate most issues in the political realm, from national security to the particularities of Israel's democratic system. The elected parliament, called the Knesset, is open to all citizens of Israel, including Druze and Arabs, both Muslim and Christian. But Israel's non-Jewish citizens—mostly Muslim and Christian Arabs but also Druze—are not given rights equal to those of Israel's Jewish population, which lends force to the claims of those who view conflicts in the region as religious in character.

Strongly Islamic States

Israel was not the first state in the modern Middle East created in the name of religion; both Saudi Arabia and Iran were established in the twentieth century as religious states. The flag of Saudi Arabia includes the Islamic profession of faith, or *shahada* ("There is no God but God, and Muhammad is his Messenger"); the Iranian flag includes the phrase *Allahu Akbar* ("God is great") twenty-two times. But states like these may be described as "strongly Islamic" not only because they claim their legitimacy to rule on religious grounds, but also because they give religious leaders high levels of power and the authority to exercise control over certain spheres of governance and social practices. What this means in practice varies considerably.

The Kingdom of Saudi Arabia was established by the House of Saud in 1932 as an Islamic state. Although perhaps a marriage of convenience, the Saudi monarchy was formed through an alliance with a very conservative Sunni revival movement, Wahhabism, which called for a return to the letter of the Quran. King Abdul Aziz ibn Saud swept to power with the support of bedouin and Islamic extremists, whose fearlessness and commitment to an Islamic vision led them to conquer village after village. Indeed, these early extremists, called the Muslim Brethren (no connection to the Muslim Brotherhood discussed later), were more zealous than Abdul Aziz in terms of religion and the desire for political conquest. In 1929, Abdul Aziz was forced to fight his own Muslim Brethren forces in order to stop their continued conquest of lands controlled by the British. Today the Wahhabi establishment in

Saudi Arabia exerts near-absolute control over decisions relating to sharia, and it fully oversees the Islamic holy sites located inside the kingdom, including Mecca and Medina. But unlike in Iran, the Wahhabi clerics do not hold formal positions of state power, which remain fully in the hands of the Saudi monarchy.

Iran is also a strongly religious state. The revolution of 1978–1979, which brought the Islamic regime to power, is conventionally understood as Islamic because of its symbolism, rhetoric, and the prominent role played by clerics and the mosques. The massive mobilization that brought down the regime of Mohammad Reza Shah Pahlavi, however, was realized only through a broad alliance of bazaar merchants, clerical elites, nationalists, intellectuals, feminists, students, and laborers (among others). More than a year passed before the clerics, under the leadership of Ayatollah Ruhollah Khomeini, emerged triumphant against the nationalists and established the Islamic Republic of Iran. Clerics further solidified their power through their control of the Council of Guardians, which passes judgment on all political matters by declaring whether policies are in line with sharia. In this sense, Iran is the only country in the Middle East directly ruled by the clergy.

Although Iran has a democratically elected president and legislative body, in practice the Council of Guardians uses its power to exert extreme control over political, social, and economic matters. The group decides what sorts of foreign investment are permissible, how citizens may dress, and even whether citizens may use contraceptives (only if married, in which case the state provides them for free). It also determines who may run for elected office, including the presidency, thus seriously limiting the range of candidates and rendering elections far less democratic than they might be. In addition, any legislative reform passed through the national assembly must be approved by the Council of Guardians. Of the hundreds of reforms passed by the popularly elected assembly during the term of reformist president Mohammad Khatami from 1997 to 2005, not a single one was approved and implemented. For example, the assembly had passed several laws expanding the rights of women in divorce and child custody matters, but in each case the Council of Guardians vetoed the new laws as contrary to sharia.

The supreme authority in Iran belongs to the *velayat-e faqih*, an individual possessing superior religious knowledge in the absence of the twelfth imam, whom Shi'a believe to be in occultation: he has not died but is absent on Earth and will one day return to fill the world with justice. The office of the *faqih* was created after the 1979 revolution and was occupied by Ayatollah Khomeini until his death in 1989. The *faqih* is selected by the Assembly of Experts—composed of eighty-six clerics elected every eight years, with the Council of Guardians determining who may run for the seats—but holds his position for life, acts as the final authority in all political matters, and is not accountable to the public or any other authority. The *faqih* appoints half of the Council of Guardians as well as the head of the judiciary, who in turn supervises the election by parliament of the remainder of the Council of Guardians. In this sense, clerical rule in Iran is virtually absolute, with a range of mechanisms used to systematically exclude challenges to their rule.

One of the stated goals of the early Islamic Republic of Iran was the export of the revolution: to encourage and indeed support Muslims in other countries to rise up against their regimes and establish Islamic states in their wake. This objective met with overwhelming failure, although the impact of this policy (which was largely pushed to the back burner following the death of Khomeini in 1989) continues to be felt in terms of the support Iran provides to a few Islamist groups, notably Hezbollah in Lebanon. Iran is also rumored to play a role in supporting Shi'i factions in postwar Iraq and a minor Shi'i movement in Yemen (the northern-based al-Huthi who are members of the Zaydi sect), though these connections have not been indisputably established.

Nominally Islamic States

Most other states in the Middle East accord some formal status to religion, often stipulating Islam as the official religion or requiring the president to be Muslim. Turkey is the notable exception: when Mustafa Kemal (later called Atatürk) established the modern state of Turkey in 1923, he advocated a program of forced secularism that included dismantling religious courts and outlawing religious or traditional dress. Most regimes in the region, however, actively embrace an Islamic identity. The monarchs and emirs of Bahrain, Jordan, Kuwait, Morocco, Oman, and the United Arab Emirates (UAE), like their counterparts in Saudi Arabia, all claim authority to rule based in part on their direct descent from the bloodline of the Prophet Muhammad. The monarchs of Jordan and Morocco, however, rest more of their legitimacy on religion than do the others. Jordan's King Hussein, for example, called himself "Keeper of Islam's Two Holy Places in Jerusalem" (the Dome of the Rock and Al-Aqsa Mosque, both on the Haram al-Sharif), a title that proved embarrassing when Jordan lost control of East Jerusalem to Israel in the 1967 Six Day War. In a similar reference to Islam, the king of Morocco refers to himself as "Commander of the Faithful."

Many republics too have established Islam as the official state religion and sharia as a source of law and legislation, including Algeria, Egypt, Syria, Tunisia, Yemen, and prewar Iraq. What this means in practice varies considerably. Certainly the president must be a Muslim, and it is not unusual on high Muslim holidays or during times of domestic or regional turmoil to see the president and other state officials praying prominently, televised for all to see. (US presidents, it should be noted, almost universally end their public addresses, in times of both war and peace, with the words "God bless America.") During the Gulf War of 1990–1991, Saddam Hussein even added the words "God is great" to the Iraqi flag: although his religious credentials were thin at best, he perhaps thought that the phrase might give him greater legitimacy and, in particular, greater support from other Muslim countries.

In Egypt the office of mufti has long been filled by a prominent cleric from Al-Azhar University; his job is to judge whether state policies are in adherence to sharia. Unlike Iran's Council of Guardians, under Husni Mubarak's rule this office (like similar ones in Jordan and elsewhere) was little more than symbolic; nevertheless, the regime's need to at least *appear* to conform to sharia underlines the power of Islamic symbolism in sustaining the state's authority to rule. As Egypt transitions into a post-Mubarak era, it remains unclear whether the mufti will remain a rubber-stamp position or will gain more power—or whether the office of mufti will be retained at all. Likewise, vibrant debates have emerged around the wording of the new constitution and whether Islam will be accorded a more substantive role in both word and practice. The clerics, or ulama, from Al-Azhar University continue to function as a conservative (but not extremist) force in Egypt; they control the religious courts and provide imams (prayer leaders) to each of the country's tens of thousands of mosques. Religious parties explicitly outlawed under Mubarak were legalized after the revolution. As we will see below, the long-established but previously illegal Muslim Brotherhood has emerged in the post-Mubarak era as a powerful political party, although it faces challenges from even more conservative Islamist groups that entered the political scene after the revolution.

Overall, the vast majority of states in the Middle East accord some official status to religion. Some regimes use religion to expand the perceived legitimacy of their rule, while others maintain an official status for religion out of popular pressure. In the early 1970s, for example, Syrian president Hafiz al-Asad tried to remove from the constitution the condition that the president be Muslim; he abandoned this aim in large part due to strong societal pressure. Since the Arab uprisings, the role of Islam in the new regimes and constitutions has been a hotly debated issue and is likely to continue to be, as a range of religious and nonreligious political actors struggle over what the new political institutions will look like.

Religious Revivalism

The contemporary Middle East has seen an expansion of religious revivalist groups, in part inspired by anticolonial struggles and the desire for a politics

Is Lebanon a Religious State?

Lebanon is a confessional state, meaning that seats in parliament and the offices of president, prime minister, and speaker of parliament are distributed according to sect, an affiliation based on membership in a confessional community. Lebanon's confessional system, which was established in 1942 as a means of preventing sectarian conflict by ensuring representation of all communities, also works to preserve (rather than overcome) sectarian differences of the sort that tore the country apart during its fifteen-year civil war beginning in 1975. That conflict formally ended with the Ta'if Accord, signed in 1989, which expanded parliament from 99 to 128 seats; these seats are now evenly divided between Muslim and Christian sects (the previous allocation provided for 54 Christian and 45 Muslim seats). This system ensures broad representation in government, but also affords Christians a disproportionate number of seats, as the demographics have changed: Muslims are estimated to now make up at least 60 percent of the population. Ironically, the adoption of a similar confessional system in post-Saddam Iraq has exacerbated sectarian tensions by institutionalizing sectarian divisions in the structure of the parliament.

Executive branch
President: Maronite Orthodox Christian
Prime minister: Sunni Muslim
Speaker of parliament: Shi'i Muslim

Parliament

Muslim seats	64
Sunni	27
Shi'i	27
Druze	8
Alawite	2
Christian seats	64
Maronite	34
Greek Orthodox	14
Greek Catholic	8
Armenian Orthodox	5
Armenian Catholic	1
Protestant	1
Other Christian	1

that can be locally recognized as authentic. Much of the Arab world remained under Ottoman control in the late nineteenth century, although the farther reaches of the empire were gradually gaining local autonomy. For many parts of the Middle East the spread of European colonialism meant the exchange of one foreign occupier (the Ottoman Turks) for another (France, Great Britain, or Italy). The lack of Arab autonomy was viewed both as humiliating and as the cause of innumerable economic and political hardships, and it was in this context that a diverse range of revivalist movements emerged, first in the early twentieth century and then in a broader wave beginning in the 1970s. In much of that century, the dominant political narratives in the region were Arab nationalism, socialism, and Islamic revivalism; each offered a means of imagining alternative political arrangements in which Arabs would regain dignity through control of their own destinies.

Islamic revivalism took many forms, but a common theme was that Muslim peoples had diverged too far from their faith and that a return to the core values of their religion would restore the community's rightful dignity—along with political, social, and economic control of their lives. This narrative gained popularity as more or less secular regimes—many espousing the language of socialism and Arab nationalism—failed to provide economic prosperity, meaningful political participation, or even a sense of pride and dignity. In the face of such ignominious military defeats as the 1967 Six Day War—which saw the routing of the Egyptian, Syrian, and Jordanian armies and the loss of much Palestinian land, including East Jerusalem, to Israeli control—Islamic revivalist groups provided an alternative vision to that of state socialism and Arab nationalism and saw their numbers swell over the next decade. Islamic revivalism took diverse forms, ranging from legal political parties that sought to contest elections to underground militant groups that aimed to use arms to defeat incumbent regimes. Jewish religious revivalism also took several forms but was primarily framed in relation to Zionism and the need to establish (and later defend) the State of Israel as a national homeland for Jews.

In the broadest terms, religious revivalist movements seek to reform or replace existing political structures and social practices with those viewed as more in line with core religious values. But how is this change to be realized? Most revivalist groups seek to enact change gradually, by working within existing political structures and through education and socialization programs. Other groups are characterized by their full rejection of existing regimes, which they seek to overthrow, if necessary through the use of political violence. The following sections examine the dominant trend of seeking gradual reform, the minority trend of advocating the immediate overthrow of existing regimes, and the new trend of working with a range of political actors to shape the post–Arab uprisings regimes. The leaders of the Islamic revivalist movements hail from diverse social and economic backgrounds, though they most frequently have strong middle-class and professional roots: they are engineers, doctors, lawyers, teachers, and civil servants. The social bases of those who support Islamist revivalist groups are likewise diverse, ranging from the disenfranchised poor to the social and political elite. But in all cases, the educated middle class makes up a significant portion of group leadership and the rank-and-file.

Islamist Groups Working Within Existing Regimes

Even prior to the Arab uprisings, the vast majority of Islamist revivalist groups sought to realize their visions for a more Islamic society by working within existing regimes, often by fielding candidates in local, municipal, and national elections, and by forming local nongovernmental organizations to advocate change at the grassroots level through education and social services. In this sense, most religious political activism in the Middle East can be readily characterized as moderate rather than extremist. In fact, the region is flush with religious revivalist groups from all the Abrahamic faiths that advocate gradual reform, organize political parties (and strive for legal status), and cooperate with groups across the ideological spectrum. In much of the region, for example, Islamic groups routinely cooperate with communists, socialists, liberals, Christians, and nationalists. Indeed, the range of religious activism is so diverse that this chapter could not possibly mention every group and examine every dimension of religion and politics.

Islamist groups that work within existing regimes justify their gradual or integrative approach on Islamic terms. Many believe that, as long as one adheres to the spirit and values of the Quran and the hadith, a wide range of political systems, from socialism to liberal democracy to monarchy, are acceptable. Contemporary justifications for gradual reform and for participation in pluralist or democratic political systems frequently reference the thinking of Hassan al-Banna (1905–1949), who founded the Muslim Brotherhood in Egypt in 1928. Al-Banna was a schoolteacher who advocated a return to Islam's core values through reading and study groups and by working within existing political structures. Rather than focusing exclusively on political participation, for example, the group was an early advocate of literacy programs for men as well as women to ensure that all Muslims are able to read the Quran and thus produce a more robustly Islamic society.

Since at least the 1990s, most debates among Islamists about political participation have found sufficient overlap in democratic and Islamic notions of participation so as to have little or no difficulty justifying participation in pluralist politics, particularly democratic elections. Branches of the Muslim Brotherhood in Egypt, Jordan, Tunisia, and Yemen have for decades sought to participate in multiparty elections—with varying degrees of success and regime permission. In Yemen, the Brotherhood has participated in elections as a segment of the legal Yemeni Congregation for Reform, or Islah party, since 1993. Though Brotherhood members are sometimes at odds with other trends within the Islah party, they strongly support pluralist politics and held numerous cabinet positions in the mid-1990s as a result of the party's success at the polls and its alliance with the ruling party, the General Popular Congress (GPC). With the defeat of the Yemeni Socialist Party during the 1994 civil war, the Islah party saw a decline in its political influence, as the ruling GPC of then president Ali Abdullah Salih dominated the political field much the way the National Democratic Party did in Egypt. The Islah party subsequently became a strong partner in the Joint Meetings Party (JMP), a bloc of secular as well as religious parties that emerged in the early 2000s in opposition to the GPC. The JMP has played a formal role in Yemen's transition since the 2011 uprising, although as a part of the formal opposition it has remained distant from much of the popular opposition mobilization on the street. 2011 Nobel Laureate Tawakkul Karman was herself an Islah member who had been elected to that party's primary governing body, or Shura Council.

In Jordan, the Muslim Brotherhood has been engaged in electoral politics since the 1950s, and since the 1970s several of its prominent leaders have held cabinet positions. With the first full parliamentary elections in two decades held in 1989—the assembly had been suspended following Jordan's defeat in the 1967 war until 1984—the Muslim Brotherhood fielded candidates and together with some independent Islamists won twenty-seven seats (out of eighty), or 40 percent of the assembly. In the early 1990s the group was granted five cabinet positions, largely in recognition of its success at the polls. When political parties were legalized in 1992, many of its prominent members joined forces with independent Islamists to form the Islamic Action Front (IAF) party. The IAF, now dominated by the Muslim Brotherhood, competes regularly in local and national elections and has forged strong relations with other opposition parties, including nationalists, communists, socialists, and liberals. Like Yemen's Islah party, the IAF also engages in democratic practices internally and has seen prominent party leaders defeated in their bids to retain top party offices.

Islamist parties in Turkey have participated in elections since the 1970s but only recently have become a strong political force. This development has come in the context of a process wherein Turkey's Constitutional Court repeatedly closed down Islamist parties for threatening the state's secular foundations. In the face of this repression, Islamists moderated in order to be permitted to participate in elections and parliament. After winning only 7 percent of the vote in 1987 (Turkey's proportional representation system requires parties to win a minimum of 10 percent of the vote to gain seats in parliament), the Islamist-oriented Welfare Party reached out to conservative and pious middle-class Turks who were hurt by economic liberalization. The party continually gained strength, winning 17 percent of the vote in 1991 and 21 percent in 1995, all under the leadership of longtime Islamist leader Necmettin Erbakan, who became prime minister in 1996. The Constitutional Court outlawed the party in 1998, however, and the Virtue Party emerged in its place. It did not fare well in the 1999 elections, and the party suffered from internal divisions about the direction of the party, particularly concerning its commitment to democratic and pluralist norms. The Constitutional Court closed Virtue in 2001.

The Virtue Party was replaced by the Justice and Development Party (AKP), whose commitments to European Union (EU) membership and pluralism are viewed by many Islamists as having strayed too far from core Islamic beliefs. The party proved highly popular, however, and won 34 percent of the vote in 2002, securing two-thirds of the parliament with 363 of 550 seats (only one other party surpassed the 10 percent threshold). After a contentious presidential election in 2007 in which AKP leader Abdullah Gül was victorious, the AKP continued its trend of dominating the political scene by winning a remarkable 47 percent of the vote and winning 341 seats (fewer than in 2002 because another party passed the 10 percent threshold). The AKP currently dominates Turkish politics, with control of the parliament, presidency, and prime ministry, but its advocacy of EU membership, neoliberal economic reforms, political pluralism, and human rights is a far cry from the policies of Erbakan in 1996, who began his premiership with official state visits to Iran and Libya and a call for an integrated Muslim economic bloc. The AKP thus stands as an important example of the diversity of even moderate Islamist revivalists, whose policies are sometimes more akin to liberal democracy than to religious conservatism.

What do these examples have in common? Beyond the language of Islam as a frame for political opposition, each of these groups works to bring gradual change to a nondemocratic regime. In this sense, the degree of state repression or openness can almost always explain far more about the character of an Islamist revivalist movement than can Islam per se. The experiences of the Muslim Brotherhood in various countries are in many ways typical of other Islamist groups that seek to realize their reforms gradually and by working within the existing political systems. Some of these parties have been outlawed (e.g., an-Nahda in Tunisia until the 2011 revolution); some function but do not have legal status (e.g., the Muslim Brotherhood in Egypt until the 2011 revolution); and some are legal political parties (e.g., the Islah party in Yemen, Hezbollah in Lebanon, and the IAF in Jordan). Kuwait has multiple Islamist groups that hold seats in its parliament, and Islamist groups are active in parliamentary politics in Iraq, Turkey, Algeria, and Morocco.

In addition to formal participation in elected national assemblies and local elections, moderate Islamist groups are known for their provision of social services, particularly where state services are nowhere to be found. Hezbollah provided significant services in southern Lebanon during the civil war and after; Egypt's Muslim Brotherhood provided earthquake relief in 1992 in the face of a state that did not know where to begin. Most moderate Islamist groups are also engaged in literacy programs and schools, although the curriculum is carefully controlled. Islamist groups also frequently carry out charity work and provide health care services. Some scholars have questioned the depth and effectiveness of these social programs, arguing that they are championed for public relations purposes but in practice are far less effective. One study shows that Muslim Brotherhood–run health clinics in Cairo, for example, are seldom staffed by a medical doctor (Clark 2004). Nevertheless, these moderate Islamic activists—those who have sought to participate peacefully and legally in economic, political, and social realms—constitute the vast majority of Islamic revivalist movements. Their popularity largely stems from the fact that they provide an alternative—ideologically and substantively—to the corruption, ineffectiveness, repression, and failed economic projects of incumbent regimes.

Islamists Who Entirely Reject Existing Regimes

Even though they make up a tiny proportion of Islamic revivalist groups, extremist religious groups garner the most headlines and the impact of their activities can be profound. The term *extremist* is used here to refer not to ideas that fall well outside the norm but, more specifically, to those who adopt militancy as a strategy for redressing their grievances. Extremists tend to emerge out of the most repressive contexts and aim to achieve political change by directly attacking those in power. Their targets include foreign agents—including troops and diplomats, but also foreign-owned businesses and tourists—as well as regimes they believe to be illegitimate. The latter includes those they see as having been imposed by colonial and imperial powers (Israel would be an example) as well as regimes deemed to have abandoned Islamic values and teachings.

In Egypt, the Muslim Brotherhood supported Gamal Abdel Nasser and the Free Officers movement, which overthrew the Egyptian monarchy in 1952. When Nasser sought to consolidate his power, however, he viewed the Muslim Brotherhood as a primary threat and outlawed the organization in 1954 after accusing its members of attempting to assassinate him. From that period until Nasser's death in 1970, thousands of its members were jailed and many were executed. Among them was Sayyid Qutb, whose experiences of repression led him to abandon al-Banna's commitment to working within existing Muslim regimes to realize change. In his book *Signposts Along the Road (Ma'alim fi-l-Tariq),* Qutb argues that, contrary to a common interpretation of sharia, Muslims are not obligated to accept the legitimacy of the leadership of Muslim rulers if those leaders are not

ruling in accord with Islam. Emancipation of Muslim communities must
come through movement, he argued, rather than through works (teaching)
alone. This position was radical because it justified, on Islamic grounds, attacking and overthrowing Muslim regimes. Qutb was executed by hanging
in 1966 along with two others for allegedly plotting against Nasser's
regime; many viewed these charges as a setup. Regardless, the impact of
Qutb's teachings and his martyrdom at the hands of the Egyptian state has
been profound.

Indeed, Qutb inspired the emergence of extremist groups in Egypt and
later throughout the Muslim world. In the early 1970s, Egyptian president
Anwar Sadat released hundreds of Muslim Brotherhood members from
prison as part of his effort to distinguish his rule from that of Nasser, who
had imprisoned thousands of political opponents, including many Islamists.
Among the hundreds of Muslim Brotherhood members released over the
course of several years were a number of Qutb followers, who formed small
groups that advocated the violent overthrow of the regime. These included
the Islamic Group (Al-Gama'a al-Islamiyya) and Islamic Jihad (Jihad al-Islami). In 1981, Islamic Jihad member Khalid Islambuli assassinated Sadat,
hoping that his death would spark an Islamic revolution in Egypt and the
Arab world, following the one in Iran just two years earlier. No popular uprising emerged, however, and Islambuli and his co-conspirators were arrested. Islambuli was executed but a number of others were exiled, including several who found refuge in Afghanistan and later joined al-Qaeda. In
Egypt, the Islamic Group and Islamic Jihad regrouped and mounted a series
of violent acts throughout the country, culminating in the 1997 massacre of
tourists in the Valley of the Kings, which claimed the lives of four Egyptians and fifty-eight foreign tourists (along with six responsible for the attack). Islamic Jihad leaders who were already imprisoned at the time dissociated themselves from that attack, condemning it and formally disbanding
their organization. Egypt has experienced little extremism since then,
though the potential for a revival of religious extremism remained considerable while the Egyptian state was repressive and nondemocratic in nature.

Egypt is not the only country that has suffered from domestic Islamic
extremism. Algeria experienced a virtual civil war by and among Islamist
groups in the 1990s, although notably this bloodshed began after the Islamic Salvation Front (FIS) won parliamentary elections in 1992 that the
military quickly annulled. Yemen has seen violence by extremists against
tourists and missionaries, as well as against the holy shrines of minority
Muslim groups and a former brewery in the south. Beginning in the 1970s,
Islamist extremists from North Yemen assassinated hundreds of socialists
from South Yemen; even after unification in the 1990s, assaults against socialists continued, particularly as the 1993 elections approached. Although
these attacks subsided somewhat during the remainder of the 1990s, in

2002 the prominent socialist leader Jar Allah Umar was assassinated: he was shot point-blank as he left the stage after addressing an assembly of the Islamist Islah party's general membership. In recent years, a group calling itself al-Qaeda in the Arabian Peninsula has launched several attacks, including the 2009 murder of four Korean tourists in Yemen and the failed Christmas Day attack on an airplane bound for Detroit that same year.

Islamic extremists justify their use of violence as jihad, a legitimate use of force necessary to defend one's faith against threats. Conventional wisdom in the West holds that holy war is specific to Islam in the contemporary period, although it was famously waged by Christians during the Crusades, and the idea of holy war also emerged early in Judaism and continues to exert a strong influence in Israeli political affairs. Some Zionist groups believe that they are obligated to use violence if necessary to bring about God's desire for all Jews to return to the Holy Land (modern-day Israel, including the West Bank). In February 1994, for example, an Israeli American named Baruch Goldstein opened fire on a crowd of Muslim worshippers in a mosque at the Cave of the Patriarchs, a site in Hebron (known to Arabs as Khalil) that is sacred to Jews, Christians, and Muslims alike. At least 39 Muslims were killed and 125 were injured. Goldstein was a member of the recently outlawed Kach party, which along with a spin-off group, Kahane Chai, is considered a terrorist organization by Israel and many other nations, including the United States.

Islamist Groups Since the Arab Uprisings

The Arab uprisings that began in southern Tunisia in late 2010 have changed the equation for many Islamist groups by creating opportunities for meaningful participation in governing institutions. Tunisia's president Zine el Abidine Ben Ali was the first regional dictator to fall, on January 14, 2011. The banned an-Nahda movement, while not a central player in the protests, reconstituted quickly with the return of its leader, Rachid Ghanouchi, who for decades had been exiled to London. A moderate revivalist group, an-Nahda had long espoused support for a democratic and liberal political system but, like all opposition, had been outlawed by Ben Ali. In Tunisia's first free elections for its Constituent Assembly in October 2011, an-Nahda won 37 percent of the seats—the largest bloc—and party member Hamadi Jebali was appointed Tunisia's first postrevolution prime minister.

In Egypt, the Muslim Brotherhood was long the most important nongovernmental group in the country, able to mobilize thousands for (largely) peaceful protests against the regime's policies and the dominance of the National Democratic Party in national politics. Under Mubarak's regime it remained an illegal organization, although it frequently fielded "independent" candidates for the People's Assembly as well as in local elections.

After years of winning few seats, during the 2005 elections it won eighty-seven seats (nearly 19 percent of the assembly). During Egypt's January 25 revolution in 2011, the Brotherhood did not emerge as a significant actor until the protests had reached revolutionary levels. In fact, the group had first instructed its followers not to join the protests at all. With Mubarak's resignation and the ensuing struggles over what the new Egypt would look like politically, the Brotherhood emerged as a major player. This is not surprising given the group's decades-long presence in communities and its institutional resources. It formed the Freedom and Justice Party in April and won 47.2 percent of the seats in parliamentary elections held between November 2011 and January 2012. Although the group had previously declared that it would not field a candidate for president, it revised its position and in June 2012, Muslim Brotherhood member Mohamed Morsi won Egypt's first free presidential elections.

Thus in two states that saw regime change through popular uprisings, Islamist movements won the largest blocs in freely elected national assemblies and assumed the highest governing office (prime minister in Tunisia and president in Egypt). These events mark a sea change in the region. While moderate Islamists had gradually worked their way into power in Turkey, here were two cases in which old regimes were replaced by Islamist revivalists through democratic elections. In both cases, it is important to note that other political parties also won seats, and in Tunisia in particular, an-Nahda worked with two center-left parties to share the three highest offices (those of the prime minister, the speaker of parliament, and president).

The success of Islamist parties after the uprisings is not surprising. In addition to possessing established constituencies, these groups presented stark alternatives to the corrupt regimes of Ben Ali and Mubarak. Islamists are often seen as highly moral and, owing to years suffering under severe state repression, unconnected to the old regime. The coming years will tell whether these newly powerful parties will adhere to their commitments to uphold democratic rule. In the meantime, they face the challenge of rebuilding crumbling economies and must contend with other strong political forces vying for power, such as Egypt's Supreme Council for the Armed Forces (SCAF), that have their own agendas and priorities for reform.

In addition to these moderate revivalist Islamists, Tunisia and Egypt have seen Salafi groups emerge onto the political scene since the uprisings. The term *Salafi* refers to a broad category of Islamist revivalists who seek to adhere closely to the practices and beliefs of the earliest Muslims, or *salaf* (meaning ancestors or predecessors). Salafi groups exist across the region and are not a united or cohesive movement. In many states, such as Jordan, Salafi groups have long been quiescent: they restrict their activities largely to Islamic study and take no position on the legitimacy of the ruling regime. Following the uprisings in Tunisia and Egypt, however, some Salafi groups (but not others) altered this position and formed formal political parties to contest elections. In Tunisia, Salafis have openly criticized an-Nahda for cooperating with secular groups and for not moving quickly to implement sharia. In Egypt, the Salafi an-Nour party won 27.8 percent of the parliamentary votes in the November 2011–January 2012 contest. Since most of these groups have engaged with existing regimes even less than groups like the Muslim Brotherhood, they are perceived by many as entirely pure and uncorrupt. The future role of Salafism on the formal political scene will likely continue to range from formal political engagement to quiescence.

Transnational Connections

The question of connections among Islamist groups in different countries has gained greater importance since the rise of groups like al-Qaeda, whose targets are not limited to a single state. The question of transnationalism, however, is fraught with difficulty, because the nature of "connections" among groups is highly varied. Islamist groups with similar goals, agendas, ideological commitments, or practical problems—but that hail from different countries—routinely dialogue with each other for purposes of sharing experiences, organizing conferences, building membership, and so on. A parallel would be the human rights groups based in a large number of countries that coordinate, cooperate, and share information (and sometimes resources) to advance goals shared by all the groups but that remain distinct and separate organizations. Many branches of the Muslim Brotherhood and other moderate Islamist groups conform to this pattern: they operate primarily within their own countries, but they dialogue with similar groups in other countries. Indeed, moderate revivalist groups frequently attend conferences organized by other Islamist groups, to discuss and debate such topics as elections, democracy, *dawa* (outreach) activities, education reform, and so on. Other transnational connections include those forged by both educational exchange programs and financial institutions, particularly banks that facilitate investments that do not violate the Islamic injunction against charging interest.

The primary concern with transnationalism, however, has less to do with these sorts of connections than with groups that are truly transnational—meaning groups that cross borders organizationally as well as with respect to their political objectives—particularly extremist groups. Indeed, Islamic extremism is not confined to domestic attacks, as the acts of violence that have gained the most attention internationally are those that target Israel and US troops in the Middle East, and of course the attacks of September 11, 2001, that targeted the Pentagon and World Trade Center in the United States. Palestinian militants have launched attacks on Israel since the 1960s, but it was not until the formation of Hamas in 1987 during the first intifada that Palestinian Islamist groups began using political violence. Lebanon's Hezbollah has also launched numerous attacks on Israeli troops and Israeli soil. Hamas and Hezbollah differ from many other militant Islamist groups, however, in that their attacks are aimed at ousting what they view as foreign troops illegally occupying their land. In this regard, their activities, instead of being considered transnational in nature, might better be viewed as concerned with protecting and restoring what they view as legitimate sovereign borders.

Currently, al-Qaeda is the most famous and active transnational extremist group, one that justifies attacking not only governments but also foreigners and civilians deemed responsible for perpetuating the conditions that oppress Muslim peoples worldwide. Following Sayyid Qutb, the group advocates attacking even Muslim rulers and regimes globally if they are not deemed to be acting in full accordance with Islam. While the activities of al-Qaeda represent an escalation of Islamic extremism in the scale of its tactics and the boundlessness of its targets, the movement has never enjoyed popular support within the Arab or Muslim world. Indeed, following the September 11 attacks, dozens of Muslim countries immediately expressed condolences to the citizens of the United States, and millions of Muslims worldwide organized candlelight vigils in neighborhoods and mosques in remembrance of the victims. While the extremism of groups like al-Qaeda is abhorrent in its targeting of innocents, it is crucial to remember that such fringe organizations are not the norm.

Likewise, it is important to distinguish organizations that operate legally and legitimately within their own countries and that might have connections with similar groups in other countries, on the one hand, from illegal and extremist groups that are fundamentally transnational in character, on the other. Because al-Qaeda has been so dramatically successful in launching attacks against numerous countries, other Islamist groups with transnational connections are now viewed with suspicion despite having a history of peacefully working for gradual reform.

Conclusion

Religion plays a central role in Middle Eastern politics, in part because political struggles have for centuries been understood as religious conflicts (e.g., the Crusades, colonialism's connection to Christian proselytizing, Western support for Israel, and the targeting of Muslims in the "war on terror"), and in part because of the intimate ties of the three Abrahamic faiths to the region. The great diversity of religious experiences and practices—from whether minority religious communities enjoy inclusion or endure repression, to the ways in which states accept or reject religious political parties, to the diverse means of invoking religious symbols and rhetoric in expressions of dissent—is a core feature of the region. Religion will undoubtedly continue to be a central component of politics in the Middle East for decades to come. As some recent trends of inclusion and tolerance illustrate, that reality need not necessarily entail violence.

As this chapter has illustrated, the fact that religion and politics have a long history in the Middle East does not mean that religion is always, or even most of the time, a crucial factor driving political conflicts. Indeed, most conflicts are classically political in character, in that they are at the most basic level conflicts over control of land, resources, or peoples. The Crusades were about the conquest of empire, not about core religious beliefs. The Arab uprisings that began in late 2010 also underline that while religion plays a role in political debates, popular political struggles more often concern demands for freedom, economic equality, and justice. This is not to suggest that religious motivations are superficial but to draw attention away from religion as a primary explanatory factor—as in "these religions have been fighting each other for centuries!"—and toward more complete understandings of struggles for power in the Middle East. In this regard, the expanding role of moderate Islamist revivalist groups in electoral politics—even within nondemocratic regimes—merits at least as much attention as do the exceptional extremist groups of the likes of al-Qaeda.

7

Identity and Politics

David Siddhartha Patel

Abbas Haydar lives in Basra, a city in southern Iraq. In the turbulent period following the US-led overthrow of Saddam Hussein's Baath regime in 2003, numerous groups tried to gain Abbas's support by telling him how he should think about Iraqi politics and his own identity. A local judge promised to represent "the people of Basra" and use revenue from nearby oil fields to develop the city. Several new political parties told Abbas to think of himself, first and foremost, as an Iraqi. One of these parties flew an old Iraqi flag with a design that had not been used since 1963. Other parties said that he was a member of an Arab nation of more than 300 million people that stretches 3,000 miles west from Iraq to Morocco. On Fridays, a preacher in the local mosque reminded Abbas that he was a member of the Islamic *umma,* the global community of more than 1 billion Muslims. Previously banned political movements said that the Shiʻite Muslim clergy knew what was best. Abbas's granduncle reminded him of his responsibility to support his extended family, including his distant cousins.

Like all people, Abbas has multiple identities. His religion (Islam), his sect (Shiʻism), the language he speaks at home (Arabic), his lineage (al-Kanaan clan of the Banu Tamim tribe), and the country (Iraq) and city (Basra) in which he lives are each a characteristic that he shares with some people but not others. Each characteristic and the group it defines could conceivably be important for Abbas's political choices, including for whom he votes, to whom he turns when he needs government services, and for whom he might willingly die or even kill. These political communities are "imagined," because Abbas will never meet, or even hear of, most fellow members (Anderson 1991). Yet they matter. In the parliamentary elections in 2005, Abbas ignored appeals from Arab nationalist, tribal, and regional

candidates and joined the vast majority of Iraqi Shi'ites in casting his ballot
for an electoral list dominated by Shi'ite Islamists. That election ensured
that ethnic and sectarian cleavages would play an important role in Iraq's
nascent governing institutions, and Shi'ite Islamists have dominated the
government ever since.

This chapter will help us make sense of Abbas's and the Middle East's
multiple identities (Lewis 1998). We will assume that an individual's political identity is not fixed but is socially and politically constructed; it can
change over time through manipulation or perhaps individual choice. In
other words, we will reject the assumption that ancient and "essential" religious antagonisms and mentalities characterize Middle Eastern politics.
This might be controversial, because the language we use to discuss the
Middle East often assumes that some identities inherently matter more than
others. For example, calling a region "the Holy Land" automatically implies that religion is important for its politics. When newspapers describe
diplomatic relations between "Shi'ite Iran" and "Sunni Saudi Arabia," the
adjectives condition us to believe that sectarian differences explain relations between these states when perhaps disagreements over oil policy offer
a better explanation.

All societies possess multiple lines of ethnic and religious division
along which political competition and conflict might occur. Most of these
divisions are politically unimportant; intergroup coexistence is always far
more common than intergroup conflict. We want to understand variation in
the political importance of particular identities within countries, between
countries, and over time. In Jordan, for example, Transjordanian voters
have tended to vote for family members or tribal candidates while Palestinian-Jordanian voters have been more likely to vote for Islamist candidates
(or not vote!) than for tribal ones. Why? Although bloody fighting occurred
between Sunni and Shi'ite Arab militias in Iraq from 2004 to 2007, sectarian violence was very rare in twentieth-century Iraq. Why did many Sunnis
and Shi'ites in Iraq come to see members of the other sect as enemies? Why
did sectarian violence between Shi'ites and Sunnis in Iraq not "spill over"
into neighboring states? Why did relations between Sunnis and Shi'ites remain relatively peaceful in Kuwait, Iran, Bahrain, Syria, and Saudi Arabia
while fighting occurred in Iraq? In the 1950s and 1960s, Arab and pan-Arab
nationalist movements grew dramatically and either came to power or
formed the most powerful opposition movements in and across most Arab
countries. Yet the political saliency of Arab nationalism declined quickly;
many scholars and observers now consider it "dead" or at least unable to
consistently mobilize large numbers of Arabic speakers. What explains this
change? The purpose of this chapter is to provide a framework for understanding identity and intergroup relations in the Middle East. It describes

these divisions and presents theories that might account for why countries differ with regard to which identities are most important for political behavior.

Ethnic and Religious Cleavages in the Middle East

Identity Groups and Identity Categories

It is useful to differentiate between identity groups and the categories those groups fit within (Sacks 1992; Posner 2005). Identity groups are the specific labels that people use to define who they are. Depending on the context, Abbas Haydar might describe himself as "Muslim," "Shi'ite," "Arab," "Iraqi," "member of Banu Tamim tribe," "member of al-Kanaan clan," "Basrawi," or "resident of al-Fursi neighborhood." Each of these is an identity group for which a specific imagined political community *could* exist. Identity categories, by contrast, are the broad cleavages of social division into which these identity groups can be sorted, such as religion, sect, native language, country of origin, tribe, clan, city of origin or residence, and neighborhood. Individuals can be assumed to have one identity group (e.g., one form of religion) from each identity category.

It is often claimed that Iraq today is divided among Sunnis, Shi'ites, and Kurds. As this framework immediately makes clear, however, this description conflates two identity categories. The identity group "Kurds" is part of the identity category of language; the identity groups "Sunnis" and "Shi'ites" are in the identity category of sect. Since most Kurds are also Sunni Muslims, the identity group "Sunnis" should include them. What people who make this claim *mean* to say is, "Iraq today is divided politically among Arab Sunnis, Arab Shi'ites, and Kurds of all sects." This is an important clarification, because it reveals how political alignments in Iraq might change in the future—perhaps Arab Sunnis and Kurdish Sunnis could ally along their shared sect, or perhaps Arab Sunnis and Arab Shi'ites will put aside their sectarian differences and align along their shared language as Arab Iraqis, a possibility that many Kurdish Iraqis fear.

Membership in a particular identity group might differentiate someone from other people in the same country, but not necessarily. Abbas and an Iraqi Christian share a nationality, but not a religion. Abbas speaks Arabic; other Iraqis speak Kurdish at home. Abbas traces his lineage to the Kanaan clan of the Banu Tamim tribe, while most other Iraqis are from different tribes or from other clans within the Banu Tamim tribe. For some countries, there is only one group in a particular category. Arabic is the native language of almost all citizens (but perhaps not all residents) in Egypt, Jordan, Saudi Arabia, Qatar, the Palestinian territories, Yemen, and Tunisia, and it is the overwhelmingly dominant and official language in several other states. Similarly, the government of Saudi Arabia presumes that all of its citizens are Muslims. The identity category of religion encompasses all Saudi citizens, but other categories could divide them. The category of sect would divide Saudis into Wahhabis, non-Wahhabi Sunnis, and Shi'ites. The category of regional identity might differentiate Saudis from the Hijaz, Najd, 'Asir, and the coast of the Persian Gulf. Citizenship, of course, divides Saudi citizens from the approximately 20 percent of the Saudi population who are noncitizens.

The Multiple Identities of the Middle East

The people of the Middle East differ in a number of ways that do matter, have mattered, or in the future could matter for politics. We turn here to exploring the cultural diversity of the Middle East in the framework of identity categories and groups, focusing on identity groups larger than family for which some sense of political community *could* exist. Each group might have associated cultural practices, such as cuisines, personal or family names, idioms, or art forms. Although not described here, these cultural practices often form the boundaries of group membership and help individuals identify who is and who is not a member of the group.

Ascriptive identity categories in the Middle East fall under four broad headings: religion and sect, language, lineage (tribe, clan), and geographic homeland (city, region, country). It is easier for individuals to move between groups in some categories than it is in others. Categories based on shared descent or ancestors' residence are probably the most difficult to change, although tribes do occasionally "re"discover lost lineages. An individual can change his language or religion; this can be difficult, but it occurs. Also, minority religious and linguistic groups in the Middle East are often concentrated in mountainous areas, such as Lebanon. This is unsurprising. Homogenizing pressures are less likely to affect communities in difficult-to-access mountains and isolated areas.

All population numbers presented here are estimates. Governments often manipulate demographic data for political reasons, especially when the size of identity groups is sensitive. Lebanon, for example, has not conducted an official census since 1932 because a new one would undoubtedly reveal that the Shi'ite Muslim proportion of the Lebanese population has increased relative to the Sunni Muslim and Christian proportions. Since the Lebanese political system allocates government jobs according to sect, acknowledging demographic changes would upset the existing agreed-upon balance. Similarly, the Jordanian government does not release data on the size of the Palestinian-Jordanian or Transjordanian populations. King Faisal of Saudi Arabia purportedly doubled the estimate of his kingdom's population after seeing the results from the country's first census, in 1969 (Wright 2006: 176); demographic data on Saudi Arabia have been inflated ever since.

Religion and sect. The Middle East is much smaller than the Muslim-majority world. Although approximately 92 percent of the residents of the Middle East are Muslims, 70 percent of the world's Muslims live outside the region. Indonesia, India, Pakistan, and Bangladesh have the four largest Muslim populations in the world; none is in the Middle East. Yet Islam remains closely associated with the Middle East because Islam's most sacred sites are in the region and Arabic is the sacred language of the Quran. All countries in the Middle East except Israel have Muslim majorities. Shi'ite Muslims are a majority in Bahrain, Iraq, and Iran. They are a plurality in Lebanon and a sizable minority in Yemen, Kuwait, Syria, and the United Arab Emirates (UAE). With the possible exception of Oman, Sunni Muslims predominate in the other Muslim-majority states of the Middle East. Few Shi'ite Muslims live in North Africa.

Christians constitute a significant minority in Lebanon and smaller communities in several other states. Although the percentage of indigenous Christians in the region has declined in recent decades as a result of emigration and relatively low fertility rates, many Christians have come to the region in recent decades as foreign workers, as noted in Chapter 6. Jews were a significant minority in several Arab countries before the founding of the State of Israel. For example, Jews constituted 35 percent of Baghdad's population at the turn of the twentieth century (Batatu 1978: 248). From 1948 until 1972, perhaps 800,000 to 1 million Jews left Egypt, Iraq, Iran, Yemen, Syria, Lebanon, Turkey, and North Africa and settled in Israel. Today, sizable Jewish populations remain in Iran, Turkey, and Morocco.

Language. The Middle East is much larger than the Arab world. Almost 50 percent of the approximately 465 million residents of the Middle East speak a language other than Arabic at home, such as Turkish, Farsi, Kurdish, Azeri, Hebrew, or Berber (see Table 7.1).

Arabic is an official or national language of every country in the Middle East except Turkey and Iran; Arabic shares its official status with Hebrew in Israel, English in Sudan, English and French in Lebanon, and Kurdish in Iraq. Modern standard or "formal" Arabic is a modernized version of the "classical" Arabic of the Quran; it is used for formal speeches, for official documents, and in most written books, magazines, and newspapers throughout the Arab world. News broadcasts are in modern standard Arabic, which is why both Moroccans and Iraqis can understand pan-Arab satellite news channels such as Al-Jazeera and Al-Arabiyya. Yet this masks tremendous linguistic variation among the 206 million first-language speakers of Arabic. Most educated Arabs can understand and many can speak

Table 7.1 Languages and Religions of the Middle East

Country	Population	Languages	Religions
Algeria	37,367,226	Arabic (majority) 14% Berber languages Kabyle (2.5 million) Tachawit (1.4 million)	99% Sunni Muslim 1% Christian and Jewish
Bahrain	1,248,348 (includes 235,108 nonnationals)	Arabic (majority) Perhaps 50,000 Farsi speakers (not including nonnationals)	70% Shi'ite Muslim 29% Sunni Muslim 1% Other (not including nonnationals, many of whom are Christian or Hindu, perhaps 20% of the total population)
Egypt	83,688,164	Arabic	Approximately 90% Sunni Muslim <1% Shi'ite Muslim 8–12% Christian
Iran	78,868,711	50% Farsi (39.5 million) 22% Azeri and Turkmen (17 million) 10% Kurdish (8 million) 7% Mazanderani and Gilaki (5.5 million) 6% Luri (4.7 million) 2% Arabic (1.5 million) 2% Balochi (1.5 million) 1% Other	89% Shi'ite Muslim 9% Sunni Muslim (mostly Turkmen, Arabs, Baluchs, Kurds) 2% Other (mostly Bahai and Christian and small communities of Zoroastrians and Jews)
Iraq	31,129,225	Arabic (majority) 20% Kurdish 2% Azeri 1% Farsi 1% Turkmen	60–65% Shi'ite Muslim 30–35% Sunni Muslim 5% Other (mostly Christian, but also small communities of Yezidis, Sabean-Mandaeans, Bahais, etc.)
Israel	7,590,758 (includes settlers in the West Bank, Golan Heights, and East Jerusalem)	Hebrew (majority) Arabic (1.4 million) Russian (750,000) Romanian (250,000) Yiddish (215,000)	76% Jewish 16% Muslim 2% Christian 6% Other (Druze, Bahai)

(continues)

Table 7.1 Cont.

Country	Population	Languages	Religions
Jordan	6,508,887	Arabic	93% Sunni Muslim 6% Christian
Kuwait	2,646,314 (includes 1,291,354 nonnationals)	Arabic	65–70% Sunni Muslim 30–35% Shi'ite Muslim (real numbers unknown; many nonnationals are Hindu or Christian)
Lebanon	4,140,289	Arabic (majority) Armenian (234,600) Kurdish (75,000)	28–45% Shi'ite Muslim 28% Sunni Muslim 22% Maronite 8% Greek Orthodox 5% Druze 4% Greek Catholic 5% Other Christian denominations (all figures are estimates as no census has been taken since 1932)
Libya	5,613,380 (includes 166,510 nonnationals)	Arabic (majority) 3% Berber dialects	97% Sunni Muslim
Morocco	32,309,239	Arabic (majority) 23% Berber languages Tachelhit (3 million) Tamazight (3 million) Tarafit (Rifi) (1.5 million)	99% Sunni Muslim 1% Christian <1% Other (mostly Jewish)
Oman	3,090,150 (includes 577,293 nonnationals)	Arabic (majority) Balochis (130,300)	Unknown, but most Ibadhi or Sunni (estimates vary widely regarding which is a majority) <5% Shi'ite (in capital and along northern coast)
Palestine	4,332,801 (1,710,257 in the Gaza Strip, 2,622,544 in the West Bank, not including Israeli settlers in the West Bank and East Jerusalem)	Arabic	Gaza: 100% Sunni Muslim West Bank: 90% Sunni Muslim, 10% Christian

(continues)

Table 7.1 Cont.

Country	Population	Languages	Religions
Qatar	1,951,591 (includes many nonnationals)	Arabic (majority) Farsi (73,000)	95% Sunni Muslim <5% Shi'ite Muslim Many nonnationals are Christian or Hindu
Saudi Arabia	26,534,504 (includes 5,576,076 nonnationals)	Arabic	90% Sunni Muslim 10% Shi'ite Muslim
Syria	22,530,746 (not including approximately 40,000 Arabs in the Israeli-occupied Golan Heights)	Arabic (majority) Kurdish (938,000) Armenian (320,000)	74% Sunni 14% Alawite and Ismaili 3% Druze 9% Christian
Tunisia	10,732,900	Arabic	99% Sunni Muslim 1% Shi'ite Muslim
Turkey	79,749,461	Turkish (majority) Kurdish (10–20 million) Arabic (1 million) Other (several million)	99% Muslim (mostly Sunni, but an unknown number of Alevis) <1% Other (mostly Christian)
United Arab Emirates	5,314,317 (includes many nonnationals)	Arabic (majority) Pashto (126,000) Balochi (100,000) Farsi (80,000)	85% Sunni Muslim 15% Shi'ite Muslim
Yemen	24,771,809	Arabic (majority)	Unknown 45% Zaydi Muslim 55% Sunni Muslim <1 % Other (Jewish, Christian, and Hindu)

Sources: Population: Central Intelligence Agency, *World Factbook* (Washington, DC, December 2012). Languages: Principally, Raymond G. Gordon and Barbara F. Grimes, eds., *Ethnologue: Languages of the World*. 15th ed. (Dallas: SIL International, 2005). Religions: Principally, National Geographic Society, *Atlas of the Middle East*, 2nd ed. (Washington, DC, 2008); Vali Nasr, *The Shia Revival: How Conflicts Within Islam Will Shape the Future* (New York: Norton, 2006); and Vali Nasr, "When the Shi'ites Rise," *Foreign Affairs* 85 (4) (2006): 58–74.

modern standard Arabic, but it is awkward for everyday conversation. It would be equivalent to a modern English-speaker using Shakespearean English in his or her daily life. Instead, Arabs speak colloquial or "informal" Arabic vernaculars that can be unintelligible across regions in the Arab world. Linguists disagree on how to categorize Arabic dialects, but generally, the closer two Arabs live to one another, the more likely they are to understand one another. Unless they spoke modern standard Arabic, it would be very difficult for a Tunisian and a Jordanian to understand one another in Arabic. Because of the popularity of Egyptian movies, however, our Iraqi friend Abbas might understand most of what an Egyptian says, but an Egyptian would probably understand less than half of what Abbas said in his Iraqi-Arabic dialect. Cities and villages within countries often differ in pronunciations and vocabulary, which means that dialect often overlaps with another identity category—city or region of origin. Abbas's Basrawi accent would mark him as a southern Iraqi if he traveled to Baghdad.

Although Arab nationalism was a powerful political force in the 1950s and 1960s, it is not readily obvious why Arabic should have generated an imagined political community. In the early twentieth century, calling a resident of Cairo an "Arab" would probably have been interpreted as an insult. At the time, the vast majority of Egyptians did not see their political fate as linked to residents of the Levant or Arabian Peninsula, much less residents of Morocco. Yet Arab nationalism, a political ideology directed at Arabic-speakers, emerged as one of the region's most powerful political identities.

With over 46 million speakers, Turkish is the second most spoken language in the Middle East. Although Turkish is rarely spoken in the Middle East outside of the Republic of Turkey, 2 million Iranians and perhaps 200,000 Iraqis speak related Turkic languages. Turkish was written in a variant of Perso-Arabic script until 1928, when Mustafa Kemal Atatürk replaced the Arabic script with a modified Latin script and purged many Arabic and Persian terms from Turkish. Today, therefore, the vast majority of Turks cannot read Arabic or the Ottoman Turkish script of their ancestors that was used for centuries in the Ottoman Empire.

The Iranian plateau is by far the most linguistically diverse region of the Middle East. As shown in Table 7.1, more than a dozen languages are widely spoken in Iran. Persian, or Farsi, is the most common language, although more than 50 percent of Iranians speak a distinct dialect of Persian or a different first language, such as Azeri, Kurdish, Gilaki, or Domari.

Modern Hebrew is a revived form of an ancient language that had largely vanished as a spoken language but had survived as a written language due to its religious importance. Its revival and spread were a result of efforts by members of the Jewish nationalist movement in the nineteenth century. Within the Middle East, modern Hebrew is spoken in Israel and among Jewish settlers in the Occupied Territories. Although not all Israeli

Jews speak Hebrew (especially since the post-1989 influx of almost 1 million Russian or Romanian speakers from the Soviet Union and post-Soviet states), it plays an incredibly important role in uniting Jews who emigrated to Israel speaking different first languages.

Arabic and Hebrew are related Semitic languages, and there are numerous similarities across the two. The term *Semitic* refers to a language group and is not a racial designation. Therefore, it is inaccurate and meaningless to claim that "Jews and Arabs are both Semites," although it is correct to say that "Hebrew and Arabic are both Semitic languages" (Lewis 1998: 46–47).

European Jews who came (or whose ancestors came) to Israel (or to Palestine, if they arrived before 1948) initially spoke different languages than Jews who came from Arab and Muslim lands. Differences between Ashkenazi Jews from western, central, and eastern Europe, and Sephardic and Mizrachi Jews from southeastern Europe, northern Africa, and the Middle East, are now more akin to a racial divide within Israeli society than to a linguistic one. Like many racial cleavages, this one overlaps with class. Although Sephardic and Mizrachi Jews are culturally and socially heterogeneous, they tend to be less well-off than their Ashkenazi compatriots.

Although Berber is often considered a single northern African language with many dialects, it varies enough to be mutually unintelligible across most dialects. Berber dialects are spoken by millions of Moroccans and Algerians and tens of thousands of Libyans and Tunisians. Approximately 23 percent of Moroccans speak a Berber dialect, the most important of which are Tamazight (3 million speakers in central Morocco), Tachelhit (3 million speakers in the High Atlas region), and Tarafit or Rifi (1.5 million speakers in the Rif mountains). Approximately 14 percent of Algerians are considered Berber-speakers; the two largest dialects are Kabyle (2.5 million speakers in northern Algeria) and Tachawit (1.4 million speakers in southern Algeria).

For centuries, speakers of Kurdish have lived in the mountains and plateaus where the modern states of Turkey, Iraq, Iran, and Syria meet. There are two main Kurdish dialects that are grammatically distinct from one another: Kurmanji (spoken by northern Kurds) and Surani (spoken by southern Kurds), and several smaller ones, notably Gurani and Zaza. Worldwide, there are perhaps 25–30 million Kurds; in comparison, there are approximately 14 million Jews and 11 million people of Palestinian descent in the world. Although estimates vary widely, about 12 million Kurds live in Turkey (constituting about 17 percent of the population of Turkey). Another 6.6 million live in Iran and 5.6 million in Iraq, constituting 10 percent and 20 percent of those countries' respective populations. The overwhelming majority (about 75 percent) of Kurds are Sunni Muslims; the rest follow varieties of Shi'ism. Kurds have increasingly thought of themselves as a distinct ethnic community since World War I, and Kurdish national identities continue to evolve among populations both within and across

Turkey, Iraq, and Iran. The Kurdish-majority region of Iraq has been de facto autonomous from the Iraqi central government since 1991 and has been stable and prosperous since the US-led invasion in 2003.

Lineage (tribe and clan). Kinship ties are often the basis of social and political solidarity. Yet the size, structure, coherence, and modes of livelihood of tribes vary across place and over time in the Middle East. Tribes usually, but not always, share some common imagined ancestry and territoriality. In general, tribes are pyramidal and segmentary. Family units aggregate into larger clans, lineages, tribes, and tribal confederations. Yet each unit or segment of the tribal structure could be an identity group and become a distinct political community. Ties to siblings and cousins tend to be strong and robust, while ties to more distant relatives are less likely to mobilize.

Before the rise of states, kinship or "tribal" forms of organization were a principal way in which individuals defended themselves and jointly provided other public goods. Tribal ties are often seen as being at odds with an individual's obligations to the global community of Muslims or patriotic loyalties to modern states. Yet some regimes use the image of tribes and familial relationships to reinforce their rule. Hafiz al-Asad of Syria, for example, was often portrayed on billboards and in the state-controlled media as the "father" of the Syrian people and, occasionally, of the Lebanese and Palestinians. In Saudi Arabia, the Saud family portrays itself as the head of a vast confederation that encompasses all citizens of the country. Kinship-based social and political organization and symbols associated with "tribes" remain important in many Middle Eastern states.

Geographic homeland (city, region, and country). The Arabic term *watan* means homeland, country, or place where one's family historically resides. Yet the idea of "place" in the Middle East has changed over time. Before the rise of nation-states in the twentieth century, *watan* could refer to a village, town, neighborhood, or province, but not to a "country" in a modern sense (Lewis 1998: 57). Boundaries were not always strictly demarcated; many of today's state borders are a colonial legacy. Since the writ of the decentralized Ottoman Empire often did not extend far beyond major cities, some provincial towns operated as de facto city-states. Powerful families and locality-based organizations provided order and public goods, and neighborhood-level affiliations could be politically important. Urban quarters in medieval Iraqi and Iranian cities, for example, were often controlled by neighborhood gangs or, as described by Juan Cole and Moojan Momen (1986), local mafias.

The breakup of the Ottoman Empire and emergence of modern Middle East states not only redrew the regional map, but also redefined the identities available to the residents of those lands. These new states, often under colonial "tutelage," wrote laws that defined nationality and citizenship. People living within a new country's demarcated boundaries were told that they were now citizens of that state. A resident of the town of Irbid in the 1920s, for example, would eventually learn that he or she was now a citizen of the newly created Emirate of Transjordan. A trip north to Damascus or west to Haifa soon involved crossing an international border to Syria or Palestine. Furthermore, this resident was told to direct any grievances and aspirations to the new capital of Amman and the British-installed king who governed from there.

The new states of the Middle East differed in how they cultivated national identity among their citizens. This national patriotism or civil nationalism *(wataniyya)* contrasts with other conceptions of political community based on descent-based identity categories, such as pan-Arab nationalism (often called *qawmiyya*). Throughout the region, the rise of national identities was controversial. State officials often used pre-Islamic civilizations to create a distinct "modern" patriotic identity (Lewis 1998). The Egyptians, for example, used the history of the Pharaohs to cultivate an Egyptian identity, and the Iraqi state rediscovered Babylon.

Country of origin is not necessarily the same as citizenship. For example, the term *Palestinian-Jordanian* commonly refers to the 60–70 percent of Jordanian citizens who trace their origins to (extant or destroyed) towns and villages west of the Jordan River in what had been the Palestine Mandate. Transjordanians, by contrast, are Jordanian citizens who trace their origins to groups considered native to lands east of the Jordan River. Despite efforts to create a "Jordanian" identity that unites Palestinian-Jordanians and Transjordanians, country of origin arguably remains the most salient identity category in Jordan. Since at least the early 1970s, Transjordanians have dominated government jobs and the military. Furthermore, the gerrymandering of electoral districts results in severe underrepresentation of Palestinian-Jordanians in the lower house of the Jordanian parliament. Despite being a majority of the population, only 14 of the 110 deputies who served in the Jordanian parliament from 2003 to 2007 were Palestinian-Jordanians.

Explaining the Political Importance of Identities

Why do some identities, but not others, become the axes of political competition and conflict? Why do individuals "choose" one identity from their repertoire rather than another? Abbas Haydar voted for a sectarian (Shi'ite) political list instead of one based on Arab nationalism, local or provincial interests, or tribal ties. Why? There are several perspectives that may give us some leverage over these questions.

Primordialism

Perhaps some identities garner inherently deeper and more emotional attachments than others. Theories of primordialism, or "essentialism," imply that "so profound are the sentiments of peoplehood, so securely are identities and loyalties transferred between generations, that even when they appear to subside they can readily be reignited" (Esman and Rabinovich 1988: 12). Journalists often describe Middle Eastern politics in primordial terms. Thomas Friedman, for example, once partly attributed authoritarianism in the region to the "primordial, tribe-like loyalties [that] governed men's identities and political attitudes so deeply" (1990: 91). Primordialism is frequently used either to account for the continued relevance of identity categories that might appear to have become less important over time in Western industrialized societies, such as tribe, religion, and sect, or to explain contemporary antagonisms as the continuation of conflicts that occurred centuries ago or even in "biblical times."

Lisa Anderson points out that many advocates of democracy assumed that the failure of the Middle East to embrace it (until recently, anyway) could be "explained by assigning some kind of handicap or immaturity to the people themselves" (1995: 77). Such arguments often rely on uninformative tautological reasoning, such as the claim that "tribalism remains important because people have deeply held loyalties to tribes; we know people have deeply held loyalties to tribes because tribalism remains important." There is a powerful tendency to look for mysterious (and often unfalsifiable) primordial "essences" that prevent democratization rather than to investigate verifiable factors that promote or hinder this process (Sadowski 1993). Similarly, journalists often describe contemporary conflicts as a continuation of age-old rivalries between groups. References to Cain and Abel, for example, are far too common in analyses of conflict between Israel and the Palestinians.

Aside from being circular, often unfalsifiable, and overly simplistic, primordialist perspectives cannot explain change or variation. Identities *do* change over time for individuals and societies. Abbas Haydar's ancestors were nominally Sunni tribesmen in southern Iraq who settled in towns in the mid–eighteenth century and converted to Shi'ite Islam. The most salient identity for Abbas (his Shi'ism), therefore, would be deeply alien to his great-great-great-grandfather, who was not a Shi'ite and would have relied on his tribal kinsmen for most social, economic, and political needs. The area that is now known as Iraq probably did not have a Shi'ite Muslim majority until the late nineteenth or even early twentieth century. Similarly, sectarianism appears to be a fairly recent political cleavage in Lebanon (Makdisi 2000). Yet these facts do not stop scholars and journalists from describing sectarian conflicts in those countries as continuous intra-Muslim conflicts that date to the seventh century. A final shortcoming of primordialist perspectives is that they overpredict conflict: that is, they cannot explain why intergroup coexistence is much more common than intergroup conflict.

Modernization and Socioeconomic Conditions

Another set of perspectives links identity to the socioeconomic conditions in which people find themselves and portrays "traditional" and "modern" identity categories as competing for the loyalty of individuals. Modernization theory, for example, posits that traditional parochial loyalties, such as to religion and tribe, gradually lose their salience as occupational and class differences become more important. Tribalism is seen as an anachronistic remnant of a previous age; it was an effective form of social organization only until centralized state governments were able to regulate economic, social, and political relations.

Urbanization and education are often linked to the weakening of tribalism and the strengthening of nonkinship identities. Although cities have long dominated the Middle East, urbanization has increased dramatically in recent decades. Today, as Table 1.1 indicates (see Chapter 1), only Yemen and Egypt have more than 50 percent of their populations living in rural areas. In many countries, the proportion of people living in urban areas is in the range of 75 to 95 percent. Despite stereotypes, pastoral nomadism is now exceedingly rare. Educational opportunities and literacy rates have also increased dramatically. Yet despite the predictions of modernization theory, tribal and religious identities appear to have strengthened in some societies. Puzzlingly, support for Islamist movements is often strongest among the most "modern" citizens in Arab societies—young, upwardly mobile university students and professionals (Wickham 2002). Survey evidence strongly suggests that support for democracy is not necessarily lower among individuals with the strongest Islamic attachments (Tessler 2002). Similarly, tribes play prominent roles in elections in several countries, and tribal identities can coexist and even thrive in democratic settings.

A related perspective comes from fourteenth-century scholar Ibn Khaldun, one of the forefathers of social science, who developed an explanation for changes in the saliency of tribal identity in a group over time. In his work *Al-Muqaddimah* (literally, "The Introduction" or "The Preface"), Ibn Khaldun describes how nomadic individuals living in harsh desert environments are driven to develop social bonds and a group solidarity or consciousness that he calls *'asabiyah*. United by *'asabiyah,* these bedouin conquer and replace sedentary city-dwellers. Within a few generations, they acquire wealth and adopt a life of ease and luxury that corrupts and undermines their group solidarity. Soon, another nomadic group united by *'asabiyah* arises to conquer the city, and the cyclical rise and fall of dynasties continues. Ibn Khaldun's argument focuses on variation in the importance of tribalism and says little about when we would expect an identity category other than tribalism, such as religion, to become salient.

These perspectives share certain claims, most notably that some identity categories (especially lineage-based or "tribal" identities) will weaken as states come to dominate people's lives. The persistence of kinship-based forms of mobilization, however, suggests that other factors, such as state policy or institutions, also play a role.

Historical Legacies

Perhaps history can bestow a hegemonic status on a particular identity group for an individual or on an identity category for a society. Many scholars argue that the saliency and resiliency of religious, linguistic, or tribal identities are a legacy of Ottoman-era institutions and policies or of European colonial efforts to "divide and rule" the people of the Middle East.

The Ottoman Empire was a vast, multiethnic, multireligious, Islamic polity ruled by a Turkish dynastic family. The subjects of the Ottoman sultan were organized into religious communities called *millets*. Muslims, Christians, Jews, and Druze were each given a significant degree of autonomy and had their own courts to administer religious and family law (e.g., marriage, divorce, custody, inheritance). Although not equal to Muslims under the *millet* system, local non-Muslim religious leaders enjoyed considerable leeway to manage the affairs of their co-religionists. Access to different legal infrastructures under this system gave the Middle East's indigenous Christians and Jews significant economic advantages compared to Muslim subjects of the sultan, which helped them dominate new economic sectors such as banking and insurance (Kuran 2004).

Kemal Karpat (1988) and others argue that the primacy of religious identity over ethnic or linguistic group solidarity in the Middle East is a function of Ottoman state policy. In other words, residents of the region think of themselves and others, first and foremost, as Muslims, Christians, Jews, and the like, because that is how their ancestors' lives were structured in Ottoman times. However, the *millet* system varied considerably across groups and regions and changed over time; the Ottomans did not attempt to create an empire-wide *millet* structure until the nineteenth century, and the Young Turks formally abolished the *millet* system in 1909. It is unclear why we should expect the Ottoman *millet* system to continue to have such a profound influence 100 years later, after the dissolution of the Ottoman Empire, the rise of territorial states, Arab nationalism, industrialization, and the promotion of patriotic identities based on citizenship.

Other scholars look to the colonial era to account for the resiliency of particular identities and identity categories. Many boundaries of today's Middle Eastern states were drawn with little regard for tribal, religious, and linguistic groups. The Kurds, for example, are divided among Iraq, Iran, Turkey, and Syria. The Druze are divided among Lebanon, Syria, Israel, and Jordan. Several tribes and clans straddle the porous border between Syria and Iraq. Smugglers used these cross-border tribal connections to move goods into and out of Iraq during the sanctions period from 1990 to 2003, and insurgents fighting the US-led occupation of Iraq in 2003–2007 utilized these same cross-border tribal connections to move fighters, money, and arms into the country. These flows reversed themselves in 2011 as men and military equipment flowed to Syrian rebels after the civil war began in that country.

The predicted effect on identity of artificially dividing groups across borders, however, is unclear. Is a coherent Kurdish national identity more likely to develop if Kurds are united in a single "Kurdistan" or if they share the grievance of having their homeland divided and living as disadvantaged minorities in different states? Perhaps the size of the identity group relative to the overall population matters. Maybe mobilization as Kurds is more feasible for Iraqi Kurds than for Syrian Kurds, because the former constitute 20 percent of the Iraqi population while the latter constitute less than 5 percent of the Syrian population. Since Kurds constitute a small portion of the Syrian population, maybe they are more likely to assume identities that would allow them to more readily assimilate into Arab-dominated Syria compared to their more numerous kin elsewhere.

In addition to drawing borders, colonial powers sometimes pursued "divide-and-rule" policies that might have effects that resonate today. Colonial legislatures frequently reserved seats for religious minorities, a practice that continues in several contemporary legislatures. For example, seats are reserved in the Jordanian lower house of parliament for Christians and Circassians/Chechens. In the mandate period, the French established autonomous states for the Druze and Alawite religious minorities in what is today Syria; the State of Jabal Druze (previously the State of Suwayda) and the State of Alawites existed from 1921 to 1936 and from 1923 to 1936, respectively. The political instability that characterized postindependence Syrian politics and the rise of the Alawite-dominated military regime are often linked to these colonial-era policies.[1] Similarly, Arab Sunni domination in twentieth-century Iraq is often linked to Ottoman and British policies that favored Sunnis for administrative and military positions. In some cases, colonial policies "invented" tribal and linguistic identities that survived past independence; colonial administrators' understandings of tribal organization were codified and disseminated in ways that made them "official."

French administrators in Morocco and Algeria, for example, emphasized the distinctiveness of Berber identity from Arab and Muslim identities (Gellner and Micaud 1972; Eickelman 2002: 205).

These perspectives suggest that identities are "sticky" and not a result of individuals' choices; the broad axes of societal division are difficult to change once established. Colonial policies and decisions made during the process of state formation shape a society's trajectory. Either individuals do not choose their identity, or the past determines the choices available.

State Institutions

If rulers promote identities that enable them to maintain their authority, perhaps different types of regimes promote different types of identities. Alan Richards and John Waterbury (2008: 291–316) argue that the socialist republics of the Middle East deliberately fostered different identities than did the region's monarchies. In general, the socialist republics have been "purposeful states" bent on development and military might. They have emphasized unity and cohesion among citizens and often repressed religious or linguistic minority movements for autonomy or group rights, especially in the early years of state formation. Atatürk, for example, promoted Turkish nationalism and ruthlessly crushed a Kurdish rebellion in 1925. The Turkish government for decades officially referred to the Kurdish minority as "mountain Turks."

Richards and Waterbury argue that, in contrast, most monarchs in the Middle East have handled diversity and pluralism differently than the socialist republics. Monarchs rule by dividing and balancing competing interests. Richards and Waterbury write, "Monarchs speak in terms of the nation and decry the fractious elements in society that impede national unity, but they do not deny these elements legitimacy so long as they behave according to the rules of the game as the monarchy defines them. What the monarchs want is a plethora of interests, tribal, ethnic, professional, class-based, and partisan, whose competition for public patronage they can arbitrate" (2008: 312). Successful monarchs position themselves above competing identity groups in such a way that those groups fear chaos if the monarch is overthrown. The Jordanian and Saudi monarchies, for example, are often described as balancing competing tribal and bedouin loyalties.

Finally, states might delegate some government powers to the leaders of identity groups, which privileges certain identity categories over others. Religious authorities, for example, oversee personal status law (marriage, divorce, inheritance, and custody) in Israel and Lebanon. Arab nationalists and political Islamists have played prominent roles in designing or reforming educational systems. All of these perspectives suggest that state policy can influence how individuals think of themselves.

Political Entrepreneurs and Political Violence

As Abbas Haydar learned, aspiring political entrepreneurs seeking to develop a political following often try to convince people that one identity matters more than others. Maybe some individuals are craftier or more charismatic than others and therefore more likely to mobilize people around a particular identity. This line of argument implies that grievances alone are insufficient for mobilization, which also requires intellectuals and charismatic leaders who can articulate group demands and organize a vanguard of the masses. This makes sense. Grievances and unfulfilled aspirations are ubiquitous, but mobilization is not. The rise of Arab nationalism, for example, is often referred to as an "awakening" or "renaissance," which implies that mobilization along linguistic lines had long been possible for the Arab subjects of the Ottoman Empire. Arab nationalists later popularized the idea that "sleeping" Turkish and Arab nations existed under the Ottomans and that the Arabs needed a linguistic and cultural intellectual revival to spark a widespread independence movement. Pan-Arabism did not gain widespread popular support until the 1950s, when it found its champion in the charismatic Gamal Abdel Nasser.

Sunni Islamists in the early twentieth century sought to organize Muslims against colonialism by appealing to Islam instead of Arab nationalism or national histories. They presented a contrasting vision of what identity category is best to mobilize around. Yet it took the organizational innovations of Hassan al-Banna and his Society of Muslim Brothers to consistently mobilize large numbers of Muslims as Muslims.

Perhaps violence leads individuals to mobilize along particular identity categories. The creation of the State of Israel in 1948, the partition of Palestine, and the defeat of Arab armies might have contributed to the rise of a shared sense among Arabs that their fates are linked. Similarly, the decline of Arab nationalism and rise of Islamism closely followed the Israeli victory in the 1967 Six Day War. Maybe military defeats delegitimize particular identities or otherwise create opportunities for political entrepreneurs to encourage mobilization along a different identity category.

Some actors might use violence to deliberately politicize a particular identity category. The radical Sunni Islamist Abu Musab al-Zarqawi deliberately tried to foment sectarian violence in Iraq from 2003 until his death in 2006 by targeting Shi'ites in ways that he hoped would provoke Iraq's Shi'ites to retaliate against Sunnis. In February 2004, US officials in Iraq circulated a letter purportedly written by Zarqawi (Coalition Provisional Authority 2004). The letter advocates attacking Shi'ites because doing so "will provoke them [Shi'ites] to show the Sunnis their rabies . . . and bare the teeth of the hidden rancor working in their breasts. If we succeed in dragging them into the arena of sectarian war, it will become possible to awaken the inattentive Sunnis as they feel imminent danger and annihilating death at the hands of these Sabeans."[2] The plan worked; sectarian violence in Iraq escalated considerably following the February 2006 bombing of the Shi'ite 'Askariyya Shrine in Samarra.

Many observers witness intergroup animosity and "hatred" during periods of violence and assume that the hatred predates the violence and explains why it began. But intergroup hatred is often a product of violence and did not exist before the conflict began. Political violence is fairly common in twentieth-century Iraq, but that violence was not sectarian in nature until 1991, or even 2003. The hatred that exists between Sunnis and Shi'ites in Iraq today is largely a result of post-2003 violence, not its cause. Similarly, after the outbreak of the Syrian civil war in 2011, the Asad-led regime quickly became reliant on Alawite-dominated military and paramilitary forces, the latter called "ghosts" or *shabiha*. The sectarian nature of the violence in Syria has made a negotiated settlement particularly difficult to imagine. How can the Sunni-dominated rebels promise not to seek revenge on the minority Alawite community after the regime falls? The Alawites, or Nusayris, follow a syncretistic religion that combines elements of different religions but is widely considered a form of Shi'ism. They fear persecution, for good reason, if Sunni Islamists come to dominate post-Asad Syrian politics.

Clientelism and Elections

If politics is about the contest for power and the distribution of scarce resources, perhaps some identities are more useful than others because they help power-holders limit access to the spoils that successful mobilization generates (Bates 1983). Writing about sub-Saharan Africa, Daniel Posner (2005) argues that group size, not depth of attachment, drives individual-level identity choice and thus determines which identity category becomes politically important at the society level. Such a perspective suggests that individuals will choose an identity that allows them to share the spoils of power with as few others as possible. Milton Esman and Itamar Rabinovich express a similar notion when they write that "ethnic and confessional solidarities survive only as long as they pay—as long as they provide more security, status and material rewards than do available alternatives" (1988: 13). In other words, individuals choose their identity based on expectations of benefits, not emotional attachments.

Tribal or religious minorities dominate several Middle Eastern regimes. The rise to power in Syria of Hafiz al-Asad, for example, allowed Alawites to enjoy privileged access to state resources and positions in the military under his regime. However, it is inaccurate to say that Alawites as a group "seized" the Syrian state. Al-Asad consolidated his power in 1970 by

ousting the two other Alawite members of the triumvirate who had shared
power with him since their coup d'état seven years earlier, and not all
Alawites benefited from the Asad regime. Furthermore, the Syrian regime
relied on the support of the Sunni urban business class. One scholar of
Syria wrote, "The [Syrian] Ba'ath recruited from all those who were outside the system of connections, patronage or kin on which the old regime
was built: the educated sons of peasants, the minorities, the rural lower
middle class, the 'black sheep' from lesser branches of great families" (Hinnebusch 1979: 17). Nevertheless, violence during the Syrian civil war has
made the conflict a sectarian one.

Finally, several Arab states have held regular competitive parliamentary elections since the early 1990s. Until the so-called Arab Spring, none
of these elections led to a transition to democracy, and they may actually
have strengthened authoritarian regimes by regularizing competition over
scarce resources. Ellen Lust-Okar (2006) argues that voters want representatives who will channel government resources to them personally. In such
a system, tribal leaders might be more effective and credible conduits of
state largesse than other candidates because of the size of tribes and the information flows among members. Tribal or other kin-based ties might make
it easier for candidates to get out the vote and give their relatives greater
faith that they will do their best to deliver jobs and services to them instead
of others. Post–Arab Spring elections offer opportunities for politicians to
try to mobilize voters along identity categories that were previously not politically salient.

Conclusion

The history of the modern Middle East is often described as a series of se-
quential eras characterized by the prominence of particular identities. Until
the twentieth century, religious affiliation was the most important identity
category for subjects of the Ottoman sultan. The breakup of the Ottoman
Empire into separate states ushered in a new identity category (state citizenship) that competed for citizens' loyalties. Pan-Arab nationalism flourished
in the 1950s and early 1960s. After 1967, however, many scholars believe
an era of political Islamism replaced the era of pan-Arab nationalism. Some
scholars argued that the region recently had moved from an era of Islamism
to something else (Roy 1994), perhaps an era characterized by local solidarities and patronage networks or sectarian cleavages (Nasr 2006a). It is as
yet unclear which identity categories, if any, will characterize the post–
Arab Spring Middle East. The one identity that remains meaningless to the
residents of the Middle East is that of *Middle Easterner,* a term that, as explained in Chapter 1, has literal and figurative meaning from a Western perspective but not from within the region.

In this chapter, I have provided a framework for making sense of the multiple identities of the Middle East, described the most important identity categories, and offered several theoretical perspectives that might account for why some identity categories—but not others—become or remain salient. The country chapters in Part 2 of this volume further describe the identity categories and groups within the various countries of the Middle East. While reading about these countries—their histories, their institutional structures, their track records regarding economic development, and so forth—consider, for each particular case, which theoretical perspective seems to best explain the nature of identity politics.

Notes

1. The cover story of *The Atlantic* magazine in January–February 2008 described how Middle East borders might change if Iraq were partitioned. The cover of the magazine showed a map with independent states called "The Alawite Republic" and "Druzistan," which suggested that the author believed these short-lived colonial states might reemerge as independent polities sixty-five years later!

2. The author of the letter uses "Sabean" as a derogatory term for Shi'ites, implying that they are not true Muslims. Some analysts argue that the letter was most probably not written by Zarqawi (see, for example, Novikov 2004).

8

Gender and Politics

Diane Singerman

Political change in the Middle East is multidimensional. In order to understand it, we need to consider such issues as changing ideological trends, executive power, institutional development, political parties and parliaments, civil society, movements, and political economy. But we also need to look at politics from multiple standpoints. This chapter explores comparative politics in the Middle East through the lens of gender, looking at how understandings of femininity and masculinity are socially constructed and institutionalized. In this sense, the chapter privileges gender as an analytic concept. Gender refers not to a fixed biological notion of sex but rather to the "appropriate" social and cultural roles that society values as normal or desirable. In every society, many factors shape gender norms and socialize mass behavior, and these norms are the result of long historical processes influenced by the state, religion, culture, law, morality, sexuality, ideology, and economic forces as well as contemporary changes and challenges. Political scientists are particularly interested in the ways in which the state, hierarchies of power, and institutions sustain and reinforce asymmetrical gender relations. An appreciation and understanding of the complex interplay among gender, politics, and the state in the Middle East will complement other perspectives on politics in this volume.

Throughout the globe and within many academic disciplines, there are raging debates about whether patriarchy, or the institutionalized domination and subordination of women, is universal or not. Many activists and scholars in the relatively young discipline of women and gender studies have asked whether women across the globe, and throughout the historical past, are subordinated in similar ways and share a similar narrative of political, economic, and literary disenfranchisement—or whether patriarchy, gender

inequalities, and discrimination against women can only be understood con-
textually, in a very particular or local fashion. The good news about patriarchy is that because it had a historical beginning in laws that institutionalized the legal, economic, and sexual subordination of women, it can also
have an end (see Lerner 1986). Men and women have waged many political
struggles to end patriarchy by transforming the institutions, norms, and
laws that have sustained it. While gender is not a synonym for women, it
has typically been the contradictions and discrimination that women face in
their daily lives that become so onerous at a certain point that they rebel to
chip away at patriarchy (Carver 1998).

At the same time, it is important to note that in the Middle East there is
a significant constituency that rejects feminist arguments about patriarchy
and the universal or institutionalized subordination of women. This constituency would argue that the ideological genealogy of formal legal gender
equality, with its roots in Western experience, the nation-state, and secularism, "taints" or compromises feminism's authenticity and relevance for
Middle Eastern societies. Another somewhat similar position is that feminism is a Western, secular philosophy and as such is incompatible with
Islam and the canon of Islamic law that regulates Muslim life.

A common religiously inflected argument in the region suggests that
men and women are not equal but instead are "complementary," each with
particular natures rooted in their biological differences, as explained in Islamic texts and institutionalized in Islamic jurisprudence. This position suggests a woman's primary duty is as a wife, mother, and caregiver and that
the interests of her family and community are paramount to her individual
needs, goals, and desires. The financial implication of this "patriarchal gender contract" is that men are the breadwinners and responsible for financially maintaining their wives, children, and elderly parents (Moghadam
2003: 41). This view shares a functionalist rationale that links women to
their reproductive roles and suggests that these "natural" attributes should
define women's lives. The biological determinism implicit in this position
is not limited to the Muslim world, but is found in other religions, including
Christian and Jewish perspectives on gender, as well as in gender ideologies that move beyond religion to identify women with their reproductive
and maternal roles.

Norms of masculinity and the appropriate role for men in society are
also deeply rooted gendered conventions and are institutionalized in various
ways in the Middle East. For example, while many Muslim women wear
modest garments to veil or "cover" themselves (as they are legally compelled to in Saudi Arabia and Iran), men typically wear what is considered
national clothing. In Saudi Arabia, Qatar, the United Arab Emirates (UAE),
and Kuwait, this is a version of a long white *thaub* or *dishdasha* (ankle-
length tunic), a *ghutra* (head scarf), and an *aqal* (head rope). While men are

not legally compelled to wear indigenous clothing, strong social norms and expectations result in a very conformist pattern, and national dress is de rigueur in official spaces. In urban Egypt, men wear Saudi-like *thaubs* to denote education, cosmopolitanism, wealth, and piety. Like female clothing, "authentic" and indigenous male clothing can also convey rural or lower-class origins to distinguish the wearer from those who clothe themselves in more expensive Western styles (see Fandy 2005).

Men are also defined and entangled by common expectations of their power vis-à-vis female relatives and the family. The concept of "honor" and the way in which a woman's honor is tied to the reputation of her male relatives in her household and the extended family remain extremely important in the region and are, more symbolically, linked to the honor of the ruling family, if not the honor of the entire nation. The manners and comportment of women (and their romantic interests) reflect on the entire family, and men are expected to "police" female honor and family honor. In Islam, sexuality is housed in marriage; premarital sexual relations are discouraged and legally proscribed. A constant debate about morality and propriety, particularly concerning the sexual and moral behavior of women, characterizes everyday life and provides fodder for sensationalized public debates about female honor, hedonistic and immoral young people, and the negative and undifferentiated influence of "the West" on morality in the region (see Singerman 1995, 2006). While much of the research on domestic violence and "honor killings" of women is rightly concerned with the women who experience violence, abuse, and exile from their families—women typically suffer far more than men if they are perceived to transgress social norms—gendered norms and expectations also influence male behavior in these confrontations. Women's movements in the region have attempted to detach socially constructed norms about "honor" from an exclusive association with sexuality and the bodies of women.

There have been countless struggles in the Middle East, involving women as well as men, to strengthen gender equality and to contest the gender ideologies that legitimize inequalities; some of these activists have succeeded, and some have failed. At the same time, larger structural changes, state policy and state capacity, technological innovations, historical circumstances, nationalism, war, revolution, and demographic trends have also deeply affected women and gender in the region, beyond intentional attempts to change or transform particular obstacles to gender equality and fairness. To name just a few examples, state-led industrialization and the building of a large public sector have offered "safe" or "legitimate" employment opportunities to women, and related processes of urbanization, revolution, education, globalization, war, and the availability of birth control have also had profound intended and unintended consequences on women in the Middle East.[1]

Measuring Gender

Many attempts have been made to measure gender equality, often as part of global efforts to improve the status and well-being of women. Standardized benchmarks are deployed to define gender equality before nations are compared universally. A prominent example of a universal approach to analyzing the inequality between men and women is the 2006 *Global Gender Gap Report,* which ranked 115 countries using economic, educational, health, and political criteria. Overall, the Middle East region ranked lowest (and Nordic countries highest), with women having just over half the resources and opportunities available to men (Hausmann, Tyson, and Zahidi 2006: 12). More specifically, the Middle East region (comprising, in the 2006 analysis, Egypt, Israel, Jordan, Kuwait, Israel, Tunisia, the UAE, Yemen, Saudi Arabia, and Bahrain) ranked last in terms of economic participation and opportunity for women as well as in terms of political empowerment, and second to last in terms of educational attainment. The Middle East region had improved most significantly in terms of health and survival, ranking third from the bottom. Kuwait (85th out of 115) was the highest-ranking Arab country, while Saudi Arabia (114) and Yemen (115) were the lowest-ranking; Israel ranked 35th.

Universal comparisons of "gaps" in gender equality point to some of the successes Middle Eastern countries have had in improving the education and health of women. They also highlight that women in the region have had only minimal success in gaining political office, still have very low labor-force participation rates (although this has been improving in some countries), and suffer from high unemployment. Yet such universal measures and comparisons of gender inequality do not tell us *why* gender gaps remain or what they mean within a local context. Furthermore, universalizing analyses that unite different societies by their similarities fail to acknowledge and account for their differences. In other words, universal measures are descriptive but offer few analytic insights or explanation.

They also have the effect, perhaps unintended, of making the "referent" for an observation the most "liberated" countries, in this case those in Western Europe and North America. The "rest" or the "worst" are then expected to "progress" toward the achievements of the referent countries. Abdellah Labdaoui argues that universalist norms "impos[e] criteria of classification regardless of local will and interests. It is a grammar which crosses national frontiers and which is scornful of national, cultural, or political considerations" (2003: 148). Because many non-Western parts of the world have experienced centuries of colonial domination, universal comparisons concerning women's status obscure important historical circumstances that partially explain why resistance to the idea of formal legal equality for women—as well as many other remaining obstacles to gender equality—still exist.

Women, Colonialism, and Islam

The degradation of women in the East is a canker that begins its destructive work early in childhood, and has eaten into the whole system of Islam.
—Stanley Lane-Poole, 1908 (quoted in Earl of Cromer 1908: 134)

America's message to other women in the Middle East is this: You have a great deal to contribute, you should have a strong voice in leading your countries, and my nation looks to the day when you have the rights and privileges you deserve.
—US president George W. Bush, 2008

In the nineteenth century, the intellectual and political roots of feminism and activism for equal rights for women were appropriated by Western colonialists and Orientalists, whose public discourse as "reformers" suggested that Westerners needed to "rescue" Middle Eastern women because of their supposed subordination and degradation by Islam and "Oriental Despotism" (Ahmed 1992: 152). Whether in the rhetoric of George W. Bush in 2008 or in that of Stanley Lane-Poole (a famous Orientalist) a century earlier in 1908, historians point out that Europeans and more recently Americans have utilized the "question of women" to legitimize foreign intervention, occupation, and influence in the region while promoting their "civilizing mission" through the rhetoric of progress, development, modernization, economic growth, and neoliberalism (Ahmed 1992; Abu-Lughod 2002). After all, the material and political motives of foreign powers for acquiring land, oil, resources, and influence are not nearly as laudable as the "noble" desire to rescue a supposedly oppressed part of the population.

Yet many of these same colonial officials never supported the liberation of women or women's rights in their own societies. When Lord Cromer, a British colonial official, returned from his diplomatic post as consul-general in the Anglo-Egyptian Condominium, he became a founding member and officer of the Men's League for Opposing Women's Suffrage in England. And his policies as consul-general actually restricted the educational and professional opportunities of women (Ahmed 1992: 153). It thus was ironic that colonial feminism needed "white men [to] sav[e] brown women from brown men" (Spivak 1988: 297). George W. Bush certainly was not a feminist icon during his presidency (2000–2008), yet he partially justified the US intervention in Afghanistan after September 11, 2001, in terms of liberating Afghan women from the yoke of the repressive Taliban.

If colonialists raised the "question of women" and spoke about the need to educate women, to employ them, to "unveil" them, and to break barriers of gender segregation in public spaces, these ideas and policies were perceived locally by many people as inauthentic, externally driven, and politically suspect. The actions of French generals to publicly unveil women in colonial Algiers offended many Algerians, not only because these actions represented a critique of a religious custom, but also because the French had decided that the veil was the cause and symbol of women's oppression. Yet the French, and other colonial powers, were hypocritical in their supposed concern for women's well-being. They spent little on public education for women, while the colonial occupation caused violence, economic crisis, and instability—disproportionally hurting women economically and socially (Lazreg 1994).

Colonial history in the Middle East has thus complicated the struggle for gender equality in important ways. Beginning in the late nineteenth century, Western elites "captured the language of feminism and redirected it, in the service of colonialism," and it was "in the combining of the languages of colonialism and feminism that the fusion between the issues of women and culture was created" (Ahmed 1992: 151). At the same time that Westerners used feminism to defend colonialism, indigenous leaders, intellectuals, and the ulama (clerics) viewed external attacks on veiling, gender segregation, and other indigenous cultural practices as attacks on Islam. As a result, women, morality, and culture were a means by which resistance to colonial domination could be waged. As Parvin Paidar explains, "The family and women [became] the subject of a power struggle in the battle between the Western intervening powers and indigenous resisting forces. In this setting, women have become the bastions of Muslim identity and preservers of cultural authenticity" (1995: 23). The burden of "bearing" national identity and being the symbol of cultural and religious authenticity often meant that as women tried to change these norms, they were seen as attacking or altering their culture and religion, particularly Islam.

One result of this has been that those seeking to change gender norms and grant women increased equality and opportunity have found it necessary or strategic to assert that oppressive practices in the Middle East are not rooted in Islam (Kandiyoti 1991). That way, they cannot be accused of assaulting the faith itself. For example, the early Muslim reformer Mohammad Abduh (1849–1905) called for the elevation of women's status and legal reforms in divorce laws and polygamy. As he did so, he argued that Islam was not responsible for the oppression of women—indeed it recognized the "full and equal humanity of women" in its "ethical voice." Abduh also argued that Islam had given women important legal protections such as the right to own property (Ahmed 1992: 139–140), but that the "practice" of Islam—reigning interpretations, customary practices, and local cultures—had prevented women from claiming the rights they had within Islam. Throughout this reformist discourse, which continues today, many scholars and activists blamed local cultural or customary practices, not the canon, laws, and message of Islam, for discrimination against women (see Sonbol

2003). Abduh, and many of his contemporaries, argued that reforming Islam from within and "restoring" the rights for women that Islam provided, rather than imitating Western ways and ideologies such as secularism or feminism, would strengthen Egyptian and Muslim societies.

Not all activists have taken this approach, however. The early women's movement in Egypt fought for women's rights not from within a religious framework but rather from within a secular and liberal framework concerning women's rights, equality, modernization, and development. When Huda Sha'rawi (1879–1947), a wealthy Egyptian woman and wife of a prominent political figure, founded the Egyptian Feminist Union in 1923, its main agenda was to fight for suffrage and other legal rights. Britain had granted nominal independence to Egypt in 1923, but the nationalist party, the Wafd, did not give women the right to vote when it came to power. Soon, the Egyptian feminist movement's public and substantive identity was enmeshed in symbolic struggles over Muslim identity as Sha'rawi publicly "de-veiled" at a train station upon her return from an international feminist conference in Rome. She and her colleagues built a cohesive women's movement that fought alongside other Egyptian nationalists to end British control of Egypt, but they primarily fought for women's rights, encouraging the growth of female leadership of and participation in charitable and literary societies, the media, political movements, political parties, and nongovernmental organizations (NGOs).

Indeed, ending gender segregation, educating women, enhancing opportunities for employment, and legislating more equitable marriage and divorce laws were objectives taken up by nascent feminist movements throughout the Middle East, from Morocco to Lebanon, from Turkey to Iran. As they did so, they would be forced to contend with Islamic religious authorities who took a conservative stance on these issues and who were reluctant to yield their power over such domains. While public schools were growing in popularity, until the advent of colonialism, schooling had been organized by religious authorities, while Islamic law had governed the intimate spheres of morality, sexuality, marriage, inheritance, child care, and family (or personal status). Thus, to change personal status law meant engaging, if not confronting, religious authorities, jurists, legal scholars, and court officials. Even though most legal systems in the Middle East had already adopted European civil, commercial, and criminal codes, personal status law remained much closer to Islamic law. Given that religious officials had already lost so much power to colonial authorities and to their own modernizing elites in the nineteenth and twentieth centuries as education was secularized and regulated by the state, they jealously guarded their severely reduced legal sphere of influence (see Paidar 1995).

We can see this dynamic playing out in dramatic fashion in early twentieth-century Iran. As far back as the Safavid Empire (1502 to 1722), religious leaders had established a monopoly over the domain of lawmaking, "while the political power of the state was there to *enforce* their laws" (Hoodfar and Sadr 2009: 5, emphasis added). As Iranians resisted Russian influence and new British taxes on tobacco in 1887, a constitutionalist movement emerged that demanded popular participation rights from the Qajar dynasty (1794–1925). European influence also sparked campaigns for modern education, secularism, and citizenship rights; yet the ulama were vehemently opposed to these ideas, since they threatened their sphere of influence and their control of education and law. Women joined protests against the state and its foreign indebtedness, started to publish in literary journals and the media, and supported public education for women. This movement succeeded in limiting the power of the Qajar monarch by establishing a constitutional monarchy and an elected parliament in 1905.

The "question of women," however, reached a critical juncture in Iran when religious leaders blocked the extension of women's rights, even though there had been much public debate about women, fueled in part by the unusual participation of women in public demonstrations. "They, along with children, criminals and the mentally unfit, were deprived of the right to elect and be elected since women's participation in politics was supposedly against Islam" (Hoodfar and Sadr 2009: 8). Despite their supposed commitment to secularism, "in the end [the reformers of the 1905 constitutional movement] agreed to the insertion of a clause in the constitution that demanded that no laws be passed by parliament that would contradict Islam and that there should be a committee of five *mojtaheds* (high ranking *'ulema* who have the right to issue religious decisions) who would over-see the laws" (Hoodfar and Sadr 2009: 8). As in many other countries, and during many other nationalist, anti-imperialist, and anticolonial struggles, in Iran the constitution now had a religious character and "significant compromises . . . were made in order to save the coalition of modernists and *'ulema* against the Monarchy . . . *at the cost of women*" (Hoodfar and Sadr 2009: 8, original emphasis). In the end, the ulama still had a legitimate role to play as lawmakers, and their strongest authority lay in the realm of personal status law.

Public and Private

Political struggles across the globe are often contests over the boundaries between what is public and what is private. As Seyla Benhabib has argued, "All struggles against oppression in the modern world begin by redefining what had previously been considered private, non-public, and non-political issues as matters of public concern, as issues of justice, as sites of power" (1992: 84). One example of this phenomenon unfolded in the region after Mustafa Kemal Atatürk successfully led the Turkish "War of Liberation" against European attempts to carve up the Ottoman Empire into its own spheres of influence in 1920. He was intent not only on building Turkish nationalism and the Turkish republic but also on dismantling the power structure and influence of the Ottoman elite and its institutions, including the ulama. Thus he embarked on a path of radical secularization, or laicism, which subordinated religion to the state and dispatched Islam from the public sphere into the realm of private observance. Turkish women were not allowed to appear in public institutions veiled, personal status law was rejected in favor of civil marriage and new divorce laws (giving women the right to initiate divorce), polygamy was forbidden, suffrage was extended to women, and the power of the Muslim order was diminished further as the caliphate was abolished. Islamic brotherhoods and Quranic schools were dissolved, the Arabic alphabet used for the Ottoman Turkish script was replaced by the Latin alphabet, men could no longer wear the Turkish fez but instead had to wear a European hat, and even Turkish and indigenous music was banned on the radio for many years as classical and European music replaced it.

In barring women from veiling in public institutions (along with banning fezzes for men), Atatürk was redefining what had been private, nonpolitical practices as unacceptable or unjust according to the tenets of his own new radical political ideology. Yet today a new generation of Turkish women, hailing largely from provincial, rural areas or who are recent migrants to the cities, are "covering" and wearing head scarves *(tesettür),* often accompanied by a long coat *(manteau)* (Saktanber 2002; Gole 1996). "Head-scarved" women have supported the conservative Justice and Development Party (AKP), which has Islamist roots and which rose to power in Turkey aided by legions of covered women working on its behalf (White 2002; Arat 2005). Currently, "covered" women in Turkey are trying to lift the restrictions that bar them from public institutions such as parliament, the courts, universities, and state offices, but these initiatives are extremely controversial, as secularists (called Kemalists in Turkey) and the secular women's movement, which is also quite strong in Turkey, object strenuously. Ironically, women in Turkey who cover their heads as a symbol of their religious piety and identity are using a Western liberal "rights" discourse to demand freedom of religion and the right to dress as they wish, as they seek to redraw Turkish laicism—and they have taken their fight to the European Court of Justice.

The "question of women" has now become an issue of human rights within discussions of Turkey's potential membership in the European Union (EU). And the fight over women's bodies continues to suggest that "women are the touchstones of this Islamic order in that they become, in their bodies and sexuality, a *trait d'union* between identity and community. This implies that the integrity of the Islamic community will be measured and reassured by women's politically regulated and confined modesty and identity (such as compulsory veiling, restricted public visibility, and the restrained encounter between the sexes)" (Gole 1996: 18). When analyzing these tensions in Turkey, it is essential to keep in mind that they are a product of their own history as well as the ways in which "unveiling" was explicitly constructed as the quintessential symbol of modernity and Westernization and was unapologetically embraced by Atatürk and his supporters. As Nilufer Gole suggests, "No other symbol than the veil reconstructs with such force the 'otherness' of Islam to the West. Women's bodies and sexuality reappear as a political site of difference and resistance to the homogenizing and egalitarian forces of Western modernity" (1996: 1).

Gender, Political Islam, "Counter-Publics," and Public Space

As in Turkey, Islamist parties and organizations in many countries of the Middle East are using a combination of rights discourse (freedom of speech, freedom of association and assembly, suffrage rights, and legal protections) and Islamist religious discourse to fuel social and political movements that critique secular, nationalist, and monarchical regimes. As many secular rulers, such as Saddam Hussein in Iraq, Muammar Qaddafi in Libya, and Husni Mubarak in Egypt, wrapped their regimes defensively in Islam to counter religiously inspired radicals who were taking up arms against them, "rightful resistance" among moderate Islamist activists became even more popularly legitimate, with more *muhaggabaat* (or veiled women, in Egyptian colloquial Arabic) everywhere in evidence (O'Brien 1996). These efforts to resist authoritarian regimes contributed in 2011 to the Arab Spring, which swept men and women across ideological camps into the streets to demand freedom, social justice, and dignity, with varying degrees of success. Women were leaders of and innovators in these movements, as well as participants and supporters—risking their lives at times to build a new political order and minimize political violence (see more on this later in this chapter). Indeed one of the leaders of the Yemeni opposition movement, a journalist who had been long active in the Islah party, Tawakkul Karman, was the youngest person ever to receive the Nobel Peace Prize in 2011 (along with Ellen Johnson Sirleaf, the president of Liberia, and Leymah Gbowee, a peace activist in Liberia).

     Islamist activism is certainly not new—its roots lie in the creation of the Muslim Brotherhood in Egypt in 1928, a movement dedicated to anticolonialism, anti-Zionism, and religious renewal. Islamist politics is discussed more extensively in Chapter 6, but it is important to recognize the vital importance of gender and women to these regional and transnational movements (transnational because many of them cross borders and are active among diaspora communities and global networks). A movement of "re-veiling" began in the Middle East after Israel's defeat of the Arab armies in the 1967 Six Day War. The defeat and humiliation not only of Egyptian president Gamal Abdel Nasser, but also of his vision of (secular) pan-Arab nationalism, provided the catalyst for a reexamination of politics and a new commitment on the part of many Egyptians to Islam and an Islamic state. Egypt has often been a "trendsetter" across the region, and the "re-veiling" movement spread to many other countries.

When President Anwar Sadat succeeded Nasser after his death in 1970, he quickly freed jailed Muslim Brothers who had been ruthlessly repressed by Nasser (the Islamists provided a useful counterweight to still-powerful Nasserist and leftist elements in Egypt). The Muslim Brothers made new inroads recruiting young university students, and new, more radical groups such as Al-Gama'a al-Islamiyya (the Islamic Group) and Repentance and Holy Flight soon won student elections and mobilized more followers throughout the population. Egyptian women had a strong presence in higher education, and one of the most potent and visible signs of growing piety and Islamic activism in Egypt was when young women decided to veil, typically wearing a scarf and loose top that covered their chest and waist (called the *khimar*)—although the most religious women would wear a niqab, or face veil, as well, which had not been seen in Egypt for many decades and was more associated with Gulf countries such as Saudi Arabia.

In general, these women self-consciously and intentionally adopted *zayy al-Islami,* or Islamic dress, as a symbol of their piety, but it also was clearly a marker of political support of, or at least sympathy with, the post-1967 Islamist movement of the 1970s and early 1980s (after that, *zayy al-Islami* became ubiquitous and thus a somewhat pedestrian fashion norm, increasingly adopted with less self-conscious ideological intent). This phenomenon spread to many other nations, since the Muslim Brothers and their derivatives were already a transnational movement, and slightly new adaptations of "traditional, modest" female dress could be seen in Iran, Turkey, Jordan, Syria, Lebanon, Morocco, Algeria, Sudan, Palestine, and elsewhere. It is critical to remember that this new type of dress was not the modest dress that uneducated, provincial, rural, or lower- or middle-class urban women typically wore in Egypt and elsewhere. In Egypt, many women from the lower and rural classes wore a *milayya liff* (a large piece of black fabric) over their clothes when they would go out, and they would often cover their head with a scarf. In contrast, the new style of the *muhaggabaat* (veiled women) symbolized a more middle-class, educated sensibility and, at least initially, sympathy for newly resurgent Islamists.

While veiling in the Middle East continues to signify "otherness" or "oppression" in the minds of Westerners, in the Middle East it expresses a political and religious identity and signals to others that a woman is modest, pious, and honorable. Furthermore, veiling was (and still is) a public, obvious symbol, a bellwether or clear evidence of a movement associated, at least for several decades in many countries, with opposition to secular, nationalist, and monarchical regimes. Islamist groups needed this public display of empathy and sympathy with their movement because, due to authoritarian and repressive policies pervading the region, it was so difficult (until very recently) to organize, form political parties, hold meetings, raise money, mobilize support, and institutionalize their movements in the region. Despite the dreams of leftist, Islamist, democratic, or liberal women (and men), they cannot wake up outside of their historicity—they are embedded within their particular social, political, and economic order. For decades political freedoms were extremely limited in the region, while regime practices of political exclusion, indiscriminate repression, co-optation, and patronage rendered civil society fractured, personalistic, and weak. Yet while the political deck was, in this respect, stacked against Islamists in many Middle Eastern countries, the ubiquitous symbol of vast numbers of "covered" or veiled women conveyed to governments that Islamist movements, such as the Muslim Brothers, Hamas in Palestine, the Justice and Charity Party in Morocco, Hezbollah in Lebanon, and the Islamist Action Front in Jordan, were still popular.

Some of these movements have come to power electorally following the Arab Spring, including Al-Nahda in Tunisia and the Muslim Brothers and various Salafi parties in Egypt; others have grown in strength. They may be able to implement their ideas about gender relations, morality, and sexuality through legislation, education policy, administrative law, the media, and other vehicles of public and private influence. At the same time, women's movements and secular and leftist parties fear the gendered conservative voices of the Islamist movements and parties, and they are strategizing and organizing to defend the limited reforms that they have won over the past few decades and strengthen women's rights and gender equality in the region.

Education, Work, and Gender

In the last quarter of the twentieth century, women's studies in the Middle East exploded, producing a profusion of scholarship, reports, and surveys on the "question of women." Scholar-activists and intellectuals searched historical archives and reinterpreted legal and religious texts to analyze the position of women from their standpoint and their experiences. Reexamining and challenging long-held male-centric histories, reinterpreting sacred texts and religious law, and reimagining political possibilities infused intellectual debates about gender and the history of women in literary salons, universities, literature, and public discourse—at the same time fueling political activism in civil society, social movements, legal activism, and other venues. This chapter draws from some of this pioneering scholarship.

One of the most common strategies to improve the position of women, across the globe, has been via education, and in the Middle East this has been extremely important. Uneducated women are often at a disadvantage, whether they are working inside the home, trying to rear and educate their children, or seeking salaried employment outside the home in family enterprises, agriculture, the civil service and public sector, or the private sector. Progress in increasing basic literacy and girls' education at all levels has been impressive in the Middle East and North Africa (MENA) region in the past few decades (see Figures 8.1 and 8.2), largely because the gender differential between men and women had been so great and because postcolonial governments (and international institutions) have invested heavily in girls' education—as well as public education more generally. Today, education is simply a requirement for many jobs, and regional trends in girls' education and female literacy have been very positive. According to a recent report, "the ratio of girls to boys in primary and secondary education was 88 percent in 2000, 92 percent in 2004, and almost equal to the world average in 2006" (Livani 2007: 10). At the same time, large variations within the region remain across countries, due to different starting baselines, as well as within countries. In rural areas of Morocco, for example, female illiteracy remained very high at the turn of the millennium (87 percent) and primary and particularly secondary enrollment rates for girls at this time were very low (10 percent) (Combe 2001 as quoted by Maddy-Weitzman 2005: 398).

Figure 8.1 Average Years of Schooling for Women in Middle Eastern Countries, 1960–2010

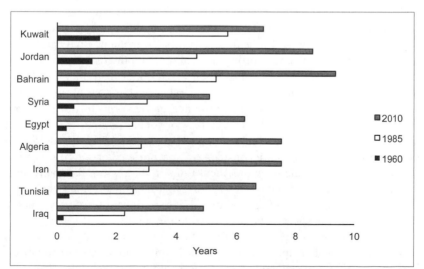

Source: The World Bank, "Education Statistics," 2012, http://data.worldbank.org/data-catalog/ed-stats.

Figure 8.2 Gains in Female Literacy in the Middle East and North Africa, 1980–2010

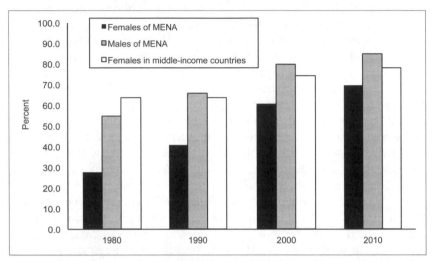

Source: The World Bank, "Education Statistics," 2012, http://data.worldbank.org/data
-catalog/ed-stats.

The greatest success in education for women has been in tertiary or higher education, where women now outnumber enrolled men in most Middle East countries. Indeed, in 2004, female enrollments in higher education in Gulf countries such as Qatar, Kuwait, Bahrain, Oman, and Saudi Arabia dwarfed male enrollments by over three times in some cases. But while these are significant achievements, there are important ways in which they reflect constraints on women's opportunities as much as they reflect a commitment to equality of educational opportunity for women. High enrollment rates for women in the Gulf, for instance, stem from the fact that protective families are far more likely to allow their sons, rather than their daughters, to attend prestigious universities abroad, because they fear allowing their daughters to live alone and also the influence of the norms of European and US society (Livani 2007: 11). The disproportionate number of women in higher education is also due to very low female labor-force participation rates, the lack of jobs that are considered "appropriate" or safe for women, and skyrocketing female unemployment rates in the region. For many, university and graduate education has become a goal in itself, not necessarily a means to an employment-related end. Higher education offers women a socially acceptable space to venture outside the home.

Gains in female education in other global regions have been associated with gains in female employment more so than in Middle Eastern countries. In a sense, public investment in education may not be paying off in economic terms, as women are not as engaged as men in the economy and thus are also not earning wages and salaries. As neoliberal reforms in the 1980s and 1990s in many Middle East countries cut public sector employment, female unemployment and withdrawal from the labor force greatly increased. According to one recent analysis, "women's participation in the labor force can significantly improve the level of household income (by 25 percent) and bring many families out of poverty" (Livani 2007: 6). Yet if women predominate in low-wage labor and if child care is expensive, the economic benefits of working outside the home are less appealing and it is thus understandable why many conservative men as well as women themselves support a "complementary" vision of female gender roles as "caregivers" and mothers. When economic recession and high male unemployment hit the region, conservative gender ideologues redoubled their message that women should "stay at home" for their children and families, so that men can fill the scant jobs and support their families.

In 2004 in Egypt, the female unemployment rate was almost four times the male unemployment rate; in Syria and Qatar it was almost three times as high; and in Saudi Arabia, Jordan, and Kuwait it was almost double (UNDP 2005). Highly educated and unemployed young women invested some of their free time in political activism in 2011 as they joined others in protesting against reigning regimes. For example, Asma Mahfouz in Egypt and Lila Ben Mhenni in Tunisia utilized social media courageously and innovatively to mobilize others and transform their governments.

In Iran, on the other hand, the success and predominance of women at universities led the government of President Mahmoud Ahmadinejad to quietly limit women's access to the most prestigious engineering fields and set a quota of 40 percent for male university engineering students. These new policies were enacted out of fear that women's access to "traditionally" male fields of medicine, science, and engineering would distort "the 'gender equilibrium' in the labor market and at home" and produce "less stable families" (Hoodfar and Sadr 2009: 24–25).

The Iranian case also brings up a different kind of education that women have been pursuing lately: formal religious education and classical religious legal training in order to become ulama, religious teachers and educators, or *shaikhas* (female religious leaders). Under the Islamic Republic, the state has tried to counter secular and feminist women and their agendas by building a countermovement produced, employed, and staffed by the new graduates of women's seminaries, or Houzeh Elmieh, in Qom (the center of Shi'i learning), steeped in a traditional religious curriculum. Although the first theological training course for women in Qom dates to only ten years before the 1979 Islamic Revolution, such schools are now very common throughout Iran and number close to 300, and from 2003 to 2007, they enrolled 20,000 to 30,000 female students. Some of these women have become *mujtahids,*

high-ranking ulama who can interpret religious law and issue fatawa (although they cannot become judges or lead mixed prayers in Iran). Many of
them have become even more dedicated supporters of the regime and staff
government-run women's centers and leadership programs, getting out the
vote and influencing their fellow female voters at election time (Hoodfar
and Sadr 2009: 57). It remains to be seen what effect these new graduates
will have on gender struggles and democratization in Iran, but clearly the
regime is investing in women as a constituency and hoping to make them
loyal allies.

The Women's Movement in the Middle East

After the Iranian revolution of 1979 and the institution of state-mandated
compulsory veiling, gender segregation in public places, and the policing of
morality, a strong contingent of Iranian women protested new laws and
practices that restricted their access to divorce, lowered the marriage age,
weakened maternal rights to child custody after a divorce, and severely
weakened their equality before the law and participation in the judiciary.
Particularly during the reformist era of President Mohammad Khatami's rule
(1997–2005), when civil society was strengthened, some of the important
daughters and disciples of the revolution began to work more closely with
secular Iranian women activists and organizations. These hyper-educated
Iranian women (educated both theologically and secularly) had become disaffected by the revolution and its harshness, militarization, corruption, and
"deafness" to the concerns and predicaments of women, including its strong
reach into the intimate sphere and the home. These women, who were an
important constituency for the revolution and had supported it, began to critique the revolution from within, since it was supposed to be representing
the highest ideals of Islamic social justice and fairness.

Homa Hoodfar and Shadi Sadr (2009) have asked whether Iranian
women can or will act as agents to democratize theocracy. They suggest
that there is some evidence that the interests of secularist activists and Islamist disciples of the revolution are converging and that—though these activists and disciples may disagree about formal legal equality, secularism,
and feminism—the crux of their concerns and the target of their activism is
the reform of personal status law. In particular, while secular activists have
continued to fight their battles in the media, in the blogosphere virtually,
and through legal activism, President Ahmadinejad has largely shuttered
their institutional base; for there to be further change in Iran, they need the
numbers, the constituency, the leadership, and the legitimacy that some of
the female internal critics of the revolution can provide.

In the Middle East, coalitions are absolutely key to negotiating the very
narrow legal and political space that women (and their male sympathizers)

often must enter in order to raise the consciousness of women and struggle against pervasive patriarchal gender codes and inequities. What the new female revolutionary generation has done in Iran is to compel the Shi'i religious establishment to acknowledge women as a major constituency and to consider the interests of women when they make policy. Moreover, when these coalitions agitated for reforms to allow Muslim widows to inherit real estate, to increase alimony for women in divorce, and to reinterpret criminal law to fight domestic violence, they strategically "frontloaded" their activism. *Before* they took their fight to the more conservative parliament under Ahmadinejad, they made alliances with key, sympathetic members of the Shi'i clergy who had strong institutional ties to the government. The big question is whether women can become a *party* to lawmaking in Iran and elsewhere, as opposed to always having to lobby for legal changes from the outside (Hoodfar and Sadr 2009).

Throughout the region, even though women have not been very successful in winning elective office or high government positions, and currently have the lowest political representation in the world (see Hausmann, Tyson, and Zahidi 2006), activists are constantly engaged in "conference politics" and in networking with local NGOs, political parties, international institutions, and regional and transnational groups such as the Women Living Under Muslim Law Network, which engages in scholarship, activism, and policy-making to improve the rights and status of women throughout the globe who are subject to Muslim legal traditions and law (Al-Ali 2000). Initiatives that meet with some success are soon copied by other groups elsewhere.

For example, in 1992 a coalition of Moroccan women and their organizations launched the "Million Signatures Campaign," prodding King Hassan II to reform personal status law and undo the contradictions between Moroccan constitutional guarantees for gender equality and the inequities present within personal status law (called the *Mudawwana* in Morocco). Within a year they succeeded in gathering a million signatures to present to the king, but he made only minor changes to the *Mudawwana* and appointed only one woman, a conservative *'aalima,* to a royal commission to propose changes (Maddy-Weitzman 2005; Buskins 2003). Still, the campaign demonstrated the popularity of personal status reforms and strengthened the political learning and efficacy of the organizations involved. Following his father's death in 1999, the younger King Mohammad VI convened a new royal commission with three female members and a more pluralist balance of religious clerics after renewed activism from Moroccan women and with prodding from the newly democratized parliament (whose leadership was committed to a national action plan to integrate women's initiatives). Following the king's recommendation, in 2004 the Moroccan parliament enacted a much more serious package of reforms that eliminated male guardianship *(wali)* over women, enhanced women's access to divorce and right to child custody, limited universal male divorce, placed divorce cases more centrally in the courts, and made polygamy more difficult.[2] Yet, the Moroccan women's movement still organizes to improve the implementation of these reforms throughout the country while other conservative or Islamist forces try to work legislatively and publicly to weaken those reforms.

Iranian women, inspired by the initiative of their Moroccan sisters and the idea of using a public referendum as a consciousness-raising tool, launched their own "Million Signatures Campaign" (also known as the Change for Equality) in 2006.[3] They fanned out into public parks and streets to engage in face-to-face contact with Iranian women about the negative consequences of legal discrimination against women for all segments of Iranian society, not only women. Despite international solidarity efforts and publicity for their campaign, the regime has arrested many of the campaign's activists, so they are taking their struggle to the virtual sphere rather than continuing to organize public demonstrations, which have been easily repressed and overwhelmed by the security police (see Hoodfar and Sadr 2009). Since the demonstrations and violence after the contested reelection of President Ahmadinejad in June 2009, most of the Change for Equality activists have been forced into exile or arrested, and civil and political society, in general, has been tightly restrained.

Clearly, women's movements confront significant obstacles to their objectives and meet with varying degrees of success in the Middle Eastern context. At the same time, as Western feminists and social scientists highlight the limited opportunities and exclusion of women in the third world, they should not forget that many *men* in third world nations have also been historically excluded from political life (Haniff 1991). Consider the case of women in the Kingdom of Saudi Arabia, which is the only Arab country where women have not yet exercised suffrage—although King Abdullah announced in 2012 that women will be allowed to campaign in and contest municipal elections in the kingdom in 2015 (Kuwait, the UAE, Qatar, and Oman have allowed women to vote only recently). Saudi men, too, have extremely limited political rights, voting only occasionally for a portion of municipal council seats in 2005 and 2011. While it certainly matters that Egyptian women have the right to vote and Saudi women do not yet, Saudi men also have few electoral rights. Saudi men can drive, work, seek an education, and travel without needing the permission of their wives, but they also live under (and some would argue suffer from) the same strict restrictions of gender segregation in the workplace, government, marketplace, and schools. It is extremely important to understand the ways in which women's access to power differs from that of men—yet at the same time, we should remember that elites restrict the boundaries of political life for both men and women to serve their own ends.

The Arab Spring in 2011 produced greater political space and electoral opportunities, and women now may be able to organize, mobilize, engage in public discourse, and raise funds more publicly and openly in some countries. Even in Saudi Arabia, which averted mass protests through large public spending programs, female activists such as Manal al-Sharif and Wajeha al-Huwaider launched the June 17 Movement to fight against the ban on female driving—though it is still in place, along with other state policies enforcing male "guardianship" over women. While women were politically mobilized during the Arab Spring, electoral quotas for women were withdrawn in the 2011 Egyptian parliamentary elections, while they were reinforced at the party level in the 2011 Tunisian elections for a new Constituent Assembly. Each women's movement across the region faces particular challenges in maintaining previously won rights as well as continuing an upward battle for political and economic gender parity. At the same time, conservative forces also take advantage of the same political space—and their constituencies are often larger, more national in nature, better funded, and able to bring quick electoral gains.

Conclusion

The struggle for gender equality and women's political participation and representation in the Middle East is diverse, complex, and deeply influenced by a range of factors. Creative and dedicated activists, intellectuals, professionals, and government personnel deploy their resources and skills within the art of what is politically possible. In the past few decades, public education has expanded women's access to knowledge, knowledge creation, and theorizing about their lives, but political campaigns were often risky and illegal, and economic difficulties and the lack of financial resources for political struggles made radical success elusive. The regional change in 2011 offers both opportunities and challenges to activists, as electoral competition will determine political power to a larger extent and thus women's movements will have to move out of the main cities to build national electoral strength. Women continue to expand their "voice" as writers, bloggers, bureaucrats, politicians, intellectuals, journalists, religious leaders, media pundits, novelists, and poets across a range of media, particularly the new media facilitated by the Internet and satellite television. Understanding the history of the women's movement and the construction of gender in its diversity throughout the region contextualizes these struggles and hopefully allows us to understand them better. As we saw in 2011, change often comes from unexpected quarters. When longstanding injustices are framed in legitimate ways and resonate deeply in society, and activists have a political "opening" to exploit, previously subdued forces in society may find their voice, and more.

Notes

Homa Hoodfar; my research assistants Anna Olsson, Korneliya Bachiyska, Mayy el-Sheikh, Tofigh Maboudi, and Kelly Nielsen; as well as students from my spring 2009 seminar at American University on gender and politics in the Middle East assisted me with this chapter, and I am very grateful for their help.

1. Jobs considered "safe" are those in which women are unlikely to be sexually harassed. Jobs considered "legitimate" are those through which women can help to further national development.

2. It is important to note that women were on both sides of the debate in Morocco, as they are elsewhere. One of the most public opponents of the 2004 reforms was Nadia Yassin, the famous daughter of Shaikh Abd al-Salam Yassin, founder of the Hizb al-Adl wal-Ihsan (Party for Justice and Charity). The counterprotests of the Islamist camp had gathered tens of thousands of people in a duel of demonstrations, and women joined these protests in large numbers. However, the 2003 bombing by Islamic radicals in Casablanca heightened the courage of the reformers to continue their support, and also resulted in the government clamping down on Islamist opposition movements in general.

3. For more information on Change for Equality, see the campaign's website, http://www.4equality.info/english.

Part 2

Cases

9

Algeria

Yahia H. Zoubir

Algeria, the largest country in Africa (since Sudan's partition in May 2011) and tenth largest in the world, dominated the news twice in its contemporary political history. The first event was the seven-year War of National Liberation against France (November 1954 to July 1962). The war resulted in the death of hundreds of thousands of Algerian Muslims, victims of one of the most intensive settlers' colonizations in modern times. The colonial period (1830–1962), which reduced Algerians to second-class status, and the war of liberation remain the determining factors of national identity. The nationalist movement that emerged in the 1920s and the war of liberation have also been instrumental in shaping the postindependence political system, in which the military has played a key role. The second, more recent event spanned the 1990s. This was a civil conflict that pitted the regime's security forces against armed Islamist groups. This period witnessed gruesome massacres committed against the civilian population by Islamist extremists and harsh repression by security forces responsible for the disappearance of hundreds of individuals. The Algerian "red decade" of the 1990s finds its roots in the intricacies of the war of liberation and the nature of the political system that the nationalists instituted following independence.

Historical Background and Contemporary Political Structure

Algeria's history, though complex, is extremely rich. The country, whose native inhabitants are the Berbers (or Amazigh, meaning "the free"), has

189

been prey to numerous foreign invasions, including by the Phoenicians, Romans, Vandals, Byzantines, Arabs, and Ottoman Turks, who were succeeded by the French. However, the Arab-Islamic culture had the largest impact and would play a critical role in unifying the local Arab-Berber population against French colonial domination. In fact, Algerians considered the war against the French a jihad (holy war) and the combatants were called mujahidin (holy warriors). At the same time, French culture also played an important role in shaping the nationalist movement, most of whose leaders were francophone.

French colonization had devastating effects on Algeria (Ruedy 2005). Though it claimed to have a "civilizing mission," France uprooted entire populations, dispossessed farmers of their lands and gave them to European settlers, transformed mosques into churches, and provided education only to the children of local notables. Access to education improved over time but ultimately remained very limited. The famous French political philosopher Alexis de Tocqueville asserted that the rate of literacy among Algerians was quite high prior to colonization. Yet after 132 years of French control, the overwhelming majority of Algerian Muslims at independence were illiterate. The injustices and blatant discrimination colonial France was responsible for explain Algerians' stiff resistance to foreign domination. Indeed it took France decades to establish its total control over the territory and crush the resistance of the very first nationalists.

On November 1, 1954, the newly created National Liberation Front (FLN) began the Algerian war for liberation against French occupation (Horne 2006). The FLN and its armed wing, the National Liberation Army (ALN), fought a bloody, eight-year war against a very strong enemy, ultimately achieving Algerian independence in 1962. The price, however, was very heavy, as hundreds of thousands of Algerians lost their lives. The war would also have concrete political consequences for the shape of postindependence Algerian politics. During the war, all other existing political parties, such as the Democratic Union for the Algerian Manifesto (UDMA), the Algerian Communist Party (PCA), and the influential Association of Algerian Muslim Ulama, were forced to dissolve their organizations and submit to the authority of the FLN. Their integration into the FLN came not as parties but as individuals. In other words, the war of independence led to the creation of a nationalist political party with hegemonic status and ambitions.

After independence, an authoritarian political regime emerged in which the FLN became the sole legal political party. In August 1963, Decree 63-297 prohibited political associations other than the FLN from forming. The country's presidents came from the FLN, and FLN members dominated the bureaucracy while they monopolized parliament. The regime distrusted autonomous associations whatever their nature; even the Boy Scouts fell under the control of the state. Thus the bureaucracy and the FLN—two key pillars of the postindependence regime—absorbed most independent or potentially independent associations. The few remaining autonomous associations were restricted to athletic, parenting, or religious activities. The media, too, were subordinated to the state and the single party and served as a propaganda tool for the regime.

True power in the postindependence Algerian political system lay in the hands of the military, the third but most important pillar of the regime. The FLN was a subordinate, minor apparatus relative to the military and its overpowering hegemony (Roberts 2003). Still, although constituting the backbone of the system, the army did not rule directly. Instead it acted as the guardian of the regime, defending Algeria's borders but also watching over the FLN and the domestic political arena. Algeria's military saw itself not just as an institution designed to ensure national security from foreign attack but also as one that needed to take the lead in developing Algeria's economy and society in the postindependence era.

For the next three decades the authoritarian Algerian regime presided over state-led economic development and the creation of a generous socialist welfare state. But it came under great stress in the 1980s as Algerians increasingly accumulated grievances against the regime. Many were angered by the regime's complete domination of state and society—specifically its repression of opposition to its rule, and the influence of the FLN. Meanwhile, state-led economic development failed as a strategy, and inflation and unemployment began to mount at the same time that the government was forced to cut back on the welfare state as it pursued economic liberalization policies. A scarcity of affordable housing, as well as food and medicine shortages, also plagued the country. Corruption, incompetence, nepotism, and inefficiency permeated the economy and the political sphere. Finally, while many Algerians' grievances were economic in nature, others criticized the regime for its secularism and demanded the Islamization of the public sphere.

During the presidency of Colonel Chadli Bendjedid, political opposition came to a head. Lacking democratic channels to express their demands and grievances, Algerian dissident groups organized protests that the authorities severely repressed. The most influential such event occurred in October 1988 when widespread riots—met first with repression—eventually moved regime elites to open up the political system and institute a modicum of political liberalization. A key reform was a constitutional amendment that legalized the creation of political parties other than the FLN. This amendment ushered in the establishment of a multiparty system, theoretically terminating the FLN's hegemony and making the FLN *un parti comme les autres* ("a party like any other"). Henceforth, numerous political parties emerged into the political arena.

The regime had hoped that its liberalizing reforms would provide a democratic facade for incumbent rulers, increasing their legitimacy. It counted on none of the new parties being able to amass sufficient support to truly challenge the military-backed FLN. But it had miscalculated, for an Islamist party, the Islamic Salvation Front (FIS), was organizing itself and rapidly increasing its support base. After winning the municipal elections in 1990, the FIS performed so well in the first round of multiparty parliamentary elections in December 1991 that it looked to be poised to form a majority after the second round. But the second round was never held. The military stepped in and annulled the elections, because it was not willing to tolerate an opposition party actually taking power in parliament—especially not an Islamist party whose rhetoric regarding its ultimate political ambitions often was illiberal and hegemonic.

This cancellation of the civilian elections pushed Algerian politics into a showdown between the regime and its primarily Islamist opposition. The military forced the resignation of President Bendjedid, dissolved parliament, appointed a new president (Mohammad Boudiaf, a historic figure during the War of National Liberation brought in from exile in Morocco), and declared a state of emergency, which was not lifted until February 2011 after the Arab uprisings swept through the region. In the wake of the annulment of the elections and in response to the military's actions, various Islamist factions turned to violence against the regime. The regime's security forces responded in kind, and the result was that Algerian politics for much of the 1990s was characterized by what some call civil strife (others refer to it as civil war). This was an era of high instability, assassination campaigns, disappearances, and grave violations of human rights by Islamists and security forces. Tens of thousands of Algerians lost their lives while the country also suffered the massive destruction of infrastructure and factories.

In the new millennium, Algeria began to emerge from this crisis environment. A constitutional revision in 1996 initiated new institutional arrangements that form the basis of Algeria's contemporary political structure. Algeria now has a bicameral parliament, encompassing a directly elected 462-member lower house, the National Assembly, and a partly appointed and partly indirectly elected upper chamber, the Council of the Nation. Local and regional assemblies elect two-thirds of the membership of the Council of the Nation; Algeria's president directly appoints the remaining third. The security services and segments of the military hierarchy remain key, pivotal actors behind the scenes of politics, however. With the support of the military, in 1999 former foreign minister (1963–1979) and FLN candidate Abdelaziz Bouteflika was elected president in a campaign that, while rich in political debate, was not truly competitive. Anticipating that the election would be rigged, Bouteflika's six other competitors withdrew from the race as it unfolded, leaving Bouteflika as the sole candidate and thus delegitimizing the outcome.

Bouteflika's major challenges were to bring about political stability (Mortimer 2004), reestablish security in the country, revamp the economy, and break Algeria's international isolation. In order to reduce the level of violence, Bouteflika initiated an amnesty law, which the population approved through referendum in September 1999. The objective of the law was to encourage Islamist groups to renounce violence and lay down their arms. The law exonerated individuals from legal proceedings, reduced the terms of existing sentences, imposed probation or the annulment of civic rights rather than prison sentences, and so forth—all at the discretion of the authorities. Although two Islamist groups accepted the amnesty, two others did not (although one was subsequently eradicated in 2002). Notwithstanding the fact that the law resulted in the surrender of hundreds of armed Islamists, large sections of civil society saw the law as a betrayal, especially since it granted "legal impunity" to the perpetrators of atrocities. But from the government's perspective this was the only means to end the civil unrest. The law was also meant to protect security forces from prosecution for abuses they might have committed.

Following his reelection in 2004, Bouteflika initiated yet another amnesty law, inscribed in the Charter for Peace and National Reconciliation and approved by referendum in 2005, which became effective in 2006. The text provides the terms of financial compensation to the families of the victims on all sides, as well as amnesty for security forces accused of human rights abuses and for Islamist groups implicated in terrorist activities. This prompted severe criticism from national and international human rights organizations, which argued that crimes against humanity should not go unpunished. Furthermore, the fact that the charter forbade any questioning of the terms of the law—be it verbally or in writing—was in direct contradiction to the country's constitution, which guarantees freedom of expression. Victims' families on both sides felt that the charter not only amnestied the perpetrators of crimes but also denied the right to truth and justice concerning the thousands of massacred and disappeared. Again, however, others felt that such an amnesty was the only way to move Algeria forward from the violence of the 1990s.

The 1996 Algerian constitution limited presidential mandates to two terms. However, Bouteflika introduced amendments to the constitution, adopted overwhelmingly by parliament in 2008, that removed the limit on the number of presidential terms in office (see Figure 9.1 for a political cartoon inspired by this maneuver). This allowed Bouteflika to run for and win another term in 2009 despite his age, poor health, and the mixed results of his presidency. Given the means at his disposal and the support of the parties that dominated the parliament, no one doubted who the winner would be. Bouteflika generally uses the parliament as a rubber stamp for his policies.

Figure 9.1 Spoofing the End of Term Limits for the Algerian President

"Draft constitutional amendment adopted by Parliament"
"Caesar for life!"
Dilem, *Liberté* (Algeria), November 15, 2008 (used with permission)

Still, to ensure support for the constitutional revisions and for his candidacy for a third term, parliamentary deputies—and later governors and high government officials—received a 300 percent salary increase two months prior to the election, even though their salaries and benefits were already considerable compared to those of the average citizen (the cartoon in Figure 9.2 satirizes this). Opposition political parties—secular and religious—exist, but they have no aspiration to accede to power. They are content with having representatives in the parliament in part because a portion of their salaries goes to the parties' coffers. The population at large has lost all hope of seeing political parties play a consequential role in politics or bring about any real change; the low turnout for the May 2012 legislative election illustrates (and confirms) this pessimism toward the political system and its capacity to effect consequential transformation. Furthermore, Bouteflika has attempted to tame civil society and tolerates only those associations that support the incumbent president.

**Figure 9.2 Satirizing the Algerian Parliament's Willingness
to Extend the Presidential Term in Office**

"The deputies vote"
Deputies vote in favor of the revision of the constitution to allow President Abdelaziz
    Bouteflika to seek a third term in office (in return for raises).
Dilem, *Liberté* (Algeria), November 16, 2008 (used with permission)

Religion and Politics

Politics and religion in Algeria have always been intertwined; the Islamic
religion and its traditions permeate both civil society and the state. Islam in
Algeria constitutes the basis of identity and culture, and Islamic norms to a
large extent govern social relations. Despite its secularist inclinations, since
independence the state has always resorted to Islamic symbols to establish
and reproduce its legitimacy. Paradoxically, social movements and the religious opposition have used Islam not only to wage their struggles against
the established regime, but also to challenge the religious claims of the
state. By denying the state one of its fundamental bases of legitimacy, radical Islamists in particular have sought to delegitimize the state and the
elites in charge of governing the country. Islam and Islamic references,

rather than "imported," foreign ideologies, have been the source of identity and authenticity. Here lies one of the main reasons for the emergence of radical Islamism and its popularity in the 1980s and early 1990s.

Neither Islam nor the Islamist phenomenon can be dissociated from the history of the country's nationalist movement. It would be no exaggeration to assert that the Islamist movement is one of the belated progenies of colonial rule in Algeria. While the movement is the product of the socioeconomic failure of the 1980s, its doctrinal aspects draw partly from the crisis of identity caused by 132 years of colonial rule. The colonial authorities did not content themselves with exploiting Algeria's natural and human resources. They also targeted the principal local religious institutions: mosques and religious schools were closed, religious lands were expropriated, and Islamic culture was projected as inferior to Western Christian civilization. In other words, the colonial state carried out a systematic uprooting of Arab and Islamic culture. Algerians lived in poverty and were denied basic religious, cultural, political, and economic rights—rights that Europeans, albeit a minority in the country, enjoyed. This explains why Islam became—and still is—the most salient component of Algerians' national identity as they sought—and still seek—to regain what European imperialism tried to destroy.

Islam, Nationbuilding, and Statebuilding

Soon after independence, the authorities manipulated Islam for political and ideological purposes. In order to build a modern identity and gain legitimacy, successive governments sought to integrate what they defined as a modern type of Islam into revolutionary, vanguard perspectives. Thus, Islam, understood in its modernized form, was decreed the religion of the state in the 1963, 1976, 1989, 1996, and (amended) 2008 constitutions. State elites conceived of Islam as the foundation of the identity of Algerian citizens. They encouraged the construction of mosques, the teaching of the Arabic language, and the creation of a multitude of religious institutions. The state established a monopoly over religious life and repressed interpretations that deviated from the official norms that the state propagated. In sum, the authorities incorporated Islam as an essential component of the ideological and political apparatus of the regime. That tactic was part of a broader vision to build a modern nation-state through a developmentalist strategy. In this context, Islam as a system of values, or a set of rational principles, was to coexist with modernity in a model that French sociologist Henri Sanson defined as *laïcité islamique* (Islamic secularism).

It was in this context, then, that largely secularist elites held a monopoly of power in postindependence Algeria. Yet Islam played an ever greater role with respect to the legitimacy of successive governments. The regime used Islam not only as an instrument of national integration in an ethnically heterogeneous society, but also as a tool of political legitimization. Over time, the importance attributed to Islam in the country's sequence of constitutions paved the way for the emergence of competing interpretations of Islam's proper role. While some elites saw Islam as a religion open to modernity, others viewed it through a traditionalist prism, resulting in very conservative interpretations of Islam's proper role in state and society. Conservative forces, including those within the regime itself, constructed a discrete interpretation of Islam that was at loggerheads with the socioeconomic and cultural policies espoused by dominant (secular) elites. In other words, the ostensibly secular state and its various structures actually incorporated many Islamists—including some influential ulama (Muslim legal scholars). Faced with an internal ideological struggle between secular "progressives" and Islamists, the regime sought to achieve a balance between two irreconcilable visions, contenting itself with excluding the most extreme Islamists in order to preserve national unity and depict the regime as an indispensable arbitrator.

The Islamist Challenge to the State

Islamist organizations have challenged the regime at various periods and to different degrees since the country's independence. Thus it would be erroneous to attribute the emergence of Islamism to late twentieth-century socioeconomic factors alone, though the latter undoubtedly contributed to its eruption. Islamism can also be situated in the context of colonization and decolonization, in that one can view Islamism in Algeria as the latest reawakening against Western domination and Western-inspired modernity following the failure of postindependence authorities to create a prosperous Muslim society.

The early Islamist organizations challenged the state on the socialist options it had chosen. The first such opposition organization was El-Qiyam al-Islamiyya (Islamic Values), founded in 1963—just one year after Algeria's independence. It was tolerated until 1966 but then banned by the government. El-Qiyam and religious personalities such as Shaikh Ahmed Sahnoun put forth demands that future Islamists would include in their agendas, like the full implementation of the sharia (Islamic law). They also advocated the closure of stores during Friday prayers (a demand satisfied in 1976) and called for a ban on the sale of alcohol, the exclusion of non-Muslims from public jobs, the separation of beaches into men's and women's sections, the introduction of religious teaching in schools (instituted in 1964), the interdiction of women's participation in sports, as well as parades celebrating national holidays. They later compelled the government to establish the weekend as Thursday and Friday rather than as Saturday and Sunday. To

the relief of the business community in its dealings with international partners, however, in 2009 the authorities decided—without debate—to change
the weekend to Friday and Saturday.

The authorities tolerated some of the Islamist organizations but then
eventually banned them. Yet many of their members remained anchored in
the system, exerting pressure to extract further concessions from the state
on moral, socioeconomic, and cultural issues. In response to those demands, the state launched its own campaign to "prevent the degradation of
morals" resulting from the loosening of mores, alcoholism, and Western influence in the country. In other words, the state decided to contribute to the
"re-Islamization" of Algeria and to the rehabilitation of the Arab-Islamic
identity that the French colonial state had denigrated. As a consequence,
francophone intellectuals and Westernized elites, particularly women,
would become the main targets of Islamist attacks. Moreover, Islamists'
ideas affected the state's legislative agenda with regard to language policy
(in the early 1970s it ruled that all university education would be administered in Arabic rather than French) as well as with regard to gender matters
(in 1984 it enacted a new personal status code that sharply constrained
women's rights in marriage, divorce, and the like). At the societal level, Islamist ideology influenced the dress code of Algerians. Beginning in the
late 1970s, Algerians increasingly abandoned Western clothing styles, with
women donning the hijab while men wore the *khamis* (a traditional loose,
flowing, floor-length robe).

The Radicalization of Political Islam

In the absence of democratic channels, marginalized Algerian youth, feeling
betrayed by the state, found in the mosque a moral substitute for alcohol,
drugs, and violence, which had constituted their main pursuit hitherto.
Alienated youth in the 1980s communicated with the state through violence, expressed in the form of cyclical riots. In general, the state lost its
authority and its raison d'être in the eyes of a disenchanted population. The
almost total failure of social, economic, and cultural modernization was one
of the main reasons for the rise of radical Islamism—without discounting
the painful colonial history whose effects continue to influence the evolution of Algerian society. Secularist elites, like those in many other Arab-
Islamic countries, understood modernization in its material sense only, failing
to take into account the necessity for a parallel process of secularization,
which, despite Islamist claims to the contrary, is not necessarily antithetical
to Islamic values.

So long as Islamists did not threaten the survival of the system, the
regime allowed them to freely operate and even encouraged them in order
to curb the secularist left, which also had its allies, albeit less powerful,

within the bureaucracy. Whenever it opposed the Islamists' ideology, the regime did so in the name of Islam, because religion was a necessary, even though increasingly contested, component of its legitimacy. In fact, the regime facilitated the spread of Islamist ideology not only by allowing the building of thousands of public and private mosques, but also by establishing Islamic institutes, flooding television with religious programs, and allocating substantial resources for hosting international seminars on Islamic thought. Secularist state elites were unwilling to leave religious activities to the realm of civil society; instead, they wished to control the terms of religious discourse. To have permitted the existence of a public sphere independent of the state would have curtailed the power of the regime and diminished its hegemonic rule.

In the 1980s, violence was present in the universities, with bloody encounters between Islamist students who mobilized around cultural, linguistic, and moralistic themes, on the one hand, and leftist or secular students, Berberists, and others who did not share the Islamists' interpretation of Islam, on the other. Ironically, it was the state's acceleration of its Arabization campaign in the public education system that led to further contestation, owing to the growing cultural distinctiveness and absence of professional opportunities for Arabic-educated emerging elites relative to francophone Algerians. Islamist groups couched their socioeconomic demands within an ideological discourse garbed with religion. Various (small) armed groups targeted bars, breweries, police stations, and Soviet citizens and interests in Algeria. They represented a real challenge to the state, which responded with equal violence. But to confirm its religious credentials, the state also responded with an expansion of religious programs and the introduction of Islamist-inspired legislation. The objective of Islamists, of course, was to take Islam away from the regime in order to undermine one of the essential pillars upon which it had built its legitimacy.

By the late 1980s, the FIS had emerged as the party that represented oppositional Islamist sentiment in Algeria. When the regime pursued political liberalization by legalizing the formation of parties other than the FLN, the FIS was the main beneficiary. It was successful because its leaders presented the party as the only potent alternative to the FLN-dominated system, even claiming that it incarnated the true, historical FLN of the war of national liberation, thus delegitimizing the postindependence FLN. The FIS convinced major segments of society that the postindependence FLN had usurped and betrayed the nationalist movement—and its Islamic principles—in the pursuit of power and self-enrichment. And because it identified itself with Islam in a profoundly Muslim society, the FIS was able to repudiate the secular pretensions of the parties that resisted its ambitions and its societal projects. By the June 1990 municipal and departmental elections, it became apparent that the other parties, whether secular or (moderate) Islamist, could not halt the ascension of the FIS. These parties failed to establish a common strategy or united front with which to meet the FIS's challenge.

Political liberalization in Algeria in the late 1980s and early 1990s would not lead to democratization, therefore, in part because of the actions (or lack thereof) of the non-FIS parties in the new, multiparty political arena. But the FIS, too, bears significant responsibility for derailing prospects for a genuine democratic transition. While part of the FIS's leadership was moderate and publicly supported the ideal of pluralistic political competition, a significant segment of the party sought to impose the party's hegemony and delegitimize the existence of any other party. FIS leaders contended that they expressed the general will of the Algerian people and promised to implement Islamic law once in power. Such a promise implied a disregard for the republican constitution and inaugurated the "divinization" of politics, hence implicitly precluding the expression of secular views and the development of a democratic polity. The claims of its leadership to represent the only legitimate path did not bode well for the future, especially for the Westernized middle class and women. Furthermore, promises of radicals within the party to create popular tribunals and to punish the "enemies of Islam," and even to punish those opposed to the FIS, scared not only officials in the regime but also secular intellectuals and ordinary citizens. This is why large segments of society did not oppose—indeed they even encouraged—the banning of the FIS after its democratic victory in the first round of the December 1991 legislative election.

Although the FIS was banned in 1992, and despite the violence that then unfolded, many of the ideas the FIS propagated continue to be advocated today by moderate, legal Islamist parties like the Movement of the Society for Peace (MSP), the National Movement for Renewal (Islah), and the Islamic Renaissance Movement (En-Nahda), which grouped together in the spring of 2012 under the Alliance of Green Algeria—along with two more recently formed parties, the Justice and Development Front (El Adala) and the Front for Change (FC). These parties are currently or will be represented in the parliament and in the executive branch; the two new parties (El Adala and FC) gained eight and four seats, respectively, in the May 2012 election. Today's remaining armed groups have lost popular support; their violent campaigns have discredited them in the eyes of the population. The main armed group, al-Qaeda in the Islamic Maghreb (AQIM), which in late 2006 grew out of the Algerian Salafi Group for Preaching and Combat (GSPC), carried out some spectacular attacks against government structures and innocent civilians in 2007, but it has been weakened by the security services and forced to establish its base in northern Mali along the border with Algeria. The few operations AQIM occasionally executes are now limited to the Sahara desert and the mountains in Kabylia in the north. And while disgruntled youths feed its ranks to some extent, a popular new strategy for today's alienated youth is to emigrate illegally to Europe by crossing the Mediterranean Sea in nonseaworthy vessels, at great risk to their lives.

Government and Opposition

While at the outset some hoped that Bouteflika's tenure in power would bring about democratization, instead Algeria has undergone a transition from military authoritarianism to presidential authoritarianism. Although Bouteflika was elected in 1999 because he was chosen by the military hierarchy and the intelligence services, he gradually managed not only to gain a degree of autonomy from the military but also to remove some of the most influential senior officers in the military hierarchy from office, usually through forced retirements or by replacing them with officers loyal to his person. Bouteflika now serves as both commander in chief and minister of defense. Following his reelection in 2004 to a second term, Bouteflika strengthened his control over the armed forces by appointing a close associate as secretary-general of the Ministry of Defense and appointing other loyalists as heads of Algeria's six military regions. In addition, the Algerian armed forces have recently distanced themselves from politics and concentrated on professionalization and modernization.

Yet these hopeful developments have not translated into civilian control over the security services, whose power has been strengthened by the domestic war on terrorism as well as their collaboration in the global war on terrorism. This international cooperation has provided them with additional power. Traditionally, the security services, collectively known as the Department of Intelligence and Security (DRS), have had great influence over the appointments of ministers and ambassadors. They are said to determine elections by manipulating the private and public media as well as political parties. For example, whenever a political party splits, the opposition accuses the DRS of having stage-managed dissent within the party in order to break up the organization. The security services continue to have considerable weight in state affairs. Any president has to bargain with their leaders over policy issues and about the extent of his prerogatives. Thus, while the political role of the armed forces has greatly diminished, elected officials—including the chief executive—do not have final say over legislation and policy, given the political weight of the DRS.

What of parties and parliament? We have already seen that the security forces exercise important, undemocratic influence over parties and elections. The regime also has set up a multiparty system in which parties play the role of mediators between their constituents and the authorities—but have no aspiration to come to power and replace the current system with a new, more democratic polity. From 2004 until 2012, the party system was dominated by three parties, referred to collectively as the "Presidential Alliance" because they supported Bouteflika and his political agenda. These included the nationalist FLN (136 seats) and the technocratic-modernist Democratic National Rally (RND, 61 seats), which some call a clone of the FLN because both it and the RND receive massive support from the state administration, are present throughout the country, and have considerable means at their disposal—and thus one can see little difference between the two. The third party in the alliance was the moderate Islamist MSP. It withdrew from the alliance in January 2012, four months before the approaching May 2012 legislative elections, accusing the other two partners of having emptied Bouteflika's reforms of their substance (Zoubir and Aghrout 2012).

In the run-up to the 2012 legislative elections, the regime allowed the formation of twenty-one new political parties, resulting in the participation of forty-four parties in the election. Given the staunch refusal by the authorities to authorize any new party under Bouteflika's rule (with one exception in 1999), the shift was most probably caused by the Arab Spring, official statements to the contrary notwithstanding. The proliferation of political parties was also intended to increase participation and to thwart the emergence of a powerful, genuine opposition party that could challenge the incumbent as the FIS had in 1990–1991. In the 2012 election—against the trend in neighboring countries, where Islamist parties were victorious in recent elections—the government parties took nearly 63 percent of the seats. The FLN obtained 221 seats while the RND obtained 70; both thus enjoyed an increase over their 2007 representation. The Alliance of Green Algeria led by the MSP, by contrast, obtained a mere 47 seats in the election, though in 2007 the MSP alone had garnered 52 seats. A number of other, smaller parties allowed to form in fall 2011—many of which hitherto were practically unknown to the public—also "earned" seats in parliament (Dessi 2012). The key dynamic to understand here is that the regime essentially decides ahead of time how many seats each party—including even those in the Presidential Alliance—will win. The regime uses parliamentary seats to reward individuals and parties that are loyal to the political status quo; it also seeks to provide the illusion of genuine pluralism.

The regime does permit Islamists to participate in this pseudo-multiparty system. A number of "acceptable" Islamist parties, including the MSP, Islah, En-Nahda, El Adala, and the FC, thus hold seats in parliament. Though critical on some issues, these parties are tamed organizations relative to what the FIS represented in the 1990s. They use their involvement in national political institutions to advance the interests of their constituents: mainly urban arabophone (i.e., solely Arabic-speaking) teachers, many of whom were educated in Middle Eastern universities, and civil servants who belong to the middle class. Their moderation and participation in the system have been

exploited by the regime to demonstrate that Islamist parties that are opposed to violence, and that do not aspire to replace the incumbent regime,
are welcome in the state's institutions—inside of which they can act as
pressure groups to advance their demands. And while the current regime
does not give in to demands for democracy, it has made concessions on
moral issues that the MSP and En-Nahda have raised in parliament, such as
with a ban on alcohol imports. In sum, legalist Islamist parties have been
co-opted and now serve as support for the regime's facade democracy.

Other non-Islamist, democratic, secularist parties of note include the
Front of Socialist Forces (FFS, 21 seats, the fourth most important party in
parliament); Independents (19 seats); and the Workers Party (PT, 17 seats),
led by the charismatic (female) Louisa Hanoune. The FFS had boycotted all
national elections for fifteen years over their allegedly fraudulent character.
By contrast, the Rally for Culture and Democracy (RCD), which held 19
seats in the 2007 parliament, boycotted the 2012 election. These parties
represent important minorities. They are made up of francophone and
Berber members, many of whom are employed in the liberal professions
(law, medicine, engineering, etc.) or serve as cadres in the various structures of the state. Even though they are critical of the regime, with the possible exception of the FFS, they have often played into the hands of the
regime and have allowed themselves to be co-opted on occasion. They con
stitute no real threat. The PT, for instance, supported the constitutional
amendment that permitted a third presidential term for President Bouteflika
while its leader, Louisa Hanoune, ran as a candidate in the 2009 presidential election, in which she garnered just over 4 percent of the votes.

Given the ongoing role of the security services behind the scenes of the
political arena and the rigged nature of a party system that contains within
it no real, active political opposition, it is not surprising that Algerians are
increasingly indifferent to parties and politics in general. This sentiment
was illustrated in the 2007 legislative election, which elicited very low
turnout—with 35 percent of voters officially reported as having shown up
at the polls. This was the lowest ever in Algeria's independent history, and
one can assume that the real turnout was even lower than the official figure.
The authorities declared that participation in the 2012 election reached 43
percent; most observers concur that the reality is about half that figure or
even lower. The fear of Arab Spring spillover into Algeria resulted in calls
from some political parties, from the FFS to the FLN, for increased participation. They warned that low turnout at the polls would cause chaos and
threaten the unity of the country—possibly triggering foreign intervention
such as that which occurred in neighboring Libya. In a speech on May 8,
2012, Bouteflika himself warned of such a scenario. Regardless, polls have
shown that Algerians are disillusioned with political parties whose leaders
have been co-opted and whose roles consist of rubber-stamping the president's

policies. Deputies derive considerable status and perquisites from their positions, thus precluding them from contradicting the regime's policies, because to do so would be to jeopardize their own material interests.

Civil Society

Although severely restricted, an Algerian civil society existed under French colonial rule. Countless civic, religious, sports, and even political associations animated organizational life throughout the country. However, after independence, except for sports or parents' associations, all other autonomous organizations were absorbed by the nationalist party, the FLN. Yet regardless of the repression used to muzzle dissent and the emergence of autonomous associations, independent organizations blossomed throughout the country to advance the interests of a wide variety of citizen-driven concerns (Zoubir 1999). These included cultural organizations (e.g., the Berber Cultural Movement), feminist groups (e.g., the Association of Independent Women), unions, human rights groups (e.g., the Algerian League of Human Rights), trade groups, and Islamist associations (e.g., Orientation and Reform [Al-Irshad wa'l Islah]). This development, coupled with cyclical revolts, forced the regime to pay more attention. Thus, a year before the 1988 riots, the government acknowledged the right of citizens to create nonpolitical associations around a number of issues, such as consumer defense and cultural activities (Zoubir 1995).

The emergence of a genuine civil society occurred in 1989 following the approval of a new constitution in February of that year. Literally thousands of associations sprang up, publicly expressing their opposition to such practices as the torture and imprisonment of individuals without due process of law. Other associations, whose members focused on such concerns as ecology, religion, and consumer protection, multiplied throughout the country. Women created associations to proclaim their right to full citizenship and to demand the abrogation of laws they felt were discriminatory, like the 1984 Family Code. Trade associations, such as the Association of Chief Executive Officers, the General Confederation of Algerian Economic Operators, and the Algerian Confederation of Businessmen, also emerged. Even retired military personnel created their own association. Artists, writers, and peasants also forged specific organizations to advance their interests.

Although some of the autonomous associations gave birth to political parties—as the Berber Cultural Movement and Al-Irshad wa'l Islah did to the RCD and MSP, respectively—most of them today do not necessarily have a political nature. Instead they tend to react to the various societal problems that the country has faced (unemployment, the promotion of market economics, and the advancement of the Arabic language, for instance).

The regime, however, has sought to undermine or co-opt these associations. For instance, it tries to mobilize them to support the election of the president; in return, co-opted associations receive financial support. Today, civil society lacks both the means and the opportunity to hold discussions on the revision of the constitution or other matters of national interest. In order to hold a public meeting, for instance, an association needs an authorization—which is refused in most cases, unless the nongovernmental organization or association in question is close to the government. Other serious handicaps for the close to 100,000 associations that exist are their lack of democratic experience, lack of adequate funding, and for most of them, dependence on the regime for survival.

Although there is an independent press, President Bouteflika has sought to discredit it and has shown that he will not tolerate harsh criticism of himself or his government. The authorities have used various means to intimidate journalists, including imprisoning them under the pretext of their alleged defamation of officials. Journalists also engage in self-censorship on issues that could implicate powerful members of the regime, in order to avoid trouble with the law. Algerian television, watched in practically all households, is an important political medium through which the president propagates his views and policies—unobstructed by opposition perspectives. Algerian television is virtually the voice of the government and it is no surprise that the government long opposed the creation of private television stations—something it reluctantly approved only in 2011. As a result, most Algerians turn to European—mostly French—channels, through satellite dishes.

Political Economy

In the mid-1960s the regime of President Houari Boumedienne inaugurated an ambitious economic program that gave priority to industrialization and heavy industry, while encouraging the creation of socialist, agricultural villages. The main objective of the regime was to get Algeria out of its underdevelopment as rapidly as possible. To achieve that goal, the authorities launched a widely acclaimed model of "industrializing industries," following a theory developed by French economist Gérard Destanne de Bernis. State-owned enterprises (SOEs) in sectors such as mining, hydrocarbons (oil and natural gas), banking, insurance, iron and steel, and construction materials constituted the vehicle for the industrialization effort. The state also nationalized a number of foreign assets to assert its economic independence. It established control over foreign trade and retail networks while nationalizing nearly all industries and businesses. SOEs run by Algerian executives, known as cadres, in cooperation with foreign nationals, covered most important industries. The authorities established multiyear economic plans, and the financing of capital-intensive industrialization was made possible thanks to Algeria's hydrocarbon revenues. Finally, the institution of free health care and free education allowed the regime to rule unchallenged.

Boumedienne was convinced that heavy industry would be the locomotive that would haul behind it agriculture and other light industries. The initial results in education, health, and many other areas were impressive. Industrial growth from 1970 to 1979 was higher than growth of gross domestic product (GDP) (11.7 percent compared to 6.9 percent); in the same period, industry outside the hydrocarbon sector created 15 percent of the total number of jobs in the national economy. Indeed, from 1970 to 1980, 250,000 jobs were created every year.

Unfortunately, this model of development presented many problems, due largely to its reliance on capital-intensive technologies. Industry became a predator that devoured all available resources. The other sectors, especially agriculture, were sacrificed on the altar of modern industry. Under inducement from the authorities, a great number of peasants gathered into collective farms. This socialist experiment ultimately proved disastrous, however. Other peasants left their meager lands and settled in the already overcrowded major cities or their peripheries. The agricultural sector suffered from insufficient funding and the irrational use of scarce water. In part because of failures in the agricultural sector, but also due to a demographic explosion, Algeria continues to this day to import more than $8 billion worth of foodstuffs per year.

Meanwhile, unemployment remained high, disillusioning those who had moved to the cities and their vicinity in the hopes of attaining higher living standards. Living conditions were simply miserable. The good intentions of Boumedienne notwithstanding, demographics aggravated the socioeconomic shortcomings of his chosen development strategy. Furthermore, although many planners became aware of the necessity of involving the private sector in agriculture and in light industry, for political and ideological reasons the regime failed to encourage that sector to partake in the process of development. This is not to say that a private sector did not exist; on the contrary, such a sector existed and benefited from state-determined, artificially high prices for its goods. But the private sector played a parasitic rather than a productive role in the strategy of development.

So despite initial euphoria about the "industrializing industries" projects, reliance on heavy industry did not produce the expected effects. The country failed to produce a diversified economy capable of sustaining long-lasting development. Moreover, reliance on hydrocarbon revenues to finance this ambitious development project meant that the strategy was vulnerable to fluctuations in oil prices. The authorities were inspired by economic nationalism and hoped that it would reduce their dependence on the capitalist economies. Unfortunately, fluctuations in the price of oil, the need for foreign (capital) assistance, and a lack of skilled labor—coupled with the cost of the welfare state (free education and free health care)—had dire consequences. The failure of the economic strategy and the socioeconomic problems that arose from this failure compelled the regime of Chadli Bendjedid to initiate economic reforms.

Increasing debt and failure of the authorities to sustain public investment compelled the government to introduce reforms intended to give Algeria a market-economy orientation. But the reforms were quite timid, hampered by a nationalist ideology that still disapproved of large-scale privatization of the economy, especially in sectors deemed strategic. The regime dismantled state-owned enterprises, breaking them down into smaller units—but this did not translate into their privatization. The way this pseudo-liberalization was effectuated resulted in social and political upheavals. Liberalization was also hampered by the unwillingness of the population to give up the welfare system, which had hitherto provided a respectable degree of social justice, as well as by popular perceptions of the regime as corrupt and inefficient. Rising discontent in the mid-1980s was an indication of the turmoil that was yet to come. Indeed, the decline in oil prices in 1986 and the socioeconomic crisis that ensued provided the ammunition for the riots that occurred two years later. In the aftermath of the riots, the regime had no choice but to initiate political liberalization, but it also introduced additional economic reforms.

To this end the regime called on technocrats capable of managing a transition to a market economy. However, transforming the economy was no easy task in view of Algeria's balance of payments. The country, which imported most of its needs and was also trying to finance its growth investments, was now incapable of paying the required installments on its foreign debt. The political instability of the late 1980s, aggravated in the 1990s due to the armed Islamist uprising, resulted in the near-bankruptcy of the state. In 1994 the Algerian government concluded an International Monetary Fund (IMF) agreement and a Paris Club rescheduling of $5.3 billion. A year later, the central bank rescheduled its commercially held foreign debt. Under its extended fund facility, the IMF agreed to a $1.8 billion structural reform credit for a three-year period (1995–1998).

IMF-inspired economic policies continued under the presidency of Bouteflika. By 2000, macroeconomic indicators were quite good and enticed some foreign investors outside the traditionally attractive hydrocarbon sector to explore the Algerian market. By 2005, inflation was down to 3 percent. At the same time, high oil prices helped Algeria overcome its budget deficit and contributed to the trade balance tilting in the country's favor. In 2005–2006, owing to huge hydrocarbon revenues and impressive external reserves (estimated at $80 billion at the end of 2006), Algeria made the strategic decision to repay its external debt. The government made early debt repayments of $10.5 billion, including to Paris and London Club creditors; this helped reduce Algeria's external debt-to-GDP ratio from 17 percent in 2005 to 4.5 percent in 2006. In 2012, Algeria's debt was less than $5 billion, around 2.4 percent of GDP. By way of comparison, in 1994 the total external debt was close to $30 billion, corresponding to 70 percent of the country's GDP.

The main fear, of course, is that Algeria remains a one-commodity producer and thus its economy is dependent upon the price of and demand for oil. Although this commodity may be finite, the national oil company, Sonatrach, discovered eighteen new oil sites in 2006 alone and others in 2007–2008. Given the importance of oil, it is not surprising that Algerians decided in July 2006 to reverse an April 2005 law on liberalization of the oil sector that had allowed foreign ownership up to a maximum level of 70 percent. The new law, voted in October 2006, compels Sonatrach to have the majority share (51 percent) in all contracts relating to research, exploitation, and refining. In addition, an amendment to the law passed in October imposes a tax of between 5 and 50 percent on exceptional nontaxable benefits, to be applied to partnership contracts when the price of oil surpasses $30 a barrel. This would represent additional revenue to the state of $1–2 billion a year.

At the end of 2006, Algerian authorities emphasized the need to lessen dependence on hydrocarbons. They decided to launch a debate on a new industrial strategy, to begin in 2007 (Aghrout 2008). In the meantime, in order to avoid social conflicts resulting from the liberalization process, an economic and social pact was signed in October 2006 by three actors: the government, the private sector, and the national trade union (General Union of Algerian Trade Workers [UGTA]). The rationale for this pact was that in order to give time for reforms to bear fruit and ignite the economy, an understanding among all parties needed to be reached so that the reforms were not undermined. Under the terms of this agreement, the government pledged to work toward improving workers' employment opportunities, incomes, purchasing power, and legal rights; the private sector promised to increase competitiveness and reduce corruption; and workers agreed to refrain from striking or creating "social tensions" in any industrial sector, or demanding raises—all for a four-year period.

In 2007, GDP growth remained at around 5 percent, again owing mostly to hydrocarbon exports. But growth in the nonhydrocarbon sector also progressed noticeably in 2007, reaching 11 percent, largely due to the booming construction sector. Algeria's foreign currency reserves reached $110 billion at the end of 2007 and $205 billion by mid-2012, making Algeria the country with the second-highest reserves in the Arab world (after Saudi Arabia). Because this circumstance owed primarily to hydrocarbon revenues, Prime Minister Ahmed Ouyahia declared in September 2008 that a drop in the price of a barrel of oil below $70 would prove catastrophic, especially since Algeria continues to import not only capital goods but also food products. However, the ensuing, momentary drop of oil prices to $40 a barrel did not impact the Algerian economy. The authorities remained quite worried about high levels of imports, especially of consumer products. In 2008, imports of foodstuffs amounted to over $6 billion, a 70 percent increase over foodstuff imports in 2007. This situation compelled the government to devalue the Algerian dinar to discourage imports. This was relatively successful; indeed, Algeria's food import bill amounted to $4.53 billion in the first nine months of 2009 compared to $6.15 billion during the same period in 2008. In 2012, the figure reached close to $9 billion.

Identity and Politics

Out of a population of nearly 35 million, the Berber-/Amazigh-speaking people represent about 6 million (17 percent). The Berbers are the native inhabitants of North Africa, concentrated mostly in Morocco, Algeria, and Tunisia. In Algeria, they are found primarily in the Kabylie and Aurès mountains, and in the Mzab and other Saharan oases. The most famous Berbers are Saint Augustine and today the soccer player Zineddine Zidane; the most famous Berber dish is couscous, which in the Berber language means "well-rolled," in reference to the semolina of which it is made. During the colonial era, many leaders of the nationalist movement were Amazigh. However, successive regimes have refused to recognize either the Berber language or the Berber identity—allegedly in the name of national unity. Algerian Berbers seek this recognition. They have protested both their lack of political influence and the state's disregard for their culture and identity, particularly concerning the place of the Amazigh language in Algerian politics and society.

   Amazigh militancy in Algeria has had a long tradition. In the spring of 1980, Berber militants called a general strike, first in Tizi Ouzou and then in the entire region of Greater Kabylia. In the ensuing days, the populations of surrounding Berber villages joined the protests in Tizi Ouzou, building barricades to confront the police. In response to this "Berber Spring" upheaval, the government launched a military operation to regain control of Tizi Ouzou; harsh repression was exerted against Berber students and workers. The government also blocked roads and isolated the region from the rest of the country. Many students, workers, and activists were arrested. To appease the situation going forward, the government took a number of measures and promised to support Berber culture, including through the creation of university chairs of Berber studies. These promises were not realized, however, though the status quo lasted for quite some time owing to diversionary tactics on the part of the government, which encouraged and created conflict between Islamists and Berberists.

The political liberalization launched in 1989 resulted in the mushrooming of hundreds of Berber associations focused mostly on their locality around issues such as language, village history, archaeological research, ancestral poetry, handicrafts, and music, as well as the organization of cultural festivals and galas. Their objective was to raise the consciousness of Berbers and assert their identity. But it would be erroneous to see the movement solely in its cultural dimension; Berbers have substantial political demands, as they feel discriminated against not only culturally but also politically and economically. Although many political parties include the Amazigh question in their platforms, two parties draw their primary support from the Berbers: the FFS and the RCD. The Movement for Autonomy in Kabylie (MAK), a more extremist, insignificant wing of the Berber movement that attracts few people, has called for the autonomy of or even independence for the Kabylie region.

In the decades after independence, with few exceptions, regime authorities claimed that Algerian identity rested solely on Arab-Islamic oneness. Thus they denied the multiplicity of other factors that also contributed to Algerians' identity—such as Berber, African, and Mediterranean influences. For decades, state elites did not seem to discern the obvious contradictions within their ideology. On the one hand, they held a secular, modernistic, and socialistic discourse. On the other hand, they held a political-religious discourse that rested on an ideologized Islam that they sought to impose upon society. Basing Algerian identity in large part around Islam was part of that discourse, and it undermined the regime's secular principles while encouraging the emergence of Islamist opposition forces. Perhaps not surprisingly then, Islamists mirrored regime elites in the 1980s and 1990s in that they, too, denied the Berber, African, and Mediterranean components of Algerian identity.

In more recent years the government has addressed some Berber grievances, creating, for instance, the High Commission for Amazighity in 1995, which introduced measures supporting the teaching of and training in the Berber language in Berber areas. The 1996 constitution also recognized Tamazight as one of the three constituent elements of Algerian identity in addition to its Arab and Islamic components. But Berbers felt that this was an administrative measure designed to deflect the Berbers' main demands: the recognition of Tamazight as an official language (i.e., that of official documents, speeches, correspondence, etc.) and as a national language (i.e., one that can be taught in Algerian schools). While the government eventually acceded to the second demand, it continues to reject the first one. Furthermore, many Algerians consider that the Algerian dialect of Arabic, the Berber dialects, classical Arabic, and French are *all* part of their cultural heritage and they thus resist the regime's policy of Arabization, wherein it gradually eliminated French and made Arabic the sole language of instruction in Algerian primary, secondary, and tertiary education.

In April 2001, another crisis erupted after the death of a secondary school pupil in police custody close to Tizi Ouzou. His death resulted in an important protest movement, notably among youth frustrated by difficult economic conditions. The repression of these protests resulted in a hundred deaths and led to an Amazigh revolt that spread to several parts of the country (Algiers, the Aurès region, Annaba, and Biskra). The protesters made various demands, including the recognition of Tamazight as an official language (Willis 2008). They also protested against the lack of economic opportunities in the region and growing governmental hostility. A fifteen-point platform, adopted in June 2001 by the local movement Coordination des Archs, Dairas, et Communes (CADC),[1] served as a basis for dialogue with the authorities.

Notwithstanding divisions within the CADC movement between *dialoguistes* (those willing to negotiate with the government) and *non-dialoguistes* (those opposed to dialogue), the government succeeded in holding a series of meetings with those who were willing to talk. The dialogue produced positive results, such as the recognition of Tamazight as a national language in March 2002 and the holding of partial new local elections in November 2005. The framers of the platform avoided regional particularism other than the language issue; generally, their demands related to national issues, including good governance and the democratization of political life throughout Algeria. The government's agreement to the CADC's demands helped ease tensions in the region; however, questions related to the status and mission of the CADC delegates remained unanswered. Will CADC delegates continue their action on other issues of contention, such as making Tamazight an official language? President Bouteflika has rejected this demand, arguing that recognizing two official languages is neither rational nor possible (despite the fact that numerous countries in Africa, Asia, and Europe have more than one official language).

Gender and Politics

Despite their active role in the war of liberation, even as fighters *(mujahidat),* Algerian women did not obtain the status that they anticipated in postindependence politics. Not only did traditional values weigh on that status, but also the state did relatively little to create opportunities for them. The state has encouraged the education of women, though: in 2004, 90.9 percent of girls between six and fifteen years old were educated and 65 percent of baccalaureate graduates were females. In 2007, two-thirds of university students

were women (compared to only 39.5 percent in 1991), and while in 1966
the rate of illiteracy among women was 85 percent, that figure had dropped
to 35 percent in 2002 (Dris-Aït-Hamadouche 2008). However, in spite of
this progress in the education of women, laws passed by the state reduced
their role to that of minors.

A case in point was the Family Code of 1984, which restricted the
rights of women, especially divorced women, who lost their right to the
conjugal residence regardless of whether they had custody of the children.
In addition, while men could easily initiate and obtain a divorce, women
did not enjoy that right. Women in Algeria have demanded the abrogation
of that law ever since parliament passed it. In fact, even some women's associations affiliated with Islamist parties have sought its dissolution, because they have found it to be contrary to Islam. The women's associations
that mushroomed in the post-1989 era made abrogation of the Family Code
one of their main demands. Facing pressures to democratize and in its fight
against radical Islamism, the government has endeavored to improve the
status of women of late. Specifically, in 2005, authorities revised the text of
the Family Code. Although the revised text does not meet all of the demands that women's associations have made, the new code makes polygamy more difficult, forces divorced fathers to pay pensions to their former
wives and their children, compels them to secure housing for mothers who
retain custody of their children, and confers upon the mother the status of a
parental authority, which was denied to her hitherto.

What of the economic and political realms? In terms of employment,
notwithstanding the relatively high rate of literacy among women, the labor
market remains rather discriminatory toward women. According to the 2005
Arab Human Development Report, women's activities constituted 31.6 percent of all economic activity in Algeria. The government did pass legislation
in 2005 to protect women in the workforce, ensuring that women receive
pay equal to that of men for equal levels of qualification and performance.

In politics, too, the representation of women remains limited, although
some progress has been made in recent years. Today, more than one-third of
judges are women. But women represented a mere 7.7 percent of members
of the National Popular Assembly elected in 2007 and less than 5 percent of
the Senate. In the executive branch of government, the percentage is at 7.2
percent. The Inter-Parliamentary Union had ranked Algeria 117th in the
proportion of women in parliament in 2011. This, however, changed when
the government introduced new legislation to increase women's participation in elected bodies. Thus, in the 2012 election, a record 146 women were
elected, making Algeria the first and only Arab country where women hold
more than 31.4 percent of the seats in parliament, as opposed to 7.7 percent
in the departing chamber. The Organic Law passed in November 2011 requires that 20–50 percent of the seats on party lists be reserved for women

so they cannot be excluded from the ballot. This law, resisted by some parties, came as part of a package of reforms that Bouteflika introduced following the uprisings that shook the Arab world.

In the 1990s, Westernized and secular women were the target of radical Islamists. Some leaders of the FIS argued that working women were responsible for the high rate of unemployment, while others argued that women should stay at home to raise children. Women fought very hard against Islamist extremists, organizing impressive demonstrations. However, not all Islamists are misogynistic. The MSP, especially under its previous leader, Mahfoud Nahnah (1943–2003), encouraged the participation of women in all areas of professional and societal activities—within the context of Islamic values, of course.

The Impact of International Politics

Over the course of the 1990s and 2000s, the main vector by which the international arena influenced Algerian politics was Western reactions to the cancellation of the second round of legislative elections in Algeria in early 1992. Divisions existed within European governments as well as inside the US administration as to how to deal with the Algerian political crisis (Darbouche and Zoubir 2008). The Islamists' distrustful attitude toward the West, on the one hand, and the West's skeptical perspective on the Islamists, on the other, not only resulted in mutual antipathy, but also forced many Western powers to adopt contradictory postures. In Europe, Islamism has never been a question of foreign policy, as it is in the United States, but it might well be considered a domestic issue, not only because of the presence in Europe of millions of Muslims, but also because of the prospect (at the time) of floods of new immigrants "marching" into Europe. Their democratic credentials notwithstanding, most Western countries, in varying degrees and with various reservations, were supportive of the cancellation of the electoral process in January 1992 by the Algerian military. The US government's initial reaction was one of "concern," but it did not condemn the cancellation as such. Thereafter the United States modified its declaration on Algeria in order to assert its neutrality in the conflict between the Islamists and the regime.

By 1995, the main initiative taken by France, the former colonial power that dominated policy on Algeria within the European Union (EU), consisted of urging the EU to infuse massive economic aid to Algeria, while at the same time finding a way of bringing together all the various Algerian political forces that were favorable to a democratic process. Fearful of Islamism, the EU's northern Mediterranean countries (France, Italy, and Spain) in particular expressed support for the Algerian regime by advocating macroeconomic assistance as a remedy for what was viewed as a crisis essentially emanating from socioeconomic roots. Thus the main European policies focused on rescheduling Algeria's debt through an IMF structural adjustment program and supporting the Algerian regime in its fight against *les intégristes* (radical Islamists), while at the same time advocating dialogue with those political forces outside of the regime that renounced violence.

For its part, the Algerian government promptly engaged in talks with the IMF that culminated in the "re-profiling" of Algeria's debt in April 1994, reducing its external debt-servicing ratio by about two-thirds from where it then stood—at around 95 percent of its foreign currency income. The government also engaged in macroeconomic reforms imposed by the IMF, reforms that resulted in an increase in unemployment and socioeconomic hardship (due to the elimination of subsidies on staple goods, the closing of inefficient state-owned enterprises, etc.). Indeed, both France and the EU conditioned the release of allocated financial assistance to Algeria on its conclusion of an IMF agreement. The EU went a step further by initially giving only a lukewarm reception to Algeria's request for the opening of negotiations toward an association agreement in the framework of the European Community's Euro-Mediterranean Partnership (also known as the Barcelona Process). This is an EU initiative that seeks, through diplomatic engagement and trade agreements, to increase prosperity, good governance, cultural exchange, and security in the EU-Mediterranean arena.

Although the necessity of democratization was part of the EU's discourse, European governments were careful not to allow the Algerian government to collapse. Thus they extended support to the regime while urging it to introduce economic reforms and undertake dialogue with a variety of Algerian political forces, including "moderate" Islamists. The United States also pushed for a compromise between "moderate" Islamists and the authorities. To that end, Algeria's main opposition parties—including the FIS, FLN, and FFS—met in Rome under the auspices of the small Catholic community Sant'Egidio in November 1994 and then again in January 1995. They agreed on a joint platform for peaceful political resolution of the Algerian crisis. The platform, deemed constructive by the international community—particularly the United States (Zoubir 2002)—set out a roadmap for a return to the electoral process and the renunciation of terrorist violence. But the Algerian government resisted the initiative and decided to proceed with its own policy of reforms and reconciliation. Under Bouteflika's presidency, the government launched a process of civil concord in 1999 and a law on national reconciliation in 2005 (Tlemçani 2008). Thus the pressure applied by the United States and the European Union resulted in the Algerian government's integration of moderate Islamists, who have now become part of the political system, garnering numerous seats in the parliament.

Since the events of September 11, 2001, Algeria has been co-opted into the security system that the United States launched in the Maghreb-Sahel region in order to fight the presence of armed Islamist groups who have settled there (Zoubir 2009). September 11 represented a significant event that focused US attention on the Maghreb in general and on Algeria in particular, as some perceive the latter as a pivotal state in the region. There is considerable concern among some US and European government officials that the Maghreb, and by extension the Sahel, will become an al-Qaeda recruiting area and a potential backdoor into Europe, particularly since many members of the al-Qaeda terrorist network, the so-called Arab Afghans, are of North African extraction. A number of events in the Sahel region, which borders the southern extremities of the Sahara, provided further justification for the US presence in the area. The existence of al-Qaeda in the Islamic Maghreb since 2007 also strengthened the rationale for the Pan-Sahel Initiative (PSI), launched by the US government in the aftermath of 9/11. The Trans-Sahara Counterterrorism Partnership (TSCTP), which succeeded the PSI in 2003, is made up of Algeria, Chad, Mali, Mauritania, Morocco, Niger, Nigeria, Senegal, and Tunisia. Although Muammar Qaddafi's Libya did not formally join the TSCTP, the new Libya will assuredly join up. Algeria has thus become an important partner in the global war on terrorism.

However, Algerians in general were not supportive of their country's involvement with the United States in the "war on terror" initiated under the administration of President George W. Bush. Algerians' hostility toward such cooperation stemmed from their perception of the United States as an enemy of the Muslim world due to its overwhelming support for Israel and the unjustified war in Iraq. Furthermore, many Algerians now believe that the regime's close security cooperation with the United States has been an impediment to genuine democratization, because Washington needs Algeria to combat terrorism globally and thus will not be likely to pressure the regime to pursue genuine democratic reforms. Under the administration of President Barack Obama, relations with Algeria, particularly in the military and security realms, have developed exponentially. Events in northern Mali since January 2013 have further strengthened Algeria's cooperation with the United States in the fight against AQIM and other terrorist groups, such as the Movement for Oneness and Jihad in West Africa (MOJWA), and against drug traffickers in the region. Furthermore, the United States has praised the reforms, especially with regard to participation of women in political life, that Algeria took following the Arab uprisings despite the fact that there is no evidence yet that those reforms are authentic.

Note

1. *Archs* are traditional clans or tribes; *dairas* are administrative units at the subprefectural level; and *communes* are local village councils.

10

Egypt

*Nathan J. Brown, Emad El-Din Shahin,
and Joshua Stacher*

Until eighteen days of mass protests resulted in the military
forcing Husni Mubarak to resign on February 11, 2011, Egypt was governed by an authoritarian system, dominated by a strong executive. Other
wings of the state apparatus such as the judiciary, parliament, and the bureaucracy were subservient to Egypt's president to varying degrees. While
power relationships between these moving parts were constantly being redefined and agents from these quarters possessed a limited ability to contest
each other, ultimate authority was highly centralized in the presidency. The
2011 uprising, or "revolution" as some call it, has not only produced popular mobilization and more competitive political interactions, but also allowed new actors to emerge or reemerge while some established elites have
watched their political fortunes sour.

Change in Egypt after the uprising appears to be everywhere—from
fair elections delivering an elected president from a previously banned organization to high officials of the Mubarak years, including Mubarak himself, being tried and convicted for crimes during the uprising as well as for
corruption. The pressure from the protests has produced some unimaginable
political spectacles. The demonstrations also disrupted the state apparatus
and its networks. Yet the basic institutions of the state continued to function, many with little change. Some were thrown into disarray but recov-
ered; others are changing only slowly. Autocratic displays of power continue to occur frequently since the uprising. Egypt has clearly experienced
a leadership change, an entirely new constitution, a former president jailed,
and a former prisoner now serving as president. But it is not yet certain if
there is a full change of regime or even what the shape of the regime is. It
may be some time before it is clear whether Egypt is in transition to democracy, a reconfigured authoritarianism, or some new blend.

Historical Background and Contemporary Political Structure

In 1952, a group of army officers overthrew a king whose family had governed Egypt since the beginning of the nineteenth century. When the army officers abolished the monarchy, they were not overthrowing an absolute ruler. In fact, Egypt's political evolution over the previous century and a half had left a strange mix of political arrangements. A family of Albanian origin held the monarchy and had tried to rule Egypt independently since the early 1800s even though the country was then—and continued until 1914 to be, at least in theory—a province of the Ottoman Empire. Some rulers from the family had ambitious plans to govern and develop the country, introducing new institutions such as a military, constructing railroads and digging canals, and encouraging profitable new crops in Egypt's dominant agricultural sector. But by the late 1870s the country had borrowed more to finance these plans than it could repay. This bankruptcy led to domestic criticism and even unrest. Egypt's debt holders in Europe successfully insisted that European officials be given a role overseeing Egyptian finances—a step that only brought more domestic criticism and unrest. In 1882, Great Britain occupied the country to put down an Egyptian rebellion, but it kept the ruling family and declined to break the tie with the Ottoman Empire, preferring to administer Egypt behind the scenes. During World War I, Britain finally declared a protectorate over Egypt, detaching it from the Ottoman Empire, and British officials considered absorbing Egypt more fully into their own empire at the close of the war. But another nationalist uprising convinced them that this would be too costly.

The leaders of the 1919 uprising formed a political party, the Wafd. The British tried to negotiate with the Wafd and, when those negotiations failed, simply ceded limited independence to Egypt while keeping it in Britain's sphere of influence. In 1923, one year following the British decision, the Egyptian king issued a constitution that allowed for an elected People's Assembly—a parliament that was generally dominated (when elections were fair) by Wafd leaders. As a result, from 1922 to 1952 Egypt combined democratic and monarchical features; it was legally an independent state, but the British continued to play a strong role. The resulting system led to a constant rivalry among the British, the Wafd, and the king. Politics grew even more complicated over time as new actors emerged. By the 1930s and 1940s, several new mass political movements—such as the Muslim Brotherhood (est. 1928)—joined the fray.

In 1952, a group of military officers seized power. They decided not only to depose the king but also to abolish the monarchy altogether as well as the parliament. They criticized the old system as corrupt and weak, allowing political interference by outside actors. After a brief interlude, the

military's leadership also moved against many other independent political
and social organizations, ranging from the Muslim Brotherhood to labor
unions. They established Egypt's highly centralized presidential system
with a single political party (the Arab Socialist Union). But while the new
regime was repressive, it also catered to popular needs in order to build
governing legitimacy. The new rulers did this partly on a symbolic level—
by abolishing titles and claiming to be much more egalitarian—but also on
a policy level, eventually adopting a populist state-led economic approach.

Inclusive Populism and Exclusivist Reform

The new post-1952 political system was not built all at once, and Egypt's
rulers have continued to tinker with it. The officers first put up their most
senior member, Mohammad Naguib, as president, with his junior Gamal
Abdel Nasser serving as prime minister. But they split over how extensively
to restructure Egyptian politics. Nasser's faction, which favored rule by the
officers, won in 1954. He deposed Naguib and assumed the presidency
himself in 1956. Nasser turned the executive office into an unchecked authority vis-à-vis civilian politics. He drew many of his top appointments
from the military. Oddly, though, it was the military that retained the most
autonomy from the presidency. At least until Egypt lost a disastrous war
with Israel in 1967, the military seemed to be a "state within a state."

Nasser reconvened parliament but allowed only one political party,
which remained under his control. Under the banners of nationalism and socialism, the Egyptian state came to control much of the economy. This allowed Nasser and his closest allies to sideline political and economic leaders from the pre-1952 era. It also allowed the new regime to pose as the
champion of previously unrepresented masses such as farmers and members of the lower middle class.

Nasser continued in office until his death in 1970, when Vice President
Anwar Sadat, another officer, became president. Sadat proclaimed a "corrective revolution" in May 1971 and gradually reformed Nasser's system.
Sadat claimed to be moving against those who abused Nasser's system by
developing "centers of power" in the sole political party or the security apparatus. So he allowed a few independent political parties and even tolerated (without legally recognizing) the reemergence of the Muslim Brotherhood. He moved as well to de-emphasize socialism and promote limited
economic liberalization.

Although he liberalized the system slightly, Sadat still ran Egypt from
the presidency. His corrective revolution seemed aimed as much at eliminating rivals as it was about ending authoritarianism. Sadat governed in
some ways that differed from Nasser. He marginalized many of his civilian
opponents in Nasser's single party before eventually dismantling it in favor

of party pluralism. Yet, when the multiparty experiment began, all the off-spring parties and their leaders were weak; if they became too independent he could move against them. He also founded his own ruling party that dwarfed the tiny new independent parties he allowed; Sadat utterly dominated his National Democratic Party (NDP) with his own shifting policy preferences and personality. Sadat also moved to phase out most military officers from serving in political capacities such as the cabinet. He did this through a constant reshuffling of the armed services' high brass during the 1970s. By the end of Sadat's term, the military's leadership that had played such a visible political role in Nasser's Egypt had been reduced to being a sounding board for Sadat's policy initiatives. Officers were not eliminated—Sadat turned to the air force commander, Husni Mubarak, when he selected a vice president—but their role was diminished to those who were loyal to him.

The way that Sadat reformed Egypt also led to his rolling back many of the inclusive social measures that Nasser introduced. Thus, by the end of his presidency, Sadat had many opponents inside and outside the formal political establishment. To contain the mounting dissent and criticism, the president launched periodic crackdowns even though he claimed to be less autocratic. In the midst of one of those crackdowns, a member of the violent Islamist al-Jihad movement, who also was an army officer, assassinated Sadat during a military parade in October 1981.

Vice President Husni Mubarak, whose entire career had been spent in the air force, became the new Egyptian leader. Under Mubarak, whose presidency lasted nearly thirty years, Egypt passed through cycles of political liberalization and crackdown without any fundamental changes in the system. Mubarak inherited, but did not innovate, Sadat's structural design as he sought to maintain the executive's unmatched hegemony. He seemed to do this successfully for three decades, even allowing some evolutionary changes (such as greater media diversity, though always within limits enforced by the regime). Perhaps Mubarak's biggest weakness was that he was unskilled in directly negotiating with opposition forces or meeting the demands of his population. These deficiencies ended his presidency after demonstrators overwhelmed his security forces and left him unable to stop their mobilization during the 2011 uprising.

Centralized Executive Authoritarianism

In the aftermath of the 2011 uprising, Egyptians confronted the challenge of changing a political system that had a powerful legacy of presidents with highly centralized authority. The state was the only organization in Egypt that penetrated society nationally; no social actor or political party could organize openly nationally (with the Muslim Brotherhood only a limited exception to this rule). All of the state's chains of command, communication, and implementation led to and from the president's office. The ministries and state bureaucracy were predicated on centralized autocratic logics in their operations as well. These internal hierarchies and lines of power within the state apparatus emerged intact despite the disruptions that the popular mobilization initially caused in 2011.

The state had also been supported by a series of dominant political parties, all founded by the president. The NDP operated only to serve the presidential will (leading Egyptians to joke that it was a triple lie—it was not national, not democratic, and not a party). Presidents controlled the party's membership and dictated its policies rather than being selected or constrained by it. There were some attempts in the late Mubarak period to build up the NDP so it could develop its own ideology and programs rather than simply reflect the president's edicts. Yet, given that Mubarak's son Gamal led the efforts, many saw the party's reform as an attempt to build a new power-base from which to direct a hereditary presidential succession.

There were regular elections and a parliament in Egypt, but neither diminished the authority and centrality of the presidency before Mubarak's removal. Presidential elections were held under restrictive conditions. Until 2005, Egyptians were only given the choice of voting "yes" or "no" regarding a nominee presented to them by the parliament—a body closely controlled by the incumbent president's ruling party. Mubarak yielded to pressure to allow competitive presidential elections in 2005, but only under conditions that made it hard for a viable competitor to run.

Parliamentary elections also were held regularly. Unlike under Nasser, independents and opposition parties were allowed to compete. In other words, Egypt no longer was a one-party system—on paper. But even if multiple parties were allowed, they were hampered in all kinds of legal ways. In addition, elections were overseen by the interior ministry and by election commissions that intervened to keep opposition candidates out. Independent judges were given some role in election oversight as stipulated in Egypt's constitution. For a brief period in the mid-2000s, the judiciary was able to pry the process open slightly. But then the constitution was amended in 2007 to bring independent judicial oversight back under executive control.

In short, prior to the uprising, the Egyptian political system had all the hallmarks of a constitutional and democratic political system—a parliament and a president, both elected by the people, and a judiciary able to ensure that the law is applied equitably and fairly. But in practice, a variety of devices—including skewed elections, restrictions on freedom of organization, and broad presidential appointive powers—created a system in which all lines of authority ultimately led back to the presidency. Additionally, the interior ministry's extensive security apparatus monitored and harassed opposition figures and groups in order to defend the status quo and the president's dominance. The system was not as openly authoritarian as it was in the 1960s—some opposition parties were allowed, the press was more open, and the judiciary was more independent—but there was no likelihood that political power would change hands as the result of an election. Furthermore, the notion that political officials would be held accountable to anyone other than the president and his coterie of close advisers was unthinkable.

This centralized presidential structure has changed in the wake of the uprising. Unlike 1952, when a group of officers seized control, this time the military as an institution—led by its high command, the Supreme Council of the Armed Forces (SCAF)—grasped the reins of power, eased Mubarak out, and began ruling itself. It also retired the powerful former head of Egyptian intelligence, Omar Suleiman. The SCAF, which was led during the transition by Field Marshall Hussein Tantawi, was responsible for key appointments, oversaw the cabinet, issued an interim constitutional document, and made key decisions such as the transition's sequence. The SCAF promised timetables and appropriated the language of the revolution. But the generals did not share the revolutionaries' agenda, showed some authoritarian tendencies, and could be politically clumsy as they commanded the bureaucracy during what turned out to be a contentious, unconstructive, and periodically violent transition. The SCAF's most egregious behaviors included the overreliance on military trials for civilians, virginity tests on female protesters, using force against protesters, and issuing constitutional decrees that continually changed the rules of the political game as it was being played.

But the SCAF also moved quickly on elections, which allowed the Muslim Brotherhood to benefit from Mubarak's forced departure. The popular mobilization that overthrew Mubarak had culminated in dramatic mass demonstrations in public squares throughout Egypt, most famously in Cairo's centrally located Tahrir Square. While initially standing on the sidelines, the Brotherhood joined the protests at crucial times to protect the squares from assault, such as during the infamous "battle of the camel," in which Mubarak's supporters attacked demonstrators while wielding swords and riding on horses and camels. The Muslim Brotherhood, with its deep and disciplined reach across Egypt, also was quick to negotiate with the exiting Mubarak regime as well as the incoming military leaders. Thus the Brotherhood came a bit late to the uprising, but its support was critical.

After Mubarak was overthrown, the revolutionary coalition began to unravel. In the post-Mubarak maneuvering, the Brotherhood's leaders were confusing actors, sometimes forming alliances and sometimes breaking them in a manner that spawned distrust and charges of opportunism. Yet, opportunism or not, the Brotherhood realized early on that the centralized edifice of Egyptian politics was changing and that they—perhaps more than any group—would stand to benefit the most if the SCAF miscalculated.

They also realized that the sooner Egyptians went to the polls, the better they would do. Elections became the currency by which the Brotherhood expressed itself. After years of campaigning and competing in Mubarak's rigged elections, no other group was as prepared to run professional parliamentary or presidential election campaigns. In fact, the Brotherhood's first worry was that it would appear so imposing that nobody would want to have elections. So it tried to form electoral alliances, considered running for a smaller number of seats, and stated it would not seek the presidency. During the legislative elections, which were held between November 2011 and January 2012, a Brotherhood-led alliance won 47 percent of the seats—the highest of any group. It would have likely won more had it not intentionally restrained itself.

When the Brotherhood arrived at the parliament, it found the institution's tools were limited. Its leaders could not make policy or determine who was in the cabinet. Even if they passed a law, it needed the SCAF's approval. Suspecting that the SCAF was not an honest broker, the Brotherhood's leaders decided they needed to make a stronger bid for power and reversed their decision not to run a candidate for president. Showing tactical acuity, they ran two candidates (realizing that the legal requirements for running were so stringent that their top pick might be disqualified). This was precisely what occurred, which left the Brotherhood with its second choice (termed by Egyptians the "spare tire"), Mohamed Morsi. Morsi was elected in a runoff election against former military officer and Mubarak loyalist Ahmed Shafiq. On June 24, 2012, the head of the Presidential Elections Commission announced that Morsi had won 51.7 percent of the vote.

The Brotherhood could not immediately celebrate the victory because of two surprising developments. First, the country's Supreme Constitutional Court had just ruled that the parliamentary election law had discriminated against independents and that the new parliament was therefore illegal. Second, the SCAF issued a new constitutional declaration, taking away some critical powers of the presidency as well as giving the generals legislative authority in the absence of a parliament.

For some, Morsi was now president in name only. The SCAF, the courts, and the bureaucracy seemed to be lining up to limit his authority. Yet Morsi found the Egyptian presidency still to be a powerful institution. Rather than clashing with the SCAF or occupying a hollow office, Morsi used his new position to work out a relationship with the military that was more cooperative. In order to do so, he negotiated a reshuffle of the top command, retiring Tantawi and some other senior officers and promoting those more willing to work with him. And he took back temporary legislative authority. Subsequently, Egypt seemed to be governed by an arrangement between the president and the military.

Morsi used his strengthened position to push through a new constitution. Before it had been disbanded, the parliament had selected a 100-member committee to draft a document, as the country's transition plan had provided. Because Islamists dominated the parliament, the committee had an Islamist majority and attempts to work out a compromise between Islamists and non-Islamists broke down. As the committee worked in the summer and fall of 2012, non-Islamists grew increasingly critical of the process, claiming that Islamists were shutting them out. Islamists complained in response that no compromise would be acceptable to their opponents and the fundamental problem was the opposition's failure to accept that they had lost the elections. When Morsi began to fear the courts would upend the entire process, he issued a decree that shut the courts out, causing great outrage among the opposition and a wave of popular demonstrations. The move allowed the committee to finish its work, and the draft constitution was approved in a plebiscite in December 2012. Islamists now claimed that Egypt had an established democratic order; their opponents complained that Morsi was acting like Mubarak.

But Egypt has not simply switched Mubarak for Morsi; deep societal changes make politics operate differently. First, while Egyptians under Mubarak, Sadat, and Nasser suffered at the hands of a powerful presidency, now the authority of state institutions is being contested by all kinds of formal and informal popular actions. Second, while the protesters and revolutionaries so successful in January and February 2011 may be sidelined for now, they continue to be a wild card as potential actors. If Egypt used to be characterized by centralized executive authority, it is now in the process of redefining itself. Competition continues between and among an economically powerful military, a politically savvy Islamist group, a bureaucracy that resists change, a set of patronage networks that may have survived the fall of the old NDP, and the protesters. It is unlikely that the political system will settle in the near future and unclear what shape it will take when it does.

Government and Opposition

Many Egyptians pressed to reform the centralized presidential system and its unrepresentative institutions, but their political opposition was ineffectual until the January 25 uprising. Three sorts of opposition existed before 2011: legal opposition parties, open but not legally recognized opposition movements, and underground opposition.

In the first category, legal opposition parties began under Sadat and grew in number during Mubarak's presidency, but most remained narrow shells without much popular following. This is because parties had to be approved by a politicized committee that doled out licenses very sparingly. But even parties that were allowed to form showed little ability to build grassroots bases or maintain internal party discipline. The Wafd party, for example, reemerged under Mubarak. But it was unable to mobilize a large number of supporters, and its leaders focused more attention on fighting each other for control of the barely viable party than they did on opposition politics.

The most viable opposition movement before Mubarak was overthrown, the Muslim Brotherhood, fell into the second category. Before the uprising, the Brotherhood did not legally exist—its permit to operate had been revoked early in the Nasser years and never restored. During the 1950s and 1960s the group was harshly suppressed, but it was allowed informally to rebuild itself when Sadat loosened some of the restrictions in the 1970s. While Sadat allowed the Brotherhood to reemerge—partly to serve as a counterweight to the left—the regime was more tolerant of the Brotherhood's social contributions than its political activities. Initially, the reestablished Brotherhood concentrated largely on educational, charitable, and religious work. Still, it did show some interest in politics. In the 1980s, it began running candidates for parliament either as independents or on the slates of other parties. The Brotherhood never applied for a license before the uprising, assuming that it would be refused. Indeed, at key points when the movement demonstrated real strength and ability to mobilize its base, the Mubarak government responded harshly, even trying Brotherhood leaders in military courts.

The Brotherhood was the largest and most sustained opposition movement, but there were others. In 2004, a broad coalition of opposition activists formed a group to combat Mubarak's reelection as president for a fifth term and the possible hereditary succession of his son Gamal. The Egyptian Movement for Change, often simply called Kifaya (Enough), quickly gained a reputation for crossing all red lines in its rhetoric and activities—it organized street demonstrations, mocked the president, and explored the use of new information technologies—to capture attention. But if imagination was its strong suit, organization was its Achilles heel. The movement fragmented under sustained regime pressure. Yet, some other spontaneous movements, such as April 6 and We Are All Khalid Sa'id (named after an Egyptian who had been beaten to death by the police), arose out of Kifaya. These new groups began to tackle such issues as economic inequalities and police brutality.

While Kifaya appeared, at times, almost deliberately clownish (it found humor an effective way to communicate its message), the group's legacy was to establish platforms for those who felt the formal opposition was too close to the regime or were not comfortable with the Muslim Brotherhood's religious activism. Kifaya introduced activism to many Egyptians, who often broke off to form their own groups. These various groups represented the un-included opposition. The activists would network online and in small groups away from the glare of the media's spotlight. They provided the backbone of mobilization during the uprising and helped formulate the enduring demands of the uprising—"Bread, Freedom, and Social Justice."

The labor movement falls in the same category. Labor unions were officially sponsored and, therefore, were policed by the regime. This left union leaders caught between representing their constituency and seeking to maintain the official line. The unions' often ineffectual results led to wildcat activity outside official unions. In fact, Egypt experienced its largest wave of labor activism in over five decades between 2004 and 2011. Over 1.7 million workers participated in more than 1,900 strikes between 2004 and 2008 alone. Industrial strikes and wildcat protests became routine events in large part as a response to the regime's liberalization policies. Other working-class and public-sector groups, such as tax collectors, protested by forming their own unions independent of the state's corporatist structures. Labor opposition functioned as a key node that increased the power of the uprising's mobilization.

Finally, there was an underground opposition. Salafi Islamism, an approach that insists on narrow and literal readings of original Islamic texts, grew gradually in Egypt beginning in the 1970s. Many Salafi groups are informally organized and uninterested in politics. But a minority stream has taken up interpretations of Islamic law that lead them into conflict with the state. In the 1980s and 1990s, a conservative Islamist underground movement, al-Gama'a al-Islamiyya, dominated some neighborhoods and even launched an insurgency against the state before it was routed. With the defeat of the Gama'a and similar groups, radical Salafis posed only a feeble challenge—a minority of these activists joined al-Qaeda and set their sights outside Egypt, while a majority repudiated their earlier violent activism and joined those who left politics.

In the face of this broad but shallow range of opposition groups, the state under Mubarak deployed considerable strengths. First, it had a variety of legal and constitutional tools: it prevented parties from forming, wrote restrictive laws, and forbade demonstrations. It also used carrots. The state rewarded allies and friends with access to state officials and business contracts (while it denied these perquisites to its opponents). In the late Mubarak period, some prominent Egyptian business leaders gravitated increasingly toward the National Democratic Party to achieve greater power and influence.

If these tools failed, the security establishment supported the regime by coercing its opponents. The 1.5 million–person security apparatus monitored, harassed, and even openly intervened on the state's behalf. For instance, in the parliamentary elections of 2005, security services openly prevented voters from reaching the polls in districts where the opposition was strong. Newspaper readers around the world were treated to startling photographs of helmeted security forces mobilized *against* would-be voters, shamelessly surrounding polling places. This may have led to bad publicity for Egypt, but as a senior legal official said: "It is not good to prevent people from voting, but this was a mission of state."[1] Any opposition would be hapless in the face of such tactics.

The military's role in politics had diminished since the 1952 coup, but its role as a potential political actor remained evident on the eve of the uprising. Until the election of Mohamed Morsi, all of Egypt's presidents had come from the military. At key moments (such as when large-scale rioting over economic grievances engulfed Cairo and other cities in 1977 and 1986), the military came out to impose order. It is unsurprising, then, that the army intervened when the Mubarak government and security apparatus were unable to curtail the continued mobilization after January 25, 2011, when the Egyptian uprising began. As the security forces were beaten into submission by the protesters, the NDP imploded, and Mubarak's belated concessions failed to peel away protesters from the country's squares. The military leadership tried to salvage what it could—including broad and deep economic perks—from the old regime. Yet, in the process, the SCAF was forced to abandon any support for civilian leaders from the NDP, crony capitalists, and even Mubarak and his family.

Other groups that have gained a foothold since the uprising include the Salafis, who won nearly 25 percent of the parliament before the body was disbanded in June 2012. Salafis have been divided, but their decades of social involvement and preaching have created receptivity to their ideas, and they seem poised to continue playing a role in politics. Non-Islamist groups, such as the Free Egypt Party and Egyptian Social Democratic Party, also gained parliamentary seats, but—given their 8 percent slice—they are still struggling to build bases in an open electoral arena. Other actors include the groups that comprise the old NDP. Although a court dissolved the NDP in March 2011, its members have regrouped into numerous offshoot parties such as the National Egypt Party. While these groups failed to do well during the parliamentary contests, they rallied around Morsi's competitor, Ahmed Shafiq, during the presidential runoff election. Their uncharismatic candidate garnered over 48 percent of the vote. The country utterly rejected the NDP during the uprising, but the fact that some sectors of society pine for security and the repressive predictability that the NDP afforded suggests that these old networks still are relevant.

The revolutionary activists—such as those encompassed by the April 6 and We Are All Khalid Sa'id movements—also constitute a new force on the political scene. Ironically, the activists that agitated for the drastic changes since 2011 have largely been unsuccessful in gaining meaningful representation in the state's institutions. Although they were unorganized, when they came together in protest they were able to constrain the ability of political elites to make decisions. Yet, if numbers were their strength, organizational resiliency proved to be their weakness. After the revolutionaries left the square when Mubarak resigned, some made clear that they were not interested in formal politics or running for office. For those who did run, youth and inexperience proved to be too much to overcome in parliamentary elections. Many of their parties and candidates were unsuccessful, which demonstrated that popularity and national electoral potential were different specialties. But even if they are weak organizers of political parties, their organizing skills should not be discounted. In the 2012 elections, they pushed two candidates up to third and fourth place in a closely fought race; if they failed in attempts to build their own parties, they still could rally around well-known figures in an effective manner.

The revolutionaries have also wrestled with the choice of being included or remaining outside the government's structures. Many have opted not to be included, but their exclusion comes at the cost of not being heard. For better or worse, the revolutionaries have not abandoned street politics. Protests remain frequent and the movements were able to extract unimaginable concessions from the transitional leaders. But many Egyptians seem to be tiring of protest politics. The revolutionaries' role may depend on whether this nascent constituency develops into a well-oiled political machine or remains a wild card in determining the direction of Egypt's political future.

Civil Society

Civil society in Egypt has deep origins, yet it is constantly evolving to respond to political limitations, domestic needs, and global influences. Needless to say, civil society will likely proliferate further in the wake of the 2011 uprising. According to estimates from the Ministry of Supply and Domestic Trade, Egypt had over 18,000 nongovernmental organizations (NGOs) before the overthrow of Mubarak. But this figure does not reveal the diversity within Egyptian civil society. Officially registered organizations include faith-based, charitable, professional, advocacy, and development-related organizations.

While the term *civil society* is new in Egypt, the practice of forming both formal and informal associations in response to religious doctrines and socioeconomic needs is old. Islamic and Coptic Christian charities, the Sufi orders of Islamic mystics, and the guild system for those in certain trades and professions were all active organizations that provided members of society with religious, social, and economic services. The Muslim and Coptic system of endowments *(waqf)* provided financial support to numerous activities such as building and maintaining mosques and churches, financing educational centers, running hospitals, and sustaining philanthropic activities.

Sufi orders performed social and economic functions that enhanced social solidarity and addressed the welfare of members of the community. These organizations, which are still functioning today, have been financed by alms *(zakat)* and private donations.

In the nineteenth century, a new breed of formal and modern associations joined these traditional entities. Most of these newer organizations emerged because local elites autocratically modernized the state's administrative structures. Civil society's development also was influenced by the presence of foreign minorities and the influence of European associational practices. These new entities focused on the protection and promotion of their members' professional interests. Among the first associations to be formed were the Greek Association (1827), the Egypt Association (1859), the Geographic Association (1875), the Islamic Philanthropic Association (1878), and the Coptic Charitable Efforts Association (1881). Women's and professional associations also emerged during this period.

During Egypt's liberal phase (1923–1952), modern civil society organizations operated under a permissive political environment. The 1923 constitution granted Egyptians the freedom to form civic associations and recognized the groups' legal rights. Upon notification of establishment, the state recognized such organizations as legal entities and limited its interference into the affairs and management of associations. Under such conditions, civil society flourished. Egyptians established a diversity of civic associations and societies that spread across charitable and philanthropic, professional, and unionist objectives. One of the reasons civil society organizations were given such a wide berth was because many were being drawn into the country's struggle for independence from Britain. Ironically, full independence would stunt civil society's growth.

The leaders of the 1952 revolution rolled back and disempowered Egypt's budding civil society. The officers asserted the state's hegemonic role as the main change and development agent in society. Embracing a socialist ideology and a statist economic orientation, the 1952 regime autocratically sought to establish control over all sectors of society. After the initial crackdown during the 1950s and early 1960s, Nasser's regime then legalized its repression. Law 32 of 1964, the Associations Law, placed severe restrictions on the formation, activities, and freedoms of civil society groups. The law granted the executive branch full control over the licensing of new civic associations. The law also allowed the state to define their activities and close groups down if it deemed necessary. The number of NGOs dropped sharply and many were folded into state institutions. State control over NGOs, which lasted for almost five decades, weakened the traditions of private initiative and the further development of civil society. Yet authoritarian rulers were less successful in asserting their control over older forms of charity and endowments. Charitable and faith-based associations

(Muslim and Coptic) continued to provide apolitical services to the needy segments of society.

While they were all authoritarian, the presidencies of Nasser, Sadat, and Mubarak showed some differences in their treatment of civil society. The Nasser years were the most restrictive. Wishing to attract foreign investment and preferring that his opponents organize openly rather than underground, Sadat, in a reversal of Nasser's authoritarian and socialist approach, started a policy of opening that gradually pluralized Egypt's political and economic structures. This transformation revived civil society and associational life. Law 32/1964 from Nasser's day remained on the books, but the state allowed new associations to form and many, such as those for lawyers and doctors, began to assume political roles. As the Islamist trend grew in the 1980s, many members of the Muslim Brotherhood were able to win seats on the boards of the country's professional syndicates. The syndicates became political because they were platforms from which the Brotherhood provided various types of social, medical, and professional services to their members. In the 1990s, the Brotherhood gained elected control of the associations for doctors, engineers, pharmacists, and lawyers. Each new set of government restrictions produced a response by these groups. Many of the syndicates and other civil society groups pushed for reform and articulated specific political demands for ending the state of emergency, granting the freedom of assembly, and holding cleaner, fairer, more transparent elections. They also opposed some of the state's foreign policies, particularly its positions vis-à-vis the Palestinian intifada, the Gulf War, and relations with Israel.

As the initial economic liberalization of the Sadat years ran out of steam, the Mubarak regime adopted a more aggressive neoliberal economic policy that forced the state to retreat from providing certain social and economic services. This allowed development-related and advocacy associations to thrive. Economic crisis also facilitated the growth of Islamist associations because they addressed the needs of those harmed by economic liberalization and fought for the meaningful promotion of individual, political, and public rights. Consequently, civil society witnessed an expansion all the while operating under the state's watchful eyes. In 1999, the number of NGOs increased to 16,000, compared to 7,593 in 1986 (Kandil 2006: 47). Though a quarter of these associations maintained a traditional role of providing charity and direct assistance, many also focused on such issues as poverty alleviation, unemployment, women's empowerment, street children, microeconomic projects, training, and development. Several advocacy associations were formed—many as nonprofit organizations in order to avoid restrictive association laws—to promote human rights, civic culture, and education. In addition, the number of business associations increased substantially, from twenty-one in the 1980s to sixty-four in 2008 (UNDP 2008: 65).

In the 2000s, domestic and external pressures for political reform resulted in other promising trends. Civil society associations in Egypt increased their engagement, dynamism, and experience. Many advocacy organizations focused on democracy education, promoting civic culture, political rights, and citizenship. During the 2005, 2010, and 2011 parliamentary elections, a concerted network of human rights and advocacy associations played an effective monitoring role. There was also a growing tendency at the domestic and international levels to engage civil society organizations in development programs. External donors have focused on empowering development as well as advocacy and women's organizations, which has contributed to growth in these areas.

Despite these gains, and even after the fall of Mubarak, distrust still shapes the relationship between the Egyptian state and the organizations of civil society. Under Mubarak, a new NGO law was finally passed, but it was far more restrictive than activists wanted. They therefore looked to the post-Mubarak era with great hope. Despite tolerating civil society's charitable and development-related associations, during the transition the state continued to view certain types of organizations, particularly human rights and advocacy groups—and even some women's groups—with suspicion. It portrays them as pawns advancing foreign agendas and influences within the country, thus characterizing them as threats to national security and political stability. Civil society organizations, on the other hand, are critical of the state's eclectic policy for dealing with civil society and of the security apparatus's use of repression against them. Possibly worried about losing its grip over civil society, the state continues to use legal constraints and security measures to curb the potential and healthy growth of such groups.

The current law for NGOs (Law 84 of 2002) still grants the executive branch control over civil society associations. Charitable organizations and advocacy organizations fall under the control of the Ministry of Social Affairs while unions are under the Ministry of Labor. When the first postrevolution parliament met in January 2012, one of the first issues it addressed was the restrictive law for NGOs, but the parliament was dissolved before it could pass its more liberal version.

Civil society organizations that emerge in the shadow of an autocratic state's restrictions tend to face serious internal challenges, as Egypt's experience has shown. The vast majority of civil society organizations are organized around a leading energetic personality and therefore are not truly membership based. This creates a serious problem for them at the grassroots level, as well as with regard to their financial capacities, as the most prominent ones rely on foreign funding as their main source of revenue. Many, particularly advocacy and women's groups, are not in tune with the country's prevailing cultural norms—particularly in the countryside—and, thus, are alienated from the environment in which they operate. Their financial reliance on external donors makes them vulnerable to their critics' accusations that they are tools for implementing foreign-driven agendas. Finally, many civil society organizations lack internal democratic practices and operate according to elitist and autocratic styles of management.

Despite these shortcomings and the existing legal constraints, the future of civil society in Egypt remains bright—particularly following the 2011 uprising. Civil society organizations in Egypt are increasing in number and are becoming more diverse and more specialized, covering a wide spectrum of areas. They have been emboldened by the domestic environment and are extending the boundaries of what is politically acceptable. As the uprising has shown, there is a limit to how much the government can police society. While formal organizations can be licensed, banned, regulated, audited, and monitored, Egyptian society is rich in social ties that are more difficult to manage, including family and neighborhood connections, as well as friendships and factory relationships. These give Egyptians the ability to act in ways that are spontaneous and loosely organized but still striking—as the January 25 revolutionaries, the labor movement, and the emergence of neighborhood popular committees have shown. Nasser, Sadat, and Mubarak were very effective at preventing organized political forces from connecting to these less formal movements. However, this did not eliminate political, economic, and social resistance to how they governed. Rather, it shifted the way in which people challenged the state from organized formal politics to spontaneous protest. As is well known now, this proved to be Mubarak's undoing. One of the most exciting arenas to watch in the coming years will be how Egypt's diverse and rich civil society will morph and transform under a state led by a freely elected president. While elites continue to initiate plans and programs, for certain, the population will respond.

Political Economy

In Egypt, political considerations have always dictated economic decision-making. This was the case under Nasser, Sadat, and Mubarak, and also under the SCAF during the transitional phase to civilian rule. Since the presidency of Sadat in the 1970s, Egypt's rulers have claimed to be gradually transforming from a socialist, state-controlled system to a market-based one. But progress has been slow and the 2011 uprising has brought the approach into question. Meanwhile, the uprising and the associated political instability led to short-term economic decline. For Egypt's new leaders, the stakes of producing equitable growth, jobs, and development could not be higher.

Throughout the first half of the twentieth century, Egypt's economy was primarily agrarian, with cotton as its main cash crop. Cotton production accounted for 90 percent of the country's exports in 1914. The British deliberately stalled Egypt's industrialization with a policy that aimed at keeping its market open for British goods while the colony fed its need for raw materials. This policy benefited a handful of Egyptian landed aristocrats, who preferred to acquire more agricultural lands, rather than reinvest their capital in other domestic sectors. The royal family, for example, owned one-tenth of the country's agricultural land and had no interest in redistributing any land. The wealth gap between the landed aristocracy and the peasantry was huge. The latter suffered from endemic poverty, diseases, and malnutrition, and the majority of the population was poor. Foreign minorities and residents also played a contributing role with strong holdings in certain sectors of the economy (banks, trading companies, hotels, and some manufacturing companies) during this period.

From the 1920s to the 1950s, local elites adopted an import substitution strategy that aimed to increase Egyptian control over the national economy. As nationalist sentiments rose in the 1920s and 1930s, industrialization became a flash point in the struggle against the British for independence. Several Egyptian industries and conglomerates emerged. The most noted of these was Bank Misr, which established several viable enterprises and industrial companies. The success of Bank Misr encouraged other Egyptian capitalists to invest in industry, including textiles, glass, transportation, food processing, building materials, and insurance. The state reformed tariffs in 1930 to impose additional duty on imported goods, which proved to support its emerging industries. However, by the early 1950s, the industrial sector's contribution to the economy still failed to exceed 10 percent, foreigners remained dominant, and the majority of Egyptians continued to suffer from poor living conditions. Some reform-minded leaders pursued projects to redress these conditions (such as imposing rent controls in urban areas and abolishing tuition in state universities), but more comprehensive changes would have encroached on the interests of Egypt's wealthy political elite.

The officers who seized power in 1952 were less beholden to this elite, however. Though they did not possess a coherent ideological vision, the officers declared their intention to eradicate feudalism and foreign capitalist domination before establishing social equality. As time wore on, Egypt's new rulers proclaimed that they were fully socialist and would build a state-planned economy that would achieve self-sufficiency and social justice. From 1952 until 1974, Egypt adopted an inward, state-led strategy of economic growth. The regime embarked on a policy of nationalization of major economic enterprises. These included the Suez Canal, the banking system, as well as hundreds of industrial, insurance, and commercial companies. Nasser also conducted a series of land reforms, where the state confiscated much of Egypt's agricultural land and redistributed it in small chunks to poor peasants.

   The regime deepened the pre-1952 import substitution policy by implementing central planning, five-year plans, and heavy industrialization at the expense of agricultural development, light industries, or efficiency. It erected a massive public sector to run state-owned enterprises and an expansive bureaucracy to deliver the objectives of the five-year plans. Under this system, the private sector was discouraged from contributing substantially to the economy. This calculation was primarily based on a political, rather than economic, logic. The regime distrusted the private sector and portrayed it as exploitative big business. By controlling the economy, the state could influence political loyalty as well as control dissent.

   Pursing a command economy, however, produced numerous negative consequences. The import substitution strategy drained much of the country's resources and led domestic manufacturers to produce commodities that were not of competitive quality. Therefore, Egypt could not export its products. The public sector was inefficient and became responsible for rampant corruption, mismanagement, and waste. Consequently, private and foreign investors were reluctant to invest their capital in Egypt. Difficulties in exporting and the lack of investment produced a capital accumulation crisis. The lack of cash forced state elites to borrow in order to finance the five-year plans. Later, they sought further loans to make good on their promises and meet the population's basic needs. Though these policies benefited large segments of society, social equality did not result, as a new state business class emerged and controlled the country. By the early 1970s, Egypt suffered from shortages in foreign currency, food, and housing. The economy was not growing fast enough.

   Sadat was forced to adopt a new economic strategy. While he did not want to reverse everything that Nasser had done, Sadat wanted to attract foreign investment, reduce the growing burden of welfare expenditures, and allow the private sector more room. The new economic strategy, called *infitah,* began in 1974 and aimed to liberalize the economy through structural reforms. Sadat enacted laws that encouraged private and foreign investment, allowed for joint ventures of domestic and foreign capital, as well as established free areas for trade, industry, and finance.

   While the policy was unleashed to much fanfare, *infitah* failed to immediately address the economy's core problems. The liberal policies attracted limited investments from some oil-rich Gulf states, but failed to attract investment interest from the United States, Europe, or Japan. Egyptians developed an increased perception of inequality and hardship. They resisted the reforms and criticized Sadat for selling off the country's assets to foreigners. Workers and farmers also complained that they were being marginalized. Because of the criticism, the implementation of these reforms became piecemeal. Nevertheless, Sadat pressed on until the food riots of 1977 undermined any commitment to drastic change. The so-called Bread

Riots, which were one of the first International Monetary Fund (IMF) revolts anywhere, broke out following the government's decision to remove subsidies on several basic commodities. The army suppressed the revolt, but the population had demonstrated its deep dissatisfaction with the state's new economic orientation. Sadat reconsidered the pace of the reforms and, thus, made little progress before he was assassinated in 1981.

As a consequence of the sporadic and half-hearted pursuit of reform, Egypt's economy became trapped in an economic wasteland. It was neither socialist nor liberal. The country increasingly suffered from several gaps: between domestic savings and investments, between imports and exports, and between government revenues and spending. Meanwhile, the state continued to prop up its huge and inefficient bureaucracy. The economy continued to survive on borrowing from abroad and foreign grants. Given that political loyalty to the regime was the major prerequisite for being allowed to conduct business, the capitalist class that emerged lacked an entrepreneurial spirit. Egypt's new *infitah* capitalists were influential and visible but mostly consumed with obtaining favorable contracts from the government rather than building productive enterprises. This led the population to complain, dubbing them "fat cats" or "hit-and-run businessmen," as the newly rich flaunted their wealth. The capacity for domestic production, export, and efficient taxation remained limited. As a result of persistent revenue shortages, the state could not afford to invest in upgrading the country's deterio rating infrastructure. The economy was clearly in shambles.

Peace with Israel became a way out of Egypt's economic morass. As a reward for signing a peace treaty with Israel in 1979, Egypt became and remains the second-largest recipient of aid from the United States. Though total amounts have declined in recent years, the United States provides an annual package of around $1.3 billion in military aid and $815 million in economic aid. After more than three decades, Egypt has received a total of over $60 billion from the United States, which has been allocated mostly to military assistance. A smaller portion has funded development and infrastructural programs, health and education initiatives, and recently good governance and democracy promotion. Despite the foreign aid inputs, the country remained mired in deep financial trouble by the end of the 1980s.

As economic policies continued to be only halfheartedly implemented, international pressure mounted on Egypt to embark on a far more serious liberalization program. Finally, in 1991, Egypt traded forgiveness on about half of its international debts for an IMF agreement to stabilize and restructure its economy. The reforms focused on adopting sound macroeconomic policies, including measures to reduce government spending, eliminate subsidies on consumer goods, and allow market forces to determine prices. The reforms also would liberalize import policies, revise labor laws, and privatize state-owned enterprises. In the first half of the 1990s, hopes for a complete recovery and even a takeoff arose. In 1996, Mubarak pledged that Egypt would become a "Tiger on the Nile" (Golia 2007: 40–42). But growth then stalled. The obstacles were all too familiar: serious economic reform not only would alienate key groups at the regime's apex but also potentially expose those at the bottom to even greater poverty. The Egyptian government promised more economic liberalization but lacked the will to pursue it. By 2003, the economy grew by only 3 percent, much lower than the rate of inflation (21.7 percent in 2004), and only slightly higher than the rate of population growth (1.9 percent in 2004) (Economist Intelligence Unit 2007: 17). The more things had changed, the more they had stayed the same.

Beginning in 2004, a younger group of politicians led by the president's son Gamal began to set Egypt's economy on a new path that improved the country's macroeconomic indicators. The new government of Prime Minister Ahmad Nazif introduced a series of measures that gave a strong boost to the economy. It reformed customs tariffs, reduced personal and corporate taxes, and rationalized the distribution of subsidies. Nazif's government reduced government spending and sped up the process of privatizing the public sector. Growth rates increased from 4 percent in 2004 to 7.1 percent in 2008; exports jumped from $7 billion in 2001 to $34.5 billion in 2008 (Economist Intelligence Unit 2008: 8); and the budget deficit decreased from 9.6 percent of GDP in 2004–2005 to 8.2 percent in 2006–2007 (Alissa 2007: 11). Egypt attracted $11 billion in direct foreign investment (a huge increase from $400 million in 2004) and the country's exports grew by 20 percent. The economy was growing steadily and showed signs of a sustained recovery. During this period natural gas exports, increased revenues from the Suez Canal, the one-time sale of state-owned enterprises, increased inflow of remittances, and a booming real estate sector drove the growth.

Despite these improvements, Egypt faced serious structural challenges that prevented it from achieving sustained economic growth. The country's leadership failed to build a healthy and attractive business environment. Despite the issuance of new laws, problems of transparency, consistency, and implementation remained. Legal codes continued to be extremely complicated and courts were slow when deciding cases. All of this tended to make investors feel insecure. In addition, rampant corruption and bureaucratic red tape remained. Egypt ranked 98th out of 178 countries on Transparency International's Corruption Perceptions Index for 2010. The economy never diversified its industrial base so as to be able to sustain manufacturing exports. It also suffered from soaring inflation, which reached 17.1 percent in 2008, and high unemployment, which reached 20 percent at the end of 2006 according to government estimates. The Mubarak regime needed to provide 600,000 new jobs each year to employ new entrants to the job market, which proved to be too tough a challenge to meet. Egypt also continues to confront the major challenges of a collapsing educational system and a workforce that is lacking in competitive skills. Unsurprisingly, unemployment among university graduates remains high, averaging around 40 percent for males and 50 percent for females (Economist Intelligence Unit 2007: 32). Public debt, which soared to 100 percent of GDP in 2007, and a trade deficit that amounted to $60.8 billion in imports compared to $34.5 billion in exports in 2008, also plagued the economy's fundamental structures (Economist Intelligence Unit 2008: 8).

In the meantime, the economic reform process rewarded some and punished others. Certain business people, who were loyalist cronies of the regime, were the main winners. These individuals, such as steel-magnate Ahmed Ezz, were closely associated with the ruling party and generated wealth from privatization, business monopolies, and financial privileges (bank loans, real estate, and tax exemptions). Yet reform hurt workers, the poor, the middle class, and people in rural areas. The process put many Egyptians out of work and resulted in skyrocketing prices that crushed the majority of the population. Statistically the Egyptian economy was doing well in the late Mubarak period, but clearly the majority of Egyptians were not. Poverty rates actually *increased* between 2005 and 2009 (and over 40 percent of the population were reported to be under the poverty line). Income disparities and differences in lifestyle became huge and alarming during the Nazif government's tenure. In parallel to the strong macroeconomic indicators, the same period also witnessed recurring strikes by workers in protest of stagnant wages and government ambivalence about their increasing hardships. By late 2010, many columnists in Egypt had warned the political and economic elites that the situation was similar to conditions in the pre–1952 revolution period. Thus, it is unsurprising that the 2011 uprising prominently included economic demands for food and social justice.

Many of these fiscal challenges grew worse during the transition under SCAF, which seemed utterly ignorant about managing the national economy. The uprising had a profoundly negative effect on national growth. According to Egypt's central bank, Egypt saw $6.4 billion of foreign direct investment (FDI) inputs in 2010, but that fell to $482.7 million in 2011. Despite recording a $1.3 billion surplus in 2010, Egypt ran an $18.3 billion deficit in 2011 (Shahine 2012a). This would have been bad enough, but the state also leaned on its foreign reserves, which dipped from $35.5 billion in November 2010 to $15 billion by the end of January 2012. Some, such as analysts at the Cairo-based investment bank CI Capital, suggested that growth was as low as 0.8 percent during 2011. Tourism, which is one of Egypt's main revenue earners, shrank by 10.4 percent. Manufacturing contracted by 3.3 percent and construction decreased by 2.8 percent (Shahine 2012b).

None of these indicators, much less the inherited and existing structural poverty endemic to the Egyptian economy, are hopeful signs for President

Morsi, who in many respects faces the same economic challenges that
Mubarak faced. How Morsi handles the economy will greatly impact
whether he becomes Egypt's first-ever one-term president. He has promised
improved economic performance, but it is not clear how much room for
maneuvering he has. In many respects, Egypt's new president is a prisoner
to the economic cage he inherited. For instance, Egypt's military has mo-
nopolistic stakes within some economic sectors that it will be reluctant to
share or surrender. It remains unclear how far Egypt's leaders will proceed
with economic liberalization or how much they will be able to spread its
promised benefits to what remains a poor society. Egypt has always suffered from acute economic crisis caused by mismanagement, increasing
population pressure, collapsing educational and health systems, and corruption. The 2011 uprising did not sweep these problems away. Nor have previous periods of economic reform delivered liberalization's purported benefits to a majority of Egyptians.

Religion and Politics:
Official and Unofficial Roles for Islam

The 2011 revolution was motivated by many concerns, but religion was not
prominent among them. Still, the more permissive social and political environment of the revolution's aftermath encouraged various religious groups
to become more involved in politics. Most prominent, of course, was the
Muslim Brotherhood, which was finally able to secure a measure of legal
recognition (not for the main organization itself, but for a political party it
founded, the Freedom and Justice Party). Members of Salafi movements,
who focus on studying foundational Islamic texts in an effort to find the
correct practices to follow in their daily lives, had established an extensive
social presence during the Mubarak years but found the political realm un-
promising. After the revolution, they quickly concluded that political activity (such as forming political parties and running for parliament) was open.
    The result was that the relationship between religion and politics be-
came a central issue in Egyptian public life. The main lines of debate, however, were not between religious movements and secularists (who wish to
separate religions and politics). Most Egyptians accept that religious values
should play a role in public life. Indeed, few would accept the "secular"
label—those opposed to Islamists have begun to call themselves "civil" instead, to make clear that they do not want to evict religion from politics.
The real lines of debate are about how much religion and politics should interact, in what ways, who has the authority to interpret religious values, and
what the place of non-Muslims should be.
    At the official level, Egypt makes no pretense of being a secular state.
The 1971 constitution proclaimed that "the principles of the Islamic sharia

are the primary source of legislation." When the country received an interim "constitutional declaration" in 2011, the phrase "Islam is the religion of state" was retained. When it came time to write the 2012 constitution, opposition to the clause had grown very weak. The drafting committee actually seemed to strengthen the clause as part of a complex bargaining process in which Islamists argued for stronger language and their opponents sought to craft language that would prevent the clause from being used for a wholesale Islamization of Egypt's laws. In the end, complicated provisions were added that seemed to offer the Islamists a stronger hand though their precise effect remained unclear.

The official role for religion is expressed in a number of ways. First, "personal status law"—which governs areas such as marriage, divorce, and inheritance—is determined by one's religious community. Muslims are governed by a law that is derived from Islamic sources; Christians are governed by one that is based on the teachings of the Egyptian Coptic Church. Other areas of law—everything from employment to theft—are not directly Islamic in origin; Egypt converted to a French-style civil law system in the nineteenth century. But parliaments have sometimes tried to draw on Islamic sources in writing laws and there has been pressure in recent decades to live up to the constitution's promise to draw on sharia principles. Such pressure has yet to have much effect on the content of Egyptian laws, however.

Second, there is a religious establishment supported by the state. The chief center of Islamic learning in the country—and one of the most important in the Muslim world—is Al-Azhar, a public mosque-university complex that dates back over a thousand years. Al-Azhar often tries to assert its role as the authoritative voice of Egyptian Islam, a role that was given firm legal grounding in the 2012 constitution. Another institution is Dar al-Ifta', a bureaucracy that was established in the nineteenth century to give guidance to Egyptian rulers on Islamic legal questions. It regularly responds to requests from government officials and private Egyptians on sharia. In addition, the Ministry of Religious Endowments oversees trusts and foundations, especially those with a religious orientation.

Third, the Egyptian state promotes Islam in public life. Religion is a mandatory subject for Egyptian school students, with Muslim students learning an official version of Islam and Christian students attending separate classes on their religion. State-run media also carry some religious programming.

How does this heavy dose of Islam affect those Egyptians (approximately one in every ten) who are not Muslim? Egyptian Copts pride themselves as constituting one of the oldest Christian communities in the world; they also note that the words *Copt* and *Egypt* have the same etymology. But while Egyptian Christians often complain of marginalization, few call for the complete separation of religion and state. There is no doubt that Islam takes primary place in Egyptian public life, and many Copts complain of discrimination in some fields. But the existing system also allows them some autonomy in their own affairs, as it allows Copts to be governed by their own personal status law. Thus the Coptic religious establishment presses not to abolish any official role for religion but instead for more favorable terms.

It is not only Christians who have doubts about the current state of religion in public life. The relationship between religion and state can seem to lead to the state dominating religion rather than the other way around. Official religious institutions, like Dar al-Ifta', are sometimes accused of being too willing to sanction whatever the regime wishes. From the perspective of Egyptian society, there are a variety of sources of religious knowledge and practice outside the state. Religion-based organizations (such as brotherhoods of Sufis or Islamic mystics) have always existed. In the 1920s and 1930s, a new kind of social organization arose: an Islamic society. These societies tended to be led not by religious scholars but by educated professionals who wished to encourage the spread of religious values. They focused on a wide variety of activities: education, community projects, charity, and self-improvement.

The most successful of these new societies, the Muslim Brotherhood, was founded by Hassan al-Banna, a provincial schoolteacher, in 1928. Al-Banna devised an ideological and religious message that proved very appealing to younger and newly educated Egyptians, focusing on righteous personal conduct, social consciousness, charitable work, and education. He also devised an organizational model that proved extremely effective (not only in Egypt but also in other countries where the Brotherhood example was copied): members formed small cells or groups in which they supported and educated each other, so that Brotherhood activists quickly formed not merely a society but also a set of tight personal bonds. And because the Brotherhood's goals were very general, its organizational structure could take many forms—charitable society, mass movement, self-help group, educational apparatus. This allowed the Brotherhood to transform itself: what began as one of many smaller Islamic societies became Egypt's most sustained mass movement.

The movement grew so quickly that by the 1940s it was a major presence in Egyptian society. Initially it only dabbled in politics, focusing instead on education and charitable work. But it became increasingly powerful, and ultimately clashed with a series of Egyptian governments—with the result that its license was revoked, depriving it of legal status. The movement repaid repression in kind. It had established a paramilitary organization initially to fight the British (who still played a role in Egyptian politics during this period) and to support Palestinians in their brewing conflict with Zionism. But in the late 1940s, the conflict with the government turned deadly: the Brotherhood was charged with assassinating a prime minister and al-Banna was himself assassinated, presumably by Egyptian security forces.

When the new regime came to power in 1952, the Brotherhood reacted with hopefulness, especially since many of Egypt's new rulers had been Brotherhood members (including Anwar Sadat). But the new regime proved unwilling to tolerate any independent social or political movements. After one of its members was accused of attempting to assassinate President Nasser (a charge that movement leaders denied), the Brotherhood was exposed to a prolonged wave of harsh repression. Its activists suffered greatly: some were arrested and tried in special courts, with many tortured and a few executed; others were driven into exile. Not until the 1970s was the Brotherhood allowed to reemerge openly (though it remains without a legal permit to this day).

Beginning in the 1970s, a wave of religiosity swept parts of Egyptian society—especially provincial towns and college campuses. New grassroots movements arose that worked for diverse causes. Some were directly political, demanding Egypt be ruled in accordance with Islamic law. Others were oriented toward social service or enhancing religious observance. Still others retreated from society, convinced that the best way to be a good Muslim in Egypt was to build a small community of pious people, far from the corrupting pressures of the broader society. The Muslim Brotherhood was able to draw some of the new generation of activists into its own ranks, rejuvenating the organization. Others were attracted to more revolutionary groups, one of which assassinated President Sadat. The most radical of the groups eventually concluded that the Egyptian government was not the best target and that it was instead necessary to attack the United States and Europe, since they were the ultimate supporters of the current un-Islamic world order in general and the Egyptian government specifically. It was such groups—the radical fringe of the Islamist movement—that helped form al-Qaeda in the 1990s.

But the bulk of Egypt's Islamist movements did not gravitate in such a radical direction. In fact, the growing interest in religion in Egyptian society took many different forms—from popular religious broadcasters on television, to small local groups of pious Egyptians who met to study or pursue charitable projects, to circles who gathered around official and, increasingly, unofficial teachers and preachers. A particularly notable trend was the Salafi movement, composed of Muslims who gathered around leading teachers to try to understand fundamental Islamic teachings—Salafi Muslims hold that Islamic teachings can inform all aspects of life but original sources (such as the Quran) have to be studied intently because so many misinterpretations and misreadings have crept in over the years. The broad interest in religion has spread to many levels of society—from wealthy Egyptians who donate to charity, to professionals who follow American-style

televangelist Muslim preachers, to residents of working-class neighborhoods who seek to study religious texts and serve as models of exemplary
Islamic behavior.

By the first decade of the twenty-first century, Egyptian religiosity was
as likely to take the form of piety as of political activism. Most of the radical groups either had been suppressed or had abandoned political violence.
What remained was the Muslim Brotherhood—an organization dedicated to
increasing the role for Islam in society but also promising to use only
peaceful methods. But as the Brotherhood rose to prominence, the Mubarak
regime was increasingly inclined to treat it as merely a softer face of the
more radical forms of Islamist movements; it took harsh measures (such as
arrests and military trials) against the Brotherhood's leadership, though it
stopped short of moving against the movement in a systematic way. For its
part, the Brotherhood sharply criticized the regime but shied away from full
confrontation. It was perhaps that caution that allowed the movement to
survive the Mubarak years, emerging quickly after the uprising to play a
role in governing Egypt for the first time in its history.

Identity and Politics

When a wave of uprisings hit Arab societies in 2011, some (such as Bahrain
and Syria) showed very strong signs of sectarianism, and tension mounted
among various social groups. While Egyptian politics was often chaotic
after 2011, it did not follow a similar pattern. Some Muslim-Christian tension existed (occasionally expressing itself in violent forms), but by regional standards Egypt seemed relatively harmonious. Indeed, Egyptian
politics has long stood out in the Middle East for its low level of ethnic and
sectarian conflict. Egyptians themselves seem unsurprised at this: they will
often describe their nation as homogeneous, and many bristle at the idea
that there are any "minorities" in the country—even those groups who differ in some way from the majority lay claim to being fully Egyptian and
often resent the "minority" label.

This protestation does have some basis—ethnic and sectarian differences do tend to be less pronounced in Egypt than in many neighboring
countries. Just as notable, however, is the way in which the differences that
do exist have not become politicized; where Egyptians do differ, they do
not always bring these differences into the political realm. In short, the
weakness of ethnic and sectarian conflict in Egypt needs to be explained. It
is not inevitable and in fact some divisions have become politically significant. A century ago, native Egyptians and those with foreign citizenship
formed different (and not always mutually respectful) political identities; at
the present time there seems to be a significant rise in resentment by Egypt's

small bedouin minority as well as the risk of greater Muslim-Christian tension. Why do these identities become politically relevant, and why do they sometimes remain latent?

From an ethnic and linguistic perspective, Egypt is fairly homogeneous. In earlier times, significant ethnic minorities were found especially in Egypt's most cosmopolitan cities (Alexandria and Cairo). Substantial Greek, Italian, and Jewish communities not only prospered but did so often while being exempt from Egyptian laws (under a system known as the "capitulations," the Egyptian government was forced to allow foreign citizens to be governed by the laws of their home countries). Smaller communities of Armenians, Lebanese, and others enjoyed similar status.

The existence of small communities of economically and legally privileged foreigners sparked resentment from Egyptian nationalists. Political leaders used the continuation of this system as a barometer of the country's sovereignty. The communities themselves often regarded the ethnically Egyptian population condescendingly. Some communities, for instance, not only preserved their own language but also taught their children French or Italian—which they deemed more sophisticated than Arabic. Egypt's path toward independence threatened these communities. In 1937 the Egyptian government negotiated an end to the capitulations and the post-1952 regime nationalized the property of most foreigners. As a result, only remnants of these communities remain in Egypt today.

There are also regional differences in Egypt, though these have generally been fairly muted in comparative terms. Those from provinces south of Cairo speak a slightly different dialect of Arabic and sometimes find themselves the butt of jokes, but few have complained of political exclusion or marginalization. Those in outlying areas—especially the Sinai Peninsula and, to a lesser extent, Nubia in the extreme south—have had more serious complaints.

In the Sinai and other desert regions, much of the population regards itself as bedouin and the Egyptian government as alien, which has led to tension in recent years. This is connected not merely to culture but also to security and terrorism, as a series of bombings in the Sinai Peninsula from 2004 to 2006 (and the strong suspicion that these were perpetrated by affiliates of al-Qaeda) led to a continuing series of intrusive security measures. Sinai also borders the Gaza Strip, a territory of deep concern to Egypt under Mubarak after it came under the control of the Palestinian Islamist group Hamas in 2007. Because at that time the Egyptian regime was dedicated to containing and repressing its own Islamist movements, tight security measures were imposed in Sinai. This led the population of the peninsula to feel closely scrutinized—and some residents of the area made clear that they regard the government in Cairo as aloof and unresponsive.

But if ethnic and regional differences are only occasionally politically salient, religious differences have sometimes led to two sorts of problems.

The first is related to the system in which Egyptians are governed according to religious community in matters of personal status. Those who are not members of accepted religious communities—such as Bahais (a group formed from an offshoot of Islam) or other unorthodox groups—simply do not fit in. Shi'i Muslims—a small group in Egypt—are often the target of suspicion as well. Some Christians have felt that the system encourages members of their community in troubled marriages to convert to Islam only to obtain a divorce (divorce is extremely difficult for Egyptian Christians but far easier for Muslims). While these problems often cause legal complications and communal tensions, they tend to cause arguments and outrage more than violence.

The second sort of problem is related to Christian-Muslim tension. Christians are a substantial minority dispersed throughout Egyptian society. In some locations there have sometimes been clashes; the rise of radical Islamist movements in the 1970s, for instance, seems to have sparked some anti-Christian violence. The severity of this problem is a matter of controversy among Egyptians, however. As with race relations in the United States, individuals in Egypt differ greatly in the extent to which they view religious tensions as a problem.

With the wave of religiosity that has swept Egyptian society since the 1970s, religious tensions seem closer to the surface. Both Muslims and Christians have participated in this tendency. While many members of both religious traditions seek to manage any resulting conflicts, small incidents—a rumored forced conversion, a squabble among neighbors—can set off tensions and even violent clashes. Egyptian Christians themselves have often debated how to react, with some insisting on a very assertive stance but others calculating that a minority only endangers itself by making its case too publicly. In the wake of the Egyptian revolution, several attacks on churches caused great alarm among Egyptian Christians; while most Muslims denounced the attacks, many also viewed them as local incidents that should not be blown out of proportion. Christians complain that they are excluded from certain fields—such as the security sector or the diplomatic corps. With a few exceptions, there is no legal discrimination in Egypt against Christians, but there do seem to be informal barriers to their entry into some parts of the society.

Gender and Politics

Egyptians often take great pride in the strength of their family structures. Most Egyptian families show strong paternal features, with the father as the central figure. But these generalizations mask a wide variety and set of debates—especially over the relationship between the individual and the family and the roles for men and women in society. Egyptians from different classes and backgrounds differ in their approach to such issues and, even within the family, different members will often try to shape relationships in different ways.

Schoolchildren are taught at an early age that the family, not the individual, is the cornerstone of society. They are also raised to respect family elders and abide by specific roles within the family unit. These roles are usually defined by gender, socioeconomic status, and age. Gender plays a role in defining the status and authority of each member in the family. Men and women have distinctive sets of rights and duties that are shaped by tradition, religion, and family heritage. Those rights are not equivalent, but they do allow the weaker member to make claims. For instance, husbands are expected to provide materially for the family's needs, a role that allows them some dominance but also makes it possible for wives to make demands of their husbands and even seek divorce if the husband is unable or unwilling to fulfill his obligations. The nuclear family has increasingly become the norm, but extended families are still very strong in Egypt. It is legally permissible for a husband to have more than one wife, though this is rare and there have also been attempts to discourage the practice in recent decades. There were over 29.4 million married persons (out of a total population of 78.7 million) in May 2008, underscoring the perception of the importance of the institution of marriage and of establishing a family. One name for the family in Arabic is *'a'ila,* which refers to the mutually interdependent relationship among its members. Family affiliations, or kinship ties, are a basic source of social and financial support, socioeconomic status, and power.

The 2012 constitution, like its predecessor in 1971, proclaimed the family "as the basis of society" founded on "religion, morality, and patriotism." It also promised that the state would strive to "preserve the genuine character of the Egyptian family." The preamble lists gender equality as a principle, though it gives no guidelines on implementation. Successive regimes since 1952 have included in their development objectives improved conditions for the family and the status of women. They have provided subsidized education, health care, and social support. However, this role has recently become more difficult to maintain with a rapidly growing population and deteriorating economic conditions. Stressful socioeconomic conditions make it increasingly difficult for young Egyptians of middle and low income to get married and start a family at a reasonable age. In comparison to the 1960s or 1970s, today many are forced to continue to live in the family home and remain under the tutelage of their parents, even when they reach their twenties or thirties.

It is difficult to generalize about family values and practices in Egypt. Class, size, educational level, religious values, and geographic origins shape relationships within the family and perceptions of gender roles. Among middle-class, poor, extended, and rural families, girls might not enjoy treatment equal to that of boys. They are less valued than boys and might not receive the same levels of education. They are expected to undertake the household chores and might even receive less food and medical care. Nationwide, the illiteracy level is higher among girls than boys (43.8 percent compared to 18.3 percent in 2005 among the age bracket of fifteen years and older) (Egyptian State Information Service 2008). This percentage is even higher in rural areas and in Upper Egypt (the southern part of the country). Female circumcision is not uncommon—particularly among poor, large, and less-educated families—as a tradition to curb female sexual desires. Recently, the government has been trying to eliminate this practice.

The oil boom in the Gulf states and the economic opening that began in the mid-1970s had a significant impact on the Egyptian family. Economic liberalization increased Egyptians' appetite for consumption and gradually raised the cost of living. This new economic situation strained the financial capacities of millions of families. Fathers increasingly sought an extra job or two while wives either worked outside the home or tried to engage in other economic activities to raise the family income. Millions of Egyptian workers, peasants, and middle-class professionals moved to the Gulf as expatriates to offer their labor in return for extra earnings that would improve their families' living standards. Many young men sought work abroad in order to generate enough savings to provide for a wife and family. It became common for an Egyptian family to muddle through with an absentee father who stayed away for long years as an expatriate. All this, in addition to the decline of the welfare state, has affected the values and cohesion of the family.

Over the past few decades, women have become increasingly visible in public life, but their profile is still fairly low. The workforce has been open to women since the 1950s. Yet while today women constitute 49 percent of the total population, they represent only about 22 percent of the labor force. The percentage of working women in rural areas is higher (57 percent) than it is in urban areas (43 percent) (National Democratic Party 2009). There are no discriminatory labor policies against women. It is a constitutional right for women to receive wages and opportunities equal to those of men. However, in practice, women might not receive the same opportunities. Women were granted the right to vote and run for parliament in 1956. They entered parliament beginning in 1957 and have assumed cabinet positions since 1963. However, in 2008 there were only 2 women in the cabinet out of 30 posts. In the 2005 parliamentary elections, the NDP nominated only 6 women out of 444 candidates. This reveals the fact that, despite the state-declared policy of empowering women in society, their presence in the labor force and in politics is limited.

The state has taken several measures to improve the rights and conditions of women and children. In 1989, it established the National Council for Childhood and Motherhood. The main objective of the council is to increase popular awareness of the needs of children and women and ways to meet them. In 2000, it established the National Council for Women, to empower women, integrate them into the development and political process, and address the challenges they face. Since the 1970s, several revisions have been made to the personal status code in favor of women. The code now places restrictions on the man's unilateral right to end a marriage as well as his right to take a second wife without the consent of his first wife. It also grants women the right of *khul'*, to divorce the husband after paying financial compensation. In 2009, the Egyptian parliament approved legislation augmenting its own size by sixty-four seats designated exclusively for women, guaranteeing that at least one-eighth of future parliamentarians would be female. Islamist movements called into question some of these developments. Salafi movements tended to be especially critical of these steps, with the Muslim Brotherhood more circumspect. The quota was repealed after the 2011 uprising, and in the parliament elected between November 2011 and January 2012, just 2 percent of lower house seats (or 10 of 508) were secured by women.

Despite the state's declared policy to champion women's causes, Egyptian women have publicly protested the mistreatment they received from the regime and from state security in the Mubarak years. In 2005, women's demonstrations broke out in Cairo in protest of the sexual harassment they were subjected to by undercover state security forces on the day a constitutional amendment was voted on. A year later, women participated in rallies against the mass incidence of sexual violations that took place during the Eid (a religious holiday) of November 2006. The revolution hardly brought an end to complaints. If anything, the number of sexual harassment and assaults has spiked—particularly in areas around protests. The breakdown of public security in some areas augmented the feeling among many Egyptian women that public spaces could be hostile places.

The Impact of International Politics

In the aftermath of the Egyptian revolution of 2011, the attention of most Egyptians was riveted on domestic politics; international political issues were much less of a concern. But this was not always the case. The international setting has had a significant impact on Egyptian domestic politics. In the nineteenth century, the decline of the Ottoman Empire and the rise of European imperialism gave Egypt's rulers some room to maneuver for a considerable period but ultimately led to the country's occupation by Great

Britain in 1882. In the twentieth century, the decline of European imperialism allowed Egypt to assert its independence, and the rise of the Soviet
Union and the Cold War allowed Egypt to leave the Western security orbit
and turn to the Soviet bloc for economic and military assistance. The Arab-
Israeli conflict also led to Egypt becoming a significant international
player—important international outcomes of peace and war hinged in part
on decisions made by Egyptian leaders.

In the 1970s, Egypt left the Soviet bloc, negotiated a peace treaty with
Israel, and secured an ongoing commitment of economic and military assistance from the United States. While its centrality in Arab politics lessened
in the late twentieth century, Egypt's willingness to contribute to the international coalition ousting Iraq from Kuwait in 1990 and 1991 led to another
infusion of aid from the Gulf and debt forgiveness by Western powers.

In short, Egypt has been able to parlay its strategic international position into both guns and butter. But while Egypt is a large country, its pivotal
international position is not inevitable and may indeed now be declining. Its
major international patron, the United States, appeared to have overreached
itself in Iraq, and US-Egyptian relations are sometimes rocky in any case,
partly because the leaderships of the two countries often differ on important
issues (such as the Arab-Israeli dispute). Egypt's role as a mediator and a
leader in the Arab world has often been eclipsed in recent years by other
countries (including Saudi Arabia and even tiny Qatar). And Egypt's economic performance and stultifying authoritarianism (until 2011, anyway)
made the country seem far less of a model to emulate than it was in the
1960s when it led the Arab world in promoting nationalism and socialism.

If Egypt's international role has declined somewhat, the significance of
international politics for the domestic political scene—while still real—also
generally seems to have declined over the past two decades. To be sure, certain international issues attract great domestic attention. The conflict between Israelis and Palestinians has provoked deep sympathies for the latter
among Egyptians of various political stripes, especially in 2002 as the second Palestinian intifada began to heat up. The US invasion of Iraq in 2003
similarly provoked strong feelings among the many Egyptians who saw it
as a return to the period of direct Western attempts to control the region and
occupy Arab lands. In both cases, such popular sentiments placed the
Mubarak regime in an awkward position: by placing itself firmly in the
Western security camp since the 1970s, the regime seemed to have aligned
with an outside power that most Egyptians deeply distrusted. In short, the
core of the regime's security and foreign policy proved domestically embarrassing at times of international crisis.

In the Mubarak years, there was a tie between dissent over international issues and dissent over domestic politics. In the aforementioned cases
Egyptians sought to demonstrate in support of Palestinians, and against the

US military campaign in Iraq. On both occasions the regime, normally averse to street protests and demonstrations, took a slightly more permissive attitude. It also took measures to ensure that protest over foreign policy did not spill over into domestic politics (for instance, it has released extra amounts of flour and bread at times of international crisis to keep economic grievances at a minimum). But in 2002 and 2003, the upsurge in activism laid the groundwork for a broader movement in 2004 and 2005 against the regime—activists learned how to organize, build coalitions, and make appeals to the public. For a brief time, a broad opposition coalition formed against President Mubarak's reelection. In October 2009, opposition groups formed another coalition against the possibility of transitioning power to Gamal Mubarak. These coalitions tended to fall apart under the pressure of their own ideological differences and regime pressure, but they did lead many to question whether the regime was as stable and inevitable as it had generally appeared since 1952.

As a result, it was no surprise that many revolutionary leaders of 2011 viewed themselves as having been schooled in political organization by the earlier, more internationally oriented waves of protest. But in 2011 and 2012, foreign policy issues simply seemed less pressing than those connected with domestic politics. Even the Muslim Brotherhood—dedicated to the Palestinian cause since its founding—made very clear after the revolution in both words and deeds that it would not make any short-term changes in the tense but peaceful relationship with Israel.

Note

1. Private conversation between author Nathan Brown and an anonymous official, May 2006.

11

Iran

Arang Keshavarzian

In 2009, elite conflict and social discontent in Iran merged into one after the results of the June presidential elections were announced (Ehsani, Keshavarzian, and Moruzzi 2009). Officially, the incumbent, Mahmoud Ahmadinejad, received 62 percent of the vote, with Mir-Hossein Mousavi, a former prime minister, trailing with less than 34 percent of the vote. Two other candidates, Mohsen Rezaeia and Mehdi Karroubi, former heads of the Islamic Revolutionary Guard Corps (IRGC) and parliament, respectively, won less than 2 percent each. Turnout in this ninth presidential election was a staggering 85 percent and not challenged by any of the candidates or observers. As in the 2005 election, Ahmadinejad wove together support from core institutions of the Islamic Republic, including the office of the Leader (Ali Khamenei), the IRGC, and the volunteer paramilitary forces (or the *basij*), as well as members of the urban middle class and lower middle class who were mobilized by his populist message of redistribution, nationalism, and religious moralism.

In the wake of the announcement that Ahmadinejad was victorious, Iran experienced the largest rallies and most disruptive acts of disobedience since the 1979 revolution. Supporters and participants in what became known as the Green Movement questioned the results by identifying procedural irregularities in the monitoring of the election, tallying of votes, and announcement of the results. Iranians took to the streets chanting "Where is my vote?" and demanding a new election. Unlike the Arab uprisings in 2011 or the Iranian revolution of 1979, these initial protests included key figures from the regime itself. The defeated candidates all held critical positions in the regime, and the movement had the explicit and implicit support of two

former presidents, Akbar Hashemi-Rafsanjani (ruled 1989–1997) and Mohammad Khatami (ruled 1997–2005), as well as other clerics and personalities associated with the Islamic Republic. The political rallies and protests in the
summer and fall of 2009 also had considerable mass support and sympathy.
Given the subsequent crackdown after the 2009 election, it is difficult to
identify and analyze the social backgrounds of supporters of the movement,
but the most active protesters seem to have been urban, educated men and
women under the age of forty—or in other words, a very large constituency
in contemporary Iran (see section on political economy).

Nonetheless, the regime withstood this challenge as it brutally repressed
political activists, independent journalists and lawyers, and student groups
and employed violence against street protesters. A mix of fear, apathy, and
disunity wore down the Green Movement. Iran's 2009 uprising did not cul-
minate in the political transformations wished for by many Iranians or experienced by parts of the Arab world in 2011, but the Leader lost support
among some members of the political elite and probably lost legitimacy in
the eyes of some ordinary citizens.

At the same time, the Green Movement challenged the regime by exposing the contradictions within the Islamic Republic. The movement is a
manifestation of the Islamic Republic's policies and semiauthoritarian
structure that have produced an educated, urban population with basic welfare—without meeting greater demands for political participation. Moreover, many practices and institutions, such as competitive elections, encourage participation and reflect diversity within the official political class, but
at the same time, restrictions exist on who may participate, and the power
and resources vested in the office of the Leader detract from the efficacy of
political engagement. Finally, the limited success of the uprising also illustrated the organizational power of the regime and organizational weak-
nesses of oppositional politics. In this chapter, we will explore these matters
and place them in their historical and comparative contexts. This approach
will reframe the dominant narrative presented by many observers, who treat
domestic Iranian politics as a mere sideshow to their own concern over
Iran's nuclear program or Washington and Tel Aviv's continued military
threats.

As we have seen in this book, specific histories, geographies, and demographics have often made political and social developments in the Middle East dissimilar from those in other regions; however, difference does
not mean that analytical concepts and political logics are unhelpful in analyzing Iran. In fact, what is often described as the "Persian paradox" or
"puzzle" is less perplexing if we study politics in Iran as a product of historical processes and state institutions, rather than religious ideology and
essential cultural characteristics. For on closer examination, what is striking
about Iranian politics is that it is multivocal, flexible, and contentious

despite the persistence of dictatorship, international conflict, and utopian ideals.

Historical Background and Contemporary Political Structure

For three decades Iran has been governed by a regime that is part republic and part "Islamic government," as theorized by Ayatollah Ruhollah Khomeini (1902–1989). As such, it is a radical departure both from Iran's two millennia of monarchy and from centuries of Shi'ite theology, which accepted and even legitimated the temporal powers of the shahs. To fully understand both the magnitude of this discontinuity and the social forces that fashioned and continue to mold this polity, one needs to reflect on the historical processes that generated the Islamic Republic and the persisting battles over the nature of the state and relations within society. In Iran, as in many other countries in the developing world, modern politics has been a struggle to create a state that is simultaneously effective and accountable to its citizens.

Contemporary Iran is the successor to a series of empires headed by shahs (kings) that have ruled the Persian plateau for over two millennia. As such, its current boundaries are a product of centuries of battles and negotiations with neighboring powers, including the Ottomans, Moguls, Russians, and British colonial forces in India. While it was one of a handful of non-Western states not to be formally colonized, ironically Iran's independence was due to a compromise between Britain and Russia to maintain it as a buffer between the two great nineteenth-century imperial powers. Thus Iran escaped the more direct and formalized imperialism experienced by Algeria, Egypt, or India, but great powers influenced its domestic politics and extracted economic concessions—including Britain's 1901 oil concession.

Another factor that sets Iran apart from much of the region is that the vast majority of Iranians are Shi'ite Muslims. Despite considerable ethnolinguistic and regional diversity, 90 percent of Iranians are Shi'ite (see section on Identity and Politics). Iranians did not adopt Shi'ite Islam in large numbers until after the sixteenth century, when the Safavid dynasty made Shi'ism the official religion and Sunni and non-Muslim Iranians converted to the minority branch of Islam. Over the centuries, Shi'ite clerics were willing to accord the shahs temporal authority; meanwhile the clergy maintained independent educational and legal institutions and sources of revenue. This independence from the state allowed politically oriented clerics to periodically participate in politics. So while Khomeini's interpretation of Shi'ite thought was radical, the clergy did have a history of parlaying their religious authority into political muscle. An early example of this was the Constitutional Revolution (1905–1911).

The Constitutional Revolution:
An Early Salvo Against Absolutism

After a series of military defeats at the hands of the Russians and economic concessions to Europeans, a broad but unwieldy alliance of Iranians challenged the absolutist monarch, who was increasingly viewed as incompetent and unjust. Western-educated and -inspired intellectuals joined the urban mercantile class and some clerics to confront the Shah, who was supported by pro-monarchist clerics and landed aristocrats. In local associations and newspapers, these activists accused the Qajar dynasty (1798–1925) of being unable to defend the nation's interests against British and Russian imperial ambitions and unable to implement the economic and social reforms necessary to achieve equal footing with foreign powers. Iranians began seeing constitutionalism as a means to limit the monarchy's power and improve the quality of citizens' lives. After a series of nationwide protests, the Shah relented and established a parliament (the Majles) and signed the constitution (1906). Yet internal differences within the constitutionalist camp, British and Russian opposition to the movement, and the chaos and misery of World War I colluded to mute the achievements of the constitutionalists; the monarchy gradually wrested powers from the parliament, leaving many social and economic reforms unrealized. Despite these failures, the Constitutional Revolution succeeded in establishing the principles of rule of law and participatory government. An indication of how Iran's "first revolution" has been a cornerstone of modern Iranian politics is that supporters of the 2009 Green Movement cited the goals and celebrated the heroics of these first constitutionalists.

Reza Shah:
Statebuilding and the Origins of Pahlavi Monarchy

The Constitutional Revolution may have failed to achieve its objectives, but it succeeded in delegitimizing the Qajar dynasty. As with the collapse of the Ottoman Empire and the establishment of Turkey in the 1920s, a military man, Reza Khan, came to power with the promise of bringing order and development to Iran. After heading a military coup and displacing the Qajars, the coup leader proclaimed himself Shah and founded the Pahlavi dynasty (1925–1979). The primary objectives of Reza Shah were to centralize power by suppressing powerful landowners, tribal leaders, and clerics, and to monopolize authority in the hands of the expanded army and the nascent bureaucracy in Tehran. It was under his direction that, for the first time, Iran had a centralized government with significant geographic reach and the capacity to initiate large-scale projects, such as building railroads and initiating industrialization.

To legitimate his statebuilding the Shah cobbled together an ideology including aspects of nationalism, secularism, and modernism. A national education system and uniform dress code were implemented to fashion a culturally uniform and disciplined citizenry. Iranians and Western intellectuals were recruited to promulgate and instill a partly mythical understanding of pre-Islamic Iranian history that both justified monarchy and privileged Persian language and culture while subordinating non-Persian languages. The powers and social functions of the clergy were restricted through the establishment of state-run courts, schools, and property and marriage registration offices. For the Shah and his advisers, modernization was associated with adopting Western culture as much as with replicating Western industrial models. For instance, it was argued that to modernize, Iranians must dress in the same manner as Europeans and this included a law *forbidding women from wearing the veil* (this law was repealed by Mohammad Reza Shah).

However, unlike the constitutionalists, Reza Shah did not see accountable government as essential to development and something that should be imported from the West along with factories and fashion. Instead, he ruled as an unabashed dictator and retained an exclusive grip on power, turning the constitution into a dead letter and the parliament into a rubber stamp. Yet Reza Shah's ability to enhance Iran's independence and curtail foreign interference in its domestic affairs was limited. In fact, his 1921 coup enjoyed the tacit (if not active) support of the British, and in 1941, fearing German aspirations to dominate Iran, the Allied Powers removed him from power and replaced him with his son, Mohammad Reza Pahlavi (ruled 1941–1979).

A Parliamentarian Interlude
and the Resurrection of Monarchical Modernism

Unlike his father, the young Shah was too inexperienced to suppress political debate and politicians who sought greater accountability of the monarch. From 1941 to 1953, Iran experienced more pluralistic politics, with liberal nationalists, pro-Soviet communists, conservative landlords, and others participating in various ways. Out of this mix, the National Front coalition marshaled the support of old constitutionalists, the emerging educated middle class, and merchants to control the parliament and elect their popular leader, Mohammad Mossadeq, as prime minister in 1951. One of the main issues that galvanized Iranians and endeared Mossadeq to them was his staunch opposition to British control of Iran's oil resources and to Iranians' limited input in the management of the Anglo-Iranian Oil Company (later renamed British Petroleum [BP]). Once he became prime minister and the parliament passed a bill nationalizing Iranian oil and redirecting oil profits from the British to the Iranian government, Mossadeq faced British ire. The battle over Iran's oil ended only in 1953 when the newly formed

US Central Intelligence Agency (CIA) helped orchestrate a military coup overthrowing Mossadeq and returning Iran to royal autocracy. This marked the CIA's first covert operation.

The coup was a watershed in Iranian international and domestic politics. After decades of direct and indirect British and Russian interference in Iranian domestic affairs, it was a shock to many Iranians that it was the self-proclaimed anti-imperialist United States that intervened in the most blatant manner. Through the coup, the United States wedded itself to the Shah, a weak but loyal leader of a strategically important frontline state in the Cold War and a protector of US interests in the oil-rich Persian Gulf. In return, the Shah received economic and military assistance and political patronage from the United States. At the government level this relationship was mutually beneficial, but within Iranian society the United States and the Shah were seen as two sides of the same dictatorial coin. Over the subsequent quarter century, the mutual dependence between the US government and the Shah only increased and blinded them to Iran's social reality (Bill 1988). A half century after the Constitutional Revolution sought to simultaneously build an accountable government and uphold Iranian independence, monarchy reinforced itself through foreign patronage.

The 1953 coup derailed Iran's first meaningful parliamentary government and with it an attempt at creating a competitive party system. Once the Shah returned to power he lost no time suppressing dissident groups, union activists, journalists, and politically active merchants while at the same time placing Mossadeq under house arrest for the rest of his life. In particular, secular political organizations, both liberal and Marxist, were identified as threats and subsequently suppressed and monitored by the regime. In this pursuit, the government initially curried the favor and assistance of clerics, who were equally threatened by these ideologies. Mosques and religious organizations enjoyed greater freedom than did secularly oriented politics in the 1950s and 1960s. This helped set the stage for the development of political Islam in Iran.

Some Iranian intellectuals became disillusioned with liberalism and socialism, for they failed to bring about political change. In response, a small but growing number turned to Islamic thought as a "native" and "authentic" means to challenge dictatorship, negotiate Western cultural influence, and garner greater popular support. Concurrently, in 1963 a little-known cleric, Khomeini, publicly began to criticize the Shah. The next year, his vociferous opposition to the extension of diplomatic immunity to US military personnel led to his arrest, exile, and eventual resettling in the seminaries of southern Iraq. The government silenced Khomeini, but he and his supporters did not forsake politics.

The Shah and his advisers, meanwhile, hoped that economic prosperity would mask demands for political participation. Flush with oil revenue,

Iran enjoyed some of the most impressive growth rates during the 1960s and 1970s. The primary beneficiary of this economic expansion was the urban population. The Shah developed an elaborate system of patronage to cultivate cronies and consumerism to maintain the acceptance (if not support) of the burgeoning middle class. As in the rest of the region, the urban bias spurred large numbers of landless peasants and their children to migrate to the cities in search of employment and opportunities for social mobility. While oil wealth, US aid, and the large development projects of the 1960s and 1970s may not have achieved the "Great Civilization" that the Shah imagined, they did restructure Iranian society. Iran went from being a largely rural, agrarian, and illiterate society in the first half of the twentieth century to one that by the 1970s had a predominantly urban population, an economy that was integrated into the capitalist world economy through its oil exports and imports of consumer and industrial goods, and a growing, educated middle class aspiring to enter the industrial and service sectors.

Yet this socioeconomic modernization did not come with a parallel "political modernization," or the restructuring of relations between government and the governed through the building of institutions and organizations for interest articulation and aggregation. The Shah would neither accept the formation of independent political parties, trade unions, and professional associations nor tolerate meaningful debate in the parliament or the media.

The Revolution of 1979: More Than Islamic

It was unthinkable to the Shah, political activists, and US policymakers that in the midst of economic growth the monarchy would be overthrown by a mass national movement that included liberal democrats, leftists, feminists, bureaucrats, laborers, merchants, and students and that was ultimately led by an elderly cleric (Kurzman 2004). But this is exactly what happened in the course of a little more than a year. By the time the Shah left Iran and Khomeini returned in early 1979, the well-rehearsed alliance of liberal intellectuals, *bazaari* merchants, and politicized seminarians was joined by new social groups such as university students, industrial workers, and the bureaucratic middle class. Some were motivated by economic hardship and political repression, while others were angered by the adulation of all things Western and the disregard of Iran's Islamic culture. Despite dissimilar grievances and goals, these groups realized that their coordination would lead to the downfall of monarchy.

This mobilization and politicization was made possible by the successes of the Shah's modernization policies as much as by the grievances that his authoritarian hubris generated. The building of universities and a large state bureaucracy had created an urban middle class whom many aspired to join.

Industrialization gave birth to a working class and a mercantile class aiming to expand their enterprises and share of profits. State-led secularism simultaneously inspired women who wanted more meaningful gender equality and angered conservative and religious men and women. The Shah produced these new demands, sensibilities, and social constellations, but was unwilling to accommodate them. Finally, because Iran was a rentier state, the Shah's regime depended on revenue from the world economy and was autonomous from domestic forces. However, direct access to revenue left Iran's state institutionally weak and ill equipped to monitor, incorporate, and bargain with social groups (Shambayati 1994).

The vehicles of the revolution were not opposition parties, for they had been driven underground. Instead, would-be revolutionaries inventively used the limited public space available to transform social venues, such as mosques and poetry readings, into places for gathering, coordinating, and protesting. During 1978, existing cultural practices were newly conceived for the purpose of political dissent. For instance, Middle Easterners of many faiths commemorate the fortieth day after a person's death. These are personal and nonpolitical events. However, when government troops murdered several protesting seminarians in January 1978, political dissidents who regarded the victims as "martyrs" transformed the fortieth-day commemorations into political rallies. When troops killed protesters attending these rallies, an opportunity for another commemoration cum political rally took place and a forty-day cycle of protests was unleashed.

The mobilization repertoire was increasingly religiously inflected, but so was the message. Prior to the revolution, Khomeini's theological writings were largely unknown, but his political sermons, captured in pamphlets and on cassette tapes, were brought into Iran from Iraq, where he was residing. Borrowing from the normative agenda of popular lay political Islamists such as Ali Shariati and Jalal Al-e Ahmad, who themselves had been influenced by Marxist and other Western ideas, Khomeini's message synthesized anti-imperialism and egalitarian populism with a call for political activism and sacrifice that he associated with Shi'ism. In his unforgiving speeches and writings, Khomeini blamed the overly didactic and quiescent clergy, the tyrannical Shah, and imperial forces for exploiting Iran and undermining Islam.

Yet, like all revolutions, the 1979 revolution in Iran is too complex a social event to be captured by a single adjective. It has come to be known as the Islamic Revolution because it authored a new utopian regime ruling in the name of Islam and with the mission of creating a just Islamic society. A cleric, Khomeini, became the principal face and spokesperson of this project. However, characterizing the revolution as "Islamic" threatens to misconstrue the motivations of the millions of Iranians who went on strike, marched in rallies, and distributed flyers in opposition to the monarchy. The speedy and relatively bloodless success of the revolution was due to its cross-class and ideological inclusiveness rather than singularity of will. Self-professed leftists, nationalists, and constitutionalists from almost all social classes coordinated and fashioned the revolution. Only a minority of clerics supported the revolution, and many of the high-ranking ayatollahs publicly distanced themselves from Khomeini's theories and advocated alternative understandings of Islam. The diversity of actors and political ideologies is important because even after Khomeini and his followers monopolized power (1979–1981), these forces persisted, produced many unintended outcomes, and challenged the ruling elites.

Islamic Republic: A Hybrid Experiment

While the revolutionary coalition agreed that the Shah must go and chanted "freedom, independence, and Islamic republic," it was not entirely clear what these concepts meant, who would define them, and how they would be instituted. In the end, Khomeini and his close associates were able to take advantage of the cleric's charismatic authority, along with their organizational advantage over the secular groups, to consolidate power. The seizure of the US embassy (November 1979) and the Iraqi invasion (September 1980) were critical events that allowed the Khomeinists to suppress opposition voices in the name of national unity against foreign threats. However, more liberal and non-Islamist voices were not quashed until after they were able to leave some imprint on the structure of the Islamic Republic.

In his writing in the 1970s, Khomeini rejected republicanism and instead envisioned a system of government headed by a single clerical guardian ("guardianship of the jurisconsult," *velayat-e faqih*) who would ensure that God's will, as reflected in the scripture and interpreted by religious scholars, was fully applied. For the first time in Shi'ism, this ruling jurist, known more commonly as the Leader, fused religious and worldly authority. Yet the 1979 constitution married Khomeini's concept of Islamic government with republican principles, which were championed by secular democrats and more liberal Islamists. As such, under the Islamic Republic's constitution, sovereignty belongs to God but is delegated to all humans (Article 3: 8, 57). Executive and legislative power is formally divided between popularly elected branches of government and unelected offices and councils that are entrusted with maintaining the dominion of God and the will of the Leader (see Figure 11.1). After Khomeini's death (1989), the religious standing of the Leader was greatly diminished and the disparity between mosque and state became more pronounced; consequently, the theological premise of overlaying popular sovereignty with clerical representation of God's will became more suspect.

Like democracies, the Islamic Republic includes institutions that allow citizens to participate in making and executing the rules governing their lives. Elections for various offices and levels of government (e.g., the president,

Figure 11.1 Structure of Power in the Islamic Republic of Iran

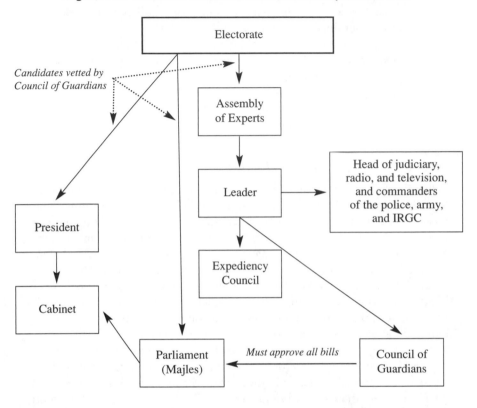

parliament, city councils, and Assembly of Experts) are regularly held and—
until the 2009 presidential election—have been largely free of violence and
allegations of vote-rigging. Even though only approved candidates can run
for office, elections are competitive and often result in surprises, such as
when Mohammad Khatami defeated the candidate aligned with the Leader
in 1997 and Ahmadinejad defeated Akbar Hashemi-Rafsanjani, a powerful
cleric and former president, in 2005. Given the populist and revolutionary
roots of the regime and the existence of universal suffrage, voter participation has become an integral means for politicians, factions, and the regime
to claim legitimacy. For instance, elections are moments when state-run
radio and television call upon citizens to be "ever-present in the [political]
arena" and demonstrate their opposition to the "enemies of the Islamic Revolution." In Iran, as opposed to many of the regimes in the region, voting is
encouraged and not thwarted. Indeed, voter participation in Iranian presidential and parliamentary elections is substantial (as high as 85 percent in
2009), even if it is uneven over time and across provinces. Iranian elections

have been a means for citizens to either punish the establishment by voting incumbents out of office or express displeasure by abstaining and implicitly undermining the popular credentials of the regime. Moreover, parliamentary debates over policies are heated and criticism of various branches of government is common, with the parliament frequently exercising its power to reject presidential appointments and censure ministers. During Ahmadinejad's first term in office, for instance, ten cabinet members were impeached and several others resigned after public criticism.

However, these democratic practices and institutions are limited by a whole host of mechanisms that mute contestation and meaningful participation. Republican institutions are straitjacketed by antidemocratic parameters. The doctrine of *velayat-e faqih* has come to be defined in personal and absolute terms, wherein the Leader (Khomeini, 1979–1989, and Ali Khamenei, 1989–present) wields extensive supervisory and executive powers.[1] The Leader is not expected to participate in everyday politics and under Khomeini acted as a father figure who remained above political squabbling and factional clashes. Yet the Leader has extensive executive powers to which Khamenei has increasingly resorted. Article 110 of the constitution stipulates that the Leader is authorized to "determine the general policies" of and "supervise over" the regime, declare war and peace as the supreme commander of the armed forces, and appoint and dismiss the heads of the judiciary and the commanders of the IRGC and police forces. While Khomeini's charismatic authority endowed this post with particular power, with the support of conservative allies in other branches of government, the less religiously authoritative Khamenei has also wielded decree powers, for example to end discussions over relations with the United States and publicly and quickly side with Ahmadinejad in the disputed 2009 election.

In addition, the Leader directly appoints half the members of the Council of Guardians; the remaining six are selected by the parliament from a list of nominees drawn up by the head of the judiciary, who is appointed by the Leader (Article 91). The Council of Guardians is entrusted with two critical responsibilities. First, it reviews all legislation to ensure that it is compatible with Islamic law and the constitution. When the Council of Guardians rejects a parliamentary bill, the legislative dispute is resolved by the Expediency Council, an unelected body composed of all branches of the government, including representatives of the Leader. Second, the Council of Guardians is authorized to supervise presidential and parliamentary elections (Article 99); it is with this approbatory power that it has vetted candidates.

Furthermore, despite constitutional protections (Articles 19–42) and claims made by public officials, political and civil rights (e.g., freedoms of assembly, speech, and the press) are routinely violated by administrative regulations and extralegal practices. A complex and opaque court system has developed to convict political activists, journalists, academics, artists,

and even members of the government whom hard-liners deem as threats to
the regime or their individual interests. These legal and administrative im-
pediments to free and fair public participation in politics are reinforced by
the use of targeted violence and indiscriminate intimidation by vigilante
squads and a multilayered law enforcement apparatus. These methods were
critical in combatting the so-called Green Movement that emerged in the
wake of the 2009 election.

Therefore, the heterogeneity of the revolution laid the foundation for a
unique attempt to accommodate God's will and popular sovereignty in a
single regime. More generally, Iran is governed by one of the growing number of "hybrid regimes" that combine democracy and authoritarianism. The
Islamic Republic of Iran is not accountable to its citizens, although it can be
responsive.

Government and Opposition:
Fragmented Elites and Their Disjointed Opponents

With its dualism in sovereignty, Iran's hybrid regime is coupled with an
equally pervasive fragmentation of power that has led to a contradictory
outcome. On the one hand, the fragmentation of state institutions makes rivalry and conflict, even among regime supporters, endemic and public.
However, the balance of power is such that neither reformers within the
state nor opponents in society at large have been able to push through radical changes using social protest or by unifying in order to bargain with
hard-liners to extract compromises and regime-led democratization.

The Architecture of Governance

A patchwork of parallel institutions creates overlapping authorities, competing interests, and checks and balances in the Islamic Republic. In sharp
contrast to the highly centralized Pahlavi monarchy, the postrevolutionary
state consists of multiple and competing bodies. Below the office of the
Leader a disjointed bureaucratic grid persists, engendering elite competition
and allowing ideological factionalism to flourish.

For instance, paralleling one another are the army and the Islamic Revolutionary Guard Corps, the Housing Foundation of the Islamic Revolution
and the Ministry of Housing and Urban Development, the Red Crescent and
the Imam Khomeini Relief Committee, and the Organization for Islamic
Propaganda and the Ministry of Culture and Islamic Guidance. The judiciary is composed of heterogeneous courts, with alleged press violations
being directed to branches of either the revolutionary court or the press
court. Even the power associated with the office of the Leader has been

fragmented in the years since it has been occupied by the less religiously qualified and politically powerful successor to Khomeini (Schirazi 1998: 79–80). This constellation of institutions makes it almost impossible for a single ministry to decide and execute policies unilaterally or without criticism from interested parties. This elite fragmentation and contestation have continued even after the sidelining of reformists after 2005 and the purges after the 2009 election; now, divisions among the conservative forces have been exposed and sharpened.[2]

The origins and persistence of fragmented state structures emanate from the nature of the revolution and the Shi'ite clergy. The initial creation of parallel bodies was due to the revolutionaries' mistrust of the ancien régime's institutions and their decision to hastily create countervailing military, economic, political, and cultural institutions. A strong single party might have added cohesion to this decentralized authoritarianism, as the National Liberation Front (FLN) did in Algeria. Indeed, the Islamic Republic Party (IRP) was established shortly after the revolution in order to unify the pro-Khomeini forces against their rivals. Yet the party was unable to create consensus or impose a uniform platform on important issues—let alone mobilize the masses, a task that was left to local Islamic associations, Friday prayer leaders, and revolutionary-era committees. Finally, the absence of a formal ecclesiastic hierarchy and the historical independence of individual Shi'ite clerics from one another have fueled the factionalism (Mottahedeh 1985). Despite initial attempts, the Islamic Republic could not create a centralized chain of command within the clergy to link the minority of clerics working for the state with the aloof majority (Chehabi 1991).

However structurally diffuse, the regime has enjoyed considerable material and ideological resources that have allowed it to withstand domestic and international pressures. For much of the first decade following the revolution, the political establishment enjoyed and manipulated its revolutionary credentials. The mass nature of the revolution allowed the government to claim legitimacy and argue that it represented the entire nation. This position was only amplified by the Iran-Iraq War and US-Iranian conflicts. Given that the revolution and much of twentieth-century Iranian politics sought greater independence from foreign powers, the government welcomed international tension as a means to exhibit its nationalist stature and restrict domestic dissent in the name of national unity in the face of "enemies."

However, by the late 1980s this revolutionary and religious rhetoric of solidarity and sacrifice became less compelling to a growing number of Iranians. Khomeini passed away and by definition his charismatic authority ended; he was replaced by Khamenei, who lacked religious stature and political gravitas. The war with Iraq resulted in enormous human and financial costs but did not achieve territorial gain or the removal of Saddam Hussein from power. Meanwhile, a whole host of pragmatic concerns such as unemployment, a deteriorating urban and petroleum infrastructure, and international isolation worried Iranians.

Beginning with the 1989 presidential election of Hashemi-Rafsanjani, the political establishment had to resort to more conventional resources to secure support, manage dissent, and demobilize and reintegrate those who fought in the war. Although diminishing in per capita terms, petroleum exports ensured that the security apparatus was funded, regime clients were cultivated through patronage, and government spending could dampen grievances by enhancing welfare, subsidizing basic goods (e.g., gasoline), and maintaining employment in the public sector. In this era in which a growing percentage of Iran's population had not experienced the monarchy, revolution, or war, politicians offered new platforms to garner votes and restructure the regime. Hashemi-Rafsanjani's presidency rolled back certain cultural restrictions and championed economic liberalism to garner greater support from the postrevolutionary urban middle class.

It is at this moment that the Islamic Revolutionary Guard Corps, which played a critical role in the eight-year war with Iraq, was encouraged to take a greater role in the postwar reconstruction effort by winning contracts for infrastructural projects. Over time the active and retired IRGC leadership expanded their activities to include banking, telecommunications, and other key sectors. Their age profile and belief that their sacrifices during the war with Iraq entitled them to a greater role in political decisionmaking emboldened them to run for elected office, take ministerial posts, and act as a lobby group with a direct line of communication with the leader. Thus, their recent political rise is reflective of a generational shift and their key socioeconomic position dating back to the 1990s rather than a political plot orchestrated and controlled by Ahmadinejad or the Leader.

If the rise of the IRGC represents one trajectory since the 1980s, the reformist movement represents a distinct alternative. In the 1990s intellectuals and technocrats proposed coupling socioeconomic liberalism with deep political reforms that curtailed the privileges of political oligarchs as well as state enterprises, but preserved the Islamic Republic as a polity. This platform helped a liberal-minded cleric, Khatami, win two terms as president while his followers were victorious in parliamentary (2000) and city council (1999) elections. The real limits of reformism were also illustrated during this era when the Leader utilized the judiciary, Guardian Council, and security apparatus (including the *basij*) to blunt legislative changes and muzzle reformist organizations, newspapers, and intellectuals.

With the reformist agenda shackled and given apathy among the reformists' social base, the stage was set for a new and younger conservative current to take center stage. Mahmoud Ahmadinejad came to power through a coalition of support from religious conservatives attracted to his avowed support for the *velayat-e faqih,* junior members of the security-military apparatus produced by the Iran-Iraq War and the conflict with the reformist movement, and members of the working class in urban and provincial areas who gravitated to his anticorruption and redistribution message. While both the reformists' message of democratization and Ahmadinejad's neoconservative message had their supporters, until recently the latter also had the personal and institutional support of Khamenei and the coercive might of the state.

Factionalism:
The Islamic Republic's Opposition from Within

The original opponents of the Islamic Republic were crushed in a series of purges shortly after the revolution. These democrats, leftists, and liberal Islamists were either imprisoned and executed or driven underground, abroad, or out of politics (Abrahamian 1999). However, the institutional fragmentation of the state and the hybrid nature of sovereignty have yielded a new category of opponents to the regime. Given the limited but real space for participation and competition, opposition to the status quo exists within the regime itself. All chief executives, from reformist president Khatami to hard-line conservative president Ahmadinejad, have faced criticisms and challenges from members of parliament (MPs), members of the judiciary, and other political elites.

The rivalries have formed into factions rather than institutionalized parties. By the 1990s these factions were typically described as comprising two blocs: hard-liners (or conservatives) and reformists. The former faction tends to support a more authoritarian interpretation of the Islamic Republic, with the Leader enjoying greater power and deference at the expense of the elected officials. These self-described "principlists" also hold a highly literal understanding of Islamic law to counter those who understand Islam in less legalistic and static terms. The members of the Council of Guardians and judiciary, the current leadership of the IRGC, and the Leader and his entourage are in this camp. Meanwhile, reformists seek to empower elected institutions, civil society, and a more pluralistic understanding of the regime. In terms of foreign affairs, they have called for improving relations with Arab and European states, while welcoming greater dialogue with the United States. The members of this camp have impeccable revolutionary credentials, as many were among the lay and clerical founders of the regime and even former members of the IRGC. Reformists can also be found among technocrats, independent-minded clerics, and intellectuals seeking to synthesize secular and religious thought. One scholar describes the reformist movement as "post-Islamist": "by embracing a fusion of faith and freedom, religion and rights, post-Islamism transcended the Islamist polity. It called for individual choice, pluralism, and democracy, as well as religious ethics" (Bayat 2007: 55). This political agenda resonates with journalists, university students, women's rights groups, and the more independently minded population. The conservative backlash during Khatami's second term and under Ahmadinejad consisted of the judiciary and the Council of Guardians clamping down on the press, disqualifying many reformist candidates, and confronting reform-oriented nongovernmental organizations (NGOs) and academics.[3]

Despite the clear conflict between reformists and conservatives, it is important to note that both groups are fluid and have profound internal differences across a number of policy areas. For instance, while currently both the legislature and the executive are dominated by the conservatives, many of Ahmadinejad's policies were rejected, modified, and criticized by conservative MPs and in newspapers. Many conservatives have viewed his economic policies as politically destabilizing and hostile to private enterprise, while his foreign policy tactics have been chastised for compromising Iran's security. Even his comments about religion and the role of the Leader in an Islamic republic have received scorn from conservatives who have labeled him and his associates as constituting a "deviant current." Meanwhile, reformists have disagreed among themselves over how to approach the imperfect electoral process, engage more pragmatic elements among the conservatives, and sequence and prioritize political, social, and economic reforms.

Currently what distinguishes the hard-liners and reformists is their access to power and resources. The hard-liners, even when they were defeated in elections in the late 1990s, wielded state power through the offices of the Leader and the judiciary as well as through the intelligence and security apparatus. In turn, the reformists have come to function as an opposition, for they have only limited access to state resources. Even when they controlled the presidency and the parliament and had the support of the vast majority of the electorate, their executive power was neutralized by the Leader and their legislative ambitions were tempered by the Council of Guardians and an activist judiciary. Still, until recently, the reformists have had something that the illegal and unrecognized opposition does not have: they enjoy personal and political credentials and relationships within the sprawling state apparatus and its appendages, and they express their views in a whole host of independent newspapers, journals, and websites. Reformists, who currently are calling for a more conciliatory tone and distancing themselves from activists in the Green Movement, seek to hold onto this status.

Thus, semiauthoritarianism remains stable because state institutions provide opportunities for factionalism and elite regeneration, but prevent coalition building between elites and social groups to ultimately democratize the system (Keshavarzian 2005). Currently the political rivalry is undergoing an unpredictable phase. Despite the fact that critical voices within the establishment are organizationally weak in absolute terms as well as relative to the regime's robust security apparatus, Ahmadinejad's polarizing policies, the ongoing conflict with the United States, and the Leader's inability or unwillingness to unify conservatives have produced deep divisions within the regime *and* society.

Opposition Outside the Regime

Given that the reformist opposition operates within the regime, its oppositional or "outsider" credentials are compromised in the eyes of a politicized society that has been disappointed with the pace and extent of changes to policies and institutions. Yet beyond the boundaries of this elite factionalism, opponents to the regime as a whole have little space or resources to either formulate clear platforms or represent them to citizens. Party formation is heavily regulated and not an option for groups unwilling to pledge loyalty to the constitution.

Yet criticism is not something heard only in the privacy of homes or with hushed voices in taxis. Government officials are taken to task by members of the inner circles of power, on front pages of newspapers, and on the floor of the parliament. When Ahmadinejad and other officials visit universities in Iran, they are routinely confronted with heckling and chants calling for the end of dictatorship. These brave acts, which have continued even after the 2009 crackdown, have not dislodged Iran's rulers or forced them to share power, but they have made government-opposition relations more polyvocal.

Opposition among Iranian expatriates living in the United States and Europe is so limited, disorganized, and unpopular inside Iran as to be almost a nonfactor. Even so, some US pundits and government officials periodically suggest that these groups (especially those with an ethnic-separatist agenda) can be bolstered to destabilize the regime. To date, these expatriate opposition groups have not threatened the regime or garnered popular support. Meanwhile, reports of the US government allocating funds to these groups allow a fearful Islamic Republic to punish any and all critics as traitors and tools of imperialism.

Political Economy: A Mixed Record

One of the chief criticisms of the Shah was that his policies did not benefit the majority of Iranians. In response, policymakers and activists in the Islamic Republic paid particular attention to human and rural development so as to redistribute resources to a larger share of the population. Because of this populist ethos, at least initially, the new regime was able to recruit young, idealistic men and women for national and local projects. Many new officials were from humble rural backgrounds, making them more attuned to local needs and giving them local clout.

In terms of basic indicators of literacy, access to health care and clean water, and life expectancy, policies have been impressive—especially considering the Iran-Iraq War, international sanctions and isolation, and declining oil revenue in real terms. Rural areas have been transformed by construction and electrification projects. In the two decades after the revolution, rural roads increased from a total of 8,000 to 59,000 kilometers, while the proportion of villages with access to electricity increased from 6 to 99 percent (Hooglund 2009). These improvements knit rural communities into the national fabric by giving villagers access to urban markets, social service facilities, and television. At the national level, education and health care have seen marked improvements. Literacy rates have continuously risen, reaching 89 percent for men and 80 percent for women by 2006, while the gap between sexes has narrowed from 1976 levels, when 59 percent of men were literate in comparison to only 35 percent of women (Elmi 2009). High school attendance for both genders has similarly increased. A system of volunteer-led health clinics has helped dramatically reduce maternal and infant mortality while increasing access to cheap and affordable vaccinations and contraception. The combination of improved access to health care and higher levels of education has lowered the fertility rate and dampened economic and political pressures associated with rapid population growth in the 1970s and 1980s. These policies and achievements garner support for the Islamic Republic among the middle and lower classes, especially those living outside Tehran (Abrahamian 2009).

There are additional burdens and persisting problems, however. This increasingly educated and young society demands greater job opportunities. Yet it faces mounting expenses associated with urban living and global competition, high levels of unemployment, and inflation. International sanctions and the lack of a transparent legal framework threaten to discourage long-term investment in productive sectors, and a lack of job opportunities undermines social welfare gains. Comprehensive and sustained development requires making the state more accountable and Iran's foreign relations less confrontational.

However, this is easier said than done, for there are profound obstacles to restructuring Iran's economy. The state has been heavily dependent upon oil exports—rather than taxing and borrowing from the domestic economy—for revenue. This has freed politicians from having to confront social classes or borrow from international lending institutions. Yet unlike small-population rentier states such as Kuwait and the United Arab Emirates, whose oil revenue per capita is extremely high, Iran has a much larger population and thus needs to diversify its economy beyond the petroleum sector to generate employment, exports, and revenue in times when oil prices decline. Like most other late-developing countries, Iran first adopted import substitution industrialization (ISI) (1950s–1980s) and later sought to liberalize and privatize its economy (1990s–2000s) as means to achieve development objectives (Ehsani 2009). Nonetheless, there are important caveats to this trajectory.

First, the oil boom years (1960s and early 1970s) ensured that Iran could import industrial and commercial goods more freely than ISI regimes could normally manage. This ensured that commercial and service sectors were profitable, with urban consumerism flourishing at the expense of agricultural and industrial production. Each round of oil price hikes has reinforced this dynamic. Politically, it meant that the private commercial community (*bazaari* merchants) has been relatively wealthier and more pivotal in Iran's economy than in Egypt, Turkey, and other large industrializing economies. These resources have made merchants important political actors, as was exhibited in the Islamic Revolution (Keshavarzian 2007).

Second, while many of the economies in the region began to adopt liberalizing economic policies as a response to budget deficits and pressure from international lending agencies in the 1980s, Iran's tight regulation of its economy persisted and even expanded in that decade. The new regime rationed hard currency, set prices for consumer goods, and distributed loans to key sectors of the economy. Policymakers were compelled to increase the state's profile because many industrialists were exiled after 1979, the regime promised to redistribute wealth, international investment had come to a standstill, and the war required the state to direct and mobilize resources for the front. Ministries, parastatal organizations, and the IRGC took on major roles in production, finance, and commerce. This resulted in multiple, sometimes competing state organizations and institutions becoming involved in the economy. Once the war ended, these vested interests resisted attempts to liberalize policies and break up oligarchies.

Still, under Presidents Rafsanjani and Khatami, limited economic liberalization was initiated with regime allies such as members of the IRGC seizing this opportunity to secure government assets and contracts. Higher oil prices since 2003 along with some policy reforms did improve growth rates and benefit certain export-oriented sectors; however, inequality and youth unemployment have persisted, while sanctions and the restructuring of subsidies have fueled inflation. Inequality helped Ahmadinejad in his 2005 presidential campaign, which championed redistribution and attending to the "real needs of ordinary Iranians," by which he meant economic livelihoods rather than political freedoms. In his time in office, however, the populist message has ushered in a series of shortsighted measures aimed at shoring up his political base, rather than meaningful policies addressing problems of welfare and employment (Ehsani 2006, 2009; Salehi-Isfahani 2008).

International sanctions, spearheaded by the United States, are another factor shaping Iran's political economy. These broad sanctions limit Iran's ability to import goods and technologies essential for manufacturing and trade. Meanwhile, oil exports have been crippled by both lack of foreign investment in the petroleum infrastructure and expanding third-party sanctions that discourage companies and countries from importing Iranian crude oil. While Iran's economy has been weakened and lives of ordinary Iranians have deteriorated, it is highly questionable whether sanctions have achieved the goal of influencing regime elites to adopt different foreign policies.

Finally, state regulations, international sanctions, and high levels of unemployment have fueled a large informal and quasi-illegal economy, including the smuggling of restricted goods and illicit commodities. This trade is reinforced by US sanctions and Iran's proximity to Dubai's commercial hub and states with porous borders and devastated economies (Iraq, Afghanistan, and the former Soviet Union). The informal economy has provided sources of income for marginalized people and ensured that Iranians have access to foreign goods, but well-placed agents and middlemen, many of them with connections to state officials, are the primary beneficiaries of this gray economy. Thus, equality and sustainable development continue to be goals, rather than realities.

Gender and Politics: Battleground for Contending Visions

The contradictions between socioeconomic accomplishments and political limits in the Islamic Republic are strikingly evident when examining gender relations. Policies toward women and the family also reveal much about the shift from the modernist and Western-oriented Pahlavi monarchy to the Islamist and populist Islamic Republic. For the Shah, women needed to be rescued from the "traditionalism" of the clergy and Islam. By reforming marriage and divorce laws and presenting an image of the ideal Iranian woman without a veil and in a miniskirt, the monarchy sought to demonstrate that Iran was "Westernizing" and hence modernizing. Similarly, the founders of the Islamic Republic believed that women needed saving; for them, Western immorality and consumerism were the blights, with women becoming symbols for Islamic authenticity and national independence. At least since Reza Shah's law that forbade the wearing of the veil, Iranian women's bodies and rights have been a battleground between contending visions of the nation and modernity.

The Islamic emancipation of women from "immorality" resulted in dramatic changes in the legal structure after the Islamic Revolution. Based on their patriarchal understanding of Islamic law, the working premise of lawmakers has been that women are principally mothers, wives, or daughters, rather than independent citizens. In order to conform to these gender roles, laws were changed to lower the minimum age of marriage for women, enhance men's powers in divorce and child custody cases, make veiling mandatory, and allow husbands to deny their wives the ability to travel abroad or work outside the home. This dramatic reversal shocked urban, educated women, many of whom had fought for these rights and used them to participate in the labor market, family decisionmaking, and the revolution itself.

Paradoxically, however, this blatant and categorical discrimination against women created a common ground for protest by women, regardless of their political attitudes, age, or religiosity (Kian-Thiébaut 2002). At first defensively, but subsequently proactively, women of different social backgrounds and generations established associations and journals to articulate policy demands as well as women-centered approaches to Islam, law, and development, replacing the earlier discourse of family, loyalty, and responsibility with one about rights, choice, and opportunity (Bayat 2007: 71–79). Iran's "Islamic feminism" has been one of the areas of dialogue between Iranian and other Muslim intellectuals.

While it would be an exaggeration to say that Iran has developed a powerful women's movement to challenge the various forms of institutionalized and societal patriarchy that exist, women activists have enjoyed political power and social presence. As Zhaleh Shaditalab, a university professor and specialist on women's affairs in Iran, reminds us: "In Iran, elections constitute one of the rare occasions when women, half the voters, can determine the fate of men" (Kian-Thiébaut 2002: 57). This power was exhibited in the electoral victories of reformists, who often highlighted many of the concerns of women, as well as the highly visible role played by women in the Green Movement.

Still, radical and socially penetrating change via political institutions alone is unlikely. Laws and policies are experienced by women in very different social and economic contexts. For instance, mandatory imposition of the veil has been viewed as a form of oppression *and* liberation because it operates differently across society. For urban and secular women, the imposition of the veil represents a public and daily instrument for gender segregation and denial of individual choice. However, for women in more religious settings in middle- and lower-class neighborhoods and smaller cities, the veil is not viewed as an alien imposition. Rather, the veil and the "Islamicized public sphere" have helped them participate in society without the admonishments of paternalistic and religious family members and their communities. After the revolution, it became more dubious for fathers, brothers, husbands, and others to tell women that they should not go to university, work, and parks, or ride buses, metros, and taxis, on the justification that these were places of irreligiosity and cultural corruption. The religious nature of the regime has simultaneously curtailed many rights and allowed larger numbers of women to access higher education and the job market, which has altered gender roles at large. This does not mean that all women support reformists or that conservative women do not exert pressure on hard-liners and clerics (Sadeghi 2009; Shahrokni 2009).

This dynamic is reflected in social indicators. Female illiteracy has dramatically declined, from 70 percent in 1975 to 46 percent in 1990 to 31 percent in 2000; less than 9 percent of fifteen- to twenty-four-year-old women were illiterate in 2000 (Moruzzi and Sadeghi 2006: 23). By 1999, an equal number of women and men were enrolled in universities (Kian-Thiébaut 2002: 63). Higher rates of literacy and education have led to Iranian women marrying later and to a declining age gap between husbands and wives (Moruzzi and Sadeghi 2006). These changes, combined with a policy shift in favor of family planning, dramatically reduced the population growth rate in the 1990s. The decline in fertility rates will ease the burden on the state and economy to provide education, health care, and jobs, and it also should help women work outside the home, something that has not increased at the same rate as educational achievement (Salehi-Isfahani 2001). Policymakers did not intend to empower women when they implemented educational and health programs, but these policies, which have often depended on the active volunteerism of women, seem to have done exactly this (Hoodfar 2009). Today, Iranian women are more educated, marrying later in life, working more outside the home, having fewer children, and struggling to make relationships within marriage more egalitarian. Not only has the behavior of women changed, but so have attitudes of Iranian women and men. Studies show that women desire to work in the labor force (even after marriage) and aspire to greater gender equality in society, in the family, and between husbands and wives (Kurzman 2008; Moaddel and Azadarmaki 2002).

Thus a widening gap has emerged between the legal system's view of women and the self-perception and social reality of women. These social changes and ideological struggles have helped women confront social norms and traditional forms of patriarchy in households. However, as a recent article concludes, women face new challenges, familiar to women around the world: "The decline of formal traditionalism has meant that gender inequality has evolved into specifically modern forms: sexual harassment on the street, gender discrimination in the workplace and sexual double standards in the bedroom. . . . If women no longer experience explicitly patriarchal authority on a daily basis, what they experience is definitely still a 'masculinist' structure of social authority: not necessarily the dominance of the father, but definitely still the preeminence of men" (Moruzzi and Sadeghi 2006: 24).

Religion and Politics: Unexpected Experiences

The Islamic Republic certainly left many of the secular and democratically oriented supporters of the revolution alienated, yet clerics and the pious also have reason to be dissatisfied. For instance, within a year of becoming president, Ahmadinejad closed a Sufi (mystic) lodge in Qom, the city where Khomeini studied and taught. The leader of the revolution himself angered clerics when he ruled that the eating and producing of caviar were permissible under Islamic dietary law, contravening the prevailing view among religious scholars.[4] Given that caviar production and exports are an important sector in the Iranian economy, it seems that once Khomeini took over the reins of the state, profits trumped purity laws. These examples force us to contemplate how religious institutions and practices have fared under political Islamism.

Khomeini's political innovation of cleric-led government has reconfigured "church"-state relations. For instance, job opportunities and income are available to clerics in the judicial system and in the ministries, and as Friday prayer leaders. Clerics and their kin, especially former students of Khomeini, have been prominent in the higher reaches of the regime, yet the actual running of the state has never been dominated by seminary graduates and their presence has declined since the 1980s. One indication is the decline in the number of clerics in parliament. In the very first parliament, almost half of the members of parliament were clerics, but by the late 1990s clerics constituted less than 20 percent of MPs. What is more, however religiously conservative and pro–*velayat-e faqih* Ahmadinejad may be, he is also the Islamic Republic's first lay president.

The majority of clerics can be found in seminaries, teaching, studying, and interpreting religious texts, and they remain indifferent and even disdainful of their peers employed by the government. In turn, the state has monitored seminaries by dictating curricula, and the Leader has used his office to support seminaries and clerics sympathetic to the concept of the guardianship of the jurisprudent and the regime's interpretations of Islam. In theory there should be no distinction between state and mosque, but in practice they remain apart despite the infusion of seminarians and religion into the state. The state can never be sure that the seminaries are producing "appropriate" clergy for the government or socializing Iranians in the official doctrine.

As the caviar example illustrates, there are tensions between religious law and the practicalities of running a modern nation-state. These conflicts were directly confronted by Khomeini at the end of his life when, after a series of disputes featuring the parliament legislating economic and social policies and the Council of Guardians striking them down in the name of Islamic law, Khomeini amended his doctrine of guardianship of the jurisprudent to allow the state to override religious law when that was deemed expedient.[5] He declared that this "absolute mandate *(velayat-e motlaq)* was the most important of divine commandments and has priority over all derivative divine commandments . . . even over prayer, fasting, and the pilgrimage to Mecca" (Arjomand 1988: 182). Needless to say, most traditional Muslims and clerics were horrified by this subordination of religion to the interests of the state, as the whole purpose of setting up an Islamic government had been the exact opposite.

Unlike in most of the Middle East, political Islam in contemporary Iran is not a movement of the opposition, but rather an ideology and policy agenda for the state. Religious tests exist for college entrance and government positions; gender segregation and mandatory veiling are instituted to maintain "Islamic dignity"; and laws, such as inheritance and criminal law, are based on Islamic doctrine. Official speeches and pronouncements are peppered with religious expressions and quotations, the calendar is full of religious holidays, and religious observance is often public and conspicuous. All of this is in order to "Islamicize" society and ensure that Iranians live in a religiously observant manner.

It is difficult to judge to what extent these policies have made Iranians (more) devout, and the limited available evidence presents a very complicated picture. While most Iranians consider themselves religious and consider religious matters and practices as important aspects of their lives, results from the 2000–2001 World Value Survey suggest many dimensions to religiosity. Based on these results, Iranians are no more "religious" than Jordanians and Egyptians, and along certain dimensions significantly less so (Moaddel and Azadarmaki 2002). Notably, in comparison to Egypt and Jordan, a larger portion of Iranians self-identify in nationalist terms. Also, while 79 and 60 percent of surveyed Egyptians and Jordanians, respectively, indicated that "religious authorities sufficiently respond to the country's problems," only 47 percent of surveyed Iranians felt this way. When considering the findings from national public opinion polls in the 1970s, we observe that levels of personal religiosity (e.g., frequency of prayer) have remained relatively constant, but participation in organized religion (e.g., attending congregational Friday prayers) has declined, reflecting a growing ambivalence toward state-sponsored public religious practices (Kazemipur and Rezaei 2003). The increasingly urban, educated Iranian society has helped generate new demands on religion and interpreters of faith. Religious belief and practice have become more individualized and personalized. This helps explain the popularity of books and lectures on meditation, self-help, and mysticism.

Finally, public opinion research shows that, on average, Iranians who attend communal Friday prayers tend to be *less* religious than those who do not attend (Tezcür, Azadarmaki, and Bahar 2006). Participation in these public and state-regulated religious events seems to be more an indication of one's political attitudes and approval of the regime than of religiosity. Since the establishment of the Islamic Republic, there also has emerged a class of Iranians that can be described as "politically dissatisfied Islamists." These people are religious and even favor clerical rule and state enforcement of Islamic law and principles, but disapprove of the regime's performance and responsiveness.

This religious disillusionment with the system is reflected in calls for reform from both those who want to strengthen republicanism and those who want to impose Islam from above more strictly. Some theologians have called for separating "church" and state—not because they advocate secularism per se, but out of concern for religious knowledge and society (Ansari 2006: 70–79). For over a century, Muslims have advocated the separation of "church" and state, but they have always been Western-oriented secularists; in Iran, for the first time, *religious* arguments are being made for this separation, on the grounds that coercively imposed religion harms religious knowledge and spirituality. These types of arguments garnered religious and clerical support for the Reformist movement in the 1990s and have spurred opposition to Ahmadinejad especially since the election debacle of 2009. Conversely, some of the pious who in 2005 voted for Ahmadinejad and against well-known clerical candidates did so in order to rebuke the regime-affiliated clergy, who are seen to have been corrupted by power.

Identity and Politics: Inclusions and Exclusions

If clerics and pious Muslims have reasons to criticize the regime's religious policies, it is not surprising that non-Muslims (approximately 2 percent of the total population) have grounds for anxiety. As small communities, Bahais, Christians,[6] Zoroastrians, and Jews have faced long-standing social discrimination and local persecution, with protection being an extension of the will of state leaders rather than legal equality. Yet for centuries these religious minorities have lived and often flourished in Iran, their identities being informed by the Persian language and history as they contributed to Iranian culture and society. The Pahlavi regime's secularist policies, emphasis on pre-Islamic history, and close ties with Western governments were reassuring for some in these confessional groups. Non-Muslim elites were more evident in the economic and cultural realms than in state institutions, nonetheless significant numbers (especially among Armenians) were involved in various political currents, including the 1979 revolution.

As the constitution of the Islamic Republic was being drafted, leaders of the Christian, Zoroastrian, and Jewish communities, in cooperation with sympathetic Shi'ite clerics, were able to acquire certain protections for religious

practices and personal matters (Sanasarian 2000). These rights are extended
because Muslims consider Islam as emerging out of the same tradition as
these religions and believe that these "people of the book" are entitled to
protections. Parliament reserves two seats for Armenian Christians and one
seat each for Assyrian Christians, Zoroastrians, and Jews. Yet the office of
the president and other top posts are exclusively reserved for Shi'ite Muslims and the penal code systematically discriminates against non-Muslims.
Finally, the law against apostasy threatens death for Muslim converts to
other faiths. Iranian Jews, the largest Jewish community in the region outside of Israel, face a particular dilemma. Since its founding the regime has
been virulently anti-Israeli and, more recently, Ahmadinejad has questioned
the veracity of the Holocaust. Yet public officials are typically careful to
draw a distinction between Judaism, which is lauded as part of the Abrahamic tradition, on the one hand, and Zionism as a political ideology of the
State of Israel, which is accused of usurping Palestinian land and oppressing
Palestinians, on the other. While this critical distinction may have encouraged some Jews to remain in Iran, where they have lived for over two millennia, it also burdens them with demonstrating their loyalty to Iran.

Unlike the "people of the book," the faith of Iran's largest non-Muslim
minority, Bahais, is unrecognized as an official religion. The estimated
350,000 Bahais living in Iran have faced social, clerical, and political discrimination since the emergence of the new faith in the nineteenth century
(Brookshaw and Fazel 2008). To Muslims, who believe that Islam is the
last revelation, the Bahai faith's belief in a new prophecy is heresy. The Islamic Republic has institutionalized this view, systematically discriminating
against Bahais; to this day they may not attend university, for instance.

The treatment of these religious minorities is and should be a concern of
Iranians and the international community; however, given that their numbers
are small and the populations are not geographically localized, religious sectarianism is not a threat to the territorial integrity or political power of the
Iranian state. By contrast, ethnolinguistic cleavages and the relatively large
Sunni population (8 percent) are potentially politically volatile. Barely over
half of Iranians are ethnically Persian. The native tongues of the remainder
are Azeri (25 percent), Kurdish (8–9 percent), Arabic (3 percent), and other
languages. While there have been instances of localized ethnic conflicts and
moments in history when separatist movements have gained traction, what is
striking about the Iranian case is the *lack* of ethnic politicization and protracted conflict that have been common in neighboring Iraq and Turkey.

Several factors have depoliticized ethnic cleavages and enabled Iranian
national identity to be inclusive of diversity. To begin with, history and,
more importantly, the understanding of history matter. As a former empire
with a polyglot and culturally diverse population distributed over a diverse
territory, Iran and Iranian identity have been constituted by history and land

as much as by language and religion. In Persian poetry, mythology, and historical narratives, "Iran" is primarily associated with a land, rather than language or religion (Kashani-Sabet 1999). Thus, nationalists have available to them a conception of Iranian identity that is inclusive of people of different languages, cultures, and religions. In addition, recent historical events have created a shared mass experience that cuts across many divides. The Islamic Revolution included and attracted the support of Iranians of all ethnic backgrounds; in fact, Kurds were particularly supportive of overthrowing the monarchy, although this enthusiasm did not lead to collaboration in the construction of the Islamic Republic. Similarly, the eight-year war with Iraq and the wartime experience of hundreds of thousands of young men from all corners of Iran helped reinforce national solidarity and consciousness. The war was also important because it forced the nascent ostensibly Shi'ite regime to simultaneously adopt a more hybrid nationalism. Given that the majority of Iraqis are Shi'ite,[7] the leaders of the Islamic Republic had to validate the war in the name of Iranian brotherhood and defense of territory, not just Shi'ite unity and duty.

Moreover, the very categories of ethnicity and religion are replete with crosscutting cleavages. While a majority of Kurds in Iran are Sunni (an additional identity setting them apart from the majority), approximately 30 percent are Shi'ite. The central government has recruited Shi'ite Kurds both as a way to reach out to the Kurdish community and as a method of divide-and-rule. The large Azeri population, meanwhile, is entirely Shi'ite, making religion a bridge with the larger Persian population. In turn, the Azeri population itself is divided geographically across large population centers in Tabriz, Ardebil, and Tehran, with noticeable rivalries and cultural differences existing among them (Chehabi 1997). While the small religious minorities tend to be united, Sunni organization and cooperation face serious challenges, since the population is fragmented into three distinct and geographically distant ethnolinguistic groups—Kurds in the northwest, Baluch in the southeast, and Turkmen in the northeast.

Unlike the Persian-centric brand of nationalism that prevailed under the Pahlavi monarchy, the current regime has initiated state policies recognizing and to some extent accommodating ethnic differences. Persian is the official language, but state law also permits and even financially supports the limited use of local languages and dialects on television, radio, and in the print media, and allows universities to teach and offer programs in the study of the Azeri and Kurdish languages. "The ethnic fact is openly acknowledged in Iran, and the central government is more willing than the previous regime to allow the expression of cultural particularism" (Chehabi 1997: 247).

Finally, economic, cultural, military, religious, and political elites increasingly reflect Iran's ethnic heterogeneity. Urban Iranian society is quite mixed, with marriage across ethnic groups common. Many Iranians acknowledge their polyglot and multiregional backgrounds and thus it is relatively unre-markable that the current mayor of Tehran is believed to be half Kurdish; a former IRGC commander and minister of defense is Arab; and Khamenei, the Leader, was born into an Azeri family.

If multiethnic coexistence is a possibility and ethnic conflict is not in-evitable, the reverse is also true. There are forces that lead to greater politi-cization of ethnic and Shi'ite-Sunni cleavages, as they have at certain mo-ments in the past. First, state policies have exacerbated as well as ameliorated ethnic conflicts. Iranian nationalism under the Pahlavi monar-chy was not as virulent as Mustafa Kemal Atatürk's Turkish nationalism or the Baath Party's pan-Arabism, yet it did alienate non-Persians because Per-sianization was frequently imposed by the strong hand of the state. That re-sentment was reflected in the rise in the 1940s of Kurdish and Azeri nation-alism and the brief creation of Kurdish and Azeri states when Iran was occupied by allied troops at the end of World War II. In the wake of the Is-lamic Revolution, Kurdish groups openly mobilized for greater autonomy and even independence—only to be suppressed through force.

The Islamic Republic's privileging of Shi'ism has overlain the existing Sunni-Shi'ite cleavage with the weight of the state. Iran's Sunni population does not have equal access to government jobs and their religious institu-tions are treated in a discriminatory manner. The Sunni population in Tehran, for instance, has not received permission to build a Sunni mosque. To date, mobilization in the name of Sunni Islam is limited in Iran, but re-gional dynamics may change this. The upsurge of sectarianism in the region and the development of transnational Islamic networks over the past three decades may enable Iranian Sunnis to envision and articulate their griev-ances in a more sectarian fashion (Ghaffari 2009). Sunni-Shi'ite strife in post–Saddam Hussein Iraq, and Sunni Arab governments speaking of a ris-ing threat from the "Shi'ite crescent," can only embolden those seeking sec-tarian violence.

These examples also allude to the role of international and cross-border dynamics. Iran's ethnic minorities live mostly in the country's periphery and all have ethnic kin across the border. Thus, Iran's ethnic dynamics are informed by the situation within and the actions of neighboring states and peoples. For instance, the formation of an independent Azerbaijan, after the collapse of the Soviet Union, strengthened Azeri consciousness and en-hanced Iranian Azeris' bargaining power vis-à-vis the central state (Chehabi 1997). Similarly, the emergence of a semi-independent Kurdish region after the 1991 Gulf War and debates about federalism and Kurdish autonomy in post-2003 Iraq have unnerved Iranian officials and may be an inspiration to some Kurds in Iran. To date, ethnic groups have been either uninterested in or unable to organize popular and resilient parties and militias; political activism has been mostly directed at acquiring greater rights and resources from the state, rather than independence. Consequently, the reformist movement was particularly popular among these groups.

The biggest cause of tension between Persians and non-Persians as well as between Shi'ites and Sunnis is socioeconomic inequality. As detailed earlier, major improvements in rural and socioeconomic development have occurred under the current regime. Yet development remains highly uneven. For instance, the provinces of Kurdistan and Sistan-Baluchestan, whose populations are largely Kurdish and Baluchi, respectively, have the lowest human development rankings of Iran's twenty-six provinces. The variation in human development across Iran's provinces is closely correlated with government expenditure, thus giving socioeconomic inequality a profoundly political dimension (UNDP and Plan and Budget Organization of the Islamic Republic 1999: 23, 156–157). Given that the central government is composed mostly of Shi'ite Persians, the disparities in rates of literacy, unemployment, and access to health care and education have politicized ethnic relations. Socioeconomic inequality, political strife, and ethnic mobilization are less pronounced in Azeri- and Arab-dominated areas, which enjoy far better standards of living, a fact that reinforces the point that development is critical for ethnic coexistence. In sum, while the Iranian polity has a long way to go to fully integrate its populations as equal citizens, critical social and political steps have been taken to imagine the Iranian community in a more inclusive manner and dampen the prospects of interethnic and sectarian violence.

Civil Society: Potentials and Limits

One of the lessons of both the revolution and contestation under the Islamic Republic is that nongovernmental organizations in civil society can be consequential. Prior to the revolution, formal associations were controlled by the state to recruit clients and co-opt elites and were not the organizations that made the revolution. Instead, a whole host of informal associations operating under the radar of the state were instrumental for social mobilization. Given that the media were restricted and professional associations were dominated by the state, informal gatherings and relations functioned as transmission belts for sharing information and forging social bonds and trust.

The mass participation in the revolution itself strengthened the sense of national engagement in politics. The Iran-Iraq War reinforced the spirit of collective participation, as large numbers of Iranians were recruited to fight and volunteer their professional expertise as doctors, nurses, and cameramen. Occurring so soon after the revolution, the war enabled the regime to redirect the politicization and mobilization of Iranians away from domestic politics and toward foreign enemies and reconstruction. Additionally, the regime demobilized civil society by integrating it into the state bureaucracy. The Islamic associations and militias *(basij)* that mushroomed during the revolution and war were gradually transformed from voluntary community-based groups into paid representatives of the Leader (Sadeghi 2009). These "governmental NGOs" were deployed by conservatives against reformists during the backlash against Khatami and against protesters since the 2009 election.

While the activities and institutionalization of political parties were limited by the regime, the two-headed nature of sovereignty and fragmented nature of the state created a space for advocacy NGOs to develop, formulate independent views, and participate in a nascent public sphere. The majority of these associations focused on various aspects of human rights and on women's issues. The Society for Protection of the Rights of the Child, created by the 2003 Nobel Peace Prize winner, Shirin Ebadi, is an example of such an initiative among legal activists. Alongside were print media covering political and social issues from a critical perspective and representing intellectual developments and debates, some of which have facilitated dialogue between secular and religious activists, who for several decades have been largely uninterested in or wary of one another.

Many of these journalists, lawyers, and activists are young university students and recent graduates and thus less encumbered by the historical weight of the revolution with which older generations grapple. Their energies have helped continue the tradition of university activism and protest. Student groups have been important in protesting the closure of newspapers and attacks on intellectuals, as well as challenging politicians more generally.

These independent NGOs and media were critical for mobilizing voters for the reformists and helped keep them relevant even after the conservatives shunted them out of government. While many of their efforts and successes came in the area of changing the terms of public debate, they have also helped push through modest legal changes, in family and inheritance law for example. These organizations are vulnerable, however, because they lack resources and are easily prevented from developing horizontal connections or transnational alliances. This is one of the main reasons why reformists have been unable to translate their clear electoral advantage into political power to negotiate with authoritarians in the regime.

The Impact of International Politics:
Real and Imagined Outcomes

Because Iran was not part of the Ottoman Empire, its main language is not Arabic, and its majority is Shi'ite rather than Sunni Muslim, the country is often treated as distinct from the Middle East. Yet regional forces have been immensely important, particularly from the 1990s to the present. This is partly related to the movement of people and goods. Economically, Iran has been trading a greater share of goods and services with countries in the Middle East and the rest of Asia than it previously did. Some of this is driven by the economic growth of East Asian economies, but it also is an outcome of sanctions and reflects the desire of Iranian leaders to participate in the world economy without being dependent on Western European and North American economies, as was the case under the Pahlavi monarchy. Additionally, commercial relations have been forged with Dubai's entrepôt economy and the war economies of Iraq and Afghanistan. Alongside this trade, weapons, drugs, and humans have been trafficked to, from, and through Iran. Conflicts in neighboring countries have also resulted in Iran becoming home to one of the largest refugee populations in the world. Finally, ordinary Iranian citizens have turned to new destinations for tourism and pilgrimage. Given tight visa restrictions for travel to Western Europe and North America, vacationers and pilgrims increasingly head to Dubai, Syria, Turkey, China, Malaysia, and Indonesia, only to encounter Iranian businessmen and politicians on their voyages. Contemporary Iran's economy and society hence are more integrated and engaged with regional dynamics than was the case during the Pahlavi era.

Iran's eight-year war with Iraq was arguably as significant as the Islamic Revolution. Its impact was felt most in the war zone along Iran's western border, but the whole society and economy were transformed by an event that mobilized over 2 million Iranians, killed and injured 1 million people, and consumed a substantial share of government resources (Ehsani 1995: 51). Politically, the impact of the war—which was officially termed the "imposed war" or the "sacred defense"—can be summed up as follows: "While the revolution brought a multiplicity of voices, at times emphasizing contradictory aspirations (e.g., submission to Islam and the spiritual leader as well as democracy and freedom), the war offered a univocal venue for both crushing domestic opposition to the newly emerging political order as well as 'sacred defense' against international aggression" (Farhi 2004: 104). Out of the war has emerged a "war generation" of young men and their families who were shaped as much by their experiences at the front as by the revolution. Now that many of these soldiers and IRGC officers are in their forties and fifties, those who have been politically inclined are demanding a bigger say in national and local politics. The tendency of these veterans has been to call for more "social order" and a greater state role in providing for the lower classes, disproportionately large numbers of whom volunteered for and perished in the war. Even though the war generation is divided politically and economically, Ahmadinejad claims to represent a large portion of this constituency by valorizing them and their sacrifices.

Yet when one thinks of Iran and international relations, one thinks primarily of international geopolitics, and for over half a century this has meant US-Iran relations. From the Shah to Ahmadinejad, from barely literate shopkeepers to ivy league–trained engineers, Iranians believe that politics in Iran can be and is altered by decisions made beyond its borders and by politicians not their own. Like most societal phobias, it is based on fact and disempowerment. As this chapter's introductory discussion of twentieth-century Iran illustrates, the facts are clear. British, Russian, and US intrigues and interests have repeatedly influenced Iranian domestic politics. Foreign forces have been involved in the toppling of rulers (e.g., Reza Shah in 1941 and Prime Minister Mossadeq in 1953) and have undermined the development of pluralism and democracy. Economically, international interests have often impinged on Iran's independence and access to technology (e.g., railroads, telegraph, and nuclear technology). Hence the Iranian government's argument that Iran has "a right to nuclear technology" resonates with much of Iranian society. International politics has not only undermined and destabilized regimes in Iran, but has also helped strengthen them, as was the case with US patronage of the Shah after 1953. US foreign policy was so important that when the administration of Jimmy Carter called for greater human rights, both the Shah and political dissidents believed that the US government had turned against the regime.

Ironically, regime leaders also benefit from US policy. The US approach to the regime, bellicose and confrontational, enables regime leaders to call for unity and smother criticism. For instance, the authoritarian backlash against the reformist movement was bolstered by the US government's decisions to invade two of Iran's neighbors, include Iran in the "axis of evil," expand economic sanctions, and threaten military action. Conservatives, including President Ahmadinejad, have used these decisions to deflect attention away from domestic woes and accuse all critics of being instruments of US imperial ambition. Thus, Iranian journalists, activists, and academic researchers have all been targeted with accusations of treason. The reality and fear of foreign meddling in Iran's domestic affairs not only exhibit Iranians' sense of vulnerability vis-à-vis more powerful foreign states but also are used by authoritarians to actually disempower Iran's polity.

Notes

I thank Greta Scharnweber for her generous help in completing this chapter. This chapter builds on an earlier textbook chapter on Iran (Chehabi and Keshavarzian 2011).

1. The Leader is selected by the Assembly of Experts, which is a popularly elected chamber of clerics with ten-year terms. In theory, the Assembly of Experts is more powerful than the Leader, since it elects him and has the power to dismiss him if it deems the Leader incapable of fulfilling his role. Yet in practice the Assembly of Experts is beholden to the Leader, since candidates for the assembly are

themselves subject to the approval of the Council of Guardians, whose members are in large part chosen by the Leader.

2. This chapter was written in 2012 and does not include the politics surrounding the 2013 presidential elections.

3. From 1997 to 2002 the courts banned 108 daily newspapers and periodicals, and from 2000 to 2003 the Council of Guardians vetoed over fifty parliamentary bills (Bayat 2007: 120, 123).

4. According to Shi'ite (and Jewish) dietary laws, fish must have scales in order to be eaten. Yet caviar is the roe from sturgeon, which have no scales.

5. This ultimately led to the creation of the Expediency Council, which is mandated to resolve disputes between parliament and the Council of Guardians. It is unelected and consists of members from various branches of government and representatives of the Leader.

6. There are several Christian groups living in Iran. The largest community is the Armenians (150,000–200,000), but there are also Assyrians, Chaldeans, and small numbers of Roman Catholics and Protestants.

7. Given that Saddam Hussein and many of the leading members of the Baath Party were Sunni, Shi'ite iconography and history were integral to the Iranian government's war effort.

12

Iraq

Fred H. Lawson

Politics in Iraq have displayed a high degree of violence for more than half a century. The officers who carried out the July 1958 revolution killed the royal family, and then fell out with one another, ushering in five years of bloody skirmishing among military commanders, Communists, Muslim Brothers, oil workers, farm laborers, and students. In the fall of 1959, President 'Abd al-Karim Qasim outlawed the Socialist Arab Resurrection (Baath) Party after its members tried to assassinate him. One of the would-be assassins was a twenty-three-year-old party activist named Saddam Hussein. Resistance to the February 1963 coup d'état, which brought officers loyal to the Baath Party to power, was crushed, and President Qasim executed. The party's militia, the National Guard, undertook to annihilate its adversaries, particularly the powerful Iraqi Communist Party.

By November 1963, the military and civilian wings of the Baath Party had begun fighting one another, which only ended when troops loyal to President 'Abd al-Salam 'Arif, who was not a member of the party, intervened. The president then created the Republican Guard, consisting of elite army units with whose officers he had close personal connections. President 'Arif was killed in a helicopter crash in April 1966 and was succeeded by his brother 'Abd al-Rahman. Fifteen months later, in a peaceful coup, Baathi officers ousted 'Arif and set up the Revolution Command Council (RCC), led by President Ahmad Hasan al-Bakr and the commander in chief of the armed forces, Hardan al-Takriti. President al-Bakr built up the Baath Party's security apparatus as a way to keep the armed forces in check and appointed his cousin Saddam Hussein to supervise the project. In July 1979, Saddam Hussein succeeded al-Bakr as president.

Historical Background and Contemporary Political Structure

Government and Opposition in Baathi Iraq

Iraq's September 1968 constitution accorded executive and legislative authority to the Revolution Command Council. The RCC was reconfigured in early 1969 to replace military officers with senior figures in the Baath Party's security forces. The new council installed party commissars at all levels of the armed forces to instill loyalty to Baathi principles and keep track of potential dissidents (Hashim 2003: 23). After an attempted coup d'état in June 1973, President al-Bakr took charge of the ministry of defense and subordinated the military's intelligence branches to the Baath Party's security apparatus. A month later, the RCC reached an agreement with the Iraqi Communist Party, which authorized Baathi cadres to take over the country's workers', students', and women's unions.

In January 1976, Saddam Hussein was awarded the rank of general, despite having no previous military experience. The Baath Party militia doubled in size; under its new name, the People's Militia, it was placed under the command of one of Saddam Hussein's protégés, Taha Yasin Ramadan. The party and its security forces then initiated a drive to impose Baathi ideology and forms of organization on the country's major institutions, most notably university campuses.

Immediately after becoming president, Saddam Hussein purged the RCC of actual and potential rivals. The resulting body consisted entirely of longtime colleagues and relatives of the new president. In March 1980, Saddam Hussein issued a law that created a 250-member National Assembly. The first elections took place that June and resulted in an overwhelming victory for Baath Party candidates (Baram 1981).

In August 1988, Saddam Hussein and his allies purged the armed forces of all commanders who showed any sign of disloyalty (Hashim 2003: 20). As part of the postwar reconstruction effort, a new ministry of industry and military industrialization was created and placed in the hands of the president's son-in-law, Husain Kamil al-Majid. The ministry was given charge over the state-run petrochemical sector, which provided it with revenues to carry out a variety of industrial and infrastructure projects. Nevertheless, the local economy continued to stagger, prompting the RCC to loosen restrictions on elections to the National Assembly. In the April 1989 balloting, independent candidates were permitted to run for the first time.

Iraq's occupation of Kuwait in August 1990 tightened the hold of the president and his closest allies over the political system. The Republican Guard and Baath Party security forces crushed the popular uprisings that erupted in March 1991. Thereafter, national politics became a family affair.

One half-brother of Saddam Hussein was minister of the interior; another half-brother headed the security directorate; a cousin took over as minister of defense; Husain Kamil al-Majid remained in his post; and another son-in-law commanded a key security force. Another security agency was put in the hands of the president's younger son, Qusai. The older son, 'Udai, became minister of information, youth, and sport.

Moves to overthrow Saddam Hussein were made by discontented military officers on a number of occasions after the 1990–1991 Gulf War. In retaliation, the Republican Guard was purged in the summer of 1995 and command was given to the president's cousin Kamal Mustafa Al Bu Sultan. Saddam Hussein's son 'Udai was severely injured in an assassination attempt in December 1996, and an attack on Qusai took place in early 1997. Nevertheless, in 2000 the president announced that Qusai would act as caretaker president in the event that he became incapacitated. In April 2001, Qusai was elected to a seat in the Regional (Iraqi) Command of the Baath Party.

As United Nations (UN) economic sanctions weakened the central administration during the late 1990s, the Baath Party apparatus distributed food and other vital goods to the population. Ration coupons issued by the party became the primary means whereby citizens acquired staples. Still, party membership dropped precipitously. The regime then turned to tribal leaders (shaikhs) to administer local affairs (Baram 1997). The shaikhs maintained public order and collected taxes in urban neighborhoods and rural districts, which were officially designated "tribal areas." Representatives of the shaikhs dominated the National Assembly after the March 2000 elections.

Government and Opposition
After the Fall of Saddam Hussein

This amalgam of family ties, party apparatus, and tribal authority collapsed in March 2003 in the face of the massive assault led by US and British troops. The Coalition Provisional Authority (CPA), which took charge of southern and central Iraq, dismantled the armed forces and prohibited members of the Baath Party from holding positions in the administration and public enterprises. The CPA instead relied on the Iraqi National Congress (INC), a loose collection of political movements headed by Ahmad Shalabi. The INC included an assortment of liberal democratic parties and three Shi'i organizations that had struggled against the Baathi regime: the Supreme Council for Islamic Revolution in Iraq (SCIRI), the Party of the Call to Islam, and the Islamic Action Organization. These organizations seized control of the INC's agenda at a December 2002 conference in London and emerged as the most powerful forces in Iraq under the CPA.

Postwar politics reflected rivalry among three factions of Iraq's Shi'i community. The most prestigious figure of the post-Baath era was Grand Ayatollah 'Ali al-Sistani of Najaf, a longtime critic of religious rule, particularly as it was practiced in the Islamic Republic of Iran. Al-Sistani urged Shi'ites not to resist the advance of US and British forces, and expected the CPA to solicit his guidance in setting up the new order. He was furious when the CPA announced that it intended to draw up a constitution. In July 2003 he denounced this course of action and asserted that an elected constitutional assembly should be formed to carry out such a momentous undertaking.

Al-Sistani's main adversary was the radical preacher Muqtada al-Sadr, who mobilized poorer neighborhoods in Baghdad, Najaf, and Kufa after the collapse of the Baathi regime, and won widespread support for his efforts to restore order and provide public services. He was contemptuous of al-Sistani for failing to stand up to Saddam Hussein prior to 2003, and was equally dismissive of Shalabi for spending his career outside the country. He insisted that Iraq be ruled by Iraqis, rather than by figures, like al-Sistani, whose family background could be traced to Iran. He advocated replacing Iraq's existing Shi'i religious hierarchy with popular seminaries that emphasized political and social activism. His followers, who formed the Mahdi Army, attacked liquor stores, video shops, and brothels, and patrolled the sprawling Baghdad suburb that took the name Sadr City.

Somewhat less powerful was Ayatollah Mohammad Sa'id al-Hakim, a cousin of the head of SCIRI, Mohammad Baqir al-Hakim. SCIRI broke with the United States in January 2003, when it announced that the CPA would run Iraq, and resumed its partnership with Iran. SCIRI's militia, the Badr Brigade, was trained by Iran's Islamic Revolutionary Guards Corps and enjoyed close ties to Iran's supreme leader, Ayatollah Ali Khamenei. US commanders warned the Badr Brigade to keep out of Iraq during the 2003 assault, but SCIRI fighters infiltrated the southern provinces anyway, and soon emerged as pivotal actors in Kut and Baquba.

In May 2003, Mohammad Baqir al-Hakim marched across the border to Basra from southwestern Iran. He called for a legal system rooted in Islam, but one that protected the rights of dissidents and women. He told supporters that the government "must be chosen by Iraqis and be totally independent. We will not," he continued, "accept a government that is imposed on us" (Macintyre 2003). A month later, the chief UN representative in Iraq, Sergio Vieira de Mello, persuaded Baqir al-Hakim to join the US-sponsored Iraqi Governing Council (IGC). His younger brother, 'Abd al-'Aziz al-Hakim, joined the council as well.

The IGC was inaugurated in July 2003. Its members were drawn from organized political parties, including the Iraqi National Congress (represented by Ahmad Shalabi), the Iraqi National Accord (represented by Iyad 'Allawi), SCIRI, the Party of the Call to Islam, the Sunni Iraqi Islamic

Party, the Iraqi Communist Party, the National Democratic Party, and the two main Kurdish organizations—the Kurdistan Democratic Party (KDP) and the Patriotic Union of Kurdistan (PUK). For the most part, these parties championed reformist, secularist programs. For that reason, and because of the IGC's ties to the CPA, they were criticized by al-Sistani, who demanded that the council be replaced by an elected government, and Muqtada al-Sadr, who charged that the council represented foreign "unbelievers."

Meanwhile, opposition to the provisional government was spreading among the Sunni population. April 2003 saw the formation of the Association of Muslim Scholars. Sunni discontent escalated when US troops fired on a crowd of protesters in Fallujah, killing fifteen unarmed demonstrators (Hashim 2006: 23). Attacks on US patrols in the area subsequently grew more frequent. At first, "the majority [of such attacks] were perpetrated by amateurs and cash-strapped individuals hired by former regime loyalists" (Hashim 2006: 33). But as less proficient fighters were killed off, more skilled guerrillas took their place.

In August 2003, Mohammad Sa'id al-Hakim was wounded by a bomb blast in Najaf. Four days later, a truck bomb exploded outside the shrine of al-Imam 'Ali, killing Mohammad Baqir al-Hakim. Several prominent Shi'ites, including Mohammad Bahr al-'Ulum, resigned from the IGC on the grounds that it was unable to protect its members or the country as a whole. The Badr Brigade then took up positions throughout Najaf, prompting the Mahdi Army to move into the city. In Karbala, Mahmud al-Hasani al-Sarkhi raised a rival Shi'i militia called Husain's Army. Competition among the militias escalated, accompanied by exchanges of fire across the barricades.

In April 2004, the CPA launched a campaign to suppress the Mahdi Army. The Sadrist movement launched attacks on US patrols and occupied government offices in Sadr City, Najaf, Kufa, and Nasiriyyah. US forces counterattacked in August and, with the blessing of al-Sistani, forced the Mahdi Army to abandon the struggle. Former Baathi activists and Islamist radicals in Fallujah proved more obdurate. Heavy fighting raged from April to December, undermining the effectiveness and legitimacy of the Interim Iraqi Government, led by Prime Minister Iyad 'Allawi, which had taken office following the dissolution of the IGC in March 2004. Sunni resistance gained traction in Ramadi and Samarra as the year went by. Sunni radicals claimed to be cooperating with a leader of al-Qaeda, Abu Musab al-Zarqawi, and took credit for attacks in the name of al-Qaeda in Iraq.

Elections to the Transitional National Assembly (TNA) took place in January 2005. The Sadrist movement orchestrated protests against the balloting and called on the authorities to restore water and electricity instead of wasting time and resources on elections. Influential Sunni movements boycotted the proceedings as well, while radical Sunnis attacked police stations and provincial offices. Candidates representing SCIRI, the Party of the Call to Islam, and the two Kurdish parties emerged victorious. The assembly named the PUK's Jalal Talebani president and the Party of the Call to Islam's Ibrahim al-Ja'fari prime minister. SCIRI's energetic minister of the interior, Bayan Jabbur, allowed the Badr Brigade to take over the security forces.

The Association of Muslim Scholars congratulated al-Ja'fari and hinted that it would help build a new political system. Radical Sunnis, however, expressed their fears of a Shi'i-dominated order through suicide bombings. The Sunni speaker of the TNA appealed to his community to give up violence and join the electoral process, to no avail (Hashim 2006: 55). Such calls were undercut by the prime minister, who refused to appoint Sunnis to major ministerial positions (Hashim 2006: 78).

Elections for the permanent Iraqi National Assembly were held in December 2005. This time, Muqtada al-Sadr urged his supporters to vote, and Shi'i parties campaigned in Baghdad and the southern provinces as the United Iraqi Alliance (UIA). Sunni parties took part as well, including the Iraqi Islamic Party, the National Dialogue Council, and the General Conference of the Iraqi People. In all, 228 parties put forward candidates (Dawisha 2009: 252). The UIA came away with 128 of the 275 seats, Kurdish parties ended up with 53, and an alliance of Sunni parties led by the Iraqi Islamic Party won 44 (Marr 2007).

UIA members of parliament nominated Ibrahim al-Ja'fari to stay on as prime minister, but objections from Kurdish and Sunni representatives led al-Ja'fari to demur. Nuri Kamal al-Maliki of the Party of the Call to Islam was named prime minister in April 2006. Of the forty-six ministers in al-Maliki's cabinet, only eleven had held ministerial posts before. The most experienced individuals were affiliated with Kurdish parties, including President Talebani, Deputy Prime Minister Barham Salih, and Foreign Minister Mushyar Zibari. Key posts were distributed along sectarian lines: since Talebani retained the presidency, a Sunni and a Shi'ite were appointed vice presidents; al-Maliki was complemented with one Sunni and one Kurdish deputy prime minister; and the speaker of the National Assembly was a Sunni, with a Shi'ite and a Kurd as deputies (Dawisha 2009: 260–262).

Prime Minister al-Maliki took steps to consolidate power in the premiership. He set up the Office of the Commander in Chief to oversee the armed forces, put it in the hands of a trusted ally, and incorporated it into the Office of the Prime Minister. He appointed his son to be deputy chief of staff in charge of the security forces; he appropriated the power to appoint district police commanders; and he used state funds to create a network of "support councils" made up of tribal leaders. In late 2008, he launched a military campaign against the Sadrist movement, pushing the Sadrist militia out of Basra and imposing the central administration's authority over Sadr

City. The campaign alienated SCIRI, now called the Islamic Supreme Council of Iraq (ISCI). In the January 2009 provincial council elections, al-Maliki formed a new alliance called the Rule of Law Coalition (RLC), which won control of all but one of Iraq's provinces.

Parliamentary elections in March 2010 pitted al-Maliki's RLC against the Iraqi List, headed by former prime minister Iyad 'Allawi. The RLC came away with 89 seats, while the Iraqi List won 91, the Sadrist movement 40, and an ISCI-led grouping 30. Al-Maliki refused to accept the outcome and ordered a recount. Wrangling over the results and subsequent political jockeying delayed the formation of a new government for almost nine months. In the end, al-Maliki retained the premiership, as well as the minister of the interior post, and put a longtime ally in charge of the ministry of national security. The government placed the previously independent Higher Electoral Commission, Integrity Council (an anticorruption agency), and central bank under the control of the council of ministers. At the same time, Sunni officers in the military and security forces were let go and replaced by Shi'ites loyal to the RLC.

Protests erupted in Baghdad, Basra, and Mosul in February 2011. The demonstrations, led by the lawyers' union and university students, demanded that the security forces respect constitutional guarantees of citizens' rights and that steps be taken to root out official corruption. After police shot into a demonstration in Kut, protesters stormed the governor's office and set it on fire. Rioting spread to Basra, Fallujah, and Tikrit. Prime Minister al-Maliki announced that plans to buy military aircraft from the United States would be put on hold to free up funds to assist the poor, then ordered a reduction in electricity rates and the distribution of food to low-income districts. In April, the security forces restricted future protests to three football stadiums in Baghdad.

Attacks against government officials persisted. Responsibility for such strikes was claimed by a clandestine organization with ties to al-Qaeda called the Islamic State of Iraq. Car bombs struck police stations in Hillah and Kirkuk in early May, then spread to the capital. Meanwhile, Sadrists organized mass demonstrations to demand that US troops leave the country by the end of the year. On a single day in mid-August, forty-two bombings took place across the country. In September, cadres of the Sadrist movement took to the streets to demand reliable public services and an end to corruption. A month later, the leadership of Salah al-Din province voted to become fully autonomous as a protest against operations by the security forces that targeted Sunni activists.

In the spring of 2012, Sadrist representatives called for the dissolution of parliament and a new election. A key Shi'i rival of the Sadrists, the Bands of the People of Truth, announced that it would give up armed struggle and take part in the electoral process (Mohammed 2012); the organization made overtures to Prime Minister al-Maliki, who allowed it to organize a rally in the heart of the capital (al-Amiry 2012). In June 2012, Muqtada al-Sadr told reporters that he would do everything he could to prevent the prime minister from pursuing a third term in office.

Civil Society

Iraq enjoyed a flowering of civic activism and public expression in the 1930s and 1940s (Davis 2005), but associational life contracted after the 1958 revolution. By the mid-1980s, regimentation and surveillance permeated the domestic arena. More than any other Arab country, late Baathi Iraq approximated a totalitarian regime: public initiatives of any kind—political, economic, artistic—were ruthlessly quashed (al-Khalil 1989; al-Khafaji 1994).

Civic activism revived fitfully after 2003 and took a distinctly sectarian form. Neighborhood and village associations that had no ties to religious parties and movements were unable to compete with the Sadrists and other Islamist groupings, particularly after the UN's humanitarian mission—which had sponsored a number of nongovernmental organizations (NGOs)—pulled out of the country in August 2003.

Industrial and infrastructure workers set up the Iraqi Federation of Trade Unions (IFTU) in May 2003. Thirteen labor unions affiliated with the IFTU, giving the federation a total membership of almost 200,000 (Tripp 2007: 298). The IFTU's efforts to improve working conditions and protect jobs attracted the attention of US military commanders, who considered worker unrest a security threat. Consequently, US troops shut down IFTU headquarters from mid-2003 to July 2004 (Tripp 2007: 299). Trade unions were subjected to further restrictions in August 2005, when the al-Ja'fari government enacted a law that allowed the newly created Committee for Labor and Social Rights to exercise authority over all aspects of worker organizations. As Charles Tripp points out, "Government attempts to interfere in union elections, as well as to retain overall control of their finances and to enforce a restrictive legal framework for their operation, indicated that the impulse to curb the potential of an independent union movement was strong in the Islamist parties of the UIA" (2007: 299).

Kurdish areas provided a more hospitable environment for civic activism. Rivalry between the KDP and PUK opened a space in which civic associations could take root (Tripp 2007: 309). Survivors of the Halabja massacre organized a demonstration in March 2006 to remind the authorities of the continuing poverty of the district, and took to the streets again that summer to protest the inefficiency and corruption of the local administration. Such protests elicited strong responses from the KDP and PUK militias, which used force to break up peaceful marches.

Civic associations in post-Baathi Iraq display features similar to those that characterized state-affiliated popular organizations during the Baathi era. NGOs survive and flourish if they enjoy close connections to state agencies or operate under the auspices of powerful external patrons but face official harassment if they do not. They are required to be licensed by the government. And their leaderships make decisions and supervise day-to-day operations in a heavily top-down fashion.

Political Economy

For most of the Baathi era (1963–2003), Iraq boasted a socialist economic program. Large estates were broken up and land was haltingly distributed to agricultural laborers. June 1972 saw the nationalization of the Iraq Petroleum Company. As oil revenues skyrocketed, state officials set up Soviet-style collective farms and constructed dams and irrigation works to support them. Both large-scale, capital-intensive and smaller-scale, labor-intensive manufacturing plants were created to form a public sector in industry. Domestic and foreign trade was subjected to pervasive state supervision (Marr 2004: 162–163).

Nevertheless, the flood of oil money ensured that planners in Baghdad could carry out socialist experiments without siphoning investment and operating capital out of private hands. The expansion of state-run enterprises in the mid-1970s accompanied the rise of new private companies, which flourished thanks to lucrative contracts with public enterprises. In 1975, the private sector accounted for three-fifths of Iraq's nonoil gross national product.

During the first months of the war with Iran, government spending remained high, due to financial assistance from Saudi Arabia and Kuwait. The value of imports jumped from $4 billion in 1978 to $20 billion in 1981. As the fighting dragged on, however, oil income plunged. Revenues that had reached some $26 billion in 1980 dropped to $9 billion two years later (Alnasrawi 1994). As a result, new industrial and infrastructure projects were abandoned. Women moved into professional and skilled positions, while Egyptian immigrants took over many unskilled jobs, particularly in agriculture and building maintenance.

By the late 1980s, shortages of revenue led policymakers to promote private enterprise. Forty-seven state-run companies were sold to private interests in 1987. Lands from the collective farms were leased to private landholders, supported by low-interest loans from the Agricultural Cooperative Bank. A fall 1988 presidential memorandum, circulated shortly after the war came to a close, recommended that government agencies encourage competition among public and private companies as a way to improve performance and increase profits. Seventy additional public-sector factories were then put up for sale.

Such measures failed to resolve Iraq's postwar economic crisis (Chaudhry 1991). State officials explored the privatization of the petroleum sector, and in a desperate attempt to create jobs for demobilized soldiers, the authorities looked the other way as hundreds of Egyptian workers died in "accidents" at worksites and factories. Baghdad put pressure on the Organization of Petroleum Exporting Countries (OPEC) to enforce production quotas. Iraqi officials complained that Kuwait and the United Arab Emirates (UAE) were robbing the Iraqi treasury by exporting in excess of their allotments and driving down world prices.

In October 1990, Deputy Prime Minister Tariq 'Aziz told reporters that Iraq's occupation of Kuwait opened the door to a bright future. The merger of the two countries would, he claimed, enable the government to pay off its debts, raise annual oil income, and lay the foundation for a major expansion of private sector activity within the borders of the "new Iraq" (Alnasrawi 2001: 208). Reality turned out to be quite different. The UN Security Council froze all Iraqi assets outside the country, imposed an embargo on Iraqi oil exports, and restricted imports. Furthermore, the 1990–1991 war destroyed almost all of the country's power plants, fertilizer factories, iron and steel works, oil production and distribution facilities, and transportation infrastructure. In March 1991, a UN report concluded that "the recent conflict had wrought near-apocalyptic results upon what had been, until January 1991, a rather highly urbanized and mechanized society. Now, most means of modern life support have been destroyed or rendered useless. Iraq has, for some time to come, been relegated to a pre-industrial age, but with all the disabilities of post-industrial dependency on an intensive use of energy and technology" (Alnasrawi 1994: 119).

UN-sponsored sanctions remained in force long after the war ended. Imports, even foodstuffs, medicine, and spare parts, continued to be in extremely short supply. By 1993 the country was suffering from severe inflation. The local economy received meaningful relief in April 1995, when the UN Security Council set up a system whereby Iraq was permitted to sell a limited amount of oil to purchase food and medical supplies (Alnasrawi 2001: 212). The first shipment of oil under the terms of the so-called oil-for-food arrangement occurred in March 1997. Indications that the arrangement was contributing to economic recovery led the Security Council to expand the program in February 1998 to allow oil revenues to be used to rebuild the transportation system. Yet, as Abbas Alnasrawi observes, "it is obvious from the data that, while the oil-for-food programme provided some relief, it failed to change the underlying conditions of a deteriorating economy. Moreover, by channeling all transactions through the government, the programme increased government control over the population" (2001: 213).

Agriculture coped with sanctions better than other sectors. Wheat and barley production, particularly in the northern provinces, exceeded pre-1990 levels (Ahmad 2002: 175). Manufacturing fared considerably worse, with food processing, metal works, and textiles registering sharp declines (al-Khudayri 2002: 210). Kurdish entrepreneurs set up profitable businesses sending truckloads of oil to Turkey and alcoholic drinks and cigarettes to Iran. Revenues from such illicit commerce provided capital for a central bank in the north, after the creation of the Kurdistan Regional Government in June 1992 (Leezenberg 2002: 307–308). Profits fueled a building boom in Zakho and Dohuk.

Out of the regulatory chaos arose a scrappy group of private business-people whom Christopher Parker and Pete Moore call "the cats of the embargo" (2007: 9–10). This group attracted risk-takers from all communities, and included midlevel state officials and party cadres along with individuals who had long resisted the Baathi regime. Operations controlled by "the cats" employed a wide spectrum of drivers, mechanics, security guards, warehouse workers, and clerks. Meanwhile, tribal shaikhs extended their hold over a wide range of economic activities. Among the most lucrative was the regulation of the major roads and highways through which products entered and left the local market (Parker and Moore 2007: 10–11).

These actors had little incentive to rally to the defense of the Baathi regime in the spring of 2003. But they faced challenges on two fronts in the wake of the US-led assault. The CPA announced plans to create a market-place built on guarantees of individual property rights (Medani 2004). The remaining state-run factories were put up for auction, tariffs and customs duties were abolished, and the banking sector was dismantled. CPA officials targeted street-corner peddlers and moneylenders, and encouraged US companies to move into manufacturing and trade. Such measures alienated "the cats" and tribal leaders alike, and posed a threat to the livelihoods of their employees.

Militias linked to the Sadrist movement and SCIRI claimed all sorts of economic activities. In the impoverished suburbs of Baghdad, Sadrists closed down shops that traded in "indecent" items or operated in an exploitative fashion. Members of the Badr Brigade and the Party of the Call to Islam oversaw the flow of Iranian goods into the south. Armed groups launched attacks against newly rebuilt petroleum pipelines in a bid to force the authorities to ship oil by truck (Parker and Moore 2007: 13). In late 2006, SCIRI activists demanded that oil-producing areas around Basra be turned over to the provincial administration, just as the oil sector in the far north had fallen into the hands of the Kurdistan Regional Government.

Officials in the Kurdish region had already signed contracts with foreign companies to increase production in the oil fields around Kirkuk. Such contracts prompted objections from the petroleum ministry in Baghdad and the Sadrists, who joined Sunni politicians in insisting that Iraq's oil resources belonged to the nation as a whole. The Kurdish administration countered that the US-sponsored 2005 constitution explicitly mentioned compensation for "the damaged regions that were unjustly deprived [of revenues] by the former regime." In July 2008, the oil ministry announced that foreign companies would be invited to submit bids for long-term contracts to rejuvenate the oil industry. The ministry also awarded short-term "partnership contracts" to Chevron, ExxonMobil, Royal Dutch Shell, British Petroleum, and Total to upgrade exploration and production facilities.

By 2011, local entrepreneurs and international investors had created a network of profitable manufacturing and financial companies. One example was the family-run Shamara Holding Company, which owned steel mills and electricity-generating plants and had begun to operate state-of-the-art petroleum refineries (Myers 2011). Another was the Iraqi branch of the British-based Hong Kong Shanghai Bank Company, which transformed the Dar al-Salam Investment Bank from a $91 million enterprise to one worth more than $400 million. Much of this private activity was supervised by the Task Force for Business and Stability Operations, an agency created in 2006 by the US Department of Defense. Ties to official institutions accompanied pervasive corruption: Transparency International in 2010 ranked Iraq the fourth most corrupt country in the world, less corrupt than only Afghanistan, Myanmar, and Somalia.

The Impact of International Politics

Iraq is intimately connected to the global economy. Yet the country's exports are concentrated in only one area, hydrocarbons. Reliance on petroleum exports actually increased between 1970 and 1985, despite the government's efforts to diversify the local economy (Lawson 1992: 191). Consequently, the country prospers when oil prices rise and suffers when they drop, no matter what kind of government is in place.

Recurrent regional conflicts have had an even greater impact on Iraq's economic and political development. The 1948 Arab-Israeli war led to the exodus of the Jewish community, which strengthened Shi'i merchants and weakened the monarchy (al-Khafaji 2000: 261). Rivalry with Egypt threatened successive post-1958 leaderships, leading them to expand the military and civilian security forces (al-Khafaji 2000: 263). Critics of the Baath Party tended to be portrayed as traitors, Zionist agents, or lackeys of Western imperialism, depending on the situation at hand.

External threats strengthened authoritarian rule by channeling an inordinate share of the country's resources into the armed forces. Military spending kept pace with oil revenue in the 1970s, and expenditures during the Iran-Iraq war eclipsed all other budgetary outlays. When the destruction of the oil facilities at Mina al-Bakr and Khawr al-'Umayyah disrupted oil income, grants and loans from Saudi Arabia, Kuwait, and the United Arab Emirates filled in the gaps (al-Khafaji 2000: 273). Once the war ended, the slump in world oil prices forced the government to carry out a rapid demobilization of troops that exacerbated the postwar economic crisis.

International conflicts gave Iraqi leaders an opportunity to weaken opposition forces and mobilize the population behind the regime. This dynamic was evident with regard to the Shi'i organizations that challenged the authorities after 1968. Moreover, as Isam al-Khafaji points out, "Iraq's position as a defender of its sovereignty once Iran turned to the offensive [after 1984] gave a significant boost to Saddam Hussein's bid to distance himself from the existing institutions and take upon himself the role of the patron of the nation. In this way, he could turn the war with Iran into Saddam's Qadisiyyah (a seventh-century battle in which Arab Muslim forces defeated Persian troops), harness military and administration institutions, give them strictly executive and professional tasks, and erode the power of other Ba'thist institutions" (2000: 281).

Iraqi politics have been profoundly affected by foreign actors in the wake of the 2003 occupation. The CPA laid the foundation for political life in the new era: it outlawed the Baath Party and prohibited party members from taking part in governmental affairs; it set up institutions and administrative agencies rooted in the principle of sectarian representation; and it discriminated in favor of Western-style political parties and nongovernmental organizations, especially ones that promoted liberal interests and ideals. Meanwhile the CPA discouraged forms of political mobilization that it deemed to be inappropriate. Whereas Baathi-era restrictions on students' and women's associations were abolished, equally restrictive regulations on workers' unions were preserved. Such moves highlighted the neoliberal ideology of the CPA, as well as the US government's commitment to remake Iraq in its own image (Tripp 2007: 289–290).

Religion and Politics

Shortly before the 1958 revolution, Shi'i notables in Najaf set up the Society of Religious Scholars to resist the spread of atheism and communism. The organization was headed by one of the most prestigious figures in the Shi'i religious hierarchy, Grand Ayatollah Muhsin al-Hakim (Wiley 1992: 31–32). Its members set up schools and clinics, supported by charitable contributions *(zakat)*. The society undertook no overt political activity, although it did protest that the proposed land reform program violated the Islamic principles that honor private property. Similar positions were espoused by the more activist Shi'i Party of the Call to Islam, which emerged in late 1957 under the leadership of Sayyid Mohammad Baqir al-Sadr, as well as by the much smaller Sunni Muslim Brothers. The latter two organizations gained strength as the Qasim regime grew more repressive in 1959–1960. They were joined in 1961 by the Islamic Action Organization, which more closely approximated a political party.

After Baath Party officers seized power in February 1963, and particularly after party radicals declared themselves Marxist that November, the Party of the Call to Islam redoubled its efforts to mobilize against the regime. The organization won widespread support after the government nationalized banks, insurance companies, and factories as part of a socialist initiative in July 1964. Activists made effective use of mourning houses *(husainiyyahs)* to recruit members, and built strong connections to Shi'i university students in Baghdad. The growing presence of the Party of the Call to Islam, and the increased visibility of the more militant Islamic Action Organization, prompted state officials to tighten restrictions on religious celebrations. The annual commemoration of the martyrdom of al-Imam Husain was subjected to intense surveillance, augmenting popular resentment against the authorities.

Religious activism revived in the spring of 1969 after the government signed an agreement with the Soviet Union to develop oil fields in the southern, Shi'i-dominated provinces, and the Baathi regime started to expel longtime residents of Iranian descent as part of a boundary dispute with Iran. Ayatollah Muhsin al-Hakim publicly decried these policies, sparking demonstrations in Najaf and Karbala. The regime dispatched Hardan al-Takriti to confer with al-Hakim, but the talks collapsed. Baathi officials then confiscated the charitable endowments of Najaf and closed the seminaries that these funds supported. These moves led to rioting in Najaf, Karbala, and Basra, which was crushed by the Baath Party's security forces. In January1970, the regime charged al-Hakim's family with collaborating with the US Central Intelligence Agency (CIA) and the Shah of Iran, and arrested and harassed the Party of the Call to Islam. Ayatollah al-Hakim responded by organizing a procession from Najaf to the shrine at Qadimiyyah outside Baghdad. Marchers were forcibly blocked by police and security forces.

Muhsin al-Hakim's outspoken opposition to the Baathi regime raised the visibility and popularity of the Party of the Call to Islam, but it was Mohammad Baqir al-Sadr's organizational skills that increased the organization's capacity to challenge the authorities. Baqir al-Sadr's efforts to mobilize the Shi'i community coincided with a series of pathbreaking lectures on religion and politics given by exiled Iranian scholar Grand Ayatollah Ruhollah Khomeini. Cells of the Islamic Action Organization were pushing for armed struggle against the Baathi regime. Before these disparate currents could converge, Ayatollah Muhsin al-Hakim died, and the Shi'i Islamist movement split between the more activist Baqir al-Sadr and the resolutely apolitical Grand Ayatollah Abu al-Qasim al-Khu'i, who succeeded al-Hakim as the most respected figure in the Shi'i hierarchy.

Members of the Party of the Call to Islam continued to be harried by the security forces as the 1970s opened. Mohammad Baqir al-Sadr himself was detained in early 1972; in 1974 five other prominent scholars were tried and executed. Many of the party's remaining leaders fled to Iran, Lebanon, and the smaller Arab Gulf states, leaving the organization severely weakened. It was therefore unexpected when mass demonstrations erupted in Najaf and Karbala in February 1977. The demonstrators, who appear to have had few links to the Party of the Call to Islam, chanted anti–Baath Party and anti–Saddam Hussein slogans. An influential scholar from Najaf, Ayatollah Mohammad Baqir al-Hakim, tried to calm the situation, but was subsequently charged with inciting the march and sentenced to life in prison.

In the wake of this protest, both the Party of the Call to Islam and the Islamic Action Organization became more active, resulting in continuous skirmishing between Islamist militants and the security forces. Popular support for these organizations deepened following the Iranian revolution. Mohammad Baqir al-Sadr even led a public celebration of the Shah's overthrow in February 1979. He was placed under house arrest that June, but demonstrations in support of the new order in Iran and against the leadership in Baghdad persisted. In April 1980, a member of the Islamic Action Organization attempted to assassinate the deputy prime minister, Tariq 'Aziz. In retaliation, Baqir al-Sadr and his sister were taken to Baghdad, tortured, and killed. Ayatollah al-Khu'i was placed under house arrest, and the endowments that were under his supervision were confiscated by the state-run Rafidain Bank.

November 1982 saw the creation of the Supreme Council for Islamic Revolution in Iraq, in Tehran, under the leadership of Mohammad Baqir al-Hakim. The organization formed a collection of armed units in Iranian-occupied Kurdistan, which carried out guerrilla operations along the border. The rise of SCIRI effectively fragmented the Shi'i community in Iraq along four axes: between Arabs and Iranian expatriates, among factions loyal to one or another of the country's senior religious scholars, over the preferred strategy to confront the Baath Party, and over the question of whether the Islamist movement should ally itself with the secular Kurdish parties.

When Shi'i districts in the south rose in revolt at the end of the 1990–1991 war, Ayatollah al-Khu'i issued a religious edict urging the population to return to their homes. SCIRI leaders openly called for the establishment of an Islamic government along the lines of the Islamic Republic of Iran. The head of the Islamic Action Organization, by contrast, held a press conference in which he denied that his followers intended to set up an Islamic republic. His words were belied by the fact that he stood under a poster of

Khomeini. When militia units loyal to SCIRI at last crossed into the south-ern provinces of Iraq, they raised banners that displayed Khomeini's image.

Simmering popular discontent in the mid-1990s led the government to embark on a campaign to promote religiosity in public affairs. A ban on the sale and distribution of alcohol was imposed in 1994; new mosques were constructed across the country at state expense, one of which was designed to be the largest in the world; women were subjected to pressure to cover themselves outside the home; and in 1997 the authorities signed an agree-ment with the Islamic Republic that reopened the shrines of Najaf and Kar-bala to Iranian pilgrims.

On the other hand, prominent Shi'i figures were systematically elimi-nated. The regime appointed Sayyid Mohammad Sadiq al-Sadr to replace al-Khu'i as the chief figure in Najaf. Sadiq al-Sadr immediately began building an underground network of religious institutions, which was super-vised by his son Muqtada al-Sadr. By early 1998, Sadiq al-Sadr had begun to give Friday sermons demanding the release of Shi'ites who had been arrested in the 1991 uprising. Such outspokenness resulted in his assassina-tion in February 1999, along with the killing of two other leading ayatol-lahs. The deaths sparked rioting in the southern cities and poorer neighbor-hoods of the capital. Still, the elimination of the country's most vocal Shi'i notables left the apolitical Grand Ayatollah 'Ali al-Sistani as the senior fig-ure in the religious hierarchy.

Religious convictions came to occupy a central place in political life fol-lowing the 2003 overthrow of the Baathi order. Those who opposed the idea of religious scholars running the day-to-day affairs of state gravitated around al-Sistani. Those who looked to Ayatollah Mohammad Sadiq al-Sadr as a source of inspiration leaned toward his son Muqtada, who in turn acknowl-edged Grand Ayatollah Qadim al-Husaini al-Ha'iri as the Sadrist movement's living source of inspiration. The chief proponent of rule by religious scholars was Ayatollah Mohammad Sa'id al-Hakim, the cousin of SCIRI's Moham-mad Baqir al-Hakim. Still, doctrinal issues often gave way to political expe-diency: Anthony Shadid reported in August 2003 that Muqtada al-Sadr had formed a tactical alliance with the Sunni Islamist Ahmad Kubaisi. Both lead-ers stood squarely against the US-backed Iraqi Governing Council and had common interests with the Sunni Muslim Scholars Association.

Rivalry among Islamist movements escalated sharply in the spring of 2004. That March, the previously unknown group al-Qaeda in Iraq deto-nated bombs outside major Shi'i shrines in Karbala and Qadimiyyah that killed more than 250 people. Four months later, the Society of Divine Unity and Struggle, a Sunni organization, took over the southern city of Samarra and attacked its Shi'i and Kurdish inhabitants. Another radical Sunni group, the Consultative Council of Fighters, forged ties to al-Qaeda in Iraq in early 2006 and probably carried out the bombing of a venerable mosque in

Samarra that ignited eighteen months of open warfare among the Islamist militias.

Armed clashes between the Mahdi Army and the Badr Brigade beginning in October 2006 culminated in full-scale confrontations in Karbala, Najaf, and Baghdad the following summer. The Badr Brigade ended up prevailing, and at the end of August 2007 Muqtada al-Sadr declared a unilateral cease-fire. The Sadrist leadership concluded a formal truce with SCIRI two months later but continued to undercut the SCIRI-backed government of Nuri al-Maliki whenever possible. Then in January 2008 the Sadrist movement joined the Party of the Call to Islam and a number of smaller Sunni organizations in releasing the Baghdad Charter, which denounced sectarianism as a basis upon which to restructure Iraq's political system. To demonstrate the sincerity of the Sadrists' commitment to national unity, that March the Mahdi Army cooperated with al-Maliki's regular armed forces in breaking up a dissident Shi'i militia, called al-Fadilah, that had attempted to exert control over oil-producing districts around Basra.

Muqtada al-Sadr returned to Iraq in January 2011 after almost four years of study in the Iranian seminary city of Qom. With remnants of the Mahdi Army, now called the Promised Day Brigade, providing protection, he told a crowd of supporters in Najaf that they should no longer target fellow Iraqis and should engage only in cultural and intellectual resistance against US forces. Three months later, al-Sadr's allies set up a new organization, named The Helpers (al-Munasirun), to push for full independence from foreign control; the organization was to be open to people of all religions.

Sectarian tensions nevertheless almost immediately escalated. Armed attacks on Christian liquor shops in Baghdad multiplied, and Sunnis in Samarra grumbled about ambitious plans to expand the newly rebuilt 'Askariyya mosque that would displace large numbers of nearby residents. Sunni tribal leaders met in Ramadi in June 2011 to coordinate their response to the resurgence of the Sadrist movement. A week afterward, radicals claiming to belong to Kataib Hezbollah, a previously unknown Shi'i group, attacked a US military outpost in eastern Baghdad. Indiscriminate bombings took place more frequently as the year went by, culminating in a wave of deadly blasts in late December. The bombings were later claimed by a Sunni group linked to al-Qaeda in Iraq, the Islamic State of Iraq.

Radical Shi'ites, who chafed at Muqtada al-Sadr's new-found moderation, filled the ranks of a rival movement, the Bands of the People of Truth ('Asaib Ahl al-Haqq), led by Shaikh Qais al-Khaz'ali. The threat of a resumption of large-scale violence by this organization prompted Sunnis living in mixed neighborhoods all across the country to relocate to religiously homogeneous districts, heightening the level of mistrust and resentment across sectarian lines. By the spring of 2012, fighting had become routine not only between the Sadrists and the 'Asaib Ahl al-Haqq, but also between supporters of Grand Ayatollah al-Sistani and cadres of Mahmud al-Hasani al-Sarkhi's militia, Husain's Army (Waleed 2012).

Identity and Politics

At first glance, Iraq appears to be made up of three distinct ethnosectarian regions: a Shi'i Arab lowlands in the south, a Sunni Arab central plain, and a mountainous Kurdish north. About 60 percent of the country's population consists of Arabic-speaking Shi'ites, while about 35 percent are Arabic-speaking Sunnis and 15–20 percent are Kurdish-speakers (who are predominantly—but not exclusively—Sunni) (Hobbs 2009: 263–264). Smaller groups of Sunni Turks, known in Iraq as Turkomans, and Christian Armenians, Chaldeans, and Assyrians can be found in the northern cities of Kirkuk and Arbil and villages scattered across the northern highlands. Finally, northwestern Iraq harbors reclusive clusters of Yazidis, an ancient sect whose beliefs derive from Zoroastrianism.

Yet even this summary masks significant distinctions. The Shi'ites of the south include cosmopolitan urbanites in Basra and Samarra, marsh dwellers along the confluence of the Tigris and Euphrates Rivers, bedouin tribespeople, and Iranian expatriates who are long-term residents of Najaf and Karbala. Similarly, the Sunni Arab population is made up of notable families (some of whose members trace their lineage to the Islamic conquest and others whose forebears arrived in 1920 with the British-sponsored Hashimi ruling family), a commercial and intellectual bourgeoisie that provided a foundation for the Arab nationalist movement of the late nineteenth century, urban factory workers and rural smallholders who formed the backbone of the early Baath Party, and bedouin tribespeople in the western desert. Kurds are divided not only into Sunnis, Shi'ites, and Alevis, but also into Kurmanji- and Sorani-speakers and, more important, supporters of the rival Barzani and Talebani clans.

Sectarian affiliation played only a minor role in politics during most of the history of the Iraqi state. Prominent Shi'ites were vocal advocates of a unified, independent Iraq in the 1920s and 1930s (Visser 2005). Nascent Assyrian nationalism was crushed in August 1933 by a coalition of Hashimi Arab troops and Kurdish auxiliaries (Husry 1974). More recently, the Shi'i population of the south not only ignored repeated appeals on the part of the revolutionary regime in Iran to rise up against the Baath Party but also stood united in defense of the Iraqi homeland during the 1980–1988 Iran-Iraq War. As late as the 1990s, the Baath Party prided itself on promoting Muslims and Christians alike to senior positions.

The exception to the rule was the Kurdish community, whose boundaries spilled over the country's borders into Turkey in the north, Iran in the east, and Syria in the west. The Iraqi Communist Party mobilized large numbers of Kurdish workers in the oil fields around Kirkuk in the 1950s, and persistent fighting between Kurds and Turkomans prompted the armed forces to crack down on the party in July 1959. Two years later, Mustafa Barzani of the Kurdistan Democratic Party openly criticized the Qasim regime and demanded an end to authoritarian rule and autonomy for the Kurdish provinces. Clashes between the KDP militia and the Iraqi armed forces erupted that fall; by the end of the year the faction of the KDP that was loyal to Jalal Talebani joined the battle. Both wings of the party welcomed the coup d'état that ousted Qasim in February 1963, and in return the new Baathi leadership hinted that it would tolerate a limited degree of Kurdish autonomy in local and cultural matters (Tripp 2000: 172).

Negotiations over the extent of Kurdish autonomy soon broke down, however, and the KDP initiated a campaign of armed struggle against the Baath Party that simmered for the next quarter-century. The most important development during these years was the break between the Barzani and Talebani wings of the KDP: in 1975 Barzani led most of his supporters across the border into Iran; Talebani then set up the Patriotic Union of Kurdistan, whose platform emphasized socialist principles. The bifurcation of the Kurdish movement set the stage for a concerted effort by the authorities to move large numbers of Kurds from the northern countryside to poorly equipped suburbs of central and southern cities (Tripp 2000: 214). During the final stage of the 1980–1988 war with Iran, Iraqi troops carried out a full-scale military offensive against Kurdish militias in the north, which culminated in the 1988 poison gas attacks against the border towns of Halabja and Sayw Senan (Yildiz 2007: 27–28).

Kurdish activists took advantage of the spring 1991 uprising in the south to seize control of Sulaimaniyyah, Zakho, Arbil, and Kirkuk ('Abd al-Jabbar 1994: 109–110). Iraqi forces recaptured the northern cities, but in April the US Air Force announced that it would enforce a "safe haven" for Kurds in territory north of the 36th parallel of latitude. Refugees from Sulaimaniyyah and Arbil flocked to the safe haven, and that October the high command in Baghdad pulled Iraqi troops out of Sulaimaniyyah, Arbil, and Dohuk provinces. The withdrawal of central authority set the stage for elections in May 1992 to choose a popular assembly, which evolved into the autonomous Kurdistan Regional Government (KRG) (Yildiz 2007: 44–50).

When the Iraqi Governing Council was created in July 2003, the CPA allocated membership on a sectarian basis (Alkadiri and Toensing 2003). Five seats were reserved for Kurds, thirteen for Shi'ites, five for Sunni Arabs, and one each for the Turkomans and Assyrians. The KDP's Mas'ud Barzani and the PUK's Jalal Talebani joined the IGC at the outset and stayed on as members of the successor Interim Iraqi Government. Talebani's appointment to the presidency confirmed the influence not only of the Kurds as a political force, but more importantly of sectarianism as the fundamental organizing principle for the new order (Visser 2008).

The Kurdish leadership's success in promoting its community's interests had a dark side. Kurdish activists took steps to annex territories adjacent to the area that was administered by the KRG, most crucially the city of Kirkuk and its surrounding oil-producing districts. Kurdish militias systematically harassed Turkoman and Arab residents of the cities under the KRG's control and tried to force non-Kurds to abandon their homes and property. As a result, leaders of the Chaldean, Assyrian, and Yazidi communities demanded that more seats be guaranteed to their respective constituents on the provincial councils that were created at the end of 2008.

Relations between the KRG and the central administration in Baghdad plummeted at the end of 2010, when Vice President Tariq al-Hashimi fled to the north on his way out of the country. Kurdish leaders who welcomed al-Hashimi took the opportunity to complain that Prime Minister al-Maliki had reverted to the authoritarian practices that had characterized the Baathi era, and at least one prominent Kurdish official declared that the time had come for Kurds to set up an independent state. By early 2012, such incendiary rhetoric had cooled down, and Kurdish leaders were working to improve relations with the governors of the provinces that bordered the KRG (Younis 2012).

Gender and Politics

Baathi socialism in principle champions the interests of women and promises to protect families from the injustices inherent in capitalist patriarchy. The Baath Party created the General Federation of Iraqi Women (GFIW) immediately after seizing power in July 1968. The organization was given responsibility "(1) to work for and fight the enemies of a socialist, democratic Arab society; (2) to ensure the equality of Iraqi women with men in rights; (3) to contribute to the economic and social development of Iraq by co-operating with other Iraqi [popular] organizations and by raising the national consciousness of women; [and] (4) to support mothers and children within family structure" (Joseph 1991: 182). The GFIW set up centers around the country to train women for skilled jobs in manufacturing, to disseminate new agricultural techniques in the countryside, and to promote literacy among poor women and girls (Ismael 1980; Rassam 1992; Al-Ali 2005). It also collaborated with the party-affiliated trade union federation to find employment for women, although as late as 1977, women made up no more than 7 percent of all wage laborers (Joseph 1991: 183).

In 1978 the authorities took what they termed "progressive" elements of Sunni and Shi'i religious law (sharia) and used them to formulate a revised personal status code. The new code permitted divorced women to keep custody of their children longer than before, and broadened the grounds on which women could sue for divorce. Suad Joseph observes that the revised code disappointed many GFIW members, who "would have preferred a direct secularization of the personal status laws (including the outlawing of polygyny), [but] the selective merger of Sunni and Shi'a laws allowed them to claim the legitimacy of the shari'a and thus enabled them to maneuver around the clerics" (1991: 184). In the 1980 National Assembly elections, nineteen women ran as candidates of the Baath Party, and women turned out "in large numbers" for the balloting (Joseph 1991: 185).

Women moved into a wide range of professional and technical jobs during the course of the 1980–1988 war with Iran. In addition, a cluster of new laws was promulgated to support those women who sacrificed family life in order to contribute to the war effort (al-Jawaheri 2008: 21–24). A female accountant recollected that "the Iran-Iraq war had a big effect on society. It showed the efficiency of women in a very clear way. Most of the men were fighting at the front. There was a great dependence on women. And women proved their strength and their resourcefulness. You could even see women at gas stations or women truck drivers. They not only took responsibility for work but also for the home and the children. Our women all became superwomen" (Al-Ali and Pratt 2009: 37). Nevertheless, wartime rhetoric generally highlighted the role of women as the mothers of prospective soldiers and glorified the masculinity of the male soldiers at the front (p. 38). Women were thus pushed out of the paid labor force once the fighting ended, and were further displaced in the aftermath of the 1990–1991 war (pp. 46–47).

State-sponsored training and literacy programs dried up during the sanctions era of the 1990s, leaving more than half of the country's fifteen- to forty-nine-year-old women illiterate by the end of the twentieth century (al-Jawaheri 2008: 57–64; Al-Ali and Pratt 2009: 47). Prostitution and family-sanctioned honor killings increased in tandem (Al-Ali and Pratt 2009: 48–49). At the same time, the regime's belated turn to purported Islamic practices imposed strict limits on the public activities of women, particularly those who had no husband or father to defend them.

When the Baathi regime was overthrown in 2003, the CPA made few overtures to representatives of women's organizations. The head of the CPA, Paul Bremer, rejected the introduction of a quota for women on the Iraqi Governing Council, although three women were eventually appointed to the body (Al-Ali and Pratt 2009: 90–91). One of these, Aqilah al-Hashimi, was assassinated in September 2003. Three months later, the IGC, chaired by 'Abd al-'Aziz al-Hakim of SCIRI, overturned the Baathi personal status code and reinstated Sunni and Shi'i religious law (Al-Ali and Pratt 2009: 93). The decree lapsed when Bremer refused to sign it. Five women were

awarded posts in the Interim Iraqi Government, and six female ministers
were appointed following the December 2005 elections. Women's rights occupied a central place in the debates surrounding the drafting of the permanent constitution, but in the end the document left personal status issues to
be determined later and in accordance with each person's "own religion,
sect, belief, and choice." Not only did the new constitution open "the way
for a Lebanese-type system, where family law is governed according to religious sect, thereby legalizing discriminatory practices with regard to marriage, divorce, child custody, and inheritance," but it also, by incorporating
notions of federalism, "devolved authority to the regions to specify family
law, thereby allowing regional differences in family law" (Al-Ali and Pratt
2009: 114).

By 2012, there remained only one female minister in the government,
the minister of state for women's affairs. This individual, Ibtihal al-Zaidi,
took over the post after her predecessor resigned in February 2009 to
protest the reduction of the ministry's budget to the token sum of $1,500. A
United Nations study concluded in March 2012 that no more than 14 percent of Iraq's women were active in the labor force, while more than half of
the women and girls in rural areas were illiterate.

13

Israel

Alan Dowty

Following the general framework of this volume, in this chapter I discuss only the domestic politics of Israel. International political dynamics, though they perhaps affect Israel more than most other nations, are considered only in the context of their impact on Israel's domestic politics. Likewise, I deal only with the territory that is juridically part of Israel and not the West Bank and the Gaza Strip, Palestinian territories occupied by Israel since 1967 and governed under the international law of belligerent occupation. (For analysis of the differing status and reality of Israeli rule in the occupied Palestinian territories, see Dowty 2001: chap. 10.)

Within this framework, Israel is a highly competitive parliamentary democracy. It has been classified as a democracy in all the major listings of democratic states (Rustow 1967; Dahl 1971; Powell 1982; Lijphart 1984, 1994); Freedom House gives it the highest ranking on political rights and the second-highest ranking (citing "deficiencies in a few aspects") on civil liberties (Freedom House 2012). There are fundamental problems in practice with the status and rights of the Palestinian Arab minority in Israel, and there are challenging issues regarding the role of religion in politics. But within its own borders, Israel meets the criteria that define competitive politics: the right to vote and to run for office, elections without a predetermined outcome, and freedom of expression. In terms of the four criteria of the "litmus test" for democracy posed in Chapter 2, incumbent parties can lose elections, the winners are allowed to form a government, the winners actually govern, and the elections are repeated at specified intervals.

One of the puzzles of Israeli politics is how the nation managed to establish and maintain a stable competitive political system. Consider the obstacles: relatively few of the Jewish immigrants to Palestine or to Israel were from countries with a viable democratic tradition; most came as refugees dominated by a sense of insecurity; and those who came were plunged into an ongoing conflict requiring total mobilization and a constant state of high readiness. The country was also plagued by serious internal cleavages, both between Jews and Arabs and within the Jewish community itself, and the economic pressures created by security demands and massive refugee flows were staggering.

In meeting these challenges, however, those who established the new Jewish *yishuv* (community) in Palestine drew upon a rich Jewish experience in politics. Numerous historical Jewish communities in different settings exercised a high degree of autonomy, governing their internal life in defense against a hostile environment. In Tsarist Russia, from which most of the early settlers came, Jewish communities held their own elections, passed their own laws, taxed themselves, had their own courts and welfare systems, and even conducted their own diplomacy. Though not democratic by modern standards, this "Jewish politics" created a foundation for the growth of competitive politics (Dowty 2001: chap. 2).

Historical Background and Contemporary Political Structure

Modern Jewish settlement in Palestine—the "Return to Zion"—began from Tsarist Russia in the early 1880s. Russia was then home to half the world's Jews and was itself in great turmoil. As a result, Jews became targets of a vicious, officially tolerated anti-Semitism. In the course of four decades (1880–1920), an estimated 4 million Jewish refugees fled to more hospitable shores. Most fled to Western Europe or to the New World, but a small handful—perhaps 2 percent of the whole—concluded that the time had come to rebuild Jewish life in the historical homeland.

Historically, Jews had often fled lands of persecution to find haven elsewhere. But anti-Semitism produced a different reaction this time, because of an important difference in context. On the eve of the twentieth century, nationalism, and the model of the nation-state, had become the dominant idea in political thinking, and had been extended from France, Germany, and Italy to the peoples of Central and Eastern Europe. But reestablishing a Jewish community in the Palestinian provinces of the Ottoman Empire, against daunting physical obstacles and the hostility of both the Turkish rulers and the Arab inhabitants, was a formidable challenge. Not surprisingly, success in the first twenty years was very limited: seventeen new settlements with a few thousand inhabitants (added to an existing Jewish community of 20,000–30,000). Had nothing changed, this would have remained a minor footnote in history. But two developments changed the course of history.

One was the emergence of the first effective Zionist political movement. The label of "Zionist" had come into use during the 1880s to identify those who supported the reestablishment of a Jewish homeland (not necessarily a state at this stage) in Palestine. This early movement lacked organization and definition, but at the end of the 1890s this lack was remedied by a very unlikely founding figure. Theodore Herzl, a thirty-five-year-old journalist and would-be playwright, was stung into action by the rise of anti-Semitism in France (where he served as a newspaper correspondent) and in his own city of Vienna. In 1896, Herzl published a hugely influential manifesto, *Der Judenstaat* (The Jews' State), and in 1897 he organized the World Zionist Organization, whose declared aim was "to create for the Jewish people a home in Palestine secured by public law" (in deference to the governing Ottoman Turks, the word "state" was avoided). This declared aim received important international support during World War I, when Great Britain announced in the Balfour Declaration (November 2, 1917) that it favored "the establishment in Palestine of a national home for the Jewish people." This support became relevant when the declaration was written into Britain's Palestine Mandate by the League of Nations.

The other new development was a renewed wave of anti-Semitism, ignited by the first Russian revolution, of 1905, which produced another wave of refugees. By the eve of World War I, Jews in Palestine had grown to an established community of about 80,000, with the organization and resources needed to absorb later influxes. This pattern repeated again and again, as each outbreak of persecution produced a new "wave" (*aliyah* in Hebrew) of settlers. Civil war in Russia in the 1920s brought the third *aliyah*. Anti-Semitic government policies in Poland in the mid-1920s led to the fourth *aliyah*. The rise of Nazi Germany and other fascist regimes in the 1930s was the force behind the fifth *aliyah*. The Holocaust—the Nazi genocide of European Jews—made Zionists out of nearly all Jews, with refugees and survivors struggling to reach Palestine. Roughly 80 percent of those who came to Israel over the years meet the standard international definition of "refugees," a fact that is basic to understanding Israeli political attitudes and opinions.

After the creation of Israel in 1948, the influx of Jews fleeing from Arab countries almost doubled the population of the country in its first decade, while the massive outflow of Arab refugees during the war that led to Israel's independence reduced the Arab population to about 19 percent within the new armistice lines—roughly the same proportion of the population as today.

There was no enforceable central authority in the Zionist movement or in the Jewish *yishuv* during the days of the Palestine Mandate (1921–1948). In Mandatory Palestine, British administration covered all areas of government, including defense, police, courts, and economic and social regulation.

Only in areas where it did not conflict with Mandatory law could the *yishuv* govern itself, and then only by voluntary consent. This reality reinforced a remarkable capacity to encompass totally opposed worldviews that could have torn the *yishuv* apart. There were revolutionary and nonrevolutionary socialists who combined Zionism with theories of class struggle, religious Zionists who demanded adherence to traditional Jewish law, and "General Zionists" who advocated Jewish statehood but rejected both socialism and traditional religion. Later on, a fourth strand, "Revisionist" Zionism, imitated militant nationalism elsewhere and advocated an expansionist territorial vision for the Jewish state. In addition, there was in Palestine an existing Jewish "ultra-orthodox" community that rejected Zionism in principle.

But Zionists of different persuasions were able to work together in a system of power-sharing that owed much to historical experience. For example, beginning in the 1930s, Labor Zionist leaders (secular socialists), who dominated at that time, made explicit arrangements with religious Zionist parties on a proportionate division of jobs and other benefits. This initiated a forty-year period of partnership between Labor Zionists and religious Zionists.

By the end of World War II, Jews in Britain's Palestine Mandate were able to maintain a level of organization and self-defense extraordinary for a community without formal government powers. This community levied and collected taxes, established an army, represented its own interests internationally, administered welfare and educational services, and set its own economic and social policies—all on a voluntary basis. The strength of this social cohesion was apparent in the 1948 war that led to Israel's independence.

During the first two decades of statehood, roughly up to the 1967 war, the basic patterns of Israeli politics were set under the leadership of David Ben-Gurion, the dominant figure from the 1930s until his resignation as prime minister in 1963. Central to Ben-Gurion's thinking was the concept of *mamlachtiut,* a term of his own devising that is best translated as "a sense of public responsibility" or "civic-mindedness." Ben-Gurion accomplished the first task of *mamlachtiut*—bringing all elements of the Jewish community under government authority—quickly and with little need for coercion. This involved important concessions to the ultra-orthodox community, which comprised strictly religious Jews who were ideologically opposed to Zionism.

Ben-Gurion centralized authority by combining the parliamentary model with centralized political parties and coalition politics, producing a government with strong executive powers. Since no single party ever captured a majority in an election, control was achieved by assembling a workable majority coalition and imposing the principle of collective responsibility. Most of the governing institutions established in the new state were based on pre-state institutions. These included a parliament (Knesset) of

120 members, elected to four-year terms by party-list proportional representation, with the entire nation as an undivided electoral district—an expression of power-sharing in perfect accord with Jewish politics. Israeli citizens thus vote for a party, not for individual candidates. The government or cabinet represents a majority in the Knesset, and since no single party has ever won a majority of the seats, all governments have been based on coalitions. The Knesset elects the president, a ceremonial head of state, to a seven-year term. Due to the lack of consensus between religious and secular parties, no written constitution was adopted, but over the years a series of "Basic Laws" that constitute most of a projected constitution have been passed.

The remarkable political stability that existed during this period was expressed in the consistency of voting behavior. In the seven elections that were held from 1949 to 1969, the Labor Zionist parties *as a bloc* consistently gained about half of the 120 available Knesset seats (from 59 to 65 seats, or 49 to 54 percent). The center-right parties (a category that combined General Zionists and Revisionists) consistently received a little less than a third of the seats (from 31 to 35 seats, or 26 to 29 percent). Religious parties received from 12.5 to 15 percent of Knesset seats, divided between the religious Zionists and the ultra-orthodox. A fourth bloc of parties included the radical left (primarily Communists) and Arab parties; they received from 5 to 9 percent of Knesset seats.

As time passed, the gap between a secular, socialist elite, mainly of Eastern European origin, and a significantly more traditional public, much of it of Middle Eastern origin, was bound to assert itself. "Traditional" in this context refers to those valuing existing family ties, ethnic identity, folkways, religion, gender stereotypes, and social roles, as opposed to the "civic" Israel—the "New Israel" created in the century since Herzl—that is more universalist, modernist, secular, liberal, and dovish. In "traditional" Israel one is usually a Jew first and an Israeli second, while in "civic" Israel the order is reversed.

In this context the 1967 war, by reviving dormant territorial issues, contributed to the rise of more ethnically assertive and nationalist forces. These trends culminated in 1977, when the inconceivable occurred and a center-right government, under prominent Revisionist Zionist figure Menachem Begin, came to power after half a century of Labor Zionist hegemony.

Government and Opposition

The "upheaval" of 1977 marked an increased resurgence of ethnicity and nationalistic thinking. There was a loss of consensus on the most basic issue: the very definition of the state that Zionism pursued. The gulf that opened between competing territorial and demographic conceptions of Israel also corresponded to a great extent with communal divisions between Jews of European and Middle Eastern backgrounds, which had been less politically significant before. Voters from Middle East countries—about half the electorate during these years—tended to be strongly anti-Arab and attracted to the more hawkish parties. This tendency was reinforced by the identification of Labor Zionism with the privileged elite and the perception that socialism was an alien, Western doctrine not linked to the Jewish tradition. After a period of incubation, alienation from the Labor establishment grew quickly among the younger Middle Eastern generation who had grown up in Israel.

Security issues—the Arab-Israel conflict—have always been the most important axis of Israeli politics, pitting hawks who favor more assertive policies against doves who advocate conciliation and negotiation. But before the 1967 war, socioeconomic issues and the secular-religious divide also were prominent and, to some extent, independent of positions on security. Some leftists on economic issues took hawkish positions on security questions, and there were parties with conservative economic positions that were dovish on security. Religious parties, by and large, were not markedly hawkish or dovish; rather, they focused on religious issues.

After the 1967 war, however, the issue created by that war—the future of the occupied Palestinian, Syrian, and Egyptian territories—came to dominate Israeli politics. Religious parties became much more predictably hawkish, and socioeconomic issues were subordinated to security issues. Choosing between parties on economic issues became more and more difficult as their positions became incoherent or indistinguishable. Israeli politics can best be described not as left-right, as in most nations, but as dovish-hawkish. In fact, since lower-income Israelis are disproportionately of Middle Eastern origin, there is even a kind of "reverse correlation": lower-income groups vote disproportionately for the "right" (hawkish) and higher-income groups vote disproportionately for the "left" (dovish).

Post-1977 Israeli politics can thus be interpreted, in large part, as a resurgence of the more "traditional" sector of society. The immediate result was polarization and deadlock between the opposed blocs; elections from 1977 to 1999 were marked by a fairly even balance between the left, dominated by a unified Labor party, and a bloc on the right led by the newly formed Likud party, with religious parties often holding the balance. Elections in 2003 and 2009 (though not in 2006) registered a distinct shift to the right, in reaction to the second intifada, the rise of Hamas, and the perceived failure of the peace process.

As Table 13.1 shows, parties of the right grew from 39 seats (of 120) in 1973 to 45 in 1977, while parties of the left fell from 54 to 33 seats (analyzing Israeli elections by blocs of parties shows patterns more clearly than a

Table 13.1 Knesset Seats by Blocs, 1973–2013

	1973	1977	1981	1984	1988	1992	1996	1999	2003	2006	2009	2013
Arab[a]	8	8	4	6	6	5	9	10	8	10	11	11
Left[b]	54	33	48	47	47	56	43	38	28	24	16	21
Center[c]	4	17	4	7	2	0	11	18	15	36	28	27
Religious[d]	15	17	13	13	18	16	23	27	22	18	16	18
Right[e]	39	45	51	47	47	43	34	27	47	32	49	43

Notes: a. Arab parties: Hadash (formally binational party whose voters are predominantly Arab) (1973–2013), Progress and Development (1973), Bedouin and Arab Village List (1973), United Arab List (1977, 1992–2013), Progressive List for Peace (formally binational party whose voters are predominantly Arab) (1984–1988), Arab Democratic Party (1988–1992), Balad (1999–2013).

b. Left parties: Alignment/Labor (1973–2013), Civil Rights Movement (1973–1988), Mapam (1988), Meretz (1992–2013), Am Echad (1999–2003).

c. Center parties: Independent Liberals (1973–1977), Democratic Movement for Change (1977), Telem (1981), Shinui (1981–1988, 1999–2003), Yahad (1984), Ometz (1984), Yisrael B'aliyah (1996–1999), Third Way (1996), Center Party (1999), Kadima (2006–2013), Gil (2006), Yesh Atid (2013), Hatnuah (2013).

d. Religious parties: National Religious Party (1973–2003), Religious Torah Front (1973), Agudat Yisrael (1977–1988), Poalei Agudat Yisrael (1977), Tami (1981–1984), Shas (1984–2013), Morasha (1984), Degel Hatorah (1988), United Torah Judaism (1992–2013).

e. Right parties: Likud (1973–2009), Shlomzion (1977), Tehiya (1981–1984), Tsomet (1984–1988), Kach (1984), Moledet (1988–1996), Ha'ichud Haleumi (1999–2009), Yisrael Beiteinu (1999, 2006–2009), Habayit Hayehudi (2013), Likud-Yishrael Beitenu (2013).

focus on individual parties, which split and merge with kaleidoscopic complexity). The fall of Labor in 1977 was accelerated by the appearance of a centrist party, the Democratic Movement for Change, whose 15 seats came primarily at Labor's expense. This, more than its own electoral success, put Likud in a position to form a government in 1977—but given prevailing trends, this would have happened one or two elections later in any event.

The 1977 upheaval was not just a change in parties but also a watershed in Israeli politics. It brought a new orientation, with new values and political symbols, into equal political legitimacy and at least equal electoral potential with Labor Zionism. It marked the emergence of a truly competitive system, with clearly opposed options, as well as Israel's first successful transfer of power between parties. The thought that the 1977 elections might have been an aberration was put to rest by the 1981 elections. Likud continued its slow but steady climb, gaining an additional five seats over 1977.

In defiance of expectations, the 1984 elections produced a balance even more delicate than in 1981, forcing Labor and Likud to embark on an era of power-sharing as a "National Unity Government," with Yitzhak Shamir and Labor leader Shimon Peres taking turns as prime minister. The elections of 1988, like those of 1984, were again a potential turning point that turned nowhere: the two blocs again emerged nearly equal in the number of seats won. As a result, Labor was forced to agree to a renewed National Unity Government on less than equal terms, with Shamir projected as prime minister for the full four-year term of office.

In early 1990 the National Unity Government finally fell, marking the end of five and a half years of power-sharing by the two major blocs. After long and intricate maneuvering, Shamir emerged as head of a "narrow" Likud-led government with a bare majority. But this government was also unable to serve out its full term. The 1992 elections produced a narrow margin of victory for Labor together with other parties on the left. On the basis of this slim edge, the Labor-led government of Prime Minister Yitzhak Rabin opened up direct negotiations with the Palestine Liberation Organization (PLO), initiating a process that led to the Israel-PLO Declaration of Principles in September 1993, agreement on Israeli withdrawal from Gaza and Jericho in May 1994, and an interim agreement on Palestinian autonomy in October 1995.

But Israel remained deeply divided between a secular, modernizing, more dovish half and a more traditional, conservative, hawkish half. This was underlined by the 1996 elections, which inaugurated an experiment of electing the prime minister directly in a vote separate from that for the Knesset. In a two-way race, Likud's Benjamin Netanyahu defeated Labor's Peres by less than 1 percent of the vote. The unintended consequence of the electoral reform was that voters abandoned Likud and Labor in large numbers in the regular party-list vote. The two major parties together gained only sixty-six seats, down from seventy-six in 1992.

The elections of 1999 continued this process of fragmentation, with Likud and Labor dropping to forty-five seats between the two of them, leading them to agree rather quickly on scrapping the direct election of the prime minister and returning to the prior system. In the meantime, however, Labor's Ehud Barak was elected prime minister in 1999 by a wide margin (56 vs. 44 percent), but then, in a specially called prime ministerial election (without a vote on Knesset seats) in February 2001, was soundly defeated (62 vs. 38 percent) by Likud leader Ariel Sharon.

Sharon also gained a solid victory in the next scheduled Knesset elections, in January 2003. But his plan for unilateral withdrawal from Gaza, in 2005, sparked considerable opposition within his own party, leading him to split from Likud and found a new centrist party, Kadima (Forward), and call new elections for March 2006. In January 2006, however, Sharon suffered a massive stroke and was succeeded as party leader by Ehud Olmert. Under Olmert, Kadima emerged as the leading party and formed the core of a new government that included Labor and Shas, an ultra-orthodox party of Middle Eastern Jews.

This was the first time in Israel's political history that a centrist party had formed a government. The center in Israeli politics has usually been weak; centrist parties have tended to make impressive debuts their first time out, gaining 10 percent or more of the vote (in 1977, 1996, 1999, and 2003), but then fading from the scene within one or two elections. Olmert's government was severely weakened by a two-front confrontation in the summer of 2006, against Hamas in the Gaza Strip and Hezbollah in southern Lebanon, in which Israel's military performance was sharply criticized. At the same time, Olmert's personal position was critically undermined by no fewer than five ongoing investigations for alleged personal corruption, forcing him to agree to elections for a new Kadima leader in September 2008. When the new leader, Tzipi Livni, was unable to reconstitute a government, elections were called for February 2009.

In the 2009 elections, against expectations, Livni managed to hold Kadima together and lose only one seat, even managing to beat Likud by one seat. For the first time in Israeli political history, a strong centrist party had actually lasted for more than one election. But the real import of the election was the clear victory of the right; in essence, the 2009 election erased the impact of the 2006 election that followed Ariel Sharon's defection from Likud and the establishment of Kadima. In 2006, center and left parties won seventy seats, while right-wing and religious parties held the remaining fifty. In 2009 the center and left were reduced to fifty-five seats, including eleven held by Arab parties, while right and religious parties grew to a combined sixty-five seats, thus reestablishing the clear majority won by these two blocs together in 2003.

The government established after elections was dominated by Likud, since together with two religious parties (Shas and United Torah Judaism) and two other right-wing parties (Yisrael Beitenu and Habayit Hayehudi), it commanded a majority. Labor, under Ehud Barak, also joined the coalition, giving the government seventy-four seats and leaving Kadima—the center party—rather illogically as the main opposition, despite its having won one more seat than Likud (twenty-eight to twenty-seven).

In January 2011 Barak and four other Labor Members of Knesset (MKs) seceded and formed their own party, Atsma'ut (Independence), which remained in the governing coalition. The remaining eight Labor MKs took Labor out of the government, which still held a majority (sixty-six seats). A new Labor leader, Shelly Yacimovich, a former journalist, was elected in September 2011.

The 2013 election showed that the center in Israeli politics was there to stay, but that center parties could change rapidly. Kadima almost disappeared, shoved aside by the new party Yesh Atid (There Is a Future), led by TV personality Yair Lapid. Yesh Atid gained much of its appeal by challenging the exemption of young ultra-orthodox Jews from military service, and following the election it formed a tactical alliance with another new party, Habayit Hayehudi (The Jewish Home), a right-wing successor to the old National Religious Party. The aim was to form a government without the ultra-orthodox parties that would curtail the exemption from the draft and reduce generous government funding of ultra-orthodox institutions. After six weeks of tough negotiation, Benjamin Netanyahu was forced to follow the script; a new government of Netanyahu's Likud-Yisrael Beitenu (still the largest party), Yesh Atid, Habayit Hayehudi, and the centrist Hatnuah (The Movement), with sixty-eight seats, emerged in mid-March. While the new government was expected to address ultra-orthodox privileges and other domestic issues, its composition made new departures on Palestinian issues highly unlikely.

Political Economy

Early Jewish settlers in Palestine had been exposed not only to the currents of nationalism and liberalism then prevalent in Europe, but also to the ideas of socialism. Labor Zionists (as socialists came to be labeled) urged Jews to move out of such accustomed trades as commerce, finance, and the professions, and to create a Jewish proletariat based on manual labor, a return to the soil, and self-reliance in all spheres of production. In the words of the Zionist slogan, Jewish pioneers came to Eretz Yisrael "in order to build and to be built in it." The establishment of the kibbutz, or rural communal settlement, was a perfect expression of these ideals.

The agrarian image of a return to the soil, as fostered by kibbutz ideology, was always exaggerated. A majority of new immigrants settled in cities; at its peak, in the 1930s, the agricultural sector accounted for less than a third of the Jewish population. The puzzle, then, is not the eventual decline of Labor Zionism but rather its long hold on power. Labor Zionists dominated the politics of the *yishuv* from the early 1930s, and socialist and agrarian thinking likewise dominated economic planning. In the circumstances of building a new society, the need for strong centralized planning was not seriously disputed, and both ideology and institutions carried over into the new state when it was established. As noted, the left-right spectrum on socioeconomic issues was not particularly prominent, being overshadowed by the Arab-Israel conflict. The roles of the public and private sectors were basically settled by the end of the first decade of statehood; there was considerable latitude for private enterprise (given the urgent need to attract capital), but in the framework of strong government direction and an extensive social welfare system.

Before the 1970s, Israel was judged to be an economic success story. With the help of reparations payments from Germany and private aid from Jewish communities, economic growth averaged around 10 percent a year. This was achieved despite the pressures of massive immigration and a level of defense spending (8 to 10 percent of gross domestic product [GDP]) heavier than that in any other democratic state. Israel did suffer from a chronic negative balance of trade, however, as well as from an overall negative balance of payments, which helped to fuel a high rate of inflation.

The wars of 1967 and 1973 ratcheted defense spending up to new levels, where it remained stuck for the time being. It rose to over 20 percent of GDP after 1967 and to 28 percent or more after 1973, peaking somewhere above 30 percent (by most calculations) in 1975 (Berglas 1983). Yet there was no offsetting reduction in governmental social spending; in fact, public services continued to expand, with real spending rising by 60 percent per capita on health and 80 percent per capita on education during the 1968–1978 decade. By 1978, Israel ranked fifth in the world in public education expenditure as a proportion of GDP, at 8.5 percent (Ofer 1986).

The results were entirely predictable. The economy's annual growth rate fell to an average of 3.2 percent in the 1976–1989 period, with a low point of 1 to 2 percent in the early 1980s. Israel was not keeping pace with other developed countries; while per capita income stood at 83 percent of the average of the twenty-three most developed economies in 1960, this figure had dropped to 48 percent by 1978. The weight of public spending in Israel had always been impressive by world standards, running at around 50 percent of GDP, but by the early 1980s this had risen to 75 percent or more of GDP by most accounts, and for some years and by some measures even exceeded the official GDP.

By the mid-1980s, inflation was running at a 300–400 percent annual rate. Despite its supposed commitment to a market economy, Likud, after its 1977 victory, found itself no more able than Labor to tame the runaway economy (indeed, Likud's base of support was disproportionately, and paradoxically, among those most dependent on a continuing high level of government subsidies and services). The need for a massive restructuring of the economy was one of the major incentives for the formation of the National Unity Government after the elections of July 1984. This forced the two major blocs to share responsibility for the unpopular steps required, thus removing the issue from politics.

After some false starts, the National Unity Government used its emergency powers in July 1985 to impose a sweeping economic stabilization plan that was, like most large economic policies, the result of hard bargaining among the government, labor, and industry. The stabilization plan included dramatic cuts in government spending and subsidies, strict price controls, severe wage restraints, and devaluation, as well as measures to encourage private sector growth and the liberalization of trade restrictions in order to expose more of the economy to open competition.

The economic stabilization plan set in motion a gradual turnaround in the Israeli economy. In the short term it accelerated the deterioration of public services and threatened to collapse the agricultural sector, but it was a textbook success in curtailing inflation and reviving economic growth. A second round of market-oriented reforms took place in 2003–2005, when former prime minister Benjamin Netanyahu served as minister of finance in the Likud-led government of Ariel Sharon. These measures included reduction of the public sector, acceleration of privatization, a more competitive banking system, and welfare reform. With these changes, Israel completed a transition, similar to many developed economies, to a market economy integrated more closely with the globalizing world economy.

By 2007, Israel had matured as a modern, diversified economy with a very strong high-technology component, as indicated by the invitation that year to join the Organization for Economic Cooperation and Development (OECD). GDP by 2011 grew to $243.2 billion, or $30,986 per capita: in terms of purchasing power parity, on a par with developed European states. The annual growth rate in 2011 was 6.6 percent not accounting for inflation (which averaged 3.5 percent in 2011) (Bank of Israel 2012). Israel ranked seventeenth in the world in 2011 on the UN Human Development Index, which the United Nations uses to measure social and economic well-being (UNDP 2011). Since 2002 Israel has been a creditor, rather than a debtor, nation, owing less than is owed to it. Its position will be further strengthened by exploitation of large natural gas reserves discovered offshore in 2010.

Globalization has been an integral feature of Israel's economic development, with a special significance because of the lack of regional economic ties. In the Swiss Economic Institute's 2012 annual globalization index, which measures a nation's integration into the world economy, Israel ranked thirtieth among the 208 countries surveyed—ahead of the United States and every other Middle East nation (KOF Swiss Economic Institute 2012). One expression of this is that Israel now has free trade agreements with the European Union (EU), the United States, the European Free Trade Association (EFTA), Turkey, Mexico, Canada, Jordan, Egypt, and Mercosur (indeed, it is the only non–Latin American partner of this South American trading bloc). Another measure is that direct foreign investment in Israel grew from $532 million in 1992 to $82.8 billion—156 times as much—at the end of 2011 (CIA 2012).

Globalization of course brings problems as well as benefits: the sharpening of internal divisions between traditional and modernizing sectors, the loss of control over social and economic policies, and the threat to local cultures. In Israel's case there has been growing concern about inequality, with roughly a quarter of the population below the official poverty line, while the country ranked 66th of 136—behind all developed nations except the United States—on a recent ranking by Gini coefficient, a measure of inequality (CIA 2012). Other analyses of the inequality issue argue that Israel ranks roughly as predicted by its level of development (Sharkansky 2004), but the issue receives considerable attention because of the obvious conflict with classic Labor Zionist ideology.

Civil Society

In analyzing Israeli politics, a focus on the formal structure and powers of institutions is misleading. Most important policy decisions have been the product of a bargaining process in which not only various branches of the government but also other public institutions and major social groups participate.

A notable feature of Israeli public life is the importance of nongovernmental public institutions performing what would ordinarily be considered governmental functions. In the past, Israel's Histadrut (Labor Federation) determined much public policy in such areas as health care, welfare, pensions, and wage policies. This is less the case today, but the Histadrut remains a key participant in broad economic decisionmaking. The Jewish Agency, which represents the World Zionist Organization in Israel and was the central Jewish body before statehood, remains active in the areas of immigration, settlement, economic development, and relations with Jewish communities abroad. The Jewish National Fund is deeply involved in the purchase and management of public lands.

Interest groups in Israel also reflect this state of affairs. There is relatively little legislative lobbying of the traditional sort, since the important decisions are not made in the Knesset. Interest groups bargain with, or pressure, the governmental ministries, parties, and other bodies that together make the important decisions. For this purpose, they not only approach decisionmakers directly, as they would in most pluralist democratic systems, but also sometimes become an integral part of the process. For example, the kibbutz and *moshav* movements, representing communal and cooperative settlements, have been closely tied to the Ministry of Agriculture; similarly, the Israeli Manufacturers Association works closely with the Ministry of Commerce and Industry. To an unusual extent, in comparison to like situations elsewhere, doctors are consulted on the policies of the Ministry of Health, bus drivers on those of the Ministry of Transport, and teachers on those of the Ministry of Education. At a minimum, many such groups are able to informally veto proposals that they consider inimical to their interests.

Another dimension of this pattern is the tendency to deal with outside challengers by trying to bring them within the system. The history of the gradual, step-by-step inclusion of the ultra-orthodox *(haredi)* community has, in a sense, been an essay in the co-optation of a potentially alienated and disruptive force. Initially the *haredim* had refused to participate in the institutions of the new Zionist *yishuv*. After the establishment of the Palestine

Mandate, there was a compromise providing for some funding of *haredi* schools, leading later to an agreement on formal cooperation in 1934. And when the state was established, Ben-Gurion gave assurances to *haredi* rabbis that Israel would not publicly violate religious law, thereby gaining their consent to join the new government on a de facto basis.

The level of political awareness and knowledge in Israel has always been high. In a study comparing Israeli "civic culture" with that of the five nations studied in Gabriel Almond and Sydney Verba's classic 1963 study, 79 percent of the Israeli respondents reported reading a newspaper at least once a week (the highest figure in Almond and Verba's study was 53 percent, in Western Germany). Also, 76 percent of the Israeli sample followed political news on radio or television at least once a week (the highest elsewhere was 58 percent, in the United States). In terms of political knowledge, 74 percent of the Israelis surveyed could name at least four government ministers and party leaders (the highest elsewhere was 40 percent, in Germany) (Golan 1977; Almond and Verba 1963).

Access to the media was more limited in the early period, since radio and television, which began in the late 1960s, were under state control, and most of the press was party affiliated. This became more pluralistic and more flexible over time, however. In 1965 the establishment of the Israel Broadcasting Authority brought more autonomy to the electronic media. A variety of viewpoints are heard, especially during election campaigns, when each party is given free broadcast time in proportion to its electoral strength. Over the years, the press has become increasingly variegated and critical, with much of the party press disappearing.

The intimate scale of Israeli politics should also be taken into account. The exposure of Israeli leaders to their own public is extensive: a prominent Israeli party leader, in or out of government, will spend many hours every week in direct and unrehearsed contact with the public in various forums, all open to media coverage. Those at the very top appear almost nightly on Israeli news programs (watched by a vast majority of the nation), either in live interviews or in films of appearances elsewhere. The aura of office is eroded to a great extent by this close contact.

The level of protest and extraparliamentary political activity was relatively low during the early years, when the political system was still able to cope with the relatively few challenges that it faced by resorting to the traditional tool of co-opting protest leaders into the system. During the 1948–1977 period, Israel ranked about average compared to other nations on indicators of political protest, and well below average on indicators of political violence (Taylor and Jodice 1983). Underneath the seeming stability, however, were signs of a basically confrontational view of politics that was only temporarily submerged. From the early 1970s there was a steep rise in direct public participation in politics. By the 1980s the incidence of protest and demonstration in Israel surpassed that of almost any other democratic regime. One analyst concluded that Israel was "the most protest-oriented polity in the democratic world today," pointing out a 1981 survey showing that 21.5 percent of Israelis had taken part in a protest event, while the highest proportion anywhere else was 11 percent, in the United States (Lehman-Wilzig 1986).

Social protest took on a new dimension with the outbreak of massive demonstrations in mid-2011. The background was the skyrocketing cost of housing, an erosion in public services, and growing inequality, coupled with the concentration of key sectors of the economy in the hands of powerful conglomerates, resulting in artificially high consumer prices. It began with a massive outcry over a huge jump in the cost of cottage cheese, but took definitive shape when residents unable to afford high rentals began pitching tents on a tony Tel Aviv street. Soon there were thousands of tents in all major cities, and hundreds of thousands participated in marches and demonstrations (the largest, in September, attracting an estimated half a million nationwide, or about 10 percent of the adult population).

The protest was similar in some respects to Arab Spring unrest elsewhere in the Middle East, including the importance of social networking, the predominance of youth, and the role of economic grievances. But the Israeli protest was primarily of domestic origin, and its demands were almost entirely economic: better and cheaper housing, changes in taxation, more free schooling, lower prices, and an end to privatization. There was less of a call for political change: while some protesters called for Prime Minister Netanyahu's resignation or a change of government, protest remained within the system. Inevitably it drew disproportionate support from the left, but at least initially it enjoyed broad public support. Here it should be recalled that, given the "reverse correlation" in Israeli politics (see Government and Opposition section), the party of the "right" (Likud) draws disproportionately from *lower* income groups likely to identify with the protesters' demands.

Netanyahu's government responded by announcing a new housing program and by appointing a governmental commission to be chaired by an academic economist (Manuel Trajtenberg). The Trajtenberg Commission took only a month to present an extensive set of recommendations covering all areas of contention. Though rejected by many protesters as insufficient, many of the recommendations were in fact enacted over the ensuing months: changes in taxation, free schooling from the age of 3, and measures to strengthen antitrust enforcement and increase competition to hold down prices. By winter, the tent encampments had been dismantled, and attempts to reestablish them in the summer of 2012 were squelched. But much of the discontent remained and promised to be a factor in upcoming elections.

322   *Cases*

Religion and Politics

Israel is a "Jewish" state, but most Jews do not understand "Jewish" to imply a state based on religious law or theocratic principles. In its broadest interpretation, Jewishness is seen as a common national or ethnic identity of a historically developed community of people with distinct cultural attributes, including a distinct Judaic religion. But nonobservant Jews are still considered Jews, and Israel demonstrates that a "Jewish" state can operate largely by secular rather than religious law—precisely the major criticism of Israel made by religious Jews.

Israel does not match the Western ideal of separation between religion and state, but neither is it a theocracy governed by religious clerics or religious laws. Israel ranks somewhere in the middle of the spectrum, together with European states that feature established, state-supported religions but strong respect, at the same time, for religious freedom. Israel does not even have a single state religion, as legally Judaism is but one of thirteen established and state-supported religions (together with Islam, Bahai, the Druze faith, and nine Christian denominations).

Thus, despite the absence of formal constitutional guarantees, the protection of minority religions is not the major issue. The main controversy involves the application of Jewish religious law to the Jewish public. Secular Israelis characterize existing arrangements (such as the orthodox rabbinical monopoly over Jewish marriage and divorce) as a form of religious coercion. Nonorthodox (Conservative and Reform) Jewish movements complain that only in Israel, among all democratic states, are they subject to legal discrimination. On the other hand, orthodox advocates argue that without protection by the state (for example, the guarantee of the right not to work on Sabbath), those faithful to religious precepts are effectively denied equal rights and full integration into the nation's social and cultural life.

This debate is complicated by conflicting readings of Jewish law, by lack of precedent on this law's relationship to the state, and by the preexisting pattern of religious governance in the Middle East—the *millet* system of autonomy for religious communities—that carried over into Zionism and the State of Israel. Furthermore, both major groups within the religious population refused in principle to recognize the supremacy of state law over religious commandments: religious Zionists did so because their Zionism was linked to the state's religious mission, while non-Zionist "ultra-orthodox" Jews disputed the state's legitimacy from the outset.

In reality there are many degrees of religious observance in Israel. In a 2009 survey, 8 percent of Israeli Jews identified themselves as "ultra-orthodox" *(haredi),* 12 percent as "religious," 39 percent as "traditional," and 42 percent as "secular" (Central Bureau of Statistics 2011: 338).

Religious Divisions in Israel

Ultra-orthodox: Strictly religious Jews who refer to themselves as *haredim,* meaning "those who tremble in awe" (before God). Historically, *haredim* were anti-Zionist or non-Zionist on religious grounds, but most participate in Israeli politics on a de facto basis.

Religious Zionists: Jews who combine orthodox Jewish religious practice with Zionism. Also known as national religious, modern orthodox, or simply "religious" *(dati).*

Traditional (masorti): Jews who follow many Jewish religious traditions, but more as custom than as law. "Traditional" describes the religious practice of many Jews of Middle Eastern background.

Nonorthodox movements: Movements such as Conservative or Reform Judaism that challenge orthodox interpretations. Such movements are small in formal membership in Israel but may overlap traditional or secular Judaism in practice.

Secular: Israeli Jews who do not follow orthodox Jewish law in their daily life, though they may observe holidays and other rituals as part of the national culture.

Most Jewish religious authorities initially rejected Zionism as a theological error and as an institutional threat. While religious Zionists came to terms with the movement by ascribing messianic significance to the Jewish state as the "beginning of Redemption," anti-Zionists turned this on its head by labeling Zionism a "false Redemption." Genuine redemption—that is, God's final salvation of the world—could not take place in a secular framework. Cooperation and accommodation with the Zionist state were regarded by many anti-Zionists as a practical or tactical necessity but did not necessarily indicate recognition of its legitimacy.

After the Holocaust, most of the ultra-orthodox came to accept the practical necessity of an independent Jewish state, even if that state was not religiously correct. Before supporting Zionist goals even on this conditional basis, however, they sought assurance that this "Jewish" state would not publicly desecrate religious law. David Ben-Gurion provided such assurance in a June 19, 1947, letter that became the basis of a "status quo" with which both sides could live. This status quo included recognizing the Jewish Sabbath as a day of rest, maintaining *kashrut* (Jewish dietary laws) in governmental institutions, state funding of religious public schools, and leaving jurisdiction over marriage and divorce in the hands of religious authorities.

Religious parties have been part of nearly every government coalition since 1948. Throughout most of this time the National Religious Party (NRP), representing religious Zionists, was the most consistent coalition partner. More recently, as the NRP has been absorbed into right-wing parties, the coalition partner has usually been Shas, the Sephardi Torah Guardians, who represent the ultra-orthodox among Jews of Middle Eastern origin (Sephardim).

Discontent about the role of religion in Israeli life is quite audible, but it needs to be seen in perspective. The status quo represents no one's preferred solution but is simply a compromise that most Israelis accept for want of a better option. Clearly the long-term goals of secularists and the orthodox are incompatible, but in the meantime the level of mutual dissatisfaction has been in reasonable balance. Despite dissatisfaction, there is little actual challenge to the basic elements of the status quo or to the general division of territory between the secular and religious spheres of life.

The primary religious arrangement that impinges on the "freedom of conscience" of a secular Israeli is the monopoly of marriage and divorce matters in the hands of the orthodox rabbinate. All Israeli Jews wishing to be married in Israel must meet the orthodox definition of who is Jewish and who is eligible to be married to whom (for example, *kohanim*—considered to be descendants of Aaron—cannot marry divorcees). On the other hand, marriages performed in other countries are recognized, providing an alternative for many secular Israelis. Most other examples of religious legislation either are matters of minor inconvenience, are unenforced, or in practice affect only religious Jews. Furthermore, there is widespread support, or at least tolerance, among secular Israelis for many of the symbolic expressions of Judaism in public life.

Strikingly, there is not even agreement on which side is gaining. Both secular and religious Israelis tend to perceive themselves as losing ground to the other side. Both sides claim defeat. This mutual dread of impending loss helps to account for some of the bitterness and desperation that characterize public rhetoric. But the major threats to the stability of secular-religious relations in Israel are the rise of ultra-orthodox influence within the religious camp and the strong link that has been forged between religious Zionism and territorial nationalism.

Religious Zionists often lament what they term the "retreat" of modern orthodoxy before a resurgence of ultra-orthodoxy. The results of the 2009 and 2013 elections were especially alarming, as two ultra-orthodox parties remained in sole possession of the religious camp, while the remnants of the National Religious Party merged into right-wing parties. There is evidence that the classic power-sharing pattern in Israeli religious politics is declining and religious-secular conflict is on the rise, in large part because of the rise of the ultra-orthodox within the religious community. There is, consequently, a more explicit rejection of pluralism as a model, and less willingness to compromise on religious issues (Cohen 2004). Others argue, however, that as Shas has taken the place of the NRP as an available coalition partner, the basic accommodation is still alive (Sandler and Kampinsky 2009).

The second major problematic aspect of religion and politics in Israel is tied to broader political issues. Many Israelis have felt threatened by orthodoxy not because of religious issues per se, but because of the linkage between religious fervor and militant nationalism. The highly charged issues connected with Israeli-Arab relations, including such questions as Jewish settlement in the territories held by Israel after 1967, are widely seen as religious issues, since many of the more fervent nationalists come from religious Zionist circles.

Identity and Politics

Israel is marked by a communal division between Jews of European background (Ashkenazim) and those from the Middle East, Africa, or Asia (Sephardim), and by an ethnic division between Jews and Arabs. In addition, a large influx of immigrants from the former Soviet Union since the 1970s has created a new subculture that seems likely to become a lasting feature of Israel's society.

The communal split in Israel developed from the reality that members of the founding generation were predominantly secular Zionists from Eastern Europe, and that most Jews from non-European backgrounds arrived after the social and political framework of the state had been established. The European elite tended to regard Sephardi Jews patronizingly, assuming that they would have to assimilate to the prevailing model. However, gaps between the two communities persisted into following generations in social, cultural, political, and (to a lesser extent) economic terms. The political awakening of second-generation Sephardim, beginning in the late 1960s, was marked by deep resentment toward the existing Labor establishment and contributed greatly to the upheaval of 1977.

But while its grip has been loosened, the Western, secular model of Zionism is still the officially sanctioned version taught widely and systematically. In addition, the categories of Ashkenazim and Sephardim (or "Western" and "Eastern") have become increasingly irrelevant as intermarriage has risen steadily. (In fact, the Central Bureau of Statistics has stopped trying to keep track of intercommunal marriages.) Officially, in 2010, 27.2 percent of Israeli Jews were born in, or had fathers born in, Asia or Africa; 33.2 percent were born in, or had fathers born in, Europe or America; and 35.5 percent were born to fathers also born in Israel (Central Bureau of Statistics 2011: 158). Remaining communal differences are likely to blur yet further.

Also, there is a strong sense of commonness among Jews in Israel; in the end, the communal split is less of a threat than other divisions (ethnic or religious), because both communities regard it as a transitory division. There is no significant opposition to integration into a common society and culture, though communal subcultures may remain.

Middle Eastern Jews, by integrating into Israeli life, have to a great extent adopted the patterns of Western society. Families have become smaller and less patriarchal, fertility rates have decreased, women have entered the job market, "Western" consumer patterns and leisure activities have been adopted, and religious observance and traditional customs have declined. Differences remain, of course: residential patterns are still segregated to some degree, religious observance and traditional gender roles are still stronger among Eastern Jews, and families are still somewhat larger.

But the "social distance" between the two communities has diminished dramatically. For example, the percentage of high school students with reservations about "intermarriage" between the two communities dropped from 60 percent in 1965 to 21 percent only ten years later; in 1991 only 6 percent of an adult sample opposed marriage of their son or daughter to someone from a different community (Smooha 1978; Levy, Levinsohn, and Katz 1993). Thus it is not surprising that communal identity is not considered very important to most Israelis; when asked to rank nine different components of collective identity, only 2.7 percent ranked their communal identity first, while 75.3 percent said it was not important at all (Kimmerling 1993).

To use Knesset membership as an index, only 6 percent (7 seats out of 120) in the first Knesset (1949) were of non-European origin, and in the eighth Knesset (1973) this had risen to only 10 percent (12 seats). With the electoral "upheaval" of 1977, this number rose to 23 seats, and thereafter increased steadily: 30 in 1981, 32 in 1984, 38 in 1988, 40 in 1992, 41 in 1996, and 40 in 2009—but only 30 in 2013. Israel has had a Sephardi president, chief of staff, deputy prime minister, speaker of the Knesset, and chairman of the Histadrut. Representation in the top echelons of the civil service, the Histadrut, party central committees, and other centers of power, while not yet proportionate to numbers in the population at large, also has increased substantially.

The Sephardi percentage of the population has actually decreased given the large influx of immigrants from the Soviet Union in the 1970s, and from the former Soviet Union after its collapse in 1991. These two groups constitute about 20 percent of Israel's population and have "changed Israel forever" (Gitelman 2004: 106). Arriving with a higher level of education than most immigrant groups, they have contributed greatly to Israel's economic advance, especially in high technology. They have also created a lively Russian subculture—newspapers, magazines, educational and cultural institutions, entertainment, shops, and so forth—that continues to thrive. Politically, the immigrants from the former Soviet Union have favored hawkish positions on security issues and secularism on the religious front. Russian parties were the first "immigrant" parties to succeed in the Israeli political system, securing several seats in elections from 1996 onward. In the 2009 election, the largely Russian Yisrael Beiteinu party, which takes a very hawkish position, won fifteen seats and emerged as the third largest party in the Knesset.

The ethnic division between Jew and Arab poses a more basic challenge to Israel as a Jewish state. The place of the Palestinian Arab minority in Israel—about 20 percent of the population—is quite different from that of any part of the Jewish population. While Arabs in Israel possess formal rights of citizenship, including the right to vote, and have access to the political system, they stand outside the sphere of mainstream Jewish politics. There has been no meaningful power-sharing with the Arab community and, despite great absolute progress made since 1948, no proportionate distribution of economic gains, government services, or other public goods. Until the early 1980s there was no independent nationwide Arab political party or organization dedicated to the vigorous pursuit of Arab rights within the Israeli political system and speaking credibly for the Arab community as a whole. In short, in the bargaining process that characterizes Israeli politics, the Arab community has not been invited to participate as a negotiating partner and has not coalesced on a strategy of pursuing this status.

Though Israeli Arabs are not partners in the political system, the overall trend has been toward gradual, if halting and incomplete, liberalization. The starting point, in 1948, was one of overwhelming suspicion and de facto domination on one side, and overwhelming alienation and demoralization on the other, with enormous economic, educational, and other gaps between the two communities. A military government established in Arab areas was phased out by the early 1970s. Expropriation of land within Israel (as opposed to the occupied Palestinian territories), beyond legitimate public need, came virtually to a halt after 1976. By the early 1990s there was visible representation of Arabs in some fields of public life, especially health, education, police, media, arts, and the Histadrut. But the peace process of the 1990s brought few tangible improvements in their position (al-Haj 2004). An "equality index," devised by the leading organization working for equality, put inequality in 2009 at 0.3361 on a scale of 0 to 1 (0 being complete equality and 1 complete inequality); this represented an increase of 6.1 percent in inequality since the index was first established in 2006. Large gaps remained, in order of increasing severity, in health, housing, education, employment, and social welfare (Sikkuy 2009).

Government policy alone does not explain such things as the underrepresentation of Arabs in the Knesset. Even though there are informal obstacles and national political organization is weak, there is no formal obstacle to Arabs voting for Arab party lists and achieving a level of representation proportionate to their share of the population. Only one proposed Arab party list—the El Ard movement in the 1960s—has been disqualified from running

in the elections (on grounds that the movement rejected the legitimacy of the
State of Israel as a Jewish state). Yet in the 2013 elections only twelve Arabs
were elected to the Knesset, as opposed to the twenty or more who could
have been elected had Arab voters all mobilized behind Arab lists.

The Arab public is politically fragmented and has consistently failed to
unite behind a single list. Some remain opposed in principle to participating
in Israeli politics, at least on the national level; the turnout among Arab voters has dropped in recent years, falling to 57 percent in 2013 (compared to
67 percent in the Jewish sector). Those who do vote remain divided not
only ideologically but also tactically, with many voting for Jewish parties
because the Arab lists are not likely government coalition partners and are
therefore not considered an effective route to influence.

Palestinian Arab citizens of Israel have recently become more assertive
in their demands for transforming Israel into a "state of all its citizens." In
an important series of documents issued in 2007, leaders of this community
challenged the basic legitimacy of a Jewish state, calling for the elimination
of all elements that reflect an ethnic character—such as the right of Jews to
return to Israel, or even the national anthem and flag. But while they may
be demanding basic changes in the political system, Arab citizens of Israel
clearly want to remain a part of the state. Suggestions that Arab-populated

---

The Islamic Movement in the Knesset

Among the movements active in the Arab sector of Israeli society
is the Islamic Movement, which sees itself as part of the Islamist
resurgence throughout the Middle East. Israeli Islamists have been
especially active in local politics and have gained control of a number of Arab municipalities. The movement debated at length
whether to run in Knesset elections, which are closed to any party
that negates "the existence of the State of Israel as the state of
the Jewish people." But beginning in 1996 the southern branch of
the Islamic Movement ran on a joint Knesset list (the United Arab
List [UAL]) with the Arab Democratic Party. Since 2003 the United
Arab List has formed an electoral alliance with the Arab Movement for Change (Ta'al); in 2009 and 2013 UAL-Ta'al won four
seats, two of them held by Islamic Movement leaders: Shaikh
Ibrahim Sarsour, head of the southern faction of the movement,
and Masud Ganaim, chair of the movement in the city of Sakhnin.
The party's eligibility to run in Knesset elections has often been
challenged; in 2009 it was disqualified by the Central Elections
Committee, but the ban was overturned by Israel's Supreme Court.

areas of Israel be transferred to a Palestinian state have met with vociferous opposition from these very inhabitants.

Gender and Politics

Classic Labor Zionist ideology included strong advocacy of women's rights, invoking the socialist image of men and women fighting shoulder to shoulder in the struggle against oppression and injustice. The image of the founding generations, especially in such settings as the progressive kibbutz movement, pictured women in frontline roles tilling the soil, driving the trucks, and even bearing arms. The Israeli Defense Forces (IDF) became the world's only army that drafted women, and Prime Minister Golda Meir was one of the first, and one of the best-known, female heads of state.

In truth there was always a considerable gap here, as in other respects, between ideology and reality. Early settlers came from societies that were still fairly traditional in gender and family terms, and they tended to continue familiar patterns; even in the kibbutzim, women were relegated to cooking, laundry, and child care. Women in the IDF were not assigned to combat duty, and in fact certain military occupations (for example, clerical or communications posts) also became "women's work," while the overwhelmingly masculine ethos of the military establishment actually worked to reinforce traditional gender roles and the subordination of women.

Israel was in the forefront as far as legal equality was concerned; legislation to date includes measures for equal pay, affirmative action, and tough penalties for violence against women. But Israel lagged behind many other states regarding de facto equality in public life, in the marketplace, and in society at large (Swirsky and Safir 1991). Even some of the advances made were rolled back as progressive ideology yielded ground to more traditional attitudes associated with growing religiosity or imported non-Western folkways. The decline of classic Labor ideology, reinforced by increasing religiosity and the large immigration from Middle Eastern societies with very conventional gender roles, led to further slippage in achieving gender equality. There was a visible revival of traditional femininity.

Religious law had always presented serious obstacles to the achievement of gender equality. In Israel, control of all marriage and divorce by the orthodox rabbinical establishment means that all women, regardless of personal beliefs, are subject to the discriminatory provisions of these laws. One ongoing problem, for example, is the plight of *agunot,* women who are "chained" to husbands who have disappeared or who are recalcitrant, but without whose consent no divorce can be granted; their number is estimated at 5,000 (Brenner 2008). In recent years the rise of ultra-orthodox influence, in particular, has led to attempts toward further segregation or restriction. For example, there are now some thirty bus routes in ultra-orthodox neighborhoods with "modesty buses," in which women voluntarily (in theory) segregate themselves in the back of the bus.

On a political level, the number of women members of the Knesset fell from twelve (10 percent) in the first two Knessets to only eight in the 1981 Knesset. Only in 1999 did the number rise appreciably, to eighteen; it rose to twenty-four in the 2003 elections, fell to seventeen in 2006, and rose again, to twenty-four in 2009, and to twenty-seven in 2013. In all Israeli governments from 1948 to 2013, only eleven women served as ministers. In 2007 the Israel Women's Network, the leading lobbying force for women's rights, submitted to the Knesset's Committee on the Status of Women a lengthy study on women in the economy. The study documented the fact that, despite legal guarantees, women are paid on average one-third less than men for the same job. This gap has remained unchanged since 1967 (Sandler 2007).

One area of relative progress was the judiciary, where by 2011 women composed nearly 51 percent of lower court judges and held five of the fifteen Supreme Court positions. Most political parties had adopted affirmative action goals for leadership positions, though this did not apply to the religious parties, whose twenty-two Knesset members were all males. In the civil service nearly 60 percent of employees were women, but they were concentrated in the lower levels of the bureaucracy (Chazan 2011).

One development that increased awareness of gender issues in Israel recently was the appearance of high-profile cases involving charges of sexual harassment and sexual crimes. The most prominent case involved the president of Israel, Moshe Katsav, who was accused of repeated sexual harassment and rape, and who was forced from office (near the end of his term) in a plea bargain that he later repudiated. As a result Katsav stood trial and in December 2010 was convicted on two counts of rape and other sexual offenses. After exhausting all channels of appeal, he entered prison a year later to begin a seven-year sentence.

The Impact of International Politics

The international context has been a dominant force in the shaping of Israeli history and politics. Events in other lands impelled the waves of immigration that created the Jewish community in Palestine. Relations between the major powers and the Ottoman Empire greatly influenced the development of this community, and the establishment of Britain's Palestine Mandate was instrumental in its consolidation. After statehood, Israel was dependent on outside powers for economic and military support; this support came from the French during the 1950s, and then from the United States in the period since the 1967 war.

In some respects, Israel's international standing is at an all-time high. In 1985 only 68 states maintained diplomatic relations with Israel; in 2012 the number was 159, including several Muslim nations. In the United States, support for Israel remains strong, with public opinion favoring Israel by a three-to-one margin (61 percent to 19 percent) over the Palestinians in a February 2012 poll (Gallup Polls 2012). Strategic cooperation—spurred by the "war on terror"—remains as high as ever. The US focus on the terrorism threat has played to Israel's advantage by strengthening agreement on the definition of common enemies.

The most important external influence, however, is regional, not global. The dominant issue in Israeli politics is, and always has been, the conflict with Palestinians and with Arab states over the creation of a Jewish state and, since 1967, over Israel's occupation of lands then forming parts of Jordan, Syria, and Egypt. In recent years this conflict has entered a new stage with the emergence of radical Islamist movements. The shift began with the appearance of Hezbollah, a non-Palestinian Shi'ite Arab movement in Lebanon inspired and supported by the Islamic Republic of Iran. This was followed by the Palestinian movement Hamas—the Islamic Resistance Movement—which came into existence with the onset of the first intifada, at the end of 1987. In 2006 this process culminated in the victory of Hamas in Palestinian elections in January, and the war between Israel and Hezbollah in July and August. And in June 2007, Hamas took over complete control of the Gaza Strip, meaning that any agreement between Israel and the Palestinian Authority would at best apply only to the 60 percent of the Palestinian population who reside in the West Bank.

In some ways the regional setting is less threatening to Israel than it was in decades past. Neighboring Arab states have, since 1967, engaged in a gradual disengagement from the Arab-Israeli conflict, and Israel now has peace treaties and normal relations with two of the four bordering Arab states. There have been no state-to-state wars since 1973; the Arab boycott of those who deal with Israel is defunct; the Iraqi threat no longer exists; and Egypt and Jordan—before the Arab Spring—had even become, in a limited way, strategic partners. But in other respects, the regional setting seems more ominous, with renewed calls for Israel's destruction from the leaders of Iran and other extremist religious figures in the Muslim world. Furthermore, Iran has developed its capacity for uranium enrichment to the point that, according to expert opinion, it could produce a workable nuclear weapon within one to two years from the moment it "breaks out" from the current contours of its nuclear activities (International Institute for Strategic Studies 2011: 120–121). Consequently, this is now the dominant issue in Israel's international relations. This is part of a bigger issue: the reality of the proliferation of weapons of mass destruction in the Middle East. Chemical and biological weapons are a part of the equation between Israel and Syria, for example. A regional "balance of terror" already exists.

The outbreak of the second intifada, in 2000, together with the rise of Hamas and the events of 2006–2007, pushed the Israeli electorate in a hawkish direction. Prime Minister Ariel Sharon, long regarded as a super-hawk, had carried out the evacuation of Israeli settlements and forces from Gaza in late 2005, and disengagement—or "consolidation"—was the de-clared objective of the government formed, under the new Kadima party, after elections in early 2006. But with the intensification of attacks and threats from evacuated areas—Lebanon in 2000 and Gaza in 2005—support for further withdrawals disappeared, and elections in 2009 confirmed a shift to the right that had already registered in 2003. Continuing rocket attacks on Israeli cities and towns near the Gaza Strip created great pressure on the government to act, leading finally to the military campaign in Gaza from December 2008 to January 2009.

The outbreak of the Arab Spring at the end of 2010 posed new chal-lenges to Israel and put greater pressure on its political system. In theory, a more democratic Middle East would work in Israel's favor by removing ag-gressive autocrats and providing a better long-term platform for lasting peace agreements. But this is the long-term view; the turbulent transition to stable democracy promised, in the short term, some rough passages.

The truth was that some autocratic regimes were less hostile to Israel than their own publics, and that this had provided some stability, over the decades, in their relations to Israel. The primary case was Egypt, which had observed a peace treaty with Israel since 1979. The fall of the Mubarak regime, and the election of an Islamist president in Cairo, rang alarm bells at all levels in Israeli public life. Though Muslim Brotherhood leaders, in-cluding the new president Mohamed Morsi, promised to maintain the peace treaty with Israel, there were already signs that Morsi would test the limits and act more unilaterally. Of special concern was the future of Hamas-controlled Gaza, where Egypt had cooperated with Israel's partial blockade; given that Hamas defined itself as a branch of the Muslim Brotherhood, it seemed likely that the new Egyptian regime would open up its frontier with Gaza and thereby undercut Israel's strategy on this critical issue.

Another case of major concern was Jordan, where King Abdullah's peaceful relations with Israel ran counter to prevailing attitudes among much of his public, a majority of them Palestinians. The Arab Spring also pushed the Palestinian Authority and Hamas to engage in serious talks aimed at unifying Gaza and the West Bank. Though none of the unity agreements achieved were immediately implemented, the specter of a re-newed Hamas presence in the West Bank gave Israeli policymakers another reason to view the Arab Spring with misgivings.

The outbreak of civil war in Syria was also a source of concern. Though the Asad regime (father and son) was among the most hostile to Is-rael, it had since 1970 avoided direct war and had kept the mutual border quiet. Should the regime fall, there was fear that what might follow—an Is-lamist government?—might be a bigger threat. Moreover, there were fears that the chaos itself would spill over into Israel, or that Syria's chemical weapons might fall into irresponsible hands.

All of this made a renewal of the peace process less likely. Israelis tended to see greater risks in the new situation, leading to support for more far-reaching security demands and less readiness for concessions (Byman 2011). In general, the Arab Spring was paradoxically pushing the Palestinian question farther down on the public agenda rather than increasing its prominence.

Since the major axis of Israeli politics is Arab-Palestinian relations, the terms "left" and "right" should be read as "dovish" and "hawkish" more than as positions on socioeconomic issues. To clarify this, let us look at the spectrum of positions toward the conflict, proceeding from left (dovish) to right (hawkish).

Arab parties support a two-state solution with an independent Palestinian state in all of the occupied West Bank and Gaza, including East Jerusalem as its capital. They also support the right of return for all Palestinian refugees to their former homes in Israel itself, or at least a "just settlement of the refugee issue." (These parties include Hadash, a successor to the Communist Party, which is formally a joint Arab-Jewish party but whose voters are overwhelmingly Arab.)

Jewish parties on the left, Meretz and Labor, also support a two-state solution but leave room for modification of the pre-1967 borders on strategic or demographic grounds. Meretz emphasizes the need for Israel to integrate itself into the Middle East, while Labor stresses defensible borders and Jerusalem remaining the capital of Israel.

In the center, Kadima supports two states "based on existing demographic realities," which implies some changes in the pre-1967 lines in order to include large Jewish settlement blocs in the West Bank within Israel's borders. Palestinian statehood would be conditioned on cessation of all claims toward Israel, including return of refugees, and demilitarization.

The ultra-orthodox religious parties historically have not taken strong positions on foreign policy and security, given their ambivalence toward the Zionist state. This is still true for United Torah Judaism, the Ashkenazi party, although it is sympathetic to the right of Jews to settle anywhere in the historical Land of Israel and its voters tend to oppose any territorial withdrawal. Shas, the Sephardi ultra-orthodox party, has opposed the Oslo peace process as well as unilateral disengagement, and is strongly opposed to any redivision of Jerusalem.

Right-wing parties oppose any unilateral territorial concessions and reject a return to the pre-1967 borders or any territorial compromise on Jerusalem. Likud has issued a highly conditional acceptance of a two-state solution, but argues that any future borders must be based on security considerations and that any negotiations must involve only "sincere" partners.

Yisrael Beiteinu, which has grown from its Soviet immigrant base to become the third-largest party, takes a somewhat heterodox view in arguing for territorial exchange rather than concessions; the party has even proposed swapping Arab-inhabited areas of Israel proper for settlement blocs in the West Bank. The smaller parties on the far right, representing primarily religious nationalists and strongly linked to Jewish settlers in the territories, continue to oppose any Palestinian state "west of the Jordan" and would offer negotiated autonomy to Arabs in the West Bank and Gaza.

In conclusion, it is important to note continuing strong support in Israel for negotiation and a two-state solution, despite the bleak prospects. A 2012 poll showed 56 percent of Israelis supporting a two-state solution—but 71 percent felt the chance of establishing an independent Palestinian state in the next five years was low or nonexistent (Harry S. Truman Research Institute for the Advancement of Peace 2012).

14

Jordan

Curtis R. Ryan

The Hashimite Kingdom of Jordan has for many decades played a regional role that would seem to belie its small size, relative military weakness, and limited economic means. Located in the very heart of the modern Middle East, Jordan is by almost any measure weaker than its neighbors: Israel, Syria, Iraq, Saudi Arabia, and even (across the Gulf of Aqaba) Egypt. Yet for all these apparent constraints, Jordan has been a vital part of Middle East politics and a central country both in regional wars and in struggles for regional peace. It remains one of only two Arab countries to have a peace treaty with the State of Israel, while also enjoying extensive ties to major global powers such as the United Kingdom and the United States. The country, like its monarchs (especially the late King Hussein and current King Abdullah II), has developed a well-deserved reputation as a survivor in a tumultuous region and as a force for moderation in an often difficult political climate.

Yet Jordan too was affected by the turbulence of the regional "Arab Spring," as Jordanians—like their counterparts across the Arab world—took to the streets demanding change. For the first two years of the Arab Spring, however, Jordanians continued to call for reform, not revolution, and most hoped that the regime of King Abdullah II would help, rather than hinder, the reform process. In many ways, and for many years now, Jordanian domestic politics has been dominated by struggles over the meaning and depth of reform in the kingdom.

Historical Background and Contemporary Political Structure

Jordan's King Abdullah II ascended the Hashimite throne in 1999, succeeding his long-serving father, the late King Hussein, who had ruled from 1953

335

to 1999. Abdullah became only the fourth king in the Hashimite dynasty, and indeed the Hashimites only came to rule the area now known as Jordan in the third decade of the twentieth century. Thus both the Jordanian state and the monarchy itself are relatively modern creations on the world stage.

Like so many states in the Middle East, the modern state of Jordan first emerged from the imperial machinations that divided the Middle East following the collapse of the Ottoman Empire in World War I. After the war, Britain, under the League of Nations mandate system, carved out Jordan's borders and set up the Hashimite regime under the Emir Abdullah (who later became King Abdullah I). The Hashimite family, however, actually hailed from Mecca in western Arabia (in what is today Saudi Arabia). During World War I, the Hashimites had allied themselves with the British, helping to launch the "Great Arab Revolt" against the Ottoman Turkish Empire. But in the years immediately following the war, the Hashimites plunged into another conflict, this time with the rival Al Saud family and its allies. The Saudis defeated the Hashimites, consolidated control over much of the Arabian Peninsula (which they thereafter renamed Saudi Arabia), and expelled the Hashimite family.

Despite their defeat and ouster from Arabia, the Hashimites, with strong British support, reemerged as the ruling dynasties in two newly created Arab states: Transjordan and Iraq. The Hashimite dynasty in Iraq, however, was overthrown and eliminated in a bloody coup in Baghdad in 1958. Yet more than fifty years later in neighboring Jordan, the Hashimite monarchy continues to both reign and rule. Following its emergence as a British mandate in 1921, Jordan evolved into the Emirate of Transjordan at the time of independence from Britain in 1946 and finally, in 1949, into its current form as the Hashimite Kingdom of Jordan (Wilson 1987). At least in its origins, then, Jordan can be seen as among the most artificial states in the modern Middle East, with a highly contested national identity (Fathi 1994; Layne 1994; Lynch 1999; Massad 2001). Over time, however, a sense of nationhood has developed within the kingdom so that the notion of "Jordanian" does carry very real meaning for most Jordanians.

From the 1950s to 1999, King Hussein was the key figure to lead Jordan's political development, creating many of its institutions and ensuring that the Western "great powers" would view the kingdom as of vital geopolitical and geostrategic importance in both the Cold War and the Middle East peace process. From the foundation of the Hashimite state onward, Jordan maintained close strategic ties to Britain. After World War II, and with the onset of the Cold War, Jordan also established increasingly strong links to the United States, as the Western powers came to view Jordan as a conservative bulwark against communism and radical forms of pan-Arabism, and potentially as a moderating element in the Arab-Israeli conflict. King Hussein, for his part, played on these concerns and his regime's conservative and anticommunist credentials to solidify ties with the United States in particular (al-Madfai 1993). From the beginning, then, Jordan has held close ties to powerful Western states and has in fact depended heavily on foreign aid from these countries to keep the economy stable and to support the survival of the Hashimite regime itself.

The regime emphasizes that Jordan is a constitutional monarchy, with the roles and responsibilities of governing institutions established in the 1952 Jordanian constitution. In Jordanian politics, executive power is invested mainly in the hands of the king, but also in those of his appointed prime minister and cabinet (the Council of Ministers). The political system also includes a bicameral legislature, with a royally appointed upper house (Majlis al-'Ayyan, or House of Notables or Senate) and a popularly elected 110-member lower house (Majlis al-Nu'ab, or House of Representatives). In addition to these national institutions, the kingdom is divided into twelve governorates, each with a royally appointed governor.

The most important change to the machinery of government in Jordan began when the regime initiated its program of limited political liberalization in 1989. Yet that process is rooted mainly in national legislative and local municipal elections, and hence has not really extended to the executive branch of government. The prime minister remains a royal appointee, and cabinet ministers are not necessarily drawn from among the elected members of parliament.

In some respects, as in many other political systems, the upper house of parliament is designed to serve as a check on the lower house. Even the leadership of the two bodies underscores this point, for the speaker of the House of Representatives is elected from and by members of the House, while the speaker of the Senate is appointed by the king. Perhaps not surprisingly, the Senate speaker tends to be a conservative royalist drawn from one of the more powerful families in the kingdom. The membership of the Senate overall, in fact, is actually constitutionally required to consist of top regime veterans. The constitution, for example, notes that Senate membership is to be extended only to former prime ministers or other ministers, ambassadors, former top military officers, and so on. As a result, the Senate often appears to be a who's who—or who was who—of Jordanian politics. In sum, this chamber remains unaffected by the political liberalization process, at least institutionally. The parliamentary effects of political liberalization, therefore, can be seen almost exclusively within the lower house.

The members of the lower house are divided among forty-five multi-member constituencies. Of that total number, the regime reserves a number of seats for specific minority constituencies, all of which have traditionally been strong supporters of the Hashimite monarchy. These include six seats for the rural bedouin, nine seats for the Christian community, and three seats for the Circassian and Chechen communities collectively. Jordanian opposition figures, especially those from Jordan's majority Muslim community, have long argued that such rules overrepresent ethnic and religious minorities. In contrast, many members of these minority communities see the reserved seats as critical to the preservation of their rights. This type of formula, originally intended to ensure religious and ethnic representation, has now also been applied to the kingdom's gender politics; in 2003, the regime added a quota of six seats to guarantee women's representation in the legislature.

Jordan's judiciary is slowly becoming a more independent entity, as the regime attempts to streamline judicial proceedings, improve the training and salaries of judges, and professionalize the court system. Yet judges remain appointees of the Higher Judiciary Council, whose members are—in turn—themselves royal appointees. The judicial system includes criminal, civil, and religious courts. The religious courts provide for separate proceedings for Muslims and Christians, in order to accommodate different religious traditions and approaches to such matters as marriage, divorce, and family law.

While Jordan did not see revolutionary fervor in 2011 or 2012, the regime did clearly feel the pressure to make changes in all the institutions and governing structures noted above. Alarmed at the sight of large demonstrations across the country (as regimes fell in Tunisia and Egypt), the monarchy dismissed the government. A series of cabinet reshuffles and changes in prime minister followed, so that Jordan had five governments from January 2011 to December 2012. The regime also responded with a series of reform measures, including a new electoral law, a new law on political parties, multiple amendments to the constitution, the establishment of a constitutional court, and an independent electoral commission. Yet many in the opposition regarded these as minimal changes and demanded far deeper structural reforms.

Pro-reform parties and movements called for a more constitutional monarchy, beyond the current model, in which the king cedes some of his powers to the elected parliament. Reformers also demanded that the Senate should be elected rather than appointed, that the judiciary should be more fully independent, and that there should be more checks, balances, and separation of powers between the government, the monarchy, and the parliament. The government itself, they argued, should emerge from parliament after elections (as in a truer parliamentary system) rather than be royally appointed, and the election law should be changed to eliminate gerrymandered districts and allow greater opportunities for political parties.

Since 1993 Jordan's electoral system has featured uneven electoral districts that overrepresent rural (and often more conservative, royalist, and East Jordanian) areas, while underrepresenting more urban (and often more Palestinian and sometimes more Islamist) areas. Jordan's opposition parties sometimes call for an end to this type of districting, but they always call for a mixed electoral system, with proportional representation to strengthen parties in the kingdom. For the 2013 elections, the government issued yet another electoral law, keeping most of the old elements, including the controversial districts, but also adding 27 seats (out of a total of 150) for national lists that would include political parties. While this was a concession to the opposition, members of the Islamist movement in particular felt that the change was too minimal, and they therefore announced that they would boycott the elections.

Government and Opposition

King Hussein, who led Jordan's political development from the early 1950s to his death in 1999, set a pattern for Jordanian politics by developing the power of the Jordanian state while also allowing intermittent and minimal levels of pluralism. Thus the Jordanian state under the Hashimite regime never developed the level of authoritarianism found in neighbors such as Saudi Arabia, Syria, or (for most of its existence) Iraq. But neither was pluralism allowed to flourish if it in any way challenged the state. For that reason, Jordan was often regarded as a semiauthoritarian or, to use a more recent phrase, a "soft" authoritarian regime. It is in that sense a "hybrid" regime, with both authoritarian features and some level of liberalization (Ryan and Schwedler 2004).

Jordan's process of political liberalization began defensively in 1989 as a then-precarious regime responded to rioting and political upheavals in many parts of the country (Brand 1992; Brynen 1992; Robinson 1998; Ryan 1998). The waves of political unrest had been triggered by an International Monetary Fund (IMF) austerity program in the spring of 1989. The kingdom had reluctantly agreed to IMF adjustment measures following a prolonged economic crisis that had featured the rapid devaluation of the Jordanian dinar, a skyrocketing national debt, and rising inflation and unemployment. But the policies intended to address the economic crisis set off a corresponding political crisis as rioting spread from the south of Jordan to parts of the capital. Reductions in state subsidies on staple foods and other goods had led to rapid price increases just as many Jordanians were already having trouble making ends meet.

Out of this sequence of negative developments, however, emerged the liberalization process itself. In the first several years of the program, liberalization included easing government controls over the media, restoring parliamentary life and electoral democracy for the lower house of the legislature, and lifting martial law for the first time in more than twenty years. In 1993—following the 1991 creation of a new national charter dedicated to pluralism, liberalization, and loyalty to the Hashimite monarchy—the regime allowed for the legalization of political parties for the first time since the 1950s. This process involved extensive intra-elite bargaining and hence underscores a key feature of political opposition in Jordan: it has tended to be peaceful and reformist, rather than violent and revolutionary (Mufti 1999). Indeed, the national charter was meant to institutionalize this long-standing idea of loyal opposition within the Hashimite Kingdom.

Since the reform program began, Jordan has seen fairly routine national parliamentary elections (1989, 1993, 1997, 2003, 2007, 2010, and 2013). Opposition in Jordan has traditionally come from two broad categories: secular, left-leaning activists (including Communists as well as Baathists and other pan-Arab nationalists) and Islamist activism. The latter category is by far the more influential and historically the best-organized opposition element in the kingdom. The Islamist movement in Jordan is based mainly in Jordan's Muslim Brotherhood, an Islamist movement as old as the Hashimite regime itself, and the movement's political party, the Islamic Action Front (IAF) (Wiktorowicz 2000b). Political parties in general have tended to be weak in Jordan, with most Jordanians having no partisan attachment. Opposition has therefore emerged institutionally not only in the form of parties, but also from within professional associations, unions, and increasingly in "Popular Movements" that have emerged in almost every town and city in the country.

For its part, the Jordanian regime heralded the political liberalization process that began in 1989 as the most extensive in the entire Arab world, and in many respects that assessment was accurate. The process began to change, however, as the kingdom secured its 1994 peace treaty with Israel. Thereafter, regime tolerance for dissent declined precipitously. The opposition had surprised regime loyalists by taking more than half the seats in parliament after the first elections, in 1989 (with Islamists taking thirty-four of the eighty seats). In response, the regime changed the electoral law for the 1993 elections, switching to a one-person, one-vote system. The previous electoral law had allowed citizens a number of votes matching the number of representatives for their respective (multimember) parliamentary districts. The new electoral law ended this practice and also featured a set of uneven electoral districts that favored rural pro-regime constituencies over the more urban bases of support for opposition groups from the secular left to the religious right.

In a sense, the regime was both mobilizing and containing political opposition. The strategy worked, and not surprisingly the Islamists as well as secular leftist parties lost seats in the 1993 elections. Jordan's opposition parties then threatened an electoral boycott in 1997 unless the electoral law was changed. When no such revision took place, the IAF led an eleven-party bloc in boycotting the 1997 elections, yielding a 1997–2001 parliament dominated by pro-regime conservatives, tribal leaders, and very few opposition voices. That parliament, pliant though it was, was dissolved by the king in 2001 in preparation for new elections. Yet the elections themselves were postponed several times, rendering the kingdom without an active parliament for more than two years. In the absence of parliament, the palace ruled by decree, issuing a series of controversial emergency and temporary laws.

In June 2003 the new elections were finally held, under still another electoral law. The new law, announced in July 2001, lowered the age of voting eligibility for men and women from nineteen to eighteen, and increased the number of parliamentary seats from 80 to 104, with new (but still uneven) electoral districts. As noted, King Abdullah later added a new decree creating six more parliamentary seats in a specific quota to ensure minimal representation for women. The 2003 elections were also important in that they were the first under King Abdullah, and they represented a return of the opposition (after the 1997 boycott) to electoral and parliamentary politics. In those elections, pro-regime conservatives, as usual, won most of the seats, but the Islamic Action Front did manage to gain seventeen seats, with five more going to independent Islamists.

The next round of elections, held in November 2007, produced a resounding defeat for Jordan's Islamist movement. But this came with considerable controversy about the process itself, as there were widespread allegations of vote-rigging. When the vote-counting was completed, the Islamists had dropped from seventeen seats to a mere six, having lost even in districts where they enjoy substantial support, such as Irbid and Zarqa. It may be that both sides—the Islamist movement and the Hashimite regime—were reacting to the 2006 electoral success of Hamas in the Palestinian territories. The government reacted with alarm and attempted to thwart any sign of a Hamas-like turn within Jordan's own Islamist movement. Yet simultaneously the IAF was inspired by the nearby elections and may have overplayed its hand (Susser 2008). The 2007 elections, in short, may have signaled a change in the regime's approach to its opponents, especially its Islamist opposition. For most of their existence, the Hashimites had pursued strategies of dividing or containing their political opponents (Lust-Okar 2004, 2006). Now there seemed to be a more confrontational tone emerging both from the state and from more hawkish elements within the Islamist movement itself (Ryan 2008). This level of mutual distrust continued well beyond the 2007 election, leading to Islamist boycotts of the national polls in both 2010 and 2013.

Despite differences in ideological or even religious orientation, opposition parties of all types in Jordan actually agree on several things. Most have been sharply critical of the peace treaty with Israel, for example. They demand that the regime cease normalizing relations with Israel, and some even demand the abolition of the treaty itself. Within domestic politics and

policy, the opposition parties also insist that future prime ministers and cabinets be drawn from parliament in a truer model of a parliamentary system,
rather than be royally appointed pending only the formality of parliamentary approval. IAF deputies are particularly engaged in this debate, arguing
that with more even electoral districts they might win 40 to 50 percent of
the vote. These Islamists remain certain that their "street" support greatly
exceeds their current parliamentary power. Thus the IAF argues that a more
truly democratic election law would allow the alleged Islamist street majority to one day become part of a governing coalition. While the Islamists do
have a point regarding the unevenness of electoral districts, they have
nonetheless never even approached a majority of the popular vote under
any electoral law—hence their arguments about their de facto "majority"
remain dubious, to say the least.

Still, whether rooted in Islam, in pan-Arab nationalism, or in secular
leftist ideas, the political opposition in Jordan has tended to struggle with
the regime over policy and the direction of the state (including demands for
greater democratization), but has not tended to challenge the nature of the
state itself as a Hashimite monarchy.

Religion and Politics

Islam is the official state religion within Jordan, with the overwhelming
majority of the population following the Sunni Islamic tradition. Throughout its existence the Hashimite monarchy has pointedly emphasized its Islamic lineage. King Hussein in particular made clear the direct Hashimite
family line descending from the Prophet Muhammad. Yet despite its Islamic familial credentials, Hashimite Jordan remains largely a secular state,
without the religious overtones that one finds in Saudi Arabia or Iran.

Jordan also has a long history of religious tolerance and support for religious minorities. Jordan's Christians, who account for perhaps 5 percent
of the country's population, enjoy full political rights, including freedom of
religion and the right to attend churches and Christian religious schools if
they so desire. The Hashimite kings have tended to rely on strong support
from Christians and other minorities, and have supported various centers,
conferences, and institutes focused on Christian-Muslim understanding.
King Abdullah II in particular has emphasized interfaith tolerance not just
on a national but also on a global level. In 2005, Jordan hosted a major conference of more than 200 leading Muslim theologians from fifty countries
and all schools of Sunni, Shi'a, and Ibadi thought. Together, they produced
the "Amman Message" against sectarianism, militancy, and questionable
practices such as Takfir (excommunication) in Islam. This was followed in
2007 by the release of "A Common Word," a message to all Christian

denominations to create greater Christian-Islamic understanding. And finally, in 2010, King Abdullah addressed the UN General Assembly and proposed World Interfaith Harmony Week, which was approved and is now celebrated in the first week of February in many places throughout the world.

Within Jordan, while many Jordanian Christians are stalwart supporters of the Hashimite regime, others have played major roles in Jordan's opposition movement, especially through left-wing political parties. It is here in fact—in the politics of opposition—that one finds the most extensive levels of religion-based activism in the kingdom. As noted, Jordan's Islamist movement remains by far the largest and best-organized component of political opposition in the kingdom, and it is indeed as old as the Hashimite monarchy itself. Unlike the Muslim Brotherhood in Egypt, the Jordanian movement has enjoyed a more cooperative relationship with the Jordanian state as a loyal opposition organization. And unlike Hamas, the IAF and Muslim Brotherhood do not have militant wings and instead focus on civilian-party and interest-group organization and remain very much a part of the pro-democratization movement in the kingdom (Schwedler 2006).

Jordan's Muslim Brotherhood therefore stands in sharp contrast to more militant and even terrorist religious organizations, such as al-Qaeda. This point was brought home in a particularly horrible way on November 9, 2005, when al-Qaeda suicide bombers simultaneously attacked several Jordanian hotels in central Amman. The attacks killed sixty while wounding hundreds, and thereafter have been considered "Jordan's 9/11." The terrorists turned out to be Iraqi nationals who had crossed the border into Jordan on the orders of Abu Musab al-Zarqawi, a former Jordanian national who became the head of al-Qaeda in Iraq. Yet most Jordanians—secular and religious, royalist and Islamist, regime supporters and opponents—united in condemning these attacks. In doing so, and despite the many divisive issues in Jordanian politics, they also underscored two major features of Jordanian political life: that the kingdom has a long tradition of moderation and tolerance between and among religions (including most Jordanian Islamists), and that opposition has rarely turned to violence or terrorism, but rather has been based in grassroots activism for reform and change.

The Impact of International Politics

When political power in Jordan shifted in 1999 from King Hussein to the current king, Abdullah II, the new regime was quickly reminded of the often intense impact of international affairs on Jordan's domestic politics and security. Indeed, the succession came at a particularly challenging time in regional politics, which would soon see the collapse of the Arab-Israeli peace process, a renewed Palestinian intifada, and US wars in both Iraq and

Afghanistan. Given its political and geographic location at the very heart of the Middle East, Jordan has for its whole existence found itself wedged between the Israeli-Palestinian conflict to the west and Iraqi and Persian Gulf tensions to the east.

Given its geopolitical position, the Hashimite Kingdom of Jordan has certainly been strongly affected—and indeed buffeted—by the tumultuous politics of the Middle East. It has been deeply affected by the Arab-Israeli wars of 1948, 1956, 1967, 1973, and 1982, and the Persian Gulf wars of 1980–1988, 1990–1991, and 2003–2009, in addition to the country's own civil war in 1970–1971. Given Jordan's long border with Israel, its peace treaty with the Jewish state, and its large Palestinian population, the kingdom has also felt the impact of Palestinian uprisings in the West Bank and Gaza from 1987 to 1993 and again after September 2000.

Jordan's very centrality in Middle East politics and geography has therefore also carried with it a real strategic vulnerability. With Israel to the west and Iraq to the east, Jordan is in many ways wedged between the main fault lines of both the Arab-Israeli and Persian Gulf conflicts. This has even led to overuse of an old English-language pun in some Jordanian political circles to the effect that Jordan resides "between Iraq and a hard place." And indeed regional conflicts, coupled with Jordan's central location, have led to repeated and massive population shifts across Jordan's borders. In both 1948 and 1967, Arab losses in wars with Israel led hundreds of thousands of Palestinians to cross the Jordan River into the Hashimite Kingdom. Even today, the kingdom includes several million Palestinians among its citizens. In 2003, the US invasion of Iraq and the severe political unrest that followed led several hundred thousand Iraqis to flee to Jordan. In 2011 and 2012, more than 150,000 Syrian refugees fled to Jordan to escape the violence of the al-Asad regime and the Syrian civil war. Each wave of refugees, whether from the west, east, or north, has put severe strains on Jordan's infrastructure and social services and sometimes its domestic security. Regional conflict, ideological challenges, and domestic regime insecurity are in many ways almost constant features of Jordan's existence as a small state in a very difficult neighborhood.

Even in the 1950s, when the kingdom was still young and viewed by many pan-Arab nationalists as an artificial "paper tiger," some Jordanian officials feared that another regional conflict might eliminate the Hashimite state entirely. In that decade, Arab politics became intensely radicalized, with the Cold War and Arab-Israeli conflicts looming large in political discourse. Radical trends from communism to pan-Arab nationalism were at their peak, challenging the legitimacy of Western-leaning conservative monarchies like Jordan. In 1957, Hussein headed off an attempted coup d'état (inspired by external radical and nationalist ideas), while in 1958 a bloody military coup overthrew the Hashimite monarchy of King Hussein's cousin, Faisal, in neighboring Iraq. The new regime in Baghdad killed the king and his family before consolidating control over the country. The effects of these ideological challenges and external events are important, because the regime reacted to them by disbanding parliament, banning political parties, and closing the door on liberalization for decades to come.

By the late 1960s, the regime was forced to focus outward once again as regional tensions escalated—especially between Israel and the Gamal Abdel Nasser regime in Egypt. Those tensions soon led to the defining event of the decade: the 1967 Arab-Israeli war. Known as the Six Day War for good reason, the conflict began when Israeli forces launched what they viewed as a preemptive strike on Arab forces in Egypt and Syria, effectively destroying the Arab air forces while they were still on the ground. With no air support, the land battles that followed produced an overwhelming Israeli victory not only against Egypt and Syria, but also against Jordan, whose forces had joined the fighting.

That fateful decision and the complete failure of the Arab war effort led to Israeli occupation of the Sinai Peninsula, Egyptian territory, and the Golan Heights, Syrian territory. More important for the Jordanians, the domestic result of the military failure in the 1967 war also was the loss of territory to Israel, specifically the agriculturally rich West Bank and the more religiously significant East Jerusalem. In addition to territorial losses, the 1967 war resulted in tens of thousands of Palestinian refugees crossing the border into Jordan, changing the demographics and ultimately impacting the domestic stability of the kingdom.

That uneasy situation exploded in September 1970, when guerrilla forces of the Palestine Liberation Organization (PLO) fought the royalist forces of the Hashimite government. This Jordanian civil war resulted in a bloody Hashimite victory and the expulsion of PLO guerrilla forces from Jordan. What looked like a particularly vicious internal struggle had become internationalized, however, when Syrian forces launched an unsuccessful invasion of northern Jordan in support of the PLO. Many feared that Israeli or US intervention would also soon follow, but those very threats, coupled with the efforts of the Hashimite army, repelled the Syrians and defeated the PLO.

In October 1973, with the kingdom still recovering from the war of 1967 and the civil war of 1970, Egyptian and Syrian forces launched an initially successful surprise attack on Israel—an event known variously as the Yom Kippur, Ramadan, or October War. Having lost all of the West Bank and East Jerusalem to Israel just six years earlier, Jordan stayed largely out of the 1973 conflict. As Egypt and Syria fought Israel on northern and southern fronts, Jordan never opened an eastern front and instead sent a small contingent of troops to aid Syria in its attempt to recover the Golan Heights.

What is perhaps most amazing about those years is that Jordan survived at all as a state and as a Hashimite monarchy despite international wars, a civil war, and revolutions toppling monarchies in neighboring states. Awareness of this strategic vulnerability led Jordanian policymakers to focus on ensuring international allies and domestic military prowess despite the small size of the state and its coffers. Many regimes fear external conflict or internal upheaval, but for the Hashimite regime these fears have been far from hypothetical.

In the 1980s the Jordanian regime became deeply concerned about the challenges posed by the Iranian revolution. Revolutionary Iran was a successful example—and indeed an active supporter—of the overthrow of conservative, pro-Western monarchies. Iran therefore seemed also to threaten the Arab Gulf monarchies (and hence Jordan's main sources of oil supplies and Arab foreign aid). When Iraq invaded Iran in 1980, King Hussein's regime supported Baghdad for all eight years of the war, and indeed Jordan came to serve as Iraq's main supply source.

Even when that war finally came to an end, however, the region would know very little peace. After a mere one-year hiatus, Jordan's now-close ally, Iraq, launched a surprise invasion of Kuwait on August 2, 1990. Once again, international affairs deeply affected Jordanian domestic politics. By this time, the kingdom's own liberalization process was well under way, and a newly energized public rallied in support of Iraq against the emerging US-led coalition. Feeling the domestic political pressure, King Hussein's Hashimite regime attempted to straddle the fence, neither aiding Iraq nor joining the coalition against it. But the result of that strategy was a sudden loss of US, British, and Gulf foreign aid; the loss of oil supplies; and the expulsion of half a million Jordanians working in the Gulf. Yet again, hundreds of thousands of suddenly displaced people descended on Jordan's capital, Amman.

That nightmarish episode has in many ways cast a shadow over Jordanian policy ever since. It was with that scenario in mind that the Hashimite regime of King Abdullah attempted to prevent its most powerful ally, the United States, from attacking Iraq once again, in 2003. But having failed in that effort, the Jordanians were determined to avoid the devastating effects of opposing the United States. Thus, after the invasion, Jordan supported Iraqi reconstruction efforts and trained police officers for the new Iraq, thereby avoiding the painful dislocations and penalties of the early 1990s. But well into the twenty-first century, the reputation of the Hashimite Kingdom of Jordan as a kind of geographic oasis of stability was challenged repeatedly by the spillover of other conflicts, including the recurrent violence of the Israeli-Palestinian conflict, insurgency and terrorism in Iraq, and civil war in Syria.

Political Economy

Given its minimal resource endowments, throughout its history the Hashimite Kingdom of Jordan has been dependent on foreign assistance to keep its economy afloat. With limited arable land and chronic problems of adequate water supply, agriculture remains a small part of Jordan's overall economy. Indeed, given the small agricultural base in the country, Jordan imports far more food than it exports. That pattern actually applies more broadly, since a chronic trade deficit is a standard feature of the Jordanian economy.

Like the agricultural sector, the manufacturing base is small, with the bulk of the economy concentrated in the service sector. The kingdom has few natural resources, but manages to exploit those minerals it does possess, particularly phosphates and potash. It also manufactures and exports cement and fertilizers. Under King Abdullah II, Jordan has moved steadily away from a state-dominated or public sector economy toward economic openness *(infitah),* increasing levels of privatization, and an overall emphasis on neoliberal economic policies.

Jordan's main resource has been and remains its people. Jordanians tend to have very high levels of education, and have therefore been able to take advantage of skilled labor and service sector job opportunities in other countries in the region, especially those in the Gulf. Worker remittances are thus a major component of the Jordanian economy. So many Jordanians work outside the country, in fact, that the kingdom is both a major labor importer and a labor exporter. Laborers from Sudan and especially Egypt, for example, work in many of the lower-skilled jobs within the kingdom, while Jordanian citizens are more likely to work in private or state businesses, in the skilled service sector, or in jobs in the Gulf states.

With foreign aid remaining a large part of state revenue, and hence a critical source of state expenditures, the Jordanian economy is highly vulnerable to regional and global tensions affecting its labor and aid partners. Jordan is, in short, a semi-rentier economy, meaning that it relies heavily on external sources of income or "rents." The rentier concept is usually associated with extensive natural resource endowments and extractive industries. But in the Middle Eastern context, with the regional political economy of oil, even nonoil states have become deeply linked to the overall petroleum economy. Jordan is thus a semi-rentier economy not because of its own minimal oil endowment (it remains an importer of oil) but rather because its major sources of both expatriate remittances and foreign aid are based in the Gulf oil states (Brand 1992; Brynen 1992).

Since 1989, when Jordan's debt crisis had triggered IMF restructuring (and political unrest), Jordan has pressed forward with its agenda of privatization and economic liberalization. King Abdullah has made clear his conviction that Jordan's future lies in economic development—including privatization of the state's companies as well as encouraging foreign investment. In doing so, he is challenging a resistant and to some extent entrenched elite of state managers. But he is also creating an alternative constituency of like-minded elites who share his enthusiasm for neoliberal solutions to Jordan's development. This has been reflected increasingly in the king's political appointments and the tendency for top cabinet posts to go to technocratic elites with experience in Jordan's industrial and trade zones.

The makeup of the government itself thus underscores the absolutely central emphasis of Abdullah's regime on economic development, continuing privatization, expanding trade, and luring international investment. With these goals in mind, the regime also aggressively pursued trade agreements with its key Western allies. In 2000, Jordan entered the World Trade Organization (WTO), and later that same year the kingdom signed a free trade agreement with the United States. Jordan also relies on extensive trade and investment from the countries of the European Union. In addition to his emphasis on free trade, King Abdullah has pushed for Jordan to become a regional center for information technology and communications.

The government's overall economic development aims are therefore clear, but restructuring remains a colossal task, and one with profound social and political ramifications. As Western stores, fast food chains, and other businesses continue to multiply in Jordan, and as the capital itself continues to expand rapidly, the larger questions that still remain are not just those of trade and investment, but also those of poverty alleviation, uneven development, and continuing high levels of unemployment. These latter questions are the focus of many opposition parties and activists, who hope to push the political liberalization process forward, in part to alleviate some of the hardships of economic liberalization. Indeed, economic grievances have led to recurrent unrest in the south of Jordan, especially among the tribal East Jordanian communities that have historically been counted on as bases of loyalty to the regime.

Identity and Politics

One of the major features of contemporary Jordanian politics is the ethnic divide between Palestinians and East Jordanians (also called Transjordanians), or between those originally of West Bank and East Bank origin, respectively, within modern Jordan. This division has sometimes been given far too much importance in writings on Jordan, especially when used as the social explanation for domestic politics, or when reduced to a "Palestinian versus bedouin" type of image. The nomadic bedouin account for less than a tenth of the kingdom's population, but they are an important part of the social construction of national identity for many Jordanians, underscoring "traditional" roots. Family, clan, and tribal links and lineages remain real and important for many Jordanians. In addition, there are other ethnic groups within Jordan, such as the Circassian and Chechen communities, who are mainly Muslims whose ancestors fled the Russian Caucasus region in the 1860s and 1870s, and who have since played prominent roles in national politics as strong supporters of the Hashimite regime.

Still, the division between the Transjordanian and Palestinian communities remains both real and controversial within national politics. While the estimated percentages vary greatly depending on one's source, it is likely that more than half the population of the kingdom today is of Palestinian origin. The Jordanian government, however, maintains that Palestinians are at most 40 percent of the population. Although this West Bank–East Bank ethnic divide is sometimes overstated, it remains a significant feature of Jordan's society and political economy, and of the Jordanian state itself. Much of the Jordanian government, public sector, and military is dominated by East Bank Jordanians, while much of the private sector is dominated by Palestinians. Before 1970, the Hashimites had regarded their monarchy as more solidly a union of the West and East Banks of the Jordan River, and had strived for some level of balance in the political system. Yet this general ethnic division of labor (so to speak), and hence of power, became more pronounced as a political issue in the wake of the 1970–1971 civil war within the kingdom.

It is difficult to imagine, in fact, a more contentious and touchy issue within Jordanian politics. Even Palestinians who were most closely associated with the Hashimite establishment are not immune from intra-ethnic controversy. In 1999, Adnan Abu Odeh, one of the most powerful Palestinians in the kingdom, a consummate insider and former adviser to King Hussein, found himself under attack from many social and political quarters for his views on Palestinian-Jordanian relations within the kingdom. Abu Odeh had published a book on the topic and then delivered a series of lectures at various venues in Jordan (Abu Odeh 1999). His theme in these writings and speeches was the ethnic imbalance of opportunities within Jordanian society and politics. Abu Odeh was thereafter asked to resign from the Senate. Similarly, in 2001, Jawad Anani, who just two years earlier had served as chief of the Royal Hashimite Court, published an editorial in an Arabic daily in the United Arab Emirates (UAE) arguing that the ethnic divide represented Jordan's main political hurdle to achieving real inclusion or democracy. Shortly afterward, Anani too was forced out of the Senate. Yet such acts of exclusion are neither systematic nor universal. For example, Taher al-Masri, a former prime minister who is of Palestinian origin, has been similarly critical of the ethnic divisions and of the limits of the political liberalization process itself. He was also one of the most prominent politicians

associated with the 1997 electoral boycott. Yet Masri has frequently been
appointed to the Senate, and for the last several years has served as Senate
president.

It is important to note that none of these prominent Jordanians of Palestinian origin are separatists; all, in fact, are integrationists, and all support
the regime. But they remain critical of specific disparities in representation—especially in government—for Palestinian Jordanians as opposed to
East Bank Jordanians.[1] The renewed attention to ethnicity within Jordanian
national identity is to some extent rooted in regional politics. With the signing of the 1993 Israel-PLO accords and the 1994 Israeli-Jordanian peace
treaty, the question of Palestinian citizenship, rights, and loyalties resurfaced within Jordanian politics. With the collapse of the peace process and
the onset of the second Palestinian uprising against Israel, beginning in
September 2000, these questions became still more intense. Waves of Iraqi
and Syrian refugees complicated Jordanian politics—and Jordanian identity—still further.

Many Palestinians clearly feel that they are second-class citizens. But
this cannot be taken in a strictly material or economic sense. For the communities do not neatly fall into an economic hierarchy that parallels the political hierarchy. Rather, in addition to impoverished Palestinians in refugee
camps (which today are usually urban neighborhoods and often slums), the
bulk of Jordan's poorest population can be found especially in rural Transjordanian communities across southern Jordan. Much of the private sector
economic elite, in contrast, is Palestinian. That said, much of the public
sector elite and most top government officials are Transjordanian. Since the
abolition of the national military draft in 1992, Transjordanian dominance
of the armed forces and the security services has only increased. Many
Transjordanians, in turn, point to the enormous wealth of many Palestinian
business families and to their lavish villas in neighborhoods like Abdun.
They point out that of all the Arab countries, only Jordan has extended citizenship to Palestinians. And they note that many of the kingdom's prominent ministers and politicians are of Palestinian origin. Accordingly, this
line of argument tends to arrive at the issue of gratitude, or perhaps more
often, ingratitude.

For their part, Palestinians—even including many who have reached
the pinnacle of the kingdom's economic and political elite—say that they
are still treated on a day-to-day basis as second-class citizens. They argue
that in interactions with bureaucrats, police officers, soldiers, and other officials, they are treated differently and negatively. Family names give much
away for anyone in Jordanian society—since the family name usually signals the owner's ethnicity and religion. Many Palestinians then argue that no
matter how long they have lived in Jordan, they still feel that they are treated
as foreigners—that despite their full citizenship status, they nonetheless do

not enjoy full political rights. They feel that they are still seen as temporary residents by many Transjordanians. And indeed, right-wing Transjordanian nationalists agree with them—at least in the sense that these nationalists see Palestinians as essentially foreign, and not as "real" Jordanians. For these nationalists, Jordanian identity is rooted in East Bank heritage, and often in real or imagined bedouin traditional values. For them, Palestinians are indeed temporarily in the kingdom, and of highly suspect loyalty. The nightmare scenario for such ultranationalist Transjordanians would be a new wave of Palestinian refugees, forced across the Jordan River in the face of an Israeli military offensive.

Thus both successes and failures in the peace process have actually exacerbated some of these domestic tensions. After the 1993 accords, the creation of the Palestinian National Authority and the possibility of a sovereign Palestinian state raised questions in Jordan about which state Palestinians would be loyal to, which state they would live in, and what any of these decisions and scenarios would mean not just for Jordan's survival as a state, but also for its very identity as a nation and as a people.

These questions are essential not just for the future of Palestinians in the kingdom, but also for Transjordanians themselves. The official line on the preceding discussion, however, tilts heavily against having the debate at all. Throughout his reign, for example, King Hussein emphasized the need for national unity. He underscored the idea that all Jordanian citizens were Jordanians, regardless of origin, and warned against an emphasis on two nationalities. For Hussein, as for the Hashimite monarchy today, there remained only one Jordanian "family" and one nationality in the kingdom. In terms of legal nationality and citizenship, that is clearly accurate. But it is also clear that many Jordanians are acutely aware of the ethnic divisions, although they differ considerably on what, if anything, should be done about them.

On this issue, as on many others, many Jordanians are looking to their leadership for hope and direction. Some point, for example, to the potentially unifying symbolism of the Hashimite regime itself, particularly in the form of Abdullah II as the Hashimite Jordanian king and his wife, Queen Rania, who is of Palestinian origin. Certainly some Palestinian Jordanians are hopeful that this translates to more than symbolism, with a king and queen literally representing a marriage of Transjordanian—and Palestinian—*Jordanians*. For his part, King Abdullah has made clear his belief that the major factor in integrating Jordanian society will be the same factor intended to dampen hostility toward normalization of relations with Israel: expanded economic development. The broader question for Jordanian politics and society will remain, however, not only one of equality of economic opportunity but also one of equality of political representation. The additional question, of course, is whether increased international investment, privatization, and trade will prove sufficient as economic solutions to social problems.

Gender and Politics

The preceding discussion of interethnic divisions within Jordan has something of a parallel in gendered divisions in Jordanian society, because here
too the emphasis is on de jure legal equality, coupled with de facto differences in empowerment. Jordanian women are not subjected to restrictive
national dress codes, as they are in Iran and Saudi Arabia; nor does one find
in Jordan the strict sex segregation and constraints on women's movement
that are so much a part of Saudi society. Indeed, women in Jordan are equal
to men before the law and have full rights to education, work, and political
participation. The state's commitment to public education for both sexes has,
for example, yielded a literacy rate among women of 82 percent (USAID in
Jordan 2010). While the legal and political systems guarantee equality of
the sexes, Jordan also remains a fairly conservative society, and hence
patriarchal norms do tend to dominate within family life and in society in
general.

Certainly the most controversial gender issue in Jordanian politics is that
of killings over "honor crimes." The reference here is to family members
killing female relatives suspected of adultery or of otherwise offending "family honor." This often amounts to little more than a woman being the subject
of rumors, wherein male family members have then acted to "cleanse" the
family's honor by killing the woman in question. This contentious issue has
received media attention globally, with specific exposure within Jordan provided by such journalists as Rana Husseini of the *Jordan Times.*

The issue has turned not only on the act of violence itself and its dubious "traditional" roots, but also on its legal status. Article 340 of the Jordanian penal code specifically allows leniency in sentencing for men convicted of murder in cases of honor crimes. While conservative nationalists
have claimed that this practice is rooted in bedouin traditions, their erst-
while Islamist opponents are actually on the same side on this issue, arguing for their part that the practice is rooted in Islamic law, or sharia. In contrast to these more reactionary positions, human rights activists have waged
a campaign to highlight this violence and to repeal Article 340. Women's
rights activists are correct when they argue that the practice is in no way
rooted in Islam, but they tend to run into a wall of tradition, in which mi-
sogyny is sometimes mistaken for tradition, culture, and religious authenticity (Sonbol 2003).

The Hashimite royal family directly joined this debate, and both Queen
Noor and later King Hussein condemned the practice. Since then, King
Abdullah and Queen Rania have lent their voices to this campaign. Even
more directly, Prince Ghazi (King Abdullah's adviser on bedouin and tribal
affairs) helped lead protests against honor killings and leniency within the
penal codes. The practice has thus been condemned by a large grassroots

movement as well as by the palace itself. It is possible, however, that the state's very emphasis on privatization and neoliberal economic reforms has unintentionally triggered a reactionary backlash among conservative Jordanians, including holding on to even the most suspect of "traditions" in the name of defending authentic Jordanian life in the face of what they see as an overwhelming pace and scale of change.

In the struggle for gender equality and social justice in Jordan, the honor crimes issue will clearly continue to be one of paramount concern in any analysis of women's rights in the kingdom. The struggle for equality also takes place, of course, very much in the public sphere, as women attempt to make their legal rights match social, economic, and political practice. In that regard, Jordanian women activists have argued that attention needs to focus also on private and public sector employment opportunities and continuing struggles for political representation.

In terms of the government itself, women are not entirely absent from top positions (such as cabinet posts), but they remain underrepresented nonetheless. This is certainly not due to a lack of qualified candidates, since Jordan, to its credit, has an extensive public education system, with a small gender gap in literacy between men and women, and one of the best-educated populations in the entire Arab world. It is precisely because of the education level of Jordan's workforce that so many Jordanians have been employed as skilled professionals in Gulf economies. Most of these migrants, however, are men. Within Jordan, despite their education levels and qualifications, Jordanian women are more often found as clerical staff, clerks, and administrators in ministries, offices, banks, and so on, rather than as ministers or directors (Brand 1998; Amawi 2000).

In terms of government positions, any student of Jordanian politics would be likely to come up with precisely the same list of prominent women in Jordanian politics—in the House, the Senate, or the cabinet—precisely because the list is so short. For most people, the aforementioned areas of public service would inevitably bring to mind people such as long-time senator Layla Sharaf or former minister of planning Rima Khalaf. Indeed, among the most prominent women in public life are princesses of the Hashimite royal family. Princess Basma, for example, has played a very prominent role as an advocate of women's rights in Jordan, as has Queen Noor and now also Queen Rania.

Jordan's women's movement scored a significant success in 2001 when its efforts to secure a women's quota for parliamentary representation finally succeeded, although not to the extent that activists had hoped for. The new law added six more parliamentary seats in a specific quota to ensure representation for women. In the previous three elections (1989, 1993, and 1997), only two women were elected to parliament.[2] The Islamic Action Front had originally opposed the women's quota, but then for the first time included a woman, Hayat al-Musayni, among its slate of thirty candidates. No Jordanian woman won a seat outright in 2003, but Musayni turned out to be the top vote-getter among women candidates overall. Thus in an ironic twist, the first woman seated in the new 2003–2007 parliament was a conservative Islamist activist. In 2010, the women's quota was increased to twelve seats, and then to fifteen for the 2013 elections.

Still, while glass ceilings have been broken in terms of educational opportunities, and despite the efforts of the prominent women noted here (in addition to the efforts of thousands of other less well-known women), the fact remains that women continue to be underrepresented in both houses of parliament, in the cabinet ministries, and in the royal court. While it is clear that women lack full empowerment with respect to the key levers of power in Jordanian public life, it would be misleading to attempt to draw a general picture of the status of all Jordanian women, given the vastly different circumstances of women's lives in the kingdom. For here the crosscutting variables of social class, ethnicity, religion, urban or rural circumstances, and so on each deeply affect a woman's status and opportunities (in both the public and private spheres). It is fair to say, however, that the various transitions confronting Jordanian society—especially in terms of the political and economic liberalization programs—each have had gendered impacts that can be disproportionately negative for women. As Laurie Brand has suggested in her study of women and liberalization, women are more likely than men to find themselves unemployed as a result of IMF restructuring programs (1998: 120).

There was some cause for optimism in the wake of the 2007 elections, however, as women made up more than 25 percent of the candidates for parliamentary office. Indeed, the 199 women who ran for office equated to four times the number who had contested the 2003 elections. Electoral success has remained hard to come by, aside from the six members of parliament determined by the women's quota. Still, in 2007, Falak Jamaani became the first woman to win a Jordanian parliamentary seat outright—without a quota. Jamaani, a career army dentist who had retired with the rank of major-general, had earned a parliamentary seat in 2003 through the quota system. When she ran for reelection in 2007 in her home district of Madaba, she earned an outright victory. Jamaani's victory was hailed by women's empowerment activists throughout the kingdom as the first major crack in a glass ceiling over women's representation.

Civil Society

When the Hashimite Kingdom of Jordan first emerged, the monarchy immediately established itself as the premier and centralized political power in the emerging Jordanian state. As the Jordanian state developed, civil society, like the economic basis for the new state, was weak. And hence the government itself almost immediately filled these gaps, establishing a large role for the public sector in the economy (a legacy undergoing transformation only today), ensuring a similarly large role for the military in backing the political regime, and finally co-opting the fragmented aspects of much of civil society into the new Hashimite political order (Brand 1995).

Civil society has nonetheless continued to emerge in Jordan, especially in the wake of the political and economic liberalization process. There are times, however, when "political society" and "civil society" in Jordan are actually difficult to distinguish from one another. In 1997, for example, after the Islamist movement led the opposition boycott of the parliamentary elections, the resulting parliament naturally proved to be overwhelmingly conservative, nationalist, and pro-Hashimite. With only six independent Islamists in the new parliament, and none whatsoever from the IAF, Islamist strength and strategy shifted away from parties and parliament toward the professional associations instead. Thus a key element of civil society became instantly politicized. In short order, Islamist candidates won the leadership posts of almost every professional association in the kingdom (e.g., engineers, pharmacists, medical doctors), thereby creating a basis for Islamist political activism outside the halls of parliament, but very much across Jordanian civil society.

Beyond the numerous legal political parties and professional associations within the kingdom, the key facets of Jordan's still-emerging civil society (as opposed to more explicitly political society) include the many nongovernmental organizations (NGOs) within the kingdom. Yet while these civic organizations are themselves independent, they nonetheless retain legal links to the state, since all NGOs register with the General Union of Voluntary Societies. State regulations also constrain the NGOs from exercising complete independence, as charitable NGOs come under the jurisdiction of the Ministry of Social Development, while cultural and social NGOs are regulated by the Ministry of Culture. Islamic NGOs are also permitted (and indeed have proliferated) in Jordan, but only if they pursue civic and social—rather than political—activism. Islamic NGOs, for example, may distribute religious literature or offer religious classes, but they may not campaign for Islamist candidates (Wiktorowicz 2002).

While NGOs have proliferated in Jordan, especially since the 1989 liberalization process began, the largest and most active organizations in the kingdom are actually royally organized NGOs—also known as RONGOs. These are organizations headed by a member of the royal family, a prince or princess who acts as royal patron of the group. These Hashimite NGOs include, for example, the Women's Resources Center (led by Princess Basma), the Arab Thought Forum (Prince Hassan), the Noor al-Hussein Foundation (former queen Noor), and the Jordan River Foundation (Queen

Rania). Thus in the Jordanian context, civic and social activism is based not only on NGOs but also on RONGOs, which in turn provide myriad services to the population, but also maintain a level of social and political control over civil society itself (Clark 2004; Wiktorowicz 2000a, 2002). Similarly, Jordanian workers are allowed to organize through trade unions, but these must then be approved and incorporated into the General Federation of Jordanian Trade Unions. In short, seemingly pluralist forms of social, economic, and civic activism are perhaps best seen as corporatist in organization, as the state both mobilizes and contains the participation of citizens in public life.

While Jordan's NGOs can be counted among the most democratic organizations in the country, at times they have been the subject of maneuvers to curb their potential influence. Since 2000 especially, the government has sometimes focused on the "foreign connections" of these groups. Most, of course, have global connections and just as obviously draw on sources of funding outside the kingdom. But some government officials, followed dutifully by many of the more pliant organs of the Jordanian media, have continued to characterize these groups virtually as foreign infiltrators. This type of maneuver is, of course, quite old in Jordanian politics. Internationalist left-wing parties, from the Communists to the Baathists, found themselves subjected to similar charges from the 1950s onward. But in the modern era of liberalization, and under a regime that openly embraces globalization, it seems particularly odd to criticize organizations for having global links. It is still odder that Jordanian Islamists sometimes fall in step with this critique themselves, despite the fact that it has also been used against them. Yet just as they tend to be suspicious of the Communist and Baathist parties, the Islamists are also suspicious of what they see as the too Western links of many NGOs, especially feminist, pro-democracy, and human rights organizations.

Another key aspect of civil society, however, is independent media, and indeed the loosening of restrictions on the media beginning in 1989 was a central pillar of the initial liberalization program. The immediate proliferation of weekly publications and the emphasis of some of them on exposing scandals apparently tried the patience of regime officials—many of whom were skeptical about the very idea of democratization. A new press and publications law in 1993 was heralded by some as a step toward democracy, since it replaced legislation in effect since 1973 and hence during the martial law period. But the law also required that journalists be members of the Jordan Press Association—a government body. Individual journalists have continually criticized this feature of the many different versions of press laws that have been handed down since 1989, since they see it as compromising their independence and hence running counter to civil society. While print media came under fairly tight restrictions, Jordan developed a regional reputation for its openness regarding the Internet. This was in keeping with King Abdullah's goals of opening the economy and making Jordan a regional center for Internet and communications technology. Yet in the midst of the Arab Spring, in September 2012, regime conservatives pushed through a new media law to restrict Internet news sites (which had proliferated) and bring them under rules similar to those for print media. In addition to the concerns regarding the stifling of news reporting in both electronic and print media, free speech advocates in the kingdom feared that the new rules might be extended to include blogs, Facebook, Twitter, or other forms of social media.

In many respects, Jordan's struggle for greater liberalization and openness seems to continually advance and retreat. But while the process has slipped since the mid-1990s, it has not yet slid backward to the pre-1989 period. Today, unlike the era before 1989, extensive polling data are produced by such impressive institutions as the University of Jordan's Center for Strategic Studies. Detailed analyses of the press, parties, associations, and other aspects of the liberalization process are produced and disseminated from the independent Al-Urdun al-Jadid (New Jordan) Research Center. NGOs such as the Arab Archives Institute now link to global human rights organizations such as Transparency International and the Euro-Mediterranean Human Rights Network. These can be counted as among the most positive and hopeful features on the Jordanian political landscape.

Within the state itself, in 2005 King Abdullah appointed the kingdom's former foreign minister Marwan Muasher as deputy prime minister for reform. In that capacity, Muasher led a broad-based committee of Jordanians (drawn from government and society) in creating an ambitious program called the National Agenda for Reform. That effort called for deep reforms within the kingdom, including changing the electoral laws, loosening restrictions on the press, expanding the rights of women, and strengthening Jordan's nascent civil society (Muasher 2008). The National Agenda, however, was met with overt hostility by many antireform hard-liners within the regime, with suspicion by the Islamist movement, and with considerable indifference on the part of a Jordanian public that seemed to have grown tired of new initiatives and new slogans. Despite its comprehensive approach to many of Jordan's problems, the National Agenda was essentially shelved in the face of conservative resistance. Today, perhaps ironically, liberal and progressive Jordanians are calling for many of the same reforms.

Despite such public cynicism and what may be called "slogan fatigue," many Jordanians are looking to a young and reformist king to tip the scales back toward liberalization and away from the conservative retrenchment that has undone much of that same reform process. Others, however, no longer count the king in the reformist camp. The lack of faith in the overall process is palpable, and was especially so during 2011 and 2012, when

Jordan reshuffled cabinets so often that it had five governments in that two-year period.

What is perhaps just as compelling about Jordan's struggles over reform, however, is the determination of many independent activists, organizations, and social movements to press on in their attempts to build civil society and more meaningful democratization. The efforts of these individuals and groups nonetheless run headlong into a core of the ruling elite who see democratization and all its trappings as a completed mission. For many regime conservatives the liberalization process already occurred, and it includes strict parameters intended to give a showy and pluralist facade to an established pattern of power and privilege. But even the cynicism on the part of old guard or hard-line elements within the Jordanian state, coupled with the trends toward backsliding and de-liberalization since 1994, should not be allowed to obscure the fact that there are real reformers within the state itself, as well as energetic democracy activists independent of the state who are working to create a more effective civil society and a return to more extensive liberalization.

Notes

This chapter draws, in part, on Ryan 2002 and Ryan 2009.

1. A detailed and thorough discussion of the public-sphere debates within Jordan over ethnicity, identity, and democracy can be found in Lynch 1999.

2. In 1993, Tujan Faysal was elected to a parliamentary seat (in a Circassian constituency in Amman), and in 1997, Nuha Ma'atah was elected in a special election called to fill the seat of the late Lutfi Barghuti.

15

Kuwait and the United Arab Emirates

Michael Herb

Kuwait and the United Arab Emirates (the UAE) stand out for their oil riches, enormous noncitizen populations, and monarchical regimes. Oil exports propelled their citizens from grinding poverty to comfortable prosperity in the span of a generation. Both countries have attracted vast numbers of immigrants but have not given them citizenship, with the result that foreign residents now vastly outnumber citizens in both places. Kuwait and the UAE are both monarchies in a world in which ruling monarchs are increasingly rare, and both have an uncommon monarchical system in which members of the ruling family hold many high posts in the state, making rule a family affair. (The UAE has seven separate ruling families, though the two most powerful are the ruling families of Abu Dhabi and Dubai.) The oil wealth of Kuwait and the UAE makes them far more important on the world stage than their size alone would warrant. Some of this international attention is positive but other attention is less so, as with the 1990 invasion of Kuwait by Iraq. And, of course, there is Dubai, one of the seven emirates of the UAE: not long ago a small village by the sea, it is now an internationally famous tourist destination complete with the world's tallest building and one of the world's busiest airports.

Historical Background and Contemporary Political Structure

Kuwait and the UAE lie along the coast of the Gulf, Kuwait at the far northern end and the UAE along the southern shore. The climate in both Kuwait and the UAE is dry with blazingly hot summers: before oil the area supported only a modest amount of agriculture and thus a small population. Those who lived on the shoreline made their living from the sea, mostly through trading and the harvesting of pearls from the offshore seabed. On land, pastoral nomads raised sheep and camels; in scattered oases, settled or seminomadic populations raised dates. The lack of population density and the absence of a large agricultural surplus discouraged the development of large, strong centralized states in the pre-oil era. We can contrast the situation along the Gulf littoral with that of Egypt, where the Nile provides fresh water for the fertile land along its banks, which in turn supports a dense population and a very large agricultural surplus. Ease of movement along the Nile facilitated the exploitation of this surplus and the construction of a relatively stronger central government. It also made Egypt a target for foreign powers. Along the Gulf shore, by contrast, there was no comparable agricultural surplus to support a large population or to attract sustained foreign interest. The hinterlands were loosely governed at best, while the seaside towns typically maintained a fair amount of autonomy, even if their rulers gave allegiance to one outside power or another.

Kuwait's modern history dates back to the eighteenth century, when a group of Arab families of Sunni tribal origin, hailing from the Nejd in what is now Saudi Arabia, settled on the site of what is now Kuwait City. The families formed the core of the Kuwaiti elite, which was a merchant rather than landowning elite as a consequence of the lack of extensive agriculture. These merchant families selected from among themselves one family, the Al Sabah, to rule (Crystal 1995). In the 250 years since, the Kuwaitis have established relationships of various sorts with outside powers, most notably the Ottoman Empire, Great Britain, and the United States. Yet throughout, the Kuwaitis have largely ruled themselves under the leadership of the Al Sabah (the exception was during the Iraqi occupation of 1990–1991). Foreign powers have typically confined their influence to matters of foreign policy: there was little economic gain to be had from a more extensive European involvement until the age of oil, by which time European empires were in full retreat.

British rule came earlier to the small emirates that later became the UAE, and this area was one of the parts of the Arab world that never came under Ottoman rule (Anscombe 1997). The British drew up treaties with local rulers (all of them Sunni Arabs), and it was as a result of this treaty-making habit that the UAE, before independence, came to be known as the Trucial Coast. Piracy was a central concern of Britain in its relations with the Trucial Coast rulers, along with prohibiting the trade in slaves, but in general the British were far more interested in maintaining order and excluding foreign powers than in exploiting the limited resources of the coastal areas of the Gulf. These treaties strengthened the authority of the ruling families against their rivals, and over time British recognition came to be a crucial element in each ruling family's claim to rule over its emirate. There were changes in the number of ruling families (and thus separate emirates) recognized by the British, but by the 1950s the current lineup of seven emirates had emerged. The southernmost, and largest, emirate is Abu Dhabi; moving north and west along the Gulf coast we find Dubai, Sharjah, Ajman, Umm al-Quwain, and Ras al-Khaimah. Fujairah lies on the Indian Ocean coast. When the British announced their withdrawal from the area before independence in 1971, the ruler of Abu Dhabi feared the consequences and actually offered to subsidize British forces if they would maintain a presence in his emirate—in marked contrast to the usual enthusiasm of rulers for kicking out the Europeans. The British withdrew anyway, and the seven emirates, along with Bahrain and Qatar, entered into negotiations to form a federation. Bahrain and Qatar eventually decided to go it alone, and thus was born the UAE as a confederation of seven separate emirates, each with its own ruling family.

Oil and the Creation of Ruling Family Institutions

The Gulf monarchies today have a distinctive form of monarchical rule: members of the ruling family are found throughout the senior posts in the government and monopolize many of them (Herb 1999). This is in sharp contrast to the traditions of monarchical governance in Europe, where relatives of the king or queen were generally expected (and very often constitutionally required) to avoid holding positions in the government. Thus in the Gulf states the prime minister (where there is one), the minister of foreign affairs, the minister of defense, and the minister of interior are almost universally members of the ruling dynasties. This style of monarchical rule is new to the Gulf, if only because formal ministerial governments (those with ministers of foreign affairs, defense, interior, and so forth) did not exist in the Gulf before the oil era. Before oil, and before the possibility of the construction of large states, the ruler shared little power with other members of his family. Sometimes he would send a male relative to rule distant dependencies. For example, in 1946 the ruler of Abu Dhabi sent his brother to govern the oasis of Al-Ain, about a hundred miles away across the desert. And the ruler might have a trusted lieutenant or two from among the members of his family. The rest of his relatives, however, lacked formal offices in the state.

The modern sharing of high posts in the government among members of the ruling dynasties emerged first in Kuwait in 1939. In the previous year the Kuwaiti merchant elite, drawn from Sunni Arab families who had migrated to Kuwait with the Al Sabah in the eighteenth century, held elections among themselves for members of a legislative council, or *majlis*. The Al Sabah had ruled much more autocratically since the reign of Mubarak the Great, who killed his brothers and seized power in 1896, and the merchant elite sought to return to the days of merchant predominance before Mubarak. The merchant elite also wanted to use Kuwait's available resources to create a more effective set of state institutions for education, the police, and so forth, and this the *majlis* did after its members were selected in 1938.

The ruler had no desire to see his wings clipped by the merchants, however, and he closed their *majlis* in 1939 with support from his family, desert tribes, and Kuwait's Shi'a. Some shaikhs of the Al Sabah supported the *majlis* movement initially, largely because the ruler had previously refused to share power with his relatives. The shaikhs of the ruling family changed this, permanently, when they helped the ruler close down the *majlis*, for the shaikhs divided up among themselves the various departments (which would later become ministries) of the Kuwaiti state. One shaikh took over the treasury, another the town police, a third the armory, a fourth the precursor to the Kuwaiti army, a fifth the department of education, and so forth. Before the *majlis* movement, the ruler ruled; afterward, the ruling family ruled.

This set a precedent in the Gulf that was followed, to one degree or another, by all of the other Gulf ruling families. Ever since, and to this day, the shaikhs of the Al Sabah have monopolized the key posts in the state, which today include the posts of prime minister, and the ministers of interior (that is, police), foreign affairs, and defense. The formation of a family regime in Kuwait, as elsewhere in the Gulf monarchies, was followed by the construction of strong, modern state institutions capable of exerting rule across the entirety of the territory claimed by the state. All of this, of course, was funded by oil, and the end result was the replacement of weak, fissiparous pre-oil states by modern states dominated by the ruling families.

In Abu Dhabi the development of a family regime came much later, in 1966. The ruler—Shaikh Shakhbut—refused to share power with his immediate relatives; he also refused to spend Abu Dhabi's surging oil revenues. The ruler's brother, Shaikh Zayid, decided to overthrow his brother and sought (and won) the support of his relatives by promising them various departments of the Abu Dhabi government. Some of these hardly existed at the time, since Abu Dhabi was little more than a dusty, if rich, village—there was, for example, but one clinic, with one doctor, in all of the town of Abu Dhabi. After becoming ruler in 1966, Zayid transformed Abu Dhabi into a modern city with blinding speed.

In Dubai a family regime was much slower to emerge than in Kuwait and Abu Dhabi: at several key junctures in Dubai's history the ruler rebuffed efforts by his wider family to share in his power, most notably in 1939 and 1954. But the lateral succession from brother to brother in 2006 suggested the formation of a stronger family regime.

The formation of these family regimes in Kuwait and the larger emirates of the UAE (and also in Qatar, Saudi Arabia, and Bahrain) helped these monarchies to survive and prosper in the modern world. Military coups have historically posed the most serious threat to monarchies in the Arab world, and the sort of family regimes found in the Gulf are hard to overthrow in a coup because there are so many members of the family embedded in key positions throughout the state. The incapacitation or death of a ruler does not threaten the regime because there are other members of the family with the necessary experience to assume the duties of rule. Moreover, the families, in effect, select the ruler from among their own number and thus can prevent unqualified rulers from coming to power—the European tradition of the eldest son always inheriting power does not apply to most of the Gulf monarchies. Finally, the families act as an informal mechanism of representation, with various members of the families talking to different groups in society. This gives groups in society the sense that they have a voice within the ruling family, though it does not substitute for formal parliamentary institutions.

Kuwait's political system. One consequence of the strength of these monarchical regimes has been a lack of pressure on rulers to share power with their people: throughout the Gulf, the ruling families have not found it necessary to liberalize in an effort to stay in power. Yet Kuwait is an exception, both in the Gulf and among Arab monarchies generally. In Kuwait the ruling family shares power with the parliament. As a consequence, political power in Kuwait is diffused among more political actors than is the case in other Arab monarchical states. The gradual increase in the authority of the parliament over time, and the corresponding loss of authority by the ruling family, makes Kuwait by far the most likely of the Gulf monarchies to make a transition to democracy in the coming years.

Why does Kuwait have a strong parliament? An important part of any explanation lies across the border, in Iraq. In two crucial periods in Kuwaiti history the Iraqi threat pushed the ruling Al Sabah family toward political reform. In 1961, Kuwait gained its independence, and Iraq immediately claimed Kuwait as its nineteenth province. The Al Sabah could not defend Kuwait against its much larger northern neighbor and had little option but to seek support from outside powers. In particular, the Al Sabah needed to join both the Arab League and the United Nations (UN), and to accomplish this the emir needed to dispel, or at least qualify, the widespread opinion outside Kuwait that the Al Sabah were oil despots ruling over a resentful population. The ruler thus appointed a well-known Arab nationalist to a leading post in what became the ministry of foreign affairs; sent a delegation of leading Kuwaitis—including opposition figures—on a tour of Arab capitals to make Kuwait's case; and held elections, in late 1961, to a constitutional convention. The emir also had a liberal streak, and his interventions ensured that the new constitution gave the parliament relatively expansive powers.

The 1962 constitution remains in effect today, without amendments. The constitution divides power between the ruling family and an elected parliament, and in this it resembles the constitutions of nineteenth-century European monarchies, written in a period when it was thought that the people should have some voice in governance but that full democracy was dangerous. These European political systems gave the king—and not the elected parliament—the power to appoint the ministers who directed the executive branch of government. These countries democratized only when the leading parties in the parliament demanded the right to appoint the prime minister and other ministers themselves, rendering the monarch a figurehead.

In Kuwait today the parliament is freely elected, but the emir appoints the prime minister, who has always been a shaikh of the ruling family. For decades the crown prince was appointed prime minister: the two posts were separated in 2003. The prime minister, with the advice of the emir and other senior members of the family, then selects the government. At least one member of the government must be drawn from among the fifty elected members of the parliament; the other members of the government become members of parliament by virtue of their government posts. The constitution limits the size of the government to sixteen total members. This arrangement allows shaikhs of the Al Sabah to hold seats in the parliament without sitting for election (the shaikhs of the family, as a matter of principle, have never subjected their authority to election); it also in effect gives the government up to fifteen wholly appointed members of the parliament, the total membership of which can rise to a maximum of sixty-five members. Since the government votes as a bloc, this gives it the ability to pass ordinary legislation even when a majority (though not a large majority) of the elected members vote against the legislation.

In standard parliamentary democracies the parliament must provide the government with a vote of confidence when it first takes office. The Kuwaiti constitution does not require this, and the practice has not emerged by tradition. Nonetheless the constitution does allow the parliament to vote no confidence in individual ministers. Members of the government cannot vote on motions of confidence and thus a majority of the elected members of parliament can dismiss a minister from his position. By contrast, ministers can vote on ordinary legislation, and thus it requires substantially more than a majority of the elected members of parliament to pass a bill over government objections. The prime minister himself can also lose what amounts to a vote of confidence. Should this happen (it hasn't yet), the emir can either dismiss the prime minister or hold new parliamentary elections. If he calls new elections and the new parliament again votes against the prime minister, the prime minister must resign.

Kuwait's Supreme Court is composed of five judges selected by the High Judicial Council and appointed by emiri decree. In practice the judiciary enjoys a good deal of independence. The Supreme Court has the power to declare laws and decrees unconstitutional. The legislative and executive branches have the standing to bring constitutional cases directly to the Court; like the US Supreme Court, the Kuwaiti Supreme Court hears cases brought by ordinary citizens only on appeal from lower courts. In practice the Court has generally avoided rulings that challenge the government, though there were signs that this might change in 2006 when the Court overturned a restrictive law on public assemblies, opening the way for large public demonstrations later that year.

The UAE's political system. The dominant political institutions in the UAE are the seven ruling families, one for each emirate. From a constitutional point of view, the federation itself is perhaps best understood as a useful device for the seven families to coordinate their control of a single sovereign state. The families, however, are not equal in stature, because some have oil and others do not, something reflected also in the differing constitutional powers of the emirates. The vast oil wealth of Abu Dhabi, some of which is redistributed to the federation and to the poorer emirates, is the glue that holds the UAE together, while Dubai's considerable economic and political resources have historically been sufficient to prevent Abu Dhabi's hegemony over the UAE as a whole.

The vast majority of the UAE's oil wealth is found in the largest of the seven emirates, Abu Dhabi. Other emirates produce oil—including Dubai, Sharjah, and Ras al-Khaimah—but their combined production in 2010 amounted to only around 5 percent of Abu Dhabi's production. Each emirate owns the oil resources in its territory. Revenues from oil exports are thus paid into bank accounts controlled by the rulers of the individual emirates and not into accounts controlled by the federal government. The federal budget relies largely on contributions from the individual emirates rather than on taxes. In practice this means that Abu Dhabi pays the bulk of federal expenses, because it owns the greatest part of the UAE's oil wealth. The poorer emirates contribute much more modest amounts, and Dubai's contribution, while larger, is not on the scale of that of Abu Dhabi.

The constitution, adopted in 1971, reflects the origins of the UAE as a loose confederation of ruling families. The dominant political institution at the federal level is the Supreme Council, which consists of the rulers of the seven emirates. The rulers of Abu Dhabi and Dubai have a veto, reflecting their predominance within the federation. One of the chief functions of the Supreme Council is to elect the president, who serves as head of state. By tradition, the rulers have always elected the ruler of Abu Dhabi to this post, a tradition that continued when Shaikh Zayid died in 2004 and his son Khalifa became ruler of Abu Dhabi, and then was elected—by the Supreme Council—to the post of president of the UAE.

Beneath the Supreme Council is the Council of Ministers: each minister heads up one of the federal ministries. The Council of Ministers includes members of each of the seven ruling families, along with some "commoners." By custom, the ruler of Dubai serves as prime minister. The federal government includes the full panoply of ministries that one would expect to find in a modern state. In practice, however, the ministries are constrained, to one degree or another, by the power and influence of the governments of the individual emirates. To give one example, the minister of defense is by tradition a member of the ruling family of Dubai, but also by tradition the minister has little power: the Emirati military is headquartered in Abu Dhabi, paid for by Abu Dhabi, and run by the ruling family of Abu Dhabi (Davidson 2007: 37–38). Some government services are provided by the individual emirates, others by the federal government. The richer emirates, especially Dubai and Abu Dhabi, tend to provide their own services, but the individual emirates enjoy substantial autonomy in many fields. Thus the federal ministry of interior pays for the salaries of police in all emirates except Dubai; the individual rulers appoint the chief of police in their emirates. In health care, Dubai and Abu Dhabi operate their own health care authorities while the other emirates rely on the federal health ministry—although even Dubai leaves prescription drugs to the federal government.

The federal institutions also include a representative body of sorts, the unicameral Federal National Council (FNC). Abu Dhabi and Dubai have eight members each on the council, Ras al-Khaimah and Sharjah have six members each, and the three smaller emirates have four members each, for a total of forty members. Up to 2006 the ruler of each emirate directly appointed the emirate's members of the FNC. In 2006, half of each emirate's delegation to the FNC was elected, but by an electorate of only 6,000 or so Emiratis, who were hand-selected by the rulers of each emirate. The method of selection was anything but transparent, and the process inspired mostly cynicism: turnout was only 63 percent even among the handpicked electorate. In 2011 the electorate was expanded to 130,000 citizens, but the elections similarly suffered from poor turnout. Press reports did not identify any elected members who could be identified as forming an opposition in 2006 or in 2011.

Compared to the Kuwaiti National Assembly, the FNC has exceedingly modest powers: it cannot remove confidence in ministers, and it has only advisory power on legislation. Its only notable power lies in its ability to publicize issues. In the 1990s, an Emirati graduate student surveyed the forty members of the FNC: thirty responded, and twenty-four of those agreed that "the FNC has virtually no powers" (Khalfan 1997). These were the views of those whom one would expect to have a positive view of the institution, having been handpicked for membership by the rulers of their respective emirates.

The UAE Supreme Court can review laws for their constitutionality, but only the emirates, the federal authorities, and lower courts have the ability to ask the Supreme Court to rule on the constitutionality of laws. The UAE has a civil law legal system that was influenced, like Kuwait's, by Egyptian practice, which in turn has sources in French and Roman law. Family law issues are heard in special courts that apply the sharia, or Islamic law; these courts are Sunni, though there is a Shi'i court in Dubai. Three emirates—Dubai, Abu Dhabi, and Ras al-Khaimah—run their own court systems independently of the federal courts. The judiciary is further weakened by the fact that many judges are foreigners working under renewable, fixed-term contracts that make them reliant on maintaining the favor of the authorities.

Government and Opposition

The Ruling Family and the National Assembly in Kuwait

In recent years Kuwait's National Assembly has increased its influence over the government, at the expense of the ruling family. The ruling family still has the dominant voice in selecting the government, for the emir has the power to select a prime minister, and the prime minister has always been a member of the ruling family. But the National Assembly has increasingly used its power to vote no confidence in ministers to assert its control over the executive branch, and there is increasing talk in Kuwait about the possibility of the appointment of a prime minister from outside the ruling family, a prime minister with the support of a parliamentary majority. If the results of elections determined who the emir appointed as prime minister, Kuwait likely would become a parliamentary democracy.

That it is even reasonable to speak of the possibility of democracy in Kuwait is remarkable, given its oil wealth. Most scholars think that oil revenues discourage democracy, and Kuwait is nothing if not oil rich: in per capita terms, it is among the world's very richest oil exporters, surpassed only by Qatar and perhaps the UAE. This is often thought to discourage demands for democracy and to strengthen the state so much that the regime can ignore what demands are made. Clearly neither is the case in Kuwait. It appears that a combination of pressure from abroad, the threat of demonstrations by citizens, and (to a lesser degree) a hesitance on the part of the ruling family to rule through repression alone, has taken Kuwait down a path that has allowed the parliament to gradually expand its prerogatives.

In past decades the ruling family has been more assertive about maintaining the limits of parliamentary power, and in some periods has sought to change the constitution to permanently limit the National Assembly's authority. The family's efforts to undo the constitution started with election fraud in 1967, which excluded leading members of the Arab nationalist opposition from the parliament. Fair elections were held in 1971 and 1975, but in 1976 the ruling family unilaterally suspended the parliament, providing as an excuse the outbreak of civil war in Lebanon, which was seen as an example of the dangers of too much participation. The Al Sabah held fair elections again in 1981, although only after a unilateral redistricting and an unsuccessful attempt to revise the constitution. Kuwaiti voters in 1985 returned a parliament much more obstreperous than its predecessors, in part because of an economic crisis involving a bubble in the stock market and in part because Islamists—who had entered the parliament in force in 1981—shifted toward the opposition. In 1985 the parliament forced a member of the ruling family from his cabinet post, and in 1986 opposition deputies directed interpellations at three prominent members of the government. In response the ruling family unconstitutionally suspended the parliament a second time.

Initial public reaction to the suspension of 1986 was muted, in part because many felt that the parliament had overstepped its bounds. By 1988, however, the opposition reemerged, circulating petitions demanding a resumption of parliamentary life. This was followed in 1989 by a series of large public gatherings at *diwaniyyas* around Kuwait, including some in the outlying bedouin areas of Kuwait City. The protests brought together the main ideological currents and identity groups in Kuwait, encompassing Sunnis and Shi'a, the nationalist left and Islamists, liberal merchants, the bedouin of the outer districts and Kuwaitis from old town families, and so forth. As the number of attendees grew into the thousands, the ruling family alternated between tolerance and repression. At one meeting, held in the outlying town of Jahra, the police beat up a number of participants, including some notable Kuwaiti figures, one in his seventies. By regional standards, however, the repression was modest. The ruling family responded to the protests by announcing elections to a new assembly, but one stripped of many of the crucial powers granted to the National Assembly by the 1962 constitution. Most Kuwaiti political figures—those who had served in previous parliaments especially, and members of organized political groups—boycotted the elections, as did many citizens. The new assembly first met in July 1990, shortly before Iraq invaded Kuwait on August 2.

After the invasion, the ruling family and much of the Kuwaiti political class wound up in exile. As the United States prepared to liberate Kuwait, its lack of democracy became awkward, and so too was the tension between the ruling family and the opposition. The United States did not want to appear to be restoring a group of despots to power. To address this problem, Kuwaitis in exile convened a conference in Jedda, Saudi Arabia, to reaffirm their support for the family. The price, however, was a promise by the Al Sabah to resume parliamentary life under the 1962 constitution after liberation. Having made this promise, and with the world watching, the Al Sabah had little choice but to hold elections after liberation, though long procrastination (a full year and a half) betrayed the family's reluctance.

In 2006, the National Assembly started to assert its authority against that of the ruling family with some persistence, resulting, by 2012, in a noticeable expansion in the power of the National Assembly and a dilution in the authority of the ruling family. In early 2006 the emir, Jabir al-Ahmad, died. The crown prince at the time, Sa'd al-Abdallah, suffered from dementia: it was said at the time that he might not have been able to pronounce the oath of office before the parliament, an oath of only twenty-six words. The obvious candidate to replace Sa'd was the prime minister, Sabah al-Ahmad, who had been the dominant member of the ruling family in the later years of Jabir's reign (Jabir himself had been very ill before his death in 2006). Sa'd, however, belonged to the Salim branch of the ruling family, while Sabah came from the Jabir branch of the family. The branches are named after two brothers who ruled in the early twentieth century, and there had been a tradition in Kuwait that rule would alternate between the branches (see Figure 15.1).

Figure 15.1 Family Tree of Al Sabah Rulers of Kuwait

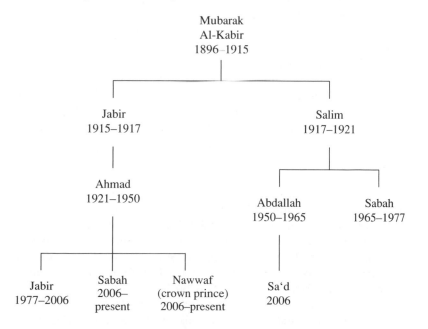

Shortly after Jabir's death, Sabah and his allies in the ruling family and in the parliament prepared to depose Saʻd. It is here that the constitution became important. Saʻd—or those in his immediate family who spoke for him—refused to resign. The ruling families of the Gulf have jealously guarded their prerogative in selecting rulers, rejecting any interference by outsiders. The shaikhs of the Al Sabah met together—absent a handful of Saʻd's diehard supporters—to proclaim their support for Sabah al-Ahmad. Yet the constitution specified that only the parliament, and not the ruling family, could depose the emir. Sabah al-Ahmad thus had a stark choice between maintaining the prerogatives of the ruling family to select the emir and following the letter and spirit of the constitution. He chose to abide by the constitution, and the emir was deposed by a unanimous vote of the parliament on January 24, 2006. The new emir, no one would forget, came to power via a vote of the parliament, and not merely by the selection of the ruling family.

A second major political crisis, a few months later, further demonstrated the ascendance of the parliament and the relative decline in the authority of the ruling family, at least in comparison with its Gulf counterparts (including the ruling families of the UAE). From the 1963 elections to the 1975 elections, Kuwait had ten electoral districts, each of which elected five members to the National Assembly. In 1980 the ruling family unilaterally increased the number of districts to twenty-five, each returning two members to the parliament. The ruling family hoped that this would make it harder for opponents of the family to win election to the National Assembly. Demands for a reduction in the number of districts grew in the years preceding 2006 and the issue came to a head in May 2006 when twenty-nine members of parliament (MPs) stormed out of a parliamentary session in protest of the government's refusal to address electoral reform. Supporters of a redistricting (who had settled on a demand for five districts) demonstrated in front of the parliament, adopting orange as the color of their movement, following the example of Ukrainian Orangist protesters earlier in the year. Opposition MPs declared their intention to interpellate and perhaps to vote no confidence in the prime minister. This was the first time that the parliament had demanded to interpellate the prime minister, and the willingness of the opposition to take this step owed much to its role in the deposition of the emir earlier in the year. The emir headed off the interpellation by dismissing parliament and calling new elections, a maneuver that was legal under the 1962 constitution. The election campaign focused on the issue of redistricting, and the opposition won decisively, building its majority from twenty-nine to approximately thirty-four seats. The ruling family, recognizing defeat, gave up its opposition to redistricting, and an electoral law with five districts was promptly passed. In addition, a shaikh with well-known authoritarian views lost his post in the new government.

Several years later, in the spring of 2009, several deputies in the National Assembly again moved to interpellate the prime minister. Fearing that this would lead to a vote of no confidence, again the emir dissolved the parliament. Before the dissolution the ruling family met and debated whether or not the suspension should be constitutional (and thus followed by elections) or unconstitutional. According to reports in a prominent Kuwaiti newspaper, the debate focused on the ability of the ruling family to "control the streets" and whether or not Kuwaitis could be ruled "in this manner" (al-Abd al-Hadi, al-Sa'idi, and al-'Aydan 2009). The consensus was that it was wiser to stay within the constitution, and a few days later the emir announced a constitutional dissolution of the National Assembly, followed by elections.

Later in 2009, the ruling family finally consented to an interpellation of the prime minister by the National Assembly and a subsequent vote of confidence. The prime minister won the vote of confidence with a solid majority: 35 deputies voted in his favor, and only 13 against. But this set a crucial precedent: the ruling family recognized that the prime minister and the government required the support of a majority in the National Assembly. When the prime minister lost majority support, he would then presumably be removed.

At the end of 2011, the prime minister did appear to lose the support of a majority in the National Assembly following a corruption scandal in which it was revealed that some deputies in the National Assembly had large sums (in the millions of dollars) in their bank accounts, and the deputies could not explain the origins of the funds. There was little reason to think that the funds were anything but bribes given in return for support for the government in the National Assembly. Faced with a lack of support for the prime minister in the parliament, the emir again dissolved the National Assembly and called new elections. He then replaced the prime minister with a different member of the ruling family.

By the summer of 2012, the Kuwaiti opposition was demanding that in the future the emir appoint a prime minister from outside the ruling family, one with the explicit support of a majority in the National Assembly. This demand was new in Kuwaiti politics but was in keeping with clear trends since 2006. Toward the end of 2012 the government pushed back against the opposition, changing the electoral law unilaterally—when the National Assembly was not in session—to allow voters to select only one, rather than four, candidates when voting. Much of the opposition, including many tribes, boycotted the elections, and turnout fell by a third compared to previous elections. With the opposition outside the National Assembly, the senior members of the ruling family won a brief reprise. This development, however, is unlikely to change the long-term trend in Kuwait's politics, which is moving toward a greater role for the National Assembly.

The change in the electoral law fell far short of the sort of rewrite of the constitution that the ruling family had sought in previous years and is the only change that is likely to interrupt the gradual ascendance of the National Assembly over the ruling family. At various times in recent years rumors of another unconstitutional suspension—like those of 1976 and 1986—have circulated, and there is no doubt that some members of the ruling family long to curb the National Assembly's power. Thus far the senior members of the ruling family have held back, calculating that the costs of closing the parliament are higher than the costs of keeping it around. In no small part this is because the parliament enjoys widespread support among Kuwaitis across much of the political spectrum. Islamists support the parliament, as do liberals. So too do the Shi'a, the bedouin, and the settled urban *hadhar* (the long-standing urban families of Kuwait town). Parliamentary elections in Kuwait are hotly contested, and those who win are the most visible and popular leaders of their communities. Each of these leaders has, by virtue of serving in the parliament, an investment in the vitality of the institution and a reason to defend it from encroachments by the ruling family.

An unconstitutional suspension of the parliament would ignite opposition from Kuwaitis of all major groups and political tendencies. This was true before the Arab Spring, and it is an even more serious threat following the precedents set in other Arab countries in the spring of 2011. Were the Kuwaiti ruling family to close the National Assembly, protests would take various forms and would include large public demonstrations. To control the situation, the ruling family would need to call on the police and even the military, but the ruling family is not well practiced at ruling through repression, having historically favored conciliation. The police and army are staffed by Kuwaitis who, in a small society like Kuwait, have strong family, tribal, and social ties to those who would take to the streets to demand a restoration of the 1962 constitution. In the end, it is not clear that the Al Sabah would be able to impose their will on Kuwait: even some in the authoritarian branch of the ruling family fear that repression would likely fail, and that the ruling family would wind up returning to the 1962 constitution in an even weaker position than it is currently. Events at the end of 2012, however, suggested that the Al Sabah might try anyway, a choice that would take Kuwait down a very uncertain path.

Political turmoil in Kuwait has led to an increasing sense of disenchantment with the parliament among economic elites and others. Much of this stems from unfavorable comparisons between Kuwait and other Gulf states: Kuwait suffers from more corruption, less efficiency in its government, and less economic diversification than its fellow Gulf Cooperation Council (GCC) states. Much of this is blamed on the parliament, and with some reason. The Kuwaiti political system gives the parliament the ability to paralyze the government through the use of interpellations. Yet the parliament does not have the responsibility of actual rule. In a fully democratic parliamentary system, of course, the government is formed by a party in the parliament, or by a coalition of parties. Those parties then have a direct stake in the success of the government. In Kuwait the ruling family—rather than political parties—in effect appoints the government. Deputies who aggressively challenge the government, however, tend to win reelection, giving members of parliament a strong incentive to make a name for themselves by interpellating ministers. The result is a political system that often seems paralyzed and that does not serve as a particularly promising model of democratic development for the other Gulf monarchies.

Ruling Families and Opposition in the UAE

While the politics of Kuwait are raucous, freewheeling, and at least partially democratic, the politics of the UAE are subdued, opaque, and not at all democratic. What accounts for this contrast? Many observers cite the UAE's oil as an explanation for the lack of a vocal opposition, but Kuwait has just about as much oil as does the UAE. Other scholars trace Kuwait's unusual level of political participation back to pre-oil political structures, including Kuwait's strong merchant class (Crystal 1995; Yom 2011). The best explanation probably lies in the political history of the two countries: the Iraqi threat has forced Kuwait's ruling family to create an open space for politics in Kuwait, and citizens have taken advantage of this to develop a vibrant and active political culture. Over time, Kuwait's freedom has become an element of its national identity and is hard to undo. The UAE, by contrast, has not faced a similar external threat. While Iran has occupied several offshore islands claimed by the UAE, overall the Iranian threat to the UAE is much smaller than the Iraqi threat to Kuwait.

Whatever the origins of the differences between the UAE and Kuwait, over the past several decades the ruling families of the UAE have maintained tight control over Emirati politics. While these regimes are not particularly repressive, neither is political activity tolerated. While Kuwaitis are free to hold political meetings *(diwaniyyas)* on a wide variety of topics, with advance notice and coverage in the press, in the UAE the police actively intervene to prevent similar sorts of political gatherings. Most citizens work for the government in one way or another, and citizens who engage in conspicuous political activity—especially Islamists—can find themselves without a position, or with their work activity restricted.

Emirati politics have not always been quite so quiet as they have been in recent years. The 1938 *majlis* movement in Kuwait was matched by a reform movement—in the same year—in Dubai. In the 1950s and 1960s an Arab nationalist movement emerged in Dubai: its criticisms focused on the

autocratic rule of the Al Maktoum ruling family and its tendency to favor
Persian merchants at the expense of Arabs (or so felt the Arab nationalists).
In the second half of the 1970s, conflict between the leading ruling families
of the UAE—the Al Nahyan of Abu Dhabi and the Al Maktoum of Dubai—
over the shape of the federation opened up a space for political participation
by Emirati citizens. The constitution adopted at independence in 1971 was a
temporary constitution (the word "temporary" appeared in the title). In the
mid-1970s, Shaikh Zayid of Abu Dhabi proposed a much stronger federation—one in which he and his family would play the dominant role—and he
had a draft constitution written that strengthened the office of the president
of the UAE (an office held by Zayid), strengthened the finances of the federation, weakened various powers held by the individual emirates (including
the veto right held by Abu Dhabi and Dubai alone), and created a national
parliament with powers similar to those of the Kuwaiti parliament.

The ruler of Dubai saw these proposals as a direct threat. A more powerful federation, especially one with a greater voice for Emirati citizens,
would constrain Dubai's efforts to develop its economy. Since Dubai had
far less oil than Abu Dhabi, the only way for the Al Maktoum to maintain
their relatively privileged place in the federation was to find a different
source of wealth, and they found this in the transformation of Dubai into a
trading entrepôt and tourist destination. This required autonomy both from
the UAE federal government and from Emirati citizens themselves, who
have never been enthusiastic about Dubai's development model. For a period both in 1976 and 1979 the rulers of Abu Dhabi and Dubai faced off
over the proposed constitution. In 1979 thousands of Emirati citizens came
out onto the streets in support of Zayid and his draft constitution. No one
demonstrated in favor of the status quo, but the ruler of Dubai nonetheless
held his ground, and the proposals to strengthen the federation came to
naught. In the end the only substantial change to the constitution to emerge
from Zayid's efforts was a decision by the rulers to remove the word "temporary" from the title of the original constitution.

After the failure to revise the constitution in 1979, there were no further efforts to reform the federal system from within. The temporary federal
arrangements of 1971 became permanent. The consequences of this were
profound. Citizens lost their best chance to gain a real voice in how they
were governed. And, in no small part as a direct consequence, Dubai preserved the necessary autonomy to pursue its own distinctive model of development. In an economic sense, Dubai has achieved spectacular success—at least up to the economic crisis of 2009—but at the cost of an
overwhelming influx of foreigners into the UAE. This has long occasioned
discontent among Emirati citizens, dating back even to the days before oil
when Arab merchants in Dubai protested the ruler's favoring of Persian
merchants. In the 1970s this was a central issue in the debate over changing

the constitution; in the 1990s it was an issue in the FNC; and today Emirati intellectuals bemoan the "irreversible" tide of immigration and what they perceive to be the loss of their country's identity. Yet while individual Emiratis often express unhappiness about the state of their country and threats to their identity, there is little in the way of a formal opposition, apart from a Muslim Brotherhood group suppressed by the regime in 2012.

The wave of protests that swept the Arab world in the spring of 2011 has had an effect on every Arab country. In the UAE there were no demonstrations in the streets, though over a hundred Emiratis signed a petition in March of 2011 demanding that the FNC be given real authority and that all citizens be allowed to vote. Later on, in 2012, additional signs of dissent emerged, albeit from a very low baseline. In the spring of 2012 the authorities initiated a series of arrests aimed at suppressing the Muslim Brotherhood in the UAE and launched a series of public attacks on the organization and those affiliated with it. Some Emiratis claimed that the group had the support of only a handful of Emirati nationals, though the group itself claimed 20,000 members. The Muslim Brotherhood is said to be particularly strong in the poorer northern emirate of Ras al-Khaimah, reflecting the increasing divergence in the privileges of Emirati citizens from the richer and poorer emirates. The vehemence of the regime's attacks on the organization suggested a deep unease among the rulers (Ulrichsen 2012a).

What explains the failure of the UAE to be swept up in the Arab Spring in any more substantive way? Many observers point to oil, and it is true that only Qatar—also rich in oil—was less affected by the Arab Spring than was the UAE. The enormous improvement in the standard of living of Emirati citizens over the past two generations has no doubt damped down the sort of dissent that is generated by economic hard times. But Kuwait also has a great deal of oil and that oil has not insulated its regime from pressures for greater political participation. One factor that does distinguish Kuwait from the UAE is the sheer number of foreigners in the UAE and their increasingly central economic role: while foreigners are a majority in Kuwait, in the UAE citizens have been reduced to a small, exceedingly privileged minority. Small, privileged minorities—especially those acutely aware that they are in fact a privileged minority—can make revolutions only very carefully.

Over time, as the economy of the UAE diversifies, the economic role of expatriates will become more and more central to the economy. The issue of democratization, or an expansion of political participation, will eventually include the question of expatriates. In Kuwait, by contrast, expatriates do not generate foreign exchange and there is no question of allowing them to participate in the political process, which is limited to citizens and citizens alone. Emirati intellectuals—in sharp contrast to intellectuals and political figures in Kuwait—today openly discuss the link between democratization and expatriates, often with a great deal of concern. The concern grows in part from fear that the Emirati demographic structure, and lack of democracy, will in the future run afoul of international norms, and the UAE will be pressured to provide citizenship to expatriates. The consequences for Emirati citizens would be profound: today they enjoy, if not political influence, a privileged claim on state resources (which is to say, on Abu Dhabi's oil wealth) in the form of state employment, free education, free health care, housing subsidies, and the like. A real democratic revolution would threaten all of this, and would threaten the Arab and Islamic identity of the country.

Identity and Politics: Citizens and Noncitizens

Kuwait

Before oil, to be a Kuwaiti was to be a resident of the town of Kuwait, or perhaps a member of one of the tribes settled in the immediate area. In the early years of oil and up to the 1980s, many bedouin in the desert hinterlands settled in the city's suburbs and gained Kuwaiti citizenship. This migration created one of the central cleavages of Kuwaiti politics—between the *hadhar,* those Kuwaitis whose families have long lived in Kuwait town, and the *bedu,* those Kuwaitis who descend from families who were until the past few decades pastoral nomads in the desert (Longva 2006). In the early years of oil the *hadhar* were better positioned than the *bedu* to exploit new commercial opportunities, and *hadhar* families built great fortunes. Less privileged *hadhar* families also had better access to education; a good education could quickly translate into a better job in the government bureaucracy. The result was a continuing class distinction that tends to echo (though never exactly) the distinction between *hadhar* and *bedu*. The *hadhar-bedu* divide also has a political component: Kuwait's Arab nationalists, who were the dominant opposition group in Kuwait from independence in 1961 to the 1980s, were almost exclusively drawn from the *hadhar,* and had difficulty winning elections in *bedu* districts. Today's liberal and nationalist candidates similarly are competitive only in *hadhar* districts. Islamists, by contrast, emerged in *hadhar* areas but have had substantial success in winning votes in *bedu* districts.

The years before and after World War II also saw the migration of a sizable Persian Shi'i community to Kuwait, and many gained citizenship when citizenship was distributed before independence. These Persian Shi'a joined a smaller number of Arab Shi'a from Bahrain and what is now the Eastern Province of Saudi Arabia. All told, the Shi'a constitute perhaps 25 percent of the total citizen population of Kuwait.

From independence up to the Iranian revolution of 1979 the Shi'i deputies in the National Assembly supported the ruling family, as they had in the *majlis* crisis of 1939. Shiʻi support of the ruling family was bolstered by Arab nationalist hostility toward the Persian Shiʻa. From 1979 forward, the Kuwaiti left moderated its attitude toward the Shiʻa, and today it is the more strident of Kuwait's Sunni Islamists who have had poor relations with the Shiʻi community.

The 1980s, after the Iranian revolution and in the context of the war between Iraq and Iran, saw a serious rise in tensions between Shiʻa and Sunnis in Kuwait and the election of opposition Shiʻi deputies to the National Assembly; the most serious incident was the attempted assassination of the emir Jabir in 1985, likely by Shiʻi militants from abroad. While Shiʻi Iran was perceived as the greatest threat to Kuwait throughout the 1980s and had a divisive effect on Kuwaiti sectarian relations, the invasion in 1990 by the Sunni Arab regime in Iraq had the effect of bringing Kuwaitis together and reducing sectarian tensions, since both Shiʻi and Sunni citizen communities in Kuwait virtually unanimously—and forcefully—rejected the Iraqi claim to Kuwait. Over the past two decades the ideological orientation of Shiʻi deputies in the National Assembly has shifted; while the Shiʻi delegation was dominated by opposition Islamists in the 1980s, in recent years the Shiʻa have returned to their pre-1979 role as supporters of the ruling family.

While there is some societal discrimination against the Shiʻa in Kuwait, they do not suffer anything like the persecution endured by the Shiʻa of Saudi Arabia or Bahrain. Neither do the Kuwaiti Shiʻa have any ambitions to remake the Kuwaiti political order, in contrast to the (relatively much larger) Shiʻi communities of Iraq and Lebanon.

The United Arab Emirates

While Kuwait is essentially a single city with its suburbs, the UAE is composed of seven emirates. The emirate of Abu Dhabi, in its origins, governance, and ethos, was very much more an emirate of the tribal desert than that of a seaside city: the *bedu* predominated. Dubai, by contrast, was resolutely centered on its port, with a desert hinterland that received little attention from the rulers. The northern emirates had substantial tribal populations, but these were tribes of the mountains rather than the pastoral nomads of the Arabian deserts. The northernmost emirate, Ras al-Khaimah, has a substantial population of mountain-dwellers, the Shihuh, who traditionally spoke a dialect of Arabic distinct from that of other Arabs in the area (Heard-Bey 1982). With the exception of Ras al-Khaimah, the emirates of the UAE are distinguished also by the fact that the ruling families come from the largest tribe in the emirate, so that the emirates are—in their origins—more emanations of the dominant tribe than is Kuwait. The consequence of this is that Emirati society lacks the clear *hadhar-bedu* cleavage that runs through Kuwaiti society, and instead is characterized by multiple regional or emirate-level cleavages. Naturalization by the rulers through the

1990s added a substantial number of Arabs from outside the borders of the UAE to the citizen population, many of them from Yemen, and these new citizens form a distinctive group within the Emirati citizen population.

UAE citizens, like those of Kuwait, are largely Arab and Sunni, with a substantial Shi'i minority, in the case of the UAE comprising about 15 percent of the total citizen population. Many Shi'a are of Persian descent, and tend to live in cities on the coast, especially Dubai. Sectarian tensions in the UAE, as in Kuwait, are muted by regional standards, and there is little overt repression of the Shi'a. Indeed, the Shi'a of Dubai have built magnificent mosques in the town and have long benefited from the patronage of the rulers.

Noncitizen Residents

The most important identity cleavage in Gulf societies is that between citizens and resident noncitizens. The latter are often referred to as expatriates: that is, foreigners who have taken up long-term residence. In Kuwait, expatriates outnumber nationals by two to one; in the UAE the ratio is an astounding nine to one. Most expatriates come from Asian countries, especially India, Pakistan, and Bangladesh; others hail from Iran, the Philippines, Europe, North America, Africa, and, of course, other Arab countries.

In many cases, what distinguishes citizens from expatriates is often not much more than the date of immigration: those who immigrated before the determination of citizenship became citizens; those who came afterward did not. It was not until just before independence that the governments set about formally distinguishing citizens from noncitizens. In Kuwait, only those whose families had lived in Kuwait since at least 1920 gained citizenship, but in practice many others also gained citizenship, and in the 1960s, 1970s, and 1980s the government handed out citizenship to many *bedu* who had settled in Kuwait. Similarly, the UAE citizenship law of 1971 gave citizenship by right to Arabs whose families had lived in the UAE since at least 1925. Others could gain citizenship by naturalization, and the UAE ruling families naturalized a very large number of Omanis, Yemenis, and others in the decades leading up to the 1990s. In Dubai, where the ruler tended to favor the Persian merchant community, many Persians and other non-Arabs gained citizenship.

Despite the variety of their origins, it is usually not difficult to distinguish citizens from expatriates. Citizens have a distinctive national dress, and often wear it. For men it is a long robe (white in the summer) and the *ghutra* (scarf) and *agal* (cord) that make up the standard headgear of the Arab Gulf. National dress is somewhat less distinctive for women; younger Kuwaiti women, for example, tend to wear their hair in a bun on the top of their head, covered by a head scarf, resulting in an identifiable Kuwaiti style. Expatriates, even Arab expatriates, do not wear attire that could be confused with that of citizens, unless they are citizens of one of the neighboring Gulf monarchies.

Today in both countries noncitizen residents have virtually no prospect of gaining citizenship. The governments of these countries distribute vast amounts of oil wealth to citizens in the form of free education, free health care, jobs, subsidized housing, marriage payments, and so forth. Bountiful oil revenues, and not taxes, pay for these state services (though Dubai is beginning to become something of an exception). Noncitizens in the Gulf receive few of these benefits. Adding an additional citizen does not increase the total amount of oil revenue available but instead increases the number of citizens among whom a fixed sum of oil revenues must be divided. In "normal" economies, by contrast, immigrants, through their labor, typically increase the total size of the economy and pay their way by paying taxes.

Living conditions for expatriates vary according to nationality and income. Expatriates who earn a substantial salary, for example, are allowed to bring their families to the Gulf to live with them, while poorer foreigners must leave their families at home. Nationality also matters: for example, I (a US citizen) was able to secure a Kuwaiti driver's license as a student, while a friend (also a student) was forced to sell his car that he had driven to Kuwait from Syria because, as a Syrian, he could not secure a Kuwaiti driver's license. The private sector also discriminates among various groups of foreigners. In Dubai especially, it is common to have separate pay scales for Westerners and South Asians, even when they do the same work, and this causes widespread resentment among South Asians and other non-Western expatriates. That said, the gap between the experiences of a Western-educated citizen of India and an Indian citizen with no education will be substantially larger than that between a well-educated Indian and a well-educated US citizen.

In the UAE, and especially in Dubai, the rulers make determined efforts to attract foreign tourists, businesspeople, and investors. To do this the governments (again, especially Dubai's) have eased visa requirements, legalized alcohol, allowed foreigners to purchase real estate, and so forth. Kuwait has not taken similar steps, and the parliament has no desire to do so, given that its electorate is conservative and would gain few economic benefits from attracting foreigners to Kuwait. Overall, the effect of these differences is to make the UAE feel much more comfortable for foreigners than Kuwait. This is most pronounced for well-off foreigners, especially those from the West, but less affluent expatriates from the Indian Subcontinent also tend to prefer the UAE to Kuwait. While there is a good deal of simmering unhappiness in both societies among less-privileged foreigners (along with an appreciation of the economic opportunities provided by both societies), in Kuwait this unhappiness is directed primarily at Kuwaitis, while in the UAE there are also complaints in the Asian community that Westerners receive preferential treatment in employment and salaries, and preferential treatment at restaurants, clubs, and other public places (Vora 2008).

Groups such as Human Rights Watch criticize the treatment of unskilled laborers in Kuwait and the UAE. To understand the context of these criticisms, it is useful to compare immigration policies in the West with those in Kuwait and the UAE. Western countries typically limit the supply of foreign labor through immigration restrictions. Limited supply of immigrant labor ensures that the price of immigrant labor (that is, wages) rises toward the price of citizen labor. Moreover, immigrants—or their children—typically can gain citizenship, and this further reduces differences in wages between immigrant and citizen labor. Gulf countries, by contrast, allow a great deal of immigration (especially relative to their small populations), flooding the labor market and holding down wages. Restrictive naturalization policies maintain a very sharp distinction between citizen and expatriate labor. Wage scales in employment formally permit lower wages for expatriate labor. The result is a vast gap between the wealth of many citizens and the poverty of their servants: in Kuwait, wage rates for live-in household servants (exclusive of food, board, and other expenses) are around $150 monthly, and often less.

Many foreign laborers arrive in the Gulf already in debt and thus prone to exploitation. Employers are legally obligated to pay the costs of transportation and visas, but many do not. The trade in visas is particularly troublesome. Foreigners entering a Gulf state to work must legally have a visa sponsor: it is the sponsor who receives permission from the state bureaucracy to import workers. Some sponsors demand a payment from workers that is above and beyond the actual cost of the visa, effectively selling to the laborer the right to work in Kuwait or the UAE. The practice is illegal, but also common and brazenly exploitative.

Workers in construction, janitorial services, and the like are often housed in large labor camps in the outskirts of the major cities. These laborers are typically in debt from the moment they arrive in the country, and often find that the job they were promised is not the one they are given. On top of everything else, employers often fail to pay their employees in a timely fashion. The consequence is labor unrest of the sort that occasionally occurs in Dubai and that led to riots in Kuwait in 2008. The end result is predictable: some effort is often made to meet the demands of the workers, but many are nonetheless deported.

Political Economy

Kuwait and the UAE are examples of what political scientists call *rentier states*—countries that depend on the sale of natural resources to fund their governments and underpin their economies. Because the oil wealth is owned by the government, it is the government that receives the natural resource income. But Kuwait and the UAE stand out from the general run of rentier states: while most rentier states—think Iran or Venezuela—annually receive a sum of rent that amounts to at most a few hundred US dollars per citizen, the annual per citizen rent income in Kuwait and the UAE is measured in the tens of thousands of US dollars. This makes them a truly exceptional sort of rentier: only a few other states are as rich, among them Qatar and Brunei, but not Saudi Arabia, Oman, or Bahrain.

How do the regimes spend all of this money? The ruling families keep a hefty amount for themselves except in Kuwait, where parliamentary oversight sharply limits the ruling family's access to the state's oil wealth. In years when the price of oil is high, these countries save vast amounts of oil income in investments abroad—Abu Dhabi's investment fund is worth hundreds of billions. The governments have also constructed elaborate welfare states to distribute some of the oil riches to citizens. Some items go far beyond what we find in Western welfare states: in Kuwait, the government gives most male citizens a loan of around $250,000 to build or buy a house. In both Kuwait and the UAE, newly married citizens receive a grant, students receive stipends when attending university (in addition to free tuition), and the state even covers the cost of a basic funeral.

The main way that the governments put cash in the pockets of citizens, however, is through jobs in the state or in state-owned enterprises. Around 90 percent of citizens who work as employees in Kuwait and the UAE work for the public sector, either directly for the government or for a state-owned enterprise of some sort. One may imagine alternatives, such as the state of Alaska's yearly direct payment of oil revenue surplus to its citizens. Kuwait and the UAE do not need all of the citizen employees they hire, but this is the main way that the regimes give citizens their share of the oil revenue. While there is a great deal of featherbedding in the government, these citizens are not wholly unproductive as a group: they do much of the business of running the state and providing public services such as education and health. They are also largely responsible for running the oil companies. In the end, however, the logic behind state employment is largely distributive.

Noncitizens also work in government but are paid substantially less than citizens are for the same work. This results not from informal discrimination but rather from the explicit creation of different pay scales for foreigners and citizens. The logic behind this is clear: expatriates' pay scales are set by the market (more or less) while citizens' pay scales are set by the political need to distribute oil revenues.

Alongside the massive public sectors in Kuwait and the UAE we also find very substantial private sectors with workforces composed almost wholly of noncitizens. Capitalists prefer to hire foreigners because they cost less than citizens, work harder, and are easier to fire. Capitalists, who are by and large citizens, generally have a jaundiced view of the quality of citizen labor as a whole: at least in economic terms, they often regard citizens as unproductive and inefficient clock-punchers. This is a result of the work culture among citizens that has developed in many parts of the state bureaucracy—though there are Kuwaiti and Emirati citizens who take their positions seriously and work hard. The average less-skilled citizen does not forget that, without the benefit of government jobs, he or she would be competing on the open labor market with foreigners from poor countries like Egypt or Bangladesh who are willing to work for wages that are very modest by Kuwaiti or Emirati standards.

Dubai's Boom

In the recent boom years of globalization the UAE, and especially Dubai, had spectacular success in diversifying its economy away from oil. The government of Dubai created an attractive business environment by building developed-world infrastructure, levying few taxes, permitting the importation of cheap foreign labor, and creating a regulatory and policy climate favorable to business. Dubai is among the most globalized economies anywhere: first and foremost it is an entrepôt, a vast trading port where merchants from far and wide come to trade. Its economy also relies on tourism and its increasing status as a regional business center. The government of Dubai—and the ruling family—profited from Dubai's growth largely through the development and sale of real estate. In Dubai, the ruler owns undeveloped land as well as land reclaimed from the sea (such as the "palms," easily visible on Google Earth, that have been built off Dubai's shoreline).

The economic crisis that emerged in late 2008 struck Dubai particularly hard. The government of Dubai, and its related companies, borrowed heavily to support Dubai's rapid growth and to finance the real estate developments that lie at the heart of the government's—and the ruling family's—wealth. When the Dubai real estate market crashed, Dubai's government, which was deeply involved in real estate, ran out of money: Dubai's government was essentially an overextended real estate developer. Dubai did not go broke, but only because it was saved by a bailout by the emirate of Abu Dhabi, still flush with oil wealth. One consequence of the crash thus was to change the balance of power within the UAE (even more) in the direction of Abu Dhabi.

Several years after the start of the economic crisis the UAE economy shows clear signs of recovery. High oil prices helped, but more important the UAE's non-hydrocarbon sectors—trade, tourism, and logistics—also showed solid growth. The real estate market, not surprisingly, lagged behind, but it is clear that there is more to Dubai's economy than real estate speculation.

The economic boom in Dubai came at a substantial cost to citizens. They increasingly feel marginalized in their own society: marginalized economically by the construction of a thriving private sector that relies very little on their labor; marginalized demographically by the flood of foreigners, many of whom are putting down roots in the UAE; and marginalized politically by their lack of voice in their own governments. While many UAE citizens enjoy the fact that their country (or at least Dubai) is now famous around the world, many wonder about the costs of this: Ibtisam al-Kitbi, a professor at the leading UAE university, points out that "[Emiratis have] been put in a situation they didn't choose. Nobody asked them, 'What do you want? Is it really, this is what you want?'" (CBS News, *60 Minutes* 2007). Thus it was not surprising that some Emirati citizens, at least initially, welcomed the economic crisis out of the hope that it would reduce the number and economic prominence of foreigners in their country.

Kuwait's Economic Paralysis

Kuwait's economy remains resolutely dependent on oil. It is not that the private sector is small in Kuwait, but instead that the Kuwaiti private sector is oriented toward providing services to citizens rather than generating foreign exchange. The Kuwaiti business sector is unhappy with this situation, and often blames it on the parliament. There is a certain logic to this: the parliament represents Kuwaiti citizens, and Kuwaiti citizens by and large work for the Kuwaiti state. They do not work in the private sector, and their government jobs do not depend on taxes levied on the private sector. They thus have little stake in the growth of the private sector, and much to lose from the sort of growth seen in Dubai (Herb 2009). Thus the Kuwaiti parliament has little desire to legalize alcohol so as to attract foreign tourists. The parliament also has little desire to sell state land along Kuwait's shoreline to private entrepreneurs so that they can build developments that would attract foreign tourists. (In Dubai, by contrast, the ruler controls land and is happy to sell it to the private sector.) In response to the global economic crisis, in 2009 the government proposed to bail out private sector firms in Kuwait. One prominent member of parliament opposed the plan on the grounds that investment companies "do not pay taxes on their income and do not participate in any way worth mentioning in . . . creating jobs for Kuwaitis" (*al-Qabas* 2009: 16). What the parliament *does* care about is distributing oil wealth to citizens, and much of what the parliament does—in economic policy at least—revolves around this. Members of parliament frequently call for increases in public sector wages, state assumption of citizens' consumer debts, no-interest loans, and outright grants to citizens from state oil revenues.

After Oil?

Is all of this spending on citizens, in Kuwait especially but also in the UAE, sustainable in the long run? The UAE has vast reserves of oil, amounting to perhaps 7 percent of the world total. It also has vast sums saved abroad, amounting to several hundred thousand US dollars for each citizen. These investments generate income. There might be a day when the UAE runs out of oil money as well as money from its investments abroad, but that day is a long way off. Kuwait has less money invested abroad, in part because it drew down many of its reserves to pay the costs of the Iraqi invasion of 1990. It also spends somewhat more on its citizens, and its in-ground oil reserves are likely smaller than those of the UAE. Thus there will come a time, someday in the future, when Kuwaiti citizens will need to find productive jobs in the private sector.

Religion and Politics

The regimes in the UAE and Kuwait have no qualms about promoting and subsidizing religion—and specifically Sunni Islam. In both Kuwait and the UAE, most Sunni mosques are funded by the government, and their imams (prayer leaders) are state employees. Shi'i mosques typically do not receive government support. Religion is taught in the public schools, and despite Kuwait's large Shi'i minority the curriculum is entirely Sunni.

In Kuwait and the UAE, as in the Arab world generally, Islamism is a potent political ideology with a substantial following among citizens. Islamists, in general, are often defined as those who wish to have their societies governed by Islamic law or, more broadly, want Islam to be the chief source of political ideology. Islamists are far more prominent in Kuwait than in the UAE, because politics in general in Kuwait are conducted in a far freer atmosphere than in the UAE. The regime in the UAE is not friendly toward Islamists, and prominent Islamists have been arrested, barred from teaching at university, and otherwise harassed by the government. Several dozen were arrested in a 2012 crackdown on the Muslim Brotherhood.

Gulf Islamists come in two main forms. The Muslim Brothers are a very well-organized political force with ties to the international movement that originated in Egypt in the 1920s. The Salafis, by contrast, are inspired by Wahhabi Islam, which is centered in Saudi Arabia. In the Kuwaiti parliament the Sunni Islamists (including the Muslim Brothers, the Salafis, and unaffiliated Islamists) form the largest single bloc, though they constitute less than a majority. The bloc lacks discipline, however, and rarely acts as a cohesive group. Sunni Islamist groups first entered the Kuwaiti parliament in force in the 1981 election, and moved over to the opposition from 1985 onward. The Islamists have had a good deal of electoral success in outlying bedouin electoral districts, and this has contributed substantially to the government's loss of majority support in the National Assembly. That said, Kuwaiti Islamists, both Sunnis and Shi'a, support the existing political order under the 1962 constitution. Kuwait and the UAE have experienced very little Islamist political violence over the past decades, especially in comparison to other Arab countries.

Civil Society

Kuwait has a vibrant civil society. In the UAE, by contrast, civil society is noticeably less active, especially with regard to anything related to politics. The most distinctive aspect of Kuwaiti civil society is the *diwaniyya,* which refers both to a physical place and to a type of meeting. The place is a large meeting room built next to, or in, Kuwaiti houses, usually with an entrance separate from the entrance to the private living quarters. Kuwaiti men hold gatherings—usually weekly—in their *diwaniyyas:* these gatherings are usually social, but often take on a political nature. Some visitors are regulars, friends of the family, political allies, business associates, and so forth. Others visit occasionally, and these can include prominent visitors from abroad: at one *diwaniyya* that I attended, the head of the largest Bahraini Islamist party made an appearance and was greeted by several prominent Kuwaiti political figures. At times the *diwaniyyas* of prominent politicians are used to host political meetings or even rallies, as for example when a member of parliament wants to drum up support for an interpellation of a minister. The times and dates of these meetings are announced in the newspapers and on the Internet. The right to hold such meetings, and the right to hold weekly *diwaniyyas,* is one that is cherished by Kuwaitis.

Traditionally, *diwaniyyas* have been an exclusively male phenomenon, and by and large remain so today. The increasing prominence of women in political life, along with their right to vote, has made female attendance at some political events more common. Some Islamist candidates for parliamentary seats have held political gatherings specifically for women.

Alongside the *diwaniyyas* we find many formal civil society organizations in Kuwait. Some of these are associated with the government, given the general expectation that the government rather than private donations will fund sports clubs and the like. Politically oriented organizations, however, generally keep their distance from government funding. Several political organizations exist for the explicit purpose of competing in elections: these are nascent parties. Other organizations advocate a wide variety of causes: the Kuwait Transparency Society is concerned with corruption, the Chamber of Commerce is a powerful advocate for business interests, and so forth. The universities have elected student governments. Each Kuwaiti neighborhood (or district) has a cooperative movement that runs its supermarket and shopping area, which is usually found at the center of the district. The boards of these cooperative societies are elected, and can serve as stepping-stones for citizens interested in running for parliamentary seats.

Kinship organizations also form an important part of civil society in Kuwait. We see this clearly in the tendency of Kuwaitis to vote for members of their tribe or family in elections. These kinship organizations can employ very modern technologies in building a common identity, constructing a common history, and maintaining communication among members. The larger tribes and families, for example, have their own websites.

The Kuwaiti press is both relatively free and extremely active, with the country supporting over half a dozen Arabic-language daily newspapers. The press reports extensively on Kuwaiti politics, though criticizing the emir is prohibited. The press, however, will freely criticize other members of the ruling family, and especially ministers who have run afoul of parliament. Personal lives of political leaders, and indeed of most others, are usually off-limits. Overall, the contrast with the press in the rest of the Gulf—and especially in the UAE—is sharp: the Kuwaiti press is interesting to read and provides excellent coverage of politics in the country, while the press in the UAE focuses on business news and politics in other countries.

Civil society in Kuwait—and in the Gulf generally—differs from that in other parts of the developing world in that it receives little funding from abroad, and especially from the West. The consequence of this is that the agendas of civil society groups in the Gulf are driven by local concerns. Nonetheless, some international nongovernmental organizations (NGOs) have branches in the Gulf. For example, Kuwait has a particularly active branch of Transparency International, an international NGO that focuses on fighting corruption. Numerous Kuwaiti businesses sponsor the organization.

Many of the same sorts of civil society groups found in Kuwait are also found in the UAE. Chambers of commerce are particularly active, as are sports clubs and professional organizations. Political organizations, however, are much less active. There are no equivalents to the blocs that operate in the Kuwait parliament, or to the groups that compete in Kuwaiti elections. While UAE citizens hold gatherings at their homes that somewhat resemble Kuwaiti *diwaniyyas,* the government does not allow these gatherings to become public political events.

Gender and Politics

Three models of women's place in society compete in Kuwait and the UAE. The first is the recent memory of gender relations in the era before oil, in which the social roles of women were sharply delineated from those of men. The second is the Western model itself, usually associated with "liberals" in the Gulf. The economic, political, and cultural power of the West makes it a model, for better or for worse, in most spheres of life. The third is the Islamist reaction to the Western model, a reaction that claims to preserve the older traditions but that in many ways is an innovation. Thus some Islamist deputies in the Kuwaiti parliament assert that women should not be allowed to serve in cabinet posts and in other senior positions. Some Islamist women counter this by arguing that Islam gives women many more rights than conservative male Islamists recognize.

The sharp divergence between liberal and Islamist views on family and women (along with differences on religion and other cultural issues) contributes to one of the central political cleavages in Kuwaiti and Emirati society. In Kuwait, where politics are more open, important political battles have been fought over the right of women to vote, gender segregation in universities, the holding of concerts with a mixed audience, the legal framework governing the employment of women, and other issues. In more than a few ways these culture wars remind the observer of culture wars in the United States: while Americans argue over abortion and homosexuality, Gulf Arabs argue (among other things) over the role of women in public life. In the Gulf, however, the liberal tradition suffers from its perceived foreign origins, allowing the conservative side in the culture wars to make a claim to cultural authenticity. This cultural divide often has a class component: urban, well-off, and well-educated families tend to be more liberal than the poorer, less educated *bedu* families, though there are of course many exceptions.

Kuwaiti women often vote for conservative Islamist candidates for the National Assembly. We can see this most clearly in the 2006 election returns. Before 2006 women could not vote, but in that year the parliament passed a law giving women political rights. Many deputies voted against the law, however. In the subsequent elections, also held in 2006, many of these same deputies ran for reelection. Men and women voted separately, and the election returns distinguished between male and female votes. An examination of the returns suggests that women did not show any particular inclination to vote against the male deputies who had opposed giving women their political rights.

While Kuwait and the UAE have not experienced the gradual economic and social development that has led to greater equality for women in developed societies, oil wealth has had some notably positive effects on the status of women. Oil has funded an enormous expansion of educational opportunities for women and has created opportunities for employment in the state. Both Kuwait and the UAE offer free public education up to college, and enrollment rates for girls are comparable to those for boys. Literacy rates are very high for young adult women. At the university level, women far outpace men: over 80 percent of citizens who graduate from the main Emirati university are female. This is because men have alternate job opportunities in the military; teenage girls are better students given that they have fewer distractions; and men, to some degree, are more likely to study abroad.

In Kuwait the citizen labor force is around 40 percent female, a comparatively high figure by world standards. In the UAE the figure is smaller but has seen rapid growth in the past decade. The explanation for this is straightforward: as we have seen, Kuwait and the UAE have offered citizens jobs in the public sector as a way of distributing oil revenues. Citizen employees do not have to work very hard in most of these jobs, and these positions come with generous retirement benefits. Kuwaitis widely consider the work environment in public sector jobs to be appropriate for women, unlike some private sector jobs. Imported and inexpensive household labor relieves women of some of their traditional child care and other household duties. In short, there are strong financial incentives for citizen households to have women in the workforce, and few cultural obstacles to female public sector employment.

Citizen women often complain about biases against women in marriage and citizenship law. When male citizens marry foreign women, their wives can eventually receive citizenship and their children are automatically citizens, whether Kuwaiti or Emirati. When Kuwaiti or Emirati citizen women marry foreign men, by contrast, their husbands and children typically cannot become citizens. If a Kuwaiti woman marries an Egyptian man, for example, this poses a very serious problem for her children, who have a great deal of difficulty in claiming most of the manifold benefits of Kuwaiti citizenship.

Women have made some tangible gains in recent years in Kuwaiti and Emirati politics. The first female Emirati joined the Council of Ministers in 2004 as minister of economy; she is a member of the ruling family of Sharjah. In 2008 the first woman was appointed as a judge in the UAE, making the UAE the second country in the Gulf, after Bahrain, to have a woman serving in the judiciary. Women have the right to vote in both Kuwait and the UAE and, though elections do not mean much in the UAE, women are at least equal to men in this regard. Kuwait's first female minister took her post in 2005: she was Shi'a and a professor of political science. Women competed in elections in 2006 and 2008, though none succeeded in winning a seat. That changed in 2009, when four women won seats: one woman came in first in her district. But in the February 2012 elections women were again shut out of the Assembly.

The Impact of International Politics

The small, oil-rich Gulf states are both wealthy and weak. Their oil is a rich prize, and they need protection from occasionally avaricious neighbors. The United States provides this protection. Kuwait hosts several large US military installations and the Dubai port of Jebel Ali is widely said to be the foreign port most visited by US naval vessels. The United States also has major bases in Qatar and Bahrain. The United States, for its part, wants to ensure that Gulf oil remains in friendly hands. While the citizens of Kuwait and the UAE share many of the grievances of other Arabs toward the United States and the West in general, especially over the Arab-Israeli issue, this is tempered by recognition of the need for US protection. The searing experience of the Iraqi invasion of Kuwait taught the Gulf Arabs the limits of Arab solidarity, and tensions with Iran provide a reminder of the dangers of the neighborhood. As a result, Kuwaiti and Emirati public opinion quietly supports the US military presence in the Gulf and close ties to Washington. In Kuwait, especially, the close alliance with the United States is accepted virtually across the political spectrum, including all but the most incorrigible leftists and militant Islamists. This is not to say that Kuwaitis, or the Kuwaiti press, support US policy in the rest of the region: the 2006 Israeli war against Lebanon came in for vocal criticism. But Kuwaitis did not take the next step and call into question their country's close alliance with the United States.

As we have seen, the threat from Iraq has had a decisive impact on Kuwaiti politics, and provides an important part of any explanation for the existence of a strong parliament in Kuwait but not in the other rich Gulf monarchies. The UAE does not face a similar threat from either Iraq or Iran. Any Iranian military assault on the UAE would need to come over water (or, even less likely, through Iraq and Saudi Arabia). Iran lacks the military capacity to move forces across the Gulf to the Emirati mainland against the opposition of US naval and air forces in the Gulf. Nonetheless, Iran and the UAE have long been involved in a territorial dispute over several small islands off the Emirati coast in the Gulf. The UAE emirates of Sharjah and Ras al-Khaimah claim the islands, but Iran occupied them shortly after UAE independence in 1971. The issue has festered ever since, but Iran does not make territorial claims to any other parts of the UAE. The main consequence of the threat from Iran on domestic politics in the UAE has been to emphasize the differing approaches of Dubai and Abu Dhabi toward Iran: Dubai

does a great deal of business with Iran and does not want other issues to interfere with commerce, while Abu Dhabi is more concerned with the occupied islands and the larger question of the role of Iran in regional politics.

The relationship between the Shi'i communities and the regimes (and
their majority Sunni Arab populations generally) is clearly affected by
developments in Iran and elsewhere in the Middle East. The revolution of
1979 made monarchs in the Gulf worry about the loyalty of their Shi'i populations. Developments in Iraq and Lebanon in the past decade have further
heightened regional tensions between Shi'a and Sunnis. The widespread
demonstrations by Shi'a against the Sunni ruling family in Bahrain, followed by the Saudi-assisted crushing of protests, have further exacerbated
tensions. That said, the Shi'i citizens of Kuwait, the UAE, Bahrain, and
Saudi Arabia are not—as some Sunni Arabs allege—tools of the Iranian
regime; the Shi'i communities of Kuwait and the UAE on the whole have
demonstrated a strong loyalty to their respective countries over the past
decades. The sectarian problem in the Gulf monarchies is not that the Shi'a
are an Iranian fifth column, but instead that tensions between the GCC
monarchies and Iran will provide an excuse for state repression of Shi'a in
the GCC, and a corresponding alienation of Shi'i communities from their
states. So far, fortunately, this has not been as much a problem in Kuwait
and the UAE as in Saudi Arabia and Bahrain.

The condition of foreign workers in Kuwait and especially the UAE
has led major international human rights groups to pressure the regimes to
do better in their treatment of foreign labor. The position of foreigners in
the Gulf states is anomalous by world standards: no other countries have
such a high percentage of foreign residents. While vast differences in
wealth are found in many developing countries, in those countries most
poor people are at least citizens; this is not the case in the Gulf.

Western powers have generally taken a hands-off approach toward domestic politics in the UAE and (to a somewhat lesser degree) in Kuwait.
This is, of course, in no small part because the regimes cooperate with the
United States, and their oil is important enough to outweigh Western concerns about democracy. The United States did, however, press for the extension of voting rights to Kuwaiti women, and the decision of the Al Sabah to
keep open Kuwait's parliament certainly owes something to fear of the US
reaction should the family close it. Yet the United States has not pressed the
Al Sabah to allow blocs in parliament to appoint the prime minister and the
rest of the government. In the UAE, Western pressure has been even less
noticeable: the UAE is among the least democratic regimes in the world,
and Western powers take little notice. In part this is because the UAE, in
comparison to the rest of the Gulf, has created a liberal social environment:
Islamists are pushed to the margins, women feel more comfortable in public
places, and conservative Gulf social standards are relaxed compared to

norms in other Gulf states. Some Emiratis nonetheless worry that, someday in the future, the international community will exert pressure on the UAE not only to democratize but also to give foreigners the right to vote. In a country in which only 11 percent of the population are citizens (and this percentage is falling), democracy does not mean a great deal if it includes only citizens.

Note

I thank Manal Jamal for her generous help with this chapter.

16

Palestine

Nathan J. Brown

Palestine is the most contested political system in the Middle East. Even to refer to it by use of a proper noun ("Palestine") risks assuming what is not clear in reality—that there is a state called Palestine, just as there is an Egypt, a France, or a Japan.

Palestine is not clearly a state, but that is not for lack of trying. Palestinians have declared a state twice (in 1948 and 1988), and their leaders have frequently suggested that they may do so a third time, most recently accepting designation as a nonmember state in the United Nations (UN). But in the past few years, the momentum on the ground seems to be swinging sharply in the other direction. Palestine now not only lacks full international standing but also internal unity—Palestinians are deeply divided between two political systems, one based in Ramallah (on the West Bank) and one in Gaza, each claiming that it legitimately governs (see Figures 16.1 and 16.2). And the Palestinian political scene is littered with all sorts of organizations, parties, and movements with differing political agendas.

Historical Background and Contemporary Political Structure

"Palestine" historically has been the term often used to refer to the strip of land along the eastern shore of the Mediterranean Sea, south of Lebanon and north of the Sinai desert. Prior to World War I, most areas of the Arab world, including the geographical area called Palestine, were governed by the Ottoman Empire. When the empire was dismantled after its defeat in the war, Great Britain sought and won a mandate for Palestine from the newly

393

Figure 16.1 Map of the West Bank

Figure 16.2 Map of the Gaza Strip

created League of Nations. That mandate allowed Britain to govern the territory, but imposed on it two obligations that operated very much in tension: it was to foster the development of the territory for self-government but also promote the development of a Jewish national home. These terms were defined very vaguely. But if the first required that inhabitants move toward governing themselves, the second required that the territory be open to Jewish immigration—something the majority of the existing inhabitants opposed. While there was a substantial Jewish minority in the country, a large majority was Arab. And the Arab Palestinian population pressed for democratic structures and independence. (Gradually the term *Palestinian* has come to refer only to the Arab population of the area, especially after the creation of the State of Israel in 1948 led to the emergence of a new "Israeli" national identity that included all the Jews.)

After facing revolts against its policies—first by the Arab population in 1936 and then by the Jewish population after World War II—an exhausted Britain turned the Palestine problem back to the United Nations (the successor to the League of Nations). The UN recommended partition of the territory into an Arab state and a Jewish state, but it was powerless to implement its decision when the Arab population of the territory rejected it.

Timeline: What Is Palestine and Who Ruled It?

Until 1917: Geographical area of Palestine is part of the Ottoman Empire

1917–1922: Great Britain occupies Palestine during World War I

1922–1948: Great Britain governs Palestine with a mandate from the League of Nations

After 1948:

Israel

1948–present: Israel controls over three-quarters of the territory of the Palestine Mandate

West Bank

1948–1967: Jordan annexes West Bank

1967–1994: Israel controls West Bank, administers Palestinian population, and establishes settlements in the region

1994–2007: Palestinian Authority administers towns and cities; Israel controls its settlements and most other land

2007–present: Palestinian Authority splits, with president controlling West Bank

Gaza

1948–1967: Egypt administers Gaza, allows it limited self-rule

1967–1994: Israel controls Gaza, administers Palestinian population, and establishes some settlements in the region

1994–2007: Palestinian Authority governs, although Israel retains its settlements and military installations until 2005, when it withdraws completely

2007–present: Palestinian Authority splits, with prime minister and cabinet controlling Gaza under Hamas leadership

---

Fighting broke out as the British withdrew. The Jewish leadership proclaimed a state of Israel in May 1948; two months later a group of Arab leaders attempted to declare their own state of Palestine. But the effort to create a state of Palestine for the Arab inhabitants was unsuccessful. It was defeated on the battlefield, even when the surrounding Arab states (chiefly Egypt and Jordan but also Syria, Lebanon, and Iraq) entered on the Palestinian side. When the fighting ended, the new State of Israel controlled most of the territory that the British had abandoned, leaving only a narrow strip in the southwest around the city of Gaza and the western bank of the Jordan River under Arab control.

The parts of Palestine under Arab control—less than one-quarter of the territory of Mandatory Palestine—were neither part of a state for Palestinians nor even under Palestinian control. Gaza was occupied by neighboring Egyptian forces at the end of the fighting, the West Bank by Jordan. Jordan annexed the West Bank rather than creating a new Arab state of Palestine out of the remnants under its control. Egypt administered Gaza but made no effort to annex it.

Some of the Arab population who had lived in areas forming the new State of Israel fled; others were forcibly expelled, leading to a large refugee problem as well. Some remained in Israel, becoming Arab citizens of the new Jewish state.

Thus, after 1948, the Arab inhabitants of Palestine were divided. They lived under Jordanian, Israeli, or Egyptian rule but had no state or organization to represent their own interests. Some slow efforts were made in the 1950s to create new Palestinian political parties and movements, but these were monitored carefully by all concerned governments. The new movements often emerged among Palestinian communities outside Palestine (especially Cairo and Kuwait), where Palestinians had more freedom. Some began to launch guerrilla raids on Israeli targets in order to provoke a military confrontation between Israel and its Arab neighbors, successfully creating tension but also earning some international notoriety when they intentionally harmed Israeli civilians. Israeli counter-raids proved extremely harsh. The most prominent Palestinian movement, Fatah, was led by an engineer named Yasser Arafat.

In 1964, the Arab League created a new body to represent Palestinians, the Palestine Liberation Organization (PLO). But the PLO at first was more a creation of Arab states than of the Palestinians themselves.

In 1967 a new round of Arab-Israeli fighting ended with Israel in control of the West Bank and Gaza. With the defeat of their Arab allies, Palestinians now felt much more independent. Under Arafat's leadership, Fatah managed to seize control of the PLO and make it a more viable body for representing Palestinian interests. And the PLO eventually received recognition by the Arab world as the "sole, legitimate representative of the Palestinian people." But the PLO controlled no territory. Israel did not recognize the PLO, nor did the PLO recognize Israel. The PLO sought to establish its state in all of the territory of the former British mandate, most of which was now Israel. Israel rejected the PLO because of its goals and its methods (Palestinian groups belonging to the PLO targeted civilians). And on a fundamental level, Israel did not recognize Palestinians as a distinct people with a right to a state. The Israeli government allowed and encouraged its own citizens to settle in the West Bank and Gaza. The PLO was left trying to represent all Palestinians while having its headquarters in different Arab countries rather than in the territory that it wanted for a state.

In 1987, Palestinians in the West Bank and Gaza launched an intifada (uprising) against Israeli rule. The intifada gradually petered out in the early 1990s, but it led some Israeli leaders to conclude that it would be better to negotiate with the Palestinians than to rule them indefinitely. And it led some on the Palestinian side to conclude that it was time to accept Israel and create a Palestinian state only in the West Bank and Gaza. In 1988, the PLO declared independence for a state called Palestine and in the process all but explicitly accepted the partition of historically Palestinian territory between the new state and Israel. Its leadership also met US demands that it renounce terrorism. But the PLO declaration of independence came in Algeria, since the PLO could not meet in Palestine—demonstrating that much had to be done to make the declaration a reality. The new initiative did eventually make it possible to negotiate with Israel, however, at first secretly and then publicly.

In 1993, those negotiations led to limited fruition. The Israeli government and the PLO came to an agreement in Oslo, Norway, to recognize each other. They then came to a series of agreements—collectively known as the Oslo Accords—that would allow Palestinians in the West Bank and Gaza to govern themselves for a transitional period. During that period, Israel and the PLO were supposed to negotiate a permanent agreement—but almost all the details of that permanent settlement were left inchoate. In a sense, the two sides simply agreed to try to agree.

The Oslo Accords were very controversial on both sides. Israelis saw that the accords were likely to lead to a Palestinian state and to significant withdrawals from the West Bank and Gaza—a price many were not willing to pay. Some Palestinians felt that the PLO had played its only card—recognition of Israel—and would likely be left with only the right to administer a few cities rather than a real state. And some rejected the idea of a peace agreement altogether. A Palestinian offshoot of the Muslim Brotherhood, Hamas, led the Palestinian opposition to the Oslo Accords.

Beginning in 1993 and 1994, the interim parts of the Oslo Accords allowed the Palestinians to set up a body they called the Palestinian National Authority (PNA) to administer Palestinian towns and cities in the West Bank and Gaza. They used this as an opportunity to create the basis of a state—founding ministries, building a parliament, writing laws, and creating security forces. In 1996, Palestinians in the West Bank and Gaza elected Yasser Arafat as their president as well as a parliament dominated by his Fatah party. Fatah tried to convert itself from a revolutionary movement to a governing party.

But while this effort was occurring, little progress was made on a final agreement between Israel and the PLO. Only in 2000 were there serious negotiations, and those did not result in an agreement. While Israel had pledged to widen the areas under Palestinian control in the meantime, it unilaterally froze its withdrawals. Palestinians despaired that they would receive a state through a negotiated peace process and saw the emerging PNA as a corrupt body ruling a shrunken territory—an entity designed to mask rather than end Israeli occupation. They also saw Israeli settlers continuing to move into the West Bank and Gaza, leading them to believe that Israel would never withdraw. Some Palestinian groups rejected the entire process and continued to attack Israeli targets. Israel was able to impose sharp restrictions on Palestinian movement within the West Bank and between the West Bank and Gaza; obstacles to Palestinian travel inside and between the West Bank and Gaza seemed to grow far more severe even as peace was supposedly being negotiated. In short, while international eyes focused on the hope of negotiations, Palestinians began to feel that there was no prospect of a genuine settlement.

In 2000, a second Palestinian intifada against Israeli rule was launched. The intifada and the harsh Israeli countermeasures took a severe toll on the PNA. Israel regarded PNA leaders—especially Arafat himself—as responsible for the violence and terrorism directed against Israeli civilians. Israel sent its forces to surround the Palestinian president, holding him prisoner in his own office. Various Palestinian groups escalated their attacks in response to every Israeli measure. And Israel began construction of a barrier—a formidable wall in populated areas and a sophisticated fence in the rest of the territory—that protected many of its citizens in the West Bank and made it difficult for would-be attackers to reach Israeli targets. Israel withdrew from the Gaza Strip in 2005, but maintained close control on entry and exit from the territory.

The intifada gradually subsided, and Palestinians tried to rebuild their political institutions. President Arafat died in 2004, and elections were immediately held for his successor, resulting in the victory of his deputy, Mahmoud Abbas. Abbas himself had advocated returning to negotiations with Israel and had strong international backing. Arafat's death and the peaceful accession to power of a figure more acceptable to the United States and Israel seemed to be an opportunity to revive the PNA. The parliament that had been elected in 1996 was still sitting—because it had been intended to last only for a three-year period while peace was being negotiated, no second round of elections were ever held. So the new president called for parliamentary elections as a way of renewing Palestinian institutions. And because he wanted to build a strong consensus among all Palestinians, he coaxed Hamas—which had boycotted previous elections—into participating. He clearly anticipated that his Fatah party would still win, but

that Hamas would become a loyal opposition rather than a radical rejection-
ist group.

Yet Hamas won a significant electoral victory in January 2006—aided
by Fatah's reputation for corruption, squabbling, and inability to deliver
peace, as well as by an election system that Fatah had tried to rig for its
own benefit but that actually rewarded the tactically smarter Hamas. Hamas
also enjoyed a reputation for being far more public-spirited and less corrupt
than Fatah. Palestinians were certainly aware of Hamas's hard-line positions (though Hamas tried to emphasize its reform credentials rather than its
rejection of a negotiated settlement with Israel in the campaign), but since
there seemed to be no viable diplomacy occurring, even Palestinians who
wished to settle with Israel voted for Hamas. The Islamic movement was
caught by surprise by the size of its victory and realized that it would not be
accepted internationally if it formed the PNA government by itself. It therefore tried to form a coalition government with other parties (including
Fatah) but was unable to persuade them to join. In March 2006, Hamas accepted power and formed a cabinet. It was met immediately by a cutoff of
funds (the PNA depended on Europe for some funding and even on Israel
for collecting its taxes), strikes by Fatah-led unions, and attempts by hostile
Palestinian forces to keep it from governing. And since Fatah still controlled the presidency, the security services, and most top administrative
positions, Hamas found that it held only some levers of power.

In the summer of 2006, after Palestinians captured an Israeli soldier
and held him hostage, Israel retaliated by arresting many Hamas members
of parliament and even some ministers. It seemed that Hamas would not be
able to govern. Hamas itself only vaguely hinted at softening its hard-line
positions. In order to find a way out of the impasse, Hamas and Fatah
briefly came to an agreement and even jointly formed a cabinet, but Palestinian infighting did not cease, and the US and European funders of the
PNA viewed the Fatah-Hamas government with suspicion. The agreement
soon fell apart, and a civil war between Hamas and Fatah in Gaza in 2007
left Hamas in control of Gaza but ousted from power in the West Bank.
Palestinians now had two governments, but they still had not achieved their
first state.

After the split, both the Hamas-led government in Gaza and the Abbas-
led government in Ramallah rejected each other's legitimacy. While they
went through the motions of attempting to reunify (neighboring Egypt
sponsored a series of efforts), both sides preferred to dig themselves in
rather than make concessions to the other. They arrested each other's supporters and tried to show that they could rule their respective areas. In
Gaza, Hamas had to do so under an extremely strict blockade imposed by
Israel and enforced by Egypt as well; only some food and medicine could
be reliably transported (though a vast array of goods were smuggled into

Gaza through underground tunnels connected to Egypt). In December 2008, after the breakdown of an informal cease-fire between Israel and Hamas, Israel launched an invasion of Gaza that caused further economic devastation. But Hamas continued to solidify its hold on power, controlling the government and regulating the tunnel economy. On the West Bank, a respected international economist headed an effort to build a clean and efficient government; he was given extensive international support.

One possible way out of the division was new elections—and indeed, both Abbas and the parliament were supposed to have been elected to four-year terms. But when their terms expired, elections became the subject of dispute rather than a way to resolve differences: after Hamas seized control of Gaza, Abbas issued a new election law by decree that effectively barred Hamas from running, and each side arrested the other's supporters, making campaigning impossible. When Abbas announced that he wanted to proceed with elections for January 2010, nobody was surprised when the independent election commission said it did not know how it could hold them.

Palestinian public opinion grew increasingly critical of both Fatah and Hamas for refusing to bury their differences. Accordingly, the two sides sometimes agreed to vague formulas for reconciliation, but they never implemented them.

Government and Opposition

Most Arab political systems have strong governments and weak and divided oppositions. Before the upheavals of 2011, the least authoritarian Arab regimes might have had some limited democratic mechanisms—like multiparty elections and parliaments—but none allowed political power to change hands as the result of elections. While some Arab systems allowed some opposition elements to operate, this resembled more a cat-and-mouse game between government and opposition than robust democratic politics. In a few countries (most notably Tunisia and Egypt), the situation for political opposition became much more open after 2011, but the rules of democratic politics were still not well established.

By these standards, Palestine has been more open for a while, in that political opposition has existed since the beginning of the PNA. But political competition is not well institutionalized. In fact, since 2006, it has not even been clear which party is in government and which one is in opposition. So while it has a more open political system, it also has fragile, weak, and decaying institutions.

The Palestine Liberation Organization still claims to represent all Palestinians everywhere, not merely those in the West Bank and Gaza governed by the PNA. But while most Palestinians continue to respect the PLO as a symbol, in reality it has become little more than a shell. To the extent that it survives, the PLO is dominated by the Fatah party—they both have the same leader (Mahmoud Abbas). Its main body is the Palestinian National Council, which consists of leading Palestinians throughout the world, but this only meets sporadically (its last meeting was in 1999). The real work of the PLO is carried out by its Central Committee and its Executive Committee—bodies dominated by Fatah but that also include other parties and independents. The creation of the PNA in the West Bank and Gaza marginalized the PLO in Palestinian politics, however. Most leading Palestinian political figures left the PLO to join the PNA, taking most Palestinian finances with them, and the PLO was allowed to decay. The PNA does acknowledge the PLO as its overseer, and the PLO remains important as a symbol of national unity. But even in that regard its usefulness has been limited by the rise of Hamas—which has not joined the PLO and refuses to do so until it is offered a significant share of power in the body.

This has left the PNA, since 1994, as the organization that administers the West Bank and Gaza. In some areas, the PNA is allowed to go beyond administration, to control police and security, but there is a steady tug-of-war with Israel on that issue.

The PNA takes on a host of governmental functions: it oversees schools, parts of the health care system, courts of law, and business licensing, and it carries out some foreign relations. It has no military and does not issue its own currency (the Israeli shekel is used). It cannot control exiting or entering of its territory—indeed, it has no defined borders. It is not a recognized state but merely an administrative body, so it leaves most diplomatic relations to the PLO, which claims to represent the state of Palestine until that state is given territorial reality.

Since 2000, many of the PNA-controlled governmental functions have decayed under the combined pressures of the intifada, Israeli restrictions, and the rivalry between Hamas and Fatah. Generally, the health and education systems have continued to function, but other governmental services work badly if at all.

For its first eight years (from 1994 to 2002), the PNA seemed to be emerging as a state that resembled other Arab political systems of the time, even with all their authoritarian features. There was a single dominant party, Fatah. It governed in a heavy-handed manner. Dissent was often tolerated (much more, in fact, than in most Arab states), but the government could sometimes be very rough with critics. There were some democratic practices, but they were not allowed to threaten Fatah rule—for instance, local elections were not held for a long time because the PNA's leaders feared the opposition was too popular. Hamas, the largest opposition group, was sometimes tolerated, but when it launched attacks on Israel, PNA leaders sometimes cracked down hard, arresting and even torturing Hamas members.

When the second intifada erupted in 2000, the PNA began to decay. Various Palestinian groups competed with each other for their ability to "resist" Israel by launching attacks, and the PNA's ability to suppress the opposition (including Hamas) collapsed.

In 2002, a group of Palestinian reformers, supported by international donors in Europe and the United States, were able to use the weakness of the PNA to impose a series of reforms on Palestinian politics. They forced President Arafat to approve a constitution he had long resisted and to accept a law creating an independent judiciary. They also made him turn over revenue to the treasury rather than control a portion himself with no accountability, as he had done earlier. For Palestinian reformers, the plan was to rebuild the PNA on a solid and professional basis. But other supporters of reform (like the United States) saw the effort as aimed at Arafat, whom the Americans and Israelis both wished to see weakened or replaced. The combined result was the dismantling of much of the remaining ability of the PNA president to dominate Palestinian politics as an authoritarian leader.

The reformed system received its most severe test in 2006, when the opposition won the parliamentary election. For the first time in Arab history, a governing party had lost power through democratic means. In some ways, Palestine confronted the same situation that had happened in other authoritarian systems—from the Philippines to Poland—with a ruling party calling an election in order to show that it could win but then going down in defeat. But the Palestinian situation was far more difficult. First, the defeated party, Fatah, still controlled the presidency, since Abbas had won it a year earlier. And much of the governmental machinery was staffed by people loyal to Fatah. Second, Palestinian political institutions were far more fragile and untested. Third, Hamas was rejected internationally because it had targeted civilians and rejected the negotiation process with Israel.

Under this harsh domestic and international pressure, Palestinian democracy simply failed the test. After a year and a half, the PNA split into two halves, with Hamas controlling the half in Gaza and Abbas controlling the half in the West Bank. And in neither territory is dissent fully tolerated. In Gaza, Fatah activists are harassed and arrested, and pro-Fatah newspapers are barred; in the West Bank, Hamas activists are arrested and pro-Hamas newspapers are forbidden from entering. Rather than leading to a democratic transition, the 2006 elections led to a political breakdown. Neither Fatah nor Hamas seems to have a realistic way of achieving the goal of creating a real Palestinian state on any territory.

If the PLO, representing Palestinians throughout the world, has become a shell, and the PNA is split and decaying, are there any sound structures left in Palestinian political life? The political party system is very lively. But in some respects this is a problem—the parties (like Hamas and Fatah) are strong at the expense of the government. The parties often have their own militias and often seem to treat government office as a way of furthering party rather than national goals.

Palestinian party life is also complicated by the fact that the parties aim not simply to win elections and government authority but also to achieve all sorts of other goals—including national liberation and provision of services. In fact, most do not call themselves "parties" but instead "movements." Hamas, for instance, whose full name is Islamic Resistance Movement, has a military wing and remains in part an underground organization. Fatah, whose full name is Movement of Palestinian Liberation, also has militias associated with it. Hamas has managed to retain some coherence even as its leaders often disagree; Fatah, by contrast, seems to be decaying, with its leaders sometimes more concerned with outmaneuvering each other than with achieving party goals. Other, smaller parties are similarly split among electoral, propaganda, social, and military activity.

Political Economy

The rest of the Middle East has witnessed a struggle over how much the state should control the economy. Palestine is not a state, but it still seems that politics drives economics. As in much of the surrounding area, the mainstay of Palestine's economy in the early twentieth century was farming, though there was some limited manufacturing, long-distance trade, and nomadic activity as well. Economic development led to some migration to the cities, and the 1948 war left most Palestinians in the West Bank and Gaza in towns, cities, and camps. This had real effects on Palestinian society, parts of which became dependent on foreign assistance for basic services. The old Palestinian leadership—consisting of prominent landowning families—declined in the new environment, and some new leading groups, grounded in fields like medicine and business, began to become more prominent.

But the Palestinian economy never experienced the ambitious state-led development projects launched by many Arab states in the 1950s and 1960s. Gaza remained tied to Egypt as a ward rather than a focus of development efforts. In the West Bank, the Jordanian government that annexed the area focused most of its attention on the East Bank instead.

Israel's occupation of the West Bank and Gaza in 1967 radically changed the nature of the Palestinian economy. Israel eliminated economic barriers among itself, the West Bank, and Gaza, meaning that residents of those areas now could work in Israel and trade freely. Palestinians paid taxes at the Israeli rate, switched over largely to Israeli currency, and even saw Israel integrate the Palestinian telephone network with its own. Israel was a far larger and more prosperous society and it developed rapidly in the decades after the 1967 war. The result was that large numbers of Palestinians found work in Israel; some even worked in settlements that Israel built for its own citizens on the land it was now occupying in the West Bank and Gaza. Most goods for Palestinian markets came through Israeli ports, and the Palestinians found that Israel was the best customer for some of their products.

The increasingly close linkages with Israel led to an increase in living standards for many Palestinians, but it was accompanied by politically distasteful effects. First, they had no control over economic policy. Second, while the arrangement generated jobs, the lower economic and educational levels of Palestinian areas ensured that most employment for Palestinians was unskilled and poorly paid relative to that for Israelis. Third, while Israel applied the same tax system to the West Bank and Gaza that it did to its own territories, it used the revenues not to finance economic development in those territories but rather to underwrite its own costs. From a Palestinian standpoint, this meant that the West Bank and Gaza were being forced to finance the cost of their own occupation. Finally, the health of the Palestinian economy depended on access to Israeli markets and that could be closed off with devastating effect, as the Palestinians found, beginning in the 1990s.

When Israel and the PLO negotiated the Oslo Accords, the Palestinian leadership first wished to detach the economies of the West Bank and Gaza from Israel's and reorient them toward the Arab world. But they soon realized that, as attractive as this might have been on nationalist grounds, it was problematic economically. This point was driven home when, toward the beginning of the negotiations, Israel constructed a fence around Gaza in order to allow it to restrict the traffic of people and goods in and out of the small territory. Such a closure would be a mixed blessing for Israelis—they would lose a source of cheap labor (but one that could be replaced by allowing Asian and African workers in) and cheap agricultural produce (which hurt Israeli consumers but satisfied Israeli farmers). But if the closure had mixed effects for Israel, it was catastrophic for Palestinians, who were thrown out of work and deprived of both basic goods and a market for their products.

Accordingly, when negotiating the economic arrangements of the Oslo Accords, Palestinian leaders felt forced to continue the close linkage between the Israeli and Palestinian economies. The arrangements—detailed in the separate Paris Protocol—required the PNA to continue to set its tax rates at Israeli levels. Some of these taxes were even collected by Israel; since goods destined for Palestinian markets had to come through Israeli ports, the Paris Protocol provided for Israel to collect the tax and then de-

liver it to the PNA (after deducting an administrative fee). Since an efficient
tax bureaucracy is difficult to establish, this provided the PNA with an immediate and easy stream of revenue—but also one that Israel could cut off
at will. But it continued the linkage between the West Bank and Israel
(links between Israel and Gaza were more controlled, but they continued
even after the construction of the fence around Gaza). The PNA even
agreed to set the price of gasoline, which was heavily taxed by Israel, at the
Israeli price, to prevent Israelis from crossing over into PNA areas in search
of cheaper fuel.

There were some exceptions to the close linkages between the two
economies, but even these created problems. For instance, the PNA was allowed to import some commodities (such as cement) as exempt from some
taxes. But this system—proposed by Israel in order to allow the PNA some
of the supplies it would need for economic development—opened the doors
for tremendous corruption. First, it meant that PNA leaders could dole out
the right to import these cheap commodities to their friends, who often
reaped large profits; second, it meant that Palestinians could sell the cheap
commodities back to Israel on the black market, deepening the corruption.
In sum, the Paris Protocol left the Palestinian economy heavily dependent
on Israel and created opportunities for corruption that came back to haunt
PNA rulers.

The Oslo period also saw the beginning of a tremendous international assistance program to the PNA. At first, some assistance simply went to pay the
normal PNA budget, but as the tax system was established, the international
assistance program turned instead to long-term development projects. While
development projects and priorities were negotiated with the PNA, the Palestinian entity was so new and inexperienced that it had a difficult time assess-
ing its own needs without international help. The result was a system in
which donors dominated development efforts and the PNA struggled to keep
abreast of what the assistance program was doing. The PNA gradually earned
a reputation for corruption, inefficiency, and heavy-handedness, meaning that
some donors preferred to bypass the new government and work directly with
nongovernmental organizations (NGOs), frustrating PNA officials even more.

The Oslo period, even when it seemed to be working well, still saw
episodic flashes of Israeli-Palestinian violence, which in turn had serious
effects on the Palestinian economy. Israel would generally respond to any
attack (and occasionally the anticipation of attacks) from Palestinian areas
with a "closure"—not only preventing movement in and out of the West
Bank and Gaza but often movement within them as well. With goods and
workers sometimes unable to move, the Palestinian economy was hostage
to the political climate between Israel and the PNA.

The second intifada led to severe closures and thus a rapid deterioration in the Palestinian economy. Israel eventually began construction of a

wall in the West Bank to separate its territory as well as large blocs of its settlements in the West Bank from Palestinian-populated areas. And Israel stopped transferring revenues to the PNA, charging that the PNA was responsible for violence against Israel.

Some of the international sponsors of the Oslo Process (particularly in Europe) stepped in with emergency assistance to Palestinians; they also kept the PNA supplied with enough funds to prevent its collapse. Israel dropped initial objections to this assistance program, realizing that humanitarian disaster and political collapse in Palestinian areas did not serve its interest. Eventually Israel resumed transfer of the revenue itself.

But the election of Hamas in 2006 threw even these makeshift arrangements into doubt. The international supporters of the peace process were face-to-face with the reality that the government they were assisting was now partly controlled by Hamas. The initial response was drastic: Israel cut off tax transfers again, and this time the international community provided only limited funds to those parts of the PNA that were not under Hamas control (like the presidency and the court system). But the result threatened political collapse and humanitarian disaster. Europe therefore built a slightly less strict mechanism by which it would make payments to Palestinian civil servants directly without going through the Hamas-controlled Ministry of Finance.

In 2007, when the PNA split into two halves, international assistance fully resumed to the Ramallah government. And the willingness of that government to prevent any attacks on Israel led Israeli authorities to lighten some of their restrictions on movement and access for Palestinians. The result was a sustained economic recovery—but one that was dependent on a favorable political environment.

The Gaza government, controlled by Hamas, was not so lucky. Some of its employees were paid by the Ramallah government (because those in power in Ramallah wished to maintain a toehold in Gaza) and others were paid with Hamas's limited funds. But the economic closure on Gaza was extremely severe, leading not to starvation (basic supplies and international relief efforts were allowed to continue) but to massive poverty, unemployment, and malnutrition. The results were disastrous for Gaza's population. Hamas pressed hard to open the border between Gaza and Egypt (it was much less interested in opening the border between Gaza and Israel, since it wanted to reverse the close linkage between the Palestinian and Israeli economies), but was largely unsuccessful. As time went on, however, and it became clear that the economic closure was not going to bring Hamas down, that smuggling through tunnels on the Gaza-Egypt border was actually taxed by Hamas (strengthening the movement), and that the Israeli blockade generated negative international publicity, Israel relaxed the restrictions slightly. The Egyptian revolution of 2011 diminished Egypt's already weak impulse to prevent smuggling. As a result, Gaza enjoyed a limited reversal of its economic misfortune. But the election of a friendly Muslim Brotherhood leader as Egypt's president did not lead to a complete opening of the Egyptian border, deeply disappointing Hamas.

Civil Society

In the mandate period, the main structures of Palestinian society were centered on family and neighborhood, town, or village, but there were also some other associations. Chambers of commerce for businessmen formed early. And various members of the elite had begun to form other organizations, such as charitable societies and women's clubs, though these did not reach deeply into the society.

After 1948, Palestinians in the West Bank and Gaza found themselves living under authoritarian governments that tended to view independent organizations with some suspicion. Jordan was more liberal than Egypt, tolerating political parties and allowing more in the way of social and charitable organizations. The Muslim Brotherhood, for instance, was repressed in Egypt but allowed to operate as a charitable society in Jordan. Outside the West Bank and Gaza, Palestinian communities in places as diverse as Cairo and Kuwait also tried to organize community institutions.

When Israel occupied the West Bank and Gaza in 1967, those areas became more isolated from the rest of the Arab world. Accordingly, residents there made some effort to establish their own organizations. But Israel kept a close watch on organized activity. Such efforts were sometimes viewed just as suspiciously by Palestinians outside, and the PLO itself often discouraged them. The PLO was worried that if a Palestinian leadership arose in the West Bank and Gaza, this leadership would negotiate a settlement with Israel that cut out the PLO and Palestinians on the outside. For instance, when a group of Palestinians tried to establish a university in the West Bank, it took them years to convince both the Israelis and the PLO to drop any objections.

Only the Muslim Brotherhood had an easier time—at least at first. The leadership of the Brotherhood stayed away from political activity at the time, arguing that the population had to become more Islamic before they could worry about confronting Israel—a stance that made Israel look to the Brotherhood with some tolerance. The Brotherhood never accepted the leadership of the PLO, regarding it as too secular and friendly to radical political ideas (such as Marxism). Instead the Brotherhood focused on religious education and social work.

The situation for Palestinian civil society began to change in the 1980s, for two reasons. First, Palestinian leaders on the outside began to change their attitude toward organizations in the West Bank and Gaza. Each political party based in the diaspora began to fear that the others would organize the population there and thus competed to form unions, organizations, and societies loyal to the various political parties. Sometimes each party would found a rival union or youth club. At other times they would compete directly against each other for control of the same organization, most often in elections for student associations. Second, Arab states began to give much more assistance to Palestinians through a fund overseen jointly by Jordan and the PLO. Since government institutions in the West Bank and Gaza were under Israeli control, Arab states preferred to give funds directly to private groups.

When the first intifada erupted in 1987, therefore, it found a network of groups and organizations with which to mobilize the population. Meanwhile the Muslim Brotherhood dropped its reservations about politics and metamorphosed into Hamas, a movement that enthusiastically joined the intifada. Israel tried to shut down some of these organizations, but many of them survived relatively intact until the ebbing of the intifada in the early 1990s.

Ironically, the Oslo peace process forced these new NGOs to adjust more than the intifada had. The tremendous influx of international assistance, the shift in donors from the Arab world to the West, the creation of the PNA, and the change in focus from resisting occupation to building a new political system rewarded some NGOs and penalized or passed over others. Those NGOs that could professionalize their operations, meeting the organizational and reporting requirements of Western donors, did well— particularly if they could satisfy the interests of those donors (some donors focused on service provision, others favored human rights and governance, and still others sought to build people-to-people contact with Israel). Such NGOs often built impressive operations but lost touch with their grassroots Palestinian constituency at the same time. And they also sometimes chafed at the PNA, which they felt was trying to control them. In some ways, the most effective political critics of the PNA during this period came from this professionalized NGO sector.

Of course, the grassroots organizations built during the preceding periods did not disappear. But they often struggled for funds and discovered that the creation of the PNA did not make things easier for them. Some were associated with political movements and parties, including Fatah, the governing party. A large number were Islamic in coloration—sometimes gravitating politically toward Hamas and sometimes uninterested in politics—and these were largely passed over by international donors.

With the collapse of the peace process in 2000, donors shifted their attention once again to emergency relief and provision of services. Those NGOs involved in the health sector, for instance, were favored in such an environment. Others, devoted to fields such as human rights, struggled to

decide whether their primary target should be the PNA or Israel. The professionalized NGOs were a real source of pressure for political reform during this period.

With Hamas's electoral victory, many professionalized NGOs were
caught in a dilemma. Continued funding from the West depended on them
assuring donors that they had no connection with Hamas—and while most
of them did not, some resented the political restrictions on aid. But in 2007
when the PNA split, most of these NGOs swung behind the Ramallah-based
PNA and against the Gaza-based PNA dominated by Hamas. In fact, the
cabinet of the Ramallah-based PNA was drawn partly from NGO leaders—
thus they had gone from being the opposition to the PNA during the Oslo
period to dominating half of the government.

Religion and Politics

In most Arab states, Islam is relevant to politics in two ways. First, the state
dominates an official religious establishment that controls mosques, religious education, and those areas of law (like marriage and divorce) governed by religion. Second, large Islamist social movements and sometimes
political parties often form the most effective political opposition. Freer
elections often result in Islamists performing very well, as Tunisia and
Egypt showed in 2011. Thus, even though Palestine is not an established
state, the relationship between religion and politics still looks very familiar
in Arab terms.

In terms of the structures of the official religious establishment, these
were largely set up during the British mandate and continue to this day. An
institution known as the *waqf* (also the Arabic term for "endowment") administers mosques and religious properties. A set of courts, headed by a
chief judge, rules in matters of "personal status"—chiefly marriage, divorce, and inheritance. And students are required to study "Islamic education" in schools (with Christian students excused and given separate instruction in their religion).

But without a recognized Palestinian state, who runs this official apparatus? After the end of the British mandate in 1948, these responsibilities
were taken over by Egypt in Gaza and by Jordan in the West Bank. When
Israel took over these territories in 1967, it tended to leave the situation
alone. In the West Bank, it actually allowed Jordan to continue running the
religious establishment. With the formation of the PNA in 1994, there was
a brief rivalry between Jordan and the PNA over control of these institutions, but the PNA generally won out.

Just as the PNA resembles other pre-2011 authoritarian Arab states in
its management of religion, it has its own religious opposition in the form

of Hamas as well as some smaller movements—but here, as with all matters connected with Hamas, there are significant complications. First, the religious opposition does not fully accept the legitimacy of the PNA. Second, to add to the complexity, this same religious opposition controls part of the PNA (in Gaza).

Hamas was born out of the Palestinian offshoot of the Muslim Brotherhood, the movement originally founded in Egypt. For a long time, the Brotherhood in Palestine traditionally avoided political activity, so a younger group of leaders formed Hamas in the 1980s to "resist" the Israeli occupation through attacks on Israeli targets. That proved so popular among the Brotherhood membership that Hamas soon came to absorb much of the Brotherhood. Initially, Israel tolerated the Hamas leadership, calculating that they would avoid politics as did the older generation. But as soon as Israel realized that a new, radical organization was emerging, it moved to suppress the movement, though without much success. Hamas became an active participant in the first intifada. But it never joined the PLO.

Hamas presented itself as acting in accordance with religious teachings and used religious symbols and rhetoric; it also drew support from more religious segments of the Palestinian population. But the core of its program was as much political as religious. Hamas supported the use of Islamic law, for instance, but generally de-emphasized this part of its program in order to stress resistance to Israel.

When PLO leaders negotiated the Oslo Accords, Hamas criticized them for compromising on Palestinian land. Hamas's position rejected any permanent agreement with the Jewish state. Yet at the same time, the Hamas leadership recognized that the Oslo Accords had strong international backing and that resisting them would be difficult. Moreover, it realized that the creation of the PNA would allow for Palestinian elections. Hamas members debated for some time about whether to run in the elections and finally decided to boycott them, arguing that the PNA would not be allowed real self-governance and that Hamas did not want to lend legitimacy to the peace process. As a result, Hamas remained outside the PNA.

While many Palestinians regarded Hamas as a legitimate (if extreme) political actor, the PNA leadership was generally more inclined to treat it as an illegitimate opposition. For instance, realizing that Hamas might be locally popular in some areas, the PNA simply kept postponing local elections in cities and towns in order to avoid giving Hamas the opportunity to gain a foothold. Hamas was totally shunned by much of the international community. During periods when Palestinian public opinion seemed supportive of the peace process, Hamas tended to scale back its activities or reorient itself back toward its Muslim Brotherhood roots by emphasizing education and social work. But when there were problems it would often lash out with violent attacks, increasingly against civilian targets.

So when the second intifada erupted in 2000, Hamas was able to move its model of "resistance" to the center of Palestinian politics. And as the existing PNA leadership seemed to grow increasingly impotent and corrupt, Hamas's popularity grew. When local elections were finally held, beginning in 2004, Hamas decided to show off its popularity by running, and did well. In 2005, the PNA leadership decided to coax Hamas into running for parliament, hoping that such participation would help tame the movement and that Hamas could be brought inside the system. But when parliamentary elections were held in 2006, the attempt to include Hamas backfired when the Islamic movement won a majority, supported by Palestinians who viewed Fatah as corrupt and ineffective.

Thus the Islamic opposition was no longer in opposition. But the older PNA leadership and the international community were unwilling to accept a Hamas government, leading ultimately to the 2007 split in which Hamas managed to assume total control of the PNA in Gaza but lost it in the West Bank. The electoral victory of Islamist movements in Egypt and Tunisia in 2011 gave Hamas leaders the sense that they were part of a strong regional trend, but the immediate impact on Palestinian political life of the string of Islamist victories was limited.

Identity and Politics

While Palestine has had difficulty establishing itself as a state, Palestinian national identity has taken deep hold of Palestinian politics. This was not an automatic or easy achievement. Palestinians speak Arabic and most are Muslim, so they feel deep links with the Arab and broader Muslim world—yet they tend to insist that within these larger entities there is still a distinct Palestinian people. Family and place of origin still divide Palestinians and many do not forget these other identities when they think about politics—the various PNA cabinets, for instance, have been carefully constituted to make certain that each major area within Palestine feels represented. But these local ties, though real, tend to receive far less stress and public attention. Even the division between the West Bank and Gaza—and the fact that, since Israel fenced in Gaza in 1994, travel between them has usually been either difficult or impossible—are rarely discussed in public.

Strong identities often are the result of government policies, in fields like education and language, that are designed to inculcate loyalty to the nation. But the precise opposite may be the case for Palestinians—their insistence on their distinct Palestinian identity is a direct result of Palestine's political weakness. In other words, Palestinians seem to feel that in the absence of strong institutions or a recognized state to support them, an insistence on Palestinian identity is all that holds them together. Any political recognition of alternative loyalties risks splintering an already vulnerable population.

Still, there has been a subtle evolution in Palestinian identity. Over the course of the twentieth century, for instance, the Arab element in Palestinian identity, while it remained strong, showed some signs of mild decline. And in the past generation the religious element in Palestinian identity has risen significantly. The most obvious testimony to the increase in religious identity is the rise of Hamas, but there are other signs of increased religiosity in public as well (for instance, dress has become more conservative, and public consumption of alcohol—allowed by law but forbidden by the Islamic religion—has greatly declined). Of course, not all Palestinians are Muslims—there is a substantial Christian minority. But this Christian population has gradually decreased, for several reasons. First, Christians tended to concentrate in urban areas and have higher levels of education; this often leads to lower birthrates. Second, better education has also provided them with more employment opportunities abroad. Finally, as a shrinking minority, Christians find that their declining share of the population snowballs— as some Christians have left, those remaining find fewer of their co-religionists. In a society in which personal ties are often formed along family and religious lines, this makes some consider emigration themselves.

Gender and Politics

In a society striving for statehood, Palestinians have witnessed tremendous political changes, and some of these changes have strongly affected gender roles. While many fairly conservative strictures on dress and comportment related to gender apply widely, there are actually wide variations in prevailing practices and expectations. This is not only because of diversity within Palestinian society but also because of the cosmopolitan nature of some segments of the population. So many Palestinians have spent time in other societies and been influenced by them that some areas (most notably the Jerusalem and Ramallah areas) tolerate a wide variety of gender roles.

The founding of the PNA and the attempt to build a Palestinian state occasioned a series of debates about gender in Palestinian society. First, it opened up greater possibilities for women playing a role in public life. Previous generations of leaders from armed political movements had largely—though not totally—excluded women, but the new focus on institution building, constructing civil society, and writing laws seemed to open new fields that were friendlier to women's public role. Some of the barriers to women's participation that exist in other Arab states fell without battle in Palestine—there were no objections to granting women the vote, and a quota was introduced for women's representation in parliament without much controversy. Women also entered the judiciary—a field that is closed in some Arab countries (based both on prevailing conceptions of gender and on medieval Islamic jurisprudence).

Second, the new PNA was also confronted with important tasks that had a strong bearing on gender relations. For instance, it worked to develop a code of personal status to govern marriage, divorce, and inheritance—setting off discussions about what is religiously sanctioned and what are appropriate rights and obligations for men and women within the family. The PNA also had to develop the first Palestinian curriculum for its school system (earlier schools had simply followed the Egyptian and Jordanian curricula), leading to arguments about how women should be portrayed and how gender issues should be discussed in schools.

The rise of Hamas and of religiosity more generally has also greatly impacted gender roles. Hamas is not hostile to some public role for women, and it produced female candidates for its parliamentary slate without hesitation. But it is also even more strongly dominated by men than are the other already strikingly male political parties. A growing trend toward social conservatism has led to more social pressure on women to wear head coverings in public. While Hamas has not formally required any change in women's dress during its tenure in power, the increased popularity of Hamas has made some women feel less comfortable uncovered. And when it gained full control of Gaza, Hamas formed squads that encouraged women (and undoubtedly intimidated them as well) to dress conservatively and avoid socializing in public with men.

The Impact of International Politics

Perhaps no political system in the Arab world shows the sharp impact of international politics more than Palestine. The international political system helped create the political situation in which Palestinians now find themselves. And international politics help sustain that difficult situation by failing to recognize Palestinian statehood. It therefore should come as no surprise that many Palestinians feel a deep sense of historical injustice.

But the impact of international politics has produced ambitions for change as well as disappointment—indeed, many Palestinians place their hopes for redress in what they often term "international legitimacy." By this they mean that international norms and laws support their struggle for self-determination. The biggest successes of the Palestinian national movement have been connected with the international realm—the acceptance of a separate and distinct Palestinian national identity within the Arab world and, much more recently, an international acceptance of the principle of Palestinian statehood. Subsequently, in November 2012 the UN General Assembly voted to award Palestine the status of nonmember observer state, another victory in the international realm.

But the outside world is not looked to only for legitimacy. Various outside actors are very much players in Palestinian domestic politics. Iran, Syria, and some Arab states give varying amounts of support to Hamas; the European Union has bankrolled Abbas's government in Ramallah; Israel helped to undermine Arafat; and the United States has not hesitated to designate specific individuals as either absolutely necessary or completely unacceptable.

In 2011, some youthful Palestinian activists attempted to bring in international factors in a new way: they worked to emulate Egyptian and Tunisian youth by generating a new movement that would press for political change. They generated some interest in Palestinian society and even helped pressure Fatah and Hamas leaders to agree to "end the division," as their slogan demanded. But the movement fizzled over time. Palestinians still talk about the possibility of renewing what they call "popular resistance," meaning a movement based on mass action rather than small armed groups, but they have not had the energy, organization, or focus realized recently by their counterparts in some other Arab societies.

The contradictory effects of international politics go even deeper. They help explain, on the one hand, why the PNA—a nonstate entity that cannot control its own territory or its own borders—cannot establish financial independence. But if international conditions create Palestinian dependence, they also explain, on the other hand, how the PNA—and Palestinians more generally—have become recipients of an enormous amount of international financial assistance. This may be the greatest irony of Palestinian politics: the Palestinian national movement has been based on a desperate quest to make Palestinians independent actors, but the movement to realize that goal has been dependent on the Palestinian relationship with Israel and global support.

17

Saudi Arabia

Gwenn Okruhlik

The dynamics of society, economics, and governance in Saudi Arabia are complex and nuanced. Saudi Arabia is the spiritual center of the diverse international Muslim community, yet it privileges one particular way of thought in its own system. The country depends overwhelmingly on foreign labor to staff the economy, yet it suffers from high local-male unemployment and limits the full economic participation of half its population, women. It is an economic powerhouse buttressed by oil revenues, yet it has significant poverty among its citizens. Within the same week, King Abdullah was hailed as "the monarch who declared his own revolution" in a race to reform the country (Dickey 2009), and he was ranked fourth in *Parade* magazine's annual list of the world's worst dictators (Wallechinsky 2009). Variously described as moderate or authoritarian, backward or modern, spiritually or materially inspired, Saudi Arabia is all of these and many things in between. It is reviled and caricatured, praised and defended. It is easy to draw stereotypes based on superficial images. When we simplify, however, we do injustice to the reality that is Saudi Arabia, and fail to fully understand a diverse people and long-standing political system. This is an exciting time to study Saudi Arabia (Aarts and Nonneman, 2005), amid demands for political reform, aging leadership and succession dilemmas, tensions over sociocultural change, and the reverberations of the Arab uprisings.

Historical Background and Contemporary Political Structure

Historical Development

Saudi Arabia has a long, rich history given its place at the crossroads of ancient Nabatean civilizations, desert caravans, hajj (religious pilgrimage),

417

and maritime trade. The current rulers, the Al Saud family, trace their political origins to 1744 and the village of Al-Dir'iyyah, where the local authority, Mohammad ibn Saud, granted safe haven to a religious reformer named Mohammad ibn Abd al-Wahhab. He had been expelled from his hometown in a nearby oasis after criticizing the lax behavior of fellow townspeople. Al-Wahhab's strict interpretation of sharia, or Islamic law, and his efforts to rid Islam of innovation unsettled members of the village. He fled to Al-Dir'iyyah, where he and ibn Saud forged a pact through which the political authority of the Al Saud and the religious leadership of al-Wahhab were made mutually supportive. Political domination by the Al Saud family and the call for religious renewal were propagated together. For a century and a half, the partners' fortunes rose and fell together.

Historians speak of three states of the Al Saud. The first was from 1744 to 1818, when they battled the Ottomans and Egyptians for control of the Hijaz, on the west coast. This ultimately led to the destruction of Al-Dir'iyyah and the collapse of that period of rule. The second state lasted from 1824 until 1891. During this time, they battled mightily with a contending family, the al-Rashid, until eventually Abd al-Rahman Al Saud fled into neighboring Kuwait to take refuge.

The contemporary state began in 1902, with the decades-long conquests of Abd al-Rahman's son Abdulaziz, across the peninsula. He created a military force called the Ikhwan (the Brethren) to battle his contenders for power in Arabia. They conquered rulers in region after region. Most significantly, these included the Ashraf, the rulers of the Hijaz in the west. The Ashraf claimed descent from the Hashimite clan of the Prophet Muhammad and had been sanctioned by the Ottoman rulers, who themselves had inherited guardianship of the holy cities, Mecca and Medina, from Egypt. The Al Saud, together with the Ikhwan, took the eastern coast from the Ottomans in 1912. And in the Najd, or the center of Arabia, they again battled the formidable al-Rashid family for authority. By 1929, Abdulaziz, feeling threatened by the very forces on which he depended, crushed the Ikhwan at the Battle of Sibila. The current state was formally declared in 1932. King Abdulaziz ruled until his death in 1953. He bequeathed power to his sons, who maintain a firm grip on rule.

Who Rules?

Authority in Saudi Arabia remains very much "all in the family" (Herb 1999). The monarchy has passed from Abdulaziz to five of his thirty-seven sons: Saud (1953–1964), Faisal (1964–1975), Khaled (1975–1982), Fahd (1982–2005), and Abdullah (2005–present). What this means in practical terms is that Saudi Arabia has long been ruled by older men, all brothers. King Abdullah, 88, was hospitalized in November 2012 for a fourth back surgery. He has outlived his two named successors: Crown Prince Sultan died in October 2011 and his replacement, Prince Naif, died in October 2012. The current Crown Prince Salman is a relatively young seventy-seven. In February 2013, the king appointed his half-brother, Prince Muqrin bin Abdulaziz, to be second deputy prime minister. This means that there will be no power vacuum should the top two leaders die. All are sons of Abdulaziz. Two familial committees have been formed to ease the power transition, especially important should it pass to the next generation. The Family Council was announced in June 2000 to deal with succession to the ailing King Fahd. It is an internal decisionmaking body composed of eighteen senior princes, chaired by the king, which meets to discuss intrafamilial issues. Should the family want to pass the throne to the younger generation, it is thought that Muqrin will not oppose the transition.

In 2006, Abdullah instituted the Allegiance Commission to lend a more formal procedure to the selection of future kings and crown princes, which had always been done by tradition. Its members are the twenty-one living sons of Abdulaziz (or their sons if they are unable to serve). The bylaws delineate a complicated process of selection in which the king and commission go back and forth designating and rejecting candidates. Abdullah also established the Transitional Ruling Council to govern in emergencies involving health crises or assassinations. This is a positive development in the sense that at least a process is finally in place and is known to citizens before a crisis of leadership occurs. Yet it is a bit surreal, and still very much "all in the family" (Herb 1999). The Allegiance Council allows the sons and grandsons of Abdulaziz to take part in what they call the "democratic selection" of their country's future leadership from among their own ranks. This is a secret enclave with no direct public input.

How have the Al Saud ruled for so long? They have perpetuated their rule through a skillful combination of distribution, penetration, and coercion, with a legitimating dose of ideology. It is a blend of carrots and sticks, with religious underpinnings. At the end of the day, governance in Saudi Arabia is not representative, not accountable, and does not protect rights for citizens, much less for foreign residents. Basic civil and political rights are absent. Uttering public criticism, striking, joining political organizations, and spreading antigovernment ideas all are crimes. Media outlets and publishing houses are strictly watched. Websites and blogs are censored. It is now a criminal act to insult the king on Twitter or Facebook. Such coercive techniques are supplemented by cradle-to-grave distributive schemes made possible by oil revenues. The Al Saud penetrate society through business deals in every economic sector, marriages into other families, and control of all key political positions. Further, the Saudi state utilizes the symbols and the vocabulary of religion to consolidate its power.

Supporting Institutions

The Al Saud still govern in an awkward and unequal symbiosis with descendants and followers of the early religious authorities, the al-Wahhab family. Though it waxes and wanes and is hotly contested, the old pact persists, however uneasily. The Al Saud enforce a strict Sunni Hanbali Wahhabi interpretation of Islam. The ulama, or religious authorities, are important players; it is not clear that the Al Saud could maintain power without their support. But the ulama are not independent from the state; they are not superior to the family and they are not the only Islamic voices in the country. Over the decades, the ulama have been bureaucratized and made employees of the state. With their selection and financing dependent upon the state, the ulama are subjugated to it. The religious authorities include not only the Council of Senior Scholars, which issues fatawa (fatwa singular; religious opinions), but also many affiliated bureaucracies such as the *hayat* and those that administer the hajj and education. They are often vocal in their reservations about changes, particularly in the sociocultural realm. The king occasionally reminds them of their subservient position. Yet the ruling family does depend on them to justify policy decisions during crises. The ulama have issued fatawa that justified in Islamic vocabulary such matters as the use of military force in the Grand Mosque in 1979, the condemnation of Ayatollah Ruhollah Khomeini in Iran, the presence of US forces on Saudi soil during the Gulf War of 1990–1991, the permissibility of peace with Israel, and the clampdown on protests in March 2011. Such fatawa closely bind the official ulama and the Al Saud, but simultaneously lead to the erosion of the legitimacy of that relationship. Indeed contending religious scholars, not necessarily high-ranking or official, have been the source of much contemporary dissent.

The Council of Ministers, or cabinet, was first appointed by the king in 1953; it grew tremendously during the oil boom. Today it consists of the heads of twenty-three ministries that oversee the daily administration of the country. The king and crown prince preside over the cabinet, and princes hold most key posts. The cabinet's advice is nonbinding. The judicial system is primarily based on sharia. Any supplementary civil or commercial codes, of which there are many, cannot contradict or supersede sharia. The Supreme Judicial Council is composed of senior jurists. The king acts as the highest court of appeal in the country.

In the early 1990s, rancorous opposition arose to the Gulf War and the stationing of US troops in Saudi Arabia. In response to this dissent, King Fahd established a long-promised consultative assembly, the Majlis al-Shura, in 1992. The membership of the assembly now numbers 150, all appointed by the king. Members are highly skilled, but their role is advisory rather than legislative, and the king can reject their advice. In 2008, one member was summarily fired after he criticized a minister in an interview. Despite these serious limitations, members do seem to be carving out a niche and trying to expand their scope of action. Nevertheless, in May 2009, seventy-seven political activists sent a petition to the king that called for a democratically elected parliament and a prime minister who is not a member of the ruling family. In June 2012, the Saudi Civil and Political Rights Association (ACPRA) circulated an initiative that, in strong and direct language, called for an end to authoritarianism and for the implementation of constitutional governance. Its founders, Abdullah al-Hamed and Fahad al-Qatani, were sentenced in March 2013 to at least ten years in prison for setting up an unlicensed human rights organization.

In 2005, there were limited elections—the first in over fifty years—to fill half the seats on newly created municipal councils throughout the country; the other seats were later appointed by the king. Today, the councilmen remain unaware of the scope of their authority. Women could neither run nor vote in the elections. There were supposed to be new elections in 2009, but instead the government chose to extend the terms of the current council members. The postponement of elections was announced just five days after the petition calling for greater democratization was delivered to the king. When the municipal elections were finally held in October 2011, voter turnout was very low, as citizens knew the councils lacked any authority to act.

Identity and Politics: Diversity and Exclusion

While the local population is overwhelmingly Arab and Sunni Muslim, there are significant variations within it. There are followers of all four *madhahib* (schools of thought; *madhab* singular) of Sunni Islamic law as well as the tradition of official, orthodox Wahhabism. Shi'i communities comprise about 15 percent of the population. The largest Shi'i community is in the Eastern Province; there are others in Mecca and Medina. The southern region of Najran is Ismaili and there are Sufi communities throughout the country.

There are also ethnic distinctions among the local population. The economy of the Eastern Province for centuries has been related to merchant activities and, more recently, to the oil industry. Families from Iran, Bahrain, and India migrated there for work reasons. Thus, Shi'i religious affiliation is prominent there. The western region is noted for a multiplicity of ethnic identities, for two reasons: its long history as the center of commerce from the port of Jeddah and the fact that it is the site of the annual hajj. Families that came to perform religious rituals often stayed and established thriving businesses. Some of the most prominent ones are originally from Persia, Indonesia, India, as well as other Arab states. In addition, there is a notable Hadrami community in the west, originally derived from Yemen's Hadramawt region. Saudi Arabia—and especially its central region, the Najd—is also home to many local tribes. It was less common for foreign families to settle in the heartland than in the coastal regions, and as a result the Najd remained insulated from migration flows for a longer period of time.

When does religious or ethnic identity become salient and, sometimes, politicized? People, Saudi or otherwise, carry multiple identities within them at all times. An ethnic, tribal, or religious identity may rise or fall depending on the particular context. The identity that is important in one circumstance may be less so in another circumstance. A key problem in Saudi Arabia is that there are diverse religious practices in the country, yet only one is structurally empowered. Wahhabis have been rewarded with institutional and bureaucratic positions of authority—in schools, the ranks of the ulama, and the judiciary—while other sects have been largely excluded. The consequence is that private religious beliefs are diverse, but public discourse is dominated by one particularly austere interpretation, the one that is sanctioned by the state. Only in February 2009 did Abdullah appoint religious authorities from different schools of Sunni legal thought to the ulama. No Shi'a are included.

In the spring of 2009, protests occurred throughout the Shi'i communities in the Eastern Province. These followed the arrest and intimidation of Shi'a who were praying at the Prophet's tomb in Medina. The incident tapped into a reservoir of resentment at their second-class status. Shaikh Kalbani, the imam at the Great Mosque in Mecca, called the Shi'a "heretics." From 2011 into 2013, Shi'a demanded their full religious, social, political, and economic rights as citizens of Saudi Arabia. The exclusionary structure of governance fails to represent the diverse population and fuels the politicization and activism of some Saudis around their sectarian identities. Were Saudis' diverse demographics incorporated into governance, those identities might become less politicized.

There is, of late, occupational and geographic mobility in Saudi Arabia. Unlike in the recent past, there are families whose members are now distributed throughout the country. A young man graduating from college must cast a wide net in his search for employment. This mobility has helped to foster a wider sense of national identity even as other identities remain important. There remain, however, distinctions and barriers between people of tribal and nontribal lineage. Saudis of tribal lineage generally do not marry Saudis of nontribal lineage (there is intertribal marriage, however).

By virtue of oil, Saudi Arabia is integrated into the global capitalist economy and is intimately tied to its rhythms. At times it reaps windfall wealth, yet it is vulnerable to fluctuations in global demand and associated price gyrations. Its economy endures the frenzy of booms and the devastation of busts. Historically, the oil-driven economy has been far larger than the indigenous population could support. This necessitated the importation of a foreign labor force to run the day-to-day economy—from construction to clerks to service workers to accountants. Between 6.5 and, more likely, 8 million residents of Saudi Arabia are foreign workers and their families. They derive from many ethnic, national, and religious backgrounds and compose about one-quarter to one-third of the total population.

The distinctions between citizen and foreigner are evident in everything from dress and living quarters to occupations and class. The state manages the flow of foreigners within its borders through an extensive system of oversight and sponsorship. Each worker must be "sponsored" by a local citizen or company and surrender his or her passport to the sponsor. Most workers, particularly from the developing world, are closely monitored. Thus far, their ethnic and religious identities have not been highly politicized. There have been worker strikes demanding better pay and conditions, but not to the extent seen in neighboring Dubai. The system is rife with abuse and leaves workers at the mercy of their sponsors, with no protection. International human rights groups have roundly criticized the system (Okruhlik 2010).

Citizenship is tightly regulated in the country and is granted through parentage (passing through the father), not place of birth. Naturalized citizenship is extremely hard to obtain and rarely achieved (applicants must be Muslims fluent in Arabic with a decade of residency who possess advanced degrees in sought-after technical fields).

Civil Society: Fluid and Creative

The Saudi state prohibits free speech and the right to assemble. There are no unions or legal political parties, and public protest has historically been rare. Not only is collective action against the law, but the potential for collective action is further inhibited by an extraordinary social concern with discretion and privacy. Behavior in the public realm (any place outside the home) is regulated by well-defined codes of conformity; the privacy of the family unit is always "protected." There are complex expectations about conformity in dress, behavior, and decorum. They are enforced by the *hayat* and its patrolmen, the *mutawwa'in* (*mutaww'a* singular). This leads to a series of perplexing questions: When the mere act of meeting together to discuss potentially controversial issues is against the law, what then constitutes civic activism or civil society? How, where, and on what issues do people get together to express themselves? How and where are Saudis pushing the boundaries?

Because the home remains a private place into which the state rarely imposes itself, civic activism happens within this space. Historically, the *majlis* (private gathering in one's home; *majalis* plural) was the only available venue for friends and colleagues to build networks and to voice opinions on politics, society, and economics. Replete with food, coffee, and lively conversation, the weekly *majalis* remain vital. They vary from the relatively structured to the informal, and are gender-segregated. "Study groups" also meet in the privacy of Saudi homes and have proven to be a dynamic mechanism through which agendas are articulated and ideologies made coherent. They were the genesis of much early Islamism in the 1970s and 1980s and continue to be important today.

The public social space in which people can interact legally is quite limited but has increased in the past decade and a half. In Saudi Arabia there exists a small but broadening public sphere in which ideas can be traded and people can simply talk without threatening the integrity of the family unit or the state. Ubiquitous now are cafés, coffeehouses, salons, and resthouses (*istiraha*). At municipal levels there are people who meet together to improve neighborhoods and call attention to problems that authorities do not address adequately. There are a host of philanthropic organizations dedicated to charity, the environment, technology training, and welfare. There are now professional associations that represent the interests of their members in the fields of journalism, law, engineering, and medicine. An extensive network of chambers of commerce has long existed to serve private businesspeople. They are active and important sources of economic criticism, although they are partially funded by the state. Parents and teachers in the public schools seek to form associations similar to the parent-teacher organizations we are familiar with in the West.

Civic activism is alive and well in the arts, literature, and the embryonic film industry. Artistic renderings make powerful statements in the abstract that cannot otherwise be published. People are freer to express critical opinions about politics and society when the characters are, at least superficially, fictional—and the locale a composite. In March 2010, Saudi novelist Abdo Khal won the International Prize for Arabic Fiction for his novel *Spewing Sparks as Big as Castles*. It explores the relationship between an individual and the state, and is set in the excessive world of wealth and power in a palace. The government routinely bans books, but they somehow are slipped quietly into the marketplace and circulated privately. The Al-Jouf Literary Club met regularly for open discussion, but its premises were vandalized and torched in 2010. Though cinema was prohibited by law for decades and has only recently been allowed in limited and regulated venues—and is sometimes shut down—there is a small and active film community. The 2012 film *Wadjda,* by Saudi female director Haifaa al-Mansour, was filmed entirely in Saudi Arabia with Saudis. It tells the story of a ten-year-old girl living in Riyadh and how she constantly attempts to circumvent the many constraints on her lifestyle—from the clothing she wears to the bike she wants to ride to the music to which she listens. It is being feted internationally even as it cannot be shown in Saudi Arabia. Theater too is experiencing a rebirth. In Riyadh, Al-Yamamah College produced a play about contemporary social concerns called *A Moderate Without Moderation.* A fracas ensued when conservative protesters turned violent, attacking the audience, props, and actors. Most such endeavors require royal imprimatur. For example, Prince Waleed produces most films. Prince Salman allowed the college play to proceed. The interesting tension is that royal approval is needed to pursue social commentary or civic activism.

The print and broadcast media remain controlled by the state, which appoints and removes editors. Still, writers and editors try to push the boundaries on the range of issues they address. Topics once taboo have now become the subject of intense debate, including crime, drugs, the alienation and boredom of youth, poverty, spousal abuse, and women's rights. *Tash ma Tash,* a popular television comedy series that airs during Ramadan, filmed an episode about a Saudi woman with four husbands. It enraged social conservatives. Still off-limits is direct criticism of the ruling family.

Hard as it tries, the ruling family seems unable to control Twitter, YouTube, and Facebook. Social media is the site of much social activism. A few examples suffice. *Alatayer* (or *On the Fly*) is a YouTube show that publicizes and makes fun of corruption, princely land grabs ("It's All Mine Now!"), and the way a big businessman can flout the law while small, struggling businessmen are held to the letter of the law. *La Yekthar* is a homemade YouTube comedy that posts videos about, for example, the $15 million it costs to repair toilet seats in a public park. Mohammed Maki posts a miniseries called *Takki* about young men in Jeddah trying to make films and the difficulties of their encounters with women. Many episodes address the shrinking middle class in Saudi Arabia and the dearth of affordable housing. The Tweeter "Mujtahidd" regularly posts in 140 characters damning accusations of corruption at the highest levels of the ruling family. So far, most authors have escaped the retribution of the state. That is why the regime is now cracking down on new media. In 2012 the Grand Mufti of Saudi Arabia, Shaikh Abdul Latif Abdul Aziz al Shaikh, lashed out against new media, charging that it was nothing more than a tool to promote lies and trade accusations and was used by individuals to promote their own names. It was a dangerous practice to be avoided by Muslims. Curiously, he did not address the fact that many Saudi Muslim scholars now utilize Twitter and Facebook to promote their opinions among their over 1 million followers.

In the meantime, new media are creating new dynamics in civic activism. To Eman al-Nafjan, a Saudi feminist, this is welcome: "No good has come of our defensive, hide-the-dirty-laundry approach. We just come off looking more closed and isolated" (in Faruqui 2010). Cyberspace enables

Saudis to build communities of social activists without violating political prohibitions on unauthorized assembly, speech, or gender-mingling. Because meeting as a group to discuss political reform is illegal, a typical method of transmitting ideas prior to the advent of social media was through petitions that articulated political demands and were submitted to the highest members of the ruling family. In recent years, these often have been posted online, vastly multiplying the number of signatories. But now, Saudis acknowledge that petitions are passé as social media are far more effective. A blogger argues, "Asking the youth to use petitions instead of social media is like asking them to use carrier pigeons instead of mobile phones" (in Khalaf 2012).

Is there civil society? Yes. It just looks unlike what we expect. Civil society is often defined in terms of voluntary associations, business organizations, labor unions, and other entities located between the household and the state. In Saudi Arabia, it is more ambiguous but no less important. It is more fluid and less formal, and incorporates social capital, more akin to civic activism. In 1989, I interviewed a woman who specialized in teaching computing skills to young girls. She relayed many instances of women working quietly and individually to advance women's rights. I asked if they ever got together to work jointly. She replied, "Of course not. We are more effective working alone. Organization is the surest way to get squashed [by the government]." Years later, in 2007, an organization called Ansar al-Mar'ah (Supporters of Women) was planned to fight for the rights of women. Founding members included both men and women. The effort was disbanded in April 2009 because it failed to obtain the official approval it needed to operate legally. Even if people supported its goals, they were hesitant to join an organization that operated illegally. Such is the plight of civic activists in Saudi Arabia.

The state sometimes tries to mimic or to co-opt civic activism by creating duplicate associations. The Human Rights First Society is a nonrecognized organization that monitors human rights abuse and advocates for the protection of rights. Its founder, Ibrahim al-Mugateib, applied for a license in 2002 but received no reply from the government. It continues to operate without a license and maintains an active presence on the Internet. In 2004 the similarly named National Society for Human Rights was established by royal decree. The other government-recognized body is the Human Rights Commission, whose head holds the rank of state minister. It plans to open a women's branch dedicated to concerns such as divorce, rape, children, and domestic abuse. Neither of these two government-recognized bodies directly addresses democracy, expression, assembly, or minorities. The former, the National Society for Human Rights, is considered somewhat more independent of the state.

Saudis who seek to make a difference in their country face a dilemma: how to navigate the fine and difficult line between having the imprimatur of royal sponsorship and maintaining independence from the ruling family. If a prince or princess sponsors you, then you are officially recognized and can operate in public, but your ability to express critical positions is quite bounded. If you maintain your independence, your group is illegal but remains unconstrained in what it advocates.

Political Economy: The Aches of Abundance

Saudi Arabia's pre-oil economy was based on date farming, merchant trade, and revenues accrued from hosting the pilgrimage. Abdulaziz also received British arms and financial supplements. With the discovery of substantial oil reserves in 1938, he began to receive small royalty payments from foreign oil companies. As the state renegotiated its relationship with foreign companies, acquiring all shares from 1973 to 1980, it grew wealthy.

The extent and speed of the oil-driven socioeconomic transformation of Saudi Arabia are mind-boggling. In a few short years, families went from subsistence to affluence. They migrated from tiny villages to sprawling urban centers. Parents who were illiterate sent their children abroad to earn doctoral degrees in the United States or Europe. Bedouin, who once moved across territory with their herds, were housed in settled communities. Women who had not covered themselves previously did so now in their tight new urban environs where they were suddenly surrounded by men outside their family. Sleepy towns were suddenly filled with construction crews, freeway systems, and high-rises. At the port of Jeddah on the Red Sea, the line of freight tankers waiting to unload goods stretched as far as the eye could see. Workers could not unload cargo fast enough to support the construction frenzy. To get around the bottleneck, helicopters repeatedly flew offshore to bring back tons of bags of cement from the ship decks. They dropped the bags with such force that the town was often covered in a layer of cement dust. Indeed, during the frenzied oil boom, the national bird of Saudi Arabia was "the crane."

Since oil revenues flow directly to state coffers rather than corporations or individual entrepreneurs, the Saudi state mushroomed exponentially during the boom period. The state's distributive function became critical. It became provider and patron—the source of contracts, jobs in the public sector, and land grants. A cradle-to-grave welfare system was built that provided health care, education, investment incentives, land grants for housing, subsidized food and energy, easy loans, and even stipends for achieving good grades in school. Every five years, the state announced a new development plan that detailed spending priorities for the next period. The oil-driven economy was so large, and the local population so small, that the state literally imported a foreign labor force to staff the burgeoning economy. Today, decades later, the private sector labor force is overwhelmingly foreign.

Citizens who were well situated reaped the rewards of oil. When I asked a man how he had made his fortune, he said simply, "Guard rails." How can you make so much money off something so simple? I was puzzled until I learned that monopolies were granted to individuals during the boom. He had the national monopoly on guard rails as the country's vast network of highways was being constructed. This story was repeated time and again with each product (distributorships for Timex watches, Sanyo radios, Toyota vehicles, cement, etc.). Over time, successful and disciplined merchant families made the transition to become industrialists as well.

While the prosperity of all citizens increased due to oil rents, there were marked discrepancies in the way it was distributed (Okruhlik 1999). Indeed, there is worrisome poverty among citizens. Like impoverished people everywhere, poor Saudis suffer from chronic joblessness, substandard accommodations, raw sewage, and no electricity. The sprawling neighborhoods of Qarantina, Sabeel, and Handawiya in Jeddah, and Suwaidi and Shamisi in Riyadh, are among many slum areas where there is rising unemployment and crime. Rural poverty is also a significant problem. One estimate places the number of poor Saudis at 1.2 million. Unofficial figures say that 20 percent of Saudis are living under the poverty line. The *bidoon,* Arabs without citizenship, especially fell through the cracks. In Greater Medina, 14.2 percent of families live below the official poverty line of $452 per month. Poverty was a taboo subject for many years; its alleviation is now noted as a national goal. Yet in October 2011 Saudi blogger Feras Bugnah and two of his colleagues were arrested after they posted a brief, powerful video on YouTube called "We Are Being Cheated" that documents poverty in al-Jaradeya, a neighborhood in Riyadh. The video went viral.

Today, Saudi Arabia remains heavily dependent on oil. It is the world's leading producer and exporter. It is home to about 18 to 20 percent of the world's proven reserves and some of the world's lowest production costs. Oil accounts for 90 percent of the country's exports, 75 percent of governmental revenues, and 45 percent of gross domestic product. The price of oil surged to $73 in early 2010 and around $110 in 2012. For perspective, consider that in 1998, prices had plummeted to $10 per barrel. Higher revenues allow the government to post budget surpluses, using the excess to pay down public debt, increase distributive subsidies and developmental projects, and implement internal security measures.

Still, abundant oil revenues do not mean that Saudi planners have no worries. Saudi Arabia's population in 2007 by official estimates totaled approximately 24 million. The 2008 estimate was 28 million. The population is now more than triple its approximately 7.3 million people in 1975; official estimates project that total population will increase to 36 million by 2025. Population growth adds demands on spending. The Saudi state's (expensive) pursuit of internal and external security complicates the demands for expenditures on education, employment, housing, and health care. In addition, a bulge in the numbers of younger citizens adds stress on an infrastructure that is already hard-pressed to keep pace with the growing population. Official estimates suggest that 37 percent of the local population is under the age of fourteen and 51 percent is under the age of twenty-nine.

For a long period now, the three-pronged mantra of state planners has been privatization, diversification, and Saudi-ization. They have done well on the first goal. The private sector now accounts for about 46 percent of the economy, compared with around 20 percent twenty years ago. They are progressing on the second goal, even if the diversified economy remains oil driven. In Saudi Arabia, diversification has meant "moving downstream." If upstream production is the simple export of barrels of crude oil, downstream production refers to making refined petrochemical products. In real terms, going downstream means that Saudi Arabia is very involved in the daily lives of many people around the world—from the cosmetics, lotions, hosiery, and synthetic fabrics they wear to the carpet in their classrooms and the paint on their walls. Going downstream is a way to avoid the wild economic gyrations associated with dependence on the export of crude oil. The government also plans to turn Saudi Arabia into an industrial giant. The crux of this vision is a $500 billion investment program over twenty years to build several "economic cities" that will diversify the economy, promote development, and create jobs for Saudi Arabian youth. Each specializes in a particular activity and will serve as a new hub for housing and commerce.

The third goal—Saudi-ization—has proven elusive. Considerable dependence on expatriate workers corresponds with a high rate of unemployment among Saudi Arabian males. Expatriates hold at least 88 percent of the jobs in the private sector. Most expatriate labor is from Bangladesh, Egypt, India, Pakistan, the Philippines, and Sudan. Unemployment among Saudis is notoriously difficult to pin down. One official estimate is 10.9 percent for 2011. It reaches a high of 25 percent for twenty- to twenty-nine-year-olds. The number of unemployed male college graduates is a particular concern. What is clear is that after decades of state effort to Saudi-ize the workforce, unemployment remains persistently high, and highest among the younger generation. In addition, while women constitute over half of the local population, they are subject to stringent codes of conduct that inhibit their participation in many economic activities. Estimates vary widely, but women make up less than 15 percent of the Saudi workforce, mostly in education and health, even though women's employment has tripled since 1992. A recent study indicates that 78 percent of jobless women hold university degrees; over 1,000 of them hold doctorate degrees (al-Munajjed 2010).

Four of the more complicated and interesting developments to watch in the coming years are the promotion of a tourist industry in an authoritarian setting, the day-to-day operation of gender-integrated universities that focus on scientific learning in the new economic cities, efforts to alleviate poverty amid wealth, and the effort to promote what is essentially a reverse population migration. About 88 percent of the Saudi population is now urban and clustered in the major centers of Riyadh, Jeddah, and Dammam, which are now overcrowded. The state is quietly promoting migration back to the more rural areas from whence people came during the boom, in an effort to distribute jobs and infrastructure and to relieve swollen cities. Also interesting is an unprecedented debate about if and how to reconcile prayer with trading. Currently, by law, all commercial establishments must close several times a day for prayer. Some businesspeople have suggested that keeping a shop open for commercial transactions should be an option. In 2012, a Saudi Islamic scholar, Abdullah al-Owaillet, expressed reservations about the mandatory closure of shops for prayers. He argued that, in the time of the Prophet, people were not asked to do so.

Religion and Politics: Sustenance and Transformation

In Saudi Arabia, Islam is part and parcel of the overall discourse on progress, the nation, and development. It is not a spiritual addendum to conversation. Islam is used by the regime to justify and legitimate the status quo. Islam is used by critics to challenge the status quo and to offer alternatives. From above and from below, Islam is a vital component of politics. There are secularists in Saudi Arabia, to be sure. But the vociferous debate is not about making a choice between being a secular state and being a religious state. Rather, the more pertinent question concerns which manifestations of Islam will have what relationship to the state. In other words, will the broad diversity of Islam be represented in governance, or will a particular orientation continue to be privileged above all others? At heart, this is a political question.

From Above: The Political Economy of Guardianship

Islam is omnipresent in the structure of the state. Since 1744 there has been a relationship between the Al Saud and the followers of al-Wahhab. The Quran and the Sunna of the Prophet are still said to be the constitution of the country, as stated in Article 1 of the 1992 Basic Law. The ulama of the

Supreme Council issue juridical opinions on the conduct of affairs both public and private. The previous king, Fahd, changed his title from the regal "Your Majesty" to the more humble "Servant of the Holy Mosques of Mecca and Medina," in order to emphasize the centrality of Islam in governance and to wrap himself ever more tightly in its mantle.

In addition, the state has special obligations that it must fulfill in its capacity as guardian of the holy cities. These include performing *dawa* (outreach) and serving as host for the hajj. *Dawa* is a moral duty incumbent on the guardian of the holy cities. The outreach can be tangible, such as developmental assistance, humanitarian aid, infrastructural construction, or financial aid. It can also be ideational, such as the propagation of Islam through the translation and distribution of the Quran throughout the world. Saudi Arabia gives generously in both regards, to the tune of nearly 4 percent of its annual average gross national product.

Over 2 million Muslims from every corner of the world converge in the holy cities each year to perform hajj. It is meant to be a deeply spiritual experience; it is also a spectacle to behold. Efficient administration of the sheer mass and movement of people is daunting. The state oversees the technical and logistical aspects of religious rituals, including transportation, accommodation, medicine, food, water, and communications technology. In the end, the ruling family is keen to tie its legitimacy to the efficient and safe performance of religious duties. It aligns everything, no matter how big (the expansion of the mosques) or small (a bottle of water), with the generosity of the king. Sponsorship of the hajj ensures a visible role for Saudi Arabia in the *umma,* the global Islamic community. As James Piscatori argues, "Appropriation of a divinely appointed role also allows the Kingdom to assert its moral leadership in the Islamic world" (2005: 228).

Yet Islam is a double-edged sword for governing officials. While it grants them legitimacy, it also leaves them vulnerable to criticism when their behavior deviates from the "straight path." The Saudi state is generally lauded for its technical supervision of hajj, but it is also deeply criticized. It has destroyed many historic sites that date to the earliest days of the Prophet Muhammad in order to make way for luxury hotels and parking decks. Gone forever are the home of Muhammad and his wife, Khadija; the mosque of Abu Bakr, the first caliph; and tombs in Medina of close relatives of the Prophet. For many observers, these sites belong to the international community of believers, not to a particular sect. People bemoan the loss of the spiritual meaning of hajj and the introduction of class distinctions into what was intended to be an experience that highlighted the equality of all believers before God. Saudi management has also been questioned as it relates to homogenization of ritual, the fairness of access for Shi'a, and responsibility for tragic deaths that occur during hajj due to fire, stampedes, or crowds.

From Below: Resonance and Challenges

Just as Islam is used by the ruling family to bolster the prevailing order, so too is it used to challenge that order. The cultural symbols and language of Islam resonate across genders, regions, ethnicities, sects, and classes. Citizens and activists thus have legitimated their concerns through the language and symbols of religion, even though, at heart, the problems they reference are political, economic, and social. Islamists have been more coherent, powerful, and organized than other social forces in Saudi Arabia, including those based on nationalism, liberalism, regional identity, or business activity. To date, theirs has been the only movement to cut across multiple cleavages (Okruhlik 2002, 2004). Importantly, though, the current uprisings are not specifically religiously fomented.

To understand the rise of Islamism in Saudi Arabia we must go back to 1979, a watershed year. Four dramatic events unfolded: the Islamic Revolution in Iran toppled the Shah; a Sunni rebel, Juhaiman al-Utaibi, forcibly took control of the Great Mosque in Mecca; the Shi'i community rioted throughout Saudi Arabia's Eastern Province; and Saudi Arabian youth began to wage jihad in Afghanistan against Soviet Communists. After executing al-Utaibi and the rebels, the ruling family instituted ever-tighter controls over social and political life. Since al-Utaibi accused the ruling family of deviating from Islam, the Al Saud sought to bolster its own legitimacy by appropriating the power of Islam. Religious educational institutions were funded throughout the country, even during the oil bust of the mid-1980s when other projects were scaled back. There were new restrictions on women's mobility, dress, and employment. The *mutawwa'in* were granted more leeway in their oversight of behavior in the public realm. An expanded Islamic education system fostered a new generation of shaikhs, professors, and students. And, through all of these developments, a narrow Wahhabi interpretation of Islam came to dominate the national discourse. Excluded from public discourse were the many Sufi, mainstream Sunni, and Shi'i populations.

During the 1980s, an Islamic resurgence swept the country. It was not about politics nor was it directed against the regime. This resurgence was about private belief systems and the comprehensive message of Islam. Several nonviolent, nonpolitical Islamist groups took root during this time. The embrace of Islam that they advocated was about a spiritual awakening. They were not formal organizations, but they did inculcate a sense of group identity. What began as small, closed circles grew gradually into large, loose, underground groups. The resurgence was also propagated by the newly returned Arab Afghan mujahidin (holy warriors). All of this cultivated a fertile field for dissent, which politicized Islamism would soon effectively tap.

These developments culminated in the rise of an Islamist opposition movement during the Gulf War of 1990–1991. Festering anger suddenly exploded with the stationing of US troops in the country. Opposition groups organized domestically and abroad, most under the rubric of Islamism. A new generation of imams voiced strident political opinions in sermons, calling for the removal of US troops and the overthrow of the ruling family. Friday sermons became an occasion for political criticism. Tapes of sermons and underground leaflets were circulated in the streets, schools, and mosques. Opposition to the presence of US military bases reached a fever pitch. Several prominent preachers were jailed or harassed. These popular imams offered fatawa that effectively countered the fatawa of the official religious authorities. For example, when the official, state-appointed religious authorities issued a fatwa that justified the presence of US troops in Islamic vocabulary, the popular scholars responded with fatawa that condemned the presence of US troops, also grounded in Islamic vocabulary and reasoning. The popular opinions often carried more credibility than did the official opinions. The alternative religious authorities decried waste and imprudence in government expenditures; they also highlighted the absence of a capable military despite massive expenditures on weaponry. This charge resonated among the population.

During this period, several petitions were presented to King Fahd that demanded structural reforms in the kingdom. The most influential were from dissident Sunni scholars. In spring 1991 and September 1992 respectively, hundreds of religious scholars, judges, and university professors issued petitions that called for a restoration of Islamic values. The 1992 petition, known as the "memorandum of advice," was particularly important. It was bolder and more defiant than the petition drafted the previous year. Its tone was straightforward; its charges were specific. It criticized almost every aspect of domestic and foreign policy. It deplored bribery, favoritism, monopolies, the feebleness of the courts, and violations of human dignity. It called for the strengthening of the military and of Islamic judicial authority. In addition, demonstrations—largely unheard of under this authoritarian regime—erupted to demand the release of the imprisoned shaikhs. For much of the Gulf War, mosques became centers of sermons, ideological debate, and political opposition.

In response to these challenges, the Al Saud simultaneously denied the existence of an opposition movement, co-opted semi-loyalists, and initiated a massive crackdown on dissent. Today, there is no monolithic Islamist movement. Islam is a powerful voice, but within it there are multiple strands. From 2002 onward, there have been loose and ambiguous working relationships forged among activists of different political orientations (Lacroix 2004, 2011). They work together on shared concerns, and dissolve on others.

Government and Opposition: Cat and Mouse

Both government and opposition use strategies to subvert the other. How do they compete and contest for space and power? How do they make their messages known to each other? The state is wealthy, with enormous resources to deploy against challengers. Opposition must be creative and multipronged to persist in the face of overwhelming odds. There is an arsenal of available strategies in this fluid game. Importantly, not all challengers seek to actually overthrow the ruling family. Some do. But many, if not most, agitate for serious structural and cultural reforms that guarantee the accountability of governance and the protection of rights within the framework of monarchy. Even if the Al Saud remained as powerful players, they would not be above the rule of law.

Strategies of Protest

Historically, protest has come from many sources and taken many forms. Always, the *majlis* in private homes has been an important arena in which to converse, sift through contesting opinions, and articulate needs. In the 1950s, Saudi workers at Aramco, the Arabian-American Oil Company, engaged in labor strikes to protest their deplorable living conditions (Vitalis 2007). Nationalist movements found articulate leaders in the new technocratic cadre during the oil boom. There were even calls for reform from within the ruling family in the 1960s and 1970s from a group known as the Free Princes. Merchants used the auspices of the chambers of commerce to agitate for transparency in contracts, a business legal code, and the protection of private property. Throughout the 1980s, strident political criticism was voiced often in conversations in the home, mosque, and market (occasionally in the media)—but only in code words. No member of the ruling family was called by name, as that would result in retribution. Individuals and policies were critiqued obliquely, through allusion to an image or reference point that listeners understood to be a particular person or policy.

During and after the Gulf War of 1990–1991, mosques were a critical safe space in which dissenting voices were heard. Signed petitions presented concerns to the king. What other forms did political opposition and protest take? In November 1990, forty-seven women protested severe constraints on their mobility by kicking their foreign drivers out of their cars and driving themselves through the streets of Riyadh (they paid dearly for their defiance, losing their passports and jobs). In 1993, a demonstration protesting the imprisonment of dissident shaikhs took place in Buraydah, in the heartland of the ruling family's support. In a country in which public demonstrations were very rare, a videotape of the event records a procession of white cars driving through the streets. Hardly dramatic in other circumstances, it was radical in Saudi Arabia. Contemporary reform efforts also incorporate the arts, literature, and social networking sites.

In 2003 and 2004, there were street demonstrations in Saudi Arabia to demand political change. In Jeddah, the police arrived at the scene to arrest protesters. But the protesters used text-messaging to immediately inform their cohorts of the situation and to publicize the next street corner at which to meet. As a result, the demonstration took an amoebic shape, forming and re-forming in response to security and technological alerts. Today, cyberspace is chock-full of Saudi blogs, websites, and discussion groups that directly address political and social issues.

There have also been several notable violent strikes against the government. Among many others, these include attacks on oil facilities, a US military complex near Dhahran, housing compounds for Westerners in Riyadh, and the US consulate in Jeddah. There have been car bombs at security headquarters in Riyadh and a petrochemical site at Yanbu, hostage-taking at an oil company compound in Al-Khobar, frequent shoot-outs between security forces and militants, and attacks on foreign tourists.

There is a common misperception that Saudi Arabia was immune to the waves of protests in the region in 2011–2012 known as the Arab Spring. In reality, there was a wide range of protest in that time frame. Street demonstrations began in January 2011 after devastating floods in Jeddah killed between 120 and 500 people and seriously affected 95 percent of buildings and streets. The urban infrastructure was inadequate due to corruption and rigged contracts. These demonstrations were followed by numerous labor strikes by both foreign and citizen workers; the declaration of the Umma Islamic Party and subsequent arrest of its founders; regular protests in front of the Ministry of the Interior by families who demanded that their sons, fathers, and brothers be released from jail; women driving; a hunger strike in support of political prisoners; a demonstration for women's rights; intense political debate on social media; student strikes in Abha; and multiple petitions with hundreds of signatories that called for elections, an independent judiciary, and freedom of expression and assembly. There was also a much-publicized call for a Day of Rage on March 11, 2011. Over 34,000 people signed a Facebook page in support of a massive uprising in Saudi Arabia to call for constitutional governance and basic human rights. There were many "silent protests" in front of the ministries in Riyadh in which a few men stood silently for hours each day to demand livable wages. Given the political culture of privacy, these brave protesters broke the barrier of anonymity at all costs. In late 2012, Saudi Aramco acknowledged a serious cyber attack on its computers that was designed to halt oil production.

In the Eastern Province, though, protest has been sustained by a Shi'i population that wants to be accepted as full citizens of Saudi Arabia. This is especially true in the towns of Qatif, Tarut, Hofuf, and Awamiya. At least fourteen civilians have been killed. Over 700 Shi'a have been arrested. In July 2012, popular Shaikh Nimr al-Nimr was wounded by police and arrested. When pictures were posted that showed him crumpled and bleeding in the back seat of a police car, thousands of people took to the streets in protest. In September, twenty-six-year-old Khalad al-Labad and two teenage relatives were killed. Their funerals became sites of protest. The regime asserts that the Shi'i protesters are nothing more than Iranian-backed puppets doing the dirty work of Iranian theocrats. This allows it to respond with a heavy hand. In the end, civil unrest in Saudi Arabia has been important, though often overlooked as international attention focused on the larger uprisings in Tunisia, Egypt, Libya, and elsewhere.

State Strategies to Blunt Protest and Opposition

The Saudi state uses numerous tactics to blunt opposition or calls for political reform. It co-opts, channels, stifles, and coerces dissenters. Why, for example, did the Day of Rage, so wildly popular on social media, fail to materialize in the streets on March 11, 2011? Officials responded with a triad of political, religious, and coercive power to scare citizens away. The Ministry of the Interior threatened jail time for all protesters, asserting that protest contradicts sharia law and the Quran, infringes on the values and norms of Saudi society, and harms the public interest. To add teeth to this threat, an extension of the antiterrorism law made it a criminal act to criticize the king or grand mufti. The state infiltrated the "Day of Rage" Facebook group and website and spread disinformation about who was really behind the organization. Potential protesters grew distrustful of each other. They feared who was listening to the online conversations. A fatwa was issued that condemned protest as un-Islamic because it sows *fitna* (chaos and destruction). It argued that the duty of a citizen is merely to give advice to the king, which he is not obliged to follow. A circular was distributed to local imams telling them to limit their sermons to a show of loyalty to the Al Saud. There were also military tanks on every street corner, sirens screaming, antiriot police at the ready, and helicopters hovering in the skies over Riyadh on the appointed day. The state thoroughly and systematically intimidated its citizens.

As if such coercion were not enough, the state also announced wide-ranging distributive schemes that eventually totaled $130 billion. It authorized an overnight 15 percent pay raise to all public sector employees, a massive affordable housing plan, a two-month stipend bonus for all students, a grant of two months' salary to all state employees, and new unemployment benefits. It waived the repayment of housing loans for hardship families. It also promised new employment opportunities, especially in the religious bureaucracy and security services, and created 60,000 new jobs in the Ministry of the Interior alone. What if the Arab Spring had happened in

1998 or 2003, rather than 2011? Oil hovered around $10 per barrel at that time and sovereign wealth funds were not fully developed. Such massive, politically driven distribution would have been difficult.

These types of efforts to blunt protest and opposition are not new; they are deeply entrenched. For example, members of the ulama and the *hayat* are formally employees of the state, their very salaries dependent upon it. They reasserted themselves after 1979, but after 2001 Abdullah reminded them that their role was one of subservience and circumscription. In the wake of 2001, hundreds of imams at local mosques were relieved of their positions because of objectionable sermons. The rest were "tamed" and given guidelines to follow in the mosques. In March 2008, the Ministry of Religious Affairs announced a retraining program for 40,000 Saudi imams, part of a wider effort to encourage "moderation." The shaikhs who were a critical component of dissent during the Gulf War have largely been co-opted by the government. Again in 2011, the state reined in the content of Friday sermons so that they expressed loyalty to the Al Saud amid the uprisings. There is a new law that states fatawa can only be issued by the state-appointed Supreme Council of Ulama, not by any alternative imams. The state works to direct calls for reform into channels that it finds acceptable (that is, controllable), such as the state-sponsored National Dialogue Forum. It also appoints reform-minded individuals to committees that have limited jurisdiction, thereby co-opting their agency.

When advocates of meaningful and peaceful political reform put forward potential leadership, those individuals are arrested, jailed, or intimidated. Thirteen were arrested in 2004 for promoting the ideas of a constitutional monarchy and human rights. In 2007, the arrest of nine reformists followed their meeting to discuss such things as elections, freedom of expression, a culture of rights, and the formation of a political party. They were sentenced to five to thirty years in prison for forming a secret organization, attempting to seize power, and incitement against the king. Also in 2007, a political activist received a sentence of six months in prison for encouraging women to protest the state's detention of relatives. In 2008, an academic and human rights activist was held for 235 days without charge. In 2011, a professor, Mubarak bin Zuair, was arrested by secret police for calling for the release of his father and brother, who had been imprisoned without charges since 2006. As noted earlier, the trial of the founders of ACPRA resulted in the founders being sentenced by a criminal court in March 2013. Suliman al-Reshoudi, seventy-five years old, was arrested after the publication of his lecture in which he explained the legality of peaceful demonstrations in Islamic law. Mohammed al-Bajadi, a human rights campaigner, was sentenced to four years in jail. Waleed al-Khair, an attorney, was charged with tarnishing the image of the state by providing false information to a foreign organization.

When newspaper editors or talk-show hosts step over the permissible boundary of criticism, they are simply removed from their posts. In 2011, in the midst of the pro-democracy Arab uprisings, the Saudi Press and Publications Law was amended to make it even more restrictive. All published criticism must be constructive and in the public interest. It is a crime to publish anything that damages the reputation of or insults the king, grand mufti, or the senior religious scholars. It is a crime to incite division among citizens. New laws also curtail online expression. The vaguely worded law makes all electronic content, including video messaging and phone text messages, subject to regulation. The government routinely censors and blocks websites and blogs, and it arrests bloggers. Earlier, in April 2009, the Ministry of the Interior imposed draconian restrictions on the country's Internet cafés that require owners to install secret surveillance cameras and register the names and identity numbers of all users. The ministry also prohibits the use of unauthorized prepaid Internet cards, censors freedom of navigation, and requires that owners of Internet cafés be Saudi (Arabic Network for Human Rights Information 2009).

Methods of responding to violent opposition also vary. The government has engaged in a sustained antiterror campaign within its borders. From 2003 to 2006, there were often reports of shoot-outs in the cities, even in the holy cities. In 2008, officials arrested twenty-eight men who they believed were seeking to reconstitute al-Qaeda's network in the country. They also arrested about thirty men believed to be planning attacks in Mecca during the pilgrimage. Interestingly, Saudi Arabia maintains an extensive program of "reeducation and rehabilitation" in which a team of psychologists, medical doctors, sociologists, and religious scholars work with those they call "deviants" to show them the error of their ways. In March 2009, the government indicted 991 suspected militants for a long series of attacks that destabilized the country from 2003 to 2006. While the reeducation program is trumpeted, these indictments may signal its ineffectiveness. The suspects are tried in secret.

In a broader strategic sense, the state uses two strategies to blunt protest. For a long time, it successfully diverted energy away from the domestic arena and toward foreign arenas. Political and religious dissent was directed outward, toward places like Iraq, Afghanistan, or Chechnya, rather than focusing on internal issues. Legitimate domestic dissent was attributed to the meddling of a foreign bogeyman, Iran. A corollary to this strategy is the purposeful deflection of debate away from political issues to social issues. There is intense debate in Saudi Arabia about gender, globalization, the economy, and how to reform Wahhabism. Although there is some room to discuss social issues, public political criticism meets with intimidation. Still off-limits—indeed, now an act of terror—is explicit criticism of the Al Saud family or of the fusion of religious orthodoxy with the state. When reform does occur, the ironic impact is that it is designed to consolidate the centrality of the Al Saud rather than broadening meaningful participation (Okruhlik 2005).

Gender and Politics

As shown in Chapter 8, the construction of gender roles in the Middle East is complex, reflecting both culture and cultural resistance. The situation is especially complicated in Saudi Arabia, where an exclusionary religious orthodoxy and state power are fused, and the particular manifestation of religion is rigidly patriarchal. In the Saudi context, religious law, social tradition, and political authoritarianism have converged to place enormous import on outlawing situations that may lead to sex outside of marriage. In Arabic the value is articulated as *sad bab al-dhara' i '* (literally, "the blocking of the means"). It is used in legal rulings, one of which states, "The Pure Law forbids those acts that lead to forbidden acts and considers those means to be forbidden also" (ibn Baz cited in al-Musnad 1996: 310). This is a slippery slope and is the foundation upon which extensive constraints on the behavior of women have been legalized, justified, and codified (Okruhlik 2009). This is why unrelated men and women cannot mix. In January 2013, Saudi authorities ordered all shops that employ both men and women to erect separation barriers to enforce gender segregation.

It is important to recognize that while covering and segregation can be tedious, they are not necessarily the most consequential issues in Saudi women's lives. They are the most visible, for sure, and are highlighted often in the Western press. But the single biggest constraint on the lives of women is the legal requirement that they always be accompanied, or their behavior approved, by a *mahram* (guardian). A *mahram* is a husband or, in cases where the woman is unmarried or widowed, an uncle, brother, father, or son—someone whom a woman cannot marry. He must grant permission for her to travel, study abroad, seek employment, have medical surgery, get married or divorced, and request her children's school files. Indeed, he can even constrain her daily movements about town. A seventy-year-old widow cried to me regarding her son, "I bore him between my legs. And now, I cannot shop for groceries without his permission!" The idea of guardianship—that somehow a woman is not capable of rational decisionmaking—is the nucleus around which much nonsense revolves. For many Saudi women today, the overriding requirement of guardianship is absurd. They are educated, talented, and confident. People should be able to succeed or fail on their own terms; women want the same right to make mistakes that their brothers have.

Saudi women are not allowed to drive. Manal al-Sharif defied this ban in 2011 and drove a car. She posted the video on YouTube and was promptly detained for a week for being behind the wheel. The following month, forty women in Riyadh with international driver's licenses participated in a "women2drive" campaign. Women often raise several children, attend school, work at a job, and protect the social standing of the family unit—and still, they must ask a foreign driver to bring them to their daily chores. When a family cannot afford to hire a foreign driver, the husband must attend to these logistical nightmares. Another serious problem is that the ulama continue to justify new forms of marriage that supplement the traditional form. Today, there are religious rulings that legitimize various forms of short-term and obligation-free marriage, legalizing sex outside traditional marriage and placing no responsibilities on the man should children arise from these unions.

Despite these considerable constraints on women in Saudi Arabia, there have been recent advancements. Women now carry an identity card in their own name. They can check into a hotel without the permission of a male. There are shopping malls, banks, and hotels that cater strictly to women. For over two decades, women have added stipulations to their marriage contracts that they may finish school, pursue professional training, have a job outside the home, have a home separate from the in-laws, or have the right to divorce should their husbands take a second wife. Premarital genetic counseling is now required. This is significant because negotiated first-cousin marriages are common. A woman can refuse the marriage if tests indicate a medical problem. Female students can now major in law or political science, subjects that were long off-limits. Physical education classes have been approved for girls' schools, though it is not clear that they are actually instituted. In May 2008, Shaikh al-Manea, a member of the Council of Senior Scholars, said that women are not prevented by sharia from being religious scholars, issuing fatawa, or working in a consultative body. In 2011, the world's largest women's university opened outside Riyadh. It has a capacity for 50,000 students. Two women participated on the Saudi Arabian Olympic team. Abdullah promised women the right to vote and run in the 2015 municipal elections. In February 2013, the king swore in thirty women, the first ever, to serve in the Majlis al-Shura. He also announced the construction of new industrial cities in which only women would live and work. While these may help alleviate the unemployment problem for women and allow women to distinguish themselves, they would still be laboring under a segregated system. People debate whether this is indicative of emancipation or not; there are arguments on both sides.

In contemporary Saudi Arabia, women challenge and protest these continuing humiliations and constraints. Women have argued with the *mutawwa'in* that there is no quranic basis for their harassment, citing quranic verses that affirm their rights. When the *mutawwa'in* are excessive in their zeal, women have doused them with pepper spray, beat them so hard as to require hospital care, and, once, even opened gunfire on them. The excesses of the *mutawwa'in* are sometimes caught on film. A cell phone clip of a young woman being forced to leave a shopping mall because of her make-up proved wildly popular on YouTube; it received over 2 million hits. In response to outcry about the absence of female members of the *hayat,* an all-woman unit has been announced that will specifically patrol women's spaces. Women protest that young girls are forced to marry old men; that a victim of gang rape at knifepoint by seven men was sentenced to 200 lashes and six months in jail because she was alone with a man who was not her guardian at the time (Abdullah later withdrew this sentence); and that divorce can be decreed through text-messaging three times, "I divorce thee."

Women now speak out about issues that once were simply off-limits for public discussion—partner rape, domestic abuse, and divorce. They provide shelters for victims of domestic crimes. Importantly, increasing numbers of women speak out without anonymity. Saudi women now proudly attach their names to such concerns. They agitate for courts for women and for women lawyers so that they can be fairly represented. Trained female scholars are privately rewriting the many legal codes that have ossified over time. At the end of the day, for women across the spectrum, the struggle is about the girls. For most women, their lives are set; they work for their daughters and nieces. Abdullah seems to have granted quiet permission for women to continue pushing the boundaries in the realm of gender rights. Until the recent appointment of women to the majlis, he had not issued a royal decree that put the authority of the Al Saud squarely behind women. That he was timid may say something about the power of the religious authorities or about succession uncertainty. There are many promises but few tangible changes in everyday life.

The Impact of International Politics

The long-standing partnership between the United States and Saudi Arabia was considered so important to the two countries that it was deemed a "special relationship" back in 1945 when Abdulaziz and Franklin Roosevelt first met. Saudi Arabia and the United States exchange a stable supply of oil for the sale of arms to ensure the security of the regime. But the arms sales have made the regime less secure in the eyes of many Saudis. Such is the dilemma with the "special" nature of this relationship. The term has many meanings, one of which refers to lack of public scrutiny and transparency to citizens of either country. People do not appreciate opaqueness. The close relationship with, and dependence on, the United States fueled much anger during the Gulf War and beyond. In 2009, some hoped for a new beginning with the leadership of Abdullah and Barack Obama. The weight of decades will be difficult to alter (Conge and Okruhlik 2009). In October 2010, a $60 billion arms sale to Saudi Arabia, the biggest-ever US arms sale, was approved.

Saudi Arabia is also affected by the international dialogue on human rights and democracy. Indeed, it is regularly the subject of reports by Human Rights Watch, International Crisis Group, and Amnesty International. The country is singled out for its practice of the death penalty, treatment of foreign laborers, discrimination against women and Shi'a, and lack of basic civil rights. Leaders do now talk about opening and liberalization. Thus far, however, talk and implementation remain distant from each other. Saudi Arabia is a signatory to many international conventions that govern fairness and rights. When it signs on, however, it does so with a rider that states "unless this contravenes sharia law"—thereby protecting its own domestic jurisdiction. In May 2009, Saudi Arabia was elected to serve on the UN Human Rights Council—even as it is routinely ranked near the bottom of comparative surveys on the protection of human rights.

In regional politics, in March 2011 in the context of the Arab uprisings Saudi Arabia and the United Arab Emirates (UAE) sent armored tanks and troops across the sixteen-mile causeway that links the former to the tiny island state of Bahrain. Bahrain is just across the water from Saudi Arabia's Eastern Province. Fearful of a spillover effect, Saudi Arabia sent troops in order to help squelch the demonstrations of Bahrain's Shi'i majority, which rose up to demand their rights as citizens. Bahrain responded with brutality. Between 75 and 100 people have been killed. Protests are banned. Dozens of Shi'a were stripped of their citizenship. As in the Eastern Province, Bahrain's regime blames the uprising on Iranian meddling. The Al Saud and the Al Khalifa ruling families are keen to forge an ever-closer political and military union among the states of the Gulf Cooperation Council (GCC) (Bahrain, Kuwait, Oman, Qatar, Saudi Arabia, and the UAE). In all of these states, there are increased (and unwelcome) demands for reform, democracy, and human rights. The GCC monarchs invited fellow monarchical states Jordan and Morocco to participate as limited members in the GCC. What were traditionally national laws have now been extended cross-nationally. Indicative of the resurgent oppression of the GCC states (Jones 2012), it is now a crime to insult the ruler of a neighboring state. Citizens have been imprisoned for what they said on Twitter about a foreign ruler. Bahrain is also home to the US Navy's Fifth Fleet.

Saudi Arabia and Iran jockey for influence. Nevertheless, the rhetoric of a "Shi'i crescent" likely holds more weight for US and Saudi officials than it does for ordinary people in the region. It is a useful tool with which to crack down on domestic adversaries. In addition, Iraq sits on the border with Saudi Arabia. During the 2000s many young Saudi men crossed what was a porous border to fight against the United States. Clearly, Saudi Arabia does not want continued instability on its border. Also important at this time are developments with neighboring Yemen, where al-Qaeda regrouped in 2009 and from which insurgents are reported to infiltrate Saudi Arabia. The Saudi state claimed to have foiled a terror plot in August 2012 when six Yemenis and two Saudis were arrested in Jeddah and Riyadh. In 2013, a secret airfield was discovered in Saudi Arabia that suggested a covert Saudi-American war in Yemen. It is thought to be the staging ground for devastating drone attacks in the war-torn country.

Saudi Arabia has also quietly funneled arms and money to the rebel forces in Syria. It pays the salaries of soldiers who defect from the Syrian military. There are reports that Saudi men now cross the border into Syria to join the fighting. This is reminiscent of Saudis fighting in Iraq or Afghanistan. It is reported that jihadis are increasingly active in the war in Syria. This may augur a wellspring of domestic problems in Saudi Arabia down the road.

Recently there have been many subtle but significant social reforms in Saudi Arabia. However, it is important to note that a legal decree or a royal pronouncement is not automatically implemented and made real in people's day-to-day lives. There is a vast gulf between legality and life as it is lived on the ground. This is especially true for women. Recent reforms address the judiciary, the *hayat,* succession, and the ulama. It remains unclear to what extent these reforms depend on the person of Abdullah and to what extent the changes have actually been institutionalized. Still, the distribution of political power and the protection of fundamental rights remain off-limits. The more things change, the more they remain the same.

18

Syria

Fred H. Lawson

Syria has experienced many different forms of government
since it emerged from the ruins of the Ottoman Empire at the end of World
War I. Arab nationalists allied to the British set up a monarchy in Damascus
with widespread popular backing in 1919, only to have it overthrown by a
French expeditionary force two years later. French officials, acting under
the auspices of the League of Nations, installed a tightly restricted electoral
system, in which the French governor-general exercised ultimate power behind the scenes. After the French pulled out of the country in April 1946, a
broad coalition of notables, known as the National Bloc, dominated a somewhat more competitive parliamentary order and jockeyed with one another
for key positions in the council of ministers. In August 1948, critics of the
National Bloc formed a rival organization, the People's Party, to push for
strict adherence to constitutional rule, the adoption of moderate economic
and social reforms, and closer cooperation with other Arab governments
(Lawson 2010). Such liberal parties steadily lost legitimacy as the decade
drew to a close. Syria's defeat in the 1948 war with Israel, rising discontent
among rural laborers and the urban poor, and perpetual deadlock in parliament galvanized popular support for organizations that advocated more radical changes in political and economic affairs.

Beginning in March 1949, ambitious cliques of military officers carried
out a succession of coups d'état. These short-lived military regimes adopted
a wide range of platforms and policies, some designed to promote public
welfare and others intended simply to buttress the position of the leadership. The growing influence of the small but influential Syrian Communist
Party led proponents of less doctrinaire socialism to push for a merger with
Egypt in February 1958, transforming Syria into the Northern Region of the

445

United Arab Republic (UAR). The Egyptian leadership's insistence on immediately disbanding all political parties and carrying out comprehensive land reform, not to mention the high-handed way in which Egyptian officials treated their Syrian comrades in the state bureaucracy, set the stage for Syria's secession from the UAR in September 1961. Parliamentary politics resumed as well, but produced a series of short-lived governments that implemented wildly vacillating, if not actually contradictory, economic programs and generally inconsistent foreign policies.

Historical Background and Contemporary Political Structure

In March 1963, a group of military officers seized control of Syria and set out to govern the country in the name of the Socialist Arab Resurrection (Baath) Party. The Baath Party's explicitly redistributive, populist platform, combined with the dynamics of military rule, set the course for Syria's subsequent political, economic, and social development. The military-party regime at first limited the extent of land reform in the countryside and the sequestration of industrial and commercial enterprises in the cities, in an attempt to mollify the liberal nationalists who had monopolized political power since independence (Lawson 1988). But the new leadership was quickly driven in a more radical direction by organized industrial workers and farm laborers, who occupied private factories and battled large landholders in the northern and central provinces and then demanded that state and party officials assist them in putting the principles of Baathi socialism into practice. The radical wing of the party enacted a comprehensive program of property seizure and redistribution in January 1965, which set the stage for a more doctrinaire group of officers to take power in a February 1966 coup d'état. This phase of the Baathi era came to a close three years later when comparatively pragmatic military commanders led by General Hafiz al-Asad removed the radicals from key posts in the state bureaucracy and party apparatus. The shift toward political and economic pragmatism was consolidated when al-Asad and his allies finally ousted the radicals through the Corrective Movement of November 1970.

After 1970, the al-Asad regime governed Syria by maintaining firm discipline among its political allies, offering substantial incentives for pivotal actors outside the dominant coalition to acquiesce in military-party rule, and not hesitating to crush more obdurate opponents. These strategies accompanied the reinvigoration of a number of political institutions that had fallen dormant or been dismantled in the mid-1960s. In addition, the authorities attempted to manage civic activism in ways that defused and delegitimized popular discontent. Nevertheless, developments in regional and global affairs after 1990 made it increasingly difficult for the authorities to limit the scale and scope of public activism, and prompted the security forces to resort to more forceful measures to restrict the activities of civic and cultural associations.

Baathi doctrine is most authoritatively codified in the party's "Some Theoretical Propositions" statement, which was drafted for the sixth National (pan-Arab) Congress that met in Damascus in October 1963. This statement introduced the party's memorable slogan: "Unity, Freedom, Socialism." Steps to promote unity of purpose and action among the Arab countries were thus accorded highest priority. The party's concept of freedom mirrors that of Jean-Jacques Rousseau: it emphasizes the collective good of the community as a whole, and shows little if any tolerance for individual liberties or representative government. The party's third objective, socialism, has proven to be the most elastic of all. During the initial years of Baathi rule, from 1963 to 1965, the term denoted a mixed economic program that included not only policies aimed at redistributing property and equalizing income but also continuing state support for "nonexploitative" private enterprise. From 1965 to 1969, a more radical notion that envisaged state ownership and central planning prevailed. Beginning in 1969–1970, Baathi economic doctrine shifted once again to encourage the reintroduction of private ownership. The underlying flexibility of Baathi ideology has thus provided a touchstone for the different leaderships that have ruled the country in the party's name since the 1963 revolution.

Shortly after coming to power, the al-Asad regime convened a parliamentary body, the People's Assembly, and charged it with drafting a permanent constitution to replace the provisional ones that had been issued in 1964 and 1969. Delegates to the initial assembly were appointed by the president and his closest advisers so as to represent the Baath Party and four other political organizations whose programs were compatible with that of the Baath: the Arab Socialist Union, the Socialist Unionists Movement, the Arab Socialists Movement, and the Syrian Communist Party. These parties formed the Progressive National Front in March 1971. A small number of independent delegates were also included in the first assembly, along with representatives of the trade union federation, the farm laborers' union, and other Baath Party–affiliated popular front organizations. In March 1973 the People's Assembly submitted a draft constitution for the president's approval, which was then ratified in a popular plebiscite.

The 1973 constitution confers primary authority on the president of the republic. The president must be nominated by the leadership of the Baath Party, approved by the People's Assembly, and confirmed by a majority of eligible voters in a national referendum. The president serves a seven-year term in office and is authorized to appoint one or more vice presidents, as well as the prime minister and other members of the council of ministers.

The president is also empowered to dissolve the People's Assembly and assume its legislative functions until it reconvenes, to nominate judges for the high courts, and to appoint provincial governors. The popularly elected People's Assembly is granted the right to veto or amend presidential decrees by a two-thirds vote, although this provision has remained dormant in practice. In fact, for the first two decades of its existence, the assembly acted as little more than a sounding board for policies under consideration by the council of ministers, and most often as merely a rubber stamp for initiatives put forward by the president and his senior advisers.

Government and Opposition

Parliamentary elections in May 1990 signaled a subtle shift in the role of the People's Assembly. Baath Party candidates won 137 of the 250 seats, while other parties in the Progressive National Front captured an additional 31. Yet the number of independent representatives who won seats in the assembly rose to 82 from the previous total of 35. The independents included a prominent Islamic television commentator from Damascus, four other religious notables from the northern districts of Aleppo and Idlib, several tribal leaders—including the son of the revered leader of the 1925 rebellion against the French—and a heterogeneous collection of wealthy merchants and successful entrepreneurs (Perthes 1992: 17). Besides taking steps to allocate patronage among their respective supporters, the new delegates set out to "use parliament as a forum to call for economic reform and liberalization, presenting themselves as the people who know how to run economic affairs, and probably—in the long run at least—claiming that private sector representatives should also share political responsibility" (Perthes 1992: 18).

During its term in office, the assembly that was elected in 1990 debated a variety of pressing economic and social issues. In April 1992, for instance, radical Baathi and communist delegates expressed their displeasure over the government's draft annual budget. At the same time, representatives of the Baath Party–affiliated workers' and farm laborers' federations criticized planned reductions in social spending and the generally low tax rates levied on private enterprise. Eberhard Kienle notes that "on several occasions during its four-year term the Assembly even used its right to pass a vote of no confidence in individual ministers leading to their resignation" (1997: 199). The unprecedented activism of the 1990–1994 assembly prompted the local press to call it "the session of opening" (Zisser 1997: 18).

By the time of the August 1994 elections, the number of candidates running for seats in the People's Assembly had fallen from some 9,000 to just over 7,400. Nevertheless, electoral competition increased sharply, a trend that was particularly evident in districts around Aleppo, where some

1,200 candidates contested 52 openings (Zisser 1997: 11). Campaigning among rival lists of independents often became heated, even though independent candidates were prohibited from running directly against candidates of parties in the Progressive National Front. In the end, 83 independents emerged victorious, virtually the same proportion of total assembly delegates as four years before. Consequently, "while the arrangements governing the 1994 elections failed to extend participation beyond the limits set in 1990, they nonetheless confirmed and consolidated the policy of restricted liberalization" (Kienle 1997: 200). Subsequent parliamentary elections produced results virtually identical to the 1994 outcome. The Progressive National Front won all but 83 seats in the March 2003 voting, and came away with all but 81 seats four years later.

The role of the People's Assembly in Syrian politics is neatly illustrated by the course of events that was triggered by the death of President Hafiz al-Asad on June 10, 2000. The parliament immediately adopted a constitutional amendment that lowered the age requirement for the presidency from forty to thirty-four, which happened to be the age of the deceased president's eldest surviving son, Bashar. The Regional (Syrian) Command of the Baath Party then announced that Bashar al-Asad had been elected secretary-general of the party, and Vice President 'Abd al-Halim Khaddam announced that Bashar had been designated commander in chief of the armed forces. On June 13, the People's Assembly nominated Bashar al-Asad as the sole candidate in an extraordinary presidential election held on July 10. He elicited the approval of 97.3 percent of voters.

Dissident offshoots of the Baath Party have been subjected to systematic harassment and repression. Among these is the Socialist Arab Democratic Baath Party, whose membership consists primarily of former Baathi cadres who stayed loyal to the radical leadership of the mid-1960s (Lobmeyer 1994: 85). Located equally beyond the pale are the Revolutionary Workers Party, a grouping of former Baath Party radicals that was founded by former Baathi ideologue Yasin al-Hafiz, and a dissident faction of the Arab Socialist Union led by one of the Baath Party's early supporters, Jamal al-Atasi (Lobmeyer 1994: 87).

When the radical wing of the Baath Party was overthrown in November 1970, the new leadership invited the Syrian Communist Party to join the Progressive National Front. Participation in the front was encouraged by officials in Moscow, who saw overt collaboration with the new Baathi regime as a step toward consolidating a viable socialist system in Syria. Under the auspices of the front, the Syrian Communist Party fielded candidates for successive elections to the People's Assembly, winning six seats in the 1977 elections and eight in 1986.

Factions opposed to the Syrian Communist Party's historic leader, Khalid Bakhdash, regularly split off from the organization during the 1970s and 1980s. Bakhdash's longtime rival, Riyad al-Turk, headed one of these breakaway groupings, which adopted the name Syrian Communist Party Political Bureau. After al-Turk was imprisoned in 1980, this party issued a series of strongly worded manifestos but engaged in virtually no political activity. In 1986, maverick Communist Yusuf Faisal declared himself head of another breakaway organization, originally known as the Base Organization. Throughout the 1990s, international human rights monitors regularly protested the drastic measures that were taken by the security forces to root out such clandestine splinter groups as the Party for Communist Action, which drew its first members from Syria's minority Alawi and Ismaili communities.

Following the 1990–1991 Gulf War, marginal communist organizations associated with the umbrella Democratic National Gathering began to issue communiqués calling for the establishment of a liberal democratic political order (Lobmeyer 1994: 88). This fundamental ideological shift provided a basis for cooperation with dissident Baathi and Islamist groups, resulting in an unprecedented degree of unity among antiregime activists. Opposition pronouncements generally emphasized the injustices that had resulted from the perpetual state of emergency and the excesses practiced by the security forces (Lobmeyer 1994: 93). But they also tended to be, in the words of Hans Gunter Lobmeyer, "highly abstract and sometimes even purely theoretical." As a result, even though such communiqués "deal with problems that may stimulate the interest of academics, and the slogans may sound revolutionary . . . none of this affects the ordinary Syrian who tries hard to surmount the difficulties of everyday life and who is tired of political slogans" (1994: 95).

Parliamentary elections grew more combative during the first decade of the twenty-first century, as several Kurdish parties put candidates forward for seats from the eastern provinces of al-Hasakah and al-Raqqah. Nine Kurdish parties fielded candidates in the April 2007 electoral campaign, only to pull out at the last minute when state officials pressured government employees to vote for candidates sponsored by the Progressive National Front. The assembly that took office that spring nominated Bashar al-Asad for a second presidential term, which was confirmed by 98 percent of voters in a May plebiscite.

President al-Asad announced in January 2011 that the Baath Party would give greater weight to district elections in the selection of delegates to the upcoming party congress. But this small step in the direction of institutional reform was quickly overshadowed by events in Tunisia and Egypt. Small-scale popular protests broke out in Damascus in early February, followed by a larger demonstration outside the Ministry of Interior in mid-March initiated by a group of women who demanded to know the fate of imprisoned family members. Security personnel used force to break up these initial instances of popular discontent, but state officials also announced plans to create jobs for an additional 10,000 university graduates each year in a bid to dampen popular discontent.

Comparatively peaceful demonstrations in the capital were soon eclipsed by a more severe outbreak of disorder in the southern city of Dir'a. The third week of May, a group of schoolchildren scrawled the slogan "The people want the fall of the regime" on a wall, prompting police to arrest them and rough them up while they were in custody. Protesters responded by sacking the local Baath Party headquarters, and riot police backed by regular army troops shot into the crowd. The authorities in Damascus tried to defuse the situation by claiming that the commanders on the spot had disobeyed orders when they used live ammunition; Prime Minister Naji' al-'Utri promised new investments in the south to reverse years of official neglect. Despite these concessions, disorder quickly erupted in the coastal city of Latakia, where antiregime protesters clashed with armed groups of government supporters, commonly called "ghosts" *(shabiha)*.

On March 30, 2011, President al-Asad addressed the country by television. He admitted that the reform process he had originally envisaged had stalled out, but blamed the Palestinian uprising of 2000, the US-led invasions of Afghanistan and Iraq, and the 2006 war between Israel and Hezbollah in Lebanon for causing the failure. The government then set up a committee to prepare for the lifting of the state of emergency that had been in force since March 1963 and another commission to confer full citizenship rights on the descendants of 150,000 Kurds who had been excluded from the 1962 census. Minister of Agriculture 'Adil Safar was appointed prime minister, despite widespread criticism of his efforts to deal with the drought that had gripped the countryside for the previous five years.

Army units moved back into Dir'a in force at the end of April. Early May saw the beginning of severe fighting in Homs between armed protesters and security forces, accompanied by heavy machine gun and artillery barrages. Skirmishing then spread to the area around Idlib, and in mid-May the army swept into the crossroads town of Tal Kalakh, sending residents fleeing across the border into Lebanon. The military advanced on the strategically situated town of al-Rastan at the end of the month, but residents repelled the assault with small arms and rocket-propelled grenades. When police fired on a funeral procession in Jisr al-Shughur in early June, protesters stormed the main police station and confiscated weapons. In the ensuing fighting, some 120 troops were killed and a number of military and security personnel defected to the opposition. Further defections were reported around Dair al-Zur, and Lieutenant Colonel Husain Harmush declared himself head of an antiregime military formation called the Free Officers. On June 20 President al-Asad once again addressed the country, this time charging that conspiracies and vandals were behind the unrest. He further remarked that the protesters were like "germs" that would damage the health of the body politic if they were not suppressed. Protesters in Dir'a and Homs immediately raised banners that proclaimed, "The germs demand the fall of the regime."

At the end of July 2011, Colonel Riyad As'ad announced the formation of the Free Syrian Army (FSA), with headquarters outside Antakya in Turkey. Another group of deserters set up the Khalid bin al-Walid Brigade around Idlib in early September. A congress of antiregime groups took place in Antalya in mid-September, which eventuated in the formation of the Syrian National Council (SNC). The first full meeting of the SNC took place in Istanbul in early October; Burhan Ghalioun, a Paris-based academic, was elected to head the organization, whose other prominent figures included the civil rights activist Riyad Saif, the communist leader Riyad al-Turk, and the general supervisor of the Muslim Brothers, Mohammad Riyad al-Shaqfah. At the same time, a collection of autonomous militias coalesced inside Syria. Most of these named themselves after famous personages and events in Islamic history, like the 'Ali bin Abi Talib Brigade outside Idlib, the 'Umar bin al-Khattab Brigade around Dair al-Zur, and the Mu'awiyya bin Abi Sufyan and 'Ubaidah bin al-Jarah Brigades in the suburbs of Damascus.

Units of the Khalid bin al-Walid Brigade attacked patrols and convoys around al-Rastan in late September, then seized the military intelligence compound in the town. State armed forces counterattacked and expelled the militia in a four-day offensive. After abandoning al-Rastan, the Faruq Battalion of the Khalid bin al-Walid Brigade took up positions in the Baba 'Amru district of Homs, while other components of the Brigade ambushed military convoys throughout the area between Idlib and Homs. On October 27, the FSA for the first time claimed responsibility for an attack that killed nine government soldiers. Fighting escalated in early November, as the armed forces bombarded and then occupied Baba 'Amru and afterward launched a massive offensive around Dir'a. Fighting continued between the FSA and the regular armed forces around Idlib throughout December. FSA units repelled an assault against al-Zabadani in mid-January 2012, while the Khalid bin al-Walid Brigade retook parts of al-Rastan. The resurgence of opposition forces accompanied sporadic bombings of security installations in Damascus and Aleppo, responsibility for which was later claimed by the Assistance Front for the People of Syria, a group that boasted ties to al-Qaeda.

Government forces regained the initiative as February waned. Baba 'Amru was overrun after the Faruq Battalion carried out what it called a "tactical withdrawal" from the district. At the same time, the Hamza al-Khatib Battalion evacuated al-Rastan. FSA units then withdrew from areas around Idlib and Dair al-Zur, and were driven out of the towns of Saraqib and al-Qusair. As the regime steadily improved its position, President al-Asad accepted a UN-sponsored cease-fire plan, which stipulated that government troops would pull out of the cities by April 10, 2012. Colonel As'ad of the FSA promised that his fighters would abide by the cease-fire as well, so long as the regular army withdrew from all urban areas and returned to their barracks. The regime immediately riposted that it had not agreed to order troops back to their barracks, and that some continuing military presence might be necessary in the cities to deal with diehards like the Assistance Front. The FSA rejected the government's clarification out of hand, yet an uneasy calm descended across the country on April 12–13. The cease-fire did not last long. State-run media reported on April 14 that a half-dozen soldiers had been killed outside Idlib, and a day later shelling resumed at Homs. Large-scale fighting subsequently broke out west of Idlib and north of Aleppo.

By the late spring of 2012 the civil war had settled into a stalemate, with neither the FSA nor the independent militias inside Syria able to win control of crucial government strongholds and neither the regular army nor the bands of pro-regime thugs known as *shabiha* able to crush the opposition. When news came of a massacre of more than 100 men, women, and children in the district of al-Hulah in western Idlib province at the end of May, merchants in central Damascus closed their shops in disgust. Signs of discontent in the heart of the capital reinvigorated the flagging FSA, which in early July launched coordinated strikes across the suburbs of Damascus combined with raids on crossing posts along the borders with Turkey and Iraq. Regular army units quickly regained control of the towns surrounding the capital, but ran into greater difficulty in the north. Severe fighting raged around Aleppo and A'zaz throughout August, and a substantial amount of territory north and northeast of Aleppo fell into the hands of the FSA, radical Islamist militias, and the armed wing of the Kurdish Democratic Union Party.

Meanwhile, state officials in June 2011 promulgated a revised political parties law that made it easier for new parties to challenge the Progressive National Front. In the local council elections of December 2011, several candidates from minor parties in the front changed their affiliation to the newly created National Unity List. Candidates sponsored by the National Unity List won seats in the People's Assembly in the parliamentary elections of April 2012. Nine other new political parties contested the April elections as well. Paradoxically, since the practice of reserving seats for minor parties in the Progressive National Front had been abolished, the Baath Party came away with greater representation in the People's Assembly than ever before.

Civil Society

Signs of increased Syrian civic activism appeared in three different arenas during the early 1990s. First, elections to the governing councils of the semiautonomous chambers of commerce in the larger cities became more fiercely contested. Campaigning for the December 1992 elections to the Damascus council got under way a full two months before the vote was scheduled to be held, and the local press devoted considerable attention to the candidates' platforms and statements. Three years later, the campaign became even more animated (Kienle 1997: 200). One prominent investor published an open letter to the Damascus chamber's general membership that called for the creation of a stock exchange, the implementation of a unified exchange rate, and significant reductions in taxes on private companies, as well as for the immediate abolition of laws that prohibited the operation of private and foreign banks. Somewhat surprisingly, the candidate won a seat on the governing council of the Damascus chamber.

Second, Syria's workers' and farm laborers' federations expressed growing discontent over the regime's efforts to encourage private enterprise and carry out market-oriented economic reforms. Grumbling among the rank-and-file of the farm laborers' union escalated in August 1992 after Prime Minister Mahmud al-Zu'bi announced that the government planned to increase support for export-oriented projects in the private agricultural sector (Lawson 1997: 10). More important, the General Federation of Workers' Unions compiled a lengthy list of grievances concerning the adverse consequences of economic liberalization in preparation for its December 1992 congress. A restive faction inside the federation even proposed to sever the organization's connections to the Baath Party, so that workers' demands could be presented to the authorities outside the usual channels. The proposal was in the end not put forward for discussion on the floor of the congress, but it was later taken up by the People's Assembly (Kienle 1997: 202).

Third, nonviolent demonstrations occurred more frequently. A small group of women gathered in front of the presidential palace in December 1989 to demand an accounting of the country's political prisoners. The following February a larger crowd, made up of "as many as 100 women, from several Syrian cities and various political orientations, assembled in front of the Presidential Palace and asked to see [President] Asad." According to Human Rights Watch, "when officials denied their request, the women refused to disperse and some cried out in protest. Police then violently broke up the demonstration, and three women had to be taken to the hospital with injuries" (1991: 505–506). Two years later, during the course of the 1990–1991 Gulf crisis, there were persistent reports of popular demonstrations in support of Iraq in the eastern town of Al Bu Kamal. Such demonstrations were quelled after the Syrian government made the decision to cooperate with Egypt and Saudi Arabia to push Iraqi armed forces out of Kuwait.

In late September 2000, ninety-nine prominent intellectuals, academics, and artists published an open letter to President al-Asad in a Beirut newspaper. The letter urged the new president to introduce measures to expand political freedom and release all political prisoners. Other reformers circulated a broadsheet that demanded a return to "constitutional legitimacy" and the rule of law, and newspapers started to criticize government economic policy openly. The security forces tolerated such activity during the winter of 2000–2001, but in mid-February 2001 abruptly enforced new restrictions on all forms of public expression and assembly. Nevertheless, a coalition of civil society activists issued a manifesto that April that advocated the pursuit of liberal democracy as a precondition for economic growth. The document was followed by the distribution of a locally produced report on human rights in Syria (Ghadbian 2001: 638). Spontaneous popular demonstrations broke out in the larger cities in July 2002 to protest Israeli actions in the West Bank. These pro-Palestinian demonstrations soon exhibited banners and slogans critical of the Baathi regime in Damascus, prompting the authorities to organize a series of tightly controlled official rallies and marches to keep public outrage within manageable channels.

Syrian civic activism reemerged in the wake of the US military offensive against Iraq in the spring of 2003. That May, some 250 prominent dissidents signed a petition that called on President al-Asad to recommit the government to political reform, rescind the state of emergency, and curtail the prerogatives of the security services. A group of human rights advocates organized a demonstration outside the People's Assembly in March 2004; almost a hundred of the protesters were placed under arrest (Ghadbian 2006: 167). A year later, a collection of liberal activists calling itself the Committees of Civil Society openly demanded a national dialogue between the authorities and the opposition. The reform campaign culminated in a May 2005 public meeting of the Jamil al-Atasi Forum in Damascus, at which an open letter from the Muslim Brothers was read. This show of solidarity between liberal and Islamist critics of the Baathi regime prompted the security forces to close down the forum and take its leading members into custody. Still, five civic associations joined the Muslim Brothers in issuing a manifesto that October, known as the Damascus Declaration, that called on the authorities to tolerate greater pluralism in public life. The document set the stage for the formation in Paris five months later of the National Salvation Front, led by former vice president 'Abd al-Halim Khaddam.

Leaders of the Damascus Declaration movement joined the Muslim Brothers in setting up the Syrian National Council in the fall of 2011. Prominent civil rights activists who argued that internal pressure was more likely to be effective in promoting political reform than any organization that was based outside the country formed the rival National Co-ordinating Committee of Forces for Democratic Change. Successive attempts to broker a tactical alliance between the two coalitions proved fruitless. As the 2011–2012 uprising steadily evolved into civil war, proponents of nonviolent political

change found themselves increasingly alienated from the opposition camp
and subjected to harsher measures by the authorities.

Political Economy

Throughout the avowedly socialist years of the 1960s and 1970s, Syria
maintained extensive commercial and financial relations with the Western
industrial economies. More than 44 percent of the country's exports were
shipped to destinations in Organization for Economic Cooperation and Development (OECD) countries in 1970; this figure rose to over 54 percent in
1975 and then to 67 percent in 1980 (Lawson 1992: 202). Just over 50 percent of Syrian imports came from OECD countries in 1970; by 1975, the
OECD accounted for more than 60 percent of imports, a proportion that remained unchanged in 1980. Furthermore, and despite the Baathi regime's
expressed commitment to build up indigenous industry, the Syrian economy
steadily transformed into a supplier of raw materials to overseas markets.
Syria's most important primary exports—cotton and petroleum—made up
half the value of total exports in 1972; three years later, they accounted for
82 percent of the total (Lawson 1992: 191). These two items provided
around four-fifths of Syrian exports until the end of the 1970s, when their
combined contribution to export earnings began to trail off.

Increased primary-goods production accompanied a steady rise in foreign direct investment. As early as 1969, Syrian officials set up a network
of free trade zones around the larger cities in an attempt to attract outside
investors. But it was the dramatic expansion of the petroleum and phosphates industries in the mid-1970s that provided the major impetus for foreign investment. In 1977 a subsidiary of Royal Dutch Shell was awarded a
concession to explore for oil in the north-central provinces, and two US
companies were granted rights to drill in the northeastern province of Dair
al-Zur. A German firm bought into the latter concession in 1983, while US-
based Chevron, Pennzoil, and Marathon simultaneously began operating in
the eastern desert. As a result of these activities, foreign direct investment
in Syria, which had totaled $43 million in 1970, jumped to $89 million in
1975, exploded to $587 million five years later, and reached $754 million
in 1985. Unlike petroleum production, which was dominated by Western
companies, phosphates extraction and processing involved barter arrangements with Romania and other Eastern European countries.

Moreover, the state-run industrial and commercial enterprises that were
set up during Syria's socialist era operated according to capitalist principles
of profit and loss. The country's largest public sector trading company, So-
ciété Import-Export, was expected to produce a profit for the government;
when it proved incapable of doing so, it was broken up into five specialized

trading companies. In 1975, state officials chartered a parastatal construction and engineering enterprise, the Military Housing Establishment (Milihouse), to coordinate new building projects in both the military and civilian sectors. Each subsidiary of this establishment was given its own management and a high degree of autonomy with regard to investment decisions, which enabled it to operate as a virtual private company. Other state-run companies followed Milihouse's lead in relying on market mechanisms in their dealings with suppliers and wholesalers, a trend that prompted growing disaffection among public sector workers as the 1980s opened (Longuenesse 1985).

Government officials attempted to parry worker discontent by reviving public sector enterprises. A program of individual incentives was put in place for public sector employees in industry, taxes were raised on private companies, and restrictions on foreign trade were restored. In 1981 the Committee for the Guidance of Imports, Exports, and Consumption was set up. Its members included several ministers, trade union leaders, and representatives of chambers of commerce and industry. Officials then contracted with North Korean and Czechoslovakian companies to carry out land reclamation and oil exploration projects. Nevertheless, persistent coordination problems and shortages of imported machinery and spare parts plagued public sector companies. The Baath Party itself criticized inefficiency and corruption in state-run enterprises at its landmark January 1985 congress (Sadowski 1985).

Measures to boost private enterprise were undertaken as the 1980s went on. Joint-stock farming companies were authorized in 1986; the next spring, private trading companies were allowed to export a wide range of agricultural and manufactured goods, and to use the profits to finance further activities. The proportion of total trade moving through private hands jumped from 10 percent in the early 1980s to over 30 percent in 1988. The trend toward economic liberalization crested in May 1991 with the promulgation of a new investment law that permitted any projects that increased the number of jobs, reduced imports, or augmented exports to bring machinery into the country on a duty-free basis.

Syria profited handsomely from the regime's decision to join the anti-Iraq coalition in 1990–1991. A flood of loans and grants washed into the local economy from grateful Kuwait and Saudi Arabia. Improved relations with the United States and United Kingdom opened the door to greater credit and economic assistance, while the rise in world oil prices led to a surge in state revenues. Government officials earmarked some of these resources for public sector projects, but also stepped up support for private enterprise. By the mid-1990s, private capital had moved into areas that had previously been reserved for the public sector. In the spring of 1994, for example, a Greek industrial equipment company broke ground for a plant to make cranes, turbines, and electrical generators for export; that fall, the Higher Council for Investment approved the construction of the country's first private cement factory; and in November 1995, flour milling and iron and steel rolling were opened to private companies.

Friction between the public and private sectors resurfaced in the late 1990s. The marked deterioration of oil revenues after 1997, combined with two years of severe drought, created greater competition for investment funds. State officials tried to make up for declining oil income by opening the door to increased trade with Iraq. Damascus negotiated a series of commercial agreements with Baghdad that sent processed food, textiles, and consumer goods to Iraq in exchange for cash payments and oil shipments under the terms of the UN-administered oil-for-food program. This trade generated heightened production at state-run manufacturing plants and provided new opportunities for some private companies as well.

During the fall of 2000, Iraqi oil began to move across Syria in substantial quantities. Nevertheless, per capita gross domestic product began to slide, at the same time that unemployment increased, particularly in state-run industry. Government officials once again looked to private companies and entrepreneurs for relief. The return of higher oil prices beginning in late 2001 enabled the authorities to raise wages in the public sector and upgrade a number of state-owned plants, but US military operations in Iraq in the spring of 2003 disrupted the flow of oil revenues to the treasury and sharply reduced the supply of investment funds from the Arab Gulf states. As a result, the private sector became the central component of the local economy.

Private capital in present-day Syria takes four very different forms. The first, and predominant, form consists of a cluster of nominally private companies that owe their existence and ability to turn a profit to their intimate connections with the heads of state agencies, powerful figures in the Baath Party apparatus, or senior commanders in the military-security forces. The second is made up of more recent ventures undertaken by private entrepreneurs, who have taken advantage of the regime's successive economic liberalization programs to set up capital-intensive industrial plants and market-oriented commercial and transportation companies. The third includes the heterogeneous collection of small-scale manufacturing and trading establishments that managed to survive the nationalizations of the mid-1960s, and still constitute the backbone of the urban economy. The fourth is rooted in the relatively small private holdings of agricultural land that began to reemerge during the late 1970s.

Private agrarian landholding gained momentum in the wake of a February 1986 presidential decree that exempted private agricultural companies from all labor laws, foreign currency restrictions, and import-export regulations in return for giving the state 25 percent ownership. Such companies quickly replaced cereals production with cultivation of fruits, nuts, and vegetables for export, and transformed Syria's agricultural sector into a major source of hard currency by the early 1990s. In December 2000, the Baath Party began to distribute lands belonging to state farms in the north-eastern provinces to their employees as private holdings (Ababsa 2005). The plan immediately stirred up conflict between its immediate beneficiaries on one side and former state farm employees and prerevolutionary landlords on the other.

Private interests and the state have come into greatest conflict over the allocation of scarce investment funds and access to hard currency. Government officials continue to earmark a disproportionate share of public revenues to support state-run enterprises, even though persistent shortages of investment capital pose a major challenge to private companies of all sorts—large and small, urban and rural. Furthermore, the distribution of investment monies remains heavily influenced by noneconomic considerations, and it is almost impossible to anticipate which way any particular decision will go. At the same time, the procedures that one must follow in order to acquire lines of credit denominated in hard currency remain opaque, making it difficult for private companies to purchase machinery and spare parts outside the country. A presidential decree issued in July 2003 rescinded the laws that made it a criminal offense for Syrian citizens to hold or spend foreign currency. Yet the direct transfer of hard currency overseas continues to be illegal, and those convicted of doing so stand subject to substantial penalties.

Two developments in 2004–2005 heightened the importance of the private sector for Syria's economy. First, the government negotiated an economic partnership agreement with the European Union, which included provisions that mandated an accelerated shift from a state-led to a market-driven economic order. Second, the tenth Regional (Syrian) Congress of the Baath Party, which took place in Damascus in June 2005, adopted a resolution that called for the creation of a "social market economy" to supplant the existing "state socialist" system. Informed observers estimated that such a transformation would require the domestic economy to grow at a rate of 7 percent annually and obligate the private sector to generate more than 150,000 jobs each year, if an acceptable degree of social stability were to be maintained. Such projections appeared overly optimistic in light of the facts that private enterprise accounted for only about one-third of Syria's total capital formation and that no more than 10 percent of private companies employed more than five workers each.

Meanwhile, the government encouraged public sector enterprises to form partnerships with private companies (Abboud and Lawson 2012). New public-private partnerships took shape in housing, electricity generation, water and sanitation, and construction. At the same time that such ventures were injecting dynamism into the cities, severe drought gripped the farmlands of the northeast. By the fall of 2009, large areas of al-Raqqah and al-Hasakah resembled dust bowls, and the residents of towns and villages had migrated to the fringes of Aleppo, Homs, and Damascus in search of work. Problems in the countryside were compounded when yellow rust struck the wheat fields of al-Hasakah in the summer of 2010, destroying half of the harvest.

As popular unrest spread during the late winter of 2010–2011, state officials raised salaries for public sector workers and increased subsidies on heating fuel and cooking oil. In the summer of 2011 the government announced plans to revive the public sector, and the Eleventh Five-Year Plan included substantial new investment in state-run manufacturing. A General Organization for Desert Management and Development was created to manage the country's expansive wastelands. Despite such initiatives, prices for food, sugar, and other staples skyrocketed. By the spring of 2012, there were reports that farmers who had fled to the cities looking for sustenance had started to return to the countryside to escape the political turmoil.

The Impact of International Politics

External influences have played little role in shaping the overall development of the Syrian economy. The trend toward economic liberalization that gained momentum in the 1980s accompanied a sharp drop in trade and investment in the Middle East on the part of the wealthy capitalist countries (Lawson 1992: 189). Conversely, the collapse of the Soviet Union, which had become Syria's primary trading partner during the late 1980s, had only a minor impact on the local economy: Syrian products quickly found new markets in the former communist countries of Eastern Europe and the Caucasus (Lawson 1994). And foreign trade made up such a minor part of total economic activity that even major transformations in the global economic order left domestic producers and consumers alike largely unaffected. Consequently, Syria suffered less than one might have imagined from the financial and commercial disruptions that shook the world economy during the first decade of the twenty-first century.

More significant consequences can be traced to the continual state of war that engulfed Syria in the decades after 1948. Ongoing conflict with Israel, along with sporadic armed confrontations with Iraq and Turkey and the 1975–1990 civil war in Lebanon, dramatically raised the stakes of domestic politics. The apparent inability of the civilian leaderships of the late 1940s to defend Syrian territory and protect Palestinian rights severely damaged not only the legitimacy of these particular governments but also the reputation of liberal democracy in general. Defeat in the 1948 war with Israel inspired disaffected military commanders to overthrow the parliamentary system and inaugurate a single-party system. Equally important, political contestation came to be seen as a threat to national unity and thereby detrimental to the struggle against Zionism. Efforts by the People's Party and other liberal organizations to resist the imposition of military rule could therefore be framed as seditious by military leaders and more radical movements, who justified the imposition of authoritarian forms of governance on the grounds that extraordinary measures were required for national security.

Furthermore, perpetual warfare strengthened authoritarian rule by putting an inordinate share of the country's material and political resources in the hands of the military establishment. The size of the armed forces jumped from 80,000 troops in 1970 to 430,000 in the early 1990s (Perthes 2000: 152). Total troop strength reached a peak of 820,000 in 2000 (Cordesman 2006: 333). To support this massive expansion in personnel, military spending soared from approximately 10 percent of gross domestic product in the late 1970s to more than 20 percent in the late 1980s. Meanwhile, pivotal components of the "regime structure itself have been reorganized along quasi-military, hierarchical lines" (Perthes 2000: 154). Both the Baath Party and the various party-affiliated popular organizations steadily abandoned deliberative decisionmaking procedures in the 1960s and 1970s and instead started to act simply as transmission belts for directives issued from commanders at the top.

Moreover, successive Baath Party–led governments have made good use of the opportunities created by external crises to maintain their hold on power. Escalating political-economic challenges at home led the comparatively doctrinaire Baathi regime of Salah Jadid to mobilize the home front for war against Israel in 1966–1967, just as the comparatively pragmatic regime of Hafiz al-Asad responded to the growing internal problems it faced by intervening in the Lebanese civil war in 1975–1976 (Lawson 1996). In each case, military initiatives directed toward the outside world set the stage for the adoption of policies that heightened state intervention in the local economy. More important, mobilizing the populace for external combat accompanied the imposition of tighter supervision of labor activists, Islamist militants, and other dissident forces. In this way, the persistence of armed conflict with Israel has played a central role in the perpetuation of Baathi rule.

Religion and Politics

Syria's branch of the Muslim Brothers (Ikhwan al-Muslimin) traces its origins to the late 1930s, when the nationalist movement was mobilizing the country's population to fight for independence from French rule. Severe economic problems led well-to-do Sunnis in the cities to set up a variety of political and social associations. Some of these were benevolent societies, headed by religious scholars who had received formal training in Islamic law. During World War II, one of these societies moved from Aleppo to the capital, where it merged with other Islamist associations and, at a 1944 congress, rechristened itself the Muslim Brothers. In the summer of 1946, the organization elected Mustafa al-Siba'i, a prominent Islamist activist from Damascus, to be its first general supervisor.

In the beginning, the Syrian Ikhwan al-Muslimin championed a platform that called on the government to nurture Islamic morals and ethics, to reform the state bureaucracy by applying laws and regulations in an unbiased way, and to do everything it could to achieve national independence. These objectives were disseminated through schools and periodicals sponsored by the organization. The first manifestos published by the Muslim Brothers offered no detailed plan of action, but rather underscored the broad goals of combating popular ignorance, immorality, and deprivation and of establishing a fully independent Syria whose political and legal systems would no longer discriminate among citizens along sectarian lines as they did under the French.

After the 1948 war in Palestine, the organization gained a larger following in the cities and towns, especially in Damascus, where candidates endorsed by the Ikhwan consistently won a fifth of the parliamentary seats allotted to the capital and its environs during the 1950s. The Muslim Brothers competed with Communists, Baathis, Nasserists, and other movements disenchanted with the veteran nationalists who governed Syria after independence. Intense rivalry with more radical parties led the Ikhwan al-Muslimin to formulate a loose package of economic reforms in the mid-1950s that pointed in the direction of "Islamic socialism." Deeply suspicious of Egyptian-style Arab nationalism, the Muslim Brothers actively supported Syria's 1961 secession from the Cairo-dominated United Arab Republic, which had been created in 1958 at the instigation of Baathi military officers.

Following the 1963 revolution, the Ikhwan cultivated popular opposition to the economic and social policies that were adopted by the Baath Party. The policies carried out by the new regime not only undercut the country's large landowners, rich merchants, and private industrialists, but also jeopardized the livelihoods of the shopkeepers and small-scale manufacturers who formed the Ikhwan's primary constituency. Religious figures connected to the Muslim Brothers mobilized repeated demonstrations and protests against the government, particularly in Aleppo, Hama, and Homs. But in the aftermath of Syria's defeat in the 1967 war with Israel and the rise of a more pragmatic wing of the Baath in 1969–1970, a schism developed inside the organization. Militants based in Aleppo and Hama pressed for armed struggle against the regime; they were countered by the Damascus-centered followers of 'Isam al-'Attar, a religious scholar who had replaced

Mustafa al-Siba'i as general supervisor of the Muslim Brothers in 1957. The more moderate wing under al-'Attar saw a convergence of interest between the country's small-scale traders and manufacturers and the al-Asad regime's commitment to economic liberalization and willingness to solicit investments from the Arab oil-producing countries of the Gulf.

The honeymoon between the al-Asad regime and the Damascus wing of the Muslim Brothers did not last long. When the authorities issued a revised—and overtly secular—constitution in 1973, the Ikhwan orchestrated mass demonstrations, which forced the government to amend the document to stipulate that the head of state be a Muslim. During the mid-1970s, the organization's northern militants gained the upper hand over the Damascus wing and escalated the level of antiregime violence. This phase of the Ikhwan's campaign against the Baath Party–dominated political order is closely identified with the leadership of 'Adnan Sa'd al-Din, a teacher and writer from Hama who became general supervisor in a disputed election in 1971. Several factors prompted the organization to adopt a strategy of armed struggle (jihad): Syria's military intervention in the Lebanese civil war, which appeared to back the Maronite Christians against the Palestinians; the flagrant corruption that accompanied the economic liberalization program; and above all, the heightened influence of the rural Alawi community, whose economic and political gains came largely at the expense of urban Sunnis.

At first, the militants concentrated on assassinating high-ranking Alawi officials and armed forces commanders. But as the 1970s passed, the campaign expanded to include armed attacks on government facilities and symbols of Baathi rule, including local party offices, police stations, and military and security installations. The violence peaked at the close of the decade with the June 1979 killing of eighty-three Alawi artillery cadets at the military academy in Aleppo; a cluster of mass demonstrations and boycotts in Aleppo, Hama, and Homs in March 1980; and an attempt on the life of President Hafiz al-Asad later that year.

In the face of escalating violence, the authorities decreed in July 1980 that anyone found to be connected with the Muslim Brothers would be sentenced to death. The regime then cracked down on the Ikhwan with its formidable armed forces and security services, in particular the elite military and intelligence units, whose ranks consisted almost exclusively of Alawis. The Muslim Brothers regrouped under the banner of the Islamic Front in Syria, a broad alliance of Islamist organizations that took shape in October 1980. Shaikh Mohammad al-Bayanuni, a respected member of the Sunni religious hierarchy in Aleppo, became the front's secretary-general, but its leading light remained 'Adnan Sa'd al-Din, the general supervisor of the Ikhwan al-Muslimin. The chief ideologue of the Islamic Front was Sa'id Hawwa, a prolific religious scholar from Hama who, along with Sa'd al-Din, had been a leader of the northern militants who took control of the Muslim Brothers in the mid-1970s.

Six years of violence culminated in a major confrontation between the Ikhwan al-Muslimin and the Baathi regime in the longtime Islamist stronghold of Hama. There, in February 1982, militants proclaimed an armed uprising and seized control of large parts of the city. It took elite military and security forces two weeks to crush the rebellion, during which time they killed between 5,000 and 20,000 civilians and razed the central business district and historic grand mosque. The showdown dealt a devastating blow to the Muslim Brothers, and put the regime's opponents on notice that the authorities would tolerate no armed challenge to Baath Party rule.

The organization's current orientation is most clearly articulated in the manifesto of the Islamic Front in Syria, which was published in November 1980. Although it was designed to appeal to a broad range of groups opposed to the al-Asad regime, this document nonetheless includes a number of key positions that the Muslim Brothers have advocated over the years. It emphasizes the Syrian people's right to regain the basic political and civil liberties that they had enjoyed during the constitutional era of the late 1940s and early 1950s. It calls for an independent judiciary, and for representative government based on the rule of law and mutual consultation between rulers and ruled. And it emphasizes the importance of continuing jihad as a means to eliminate pervasive sectarianism, particularly in the armed forces. Many of the values and principles that are highlighted in the manifesto are not exclusively Islamic in character, particularly those that emphasize natural rights and civil liberties. In this sense, Syria's Muslim Brothers march in step with a variety of Islamist opposition movements throughout the Middle East that make individual freedoms their highest priority in the fight against persistent authoritarian rule.

After its crushing defeat at Hama in 1982, the Ikhwan al-Muslimin's prospects dimmed dramatically. The strategy of armed struggle proved to be a complete failure and severely damaged the organization's reputation among the general public. Divisions inside the leadership over whether to maintain a belligerent posture toward the regime contributed to its fragility during the remainder of the 1980s. External allies turned their backs on the movement as well. Ayatollah Ruhollah Khomeini made it clear that the Islamic Republic of Iran would take no steps to undermine the Baathi regime in Damascus, since it was the only Arab government to assist Iran in the war with Iraq that erupted in September 1980.

Desperate for allies, the Muslim Brothers formed a partnership with a wide range of groups and movements opposed to the Baath Party, which coalesced in mid-1982 as the National Alliance for the Liberation of Syria. The National Alliance's platform reiterated many of the demands contained in the 1980 manifesto of the Islamic Front, but it conspicuously dropped all mention of such explicitly Islamic notions as mutual consultation between rulers and citizens. A dissident, radical faction of the Ikhwan led by Adnan 'Uqla rejected the new coalition and the comparatively liberal platform that it espoused, but its militants remained isolated and on the run.

By the early 1990s, contacts between the Ikhwan al-Muslimin and the authorities became more frequent, and in December 1995 the organization's general supervisor, Shaikh 'Abd al-Fattah Abu Ghudah, returned to Damascus from Saudi Arabia. He pledged to refrain from any kind of overtly political activity, and settled down to teach theology and Islamic law in Aleppo. Radical activists in London then elected 'Ali Sadr al-Din al-Bayanuni to the post of general supervisor. As the decade ended, prominent figures expressed increasingly moderate sentiments. In August 1999, for example, they issued a proclamation that called on the government to abandon autocratic rule and establish democracy, freedom, and political pluralism. Such demands were repeated following the death of Hafiz al-Asad in June 2000. Shortly after the election of Bashar al-Asad to the presidency that July, al-Bayanuni told reporters that the Ikhwan did not even have to be permitted to operate legally inside Syria; it would be enough to come up with some sort of "formula" that would allow the organization to "express its views" concerning public issues.

In May 2001, the Muslim Brothers published a Covenant of National Honor, which called for the creation in Syria of a "modern state," that is, "a state of rotation" in which "free and honest ballot boxes are the basis for the rotation of power between all the sons of the homeland." The document made no mention of mutual consultation, or of instituting Islamic law. An April 2005 statement once again demanded "free and fair elections" and the termination of the state of emergency that had been imposed in 1963. General Supervisor al-Bayanuni announced in January 2006 that the organization had decided to join the opposition National Salvation Front (NSF), headed by Syria's exiled former vice president 'Abd al-Halim Khaddam, in a campaign to replace the Baathi regime with a liberal democratic political system. In taking this step, the Ikhwan al-Muslimin openly allied itself with the proponents of liberal reform who had issued the Damascus Declaration in October 2005.

Radical Islamists who were upset with the London-based leadership of the Muslim Brothers for allying with the secular organizations that dominated the NSF returned to armed struggle in an attempt to discredit al-Bayanuni and at the same time destabilize the regime. The security forces raided a house filled with weapons in May 2005, and a month later killed an alleged Islamist leader in a shoot-out in a suburb of Damascus. Armed clashes between Islamist radicals and the security forces took place in Hama that summer and outside Aleppo in December. Further raids on Islamist hideouts in the coastal mountains were reported during the spring of 2006.

In April 2009, the London-based leadership of the Muslim Brothers pulled out of the NSF. General Supervisor al-Bayanuni attributed the split to unrelenting criticism of the Ikhwan al-Muslimin on the part of liberal components of the front, as well as to fundamental disagreements inside the NSF concerning the appropriate response to Israel's 2008 invasion of Gaza. That May, an influential religious figure with close ties to the regime was placed under arrest on charges that he had held unauthorized discussions with Western diplomats. Further religious-based controversy erupted in June 2009 when the government promulgated a new personal status law that mandated greater uniformity across religious communities with regard to issues of marriage, inheritance, and child custody.

Leaders of the Ikhwan al-Muslimin at first ignored the popular protests of 2011–2012. Representatives of the movement took part in the founding meetings of the Syrian National Council, but had few connections to the network of militias that carried out most of the actual fighting. Thomas Pierret (2012) points out that established religious figures carefully avoided speaking out in favor of the uprising. By the winter of 2011–2012, the Muslim Brothers found themselves challenged by more radical Islamist groups, most notably the Islamic Liberation Party. Senior figures of the Ikhwan al-Muslimin met in Istanbul in March 2012 and drew up a revised covenant, which laid out a liberal platform that called for a political system based on the separation of executive, legislative, and judicial powers.

While the Muslim Brothers collaborated with civil rights activists under the auspices of the SNC, a collection of militant Islamist groupings came to the forefront in the struggle against the Baathi regime inside Syria (Lund 2012). Most prominent was the Assistance Front for the People of Syria (Jabhah al-Nusrah), which carried out a succession of car bombings in Damascus and Aleppo and enjoyed close links to the al-Qaeda–affiliated Islamic State of Iraq. Somewhat larger was the Brigades of the Free of the Levant (Ahrar al-Sham), which appeared around Idlib at the end of 2011. The Brigades of the Free initiated a campaign of bombings that targeted military installations around Idlib and Hama in the name of promoting a just and righteous political order.

September 2011 saw the appearance of the Hawks of Syria in the countryside around Idlib. The group's leader, Ahmad 'Isa al-Shaikh, declared its aim to be the creation of an Islamic state in Syria. As fighting raged around Aleppo throughout the summer of 2012, the Hawks were challenged by both the Ummah Division, which consisted largely of Libyan fighters, and the Dawn of Islam Movement, which included a diverse assortment of Chechens, Britons, and other foreign nationals.

Identity and Politics

Syria's mountainous coast, hardscrabble southern hill country, and far-flung northeastern plains have provided safe haven for a remarkable collection of ethnic and sectarian communities. The great majority of Syrians are Arabic-speaking Sunni Muslims. Yet Alawi, Ismaili, and Christian communities flourish in the isolated valleys adjacent to the Mediterranean Sea. The districts south of Damascus are settled predominantly by Druze, with smaller concentrations of Shi'ites and Circassians. Kurds, Turkomans, and Yazidis can be found in sizable numbers in the northeastern provinces. Kurds join Armenians, Greek Orthodox Christians, and Maronite Catholics in the heterogeneous northern metropolis of Aleppo. And a vibrant Shi'i neighborhood sits alongside a cluster of ancient Christian communities within the walls of the old city of Damascus.

Minority groups have played a crucial role in Syrian politics for almost a century. Armed resistance to the imposition of French rule immediately after World War I galvanized large numbers of Kurds in the north and Druze in the south in active defense of the nationalist leadership in Damascus (Provence 2005; Tejel 2009). After local resistance was overcome, the French imperial administration organized the country along sectarian lines during the 1920s, and set up autonomous Alawi and Druze states as a way to weaken residual Arab nationalist sentiment. More important, French military commanders recruited heavily among the relatively disadvantaged Alawi, Druze, and Ismaili populations to staff the auxiliary regiments upon which French domination rested (Bou Nacklie 1993).

At independence in 1946, the doors to the military academy were thrown open to all citizens, and Sunnis rapidly achieved a predominant position in the armed forces in general and within the officer corps in particular. Persistent discrimination against Alawis, Druze, and Ismailis in society at large nevertheless nurtured feelings of alienation and resentment among cadets and officers alike, and minority soldiers ended up gravitating toward such radical political movements as the Baath Party and the Syrian Social National Party (Drysdale 1979). It was officers from the social and geographical fringes of Syrian society who carried out the coups d'état of the late 1940s and early 1950s, and who later engineered the March 1963 revolution. And it is generally agreed that the doctrinaire socialist leadership that seized power in February 1966 was more markedly Alawi in composition than any previous collection of politically active officers. In fact, one can construct a persuasive account of the recurrent rivalries inside the armed forces that shaped Syrian politics from 1949 to 1970 in almost exclusively sectarian terms (Van Dam 1996).

Beyond the confines of the barracks, however, sectarian mobilization tended to be heavily muted. Armenians and other Christians did their best to maintain the solidarity of their respective communities, but made a point of refraining from any sort of communal political activity. This was partly out of fear of attracting the attention of the security forces, but even more out of an underlying worry that the most likely alternative to Baathi rule would be an avowedly Islamist regime that would severely restrict the economic and social opportunities they enjoyed in a broadly secularist order. In a similar fashion, Syria's Kurds generally found themselves better treated and more fully assimilated here than in any of the surrounding countries, and only rarely protested the Baath Party's efforts to convince the population to abandon "outdated" ethnic and sectarian identities in the aftermath of the 1963 revolution (Tejel 2009: 63–64).

Growing economic difficulties in the countryside sparked a series of clashes in November 2000 between the settled Druze population of al-Suwaida province and Sunni bedouin. The fighting quickly engulfed Sunni villages in the area, whose inhabitants were rumored to be sympathetic to the bedouin. Lightly armed security forces attempted to impose a curfew, but failed. It was only when armored vehicles and elite battalions from the capital intervened that order was at last restored. In three days of skirmishing, some twenty people were reported killed and another 200 injured. Members of the Druze community immediately organized public protests not only in the provincial capital but also in front of the interior ministry in Damascus. A further demonstration involved some 200 Druze students on the campus of Damascus University. Attacks on Druze farmers at the end of the month precipitated another round of protests in al-Suwaida, which prompted the provincial governor to order the release of members of the Druze community who had been detained after the initial clashes.

Some three years later, the growing influence of Kurdish nationalist organizations in Iraq emboldened the Kurds of northeastern Syria to engage in greater communal activism. During a March 2004 football (soccer) match in the city of al-Qamishli, Kurdish fans taunted the supporters of the visiting Arab team by waving a Kurdish flag and chanting slogans in support of US president George W. Bush. Some of the Arab team's supporters reacted by shouting pro–Saddam Hussein slogans, and then attacked the Kurds with makeshift weapons (Gauthier 2009). News of the clash led to rioting in nearby towns, during the course of which hundreds of Kurds were arrested by the security forces. On the one-year anniversary of the incident, Kurdish activists staged a sit-in outside the High Court in Damascus and demanded an end to the long-running state of emergency. This protest was broken up by club-wielding cadres of the Baath Party–affiliated students' federation.

When Jalal Talebani of the Patriotic Union of Kurdistan was elected president of Iraq in April 2005, Kurds in Damascus took to the streets to celebrate. A leading Kurdish figure, Shaikh Mohammad Ma'shuq al-Khaznawi, went so far as to tell Agence France Presse a few weeks later that "either the [Syrian] regime must change or the regime must go. . . . The reason I and others can speak out is because the Americans are trying to get rid of dictators and help the oppressed" (June 2, 2005). Al-Khaznawi disappeared on May 10, prompting a new round of large-scale demonstrations in al-Qamishli. The security forces responded by arresting not only those suspected of instigating the protests, but the country's remaining civil rights activists as well.

The potential for ethnic and sectarian friction was increased by the flood of refugees coming into Syria from Iraq in the years since 2003. The first wave of refugees consisted almost entirely of Sunni Arabs, including senior members of the Iraqi Baath Party (Fagen 2009: 14). Later arrivals came from Iraq's disadvantaged Shi'i community, and thus tended to be substantially poorer than the individuals and families who had come before. Syrian authorities permitted the refugees to seek medical care at public hospitals and send their children to public schools, leaving these institutions increasingly unable to accommodate the needs of Syrian citizens. Furthermore, the influx of Iraqis seeking a place to live and food to eat, particularly in and around Damascus, caused housing and staples prices to soar. The rising cost of living, combined with a notable jump in criminal activity, galvanized popular resentment and animosity against the new Iraqi residents (Fagen 2009: 19).

Sectarian conflict escalated sharply as the 2011–2012 uprising turned into civil war. Members of the Alawi community, rich and poor alike, tended to rally behind the regime, while clashes between Alawis and Sunnis in the coastal provinces and countryside around Idlib became increasingly frequent and bloody. Neighborhoods of Homs and villages scattered across the Ghab region of Hamah province split along strictly sectarian lines, disrupting economic and social relationships that had joined them together for decades.

By the summer of 2012, the Kurdish population of northeastern Syria had been drawn into the battle for the country's future. The military wing of the Democratic Union Party (PYD) took charge of towns and villages that fell out of government control from al-Qamishli in the east to 'Afrin in the west. Eleven rival Kurdish parties, including the Freedom Party (Azadi), coalesced into the Kurdish National Council in an attempt to offset the growing influence of the PYD. At the same time, the Kurdish Union Party (Yakiti) aligned with the National Coordinating Committee of Forces for Democratic Change. The Kurdish Future Movement, by contrast, initially worked with the Syrian National Council but broke away when it became clear that the SNC leadership had no interest in discussing Kurdish autonomy. A fifth movement, the People's Council for Western Kurdistan, generally collaborated with the PYD. The Kurdish Regional Government in northern Iraq set out to reconcile the disparate Syrian factions in July 2012 and managed to obtain agreement that their respective militias would be replaced by unarmed protection committees in districts abandoned by the Syrian authorities (*The National* [Abu Dhabi], July 15, 2012). Nevertheless, that October PYD activists openly criticized the "traitors" inside the Kurdish community who were cooperating with the Free Syrian Army, and

armed clashes erupted between Kurdish fighters and units of the FSA in
Aleppo.

Gender and Politics

Baathi socialism in principle champions the interests of women and promises to protect families from the injustices inherent in capitalist patriarchy.
The party's commitment to women's rights was most clearly evident during
the mid-1960s, when a network of vocational schools and child care centers
opened in the cities and towns. The General Union of Women was set up
under party auspices in 1967 to deal with issues and sponsor programs of
particular concern to Syria's female population.

Programs instituted in the heyday of Baathi socialism laid the foundation for a dramatic expansion in women's participation in the labor force.
The total number of paid female workers reached 804,000 in 2001—more
than triple the figure two decades earlier. Half of women working outside
the home were employed by the state, either in the administration or in public sector enterprises. About one-third worked in agriculture and forestry.
Private sector industry employed some 7 percent, with the remainder found
in the hospitality industry, real estate and banking/finance, construction,
and transportation/communication (Syrian Central Bureau of Statistics 2005
cited in Zaman 2006: 154, 70).

In the political arena, the number of women seated in the People's Assembly has risen steadily. The biggest increase in women's representation
was evident in the 1981–1985 assembly, which served at the height of the
struggle between the Baathi regime and the radical Islamists. In the 2003–
2007 assembly, a woman won one of the independent seats—the first time
that a female candidate succeeded in the polls without being sponsored by
one of the parties in the Progressive National Front. The same assembly
saw the first woman elected as a parliamentary officer, specifically to the
post of secretary. Women have served as government ministers since 1976,
when a female was appointed to the post of minister of culture. Fifteen
years later, two women held ministerial office, as minister of culture and
minister of higher education.

Legal obstacles to full equality between men and women nevertheless
remain firmly in place. The current citizenship law recognizes the offspring
of a Syrian man and a non-Syrian woman as a Syrian national, even if the
child happens to be born outside the country. By contrast, children of Syrian women and non-Syrian men are not recognized as citizens, even if they
are born on Syrian territory. Similarly, men enjoy the exclusive right to initiate divorce proceedings, and females are only authorized to inherit one-
half of what males inherit.

Faced with such barriers to equal treatment under the law, growing numbers of Syrian women started to look outside the political arena for inspiration and redress. One source of succor has been the Qubaisi movement, whose leader, Miss Munira Qubaisi, resides in a quiet neighborhood of Damascus. "The Miss" has attracted disciples from many of the country's wealthiest and most prestigious families, including several well-known Islamic scholars. All of the movement's preachers are unmarried females, although the Qubaisis do not discourage young women from marrying. The movement actively promotes elementary education, particularly for girls, and has sponsored the establishment of a large number of primary schools. Each one follows the curriculum mandated by the state, but supplements the official program of study with lessons in religion and morality. The exact precepts of the movement are known only to initiates, although they are said to combine the sophist ideas of Ibn 'Arabi and al-Hallaj with modern nationalist thought. Perhaps indicative of the appeal of this potent mix of religious mysticism and social activism is the fact that a prominent figure in the order is Amirah Jibril, the sister of the longtime secretary-general of the Popular Front for the Liberation of Palestine General Command.

19

Turkey

Marcie J. Patton

On November 3, 2002, 79 percent of eligible Turkish voters
stood patiently in long queues at polling stations to elect a new government.
Because Turkish law required that ballots be cast in person, many expatriates either traveled home or used one of the ballot boxes specially set up at
major airports and border points. Political parties even provided free bus
transportation from Germany to border stations. The outcome was heralded
as a political earthquake. None of the incumbent political parties passed the
10 percent threshold needed to enter parliament, whereas the recently
formed party with Islamist origins, the Justice and Development Party
(AKP), received 34.3 percent of the vote, capturing 363 of the 550 seats in
the Turkish parliament. Of the eighteen parties contesting the election, the
adamantly secularist Republican People's Party (CHP) was the only other
party to win parliamentary representation, earning 19.4 percent of the vote
and 178 seats. The AKP's landslide victory gave Turkey its first single-
party government in over a decade and, for the first time since the 1954
election, a two-party parliament.

There were other novelties as well. The AKP's roots are Islamist, but in
contrast to its banned Islamist predecessor the Welfare Party (RP), it dis-
avows an Islamist agenda and is strongly committed to pushing for membership in the European Union (EU) and integration with the world economy. Under conditions of financial crisis and rampant inflation, the AKP
was able to win a parliamentary majority in national elections just one year
after its founding without ever having been tested before voters. The AKP's
electoral success derived from its mobilization of a powerful centrist coalition that drew together a core constituency of conservative Islamist voters;
pro-democratic, liberal secularists frustrated with the performance failures

474 Cases

of the ruling establishment parties; and financial and economic elites attracted to its pro-market, internationalist outlook.

Historical Background and Contemporary Political Structure

Modern Turkey emerged out of the collapse of the Ottoman Empire after World War I and remarkably was never colonized by any Western power. The Allied Powers' intention was to dismember the empire; however, unexpectedly, a national independence movement surfaced and after two grueling years of fighting was victorious and declared a republic. Together with his followers Mustafa Kemal, the charismatic leader of the liberation struggle who was later bestowed with the honorific surname Atatürk (Father of the Turks), made Westernization the state's chief political project. As Atatürk told the nation in 1933, on the tenth anniversary of the Turkish republic, his aim was to lift Turkey to the level of the most prosperous and civilized countries of the world. To this end, Atatürk and his followers initiated a program of radical social and cultural change, modeling the new republic on nationalist, secularist, and progressive lines, similar to what they observed in Europe.

What was distinctive about Atatürk and his supporters (referred to as Kemalists) was their radical ambition to construct a state and mold a society utterly disconnected from the Ottoman past, and their belief that it was imperative for Turkey to catch up to the West in the shortest time possible. The Kemalists were in a hurry to stomp out religious reactionism, and did not hesitate to use force to suppress religious opposition. They introduced secularizing reforms not only to copy the "progressive" West but also to undermine Islamic "backwardness." Kemalist secularization has been termed "radical" or "militant" because its purpose is to exert state control over religion by excluding religion from public life (but not extinguishing personal belief), as opposed to the separation of religion and state, which is the Anglo-American understanding.

The first secularizing reform to be introduced was the abolition of the caliphate (1924), which was the spiritual symbol of power in the Ottoman Empire. This was followed by the adoption of a secular educational system; assignment of control over mosques, imams, and religious affairs to a state body; and closure of Islamic brotherhoods (tarikats). In addition, the Kemalists replaced the Islamic calendar with the European one, changed the alphabet from Arabic to Latin script, and made Sunday instead of Friday the weekly day of rest. They strongly discouraged veiling and prohibited men from wearing the traditional male headgear, the fez. The legal system too was secularized, with the Swiss civil code replacing Ottoman family law, which had been based on sharia (Islamic law).

Atatürk was impatient to unify the citizenry, but not around a Muslim national identity. Consequently Turkish nationalism replaced Islam as the unifying bonding agent. The Kemalists sought to minimize differences and maximize similarities; therefore they considered every citizen inside Turkish borders to be a Turk. Because of their uncompromising view of the indivisibility of the Turkish territory and people, they refused to acknowledge the many ethnic minorities inside the country's borders. Regarding the country's largest minority group, the Kurds, Kemalist leaders banned the Kurdish language, dress, and names. They used military conscription in an effort to assimilate Kurdish youth, and when assimilation did not work, armed repression was applied. The price of Kemalism was the imposition on Turkish citizens of a monolithic, homogeneous national identity that excluded other identities.

Until 1945, democracy in Turkey had shallow roots. To restrict opposition to the Kemalist reforms, Atatürk constructed a system of one-party rule that remained in place even after his death in 1938. However, following World War II, pressures for democratization came from two directions: externally from the West, which considered Turkey a key ally in the unfolding Cold War, and internally from pressures to liberalize the economy and to allow multiparty competition. A group of politicians split off from the Republican People's Party, the party that Atatürk had founded, and formed the Democratic Party (DP), which ended the former's monopoly on power by winning a parliamentary majority in the 1950 election. The Democratic Party identified itself as the party of the common people and promised greater religious freedom and liberal economic policies.

Although the Democratic Party was careful to emphasize that it supported secularism and was credited with modernizing agricultural production and building up the country's industrial base, it became increasingly authoritarian and restrictive of political liberties over time. It also opened itself up to criticism by changing the call to prayer from Turkish back to Arabic and boasting about the number of new mosques built and religious schools opened. After a decade in power, the Democratic Party government was toppled by a military coup.

The military holds a unique role in Turkey as guardian of the Kemalist reforms. Its pivotal position is a legacy of Atatürk, who relied on the officer corps as the main defender of the Kemalist project to construct a modern nation-state along secular, Western lines. Although the Turkish military in principle accepts the desirability of democracy and the legitimacy of civilian rule, its paramount mission is to maintain Kemalist ideas by preserving national unity and defending the country's territorial integrity.

In May 1960 the Turkish military accused the Democratic Party of deviating from Kemalist principles and seized power. Democratic civilian rule was restored the following year under the very liberal constitution of the second Turkish republic (1961–1980), which allowed the expression of diverse ideological views and spurred the growth of civil society. The two parties garnering the largest share of votes for the next two decades were the Justice Party (AP), which stepped into the shoes of the banned Democratic Party, and the Republican People's Party. Elections were hotly contested, with anywhere from six to eight parties gaining seats in the bicameral parliament. However, the new freedoms also made possible the emergence of far-right and far-left militant groups, whose violent clashes with one another and with authorities played a role in growing social fractionalization. During the 1970s, various steps were taken to check political terrorism, including a brief military "coup by memorandum" in 1971. Nevertheless, lawlessness and street killings escalated, and the economy began to stagnate. The ineffectiveness of short-lived, unruly coalition governments also contributed to the mounting political polarization and continued deterioration of the economy.

Claiming that the situation had spun out of control, the military intervened for a third time in September 1980. The generals blamed politicians for partisan squabbling and inaction, and decried the "overly permissive" civil liberties and social rights granted by the 1961 constitution. They banned all political parties, suspended the constitution, dissolved trade unions, and closed down civil society organizations—in particular women's, student, and human rights associations. Their harshest measures were directed at leftists, who suffered extended imprisonment, abuse, and torture.

The coup leaders oversaw the drafting of a new constitution in 1982, which in stark contrast to the 1961 constitution moved the regime in an illiberal direction, subordinating civil society to the state by restricting free expression and associational activities. Individual rights and liberties were subject to annulment and suspension on a range of nebulous grounds (threats to public order, national interest, national security, or public health); voluntary associations and trade unions were banned from engaging in any kind of political activity; and the education system was placed under tight state control, with universities administered by the state-appointed Higher Education Council (YÖK). The new constitution created a bounded electoral democracy by making it easy to close political parties and ban politicians from politics.

The 1983 election marked the return to parliamentary politics and brought to power the center-right Motherland Party (ANAP), which managed to maintain a majority in the government until 1993. Turkey's elections are run under a system of proportional representation in multimember districts. Only parties that have mustered 10 percent of the national vote are represented in the National Assembly. Turkish voters have typically supported center-right parties; however, after the ban on political activities by pre-1980 political leaders was lifted in the late 1980s, the party system fractured. The center right divided into two parties and the center left into three. Turkey entered into a period of coalition governments that lasted until the AKP's sensational win in 2002.

In the 1990s, frustration with the failure of centrist parties to deal effectively with economic and social problems translated into high levels of voter volatility in elections. On the one hand party competition polarized on an Islamist-secularist axis, and on the other hand the party system grew extremely fragmented, with numerous minor parties competing for office—a situation that was exacerbated by the refusal of party leaders to merge with other parties sharing similar views (see Table 19.1 for an overview of the party spectrum in Turkey). Turkish parties are overwhelmingly personality-based, so much so that party cohesion depends greatly on the charismatic appeal of the party's leader.

Only three parties passed the 10 percent threshold in the 2007 and 2011 elections. Among these was the ultranationalist Nationalist Movement Party (MHP), founded in the late 1960s. Led by Devlet Bahçeli, the MHP emphasizes a homogeneous Turkish national identity. The MHP opposes the establishment of a Kurdish state in northern Iraq and views Kurdish nationalism through the lens of terrorism. Its hard-line stance on the Kurdish and Cyprus issues enabled it to benefit from a growing anti-EU backlash to win 14.3 percent of the vote in 2007. However, in 2011 the party dropped to 13 percent and lost twelve seats due on the one hand to a sex scandal that implicated a number of high party officials, and on the other hand to AKP leader Recep Tayyip Erdoğan's success in attracting nationalist voters.

The CHP—once Atatürk's party and today's main opposition to the AKP—is led by Kemal Kılıçdaroğlu. It claims to be a left-of-center, social democratic party, although until Kılıçdaroğlu became party chairman in

Table 19.1 Ideological Distribution of Political Parties in Turkey, 2011

Name	Orientation
Peace and Democracy Party (BDP)	Left-Kurdish
Democratic Left Party (DSP)	Center-left Kemalist
Republican People's Party (CHP)	Center-left Kemalist
Justice and Development Party (AKP)	Center-right Muslim democratic
Democratic Party (DP)	Center-right Kemalist
People's Voice Party (HAS)	Right-Islamist
Felicity Party (SP)	Right-Islamist
Nationalist Movement Party (MHP)	Right-ultranationalist
Grand Unity Party (BBP)	Right-ultranationalist
Rights and Equality Party (HEPAR)	Right-ultranationalist

Note: These parties are the most noteworthy of the twenty-seven parties that registered to participate in the 2011 general elections.

2010 it was known for dogmatically upholding Kemalist secularism and nationalism. The party lost sixty-six seats in the 2007 election due to its failure to offer voters an alternative vision to the AKP, and the immense un-
popularity of its leader Deniz Baykal. Under Kılıçdaroğlu's leadership the
party underwent a makeover. In 2011, the "new CHP" ran its most successful campaign in years, abandoning its dogmatic secularism for a more conventional social-democratic, populist platform that emphasized unemployment and urban poverty. The CHP's seats climbed from 112 to 135, and its
share of the vote rose from 20.9 to 25.9 percent.

The AKP, although often identified as a pro-Islamist party, rejects the
"Islamist" label and insists that it is a pro-West, pro-EU, socially conservative, pro–free market party. It won 34.3 percent of the popular vote in 2002,
46.6 percent in 2007, and an astonishing 49.9 percent in 2011. Following
the 2007 election, the new parliament elected the party's nominee, Abdullah
Gül, to the presidency. The AKP has managed to maintain single-party rule
for three consecutive elections, although in 2011 its dominance in parliament dropped from 341 to 327 seats. This was an immense disappointment,
as the AKP had hoped to win a two-thirds majority (330 seats) that would
have enabled it to push through a new constitution and submit it to a popular referendum, which it was confident it would win. If it had won 367 seats
it could have unilaterally amended the constitution without going to a referendum. Without a supermajority, the party will have to compromise with at
least one other party in parliament to write a new constitution, making it
more difficult for the AKP to achieve Erdoğan's goal of creating a strong
presidential system in time for him to run for the presidency when his last
term as prime minister ends in 2014. Table 19.2 presents the results of the
2002, 2007, and 2011 parliamentary elections in Turkey, and shows the predominance of the center right in Turkish politics.

In the architecture of the third Turkish republic (1982–present), the
presidency was originally envisioned to be a Kemalist preserve. Presidential powers were strengthened in the 1982 constitution. Since there was an
established tradition that the president be a former military figure, no
changes were made to the previous method of indirect election of the president by parliament from among its members for a seven-year, nonrenew-
able term. This pattern was broken when General Kenan Evren's term
ended in 1989 and parliament voted in civilian politician Prime Minister
Turgut Özal; however, as long as presidential candidates like Özal affirmed
Kemalist secular traditions, their selection was uncontroversial.

Of particular importance are the president's appointive powers and
checks on the unicameral legislative body, the Grand National Assembly
(TBMM). The president is empowered to appoint the chief of the General
Staff, members of the Constitutional Court, university chancellors, and members of the Higher Education Council. These officials sit atop what once were

Table 19.2 Turkish General Election Results in 2002, 2007, and 2011

Party	Percentage of Popular Vote			Number of Parliamentary Seats		
	2002	2007	2011	2002	2007	2011
Justice and Development (AKP)	34.3	46.6	49.9	363	341	327
Republican People's (CHP)	19.4	20.9	25.9	178	112	135
Nationalist Movement (MHP)	8.3	14.3	13.0	0	71	53
Independents[a]	6.2	5.2	6.8	9	26	35
Felicity (SP)	2.5	2.3	1.3	0	0	0
Grand Unity (BBP)	1.0	—	0.75	0	—	0
Democratic (DP)	—	5.4	0.65	—	0	0
People's Voice (HAS)	—	—	0.77	—	—	0
Democratic Left (DSP)	1.2	—	0.25	0	13[b]	0
Rights and Equality (HEPAR)	—	—	0.29	—	—	0
Youth (GP)	7.3	3.0	—	0	0	—

Sources: "Turkish Elections, 1950–2007," Konrad-Adenauer Stiftung-Turkey Office, April 15, 2009, http://www.belgenet.net/ayrinti.php?yil_id=15; "Official 2011 Election Results from Yüksek Seçim Kurulu," *Hurriyet,* June 22, 2011, http://www.turkiyesecimeri.com/secim-sonuclari-2011.php.

Notes: a. The threshold system requires a party to win 10 percent of the national vote to obtain a seat in parliament. For this reason Kurdish candidates run as Independents. Although the Kurdish party DEHAP only won 6.2 percent of the vote in 2002, 8 of its members secured seats as Independents. After DEHAP was banned a new Kurdish party, the DTP, formed. DTP garnered 21 of the 26 seats won by Independents in 2007. It too was banned, and its successor, the BDP, picked up 29 of the 35 Independent-held seats in 2011.

b. The DSP entered the 2007 elections in alliance with the CHP and received 13 of the CHP's 112 seats, leaving the CHP with 99 seats.

the key institutional strongholds of Kemalism: the military, the judiciary, and the universities. These were considered the repositories of Atatürk's reforms and defenders of the secular, unitary nature of the republic. The president may veto legislation passed by parliament, submit proposed constitutional amendments to popular referenda, challenge the constitutionality of laws and cabinet decrees, dissolve parliament, call for new elections, and declare martial law or a state of emergency.

The president also convenes and chairs the National Security Council (MGK), another Kemalist stronghold established after the 1960 coup. Along with the president, the MGK includes the prime minister, a number of other ministers, plus the chief of the General Staff and the commanders of the army, navy, and air force. It was originally intended to be a forum for the military to convey its views on national security policy to the Council of Ministers; however, the 1982 constitution boosted the authority of its advisory opinions, making them into top-priority concerns, and increased the number of senior commanders so as to outweigh civilian members. Democratic reforms adopted in 2003 to align civil-military relations with EU norms have downgraded the MGK to a consultative body with a civilian majority; nonetheless it continues to exercise influence through informal, backdoor channels.

The president shares executive power with a prime minister, whom the president appoints and who is expected to lead a majority of the TBMM. The prime minister presides over the cabinet (Council of Ministers), whose members must be approved by the president. It was always expected that the president would exercise a restraining hand over both the prime minister and the elected parliament if Kemalist principles were threatened in any way. Not surprisingly, secularist president Ahmet Necdet Sezer (2000–2007) cast a record number of vetoes in opposition to AKP-proposed bills.

Similar to other parliamentary democracies, the TBMM has the power to enact, amend, and repeal laws as well as override a presidential veto with a three-fourths vote. Its 550 members are elected for five-year, renewable terms. Although the TBMM often laid claim to a popular mandate because it was directly elected, in reality it was limited in the extent to which it could exercise national sovereignty on behalf of the electorate until the AKP government rebalanced power in favor of the legislature. Civil-military reforms demanded by the EU and introduced by the AKP curbed the power of the MGK over the TBMM, and the 2007 election to the presidency of Gül, one of the AKP's founders, gave the party control over both the legislative and executive branches.

A further check on the power of the legislature had been exercised by the judiciary until the AKP restructured it through constitutional amendments approved by popular referendum in 2010. Prior to the referendum, judicial personnel had embraced hard-line Kemalist secularism and worked in tandem with the president (who was chosen based on his secularist credentials). Opponents of the AKP often sought to tie the hands of the elected government through judicial means by appealing laws and constitutional amendments to the Constitutional Court. The new changes—rather than depoliticizing the judiciary as the AKP had promised—instead enabled the top judicial organs to be populated with individuals whose views aligned with those of the AKP.

Historically, the bureaucracy was intended to be a key instrument for implementing Kemalist reforms. This role began to erode when the emergence of competitive party politics in the 1950s encouraged patronage-based appointments. The AKP is no different from its predecessors in appointing its partisan supporters to key bureaucratic posts. In 2004 the government passed a law lowering the compulsory retirement age, allowing for the replacement of the older secularist generation with pro-Islamist supporters and graduates of state-run religious high schools. Since the AKP came to power, the Islamist-leaning civil servants' union Memur-Sen has gained more members than any other public sector union—tangible evidence that the AKP has been installing its supporters in the bureaucracy. Clearly, the AKP's electoral dominance from 2002 to the present enabled it to alter the institutional balance of power in Turkey in ways that have undermined traditional Kemalist strongholds.

Religion and Politics

Moderate Islam has been remarkably successful in Turkey, a Muslim-majority country that is also a secular, democratic state. The rise of political Islam in Turkey is a consequence of its forced marginalization during the one-party period. Kemalist state builders implemented projects and reforms to reduce the influence of Islam in the everyday lives of people. Yet despite their efforts to modernize religio-cultural traditions, an Islamic identity was never extinguished among the population at large.

The shift from one-party to multiparty politics in 1946 opened the door to the emergence of political Islam. In the 1950s rapid urbanization, the mechanization of agriculture, and rural-to-urban migration produced dramatic transformations in the economy and in social interactions, generating constituencies for a politicized Islam. The electoral success of the Democratic Party in 1950, 1954, and 1957 derived in part from its skillful use of religion to attract conservative, religious voters (e.g., restoring the call to prayer to Arabic from Turkish). Necmettin Erbakan formed the first overtly pro-religion political party in 1969. After it was closed in the 1971 military intervention, he resurrected it as the National Salvation Party (MSP, 1972–1981). The MSP appealed to small-town shopkeepers, traders, and craftsmen suffering from economic dislocation as the economy modernized and industrialized. While branded an Islamic fundamentalist because of his inflammatory rhetoric, Erbakan eschewed militant Islam and situated himself in the mainstream of politics. Under his leadership the MSP participated in three coalition governments.

After the 1980 coup, a confluence of three factors gave fresh momentum to the rise of political Islam: the state's Turkish-Islamic synthesis strategy, the effects of the liberal economic policies of Prime Minister Turgut Özal, and the exceptional organizing skills of Islamist parties. The prosecular military, intent on promoting national solidarity and checking the emergence of radical Islamist groups, engineered the spread of a new ideology—a blend of Turkish nationalism and conservative Sunni Islam—through the introduction of compulsory religious education in public schools and by increasing the number of mosques and imams (prayer leaders). Unintentionally, this revived interest in religion.

Meanwhile, Özal's free market policies promoting export-led growth helped produce an upwardly mobile, affluent Muslim middle class. At the same time, the International Monetary Fund (IMF) stabilization measures that he introduced included a reduction in public expenditures that contributed to the development of an impoverished underclass, especially in urban areas. Yet both constituencies identified with Islamic activism and wanted the state to loosen constraints on the expression of religion in public life.

The Welfare Party emerged in this period as the most influential representative of political Islam. RP loyalists canvassed neighborhoods and built face-to-face relationships with Islamist constituents. The party proved to be extraordinarily effective at grassroots organizing and providing welfare services at the local level, successfully mobilizing those who were reeling from high inflation and cuts in state subsidies. Donations to the party's coffers came from religiously conservative businessmen who had profited from the opened economy and who were also financing an explosion of Islamist publishing houses, television channels, radio stations, and daily newspapers.

In the 1995 general election the Islamist Welfare Party won the largest bloc of seats in parliament; soon thereafter Erbakan became prime minister. Once in office Erbakan abandoned his wild campaign promises to withdraw from the North Atlantic Treaty Organization (NATO), to eliminate bank interest charges, and to form an Islamic Common Market. Still, the RP's populist allure and religious rhetoric frightened Kemalists. Rather than directly intervening in the political process, the military high command—in what was dubbed the country's first "postmodern" coup—engineered Erbakan's resignation from office in 1997 by pressuring him to adopt a number of policy directives aimed at clamping down on pro-Islamic activities and institutions. After Erbakan dragged his feet for several months, the True Path

Party (DYP) deputy prime minister Tansu Çiller threatened to dissolve their coalition partnership, forcing Erbakan to step down. Not long afterward, the Constitutional Court banned the Welfare Party for violating the secular principles underpinning the republic.

A new Islamist party, the Virtue Party (FP), quickly formed to step into the Welfare Party's shoes. The FP incorporated two generations of Islamists, an old guard of traditionalists loyal to Erbakan and a younger cadre of reformists. When as expected the FP was also closed, Recep Tayyip Erdoğan, the former Welfare Party mayor of Istanbul, convened a meeting of the latter and founded the AKP, while the Erbakan loyalists created the Felicity Party (SP). The AKP rapidly became a major political force, whereas the Felicity Party slipped into near electoral oblivion.

The turnabout in the fortunes of political Islam had much to do with the strategy of strategic moderation adopted by the AKP. (See Figure 19.1 for competing views of the AKP from supporters and critics.) Erdoğan and his followers believed that the Welfare Party had overplayed its hand with the secularist establishment and that a more conciliatory approach would give them a shot at gaining power. The transformation of the AKP was also influenced by the lure of membership in the EU. Erdoğan and his clique, sometimes referred to as neo-Islamists or post-Islamists, were sympathetic to Europe's strong support for individual rights and liberties. Whether their beliefs were influenced more by political calculation or philosophical beliefs is much debated; however, there is no doubt that the AKP recognized that guaranteeing freedom of religion could lead to lifting restrictions on expression of an Islamic identity in public spaces.

The AKP has proved highly popular with the electorate. Under its rule the Turkish economy rebounded from a debilitating crisis and achieved economic stability. The government's pro-growth policies have brought prosperity to the religiously conservative middle class, and its social policies, such as the delivery of free health care, medicine, food, and coal to impoverished families, have made it popular with the poor. Its early advocacy of EU membership and the associated reforms gained it the support of liberal intellectuals, although many became disillusioned with its later inertia on the EU-reform front. Opposition parties have proved to be weak in establishing links to voters, whereas the AKP has built a sophisticated voter mobilization operation with well-funded local branches.

Government and Opposition

The AKP's victory in the 2002 election was nothing less than a political earthquake. For some, the AKP's electoral landslide was a step toward normalizing democracy, in that it provided a counterweight to the powerful

Figure 19.1 What Is the Justice and Development Party (AKP)?

Defenders Say:	*Critics Say:*
• It is a conservative democratic party.	• It is an Islamist party.
• It does not make political claims on religious grounds.	• It has a hidden Islamist agenda.
• It challenges authoritarian Kemalist secularism.	• It threatens Kemalist ideology.
• It believes in social and cultural pluralism.	• It wants to impose Islamic values and lifestyle on society.

unelected Kemalist blocs that controlled the state, while for others it represented the gravest challenge that Kemalism had ever faced. The principal points of friction between the AKP government and its opponents have been secularism, the reforms stipulated by the EU for membership, the balance of power within state institutions, and the Kurdish issue.

The AKP and the Kemalists have conflicting understandings of secularism. The AKP insists that it is committed to preserving a secularist system, but at the same time it has been advancing its own interpretation of secularism. The party's view as phrased by Erdoğan is that "the state can be secular, individuals cannot be secular." The AKP's bottom line is that individuals should have the right to religious freedom.

As believers in state control over religion, Kemalists have become increasingly uneasy about the growing visibility of Islam in public life, the increasing economic power of a religiously minded business class, and the AKP's pursuit of policies that appear to promote the Islamization of society such as lifting the head scarf ban in universities, introducing regulations to discourage the consumption of alcohol, and supporting the segregation of public parks and beaches by gender. Kemalist secularists fear the imposition of a religious lifestyle and point to the prevalence of displays of public religiosity in dress and social mores. In society at large pro-Kemalist secularists have looked to the Kemalist power bloc within the state to preserve secularism.

Turkey's prospect of EU membership is another issue that pits government versus opposition. Kemalists, who were once the motor force driving Turkey's ambition to catch up to the West, have become Euro-skeptics due to their views on secularism and their abiding commitment to the unity and integrity of the Turkish nation. Adamant secularists worry that EU-mandated democratizing reforms are empowering Islamists, the nemesis of Kemalists. Kemalist nationalists fear that EU membership will entail a loss of sovereignty, and ultranationalists suspect that the EU harbors an ambition to territorially divide Turkey. Both balk at EU reforms that insist Turkey grant minority rights to Kurds, acknowledge the Armenian genocide, and make any concessions on Cyprus. Also in the Euro-skeptic category are radical, anti-imperialist leftists, as well as anti-Western Islamic militants who view the EU as a Christian club. Turkey's Europhiles favor a liberal, democratic Turkey and are opposed to Kemalist secularism. The Europhiles formed a historic alliance among liberals, moderate Islamists, and Kurds that voted the AKP into office in 2002. Their shared goal was a democratic and secular state respecting human rights.

From 2002 through 2005, the year the EU gave Turkey the green light to commence accession negotiations, the AKP government was strongly committed to EU membership. Upon entering office it immediately set about redressing the most illiberal aspects of Turkey's democracy, including restrictions on freedoms of speech, expression, and association; lack of cultural rights of minorities; and the strong influence of the military on domestic politics. Several EU-stipulated reform packages dealing with these issues were easily passed over the protestations of the CHP opposition in parliament.

However, since 2006 the EU reform momentum has stalled, and in November 2012, on the tenth anniversary of the AKP's first electoral victory, Erdoğan delivered a speech about the party's vision for the future that made no mention of the EU, making it clear that EU membership was no longer a priority for the AKP. Nor is it a top concern for the Turkish public, as popular backing for the EU bid has slumped to well under 50 percent.

As the EU process slowed, so too did Turkey's democratic reform process. Contributing to this slowdown was friction between the AKP and Kemalist state institutions. With the AKP holding a parliamentary majority (the CHP was the only other party elected to parliament in 2002), its early political battles tended to be focused on Kemalist state institutions. Specifically, one elected and two unelected Kemalist institutions acted as wardens of Kemalist secular values and influential checks on the AKP's governing capacity: the presidency, the Turkish Armed Forces (TAF), and the Constitutional Court. From the perspective of the AKP the actions of these bodies were highly politicized and interfered with the AKP's popular mandate from voters.

Relations between the TAF and the AKP were strained from the moment the AKP took office. The military was accustomed to exercising its authority over civilian politicians through the National Security Council. When the AKP sought to control the presidency in 2007, the TAF viewed this move as a major challenge to their oversight of the popularly elected legislative branch. The two sides collided in April when secularist President Sezer's term was expiring, and Erdoğan nominated his party's foreign minister, Abdullah Gül, to fill the office. Through a midnight posting on its website, the military warned that it might be compelled to step in if the

AKP did not withdraw Gül's name. However, the military's "e-coup" back-fired. The AKP called for early elections that July, and won an even larger percent of the popular vote than it had in 2002. Its win was widely inter-preted as an indication that Turkish voters opposed the military's interfer-ence in politics and wanted the government to continue with democratic re-forms. Two months later, Gül made history when parliament elected him as the country's first Islamist president. It was more than a symbolic victory, because it put the AKP in control of both the legislative and executive branches.

A second round of AKP-military discord followed in the summer of 2008 with the exposure of an alleged deep-state conspiracy implicating a clandestine ultranationalist group, called Ergenekon, which supposedly had schemed to overthrow the government. Among those arrested were several top military commanders. The investigation quickly mushroomed as link-ages were drawn to other purported plots to assassinate major political fig-ures and public intellectuals, all aimed at undermining the AKP. The arrest of hundreds of military officers (active and retired), politicians, and jour-nalists followed. In the beginning the Ergenekon arrests were praised by pro-democratic voices for exposing threats to democracy and bringing the military under civilian control. However, as the probes dragged on, the AKP was accused of pursuing a vendetta against its opponents. Its strongest detractors have accused the AKP not only of settling old scores, but also of fabricating evidence.

Although the AKP captured the presidency in 2007, it still faced a Kemalist-controlled judiciary that interfered with the AKP's reform agenda. In February 2008 the AKP government attempted to lift the ban on women wearing head scarves at universities by passing a constitutional amendment guaranteeing the right to an education. The pro-secularist Constitutional Court blocked this move, ruling that revoking the ban violated the secular principles enshrined in the constitution. While awaiting the head scarf rul-ing, Kemalist prosecutors filed a case with the Constitutional Court to close the party. Although this attempted "judicial coup" against the AKP failed when the Court ruled by a narrow margin not to ban the party, ten of eleven justices voted the party guilty of being "a center of anti-secular activities" and ordered that the party's funding from the national treasury be cut in half.

Critical to eliminating these institutional checks on the AKP's power was a successful September 2010 referendum on new amendments to the constitution. These amendments altered the appointments process for the highest judicial bodies, giving elected institutions more say—arguably in-creasing democratic control over the judiciary. Earlier legislation had made the military subject to civilian courts, meaning that the amendments re-moved assurances that the military could be protected by the judiciary since the AKP would be able to pack the courts. In essence the referendum altered the balance of power between the elected and unelected institutions. The AKP framed the referendum as a step toward further consolidation of liberal democracy because the amendments weakened the secularist-dominated judicial and military power bases. The AKP's opponents argued that the amendments paved the way for civil authoritarianism by undermining the independence of the judiciary and enabling the government to embed AKP-friendly justices and prosecutors in the judicial system. While Prime Minister Erdoğan hailed the outcome as a "turning point" for Turkish democracy, the CHP opposition declared it a civilian coup d'état.

The final point of friction between the AKP and its opponents has concerned the Kurdish issue. In its first term, over the objections of the CHP, the AKP-controlled legislature passed limited cultural rights for broadcast and education in the Kurdish language. Moderate Kurds who supported joining the EU in hopes of further improvements in cultural and human rights responded positively to the AKP's promises to deliver EU membership and continued democratic reforms. In the 2007 election the Kurdish vote for the AKP doubled from 26 percent in 2002 to 53 percent, far outstripping Kurdish support for the pro-Kurdish Democratic Society Party (DPT).

The AKP has struggled with satisfying the interests of both Kurds and Turkish nationalists. On the one hand, it does not object to strengthening Kurdish identity, which it believes falls under the rubric of cultural rights. On the other hand, it does not wish to run afoul of nationalist sentiments among the public (or within its own ranks) by appearing to make concessions to Kurdish separatists led by the Kurdistan Workers Party (PKK), who have waged a separatist insurgency against the Turkish state in the southeastern part of the country since 1984.

A hot-button issue for nationalists in the 2007 election was PKK attacks on Turkish targets from secret bases in semiautonomous Iraqi Kurdistan. The ultranationalist MHP, which ran campaign ads that featured mothers sobbing at funerals for their sons who had died fighting the PKK, won seventy-one seats to become the third party represented in parliament. Having won much of the Kurdish vote, the AKP seemed to think that it could contain Kurdish demands. However, after it lost votes to the pro-Kurdish Democratic Society Party in spring 2009 local elections, the AKP decided to launch a vaguely defined "Kurdish Opening" to address Kurdish minority rights. The initiative fizzled out quickly, and since then the AKP has adopted a more nationalist discourse and supported a crackdown on Kurds who stand outside the AKP umbrella. Late in 2009 the court closed the Democratic Society Party and nationalist prosecutors initiated mass arrests of pro-Kurdish political activists on charges of supporting the KCK (Union of Kurdistan Communities), which the AKP regards as the PKK's urban and political wing.

KCK arrests and indictments continued with an uptick after the 2011 parliamentary elections, in which the AKP gained seats at the expense of the ultranationalist MHP. Over 3,000 people have been detained as part of the anti-KCK operations, including members of the new pro-Kurdish party, the Peace and Democracy Party (BDP), who were elected to parliament, as well as journalists and academics who write on the Kurdish issue. The AKP's pandering to nationalist sentiments was not sufficient to win it the supermajority it desired in order for it to unilaterally write a new constitution. With the AKP and BDP as antagonists, it is apparent that a new constitution can be drafted and passed only if the AKP and MHP pool their votes. The one issue that divides them is adopting a presidential system, which the MHP opposes. There is no doubt that the Kurdish issue could be resolved in the context of a new constitution, but what is unclear is whether Erdoğan will opt for a deepening of democracy or for writing a constitution that will consolidate his grip on power.

Civil Society

During the period of single-party rule (1923–1950) voluntary associations in Turkey remained under strict state control due to the Kemalist elite's mistrust of the unenlightened masses (who could potentially resist the modernization project). Not until the 1960s did civil society organizations proliferate, nudged by the 1961 constitution's guarantee of the right to free speech and association. The next two decades, however, were ones of escalating instability as trade unions, professional organizations, and student associations became polarized and split into right- and left-wing camps.

Whereas the 1960 coup was carried out to protect civil society from state repression, the motivation behind the 1980 coup was to ensure the authority of the state against civil society. To this end, the 1982 constitution, drafted under the watchful eye of the military, was designed to reduce citizen participation in politics by circumscribing the exercise of individual and associational rights in the interest of safeguarding the "integrity of the state" and the "public interest."

Despite the closure of over 20,000 nongovernmental organizations (NGOs) by the military government and legal restrictions intended to hamper the revival of civil society, the number of NGOs skyrocketed to over 60,000 by the mid-1990s and continued to climb to over 88,000 by 2011. Nevertheless, associational activity in Turkey tends to be formally structured rather than taking the form of ad hoc civil initiatives, and individual participation in NGOs is small (only about 10 percent of the population participate). The vast majority of NGOs are found in urban areas, with one-third of all NGOs located in Turkey's three largest cities: Istanbul, Ankara, and Izmir. The most visible and well-known NGOs are concerned with human rights, women's and children's rights, and environmental protection.

Turkish civil society is also populated by profession-based organizations, the largest of which represent architects, engineers, physicians, lawyers, and writers. Organized labor, which is a politically weak actor, is represented by three trade union confederations in the private sector: the center-right Confederation of Turkish Trade Unions (Turk-İş), the pro-Islamist Confederation of Justice Seekers' Trade Unions (Hak-İş), and the center-left Confederation of Progressive Trade Unions (DISK). There are three umbrella organizations that represent public sector workers: the Confederation of Public Employees' Unions (KESK), which has ties to the Kurdish BDP, Memur-Sen (closely linked to the AKP), and Kamu-Sen (linked to the MHP). The 1982 constitution prohibited strikes and collective bargaining, enabling successive governments to successfully prevent wage increases and resulting in an overall decline in real wages. Business associations, on the other hand, have had an active voice in politics and are highly visible in the media. The key business groups are the Turkish Industrialists' and Businessmen's Association (TUSIAD), which represents the interests of older Istanbul-based big businesses; the Independent Industrialists' and Businessmen's Association (MUSIAD), which advocates for small and medium-sized, pro-Islamist Anatolian companies; and the Young Businessmen's Association of Turkey (TUGIAD), which is made up of young, pro-EU entrepreneurs. In terms of membership size, the largest business association is the Union of Chambers (TOBB), which has a quasi-official relationship with the state—functioning as both a public institution and a pressure group.

Most civil society groups are involved in sports, educational, and service-related activities, and there has been a significant proliferation of Islamic charitable foundations that assist the poor and needy, often working closely with AKP-controlled municipalities. There are three prominent human rights organizations, but due to different political agendas their collaboration is limited. Mazlumder (Solidarity for Oppressed Peoples) takes an interest in acts of repression against Islamists, while the Human Rights Foundation of Turkey (THIV) helps victims of torture, and the Human Rights Association (IDH) is most concerned with the treatment of Kurds.

The EU integration process has had a major impact on strengthening pro-democracy civil society organizations. The EU Commission's Civil Society Development Program has provided funding opportunities and training programs to local NGOs, and legislative reforms to harmonize Turkish laws with the EU have reduced legal restrictions on associations. The AKP government has expressed its willingness to work constructively with civil society, although it has often been criticized for selectively choosing like-minded

NGOs as partners. One noteworthy exception to this inclination was the government's collaboration with women's rights NGOs to revise the penal code to combat domestic violence against women.

A pluralistic civil society has materialized in Turkey, but it should be remembered that the state has not found it easy to let go of its habit of controlling civil society, nor should it be assumed that all civil society organizations consider the ideology of Kemalism an obstacle to democracy.

Political Economy

At the time the republic was established, the Turkish economy was overwhelmingly agriculture-based and the majority of the population lived in rural areas. A shortage of entrepreneurs, skilled labor, and capital hampered the republican elite's aspiration to achieve industrial self-sufficiency. The Great Depression dramatically disrupted economic life and led to the state assuming responsibility for developing the national economy by adopting an economic policy known as étatism *(devletcilik),* in which the state assumed a directly interventionist role with rapid industrial development as its goal. From the 1930s until 1980, the state pursued import substitution industrialization (ISI) by means of establishing state-owned economic enterprises and implementing five-year development plans.

Under ISI, Turkey achieved rapid economic growth and a substantial improvement in living standards. From 1960 to 1977, Turkey's average annual rate of growth was 7 percent, a figure much higher than that for most developing countries. Trade and exchange rate policies protected industrialists, yielding high profits. Wage-earning groups (workers and public sector employees) experienced steady increases in real wages, and programs of agricultural input subsidies and output price supports benefited larger farmers. However, the oil crises of the middle and late 1970s destabilized the economy. A large inflow of worker remittances, mainly from Germany, helped initially, but the rising costs of imports precipitated balance-of-payment difficulties. Turkey resorted to foreign borrowing but by the end of the decade faced a mountain of debt that it could not repay. In January 1980, with no foreign currency reserves remaining, the Turkish government had no choice but to abandon its ISI-based national-developmentalist strategy and agree to an IMF stabilization program that opened the Turkish economy to international markets.

The military regime (1980–1983) backed the shift from ISI to a strategy of export-led growth accompanied by free market reforms. Under the semi-authoritarian rule that followed the 1980 coup, Turkey worked closely with the IMF and World Bank to break free of the country's statist, inward-oriented development strategy and shift to export-oriented manufacturing.

Neoliberal economic policies of trade and financial liberalization, privatization, and deregulation were introduced, along with the expectation that the private sector would replace the state as the main engine of economic growth. The post-1980 development strategy of promoting manufactured exports initiated the Turkish economy's exposure to globalization, firmly integrating it into the world economy.

With the return to competitive politics in 1983, however, politicians went on a populist spending binge that triggered fiscal imbalances. They spent recklessly particularly at election time to woo voters. Throughout the 1980s and 1990s, debt-financed growth proved to be unsustainable, and a majority of the population experienced a decline in purchasing power while inflation and deficits spiraled upward. In 2001, what began as a financial crisis escalated into an economic meltdown in which the Turkish currency (the lira) plummeted in value, causing millions of Turks to lose their life savings. Seventy-five percent of the population saw their incomes halved.

Voters took revenge on the incumbent parties for double-digit inflation and uncontrolled government corruption. None of the parties from the 1999–2002 coalition government was reelected to parliament in the 2002 election. The IMF offered a bailout, conditional on the acceptance of a sweeping structural reform program, and in 2002 the AKP took over responsibility for its implementation. It placed a tight rein on public spending, boosting international confidence in the economy; accelerated a program of privatization, drawing in significant amounts of foreign investment; and dramatically lowered inflation. It also launched banking, taxation, and social security reforms.

From 2002 to 2007, the economy made a remarkable recovery, achieving an average growth rate of nearly 7 percent while inflation plummeted from its double-digit highs to single digits. The AKP's restoration of economic stability and promise of longer-term prosperity go a long way toward explaining its electoral successes in 2007 and 2011. Although the 2009–2010 global financial crisis did slow Turkish growth, Erdoğan's 2011 election campaign focused on his government's economic achievements (like tripling per capita income) and on its ambitions for the country to become one of the top ten economies by 2023, the 100th anniversary of the republic.

Economic liberalization created a more competitive economy, but the effects of economic adjustment have not been felt evenly. Privatization resulted in lost earnings for laid-off workers as well as for the reemployed, many of whom found work in lower-paying jobs. Flexible employment and subcontracting jobs pay lower wages and have fewer worker protections. The number of people working in agriculture tumbled with the dismantling of agricultural subsidies and price supports. The most economically disadvantaged have been women, as well as those living in rural areas and urban shantytowns. The benefits of economic growth have been lopsided, with 16 percent of the population living below the poverty line in 2011, 40 percent of 15–24 year olds looking for work, and the wealth gap widening. Still the AKP has thus far successfully capitalized on its strong macroeconomic performance and dangles the carrot of longer-term prosperity, vowing that boosting job creation and remedying income inequality are among its top priorities.

The economically liberal, export-oriented growth model pursued since 1980 also has another face. It gave birth to a new urban middle class and Islamist business elite, many of whose members moved from provincial towns to cities while retaining their religious values and conservative lifestyles. Whereas many big industrialists found it difficult to adapt to unprotected, competitive export markets, small and medium-sized enterprises sprang up throughout Anatolia and played a significant role in the export boom. The owners of these firms, referred to as the "Anatolian tigers," formed their own Islamic business community. Economic growth and privatization led to the proliferation of media outlets and alternative information sources catering to a religiously pious audience. Cultural interactions, economic networks, and private schools furthered the construction of an Islamic consciousness. As new economic spaces opened up, opportunities for the articulation of an Islamic identity were unleashed, and political Islam gained an important constituency. The AKP has presided over the expansion of this emergent nouveau riche class while at the same time drawing much of its support from the pious poor. As yet the AKP has not experienced any political backlash from the latter group, which identifies with its conservative values.

Identity and Politics

Since the republic's founding, the Kemalist establishment has regarded Turkey's minorities with profound mistrust and suspicion and thus has adopted a restrictive definition of who is a minority. All three of Turkey's official minorities are non-Muslim and collectively they constitute less than 1 percent of the population: Greek (Rum) Orthodox Christians (5,000), Jews (26,000), and Armenian Orthodox Christians (100,000). These non-Muslim groups were guaranteed minority status under the terms of the Treaty of Lausanne (1923), whereas the country's two largest minority groups, ethnic Kurds and Alevi Muslims, have been granted no special recognition despite the fact that Kurds make up close to 20 percent of the population and Alevis around 15 percent (10–30 percent of Kurds are Alevi; the rest are Sunni Muslim). A plethora of other ethnic, linguistic, and religious minorities also remain unrecognized by the state, including Roma (Gypsies), Laz from the Black Sea region, and Arabs.

Part of the contemporary debate over Turkish identity is connected to the Armenian genocide issue, which raises troubling questions of history, memory, guilt, and responsibility. Official Turkish historiography admits that large numbers of Armenians died in 1915 but insists that their forced deportation was not planned but rather that there were hundreds upon thousands of deaths from disease during World War I, as well as from mutual killings between Turks and Armenians. The nationalist taboo on reexamining the past kicked in when Turkish and international scholars organized a conference in 2005 to discuss the Armenian issue. Kemalists as well as the AKP justice minister accused the organizers of treason and attempted to block the conference, although it was eventually held.

The AKP has made some progress in making good on its assurances to the EU that it will respect the freedoms of religious minorities. In early 2008 the Turkish parliament signed a law to return to Christian and Jewish minority foundations certain properties (e.g., churches, school buildings) that were confiscated by the state more than three decades ago. However, external pressures, such as efforts by legislatures in Europe and the United States to pass bills regarding the Armenian genocide, have nourished the paranoid fears of Turkish ultranationalists who believe that minorities and their foreign backers are plotting and collaborating to partition the country.

Consequently non-Muslim minorities have increasingly become targets of political violence, hate crimes, and hate speech. In 2007 Hrant Dink, the widely admired Turkish-Armenian human rights activist and editor of a weekly Armenian newspaper, was gunned down in front of his office in Istanbul by a teenager reportedly acting on orders of militant ultranationalists. In addition there has been a spate of church stonings and synagogue bombings as well as the murder of several Christian missionaries and a Catholic priest. Popular culture is permeated with virulent expressions of Turkish nationalism evidenced by bestsellers, TV series, and box office blockbusters that defame and vilify Armenians, Christians, and Jews.

The Alevis, an offshoot of Shi'i Islam, are the country's largest religious minority. They have criticized the AKP for catering to the interests of pious Sunni Muslims, such as by lifting the head scarf ban. The AKP government initiated an "Alevi Opening" in 2007 to improve relations with the Alevi community. Outreach steps included symbolic gestures of national reconciliation, like attendance at Alevi *iftar* breakfasts (to break the fast during Ramadan), speeches of unity, and sponsorship of an Alevi workshop series. In 2011 Erdoğan issued an apology on behalf of the Turkish state for a 1937 massacre in the predominantly Alevi region of Dersim. Nonetheless, moves toward more meaningful change have not been forthcoming: no compensation accompanied the apology, a promise to elevate Alevi *cemevis* (houses of worship) to the status of mosques (which receive state subsidies) remains unfulfilled, and Alevi demands that the government abolish compulsory religious courses from schools' curricula have gone ignored.

On the other hand the Alevi community, which comprises nearly 300 organizations, is far from unified. Some Alevis favor representation in the

Directorate of Religious Affairs, whereas others oppose this for fear that assimilation into official structures will deprive them of a separate identity. Yet others who are pro-secular and anti-statist desire a complete dismantling of the state religious authority. More recently the prospect of a prolonged conflict in Syria between Alawites and Sunnis has raised concerns that sectarian violence could spill over into Turkey. (Syrian Alawites—like Turkish Alevis—are Shi'a, although their respective histories and religious rituals differ).

Since the republic's founding, a separate Kurdish identity was suppressed and swallowed whole by Turkish nationalism. Kemalists developed an idiosyncratic notion of Turkish nationalism that served their nation-building goals. They denied the existence of Kurds as an ethnic group, forbade the Kurdish language, and insisted that every citizen be considered a Turk. Citizenship was extended to everyone living within the borders of the republic, but "Turkishness" was the only acceptable ethnic category. This meant that although the Kurds constituted an ethnic minority, they were not recognized as such, and the use of the Kurdish language, dress, and names was outlawed. Over the years many Kurds came to hold important and high-level positions in the economy, military, and government so long as they assimilated into the mandated Turkish identity. Oppression in the wake of the 1980 coup played a key role in strengthening Kurdish identity and motivated the Kurdish separatist party, the PKK, to launch a guerrilla offensive against the Turkish state that has dragged on for nearly thirty years.

The Kurdish problem is the most urgent issue facing the AKP government at home, and it is one of the major stumbling blocks on the road to EU membership. Early in 2009, Erdoğan announced a "Kurdish Opening" in which he promised to seek a nonmilitary solution. This was followed up by an amnesty offer to PKK militants and modest cultural improvements (authorizing a state-run twenty-four-hour Kurdish language television station and legalizing elective Kurdish language courses in school). The initiative died later that year when, as reported by the media, PKK fighters returning home from their bases in northern Iraq were welcomed at the border-crossing with victory celebrations. Not long after this the government arrested more than 1,000 Kurdish politicians, lawyers, and civil society activists for their alleged support of the PKK. As mentioned earlier, these arrests blossomed into the KCK trials. In addition, the Constitutional Court banned the pro-Kurdish DPT party, although it was immediately replaced by the BDP.

Instead of working with democratically elected Kurdish officials to develop a credible response to Kurdish requests for broader political and cultural rights, the AKP government opted to criminalize Kurdish activists. Kurdish demands include recognition and protection of a Kurdish identity; making Kurdish an official language; free use of Kurdish in daily life, education, and the courtroom; plus a political arrangement termed "democratic autonomy"—which to Kurds means more decentralized governance and to most Turks spells an independent Kurdistan. The BDP has been accused of being the political arm of the PKK, and although it denies the connection and rejects the PKK's use of violence, both share similar goals, like political decentralization. The possibility of a separate Kurdistan elevates the Kurdish issue into a national security concern. As noted in Chapter 7, 30 million ethnic Kurds are geographically concentrated in a wide region where the borders of Syria, Turkey, Iran, and Iraq meet. The aftermath of the Gulf War enabled the establishment of a semiautonomous Kurdish region in northern Iraq, and the civil war in Syria has led many Syrian Kurds to envision an autonomous region in Syria. Turkey fears a contagion effect whereby a sovereign Kurdistan would be formed by Turkish, Iraqi, and Syrian Kurds. A majority of Turkish Kurds believe that Turkey's EU accession is their best hope for a future that guarantees democratic rights, ensures civil liberties, and protects minority rights; however, due to Erdoğan's authoritarian style of rule, this hope is fading.

Gender and Politics

Women's emancipation was a strategic component of Atatürk's intention to Westernize the country; however, women were treated as vehicles of modernization and not considered partners. To this day gender inequality remains remarkably high. According to the World Economic Forum's "Global Gender Gap Index" (2012), Turkey was one of the worst performers, ranking 124th out of 135 countries. Referred to as "Kemalist feminists," Turkey's first generation of "emancipated" women put service to the nation ahead of women's issues, and even after the one-party regime ended, women's activism did not extend to the formation of an explicit women's rights movement. In the 1980s, a younger generation of educated, middle-class, professional women who had benefited from the opportunities afforded to their mothers by the Kemalist reforms emerged to criticize Kemalist feminists. The previous generation believed that it was important to concentrate on improvements in public health and education for women and to combat women's illiteracy to rectify gender inequality in the public realm. The new generation of women activists argued that the Kemalist revolution had failed to address issues in the domestic sphere, and that individual rights had been suppressed after the 1980 military intervention. Whereas the former, who were attached to the Kemalist unitary state model, placed importance on the communal goal of constructing a secularized, modernized nation, the latter called for respect for individualism and individual rights and argued that women needed to speak for themselves as opposed to the state defining women's interests.

Women's rights advocates today, while drawn principally from the educated middle and upper classes, are not a unified bloc. Broadly speaking, there are three different groups of feminists whose demands are at times overlapping. Radical pro-secular feminists and Islamist feminists both stress the need for democratic reforms to protect individual rights, and both condemn the post-1980 efforts by the state to rein in and control civil society. However, they have different agendas. Radical pro-secular feminists focus on issues of domestic violence and sexual harassment and aspire to dismantle the patriarchal structure that dominates the private sphere. Islamist feminists want the state to respect religious identity as an individual right and allow them to express their religious beliefs in the public sphere.

Kemalist feminists comprise the third group. They believe that secularism should be defended because it has enabled women to gain equality with men in the public realm. They regard the state as the protector of women's rights and modernity, and consider Islam to be anti-modern and oppressive of women. They stand opposite from radical pro-secular feminists who are anti-statist and who support Islamic feminists' demand for greater religious freedom, believing that the state should not dictate personal choice.

Women's participation in politics climbed in the 1960s and 1970s as political parties established women's branches. A woman, Tansu Çiller, was prime minister from 1993 to 1995, but while symbolically significant, this did not help rectify women's unequal access to positions of political power. Even though the proportion of women in parliament jumped from 9.1 percent in 2007 to 14.2 percent in 2011—up from a fairly constant average of 4 percent in previous decades—women continue to be placed on the bottom of party lists, reducing their prospects of making it into parliament. Despite assurances made by Erdoğan, in 2011 the AKP ran only seventy-eight female candidates for parliament, who made up 14 percent of its candidate list. Of its twenty-six cabinet ministers there is one female, the minister of family and social policy, and out of eighty-one governors only one is a woman. At the local level, there are even fewer women in public office. Less than 1 percent of mayors are women and barely 1 percent of local municipal councils include women. Ironically, women have been active campaigners in elections. The Welfare Party's women activists were especially noted for their skill in getting out the vote. But there are still few women in positions of political authority.

The Impact of International Politics

The post–September 11 global war on terrorism strengthened the tilt toward the securitization of politics that had been under way since the Turkish military's 1997 "postmodern coup," which cracked down on Islamists and

Kurdish separatists. The republic's counterterrorism activities had been overwhelmingly concentrated on the PKK until, in 2003, suicide bombers targeted two Jewish synagogues, the British consulate, and a major foreign bank in Istanbul. The perpetrators were identified as homegrown terrorists with links to al-Qaeda. Over the years, many young Turkish men had joined Islamic jihadist fighters in Bosnia, Chechnya, Afghanistan, and Iraq, developing close ties with al-Qaeda operatives.

Since 2003 Turkish police have arrested a number of local militants with al-Qaeda connections and foiled one cell's plot to attack the US Embassy in Ankara in 2011. Local al-Qaeda operatives consider Turkey deserving of jihadist attacks because of its close ties to the United States and its NATO membership (under the aegis of which Ankara contributed troops to fight al-Qaeda in Afghanistan). However the civil war in Syria has introduced foreign jihadist fighters into the mix. Hard-line Islamic jihadist militants from Libya, Chechnya, and Afghanistan, many of whom have ties or affiliations with al-Qaeda, have infiltrated across Turkey's 556-mile border into northern Syria to join the civil war.

Damascus's support for the PKK led Turkey and Syria to the brink of war in the late 1990s, after which Syria's backing of the PKK ended. However, as fighting between the Turkish military and the PKK escalated domestically in 2011 and 2012, Turkish officials blamed the situation on Syria. They speculate that the Syrian regime has renewed its support for the PKK and are alarmed at the prospect of links between the PKK and the PKK's offshoot in Syria, the Democratic Union of Kurdistan Party (PYD). Others counter that the PKK has simply taken advantage of the instability in Syria to escalate its operations in Turkey. In either case, Ankara also fears that the uprising against Bashar al-Asad could present an opportunity for Syrian Kurds, like their ethnic kin in Iraq, to establish an autonomous region, which would add fuel to separatist demands within Turkey's own borders. Turkish foreign minister Ahmet Davutoğlu has emphatically stated that Turkey will not allow terrorist organizations like the PKK or al-Qaeda to establish a presence near the Turkish-Syrian border, making it clear that tensions will not ameliorate so long as the Syria crisis continues.

In the EU's 2012 annual report card on its membership readiness, Turkey was sternly rebuked for its lack of progress on meeting the political criteria for accession. The report cited "recurring infringements" of individual civil liberties (e.g., freedom of speech and assembly), due process, and restrictions on the media; it also reprimanded Turkey for failing to settle the Cyprus problem and find a political solution for the Kurdish issue. Since accession negotiations began in 2005, the EU reform process has slowed and membership no longer appears to be a foreign or domestic policy priority of the AKP. While the AKP government has made progress in democratizing Turkey's government institutions and bringing the military under civilian control, there is still much left to do—including ending censorship, reforming the judiciary to ensure due process and end improper detention practices, and revising the penal code and the 2006 antiterrorism law such that they no longer can be used to restrict freedom of expression. Whether such reforms will be forthcoming without external political pressure is an open question.

Lastly, the Arab Spring has produced problems for Turkish domestic politics, most notably Turkey's claim to be a model for Middle East and North Africa (MENA) countries in terms of democratization. Prior to the Arab revolts, Turkish foreign policy in the MENA area relied on deepening economic relations to states regardless of their authoritarian character, and close economic ties were forged with Libya, Saudi Arabia, and Syria in particular. When the revolutionary wave of demonstrations swept across the Arab world, Turkey began to articulate support for the pro-democracy protesters, hoping that an investment-friendly climate of political stability would ensue if gradual reforms were adopted. Democracy, however, took a backseat to Turkey's economic interests.

With no substantial investments in Tunisia or Egypt, Turkey quickly endorsed regime change in those countries. However, when Saudi troops rolled in after weeks of protests in Bahrain, the Turkish government stayed loyal to its Saudi trading partner and kept quiet. The situation in Libya presented higher stakes. As Egyptian-inspired unrest spread to Libya, Turkey's $15 billion in construction projects and $2.4 billion in bilateral trade (in Turkey's favor) were at stake. Erdoğan first urged Muammar Qaddafi to make concessions to opposition demands and later urged him to step down. During the early period of unrest he raised strong objections to NATO intervention and opposed the imposition of sanctions on Libya. Once it became clear that Qaddafi would fall, Erdoğan reversed his position and supported NATO intervention.

Syria has been the most problematic of all for Turkey. Since 2002 rapprochement between Syria and Turkey had become a major pillar of Turkey's "good neighbor" foreign policy. By 2011 investment by Turkish firms had reached $260 million and bilateral trade had climbed to $2.5 billion, making Turkey Syria's top trade partner and its largest investor. Similar to Libya, Turkey called first for mediation between regime and opposition, then for reforms—before abandoning ship and calling for al-Asad to step aside. Not only has Turkey been hurt by the loss of revenues, but it is also burdened with a massive refugee flow across its border that has cost the government over $600 million in humanitarian aid—more than the amount spent by the EU states combined. By mid-October 2012, the number of Syrian refugees fleeing the civil war surpassed Turkey's "psychological limit" of 100,000, and by early February 2013 that number had climbed to 180,000.

The Arab Spring has placed a critical burden on Turkey's shoulders in that it needs to live up to its image as an inspiring model of a successful democracy in the region. Yet, Turkish democracy remains unconsolidated due to the illiberal 1982 constitution drawn up by the military rulers. Extensive amendments have been made since that time, but there is a solid consensus in Turkey that a new civilian-made constitution must be written. The four political parties represented in parliament after the 2011 elections (the AKP, CHP, MHP, and the BDP members of parliament, who vote as a bloc with other Independents) agreed to form an all-party Constitutional Conciliation Committee to prepare a draft, which was expected to be completed by the end of 2012. However, the process stalled amid objections from the opposition parties, which accused the AKP of trying to rewrite the constitution unilaterally. A major sticking point is Erdoğan's preference for a strong presidential system. Since he intends to run for the presidency in 2014, the opposition feared that replacing the existing system would grant him too much power. The AKP does not have the two-thirds vote in parliament to push a new constitution through alone. Consequently, any new draft constitution likely would have to be put to a referendum. But even if a majority vote were to approve, which given Erdoğan's popularity appears likely, there would be questions about the democratic credentials of a document that primarily reflects the priorities of the ruling AKP. How Turkey will settle its struggle to balance the principles of majority rule and minority rights in a new constitution will determine whether it is a political model worthy of emulation.

Part 3

Conclusion

20

Trends and Prospects

Michele Penner Angrist

This text has covered a lot of ground. The introductory chapter presented an overview of the states of the Middle East and provided crucial historical context for contemporary political dynamics in the region. Part 1 described seven key dynamics and issues that animate politics and society in the Middle East (and indeed anywhere): government and opposition, the domestic impact of international politics, political economy, civil society, religion, identity, and gender. The case study chapters of Part 2 illustrated the ways in which each of these seven dynamics plays out with respect to twelve states of the region: Algeria, Egypt, Iran, Iraq, Israel, Jordan, Kuwait and the United Arab Emirates, Palestine, Saudi Arabia, Syria, and Turkey. The task of this concluding chapter is to reflect on this material and offer some thoughts as to what the future likely holds for the region.

The closing pages of Chapter 1 highlighted a series of key problems, dilemmas, and issues in Middle Eastern politics. The first concerned regime type. While the vast majority of political communities in the region were authoritarian for most of the postindependence period, the uprisings of the Arab Spring felled autocrats who once had seemed invulnerable, while demonstrating on the world stage the depths of citizens' grievances with the status quo. As Chapter 2 showed, the region still features more than its fair share of authoritarian politics, and yet several countries—Tunisia, Egypt, and Libya—have made important strides and joined Israel, Turkey, Lebanon, and Iraq on a journey toward a state of affairs wherein repeated competitive elections to determine who rules are the sole currency of politics. Meanwhile, citizens and politicians in Iran, Kuwait, Bahrain, Jordan, Morocco, and elsewhere have made it plain that they wish to travel this path as well.

The path is fraught with difficult obstacles, and countries can (and likely will) alternate between making forward progress and backtracking. Will Tunisia, Egypt, and Libya succeed in institutionalizing democratic governance? Can Lebanon and Iraq build on existing practices and improve guarantees of key political rights? Can Israel and Turkey preserve their systems? The answers to these questions will depend on a mix of environmental factors and leadership. Where the former is concerned, economic realities and the disposition of key external actors each could either boost or undermine these states' chances for success. Perhaps more important, however, will be party leaders' ability to build trust in one another (and one another's constituencies) and to compromise and find common ground with one another across a range of policy issues. Given the difficult experiences of many parties during earlier periods of dictatorship, and given secular-Islamist and other identity-related political divides, this is no small task. Meanwhile, Lebanon, Iraq, and Libya must also do something even more basic: build more capacious, politically neutral bureaucratic and police apparatuses that are perceived as serving the public as a whole rather than the interests of a specific constituency.

As for the region's remaining autocrats, they face a new political landscape in the wake of the Arab uprisings. Thus we should expect them to seek new tactics for retaining the reins of power to add to their traditional toolbox (i.e., rigging elections, directing patronage to key clients, arresting opponents, banning political parties, and using brute force against rivals when all else fails). Yet the post–Arab Spring terrain is not wholly discouraging for autocrats. On the one hand, they undoubtedly worry that the example of their peers' regimes crumbling, combined with the cross-border transmission of effective opposition strategies, has altered the playing field in favor of the opponents of authoritarian rule. On the other hand, two years out from the start of the Arab Spring, what has transpired in the countries most affected may give others pause regarding pushing the political boundaries. From the violent repression of protesters in Bahrain, to the fragmentation and deterioration of the security environment in Libya, to the rise of Salafi politics in Tunisia, to the ongoing disruption and uncertainty of Egyptian politics, to the horrific civil war in Syria—the Arab Spring has brought hope and exhilaration but also multiple thorny problems that in the long term might be a disincentive to the emergence of new mass protests.

In the meantime, dictators also have been learning across borders. Chapter 17 noted that when Saudi activists called for mass demonstrations in March 2011, the Saudi regime—having already witnessed two others fall—was more than ready with multiple effective interventions that stopped protests before they started. If protests caught Tunisia's president Zine el Abidine Ben Ali and Egypt's president Husni Mubarak by surprise, the Saudis (and others) were ready, and this constituted an advantage for the incumbents.

In addition, while opposition activists used Facebook, Twitter, and other social media to galvanize and organize protests during the uprisings, autocrats
in the region—and indeed globally—are becoming increasingly savvy about
using Internet technologies to shore up autocracy by tracking and deterring
dissent (Morozov 2012).

The second issue that was flagged in the introductory chapter is identity. Since the 1970s Islam has become an important—if not the dominant—element of political discourse in the Middle East. Oppositions first,
and then governments in reaction, appropriated the language and symbols
of the faith in order to frame their respective arguments and mobilize their
respective supporters. While this dynamic in its early phases entailed considerable violence—with Islamists and their government opponents both resorting to the use of force in places like Algeria, Egypt, and Syria—by the
late 1990s, oppositional Islamists had largely laid down their arms. As Chapter 6 noted, today the vast majority of oppositional Islamist movements are
moderate: they eschew violence, seek coalitions with other actors in the political spectrum, and confine themselves to working within their respective
political institutional environments for gradual change.

Chapter 7 demonstrated that the rise of politicized Islam as a major
vector of politics in the Middle East was probably not inevitable, nor is it
necessarily a permanent fixture of politics in the region. That chapter
teaches us that how citizens identify themselves in politically consequential
ways—in terms of not only faith but also language, lineage, and place—is
not a constant but rather a variable that must be explained through careful
analysis. In the 1950s and 1960s, politics in much of the Middle East was
quite secular in nature in the heyday of Arab nationalism as articulated by
Gamal Abdel Nasser and others. Pan-Arab unity, its proponents declared,
would strengthen Arab states and deliver prosperity, dignity, and victory in
the conflict with Israel. It was not until Arab nationalism was deemed to
have failed in all of these respects (the evidence was in by the conclusion of
the 1967 Six Day War) that a kind of collective regional soul-searching produced powerful Islamist leaders arguing convincingly to their followers that
"Islam is the solution."

Until peoples and societies in the Middle East determine that bringing
the ethics, values, and laws of Islam into the public sphere is *not* the solution—or not the only solution, anyway—Islamism will continue to be a
powerful dynamic in the region. There is little evidence that large groups of
political actors have reached such a conclusion. To the contrary, the success
of a number of regional Islamist movements either in obtaining some of
their political objectives (e.g., Hezbollah forcing an Israeli withdrawal from
southern Lebanon and Turkey's Justice and Development Party winning
three consecutive parliamentary elections) or in assisting large numbers of
citizens in the challenges they face in their daily lives (e.g., the substantial

charitable activities of groups such as Palestine's Hamas) no doubt sends the message that Islam still has quite a prominent role to play in politics. The impressive victories of Egypt's Muslim Brotherhood and Tunisia's En-Nahda parties in competitive elections in 2011 underscored the appeal and capacity of Islamist political parties.

However, in the wake of the Arab uprisings and as iconic Islamist parties transition from political repression to political responsibility at the helm of governments in Egypt and Tunisia—and perhaps elsewhere over time—the prospect emerges that Islamism may encounter harder times going forward. Assuming that Egypt's Muslim Brothers and Tunisia's En-Nahda do not solve their countries' many intractable policy problems and deliver on their promises in short order, the persuasiveness of the "Islam is the solution" assertion may fade over time. This has been the case in Iran in the decades that have passed since that nation's Islamic Revolution. Opposition activists in that setting now struggle to take political power *away* from clerics who are perceived by many as harming the nation as well as the faith. Much will depend on how newly empowered Arab Islamists comport themselves during what is in many respects a moment of truth for political Islamism in the region.

The third challenge facing states of the Middle East is that of generating prosperity that is broadly shared by their citizens. While casual observers often are under the impression that the region is a rich one, it is in fact bifurcated between those states that are rich as a result of oil and natural gas and those that aren't. In the latter category are countries like Egypt, Syria, and Jordan, which to varying degrees pursued state-led development schemes in the 1950s, 1960s, and 1970s that failed to yield diversified, productive, self-sustaining economies. The solution that the major international financial institutions have tended to offer countries in this situation is privatization and structural adjustment. Yet as Chapter 4 detailed, a political logic underpins deep state involvement in domestic economies, and authoritarian incumbents were reluctant to reform the political-economic status quo in substantial ways. Less state involvement in the economy means fewer opportunities to reward supporters or appease key constituencies with material perquisites. For this reason, economic liberalization and the prosperity it is supposed to generate generally have not proceeded in thoroughgoing fashion in the countries of the Middle East. Nor did these regimes invest sufficiently in education, infrastructure, communication, and technology in order to build and harness their human resources in productive ways.

Thus as the first decade of the twenty-first century drew to a close, economies across the region were facing ticking time bombs to the extent that, demographically, large portions of many Middle Eastern populations are under the age of twenty-five. This generation needs to be educated and employed if regimes are to avoid the political instability that can unfold when large numbers of young, unemployed citizens with profound material and political grievances conclude that they have little to lose from confronting their rulers. Tunisia's Mohamed Bouazizi symbolized this Achilles heel for dictators, and the political statement he made with his self-immolation attempt catalyzed a wave of instability that spread regionwide in 2010–2012. Three of the four presidents whose terms in office were ended by the Arab Spring—Tunisia's Ben Ali, Egypt's Mubarak, and Yemen's Ali Abdullah Salih—came from poorer Arab dictatorships with low per capita gross domestic products (GDPs) and comparatively little in the way of oil and natural gas wealth. Syria—where President Bashar al-Asad was fighting for his political life at the time of this writing—also fits this profile.

This is not to say that the Arab uprisings and their aftermaths were solely a function of poor economic performance. Libya has significant hydrocarbon reserves and its per capita GDP is more than double that of Tunisia and Syria, yet President Muammar Qaddafi still proved politically vulnerable. Algeria's per capita GDP was one-third less than Tunisia's, yet President Abdelaziz Bouteflika remains in power. The Jordanian and Moroccan monarchs preside over economies with worrisomely low per capita GDPs, yet they survived as well. Clearly, many noneconomic factors bore on the question of whether regimes withstood the Arab Spring. Still, economic grievances loomed large among the motivations of protesters. And the ability of post–Arab Spring regimes to improve citizens' economic fortunes no doubt will be pivotal to their survival.

In the richer Middle Eastern countries, oil and gas wealth does not exempt rulers from anxiety regarding their balance sheets. Those countries that possess significant such wealth relative to the size of their populations struggle with volatile world market prices for their commodity, for example. They also grapple with the question "What happens after oil?" and the imperative of economic diversification. From Dubai's odyssey in becoming a cosmopolitan regional trade and financial entrepôt, to Saudi Arabia's new "economic cities," to the sovereign wealth funds that Gulf governments utilize to ensure a steady revenue stream into state coffers for decades to come—these trends seem sure to remain a central reality in the oil-rich states, given growing global awareness of, consternation regarding, and activism around the link between the burning of fossil fuels and global climate change.

A fourth pivotal issue for Middle Eastern leaders and peoples is how to relate to the West, and particularly the United States. As Chapter 1 chronicled, the region has struggled with the superior economic, military, and political power of the West for centuries now—as the Ottoman Empire declined, as European imperialism became a reality, as the United Kingdom helped create the physical and political space into which Israel was born, and as, in the post–World War II era (and in a more pronounced way in the

post–Cold War era), US policies shaped global political and economic institutions. The fact of Western power is problematic for governments and peoples in the Middle East for myriad reasons. To name just a few: US policies
in the region (support for Israel, sanctions on and then war in Iraq, etc.)
generate substantial popular political hostility; the economic dependence of
poorer states that rely on international financial institutions (dominated by
the United States) for debt relief engenders resentment; and many in the region have a deep concern about the spread of Western culture and values on
the wings of globalization.

       Yet at the same time, many Middle Eastern governments are in a posi-
tion that requires productive diplomatic relations with the United States—
whether because US power helps guarantee their security (in the case of
Saudi Arabia and the smaller Gulf states), because access to US markets is
a cornerstone of economic policy (as in Jordan), because of the levels of bilateral aid the United States provides (as in Egypt), or because US pressure
on Israel will be critical to the creation of a Palestinian state if such an
eventuality is to happen in the foreseeable future (many in the Arab world
hope it will). And while many in the region dislike US foreign policy and
aspects of what they perceive as American culture (materialism, individualism, etc.), many also admire the dynamic political, economic, and educational institutions that operate in the West. Thus, for both peoples and governments in the Middle East, forces of both attraction and repulsion
condition a complicated relationship with the West.

       The fifth and final dynamic highlighted in the introductory chapter is
the impact of the first four—struggles over the right to participate in politics, economic realities, identity politics, and the region's relationship with
the West—on gender realities and dynamics. In terms of the region's pen-
chant for authoritarian politics, while dictators have the power to simply
decree (as many have) that women be placed in parliament, the cabinet, and
the like, authoritarian political arenas do not grant women (or men, as
Chapter 8 pointed out) the political space and freedom to organize as they
wish, for whatever types of policy changes they favor. Economic conditions
in the region constrain women's opportunities to join the workforce: in
wealthier societies, it is harder to make the argument that women "need" to
work; in societies undergoing economic crises or painful reforms that produce unemployment, as Chapter 8 noted, often it is women who are asked
to leave the workforce first, to preserve scarce jobs for male workers.
Meanwhile, the rise and popularity of politicized Islam tend to bring expectations that women will veil and that they will play a complementary role to
men (in the household primarily, as wife and mother). Many Middle Eastern women are supportive of such norms. For those who have a different vision, however, the strength of those norms is a significant political constraint. And to the extent that Islamists continue to play a key role in

governance in the aftermath of the Arab uprisings in places like Tunisia and Egypt, the prospect of legal changes consistent with Islamist preferences is newly concrete. Finally, the legacy of Western powers justifying their interventions in the region in terms of gender rights, combined with regional hostility toward contemporary Western policy and presence, means that those activists who choose to push for the sorts of rights and equalities women have struggled for in the West run the risk of being portrayed by their compatriots as "siding with the enemy." All of these realities will continue to shape the context in which women in the Middle East operate politically.

References

Aarts, Paul, and Gerd Nonneman, eds. 2005. *Saudi Arabia in the Balance: Political Economy, Society, and Foreign Affairs*. New York: New York University Press.

Ababsa, Myriam. 2005. "Privatisation in Syria: State Farms and the Case of the Euphrates Project." RSCAS Working Paper no. 1. Fiesole, Italy: European University Institute.

Abboud, Samer N., and Fred H. Lawson. 2012. "Antinomies of Economic Governance in Contemporary Syria." In Abbas Kadhim, ed., *Governance in the Middle East and North Africa* (London: Routledge), pp. 330–341.

al-Abd al-Hadi, Mubarak, Ibrahim al-Sa'idi, and Tariq al-'Aydan. 2009. "Al-Hall al-'aql Kalifatan Su'ud al-Muhammad al-Mansa" (The Least Costly Solution Is for al-Muhammad To Take the Stand). *Al-Qabas,* March 5, p. 1.

'Abd al-Jabbar, Faleh. 1994. "Why the Intifada Failed." In Fran Hazelton, ed., *Iraq Since the Gulf War* (London: Zed), pp. 97–117.

Abrahamian, Ervand. 1980. "The Guerrilla Movement in Iran, 1963–1977." *MERIP Reports* (March–April 1980): 3–15.

———. 1999. *Tortured Confessions: Prisons and Public Recantations in Modern Iran.* Berkeley: University of California Press.

———. 2008. *A History of Modern Iran.* Cambridge: Cambridge University Press.

———. 2009. "Why the Islamic Republic Has Survived." *Middle East Report,* no. 250 (Spring): 10–16.

Abu-Lughod, Lila. 2002. "Do Muslim Women Really Need Saving? Anthropological Reflections on Cultural Relativism and Its Others." *American Anthropologist* 104 (3): 783–790.

Abu Odeh, Adnan. 1999. *Jordanians, Palestinians, and the Hashimite Kingdom in the Middle East Peace Process.* Washington, DC: US Institute of Peace.

Aghrout, Ahmed. 2008. "Policy Reforms in Algeria: Genuine Change or Adjustments." In Yahia H. Zoubir and Haizam Amirah-Fernàndez, eds., *North Africa: Politics, Region, and the Limits of Transformation* (London: Routledge), pp. 31–52.

Ahmad, Mahmood. 2002. "Agricultural Policy Issues and Challenges in Iraq: Short- and Medium-Term Options." In Kamil A. Mahdi, ed., *Iraq's Economic Predicament* (Reading: Ithaca Press), pp. 169–200.

511

Ahmed, Leila. 1992. *Women and Gender in Islam: Historical Roots of a Modern Debate*. New Haven: Yale University Press.

Al-Ali, Nadje. 2000. *Secularism, Gender, and the State in the Middle East: The Egyptian Women's Movement*. Cambridge: Cambridge University Press.

——. 2005. "Reconstructing Gender: Iraqi Women Between Dictatorship, Wars, Sanctions, and Occupation." *Third World Quarterly* 26 (4–5): 739–758.

Al-Ali, Nadje, and Nicola Pratt. 2009. *What Kind of Liberation? Women and the Occupation of Iraq*. Berkeley: University of California Press.

Alissa, Sufyan. 2007. "The Political Economy of Reform in Egypt: Understanding the Role of Institutions." Carnegie Paper no. 5. Washington, DC: Carnegie Endowment for International Peace.

Alkadiri, Raad, and Chris Toensing. 2003. "The Iraqi Governing Council's Sectarian Hue." *Middle East Report Online*, August 20.

Almond, Gabriel A., and Sydney Verba. 1963. *The Civic Culture: Political Attitudes and Democracy in Five Nations*. Princeton: Princeton University Press.

Alnasrawi, Abbas. 1994. *The Economy of Iraq*. Westport: Greenwood.

——. 2001. "Iraq: Economic Sanctions and Consequences, 1990–2000." *Third World Quarterly* 22 (2): 205–218.

Amawi, Abla. 2000. "Gender and Citizenship in Jordan." In Suad Joseph, ed., *Gender and Citizenship in the Middle East* (Syracuse: Syracuse University Press), pp. 158–184.

al-Amiry, Kholoud Ramzi. 2012. "The Prime Minister Who Plays with Fire." *Sada*, April 19. http://www.carnegieendowment.org.

Anderson, Benedict R. 1991. *Imagined Communities: Reflections on the Origin and Spread of Nationalism*. New York: Verso.

Anderson, Lisa. 1995. "Democracy in the Arab World: A Critique of the Political Culture Approach." In Rex Brynen, Baghat Korany, and Paul Noble, eds., *Political Liberalization and Democratization in the Arab World*, vol. 1, *Theoretical Perspectives* (Boulder: Lynne Rienner), pp. 77–92.

——. 2001. "Arab Democracy: Dismal Prospects." *World Policy Journal* 18 (3): 53–60.

Ansari, Ali. 2006. *Iran, Islam, and Democracy: The Politics of Managing Change*. London: Chatham.

Anscombe, Frederick F. 1997. *The Ottoman Gulf: The Creation of Kuwait, Saudi Arabia, and Qatar*. New York: Columbia University Press.

Arabic Network for Human Rights Information (Cairo). 2009. "New Security Measures Against Internet Cafes." http://www.anhri.net/en/reports/2009.

Arat, Yeşim. 2005. *Rethinking Islam and Liberal Democracy: Islamist Women in Turkish Politics*. Albany: State University of New York Press.

Arjomand, Said Amir. 1988. *The Turban for the Crown*. New York: Oxford University Press.

Bank of Israel. 2012. *Main Israel Economic Data*. http://www.bankisrael.gov.il/dept data/mehkar/indic/eng_b04.htm.

Baram, Amatzia. 1981. "The June Elections to the National Assembly in Iraq: An Experiment in Controlled Democracy." *Orient* 22: 391–412.

——. 1997. "Neo-Tribalism in Iraq: Saddam Hussein's Tribal Policies, 1991–1996." *International Journal of Middle East Studies* 29 (1): 1–31.

Barnett, Michael N. 1992. *Confronting the Costs of War: Military Power, State, and Society in Egypt and Israel*. Princeton: Princeton University Press.

Barro, Robert J., and Jong-Wah Lee. 2000. "International Data on Educational Attainment: Updates and Implications." Working Paper no. 42. Cambridge: Harvard University, Center for International Development.

Batatu, Hanna. 1978. *The Old Social Classes and the Revolutionary Movements of Iraq.* Princeton: Princeton University Press.

Bates, Robert. 1983. "Modernization, Ethnic Competition, and the Rationality of Politics in Contemporary Africa." In D. Rothchild and V. A. Olunsorola, eds., *State Versus Ethnic Claims: African Policy Dilemmas* (Boulder: Westview), pp. 152–171.

Bayat, Asef. 2007. *Making Islam Democratic: Social Movements and the Post-Islamic Turn.* Stanford: Stanford University Press.

Bellin, Eva. 2004. "The Robustness of Authoritarianism in the Middle East." *Comparative Politics* 36 (2): 139–157.

Benhabib, Seyla. 1992. "Models of Public Space: Hannah Arendt, the Liberal Tradition, and Jürgen Habermas." In Craig Calhoun, ed., *Habermas and the Public Sphere* (Cambridge: MIT Press), pp. 73–98.

Berglas, Eitan. 1983. "Defense and the Economy: The Israeli Experience." Discussion Paper no. 83.01. Jerusalem: Maurice Falk Institute for Economic Research in Israel.

Bill, James A. 1988. *The Eagle and the Lion: The Tragedy of American-Iranian Relations.* New Haven: Yale University Press.

Bou Nacklie, Nacklie E. 1993. "Les Troupes Speciales: Religious and Ethnic Recruitment, 1916–1946." *International Journal of Middle East Studies* 25 (November): 646–660.

Brand, Laurie A. 1992. "Economic and Political Liberalization in a Rentier Economy: The Case of the Hashimite Kingdom of Jordan." In Iliya Harik and Denis J. Sullivan, eds., *Privatization and Liberalization in the Middle East* (Bloomington: Indiana University Press), pp. 167–188.

———. 1995. "'In the Beginning Was the State . . .': The Quest for Civil Society in Jordan." In Augustus Richard Norton, ed., *Civil Society in the Middle East,* vol. 1 (Leiden: Brill), pp. 148–185.

———. 1998. *Women, the State, and Political Liberalization: Middle Eastern and North African Experiences.* New York: Columbia University Press.

Brenner, Joyce Rosman. 2008. "Women's Issues in Israel." *Journal of Jewish Communal Service* 83 (2–3): 204–208.

Brookshaw, Dominic Parviz, and Seena B. Fazel, eds. 2008. *The Baha'is of Iran: Socio-Historical Studies.* London: Routledge.

Brown, Nathan. 2002. *Constitutions in a Nonconstitutional World: Arab Basic Laws and the Prospects for Accountable Governance.* Albany: SUNY Press.

Brumberg, Daniel. 2002. "The Trap of Liberalized Autocracy." *Journal of Democracy* 13 (4): 56–68.

Brynen, Rex. 1992. "Economic Crisis and Post-Rentier Democratization in the Arab World." *Canadian Journal of Political Science* 25 (1): 69–97.

Buskins, Leon. 2003. "Recent Debates on the Reform of Family Law in Morocco." *Journal of Islamic Law and Society* 10: 70–131.

Byman, Daniel L. 2011. "Israel: A Frosty Response to the Arab Spring." In Kenneth M. Pollack et al., eds., *The Arab Awakening: America and the Transformation of the Middle East* (Washington, DC: Brookings Institution Press), pp. 250–257.

Carapico, Sheila. 1998. *Civil Society in Yemen: The Political Economy of Activism in Modern Arabia.* Cambridge: Cambridge University Press.

Carver, Terrell. 1998. "A Political Theory of Gender: Perspectives on the 'Universal' Subject." In Vicky Randall and Georgina Waylen, eds., *Gender, Politics, and the State* (New York: Routledge), pp. 18–28.

CBS News, *60 Minutes.* 2007. "A Visit to Dubai Inc.: Steve Kroft Reports on a Success Story in the Middle East." Transcript of segment broadcast October 14,

2007, updated July 30, 2008. http://www.cbsnews.com/stories/2007/10/12/60
minutes/printable3361753.shtml.

Central Bureau of Statistics (Israel). 1976–1989, 2011. *Statistical Abstract of Israel.*
http://www1.cbs.gov.il/reader/shnatonenew_site.htm.

Chaudhry, Kiren Aziz. 1991. "On the Way to the Market: Economic Liberalization
and the Iraqi Invasion of Kuwait." *Middle East Report* 170: 14–23.

Chazan, Naomi. 2011. *Women in Public Life.* Jewish Virtual Library. http://jewish
virtuallibrary.org/jsource/Society_&_Culture/Women_in_public_life.html.

Chehabi, Houchang E. 1991. "Religion and Politics in Iran: How Theocratic Is the
Islamic Republic?" *Daedalus* 120 (Summer): 48–70.

———. 1997. "Ardabil Becomes a Province: Center-Periphery Relations in Iran."
International Journal of Middle East Studies 29 (2): 235–253.

Chehabi, Houchang E., and Arang Keshavarzian. 2011. "Politics in Iran." In Gabriel
A. Almond et al., eds., *Comparative Politics Today,* 10th ed. (New York: Pear-
son Longman), pp. 332–379.

CIA (Central Intelligence Agency). 2008, 2009, 2012. *World Factbook.* Washington,
DC. http://www.cia.gov.

Clark, Janine A. 2004. *Islam, Charity, and Activism: Middle-Class Networks and
Social Welfare in Egypt, Jordan, and Yemen.* Bloomington: Indiana University
Press.

Coalition Provisional Authority (Iraq). 2004. "Full Text of Zarqawi Letter." Press
release, February 12. http://www.cpairaq.org/transcripts/20040212_zarqawi
_full.html.

Cohen, Asher. 2004. "Changes in the Orthodox Camp and Their Influence on the
Deepening Religious-Secular Schism at the Outset of the Twenty-First Century." In Alan Dowty, ed., *Critical Issues in Israeli Society* (Westport: Praeger),
pp. 71–94.

Cole, Juan R. I., and Moojan Momen. 1986. "Mafia, Mob, and Shiism in Iraq: The
Rebellion of Ottoman Karbala, 1824–1843." *Past and Present,* no. 112 (August): 112–143.

Conge, Patrick, and Gwenn Okruhlik. 2009. "The Power of Narrative: Saudi Arabia,
the US, and the Search for Security." *British Journal of Middle Eastern Studies*
36 (3): 357–371.

Cordesman, Anthony H. 2006. *Arab-Israeli Military Forces in an Era of Asymmetric Wars.* Westport: Praeger Security International.

Crystal, Jill. 1995. *Oil and Politics in the Gulf.* Cambridge: Cambridge University
Press.

Dahl, Robert, A., ed. 1966. *Political Oppositions in Western Democracies.* New
Haven: Yale University Press.

Dahl, Robert, A. 1971. *Polyarchy, Participation, and Observation.* New Haven:
Yale University Press.

Darbouche, Hakim, and Yahia H. Zoubir. 2008. "The Algerian Crisis in European
and US Foreign Policies: A Hindsight Analysis." *Journal of North African
Studies* 14 (1): 33–55.

Davidson, Christopher M. 2007. "The Emirates of Abu Dhabi and Dubai: Contrasting Roles in the International System." *Asian Affairs* 38 (1): 33–48.

———. 2008. *Dubai: The Vulnerability of Success.* New York: Columbia University
Press.

Davis, Eric. 2005. *Memories of State: Politics, History, and Collective Memory in
Modern Iraq.* Berkeley: University of California Press.

Dawisha, Adeed. 2009. *Iraq: A Political History from Independence to Occupation.*
Princeton: Princeton University Press.

Dessi, Andrea. 2012. "Algeria: Cosmetic Change or Actual Reform?" *Actuelles de l'IFRI* (July 9, 2012). http://www.ifri.org/?page=detail-contribution&id=7242.

Dickey, Christopher. 2009. "The Monarch Who Declared His Own Revolution." *Newsweek*, March 30.

Dodge, Toby. 2012. "Iraq's Road Back to Dictatorship." *Survival* 54 (June–July): 147–168.

Dowty, Alan. 2001. *The Jewish State: A Century Later.* Berkeley: University of California Press.

Dris-Aït-Hamadouche, Louisa. 2008. "The 2007 Legislative Elections in Algeria." *Mediterranean Politics* 13 (1): 87–94.

Drysdale, Alasdair. 1979. "Ethnicity in the Syrian Officer Corps: A Conceptualisation." *Civilisations* 29: 359–373.

Dziadosz, Alexander. 2011. "Could Suez Be Egypt's Sidi Bouzid?" *Reuters,* January 27.

Earl of Cromer. 1908. *Modern Egypt.* Vol. 2. New York: Macmillan.

Economist Intelligence Unit. 2007, 2008. *Egypt Country Report.* London.

Egyptian State Information Service. 2008. "Al-Hala al-Ta'limiya li al-Mar'ah" (The Social Condition of Women). http://www.sis.gov.eg/Ar/Women/Society /Education/100303000000000001.htm.

Ehsani, Kaveh. 1995. "Islam, Modernity, and National Identity." *Middle East Insight* 11 (5): 48–53.

———. 2006. "Iran: The Populist Threat to Democracy." *Middle East Report,* no. 241 (Winter): 4–9.

———. 2009. "Survival Through Dispossession: Privatization of Public Goods in the Islamic Republic." *Middle East Report,* no. 250 (Spring): 26–33.

Ehsani, Kaveh, Arang Keshavarzian, and Norma Claire Moruzzi. 2009. "Tehran, June 2009." *Middle East Report Online,* June 28. http://www.merip.org/mero /mero062809.html.

Eickelman, Dale. 2002. *The Middle East and Central Asia: An Anthropological Approach.* 4th ed. Upper Saddle River, NJ: Prentice Hall.

Elmi, Zahra Mila. 2009. "Educational Attainment in Iran." In *The Iranian Revolution at 30* (Washington, DC: Middle East Institute), pp. 62–69.

Esman, Milton J., and Itamar Rabinovich, eds. 1988. *Ethnicity, Pluralism, and the State in the Middle East.* Ithaca: Cornell University Press.

European Union. 2008. "The Euro-Mediterranean Partnership." http://ec.europa.eu /external_relations/euromed/index_en.htm.

Fagen, Patricia Weiss. 2009. "Iraqi Refugees: Seeking Stability in Syria and Jordan." Occasional Paper no. 1. Washington, DC: Georgetown University, School of Foreign Service in Qatar, Center for International and Regional Studies.

Fandy, Mamoun. 2005. "Political Science Without Clothes: The Politics of Dress; or, Contesting the Spatiality of the State in Egypt." In Amira El-Azhary Sonbol, ed., *Beyond the Exotic: Women's Histories in Islamic Societies* (Syracuse: Syracuse University Press), pp. 381–398.

Farhi, Farideh. 2004. "The Antinomies of Iran's War Generation." In Lawrence G. Potter and Gary G. Sick, eds., *Iran, Iraq, and the Legacies of War* (New York: Palgrave Macmillan), pp. 101–120.

Faruqui, Fahad. 2010. "Saudi Youth Are Struggling with Their Identities." *The Guardian,* June 25.

Fathi, Schirin H. 1994. *Jordan: An Invented Nation? Tribe-State Dynamics and the Formation of National Identity.* Hamburg: Deutsches Orient-Institut.

Freedom House. 2012. "Freedom in the World: Israel." http://www.freedomhouse .org/country/israel.

Friedman, Thomas L. 1990. *From Beirut to Jerusalem.* New York: Anchor.

Gallup Polls. 2012. "Americans Continue to Tilt Pro-Israel." March 2. http://www
.gallup.com/poll/153092/americans-continue-tilt-pro-israel.aspx.

Gasiorowski, Mark, and Malcolm Byrne, eds. 2004. *Mohammed Mossadeq and the 1953 Coup in Iran*. Syracuse: Syracuse University Press.

Gause, F. Gregory, III. 1993. *Oil Monarchies: Domestic and Security Challenges in the Arab Gulf States*. New York: Council on Foreign Relations.

Gauthier, Julie. 2009. "The 2004 Events in Al-Qamishli: Has the Kurdish Question Erupted in Syria?" In Fred H. Lawson, ed., *Demystifying Syria* (London: Saqi).

Gellner, Ernest, and Charles A. Micaud. 1972. *Arabs and Berbers: From Tribe to Nation in North Africa*. Lexington, MA: Lexington Books.

Gelvin, James. 2008. *The Modern Middle East: A History*. New York: Oxford University Press.

Gerber, Haim. 1987. *The Social Origins of the Modern Middle East*. Boulder: Lynne Rienner.

Gerschenkron, Alexander. 1962. *Economic Backwardness in Historical Perspective: A Book of Essays*. Cambridge: Belknap.

Ghadbian, Najib. 2001. "The New Asad: Dynamics of Continuity and Change in Syria." *Middle East Journal* 55 (4): 624–641.

———. 2006. *Al-Dawlah al-Asadiyyah al-Thaniyyah*. Jiddah: Dar al-Rayya.

Ghaffari, Sonia. 2009. "Baluchistan's Rising Militancy." *Middle East Report*, no. 250 (Spring): 40–43.

Gitelman, Zvi. 2004. "The 'Russian Revolution' in Israel." In Alan Dowty, ed., *Critical Issues in Israeli Society* (Westport: Praeger), pp. 95–108.

Globes. 2012. "Likud Weakens, Labor Gains, Kadima Collapses." August 28. http://www.globes.co.il/serveen/globes/docview.asp?did=1000771357.

Golan, Esther. 1977. "Political Culture in Israel: A Case Study." Master's thesis, University of Haifa (in Hebrew).

Gole, Nilufer. 1996. *The Forbidden Modern: Civilization and Veiling*. Ann Arbor: University of Michigan Press.

Golia, Maria. 2007. "The Tiger on the Nile." *Middle East* 377 (April): 40–42.

Gordon, Raymond G., and Barbara F. Grimes, eds. 2005. *Ethnologue: Languages of the World*. 15th ed. Dallas: SIL International.

al-Haj, Majid. 2004. "The Status of Palestinians in Israel: A Double Periphery in an Ethno-National State." In Alan Dowty, ed., *Critical Issues in Israeli Society* (Westport: Praeger), pp. 109–126.

Halliday, Fred. 2005. *The Middle East in International Relations: Power, Politics, and Ideology*. Cambridge: Cambridge University Press.

Haniff, Nesha. 1991. "Western Feminism and Colonialism." Paper delivered at the Conference on Gender and Society in the Middle East, University of Michigan, September 21.

Harrigan, Jane R., and Hamed El-Said. 2009. *Aid and Power in the Arab World: World Bank and IMF Policy-Based Lending in the Middle East and North Africa*. New York: Palgrave Macmillan.

Harry S. Truman Research Institute for the Advancement of Peace. 2012. "Joint Israel-Palestinian Poll." Press release. June. http://truman.huji.ac.il/.upload/Joint%20press%20releaseJune%202012%20eng.pdf.

Hashim, Ahmed S. 2003. "Saddam Husayn and Civil-Military Relations in Iraq: The Quest for Legitimacy and Power." *Middle East Journal* 57 (1): 9–41.

———. 2006. *Insurgency and Counter-Insurgency in Iraq*. London: Hurst.

Hashimite Kingdom of Jordan. n.d. "The Hashimites." http://www.kinghussein.gov.jo/hashemites.html.

Hausmann, Ricardo, Laura D. Tyson, and Saadia Zahidi. 2006. *The Global Gender Gap Report*. Geneva: World Economic Forum.

Heard-Bey, Frauke. 1982. *From Trucial States to United Arab Emirates: A Society in Transition*. London: Longman.

Henry, Clement M., and Robert Springborg. 2001. *Globalization and the Politics of Development in the Middle East*. Cambridge: Cambridge University Press.

Herb, Michael. 1999. *All in the Family: Absolutism, Revolution, and Democracy in the Middle Eastern Monarchies*. Albany: SUNY Press.

———. 2009. "'A Nation of Bureaucrats': Political Participation and Economic Diversification in Kuwait and the United Arab Emirates." *International Journal of Middle East Studies* 41 (3): 375–395.

Heydemann, Steven. 2007. "Upgrading Authoritarianism in the Arab World." Saban Center Analysis Paper no. 13. Washington, DC: Brookings Institution.

Hinnebusch, Raymond. 1979. *Party and Peasant in Syria: Rural Politics and Social Change Under the Ba'th*. Cairo: American University in Cairo.

———. 2003. *The International Politics of the Middle East*. Manchester: Manchester University Press.

Hobbs, Joseph J. 2009. *World Regional Geography*. 6th ed. Belmont, CA: Brooks/Cole.

Hoodfar, Homa. 2009. "Activism Under the Radar: Volunteer Women Health Workers in Iran." *Middle East Report,* no. 250 (Spring): 56–60.

Hoodfar, Homa, and Shadi Sadr. 2009. "Can Women Act as Agents of a Democratization of Theocracy in Iran?" Final research report prepared for the project "Religion, Politics and Gender Equality." United Nations Research Institute for Social Development (UNRISD) and the Heinrich Böll Foundation. October, Geneva, Switzerland. http://www.awid.org/eng/layout/sct/print/Women-in-Action/New-Resources/A-New-Publication-UNRISD-Can-Women-Act-as-Agents-for-Democratization-of-Theocracy-in-Iran.

Hooglund, Eric. 2009. "Thirty Years of Islamic Revolution in Rural Iran." *Middle East Report,* no. 250 (Spring): 34–39.

Hopwood, Derek. 1991. *Egypt: Politics and Society, 1945–1990*. New York: Routledge.

Horne, Alistair. 2006. *A Savage War of Peace: Algeria 1954–1962*. 2nd ed. New York: New York Review Books Classics.

Human Rights Watch. 1991. *World Report 1990*. New York.

Husry, Khaldun S. 1974. "The Assyrian Affair of 1933." *International Journal of Middle East Studies* 5 (2–3): 161–176, 344–360.

IMF (International Monetary Fund). 2003. *World Economic Outlook*. Washington, DC.

International Institute for Strategic Studies. 2011. *Iran's Nuclear, Chemical and Biological Capabilities: A Net Assessment*. London: International Institute for Strategic Studies.

Ismael, Jacqueline S. 1980. "Social Policy and Social Change: The Case of Iraq." *Arab Studies Quarterly* 2: 235–248.

Issawi, Charles. 1982. *An Economic History of the Middle East*. New York: Columbia University Press.

al-Jawaheri, Yasmin Husein. 2008. *Women in Iraq*. London: Tauris.

Jones, Toby. 2006. "Rebellion on the Saudi Periphery: Modernity, Marginalization, and the Shi'a Uprising of 1979." *International Journal of Middle East Studies* 38 (2): 213–233.

———. 2012. "Embracing Crisis in the Gulf." *Middle East Report,* no. 264: 26–29.

Joseph, Suad. 1991. "Elite Strategies for State Building: Women, Family, Religion, and the State in Iraq and Lebanon." In Deniz Kandiyoti, ed., *Women, Islam, and the State* (Philadelphia: Temple University Press), pp. 176–200.

Kandil, Amany. 2006. *Al-Mujtamaʻ al-Madani wa al-Dawla fi Misr* (Civil Society and the State in Egypt). Cairo: Al-Mahrusah.

Kandiyoti, Deniz. 1991. "Islam and Patriarchy: A Comparative Perspective." In Nikkie R. Keddie and Beth Baron, eds., *Women in Middle Eastern History: Shifting Boundaries in Sex and Gender* (New Haven: Yale University Press), pp. 23–42.

Karam, Souhail. 2011. "Moroccans Protest Polls, Violence in the Capital." Reuters, October 23. http://www.reuters.com/article/2011/10/23/us-morocco-protests-id USTRE79M3ZU20111023.

Karawan, Ibrahim A. 1994. "Sadat and the Egyptian-Israeli Peace Revisited." *International Journal of Middle East Studies* 26 (2): 249–266.

Karl, Terry Lynn. 1997. *The Paradox of Plenty: Oil Booms and Petro-States.* Berkeley: University of California Press.

Karpat, Kemal. 1988. "The Ottoman Ethnic and Confessional Legacy in the Middle East." In Milton J. Esman and Itamar Rabinovich, eds., *Ethnicity, Pluralism, and the State in the Middle East* (Ithaca: Cornell University Press).

Kashani-Sabet, Firoozeh. 1999. *Frontier Fictions: Shaping the Iranian Nation, 1804–1946.* Princeton: Princeton University Press.

Kazemipur, Abdolmohammad, and Ali Rezaei. 2003. "Religious Life Under Theocracy: The Case of Iran." *Journal of the Scientific Study of Religion* 42 (September): 347–361.

Kerr, Malcolm H. 1971. *The Arab Cold War.* London: Oxford University Press.

Kerr, Malcolm H., and El Sayed Yassin, eds. 1982. *Rich and Poor States in the Middle East: Egypt and the New Arab Order.* Boulder: Westview.

Keshavarzian, Arang. 2005. "Contestation Without Democracy: Elite Fragmentation in Iran." In Marsha Pripstein Posusney and Michele Penner Angrist, eds., *Authoritarianism in the Middle East: Regimes and Resistance* (Boulder: Lynne Rienner), pp. 63–88.

———. 2007. *Bazaar and State in Iran: The Politics of the Tehran Marketplace.* Cambridge: Cambridge University Press.

al-Khafaji, Isam. 1994. "State Terror and the Degradation of Politics." In Fran Hazelton, ed., *Iraq Since the Gulf War* (London: Zed), pp. 20–31.

———. 2000. "War as a Vehicle for the Rise and Demise of a State-Controlled Society: The Case of Ba'thist Iraq." In Steven Heydemann, ed., *War, Institutions, and Social Change in the Middle East* (Berkeley: University of California Press), pp. 258–291.

Khalaf, Roula. 2012. "Saudi Whispers Turn into Online Roar." *Financial Times,* March 23.

Khalfan, Mohammed. 1997. "The Practicality of Having the Federal National Council of the United Arab Emirates Become an Elective Body." PhD diss., University of La Verne.

Khalidi, Rashid. 1997. *Palestinian Identity: The Construction of Modern National Consciousness.* New York: Columbia University Press.

al-Khalil, Samir. 1989. *Republic of Fear.* Berkeley: University of California Press.

al-Khudayri, Tariq. 2002. "Iraq's Manufacturing Industry: Status and Prospects for Rehabilitation and Reform." In Kamil A. Mahdi, ed., *Iraq's Economic Predicament* (Reading: Ithaca Press), pp. 201–232.

Kian-Thiébaut, Azadeh. 2002. "Women and the Making of Civil Society in Post-Islamist Iran." In Eric Hooglund, ed., *Twenty Years of Islamic Revolution* (Syracuse: Syracuse University Press), pp. 56–73.

Kienle, Eberhard. 1990. *Ba'th Versus Ba'th: The Conflict Between Syria and Iraq*. London: Tauris.

———. 1997. "Authoritarianism Liberalised: Syria and the Arab East After the Cold War." In William Hale and Eberhard Kienle, eds., *After the Cold War: Security and Democracy in Africa and Asia* (London: Tauris), pp. 194–226.

Kimmerling, Baruch. 1993. "Yes, Returning to the Family." *Politika* 48 (March): 40–45.

Kimmerling, Baruch, and Joel S. Migdal. 1993. *Palestinians: The Making of a People*. New York: Free Press.

Kirkpatrick, David. 2012. "Jordan Protesters Dream of Shift to King's Brother." *New York Times,* November 21. http://www.nytimes.com/2012/11/22/world /middleeast/jordan-protesters-dream-of-shift-to-prince-hamzah.html?page wanted=all&_r=0.

KOF Swiss Economic Institute. 2012. *Index of Globalization.* http://globalization .kof.ethz.ch/static/pdf/rankings_2112.pdf.

Kuran, Timur. 2004. "The Economic Ascent of the Middle East's Religious Minorities: The Role of Islamic Legal Pluralism." *Journal of Legal Studies* 33 (June): 475–515.

Kurzman, Charles. 2004. *The Unthinkable Revolution.* Cambridge: Harvard University Press.

———. 2008. "A Feminist Generation in Iran?" *Iranian Studies* 41 (June): 297–321.

Labdaoui, Abdellah. 2003. "Universality, Modernity, and Identity: The Case of Morocco." In Roel Meijer, ed., *Cosmopolitanism, Identity, and Authenticity in the Middle East* (London: Routledge Curzon), pp. 145–158.

Lacroix, Stephane. 2004. "Between Islamists and Liberals: Saudi Arabia's New 'Islamo-Liberal' Reformists." *Middle East Journal* 58 (3): 345–365.

———. 2011. *Awakening Islam: The Politics of Religious Dissent in Contemporary Saudi Arabia*. Trans. George Holoch. Cambridge: Harvard University Press.

Lawson, Fred H. 1988. "Political-Economic Trends in Ba'thi Syria: A Reinterpretation." *Orient* 29: 590–603.

———. 1992. "Economic Liberalization in Syria and Iraq During the 1980s: The Limits of Externalist Explanations." *New Political Science* 11: 185–205.

———. 1994. "Domestic Transformation and Foreign Steadfastness in Contemporary Syria." *Middle East Journal* 48 (1): 47–64.

———. 1996. *Why Syria Goes to War.* Ithaca: Cornell University Press.

———. 1997. "Private Capital and the State in Contemporary Syria." *Middle East Report,* no. 203 (Spring): 8–13, 30.

———. 2006. *Constructing International Relations in the Arab World.* Stanford: Stanford University Press.

———. 2010. "Liberal Champions of Pan-Arabism: Syria's Second Hizb al-Sha'b." In Christoph Schumann, ed., *Nationalism and Liberal Thought in the Arab East* (London: Routledge), pp. 48–65.

Layne, Linda. 1994. *Home and Homeland: The Dialogics of Tribal and National Identities in Jordan.* Princeton: Princeton University Press.

Lazreg, Marnia. 1994. *The Eloquence of Silence: Algerian Women in Question.* London: Routledge.

Leezenberg, Michiel. 2002. "Refugee Camp or Free Trade Zone? The Economy of Iraqi Kurdistan Since 1991." In Kamil A. Mahdi, ed., *Iraq's Economic Predicament* (Reading: Ithaca Press), pp. 289–320.

Lehman-Wilzig, Sam. 1986. "Conflict as Communication: Public Protest in Israel, 1950–1982." In Stuart A. Cohen and Eliezer Don-Yehiya, eds., *Conflict and*

Consensus in Jewish Public Life (Ramat Gan: Bar-Ilan University Press), pp. 128–145.

Lerner, Gerda. 1986. *The Creation of Patriarchy.* New York: Oxford University Press.

Levy, Shlomit, Hana Levinsohn, and Elihu Katz. 1993. *Beliefs, Observances, and Social Interaction Among Israeli Jews.* Jerusalem: Guttman Israel Institute of Applied Social Research.

Lewis, Bernard. 1998. *The Multiple Identities of the Middle East.* New York: Random House.

Lijphart, Arend. 1984. *Democracies: Patterns of Majoritarian and Consensus Government in Twenty-One Countries.* New Haven: Yale University Press.

———. 1994. "Democracies: Forms, Performance, and Constitutional Engineering." *European Journal of Political Research* 25 (January): 1–17.

Livani, Talajeh. 2007. "Middle East and North Africa: Gender Overview." Washington, DC: World Bank.

Lobmeyer, Hans Gunter. 1994. "Al Dimuqratiyya Hiyya al-Hall? The Syrian Opposition at the End of the Asad Era." In Eberhard Kienle, ed., *Contemporary Syria* (London: Tauris), pp. 81–96.

Longuenesse, Elisabeth. 1985. "The Syrian Working Class Today." *MERIP Reports,* no. 134 (July–August): 17–24.

Longva, Anh Nga. 2006. "Nationalism in Pre-Modern Guise: The Discourse on Hadhar and Badu in Kuwait." *International Journal of Middle East Studies* 38 (2): 171–187.

Lucas, Russell. 2004. "Monarchical Authoritarianism: Survival and Political Liberalization in a Middle Eastern Regime Type." *International Journal of Middle East Studies* 36 (1): 103–119.

Lund, Aron. 2012. *Syrian Jihadism.* UI Brief no. 13, Swedish Institute of International Affairs, September 14.

Lust, Ellen. 2011. "Morocco Elections Aren't a Model for the Arab Spring as West Claims." *Christian Science Monitor,* November 28. http://www.csmonitor.com /Commentary/Opinion/2011/1128/Morocco-elections-aren-t-a-model-for-the -Arab-Spring-as-West-claims.

Lust-Okar, Ellen. 2004. "Divided They Rule: The Management and Manipulation of Political Opposition." *Comparative Politics* 36 (2): 159–180.

———. 2006. "Elections Under Authoritarianism: Preliminary Lessons from Jordan." *Democratization* 13 (3): 456–471.

Lynch, Marc. 1999. *State Interests and Public Spheres: The International Politics of Jordan's Identity.* New York: Columbia University Press.

———, ed. 2012. *Arab Uprising: Breaking Bahrain.* Project on Middle East Political Science (POMEPS) Briefing 10. April 26. http://pomeps.org/wp-content/up loads/2012/04/POMEPS_BriefBooklet10_Bahrain_Web.pdf.

Macintyre, Donald. 2003. "Exiled Cleric Returns Home to Call for Free Islamic State." *Independent* (London), May 11, p. 18.

Maddy-Weitzman, Bruce. 2005. "Women, Islam, and the Moroccan State: The Struggle over the Personal Status Law." *Middle East Journal* 59 (Summer): 383–410.

al-Madfai, Madiha Rashid. 1993. *Jordan, the United States, and the Middle East Peace Process, 1974–1991.* New York: Cambridge University Press.

Makdisi, Ussama. 2000. *The Culture of Sectarianism: Community, History, and Violence in Nineteenth-Century Ottoman Lebanon.* Berkeley: University of California Press.

Marr, Phebe. 2004. *The Modern History of Iraq.* 2nd ed. Boulder: Westview.

————. 2007. "Iraq's New Political Map." Special Report no. 179. Washington, DC: US Institute of Peace.

Massad, Joseph A. 2001. *Colonial Effects: The Making of National Identity in Jordan*. New York: Columbia University Press.

McDowall, David. 2004. *A Modern History of the Kurds*. London: Tauris.

Mearsheimer, John J., and Stephen M. Walt. 2007. *The Israel Lobby and U.S. Foreign Policy*. New York: Farrar, Straus and Giroux.

Medani, Khalid Mustafa. 2004. "State Building in Reverse: The Neo-Liberal 'Reconstruction' of Iraq." *Middle East Report*, no. 232: 28–35.

Milani, Mohsen M. 1994. *The Making of Iran's Islamic Revolution*. Boulder: Westview.

Moaddel, Mansoor, and Taghi Azadarmaki. 2002. "The Worldviews of Islamic Publics: The Case of Egypt, Iran, and Jordan." *Comparative Sociology* 1 (3–4): 299–319.

Moghadam, Valentine M. 2003. *Modernizing Women: Gender and Social Change in the Middle East*. Boulder: Lynne Rienner.

Mohammed, Abeer. 2012. "Alarm as Shia Paramilitaries Enter Politics." Institute for War and Peace Reporting. January 17. www.iwpr.net.

Moore, Pete, and Bassel F. Salloukh. 2007. "Struggles Under Authoritarianism: Regimes, States, and Professional Associations in the Arab World." *International Journal of Middle East Studies* 39 (1): 53–76.

Morozov, Evgeny. 2012. *Net Delusion: The Dark Side of Internet Freedom*. New York: Public Affairs.

Mortimer, Robert. 2004. "Bouteflika and the Challenge of Political Stability." In Ahmed Aghrout, ed., *Algeria in Transition: Reforms and Development Prospects* (London: Routledge), pp. 185–199.

Moruzzi, Norma Claire, and Fatemeh Sadeghi. 2006. "Out of the Frying Pan, into the Flame: Young Iranian Women Today." *Middle East Report*, no. 241 (Winter): 22–28.

Mottahedeh, Roy P. 1985. *The Mantle of the Prophet: Religion and Politics in Iran*. New York: Pantheon.

Muasher, Marwan. 2008. *The Arab Center: The Promise of Moderation*. New Haven: Yale University Press.

Mufti, Malik. 1999. "Elite Bargains and the Onset of Political Liberalization in Jordan." *Comparative Political Studies* 32 (1): 100–129.

al-Munajjed, Mona. 2010. "Women's Employment in Saudi Arabia: A Major Challenge." Booz & Co., March. http://www.booz.com/media/uploads/Womens _Employment_in_Saudi_Arabia.pdf.

al-Musnad, Muhammad bin Abdul Aziz, comp. 1996. *Islamic Fatawa Regarding Women*. Jamal al-Din Zaraboro, trans. Saudi Arabia: Darussalam.

Myers, Steven Lee. 2011. "The Hot-Money Cowboys of Baghdad." *New York Times Magazine*, May 18.

Nasr, Vali. 2006a. *The Shia Revival: How Conflicts Within Islam Will Shape the Future*. New York: Norton.

————. 2006b. "When the Shi'ites Rise." *Foreign Affairs* 85 (4): 58–74.

National Democratic Party (Egypt). 2009. "The Egyptian Woman." http://www.ndp .org.eg/ar/News/ViewNewsDetails.aspx?NewsID=20389.

National Geographic Society. 2008. *Atlas of the Middle East*. 2nd ed. Washington, DC.

Novikov, Evgenii. 2004. "Baathist Origins of the Zarqawi Letter." *Terrorism Monitor* 2 (6).

O'Brien, Kevin J. 1996. "Rightful Resistance." *World Politics* 49 (October): 31–55.

Ofer, Gur. 1986. "Public Spending on Civilian Services." In Yoram Ben-Porath, ed., *The Israeli Economy: Maturing Through Crises* (Cambridge: Harvard University Press), pp. 192–208.

Okruhlik, Gwenn. 1999. "Rentier Wealth, Unruly Law, and the Rise of Opposition: The Political Economy of Oil States." *Comparative Politics* 31 (3): 295–315.

———. 2002. "Networks of Dissent: Islamism and Reform in Saudi Arabia." *Current History* 101 (651): 22–28.

———. 2004. "Making Conversation Permissible: Islamism in Saudi Arabia." In Quintan Wiktorowicz, ed., *Islamic Activism: A Social Movement Theory Approach* (Bloomington: Indiana University Press), pp. 354–384.

———. 2005. "The Irony of Islah (Reform)." *Washington Quarterly* 28 (4): 153–170.

———. 2009. "State Power, Religious Privilege, and the Myths About Political Reform." In Mohammed Ayoob and Hasan Koselbalaban, eds., *Religion and Politics in Saudi Arabia: Wahhabism and the State* (Boulder: Lynne Rienner), pp. 91–107.

———. 2010. "Dependence, Disdain and Distance: State, Labor and Citizenship in the Arab Gulf States." In Jean-Francois Seznec and Mimi Kirk, eds., *Industrialization in the Arab Gulf: A Socioeconomic Revolution* (New York: Routledge with the CCAS Georgetown University), pp. 125–142.

Organski, A. F. K. 1990. *The $36 Billion Bargain: Strategy and Politics in U.S. Assistance to Israel*. New York: Columbia University Press.

Paidar, Parvin. 1995. *Women and the Political Process in Twentieth-Century Iran*. Cambridge: Cambridge University Press.

Parker, Christopher, and Pete W. Moore. 2007. "The War Economy of Iraq." *Middle East Report*, no. 243: 6–15.

Parra, Francisco. 2004. *Oil Politics: A Modern History of Petroleum*. London: Tauris.

Perthes, Volker. 1992. "Syria's Parliamentary Elections." *Middle East Report*, no. .174 (January–February): 15–18, 35.

———. 2000. "*Si Vis Stabilitatem, Para Bellum:* State Building, National Security, and War Preparation in Syria." In Steven Heydemann, ed., *War, Institutions, and Social Change in the Middle East* (Berkeley: University of California Press), pp. 149–173.

Peters, Anne, and Pete Moore. 2009. "Beyond Boom and Bust: External Rents, Durable Authoritarianism, and Institutional Adaptation in the Hashemite Kingdom of Jordan." *Studies in Comparative International Development* 44 (2): 256–285.

Pierret, Thomas. 2012. "The Role of the Mosque in the Syrian Revolution." *Near East Quarterly*, no. 7 (February).

Piscatori, James. 2005. "Managing *God's* Guests: The Pilgrimage, Saudi Arabia, and the Politics of Legitimacy." In Paul Dresch and James Piscatori, eds., *Monarchies and Nations: Globalisation and Identity in the Arab States of the Gulf* (London: Tauris), pp. 222–245.

Posner, Daniel N. 2005. *Institutions and Ethnic Politics in Africa*. New York: Cambridge University Press.

Posusney, Marsha Pripstein. 1997. *Labor and the State in Egypt: Workers, Unions, and Economic Restructuring*. New York: Columbia University Press.

———. 2002. "Multiparty Elections in the Arab World: Institutional Engineering and Oppositional Strategies." *Studies in Comparative International Development* 36 (4): 34–62.

Powell, G. Bingham. 1982. *Contemporary Democracies: Participation, Stability, and Violence*. Cambridge: Harvard University Press.

Provence, Michael. 2005. *The Great Syrian Revolt and the Rise of Arab Nationalism*. Austin: University of Texas Press.

Przeworski, Adam, et al. 1996. "What Makes Democracies Endure?" *Journal of Democracy* 7 (1): 39–55.

al-Qabas. 2009. "Ajwa al-Tabayun al-Mustamira Hawla Mashru'al-Hukuma Da'm al-Sharikat al-Istithmariya" (Continuing Crosswinds Around the Government Plan to Support Investment Companies). February 10.

Ramazani, R. K. 1986. *Revolutionary Iran: Challenge and Response in the Middle East*. Baltimore: Johns Hopkins University Press.

Rassam, Amal. 1992. "Political Ideology and Women in Iraq." In Joseph D. Jabbra and Nancy W. Jabbra, eds., *Women and Development in the Middle East and North Africa* (Leiden: Brill).

Richards, Alan, and John Waterbury. 1990, 2008. *A Political Economy of the Middle East: State, Class, and Economic Development*. Boulder: Westview.

Ricks, Thomas E. 2007. *Fiasco: The American Military Adventure in Iraq*. New York: Penguin.

Rivlin, Paul. 2009. *Arab Economies in the Twenty-First Century*. Cambridge: Cambridge University Press.

Roberts, Hugh. 2003. *The Battlefield: Algeria, 1988–2002*. London: Verso.

Robinson, Glenn. 1998. "Defensive Democratization in Jordan." *International Journal of Middle East Studies* 30 (3): 387–410.

Rodrik, Dani. 1997. *Has Globalization Gone Too Far?* Washington, DC: Institute for International Economics.

Ross, Michael E. 2001. "Does Oil Hinder Democracy?" *World Politics* 53 (3): 325–361.

Roy, Olivier. 1994. *The Failure of Political Islam*. Cambridge: Harvard University Press.

Roy, Sara. 2007. *Failing Peace: Gaza and the Palestinian-Israeli Conflict*. London: Pluto.

Rubin, Barry. 1981. *The Arab States and the Palestine Conflict*. Syracuse: Syracuse University Press.

Rubinstein, Alvin Z. 1977. *Red Star on the Nile: The Soviet-Egyptian Influence Relationship Since the June War*. Princeton: Princeton University Press.

Ruedy, John. 2005. *Modern Algeria: The Origins and Development of a Nation*. 2nd ed. Bloomington: Indiana University Press.

Rustow, Dankwart. 1967. *A World of Nations: Problems of Political Modernization*. Washington, DC: Brookings Institution.

Ryan, Curtis R. 1998. "Elections and Parliamentary Democratization in Jordan." *Democratization* 5 (4): 194–214.

———. 2002. *Jordan in Transition: From Hussein to Abdullah*. Boulder: Lynne Rienner.

———. 2008. "Islamist Political Activism in Jordan: Moderation, Militancy, and Democracy." *Middle East Review of International Affairs* 12 (2): 1–13.

———. 2009. *Inter-Arab Alliances: Regime Security and Jordanian Foreign Policy*. Gainesville: University of Florida Press.

Ryan, Curtis R., and Jillian Schwedler. 2004. "Return to Democratization or New Hybrid Regime? The 2003 Elections in Jordan." *Middle East Policy* 11 (2): 138–151.

Sacks, Harvey. 1992. *Lectures on Conversation*. Oxford: Blackwell.

Sadeghi, Fatemeh. 2009. "Foot Soldiers in the Islamic Republic's 'Culture of Modesty.'" *Middle East Report*, no. 250 (Spring): 50–55.

Sadowski, Yahya. 1985. "Cadres, Guns, and Money: The Eighth Regional Congress of the Syrian Ba'th." *MERIP Reports*, no. 134 (July–August): 3–8.

————. 1993. "The New Orientalism and the Democracy Debate." *Middle East Report,* no. 183 (July–August): 14–21, 40.

Saktanber, Ayşe. 2002. *Living Islam: Women, Religion, and the Politicization of Culture in Turkey.* London: Tauris.

Salehi-Isfahani, Djavad. 2001. "The Gender Gap in Education in Iran: Evidence for the Role of Household Characteristics." In Djavad Salehi-Isfahani, ed., *Labor and Human Capital in the Middle East* (Reading: Ithaca Press), pp. 235–255.

————. 2008. "Iran's Economy: Short-Term Performance and Long-Term Potential." http://www.brookings.edu/speeches/2008/0523_iran_economy_salehi _isfahani.aspx.

Sanasarian, Eliz. 2000. *Religious Minorities in Iran.* Cambridge: Cambridge University Press.

Sandler, Neal. 2007. "Women Fight for Equality in Israel." *Business Week,* May 1.

Sandler, Shmuel, and Aaron Kampinsky. 2009. "Israel's Religious Parties." In Robert O. Freedman, ed., *Contemporary Israel* (Boulder: Westview), pp. 77–96.

Saudi National e-Government Portal. 2010. "Regime of the Kingdom of Saudi Arabia." http://www.saudi.gov.sa/wps/portal.

Schedler, Andreas. 2002. "The Menu of Manipulation." *Journal of Democracy* 13 (2): 36–50.

Schirazi, Asghar. 1998. *The Constitution of Iran: Politics and the State in the Islamic Republic.* John O'Kane, trans. London: Tauris.

Schmitter, Philippe C. 1978. "The Impact and Meaning of 'Non-Competitive, Non-Free and Insignificant' Elections in Authoritarian Portugal, 1933–74." In Guy Hermet, Richard Rose, and Alain Rouquie, eds., *Elections Without Choice* (New York: Wiley), pp. 145–168.

Schwedler, Jillian. 2006. *Faith in Moderation: Islamist Parties in Jordan and Yemen.* Cambridge: Cambridge University Press.

Seale, Patrick. 1987. *The Struggle for Syria.* New Haven: Yale University Press.

Shadid, Anthony. 2003. "Iraqi Clergy United in Rare Alliance." *Washington Post,* August 17.

Shahine, Alaa. 2012a. "Egypt Had FDI Outflows of $483.7 Million in 2011." Bloomberg, March 25. http://www.bloomberg.com/news/2012-03-25/egypt -had-fdi-outflows-of-482-7-million-in-2011-correct-.html.

————. 2012b. "Egypt's Economic Growth Slows as Turmoil Hurts Investments." Bloomberg, January 4. http://www.businessweek.com/news/2012-01-04/egypt -s-economic-growth-slows-as-turmoil-hurts-investments.html.

Shahrokni, Nazanin. 2009. "All the President's Women." *Middle East Report,* no. 253 (Winter): 2–6.

Shambayati, Hootan. 1994. "The Rentier State, Interest Groups, and the Paradox of Autonomy: State and Business in Turkey and Iran." *Comparative Politics* 26 (April): 307–331.

Sharkansky, Ira. 2004. "A Critical Look at Israel's Economic and Social Gaps." In Alan Dowty, ed., *Critical Issues in Israeli Society* (Westport: Praeger), pp. 129–150.

Sikkuy. 2009. "The Equality Index of Jewish and Arab Citizens in Israel." http:// www.sikkuy.org.il.

Singerman, Diane. 1995. *Avenues of Participation: Family, Politics, and Networks in Urban Quarters of Cairo.* Princeton: Princeton University Press.

————. 2006. "Restoring the Family to Civil Society: Lessons from Egypt." *Journal of Middle East Women's Studies* 2 (Winter): 1–32.

Smooha, Sammy. 1978. *Israel: Pluralism and Conflict*. Berkeley: University of California Press.

Sonbol, Amira El-Azhary. 2003. *Women of Jordan: Islam, Labor, and the Law*. Syracuse: Syracuse University Press.

Spivak, Gayatri Chakravorty. 1988. "Can the Subaltern Speak?" In Cary Nelson and Lawrence Grossberg, eds., *Marxism and the Interpretation of Culture* (Urbana: University of Illinois Press), pp. 271–313.

Susser, Asher. 2008. "Jordan: Preserving Domestic Order in a Setting of Regional Turmoil." Middle East Brief no. 27. Waltham, MA: Brandeis University, Crown Center for Middle East Studies.

Swirsky, B., and M. P. Safir, eds. 1991. *Calling the Equality Bluff: Women in Israel*. New York: Pergamon.

Taylor, Charles Lewis, and David A. Jodice. 1983. *World Handbook of Political and Social Indicators*. 3rd ed. New Haven: Yale University Press.

Tejel, Jordi. 2009. *Syria's Kurds*. London: Routledge.

Tessler, Mark. 2002. "Islam and Democracy in the Middle East: The Impact of Religious Orientations on Attitudes Toward Democracy in Four Arab Countries." *Comparative Politics* 34 (3): 337–354.

Tezcür, Güneş Murat. 2008. "Intra-Elite Struggles in Iranian Elections." In Ellen Lust-Okar and S. Zerhouni, eds., *Political Participation in the Middle East* (Boulder: Lynne Rienner), pp. 51–74.

Tezcür, Güneş Murat, Taghi Azadarmaki, and Mehri Bahar. 2006. "Religious Participation Among Muslims: Iranian Exceptionalism." *Critique* 15 (Fall): 217–232.

Tilly, Charles. 2007. "Grudging Consent." *The American Interest* (September/October): 17–23.

Tlemçani, Rachid. 2008. "Algeria Under Bouteflika: Civil Strife and National Reconciliation." Carnegie Paper no. 7. Washington, DC: Carnegie Endowment for International Peace.

Tripp, Charles. 2000, 2007. *A History of Iraq*. Cambridge: Cambridge University Press.

Ulrichsen, Kristian Coates. 2012a. "The UAE: Holding Back the Tide." *openDemocracy,* August 5. http://www.opendemocracy.net/kristian-coates-ulrichsen/uae -holding-back-tide.

———. 2012b. "Political Crisis at Critical Juncture," BBC News, October 22. http://www.bbc.co.uk/news/world-middle-east-20026581.

UNDP (United Nations Development Programme). 2004. *The Arab Human Development Report: Towards Freedom in the Arab World*. New York.

———. 2005. "Employment Statistics." http://unstats.un.org/unsd/economic_main .htm.

———. 2008. *Egypt Human Development Report: Egypt's Social Contract: The Role of Civil Society*. New York.

———. 2011. *Human Development Index (HDI)—2011 Rankings*. http://hdr.undp .org/en/statistics.

UNDP (United Nations Development Programme) and Plan and Budget Organization of the Islamic Republic. 1999. *Human Development Report of the Islamic Republic of Iran*. New York.

USAID (US Agency for International Development) in Jordan. 2010. "Education." http://www.usaidjordan.org/sectors.cfm?inSector=17.

Valenzuela, J. Samuel. 1990. "Democratic Consolidation in Post-Transitional Settings: Notion, Process, and Facilitating Conditions." Kellogg Institute Working Paper no. 150. University of Notre Dame.

526 References

Van Dam, Nikolaos. 1996. *The Struggle for Power in Syria*. London: Tauris.
Visser, Reidar. 2005. *Basra: The Failed Gulf State*. Berlin: Lit Verlag.
———. 2008. "The Western Imposition of Sectarianism on Iraqi Politics." *Arab Studies Journal* 15 (2): 83–99.
Vitalis, Robert. 2007. *America's Kingdom: Mythmaking on the Saudi Oil Frontier.* Stanford: Stanford University Press.
Vitalis, Robert, and Steven Heydemann. 2000. "War, Keynesianism, and Colonialism: Explaining State-Market Relations in the Postwar Middle East." In Steven Heydemann, ed., *War, Institutions, and Social Change in the Middle East* (Berkeley: University of California Press), pp. 100–148.
Vora, Neha. 2008. "Producing Diasporas and Globalization: Indian Middle-Class Migrants in Dubai." *Anthropological Quarterly* 81 (2): 377–406.
Waldner, David. 1999. *State Building and Late Development*. Ithaca: Cornell University Press.
Waleed, Khalid. 2012. "Clashes Spread Between Iraqi Shia Groups." Institute for War and Peace Reporting, April 19. http://www.wiwpr.net.
Wallechinsky, David. 2009. "The World's Worst Dictators 2009." *Parade,* March 22.
Waterbury, John. 1993. *Exposed to Innumerable Delusions: Public Enterprise and State Power in Egypt, India, Mexico, and Turkey*. Cambridge: Cambridge University Press.
White, Jenny. 2002. *Islamist Mobilization in Turkey: A Study in Vernacular Politics*. Seattle: University of Washington Press.
Wickham, Carrie Rosefsky. 2002. *Mobilizing Islam: Religion, Activism, and Political Change in Egypt*. New York: Columbia University Press.
Wiktorowicz, Quintan. 2000a. "Civil Society as Social Control: State Power in Jordan." *Comparative Politics* 33 (1): 43–62.
———. 2000b. *The Management of Islamic Activism: Salafis, the Muslim Brotherhood, and State Power in Jordan*. Albany: SUNY Press.
———. 2002. "The Political Limits to Nongovernmental Organizations in Jordan." *World Development* 30 (1): 77–93.
Wiley, Joyce N. 1992. *The Islamic Movement of Iraqi Shi'as*. Boulder: Lynne Rienner.
Willis, Michael J. 2008. "The Politics of Berber (Amazigh) Identity." In Yahia H. Zoubir and Haizam Amirah-Fernàndez, eds., *North Africa: Politics, Region, and the Limits of Transformation* (London: Routledge), pp. 227–242.
Wilson, Mary. 1987. *King Abdullah, Britain, and the Making of Jordan*. New York: Cambridge University Press.
Wittes, Tamara Cofman. 2008. *Freedom's Unsteady March: America's Role in Building Arab Democracy*. Washington, DC: Brookings Institution.
World Bank. 2003. "Increasing Girls' Education in the Arab Republic of Egypt." Washington, DC: Human Development Group, Middle East and North Africa Region.
———. 2004. *Gender and Development in the Middle East and North Africa: Women in the Public Sphere*. Washington, DC.
———. 2008. *World Development Indicators*. Washington, DC.
———. 2012. The World Bank EdStats Query. Washington, DC. http://data.world bank.org/data-catalog/ed-stats.
World Economic Forum. 2012. "Global Gender Gap Index 2012." http://www.we forum.org/issues/global-gender-gap.
Wright, Lawrence. 2006. *The Looming Tower: Al-Qaeda and the Road to 9/11*. New York: Vintage.

Yildiz, Kerim. 2007. *The Kurds in Iraq.* London: Pluto.

Yom, Sean L. 2011. "Oil, Coalitions, and Regime Durability: The Origins and Persistence of Popular Rentierism in Kuwait." *Studies in Comparative International Development* 46 (2): 217–241.

Younis, Ahmed. 2012. "Arab-Kurdish Rapprochement in Northern Iraqi Region." Institute for War and Peace Reporting, June 7. http://www.iwpr.net.

Zaman, Constantin. 2006. "A Review of Syrian Economy." Institutional and Sector Modernization Facility (ISMF). http://www.ismf-eusy.org/ismf_reports/Reports /E019-10-06.pdf?.

Zisser, Eyal. 1997. "Syria: Exercising Democracy? Elections to the People's Assembly, August 1994." Paper presented at the annual meeting of the Middle East Studies Association, San Francisco.

Zoubir, Yahia H. 1995. "Stalled Democratization of an Authoritarian Regime: The Case of Algeria." *Democratization* 2 (2): 109–139.

———. 1999. "State and Civil Society in Algeria." In Yahia H. Zoubir, ed., *North Africa in Transition: State, Society, and the Limits of Transformation* (Gainesville: University Press of Florida), pp. 29–42.

———. 2002. "Algeria and U.S. Interests: Containing Radical Islamism and Promoting Democracy." *Middle East Policy* 9 (1): 64–81.

———. 2009. "The United States and Maghreb-Sahel Security." *International Affairs* 85 (5): 977–995.

Zoubir, Yahia H., and Ahmed Aghrout. 2012. "Algeria's Path to Reform: Authentic Change?" *Middle East Policy* 19 (2): 65–83.

The Contributors

Michele Penner Angrist is associate professor of political science at Union College, where she teaches courses in international, comparative, Middle East, and African politics. She is author of *Party Building in the Modern Middle East* and coeditor of *Authoritarianism in the Middle East: Regimes and Resistance.*

Nathan J. Brown is professor of political science and international affairs at George Washington University and nonresident senior associate at the Carnegie Endowment for International Peace. His most recent book is *When Victory Is Not an Option: Islamist Movements in Arab Politics.*

Sheila Carapico is professor of political science and international studies at the University of Richmond. During 2010 and 2011 she spent three semesters as visiting chairperson of the Department of Political Science at the American University in Cairo. She is author of *Civil Society in Yemen: The Political Economy of Activism in Modern Arabia* and, most recently, *Promoting Arab Democratization: International Political Aid in Practice.*

Alan Dowty is professor emeritus of political science at the University of Notre Dame. He is an associate member of the Center for Jewish Studies and the Center for Middle Eastern Studies, both at the University of Chicago. Among his published works are *The Jewish State: A Century Later* and *Israel/Palestine.*

F. Gregory Gause III is professor of political science at the University of Vermont. His publications include *The International Relations of the Persian Gulf, Oil Monarchies,* and *Saudi-Yemeni Relations: Domestic Structures and Foreign Influence.*

Mona El-Ghobashy is assistant professor of political science at Barnard College. She specializes in Egyptian politics and was named a 2009 Carnegie scholar in support of her research. Her work has appeared in the *International Journal of Middle East Studies, Middle East Report,* and *American Behavioral Scientist.*

Michael Herb is associate professor of political science at Georgia State University, where his research focuses on Gulf politics. He is author of *All in the Family: Absolutism, Revolution and Democracy in Middle Eastern Monarchies.*

Arang Keshavarzian is associate professor of Middle Eastern and Islamic studies at New York University and a member of the editorial board of the *International Journal of Middle East Studies.* He is author of *Bazaar and State in Iran: The Politics of the Tehran Marketplace.*

Fred H. Lawson is Lynn T. White, Jr. professor of government at Mills College. In 2001, he was Fulbright lecturer in political science at Aden University. He is author of *Global Security Watch—Syria* and *Constructing International Relations in the Arab World.*

Pete W. Moore is associate professor of political science at Case Western Reserve University and serves on the editorial board of the *Middle East Report.* He is author of *Doing Business in the Middle East: Politics and Economic Crisis in Jordan and Kuwait.*

Gwenn Okruhlik specializes in the politics of the Arabian Peninsula, with a focus on Saudi Arabia. She is president of the Association for Gulf and Arabian Peninsula Studies, and in 2011–2012 she taught as a Brookings Doha fellow at the University of Qatar. Her work has appeared in *Comparative Politics, Middle East Journal, Middle East Policy,* and *Middle East Report,* as well as numerous edited volumes.

David Siddhartha Patel is an assistant professor of government at Cornell University, where his current research focuses on the relationship of Islamic institutions to mobilization and collective action. He is writing a book on the rise of sectarianism and social order in post-Saddam Iraq and has previously written on ethnic divisions within the Jordanian Islamic Movement, the diffusion of protest in the Arab world, and the signaling role of Islamic dress.

Marcie J. Patton is professor of politics at Fairfield University. She taught as a visiting professor at Boğazici University and was a senior Fulbright scholar at Bilkent University in 2002–2003. Her work has appeared in *Middle East Politics, Mediterranean Politics, Middle East Report, CEMOTI,* and *Comparative Studies of South Asia, Africa and the Middle East,* and as chapters in edited books.

Curtis R. Ryan is associate professor of political science at Appalachian State University in North Carolina. He has served as a Fulbright scholar and guest researcher at the Center for Strategic Studies, University of Jordan, and was twice named a Peace Scholar by the United States Institute of Peace. He is author of *Jordan in Transition: From Hussein to Abdullah* and *Inter-Arab Alliances: Regime Security and Jordanian Foreign Policy.*

Jillian Schwedler is professor of political science at the City University of New York, Hunter College and the Graduate Center. She has conducted research in Jordan, Yemen, and Egypt and has traveled extensively throughout the Middle East with support from the National Science Foundation, the United States Institute of Peace, the Fulbright Scholars Program, and the Social Science Research Council. She is author of the award-winning *Faith in Moderation: Islamist Parties in Jordan and Yemen* and, most recently, coeditor of *Policing and Prisons in the Middle East.*

Emad El-Din Shahin is professor of public policy at the School of Global Affairs and Public Policy, the American University in Cairo. In addition to coediting *Struggling over Democracy in the Middle East and North Africa,* he is editor-in-chief of *The Oxford Encyclopaedia of Islam and Politics* and coeditor of *The Oxford Handbook of Islam and Politics.*

Diane Singerman is an associate professor in the Department of Government, School of Public Affairs at American University. She has written *Cairo Contested: Governance, Urban Space, and Global Modernity* and coauthored *Cairo Cosmopolitan: Politics, Culture, and Urban Space in the New Globalized Middle East.*

Joshua Stacher is assistant professor of political science at Kent State University. He was a fellow at the Woodrow Wilson International Center for Scholars in 2012–2013 and is presently on the editorial board of the *Middle East Report.* Stacher is the author of *Adaptable Autocrats: Regime Power in Egypt and Syria.*

Yahia H. Zoubir is professor of international relations and international management and director of research in geopolitics at Euromed Management, Ecole de Management Marseille. He has coedited the book *North Africa: Politics, Region, and the Limits of Transformation* and is coauthor of *Doing Business in Emerging Europe.*

Index

Middle East and North Africa (MENA), 2–4; education of women in, 170–174, 179–180*tab*; employment of women in, 179–181; map of countries in, 3*fig*

Milayya liff, 177

Millet system, 159, 322

"Million Signatures Campaign," in Morocco, 183–184

Ministry of Social Affairs (Egypt), 107, 231

Monarchy(ies), 7–8; dividing/balancing of interests by, 39–40; economic development in, 20; in Jordan, 25, 39–41; linchpin, 39; in Morocco, 41; nondemocracy, republics compared to, 7–8; right to rule in, 20; in Saudi Arabia, 39–40

Morocco, 2, 8; monarchy in, 20, 25, 39, 41; protests of women in, 183

Morsi, Mohamed, 47, 223–224, 227, 238, 332

Moses, 122, 124

Mossadeq, Mohammad, 255–256, 282; US overthrowing, 54, 60

Motherland Party (ANAP), 476

Movement for Autonomy in Kabylie (MAK), 210

Movement of the Society for Peace (MSP), 200, 202–204, 213

MPs. *See* Members of parliament

MSP. *See* Movement of the Society for Peace; National Salvation Party

Muasher, Marwan, 357

Mubarak, Gamal, 249

Mubarak, Husni, 25, 56, 63, 118, 131, 176, 217; policies of, 220–228, 230–232, 236–238

Mubarak the Great, 361

al-Mugateib, Ibrahim, 426

Muhaggabaat (veiled women), 176–177

Muhammad, Prophet, 10, 20, 39, 75, 124–126, 130, 342, 418, 431

Munif, Abdul Rahman, 88

Al-Muqaddimah (Khaldun), 158

al-Musayni, Hayat, 354

Muslim(s), 4, 16, 124–125; definition of, 124; Egypt, Christian tension with, 242–244; types of, 125. *See also* Islam; Shi'ite(s); Sunni(s)

Muslim Brotherhood: in Egypt, 137, 139–141, 218–220, 225; founding of, 23, 134, 240–242; Hamas and, 332, 411; in Jordan, 135, 340, 343; in Palestine, 398, 408; in Syria, 461–466; tactics of, 136–137

al-Muslimin, Ikhwan, 461–466

Al-Nahda, 136, 139–141, 178, 506

Nahnah, Mahfoud, 213

al-Nahyan family, 374

Nasser, Gamal Abdel, 19, 61, 137, 162, 177, 219; policies of, 70, 219–221, 224–225, 229–235

National Action Party (MHP), 477, 479, 487–489, 499

National Agenda for Reform (Jordan), 357

National Alliance for the Liberation of Syria, 464

National Democratic Party (NDP), 106, 135, 139, 220, 226

National Dialogue of Political Forces, 114

National Liberation Army (ALN), 190

National Liberation Front (FLN), 17, 79, 106, 190; Algeria, rule of, 190–192, 199, 202–204, 214

National Religious Party (NRP), 313, 316, 324

National Salvation Front (NSF), 455, 465–466

National Salvation Party (MSP), 481–482

National Security Council (MGK), 480, 485

National Unity Government (Israel), 313–314; stabilization plan of, 317

Nationalism, 11; civil, 156; of Hussein, King, 351. *See also* Arab nationalism; Kurdish nationalism

Nationalization: civil society and, 102, 106–107; of oil, 293; of Suez Canal, 61, 81, 233

NATO. *See* North Atlantic Treaty Organization

Nazif, Ahmad, 57, 236

NDP. *See* National Democratic Party

Near East. *See* Middle East

Neo-Destour movement, 16

Netanyahu, Benjamin, 314, 316, 318, 321

NGOs. *See* Nongovernmental organizations

Nongovernmental organizations (NGOs): civil society and, 107–108, 118 in Egypt, 228–231; GONGOs, 108; in Iran, 266, 280; in Jordan, 355–357; in Palestine, 406, 409–410; RONGOs, 108, 355–356; in Turkey, 488–490

Nonorthodox Jews, 322–323

Noor, Queen, 352–353, 355

North Africa: definitions of, 2–4; map of

Washington Consensus, 56–57, 90
Waterbury, John, 161
Welfare (*khayriyyah*), 101
Welfare Party (RP), 46, 135, 473, 482–483, 496
Women: circumcision of, 246; colonialism, Islam and, 171–174; education of, in Iran, 181, 268, 272; education of, in MENA, 170–174, 178–181*tab*; Egypt, education and, 177, 246; employment of, in Egypt, 230; employment of, in MENA, 180–181; global subordination of, 167–168; Hamas and, 414; honor and, 115, 352–353; in IDF, 329; Iran, protests of, 182–183; Iran-Iraq War and, 305; Islam and veils for, 168, 171–178, 255, 270, 274; Kemalists and, 175; in Knesset, 330; *mahram* and, 439; Morocco, protests of, 183; in People's Assembly, 470; politics and struggles of, 167–186; Saudi Arabia, political rights of, 439–441; Saudi Arabia, protests of, 440–441; transnational networks for, 183. *See also* Feminism; Gender
Women Living Under Muslim Law Network, 183

World Bank, 24, 56, 90, 490
World Trade Organization (WTO), 58, 93, 348
World War II, economic development after, 76–79
WTO. *See* World Trade Organization

Yamani, Shaikh Ahmed Zaki, 84
Yassin, Nadia, 186*n*2
Yassin, Shaikh Abd al-Salam, 186*n*2
Yemen: civil society in, 103, 105; Soviet Union's relationship with, during Cold War, 63; protests in, 25, 75, 95; unification of, 14, 105, 113. *See also* General People's Congress
Yisrael Beiteinu Party, 313, 327, 334
YOK. *See* Higher Education Council
Youth Party (GP), 479

Zakat (charitable tithe), 101–102, 110–111, 229, 297
al-Zarqawi, Abu Musab, 162, 289, 343
Zayid, Shaikh, 362, 365, 374
Zayy al-Islami (Islamic dress), 177
Zionism: history of, 15, 123; Labor, 312–313, 316; revisionist, 310
al-Zu'bi, Mahmud, 454

About the Book

This cutting-edge examination of the domestic politics of
the Middle East—now thoroughly revised to reflect the events of the Arab
Spring—has quickly proven itself ideal for classroom use.

The book has been designed to give students tools that will help them
to analyze politics in the region not only during the present unsettled period, but also as events unfold. Offering insightful analyses and a wealth of
accessible information, it encourages comparative, critical thinking by students at all levels.

Michele Penner Angrist is associate professor of political science at
Union College. She is author of *Party Building in the Modern Middle East*
and coeditor (with Marsha Pripstein Posusney) of *Authoritarianism in the
Middle East: Regimes and Resistance*.